TREKKING IN
TIBET

A TRAVELER'S GUIDE

SECOND EDITION

GARY McCUE

FOREWORD BY
GEORGE B. SCHALLER

THE
MOUNTAINEERS

In Memory of Joseph F. McCue, Jr.
1928–1988

 Published by
The Mountaineers
1001 SW Klickitat Way, Suite 201
Seattle, WA 98134

Second edition, 1999

Published simultaneously in Great Britain by Cordee, 3a DeMontfort Street, Leicester, England, LE1 7HD

Manufactured in Canada

Edited by Uma Kukathas
Maps and artwork by Kathy Butler
All photographs by Gary McCue, except where noted
Cover design by Jennifer LaRock Shontz
Book design and layout by Jennifer LaRock Shontz

Cover photograph: *Prayer flags atop Drolma La pass, Mount Kailash, Tibet* © Gary McCue

Library of Congress Cataloging-in-Publication Data

McCue, Gary, 1953–
    Trekking in Tibet: a traveler's guide/by Gary McCue. — 2nd ed.
      p.   cm.
    Includes bibliographical references and index.
    ISBN 0-89886-662-6 (pbk.)
    1. Mountaineering—China—Tibet Guidebooks. 2.
Hiking—China—Tibet Guidebooks. 3. Tibet (China) Guidebooks. I.
Title.
    GV199.44.C552 T536 1999
    796.5'22'09515—dc21   99-6541
                                          CIP

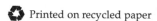

CONTENTS

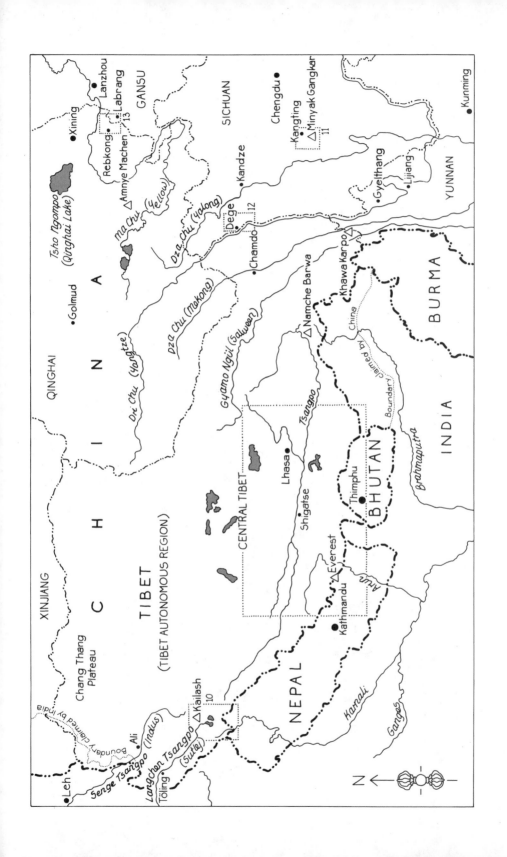

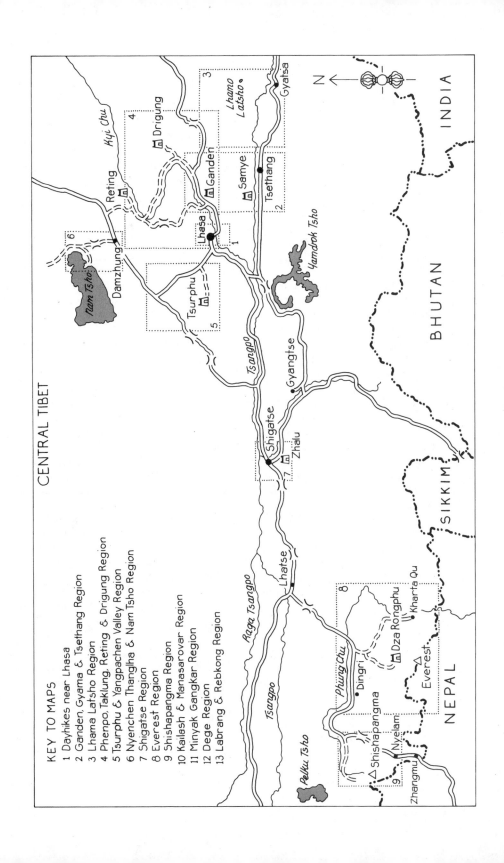

CENTRAL TIBET

KEY TO MAPS

1 Dayhikes near Lhasa
2 Ganden, Gyama & Tsethang Region
3 Lhamo Latsho Region
4 Phenpo, Taklung, Reting & Drigung Region
5 Tsurphu & Yangpachen Valley Region
6 Nyenchen Thanglha & Nam Tsho Region
7 Shigatse Region
8 Everest Region
9 Shishapangma Region
10 Kailash & Manasarovar Region
11 Minyak Gangkar Region
12 Dege Region
13 Labrang & Rebkong Region

N

INDIA

BHUTAN

SIKKIM

NEPAL

Nam Tsho

Damzhung

Reting

Kyi Chu

Drigung

3

4

Lhamo Latsho

Gyatsa

Lhasa

1

Ganden

Samye

Tsethang

2

Yamdrok Tsho

Tsurphu

5

Tsangpo

Gyangtse

Shigatse

Zhalu

7

Lhatse

Raga Tsangpo

Tsangpo

Phung Chu

8

Dingri

Dza Rongphu

Kharta Qu

Everest

Shishapangma

Nyelam

9

Zhangmu

Pelku Tsho

FOREWORD

North of India and Nepal, north of the ice rampart of the Himalaya, lie the uplands of Tibet. Long sealed to outsiders, Tibet became a land of mystery and fantasy, penetrated only occasionally by Westerners whose tales of a unique Buddhist culture and grand peaks and plains only added to the allure.

This land of contrasts and superlatives became accessible to visitors in the 1980s when China began to permit travel to various parts. I first visited Tibet in 1980, and since 1988 have returned annually to study wildlife and promote conservation with various government departments. Despite the various political upheavals it has weathered during the twentieth century, Tibet retains for me some of the aura that so intrigued the early travelers: fascinating monasteries, friendly people, and an ecological wholeness that, fortunately, still persists. There are valleys, turquoise lakes, and paths cutting through raw highlands swept by relentless winds that no expedition has ever beheld. One can record plants, birds, and butterflies whose distribution remains but vaguely known. *Trekking in Tibet* is a superb guide to this cultural and natural landscape, as well as a book to be read by anyone who dreams of adventure.

This book also serves another important function: It creates an awareness of the splendor that still lies hidden in Tibet. However, even in this relatively unspoiled land, some species are threatened with extinction and habitats are being degraded by a pervasive presence of people and livestock and an emphasis on development. Tibet has in recent years made a major conservation effort with a quarter of its land area now designated as reserves whose purpose is to preserve the region's natural heritage. But there is still a relentless attrition of wildlife. For example, Tibetan antelopes are illegally slaughtered by the thousands for their fine wool, which is woven into shawls in India and then sold worldwide under the name of "shatoosh."

How can cultural traditions and the environment best be preserved? This question should touch the heart and mind of every traveler who treasures his or her Tibetan experience. The Chinese know Tibet as *Xizang*, the Western Treasure House. Treasures are usually defined in terms of gold and jewels. However, the real treasure of Tibet is the land—with its golden vistas, its snow leopards and blue poppies, and its resilient people. *Trekking in Tibet* will, I hope, inspire a unity of effort among visitors to become advocates for conservation and to cherish and help protect these unbounded uplands or, in the words of an ancient Tibetan poet, this "center of heaven, this core of the earth, this heart of the world."

George B. Schaller is one of the world's foremost field biologists. He has spent over four decades studying wildlife in the remote corners of the world and works in association with the Wildlife Conservation Society in New York. He is the author of a dozen books and has helped establish several nature reserves, including Tibet's Chang Thang Reserve.

PREFACE TO THE SECOND EDITION

Little did I imagine in 1990 when I wrote the preface to the first edition of this book that the "many changes in Tibet" that I referred to then would now be considered rather minor compared to what has transpired over the last nine years. Like many cities in Asia, Lhasa is now almost unrecognizable from a decade ago; it is no longer a sleepy town, but rather a bustling, if small, city. Tsethang, the town to the south of Lhasa along the Tsangpo River, and Lhatse, a former one restaurant–one gas pump roadside stop on the Friendship Highway, are the runaway winners for the most-changed-place-in-Tibet award. And little ole Dingri, the trekkers' gateway to Mount Everest, now sprawls along the Friendship Highway with enough new shops and guesthouses to be in the runner-up circle.

Despite these irreversible changes, Tibet remains my favorite adventure travel destination in Asia. And it continues to be one of the most physically, mentally, and—unfortunately—politically challenging places in which to travel. The rules for entering Tibet are constantly changing, and the roads and bridges continue to be washed away each rainy season. But once you're away from the roads, walking up a broad valley of barley fields with yaks dotting the hillsides and those amazing Tibetan clouds hanging overhead in the spectacular Tibetan sky, the tribulations of getting to the trailhead are soon forgotten.

With this second edition of Trekking in Tibet, my choice of trek descriptions has expanded beyond Lhasa, Central Tibet, and Western Tibet to include walks in the old Kham and Amdo regions of the eastern part of the Tibetan Plateau (now in the Chinese provinces of Qinghai, Gansu, Sichuan, and Yunnan). I have not attempted to cover all regions of Tibet—an impossible task when you consider that the Tibetan Plateau is a third larger in size than Alaska. Instead I have chosen what I consider to be the "greatest hits" of possible walks.

A big change for me has been the decision to include a trek to such a sacred place as Lhamo Latsho, the "life-spirit" lake of the Dalai Lamas. My reluctance to describe this walk was overcome after I had an audience with Trülku Kalzang at Dzokchen monastery, in the Dege region. He was asking me about my book and which areas were included in it. When I told him I had omitted certain sacred places, including Lhamo Latsho, from my descriptions, he explained to me that the good that comes from people visiting such an important pilgrimage site far outweighs the negative impacts that may accompany tourism. As I listened at his feet, I realized I had no reason to be worried about including the walk to Lhamo Latsho in this book. However, there are still many other special places in Tibet that I have chosen not to describe here. I leave those for you to discover.

Gary McCue
Kathmandu, Nepal

PREFACE TO THE FIRST EDITION

Many changes have occurred in Tibet since I first visited in the summer of 1985. It was an exciting time, for the land border between Nepal and Tibet had just opened. It seemed as if half the people I met were journalists, guidebook writers, or photographers, and almost everybody was bent on adventure: seeking out hidden temples, hitchhiking to the forests along the southern border, trying to be the first to visit an "oracle lake" or a remote cave hermitage. During my six weeks in Tibet I went with several friends on a short trek that had already become popular, from Samye monastery to the town of Dechen Dzong, near Lhasa. It was only a two-and-a-half-day walk, but I remember thinking how amazing it would be to research a trekking book, to have the opportunity to hike throughout a country as unusual as Tibet.

I went back in 1986 for the Tibetan New Year celebrations and the revival of the Monlam Chenmo, the Great Prayer Festival. Once again I went on a short trek, this time from Tshurphu monastery to the Yangpachan Valley, northwest of Lhasa. By 1987 I had definitely decided to compile a trekking guide, and returned to Tibet for nearly four months to research routes. Tibet's trekking and travel scene had become a free-for-all by then, with tens of thousands of tourists moving through the country. I left in September that year, only weeks before the first big political demonstrations rocked Lhasa.

Restrictions were placed on individual travelers, but in 1988 I managed to spend another five months trekking in Tibet. I had grand hopes of completing my trek research in 1989, but only two weeks after I had secured a six-month visa for China, fresh demonstrations erupted and Lhasa was placed under martial rule. My visa melted into the page of my passport, unused.

As a result, people who are well versed in the treks of Tibet may notice a few gaps that otherwise would have been filled in. My dream of trekking to the four great river sources near Mount Kailas never materialized—I hope I can include it in a future edition. Also, I purposely omitted several of Central Tibet's most sacred pilgrimage destinations, which I feel should not be broadcast in a book like this; these are for you to discover.

I have walked each of the treks described; none of the route information is second-hand. Many of the place names used in the descriptions were derived from my conversations with local people. Undoubtedly changes will need to be made, names respelled, and so on. Any corrections or suggestions regarding the text will be greatly appreciated and should be sent to me in care of the publisher.

I hope this book will allow you to enjoy Tibet as much as I have. Treat Tibet kindly, and ask others to do the same. The trekking industry in Tibet is still young and impressionable, but not incapable of learning how to care for the countryside and the culture, especially where trekking and tourism are most popular. This 1200-year-old civilization is rich with unique religions, music, literature, and art. True, many of the important historical sites and monasteries have been knocked down, but like a rare book with the cover torn off, much has remained intact . . . especially in the hearts of the Tibetan people.

Gary McCue
Kathmandu, Nepal 1991

Acknowledgments

The multiyear project to update and expand the second edition of this book has once again been an energetic endeavor that could not have been accomplished without the support of numerous friends and associates. First and foremost, I again wish to thank Kathy Butler, creator of the superb maps and line drawings, my trekking companion, my best friend for the past thirteen years, and my soul mate. I would particularly like to thank wildlife biologist George B. Schaller for generously providing the foreword and for his patient help with the expanded Mammals section. Thanks also go to anthropologist Charles Ramble, for updating "The People and Their Culture" chapter and overhauling the "Tibetan for Trekkers" chapter; Robin Houston, MD, who updated the "Staying Healthy" chapter; geologist Peter Molnar, for his valuable comments on the "Geology" section; Jon Meisler, who contributed both the section "Mountaineering in Tibet" and Appendix D, "Mountaineering Peaks in Tibet"; Salik Ram, of JS Photo, Kathmandu's finest photographic printer; Karma the Khampa, guide extraordinaire and friend extraordinaire; Chris Nielsen, for his continued support and friendship over the years; Francoise M., Francoise B., and all the others at MSF in Lhasa, for sharing their "home" with us each summer; Tashi and Rigdzin, for their warmth, friendship and good food at Tashi 1 and Too; Mr. Hugh Richardson, for his valuable comments on the original text and kind hospitality during our stay in St. Andrews; Matthew Akester, for many a Saturday afternoon of information over Nepali *chiya*; Kalnam at Norbulingka, who cheerfully provided translations and other useful information; Su Ping, Jigme Wangchuk, and Dawa at TIST in Lhasa, for their continued support of my trek research; Mattieu Ricard, who provided valuable information about Kham; Dorjee Tashi, for helping me get where I needed to go; Jiang Lin in Chengdu, for his warm hospitality, and encouragement to expand this book to include East Tibet; Trülku Kalzang at Dzokchen monastery, for his kind assistance and encouragement; anthropologist Toni Huber, for providing endless replies to my endless questions; anthropologists George and Jane Collier, who led me to the Russian maps; G. T. Sonam at Windhorse, for his kind assistance over the years in Tibet; Michael Tan, for all his help in Chengdu; Nicholas Clinch, who shared his amazing library with me; Steve M., for his skill at obtaining information and maps; Jim Edwards and all the staff at Tiger Mountain; Bidur at Mandala Book Point; Bill Abbott, Marsha, and the gang at Wilderness Travel; John Ackerly, who has been most helpful over the years since I caught him reading my mail; Becky and Jennafer Kinsey, Phil Schack, Salmon Patties, Ken Fullmer, May and Tony Cann, and Nick and Lucy Howen, for sharing their homes while I researched the book; Carl R., for his assistance with maps; Thupten Gendun at Holyland Adventures; Tsultrim Palden; Carole LaBranche; Uttara Crees, for all her help in Gyelthang; David Kojo Hakam; Ann Alwyn at the old Inner Asia; Frances Howland; Wendy and Karma Lama; Ashok the Magician; Brett McCue, my car rental agent; the entire Mountaineers Books staff; the Lhasa Holiday Inn manager for dumping my stored luggage without notifying me; all the monks, nuns, and villagers in Tibet who've made my journeys so memorable; and that indomitable pillar in my life, my secretary, accountant, travel agent, stockbroker and mother, Gail McCue. And to a host of others too numerous to mention, but whom I haven't forgotten—to you I extend a hearty *thu je che*!

A NOTE ABOUT SAFETY

Safety is an important concern in all outdoor activities. No guidebook can alert you to every hazard or anticipate the limitations of every reader. Therefore, the descriptions of roads, trails, routes, and natural features in this book are not representations that a particular place or excursion will be safe for your party. When you follow any of the routes described in this book, you assume responsibility for your own safety. Under normal conditions, such excursions require the usual attention to traffic, road and trail conditions, weather, terrain, the capabilities of your party, and other factors. Keeping informed on current conditions and exercising common sense are the keys to a safe, enjoyable outing.

Political conditions may add to the risks of travel in Tibet in ways that this book cannot predict. When you travel, you assume this risk, and should keep informed of political developments that may make safe travel difficult or impossible.

The Mountaineers

The North Face of Mount Everest

ABOUT TREKKING

Pilgrims en route to Samye monastery

1
INTRODUCTION TO TREKKING IN TIBET

Tibet, the largest and highest plateau on the earth, is surrounded by the most extensive jumble of mountains found on any continent. Stretching for almost 1900 miles (3000 km) and forming its entire southern boundary is the Himalaya, and along its western extremity is the equally rugged Karakoram. Between these two ranges are found all fourteen of the world's 8000-meter peaks (26,250 feet or more), including Mount Everest. In Northern Tibet the plateau is a high, arid expanse known as the Chang Thang, the "Northern Plains," while Eastern Tibet is bounded by a succession of mountains (known in Chinese [Chi.] as the Hengduan Shan) where three of Asia's largest rivers cut deep, parallel gorges on their journey from the plateau to the sea.

Many people identify Tibet with the Northern Chang Thang—a desolate, cold, windswept desert on the roof of the world—but an unusually diverse and strikingly beautiful landscape of snowcapped summits, lush rhododendron and conifer forests, and fertile agricultural valleys also lies north of the Himalaya.

The term "Tibet" in this book generally refers to the entire Tibetan Plateau (geographic Tibet), an area encompassing over 800,000 square miles (2.1 million km²) or about one quarter the size of the continental United States. This includes the four traditional regions of Tibet: Ü and Tsang (Lhasa and Shigatse were the original capitals, respectively), which together comprise Central Tibet; Ngari-korsum, the westernmost region, which included the Mount Kailash area and extended into Ladakh; Amdo, the land of nomadic herders in the northeast; and Kham, the forested, easternmost edge of the Plateau.

The Chinese province of Tibet, the Tibet Autonomous Region (TAR), is a political entity created in 1965 that makes up half the geographic area of the Tibetan Plateau, covering 470,000 square miles (1.2 million km²). The outlying regions of the Plateau that are not part of the TAR—including large areas of the Chang Thang—are now within the Chinese provinces of Xinjiang, Qinghai, Gansu, Sichuan, and Yunnan. The ethnographic distribution of the Tibetan people, which includes Tibetans south of the Himalaya as well as those in Ladakh, Spiti, and Lahaul in India, stretches across an area twice the size of the Tibetan Plateau.

A HISTORY OF TREKKING AND EXPLORATION IN TIBET

Until the early eighteenth century, only a handful of Europeans had ever traveled in Tibet; by the dawn of the twentieth century fewer than two dozen foreigners, most of them missionaries, had managed to visit the Holy City of Lhasa. Natural and political barriers were equally formidable, sealing off Tibet from most outsiders. The aura of mystery surrounding Tibet was heightened by Western authors' romantic descriptions of this seemingly impenetrable land.

Europeans first learned of a distant land called "Tubbat" in about the ninth century from Arab traders who plied the silk routes. Marco Polo traveled near Tibet in the thirteenth century on his journey to Kublai Khan's capital in Central China. After the Mongols were driven from China in the fourteenth century, the silk routes were closed off to any further European exploration.

Two centuries later Portuguese Jesuits arrived in India and established a Catholic mission in Goa. In 1624, after hearing stories of a Christian-like religion in a land to the north called "Bhottan," two Jesuit priests, Father Andrade and Father Marques, disguised as Hindu pilgrims, set off to cross the Himalaya near the Ganges River source. They were to become the first Europeans known to enter Tibet. Their warm welcome at Tsaparang, capital of the Guge kingdom in Western Tibet, encouraged them to return the following year to establish a mission. Soon the Jesuits penetrated Central Tibet, and in 1661 Fathers Gruber and d'Orville became the first Europeans to reach Lhasa. Capuchin monks soon followed, and missions were established in Lhasa, but Rome's lack of interest forced the last of these missions to close in 1745. Over the next 100 years the only Europeans known to have reached Lhasa were an unusual British chap, Thomas Manning, and two French Lazarist priests, E. R. Huc and Joseph Gabet. The latter two travelers arrived in 1846 via the northern caravan route from China.

British India had just begun sending trade representatives to Tibet in the late eighteenth century when war broke out between Nepal and Tibet in 1791, prompting a large Chinese army to advance on Kathmandu. After withdrawing from Nepal, the army remained in Tibet, and once again the country was isolated from visitors—this time for a century. India's support of this closure eventually set the stage for a new generation of "unofficial" trekkers: adventurous European travelers, sans Bibles, on hunting trips over the Himalaya from India, or in disguise and armed with pens and journals rather than rifles. An unprecedented number of these adventurers attempted to cross the Chang Thang, some traveling solo, while others financed huge caravans with hundreds of pack animals. British, American, French, Russian, and Swedish travelers all tried their luck reaching Lhasa, but only Ekai Kawaguchi, a resourceful Japanese Buddhist who traveled in disguise as a Chinese monk, was successful.

In August 1904, Lhasa was forcibly unveiled by an invading British army led by Colonel Frank Younghusband. Fearing Russia's rapid expansion through east Asia, the British coerced the Tibetans to sign a treaty that prevented them from dealing with other foreign powers, particularly the Russians. Once the British army returned to India, the Chinese Emperor enforced the policy to prevent further unauthorized visits to Lhasa and Tibet.

With the collapse of the Manchu dynasty in 1911, the Thirteenth Dalai Lama expelled the Chinese and regained complete control of the Tibetan government. The strict closed-door policy toward foreigners was relaxed and the first climbing expeditions were soon permitted to enter Tibet. The British organized eight expeditions to Mount Everest between 1921 and 1938, all of which failed to reach the summit. During this time dozens of intrepid travelers, official and unofficial, made their way into Tibet. One notable visitor was the Frenchwoman Alexandra David-Neel, who disguised herself as a Buddhist pilgrim to become the first European woman to enter Lhasa.

Mao Zedong's Communist army invaded Tibet in 1950. For the next three decades Tibet was closed to foreigners and climbing expeditions, encouraging British and Swiss climbers to approach Everest via a newly opened route through Nepal; in 1953 the British successfully placed Edmund Hillary and Sherpa Tenzing Norgay on the summit using this approach. In 1960 a monumental Chinese expedition put several Tibetan climbers atop Mount Everest via the North Col route from Tibet.

As the constraints of the Cultural Revolution relaxed in the late 1970s, the first commercial tour groups arrived in Lhasa. In the spring of 1981 the first commercial trekkers walked to Dza Rongphu monastery and Everest base camp with photographer Galen Rowell as their group leader. In a style Rowell describes as "truck trekking," the group hiked to the base camp along the dirt road built for the 1960 Chinese Everest expedition while a truck hauled their gear to each successive campsite. Government-organized tours were the only way to trek in Tibet until September 1984, when Lhasa was officially opened to individual travelers. Suddenly the Tibetan countryside was open to anyone keen enough to carry a backpack and set off into the mountains. The number of tourists visiting Tibet quickly mushroomed, peaking at about 43,000 visitors in 1987.

The political disturbances in Tibet between 1987 and 1989 led the Chinese to close the TAR and Lhasa to tourists for nearly three months in 1989. When Tibet reopened, foreigners were again welcomed, but entering the TAR and Lhasa as an individual without a fixed itinerary became more complicated. At present, travelers can choose between trekking as an individual, trekking in a private group with its own itinerary, or joining a commercially organized trek. Each of these styles of trekking is explained in the following sections.

TREKKING AS AN INDIVIDUAL

The main options available to you as an individual trekker are carrying your own pack (backpacking) or hiring a local guide with pack animals. Because of the high elevations in Tibet, do not attempt to backpack unless you are physically fit and well acclimatized to the altitude; many people become breathless just climbing their hotel stairs in Lhasa! The best way to arrange for a guide and pack animals is to inquire at the nearest village to where your trek begins. The standard procedure is to hire one or more pack animals (yak, horse, or burro: 20 to 50 *yuan* per animal per day; in 1999, US$ 1 = 8.28 *yuan*) and a person who will tend the animal(s) (20 to 50 *yuan* per day). Usually one animal can carry the gear of two or three trekkers on a two-week walk. Since most yaks in Tibet do not have nose rings, they cannot be led by rope, nor will they remain on a trail unless they're following another yak. If you have a small group and yaks are the only animals available, you may have to hire two, even if you only need one. Remember to bargain! If the trek does not finish where you started, negotiate a price for the guide's journey home. Paying half wages for each day of his return is fair; in some regions guides insist on full wages.

TREKKING IN A PRIVATE GROUP

There are two options for a private group organizing a trek in Tibet. The first is to contact a commercial trek agency based in your home country, Nepal, or Hong Kong. Using an agency outside Tibet is especially convenient if you want all your trek details arranged ahead of time (before you arrive in Tibet). Although these companies mostly sell trekking packages, they also arrange private "free and individual tourist" (FIT) groups, book international air reservations, and can help plan your itinerary.

The other option is to deal directly with one of the trek companies operating in Lhasa or in one of the "gateway" Chinese cities such as Chengdu, Xining, or Kunming (see Appendix A, "Trekking and Mountaineering Agencies"). Queries are best made by fax or phone; email will soon be available. The price per person per day can be almost half the rate of having a commercial trek agency based in the West (or in Nepal or Hong Kong) handle your plans, but you will be doing all the secretarial work and financial transactions. Trek rates are based on double occupancy, and the larger the group, the lower the price per person. The "leader" rate is typically half price for groups larger than ten people, and free for groups of sixteen or more.

One of the great advantages of organizing your group through a trek agency in Nepal is that these outfits can provide experienced Sherpa camp and cook staff and reliable trek equipment. The price is higher than it would be if you were to book directly, but even the best of Lhasa's trek companies can't equal the services commonly available in Nepal.

To receive a price quote, advise the company of your proposed itinerary, how many days the group will be in Tibet and China, the number of trek days, the group size, and how many nights you will stay in hotels before and after the trek. Also specify whether you want the following:

- Budget, moderate priced, or "best available" hotels
- Full board (meals) at hotels, breakfast only, or meals on your own
- Full board on trek (a good idea; bring extra food to supplement their menu)
- Box lunches while driving overland (expensive and not very exciting; you're better off putting together your own picnic-type lunch)
- Sightseeing with guide and vehicle in Lhasa (or any other gateway city)
- Special sightseeing excursions, for example visiting sites outside the Lhasa Valley
- Personal tents, ground pads, dining tent with chairs and tables, kitchen tent, toilet tent, and staff tents (ask about tent quality; leaky tents are common)
- Cooking pots, utensils, and other kitchen equipment
- Pack animals pre-arranged before the start of your trek
- Single rooms or single-person tents (called a single supplement; this costs extra, whether requested or "forced" by an odd number of trekkers)

Once the trek company has this information, the quote typically includes a local English-speaking Tibetan guide, a cook, transportation to and from the airport if you fly, transportation before and after the trek, supply truck, fuel, drivers, trek staff, cooking stoves and other camp necessities, pack animals, and all necessary permits. The trek company will also arrange the groups' visa authorization at the Chinese embassy of your choice, although each member must pay for his or her own visa. Bring your own sleeping bag, inflatable sleeping pad (optional), daypack or backpack, water bottles, down jacket, and other warm clothing.

TREKKING WITH A COMMERCIAL COMPANY

The beauty of signing up with a commercial trek company is that it takes care of all your day-to-day holiday details—and typically in a very professional manner. If your time is limited, if money is not a problem (in 1999 commercial treks in Tibet rarely cost less than US $180 per person per day, not including international airfare), and if you don't want to plan your own itinerary, then a commercial trek is definitely the way to go.

Most major trek companies produce beautiful color brochures (I call them "wish books") that list the various trips they offer to Tibet, departure dates, plus information about other destinations all over the world. Their services are generally of a very high standard, though companies that don't have fancy brochures can provide fine service as well. A Western group leader often accompanies the group in addition to a local leader, one or more Sherpa guides are often brought from Nepal to assist with the trek, high-quality tents are provided, and meals are usually included once you're in Tibet or mainland China. A recommendation from a friend is one of the best ways to learn about a reputable trek company. Also, most companies have a list of former clients whom you can contact to ask candid questions about their experiences. Adventure travel directories, advertisements in outdoor-oriented magazines, and promotions on the Internet are other ways to find companies specializing in trekking.

Perhaps the biggest drawback to a commercial trek is the inflexible nature of the itinerary: Once the trip starts, you're on a fixed schedule that can rarely be altered. If you enjoy the spontaneity of adventure travel, arranging your own private group may be the preferred alternative to joining an organized commercial trek.

HINTS FOR WOMEN TREKKERS

Tibet is one of the safest destinations in Asia for female travelers. Sexual harassment is almost nonexistent, and the towns and cities are generally very safe—but it is always advisable to be accompanied if you walk after dark. Westerners are typically well accepted by Tibetans, and the culture has few taboos that might inadvertently be broken. However, there are some do's and don'ts to consider.

Your clothes are one of the first things people will notice. Modesty should be a prerequisite. Do not wear shorts or other revealing clothes; calf-length skirts or dresses, or long, loose trousers are best. Tibetan women usually wear an ankle-length dress, called a *chupa,* with a blouse and often some type of jacket.

A long skirt or dress can be convenient for a little privacy when urinating. Tibet has few toilets (most of them you wouldn't want to use), and there seems to be a chronic shortage of handy rocks or bushes to duck behind. One solution is to squat behind an open umbrella! Tibetan women simply hike up their dresses with little concern for who may be nearby. If you're wearing a long dress you can do the same, though wearing underwear makes it a bit more difficult. Trying to find somewhere private to change your clothes or having a proper wash can also be difficult once you're away from the luxury of hotels. On a commercial trek you can bathe with

The bung-gu, *Tibet's most lovable pack animal*

a wash basin in the privacy of your tent. But having a complete wash near a stream is usually not appropriate. Tibetan women in rural areas usually don't wash their bodies except during a yearly bathing festival, so there really isn't a local example to follow. Try sponge bathing; it's easier to be modest when you're washing small areas of your body at a time. Packaged moist towelettes are useful for quick clean-ups. Bring plenty of facial lotion, moisturizer, and hand cream—the combination of cold water and dry winds can cause chapping and cracked skin.

In Central Tibet women can enter most Buddhist temples, but occasionally a protector's chapel *(gönkhang)* will be off limits. Kham and Amdo are more strict; women can rarely enter a *gönkhang,* and some monasteries won't even allow women into the courtyard. Women having their period may be prevented from entering monasteries, and I know one woman who was asked to leave a home when the family learned she was menstruating. Sanitary napkins are now available in Tibet's larger cities, but tampons are not; bring enough and then some. To dispose of feminine hygiene products while trekking, wrap in toilet paper, place in a plastic bag, and carry out for disposal when you reach a large city. Animals (and people) tend to dig up anything that's buried, and burning is near impossible. Also note that it is not unusual for women to skip their period while on a trek.

WHEN TO GO TREKKING

In general the best season for trekking is from May through October. The weather during these months is surprisingly mild, with warm days and cool to chilly nights in the mountains: not very different from summer conditions in many mountain ranges of

America and Europe. July and August can be very rainy, receiving over half of Tibet's annual precipitation. India's monsoon manages to push over the Himalaya into much of West, Central, and Eastern Tibet, bringing rain (and sometimes snow) most nights and occasionally during the day. At this time of year even the most barren hills don a fuzzy green coating of grass, while up in the alpine areas the valleys become lush and speckled with wildflowers and blooming shrubs.

By September, autumn is knocking on the door. The days are cooler and the willow and poplar leaves begin turning yellow. Indian summers are not uncommon and may last into late October or early November, bringing sunny days and clear, crisp nights with temperatures often near freezing. But September and October can also bring surprise snowstorms to the mountains.

The coldest time of the year is December through February, but this is also a time when Tibet often experiences extended periods of clear, sunny weather. In the high mountain areas the snowfall is generally too great to consider winter treks. However, the regions around Lhasa, Shigatse, and Dingri in Central Tibet, and the Dege and Labrang/Rebkong regions in Eastern Tibet receive relatively little snow; while it is generally cold, the trekking can still be enjoyable.

In March the lower-altitude valleys start to warm and show signs of spring. A jacket is no longer needed on sunny afternoons and the winds start losing their chill. May and June are usually the hottest and most windy months in Central Tibet. Wind is common throughout the year in most areas of Tibet, but during these months it can be particularly bad. Billowing afternoon dust storms occasionally engulf the larger Central Tibetan valleys such as the Lhasa and Tsangpo River basins. A cotton surgical-type mask is recommended for dusty road conditions.

As in any mountainous region, the weather can change quickly and snow is possible *any* month of the year. Even in summer it is advisable to carry winter clothing, particularly if you plan to ascend above 16,000 feet (4880 m). But more often than not the weather in Tibet is fine and wonderfully clear.

Taking a break on the World's Highest Trek

2
PREPARING FOR YOUR TREK

Getting ready to travel internationally and trek in a remote region such as Tibet can be surprisingly time-consuming. The process of booking air tickets, obtaining a passport (if you don't have one or if it has expired), applying for visas, and organizing clothes and trekking gear is almost like taking on a second job. Start working on these details at least three months in advance—even then you'll be surprised at how much you haven't done by the last week before you head off. And no matter how busy you are, don't neglect getting those legs and lungs in shape.

PHYSICAL CONDITIONING

Start your physical fitness program several months before you arrive in Tibet. Walking, hiking, and backpacking over rugged terrain are the best ways to prepare for a trek. Any regular regime of strenuous aerobic exercise is also beneficial, especially running, cross-country skiing, swimming, and bicycling. Be creative. Regular sessions of running up and down multiple flights of stairs in an office or apartment building can improve fitness, and people who frequently practice more passive types of exercise such as yoga are often in excellent shape for trekking. Don't tell yourself you'll get in shape after a few days of walking. When you climb toward a high pass on your second or third day of trekking, you'll be a lot happier if you exercised regularly before arriving in Tibet.

LEARNING ABOUT TIBET

Your travels will be enhanced tremendously if you make the effort to learn about Tibet's unique culture and people (see Appendix B, "Suggested Reading"). If your local library doesn't have certain titles, try the interlibrary loan system. Other resources include university libraries (particularly schools with an Asian Studies program), mountaineering club libraries, and specialty bookstores. For extensive mail order "dream" catalogues of Himalaya and Tibet titles, contact Chessler Books, P.O. Box 4359, Evergreen, CO 80437, tel. (800) 654-8502 or (303) 670-0093, email: chesslerbk@aol.com; Yak and Yeti Books, P.O. Box 5736, Rockville, MD 20855, tel. (301) 869-5860, fax (301) 869-4438; and on the Internet try Amazon.com, www.amazon.com. Also, *The Reader's Guide to Periodical Literature*, available in most libraries, is a voluminous catalog that indexes articles from hundreds of magazines according to subject.

VISA REGULATIONS

United States citizens traveling abroad must carry a valid U.S. passport. If you do not have a passport or if it has expired, you will need to apply for a new one at least a month before your departure. Large cities have government passport agencies, and your local post office should have the proper application forms. It takes about four weeks after submitting the application to receive a new passport by mail. You will also need a Chinese visa, which is required for everyone visiting Tibet. These visas can be obtained from the Embassy of the People's Republic of China, 2201 Wisconsin Ave. NW, Washington, DC 20007, tel. (202) 262-9809; or at the Chinese consulates in Chicago, New York, and San Francisco.

Most commercial trekking companies now use expensive but efficient visa processing agencies to handle clients' visa applications. The alternative is go to the embassy yourself or call to request application forms, then submit them by mail along with your passport (not a copy) and the appropriate visa fee. To be safe, use only registered or express mail. Embassies usually know the return express mail charge, which can be included with the visa fee. Money orders or bank drafts are preferred; personal checks must clear before a visa will be issued.

For Chinese visas, note that unless the embassy or consulate has received prior authorization to issue a visa (this can only be done by a travel company based in Tibet or China), anyone planning to visit the TAR will be denied a Chinese visa if Tibet or any city in Tibet is listed in the "Places to be visited in China" section of the visa application. Either don't mention Tibet on the form, or contact your trek company to obtain the necessary authorization. If you are in a group that will enter Tibet from Nepal, consider having the visa authorization sent to the Chinese embassy in Kathmandu. The visa office is only open Monday, Wednesday, and Friday, 10:00 A.M. to 11:00 A.M. Standard service takes one week. Rush service is more costly but processed the same day. Individuals are not very welcome at this embassy, but with confirmed air tickets it has been possible to obtain a visa for travel to mainland China from Bangkok, Hong Kong, or other Asian cities, but not via Nepal to Tibet.

On your journey to Tibet you may pass through Hong Kong, Thailand, or Nepal. Each of these places will issue an entry visa good for fifteen days or more upon your arrival. India, however, does not allow travelers to enter without a valid Indian visa. You will be sent back on the next plane if you try! Even transit passengers are advised to have an Indian visa to prevent being locked in the transit lounge if their connecting flight is delayed or canceled. The Indian Embassy is located at 2536 Massachusetts Avenue NW, Washington, DC 20008, tel. (202) 939-9861; consulates are in Chicago, New York, and San Francisco.

GETTING TO TIBET

The main airline hub to Lhasa is through Chengdu, capital of China's Sichuan Province, with daily year-round flights. Less frequent connections to Lhasa from mainland China operate via Bejing, Chongqing, Xining, and Xian. The only international service to Lhasa (as of 1999) are the seasonal Saturday and Tuesday flights from April to November. During the peak tourist season (starting the first week of July), an extra plane is added on Thursdays. All incoming flights to Lhasa land at Gongkar Airport in the Tsangpo River Valley. The 56-mile (90-km) drive to the city takes about 90 minutes in a minibus, and 2 hours or more on the China Southwest Airlines (CSWA) airport bus. Note that the CSWA offices in Kathmandu and Chengdu may refuse to sell tickets for Lhasa to anyone who is not in an official group of five or more people. When this rule is enforced, individuals wishing to fly to Lhasa must first join a short two- to three-day tour sold by local travel agents before the CSWA office will issue a ticket. A second airport (Bangda) has opened near the city of Chamdo, in Eastern TAR, with year-round connections four times per week from Chengdu. In Yunnan, flights operate daily from Kunming to Lijiang, and several times per week to Gyelthang.

The principle overland route into Tibet is from Nepal along the Lhasa-Kathmandu Friendship Highway (also called the Arniko Friendship Highway). This three-day, 600-mile (1000-km) journey is a rugged but beautiful drive crossing several high passes, including the 17,025-foot (5190-m) Lakpa La pass. Commercial trek and tour groups arriving at the border town of Zhangmu (Tib., Dram; Nepali, Khasa) from Nepal are met at the Chinese immigration post by their local tour guide, who then presents the group's travel permits to the border officials. The rules for individual travelers going from Nepal into Tibet via Zhangmu are constantly changing. In Kathmandu, the best information comes from travelers who have just returned from Tibet. Or, go to the border and see if the Chinese immigration authorities will allow you to enter. If you are turned away, try again later that day or the next day. Perseverance often works!

Makalu (l.), Lhotse Shar (m.), and Everest (r.) from the Kathmandu-Lhasa flight

Several other major land routes into Tibet include the Tibet-Qinghai Highway from Golmud, in Qinghai Province, and the long, rugged Tibet-Sichuan Highway from Chengdu and Kunming, a spectacular journey that climbs over perhaps a dozen mountain ranges and crosses the Yangtze, Mekong, and Salween rivers in Eastern Tibet. From June to mid-September the less mountainous northern route from Chengdu to Lhasa via Nakchu is preferred for avoiding landslides and swollen rivers. Another access route to Tibet is the road from Kashgar, an oasis market town in China's Xinjiang Province. This route goes to Mount Kailash via Aksai Chin, an area that has been controlled by China since a 1962 border war with India. The road crosses four major passes over 17,000 feet (5200 m). Since the early 1990s it has been possible to enter and exit the Kailash region in Western Tibet via a new trek route between Purang and Simikot in Western Nepal.

MAPS

While road maps of Tibet are now available, good topographical maps for trekking are more difficult to obtain. The best maps in English are the Joint Operations Graphic (JOG) maps, Series 1501, 1:250,000 scale with 100-meter (328-ft) contours, published by the Defense Mapping Agency Topographic Center in Washington, DC; and the 1:250,000 L500 Series (China) printed by the Army Map Service (AMS), Corps of Engineers, Washington, DC. The topographical data is generally good, but the names and locations of towns and roads are prone to inaccuracies. Still, they are a useful complement to the trekking maps in this book.

The map libraries of the Library of Congress in Washington, DC, and the National Archives in Alexandria, Virginia, have most of the 1501 and L500 Series maps that have been produced (not all of Tibet was mapped in these series), but they may not allow these maps to be photocopied; you should be able to trace them. The best alternative is to visit the map library of a university with a large Asian Studies or Geography department, where photocopies are more readily obtained.

The 1:250,000 topographic maps listed below are available for Tibet. Seven maps (noted with an asterisk) are often found in large map libraries; the others are more difficult to locate. Several small corners of Tibet appear in the AMS Series U502 1:250,000 maps covering India and Nepal. Each map has a code number: NH is the region, followed by a section number (44, 45, etc.), with maps in each section numbered 1 to 36; for the U501 series, the section numbers are A–X.

Joint Operations Graphic (JOG), Series 1501 Maps: La-tzu-Tsung (west of Shigatse), NH 45-11; Zih-k'a-tse (Shigatse), NH 45-12; Tamshun (Damzhung, north of Lhasa), NH 46-5; Shunta (north of Tsethang), NH 46-6; *Lhasa, NH 46-9; Tsetang, NH 46-10; *Namche Barwa, NH 46-12.

Army Map Service (AMS), Series L500 Maps: Kang-ti-ssu Shan-mo (Mount Kailash, Western Tibet), NH 44-3; *Manasarowar, NH 44-7; *Mustang, NH 44-12; *Tingri Dzong (Shishapangma/Western Everest region), NH 45-14; *Gyantse/(Gyangtse), NH 45-16; *Yamdrog Tsho, NH 46-13.

Army Map Service (AMS), Series U501 Maps (1:253,440): Khampa Dzong (west of Gyangtse), H-45 W.

Currently the best available topographical maps of Tibet are a 1:200,000 Russian series, but they are in Cyrillic, not English! All of Tibet and China (and the world) is covered with remarkable accuracy, though data for roads and towns was last updated in the 1970s. Only a few universities with large Geography departments have these maps in their collection. Also useful are the 1:253,440 Survey of India maps produced before 1947, but their availability seems to be limited to British map collections. A more readily accessible but much larger-scale set of maps covering Tibet and Asia is the Tactical Pilot Charts, Series TPC (1:500,000). Sheets H-9B and H-10A cover most of Central Tibet; H-10B includes most of Kham; and G-8C covers much of Amdo. These are meant for aeronautic navigational use, as are the Operational Navigational Chart maps, Series ONC (1:1,000,000); sheets ONC H-9 and ONC H-10 include the southern half of Tibet, from Mount Kailash across to Kham; and ONC G-8 covers most of Northeast Tibet and Amdo. The TPC and ONC map series are available from the Defense Mapping Agency, DMA CSC, Attention: PMA, Washington, DC, 20315-0020, tel. (301) 436-6990; specialty map stores often have them in stock as well. Cordee Books and Maps in Great Britian, 0533-543579, tel., publishes several useful 1:100,000 maps for trekkers. Produced by the Chinese Institute of Glaciology Mapping, these maps include #MW227 Mount Xixabangma (Shishapangma), and #MW239 Namjagbarwa (Namche Barwa). Each of these maps has trekking and approach maps marked and helpful information on the region and how to reach it is given in English on the reverse.

EQUIPMENT AND CLOTHING

If you trek in Tibet with a commercial company, they will supply all the necessary camping equipment. Some outfits provide sleeping bags and parkas for use during the trek, a bonus that can save you hundreds of dollars if you have little use for such gear after the trek. If you are organizing a private group, ask your agent whether the necessary tents and kitchen equipment are included in the price quote (see "Trekking in a Private Group").

When planning your clothing needs for a trek, think in terms of layers. Layers of clothing will keep you warm, but can be removed gradually to prevent you from overheating. During spring and autumn the night temperatures in the mountains often dip below freezing, making warm gear essential. In summer the days can be hot, requiring light cotton clothing. Good wet-weather gear is recommended during the rainy summer months. The mountainous regions of Tibet can receive snow any month of the year; be prepared for cold weather if you plan to trek at elevations above 16,000 feet (4880 m). Below is a list of suggested equipment, clothing, and accessories for Tibet.

EQUIPMENT

Footwear. Hiking boots should have thick soles and be high enough to provide adequate ankle support. The newer lightweight boots are more comfortable but less durable than all-leather hiking boots. Consider Gore-Tex–lined boots for treks during the rainy summer months. Optional: A pair of thongs or sneakers to wear in camp.

Packs. If you plan to backpack, use a pack with a wide, cushioned waist belt and thick shoulder straps that will comfortably support weight. On commercial treks you only need a daypack to carry your daily essentials. This pack should have padded shoulder straps, a wide waist belt, and a volume of about 1,500 to 2,000 cubic inches.

Duffel bag. Long (36 inches or so), heavy-duty canvas or nylon bag that can be secured with a padlock. Waterproof by lining it with one or two thick plastic bags.

Sleeping bag. A three-season (spring-summer-autumn), mummy-style down or fiber-filled bag rated to about 10 to 15°F.

Inner sheet. A silk or cotton inner sheet minimizes the need to wash your sleeping bag.

Sleeping pad. Choose a full-length, self-inflating, or standard closed-cell foam pad.

Rain gear. Your raincoat should be roomy, mid-thigh in length, and have a waterproof hood. Rain pants can double as wind pants. Gore-Tex, Japara, or high-quality coated nylon materials are best.

Tent. A sturdy, lightweight, waterproof nylon tent with collapsible aluminum poles is best. Dome tents are heavy but well liked for their high ceilings.

Fuel stove. Choose an efficient lightweight camping stove that can burn kerosene, the most readily available liquid cooking fuel in Tibet.

Water bottle. Take along one or two plastic or metal leakproof quart or liter bottles.

CLOTHING

Thermal underwear. Bring one or two pairs of long-sleeved tops and bottoms made from wool, silk, polypropylene, or a similar synthetic fiber. Short-sleeved thermal tops are good on cool days while trekking. Avoid cotton long underwear.

Cotton underpants. Bring four or five pairs.

Socks. Have at least three pairs of wool/wool-mix socks, and several pairs of cotton socks. Hand-knit wool socks are available in Lhasa and Kathmandu.

Shirts. Bring a long-sleeved shirt made of wool, flannel, or chamois; a long-sleeved stay-press cotton shirt; and two or three cotton T-shirts.

Pants. Men should plan on taking one pair of loose-fitting wool or fiberpile pants and one pair of lighter-weight cotton pants. Women should bring several changes of mid-calf–length dresses or skirts, though loose-fitting pants are also acceptable. Shorts are not appropriate at any time in Tibet for men or women.

Sweater. Choose wool or wool mix with a high neck for extra warmth.

Jacket. A fiberpile jacket is ideal for trekking and evenings in camp.

Insulated coat or parka, with hood. A heavy-duty down or fiber-filled coat is usually not necessary from mid-May to mid-September. During other months most evenings you'll want to wear one that can fit over bulky clothing, with 14 to 16 ounces of down or 18 to 20 ounces of a fiber-fill material.

Headgear. Bring along a wool or fiberpile ski-style cap or balaclava for warmth. A lightweight brimmed hat is good for sun protection. Inexpensive broad-brimmed straw and felt hats are sold in Tibet's city markets. *Buła + Sun Hat*

Scarf. Wool or silk is best, or use a fiberpile neck gaiter.

Mittens or gloves. Wool, pile, or polypropylene are best.

Bandanna or handkerchief. Bring several.

ACCESSORIES AND EXTRAS

Many of the following items are optional. Don't try to bring everything—you would need a herd of yak to carry it all! On commercial treks the weight limit for personal duffel bags is approximately 42 pounds (20 kg).

Pocket knife. Swiss Army–style is best.

Sewing kit. One small kit. A leather sewing awl is ideal for big repairs.

Duct tape. One small roll for repairs.

Compass. For use with trail descriptions and orientation with maps.

Altimeter. Measures altitude as a function of the barometric pressure.

Maps. I wouldn't go trekking without them. See "Maps," earlier in this chapter.

Gaiters. Good for winter treks or wet trails during rainy summer months.

Insulated booties. Down or fiber-fill, for the colder months.

Umbrella. The lightweight collapsible kind for rain and hot sunshine.

Waterproof ground sheet or poncho. Can double as a tarp when it rains.

Cooking pots. Necessary only if you are trekking as an individual.

Utensils. Supplied on commercial treks. Carry your own chopsticks.

Drinking cup. For the ubiquitous butter tea offered when visiting a monastery or a Tibetan home. Carry it in your daypack.

Nylon cord. Fifteen to twenty feet for a clothesline.

Toilet paper. Stock up before the trek. Burn after using or pack it out.

Tampons or sanitary napkins. Only sanitary napkins are available in Tibet.

Cigarette lighter. Superior to matches when burning used toilet paper.

Toiletries. Use a small stuff sack to hold your toothbrush, toothpaste, comb, soapdish, dental floss, skin moisturizer, and perhaps a mirror.

Towel. Two small, thin towels are preferable to one thick towel.

Moist towelettes. For quick "tent baths."

Flashlight. A headlamp is ideal for camping. Chinese AA and D batteries are common

Fox-skin hat

but of poor quality, but AA and AAA alkalines are now available.

Plastic bags. A few of each size, from sandwich-sized to strong trash bags.

Sunglasses. For Tibet's bright, high-altitude sunlight. Dark glacier glasses with side hoods are necessary in the mountains and after fresh snowfalls.

Sun creams and lip balm. Sun block rated 15 SPF or higher is best. Use zinc oxide for a total blockout. Lip balms prevent burning and chapping.

Journal, reading book, writing materials. For quiet moments.

Camera. You'll regret not bringing one.

Binoculars. Good for observing birds, wildlife, and distant scenery.

Shortwave radio. Bring earphones so you don't disturb others.

Portable tape recorder. To bring home the music and sounds of Tibet.

Money pouch or belt. For your passport, money, and valuable papers.

Frisbee. Great entertainment; doubles as a salad bowl!

Pictures from home. Personal photographs of your children, pets, city, house, and so on are a great way to bridge the language barrier with local people.

Snack foods. Nuts, chocolate bars, granola bars, dried fruit, hard candies, beef jerky, and flavored drink mixes are much-appreciated trail treats.

Watch. Useful for pacing yourself with the trek descriptions in this book.

PHOTOGRAPHY IN TIBET

Contrary to what many people believe, a fancy camera is not necessary to take excellent photographs: The person who stands behind the camera is responsible for that. While a pocket-sized point-and-shoot camera is ideal for quick, candid photos, a 35mm single-lens reflex (SLR) camera with interchangeable lenses is the most versatile for creative travel photography. With a 35–70mm zoom and a 70–210mm zoom you can cover a wide range of photographic possibilities, though fixed focal length lenses are generally faster and allow you to shoot slower, fine grained films. Buy the best lens you can afford; don't be tempted to purchase an inexpensive lens made by an unknown manufacturer. Most of the broken or jammed lenses I've seen on treks have not been major brand names. Always test new camera gear by shooting a roll of film at home and having it processed. And read the instruction booklet. Remember you must carry your own camera gear while trekking. Don't overload yourself, but avoid packing any camera equipment in your duffel bag; it will get banged about all day in the back of a vehicle or while tied to a yak.

Dust is a big concern in Tibet's arid climate. Always keep your camera in its protective case or in a padded carrying bag, and avoid changing film or lenses in the wind. A lens-cleaning kit with a camel-hair brush is a must. In cold weather, cover your gear at night or put it inside your sleeping bag to prevent mechanical parts from seizing. Bring several extra sets of camera batteries, as they may not be available in Tibet. If you are shopping for an electronic SLR camera, consider one that operates on a manual setting without batteries.

The light in Tibet can be tricky to capture properly on film. Early mornings and late afternoons are typically best for dramatic pictures; the midday light in Tibet is often harsh, causing contrasty photos. Try using a polarizing filter to enhance colors and the sky, especially on hazy days. Dial it about one-third of a turn from dark for the best results. ASA 25, 50, 64, or 100 color slide film is best for sharp, vivid outdoor photography; 200 or 400 ASA is best for limited light situations. Ten or fifteen rolls of film for a three-week trip should be sufficient. Brand-name print film and 100 ASA slide film is available in Lhasa; try the camera shops on the street running south from the main post office, or the Lhasa Hotel.

The Tibetan people are as tough to capture on film as the high-altitude light. They can be rather averse to being photographed, or may demand money. Please, *never* pay for a photograph. Always ask permission to take someone's picture, and respect a refusal. To break the ice, have them look through the view finder (a wide-angle or telephoto lens is best), or point to the shutter and have them take a picture of you. Most Tibetans are convinced every camera will produce instant pictures. To be fair, be sure to explain that you have only film inside your camera. Phrases such as *Nga khyerang-gi par gyebna drik-gi-re-pe?* ("May I take your picture?") and *Parche nangla pingshok du. Danda par mindu* ("Inside my camera is only film; no pictures now") are worth learning.

Always ask permission before taking photographs in monasteries. Monks at the larger *gompas* are required to collect photography fees from tourists, usually a flat rate ranging from 5 to 20 *yuan* (US $0.60 to $2.50). Some monasteries and temples, particularly in Kham and Amdo, do not allow any photography. To avoid an unpleasant scene, don't try to sneak photographs. A wide-angle lens is good for capturing the feeling of temple interiors; for wall frescoes, try bouncing your flash to prevent flaring on the shiny murals.

MOUNTAINEERING IN TIBET
BY JON MEISLER

The mountains of the Tibetan Plateau represent one of the earth's last great mountaineering challenges. Since China opened its peaks to international expeditions in 1980, a surprisingly small number of climbers have ventured into the mountains of the Tibetan Plateau, mostly due to complicated logistics and a lack of knowledge regarding the potential for mountaineering.

The Chinese Mountaineering Association (CMA) in Beijing oversees all of the provincial mountaineering offices in China and can provide useful expedition information. If you have a specific peak in mind, it is often more efficient to contact the mountaineering association for the province in which the peak is located (see Appendix A, "Trekking and Mountaineering Agencies"). After deciding on the peak, the climbing route, expedition dates, and your group size, fax or mail this information to the appropriate mountaineering association along with your return address and fax number. The association will fax back regarding the peak's availability and cost estimates.

Once the decision to climb a peak has been made, fax the passport information (full name, nationality, passport number, passport expiration date, birth date, age, sex, and occupation) for each team member and any Sherpas accompanying the climb. The association will then request a cash deposit via bank transfer. The amount will vary depending on the association used; some may request the entire expedition fee at this time. A word of caution: In the last few years there have been several travel companies operating in Yunnan, Sichuan, and Qinghai Provinces which have falsely claimed they can procure permits for mountaineering expeditions. Make sure the organization you are using is legitimate before sending money.

Once the mountaineering association has your deposit or full payment, they will ask which Chinese embassy or consulate you would prefer to have process your visas. An official invitation letter will then be sent to this embassy or consulate requesting the visas to be issued.

The costs for mountaineering in Tibet depend on peak height, location (whether it is in a restricted area or not), climbing route, and length of the expedition. The association also charges a daily rate for vehicles and drivers, a liaison officer/translator, food for any accompanying staff, hiring pack animals, an environmental fee, vehicle waiting fees, and photography fees.

To help reduce mountaineering costs, chose a peak that has already been climbed, or one that is relatively close to the provincial capital where the mountaineering association is located. Expeditions are charged for the type and number of vehicles used as well as for mileage. In some cases it is not necessary to use expensive four-wheel drives; minibuses are usually adequate and considerably cheaper. Make sure the vehicle you are using is fit for the drive. Ask the association for a test drive around town at least a day before departure.

Photography fees are negotiable, and shooting stills is much cheaper than video. Cooking your own food in base camp can eliminate the need to hire a cook. If your peak is near the provincial capital, request that just one emergency vehicle remain at base camp and have all others return while you climb. This will save on vehicle waiting fees and rental costs.

Virtually any peak in Tibet or China can be climbed if the price is right, though location in a restricted area increases the cost. Each provincial mountaineering association has a list of open peaks (see Appendix D, "Mountaineering Peaks in Tibet"). If you are interested in a peak that is not on this list, send queries to the appropriate association for a quotation.

Jon Meisler is founder and one of the principle guides of High Asia Exploratory Mountain Travel Company. He lives in China.

A touching farewell from the nuns of Samtenling ani gompa, *above Reting*

3
STAYING HEALTHY

Trekking in Tibet is relatively safe despite the remoteness of trekking areas; with common sense, preparation, and some basic medical knowledge, most illnesses or injures can be treated with a properly stocked personal first-aid kit.

There is no emergency helicopter service in Tibet. If anybody becomes sick or injured and requires evacuation, he or she must be carried or ride a pack animal to the nearest road head. An emergency ambulance service (dial 120) is now operational in Lhasa and will expand to cover Central Tibet.

PRE-TREK PREPARATIONS

Prior to departure, visit your physician. Most treks in Tibet are rather strenuous and occur at elevations from 12,000 to 17,000 feet (3660 to 5200 m). People with diabetes, asthma, or high blood pressure can successfully trek in Tibet, but should check with a doctor about potential problems and precautions. Most trekking companies require all clients to submit a medical examination report signed by a physician. Also, consider having a dental checkup.

IMMUNIZATIONS

The Centers for Disease Control (CDC) in Atlanta, Georgia (tel. [404] 639-3311; automated number [888] 232-3228; www.cdc.gov/travel/html) can provide the most up-to-date information about immunizations. In some cities, specialized travelers' health clinics, university clinics, or county public health clinics offer inoculations and advice about health situations around the world. Update your diphtheria, measles, polio, and rubella immunizations, even though China and Tibet require no specific inoculations for entry. Also note the following:

Recommended Immunizations: Hepatitis A, tetanus, and typhoid (oral).

Immunizations or Protection Worth Considering: Malaria (not a concern in Tibet, unless travel plans include known malarial areas), meningitis (only if you plan to trek in Nepal), rabies.

Not Recommended: Cholera.

FIRST-AID KIT

Always carry a basic first-aid kit, even if you are with a commercial trekking company. The quantities suggested below are based on the needs of one person during a three-week visit in Tibet. Consult your doctor for appropriate dosages. A must for all trekking group first-aid kits is James Wilkerson's *Medicine for Mountaineering* (see Appendix B, "Suggested Reading").

MEDICATIONS
ANALGESICS AND ANTI-INFLAMMATORIES

Aspirin, Acetaminophen, or Paracetamol. 20 tablets (5 grains/325 to 500 mg). Aspirin is better as an anti-inflammatory.

Acetaminophen or Paracetamol with codeine. 10 tablets (325 mg plus 30 mg codeine). Good for moderately severe pain and to suppress coughs.

Ibuprofen. 10 tablets (200 or 400 mg). A good anti-inflammatory.

ANTIBIOTICS

Cephalexin. 20 tablets (250 mg). A penicillin-based drug for skin infections and abscesses, and for chest, urinary, inner ear, and sinus infections. Substitute with Erythromycin (250 mg) for those allergic to penicillin.

Trimethoprim/sulfamethoxazole. 10 "double-strength" tablets (160 mg/800 mg) for urinary infections, chest infections, and sinusitis.

Tinidazole. 4 to 8 tablets (500 mg) for intestinal parasites such as *giardia* and amebas. Substitute 15 to 30 tablets of metronidazole (200 mg).

Norfloxacin. 24 tablets (400 mg) for treating bacterial diarrhea. Ciprofloxacin (500 mg) is equally effective but expensive.

Ophthalmic antibiotic cream or drops. To relieve conjunctivitis and other eye infections.

Antibiotic ointment. May prevent slightly infected cuts from worsening.

ANTIDIARRHEA AND GASTROINTESTINAL MEDICATIONS

Loperamide or Lomotil. 10 tablets to stop diarrhea.
Antacid tablets (optional). 24 tablets for upset or acid stomach.
Oral rehydration salts. 2 packets for diarrhea.
Antiworm medication/Antihelminth (optional). 6 tablets (100 mg).
Laxative (optional). 5 suppositories or tablets.
Antivomiting medication (optional). 5 suppositories or tablets (25 mg).

ANTIHISTAMINES

Diphenhydramine (50 mg) **or Chlorpheniramine** (4 mg). 5 tablets for severe itching, rashes, or swelling from allergic reactions or for insect bites, hay fever, cold symptoms, motion sickness, and insomnia at high elevations.

DECONGESTANTS AND RESPIRATORY MEDICATIONS

Nasal decongestant. 10 tablets for relief of cold and sinus symptoms.
Throat lozenges. 10 pieces or more (hard candies are a good substitute).
Nose spray or drops (optional). 1 small bottle (0.25 to 0.50 percent solution).
Aromatic balms (optional). Used as an inhalant or a chest rub; several brands are also excellent topical anti-inflammatories for muscle pain.

HIGH-ALTITUDE MEDICATION

Acetazolamide. 10 tablets (250 mg) for prevention of AMS.
Dexamethasone (optional). 5 tablets (4 mg) for high altitude cerebral edema (emergency use only).

BANDAGES, DRESSINGS, AND BURN TREATMENT

10 adhesive strips
1 roll of 1" cloth adhesive tape or micropore tape
1 3" wide elastic bandage
2 packets of 4" x 4" sterile gauze pads
2 2" gauze rolls
5 butterfly bandages
1 triangular bandage or a large handkerchief
2 3" x 5" sheets of moleskin
2 5" x 9" sheets of sterile petroleum dressing
Aloe vera lotion for healing burns

DISINFECTANTS
Merbromine solution. A good drying agent for cuts.
Povidone-iodine (betadine) (optional). A topical disinfectant.
Alcohol pads.

MISCELLANEOUS SUPPLIES

Safety pins

Thermometer (low-reading, if possible)

Sewing needles

Cotton swabs (optional)

Scissors

Cotton masks (for dusty roads)

Tweezers

HEALTH AND MEDICAL PROBLEMS
INTESTINAL ILLNESSES

Travelers' diarrhea, one of the most common health problems facing trekkers in Tibet and Asia, is primarily due to infections from bacteria, giardia, or amebas. A stool examination is best for determining both the cause and the treatment; if you are in a remote area, weigh the evidence of your symptoms and make an educated guess regarding the proper treatment.

All drinking water should be boiled or purified with iodine (see "Water Purification") including city tap water. Wash your hands often with soap and don't lick your fingers. Peel or wash fresh fruits and vegetables before eating, and avoid food that's been left sitting out or has been exposed to flies.

BACTERIAL DIARRHEA

Most travelers' diarrhea in Asia is due to a bacterial infection. The onset is typically abrupt, and symptoms vary from mild discomfort to frequent watery stools, nausea, cramping, vomiting, or fever. Pus, mucus, and blood may also be present in the stool.

Bacterial diarrhea is often self-limiting and will usually go away within two to seven days. Treatment with an antibiotic (norfloxacin or ciprofloxacin) may shorten the duration of illness. Lomotil or Imodium is useful for limiting the frequency of movements but do not kill the microorganisms causing the problem. Avoid dehydration by drinking plenty of fluids and use oral rehydration salts (one packet to a quart or liter of purified water).

GIARDIASIS

Diarrhea with no blood or pus lasting more than a week is often caused by the protozoa *Giardia lamblia*. Giardia is usually less severe than a bacterial infection and has a gradual onset a week or more after ingesting contaminated food or water. A bloated, grumbling stomach, cramps, and sulfurous, rotten egg–smelling burps or gas are classic complaints. The diarrhea is usually not watery but moderately frequent, occurring three to five times a day. Fever and vomiting are uncommon. Unlike bacterial infections, this type of diarrhea can linger for weeks if left untreated.

The standard medication for giardia is tinidazole, which is available in most Asian countries but not in the United States. A substitute is metronidazole. Avoid alcohol while using either of these drugs.

AMEBIC DYSENTERY

Most travelers in Tibet and Asia don't contract amebic diarrhea, which is caused by the water-born protozoa *Endamaeba histolytica*. Typical symptoms are frequent bowel movements producing only small amounts of stool (blood and pus may be present), alternating with days of normal movements, or constipation in cycles lasting one to three days. Vague but chronic abdominal cramps, fatigue, and weight loss may occur if left untreated.

Diagnosing an amebic infection is not easy, even for a laboratory. Treatment is an initial three-day course of Tinidazole, followed by a ten-day course of Diloxanide furoate.

FOOD POISONING

Food poisoning is caused by eating food contaminated with toxins elaborated by certain bacteria (salmonella, staphalococcus). These microorganisms thrive in warm foods stored without proper refrigeration, such as hotel buffets. Eggs, poultry, mayonnaise, raw meat, and casserole-type dishes are most susceptible. The onset is typically abrupt and violent, often within 6 hours after eating. Primary symptoms are severe vomiting and frequent diarrhea, sometimes with blood and pus. Nausea, abdominal cramps, and fever with chills may be present. Recovery time is usually quick, with symptoms lasting 12 to 24 hours. Keeping hydrated is important, but usually medication is not necessary.

WATER PURIFICATION

Even in the mountains of Asia and Tibet, water should be either boiled or purified with iodine. Filtering will remove sediments, but may not kill certain microorganisms. Few chemical purifiers are available in Tibet.

BOILING

Water must come to a rolling boil to kill all pathogenic organisms. Although water boils at a lower temperature at higher elevations, the boiling point at 20,000 feet (6100 m) is still high enough (176°F, 80°C) to kill all the microorganisms that cause intestinal infections.

CHEMICAL DISINFECTANTS

Iodine is the best chemical treatment for contaminated water. For very cold or murky water, either double the purification time or the dosage. If a flavoring is used, add it after the iodine has had time to purify the water. A vitamin C tablet dissolved in the water removes the iodine taste.

Iodine in the form of tablets (tetraglycine hydroperiodide) is the most convenient but most expensive chemical purifier. Dissolve a tablet in a quart (liter) of water, shake the container, then wait 20 minutes before drinking.

Iodine crystals are far cheaper, last for years, and are sold at most outdoor centers. To purify water, fill the iodine crystal storage bottle with clean water and let it sit for one hour. Then add half an ounce (15 ml; about four capfuls) of this saturated iodine solution to a quart (liter) of water; avoid getting crystals into your bottle. Purification takes 20 minutes.

Iodine liquids are inexpensive and easy to use. For tincture of iodine (US) and similar solutions with 2 percent free iodine, use 5 to 8 drops per liter depending on water clarity. Stronger solutions, such as Lugols, with 5 to 10 percent free iodine, are also available; use 1 to 4 drops per liter.

Hand-operated water filters can remove sediments and unpleasant tastes as well as bacteria, giardia, and amebas, depending on filter pore size. Those without iodine incorporated in the filter system may not filter out hepatitis or other viruses. Water filters are bulky, and must be cleaned frequently.

ALTITUDE SICKNESS

Altitude sickness is an environment-related condition that can affect anyone ascending too rapidly to high elevations (10,000 feet [3000 m] or more) without acclimatizing properly. The best way to prevent altitude-related problems is to allow sufficient time to adjust to higher elevations. In Nepal, trekkers are encouraged to acclimatize gradually by ascending at a pace of no more than 1300 feet (400 m) per day, and to take one rest/acclimatization day for every 3000 feet (1000 m) of ascent. In Tibet, gradual acclimatization is difficult due to the extreme elevation of the entire country: the elevation of Lhasa Airport is 11,600 feet (3540 m), while driving to Central Tibet from Nepal or Qinghai Province involves crossing passes over 17,000 feet (5180 m).

If you fly into Tibet, go easy on the first day and allow a minimum of four nights acclimatizing before your trek. Gradually become more active and try to spend a few hours every day going for walks, preferably into the hills. If you are driving to Central Tibet from Nepal, spend a night acclimatizing in Nyelam (12,200 ft, 3720 m) before crossing Thong La pass (16,580 ft, 5050 m).

ACUTE MOUNTAIN SICKNESS (AMS)

The most common problem at altitude is acute mountain sickness (AMS), a general term for a number of high altitude–related symptoms. AMS should be taken seriously, as it may signal the onset of the more serious and potentially deadly altitude-related illnesses, high altitude pulmonary edema (HAPE) and high altitude cerebral edema (HACE). Typical signs of AMS are headache, lack of energy, nausea, insomnia (often from irregular [Cheyne-Stokes] breathing patterns), peripheral edema (swelling of the hands, feet, or face), and shortness of breath while exercising. Most people who ascend to elevations between 11,000 and 20,000 feet (3,350 to 6100 m) experience one or more of these symptoms. The severity and onset may vary, but they should be considered altitude-related until proven otherwise.

Headaches are one of the most common AMS symptoms, but may also be caused by overexertion, dehydration, or intense sunlight. A persistent headache after rest, nourishment or analgesics, or waking in the morning with a headache, especially if it persists after getting up or after taking an analgesic, is a sign of poor acclimatization. A severe or progressively worsening headache, particularly if accompanied by vomiting, lassitude (persistent weariness, or indifference to everyday events), or ataxia (loss of balance), is a danger sign and could be due to HACE (see below), making descent mandatory.

Mild AMS should be a warning that the limit of acclimatization has been reached, and further ascent should be halted until symptoms are gone, usually in a day or two. Acetazolamide (Diamox) is a sulfa drug and a mild diuretic useful in the prevention and treatment of AMS (avoid if you are allergic to sulfa drugs). Anyone with a history of AMS might consider taking acetazolamide a few hours before the flight to Lhasa, or the morning of departure from the Nepal-Tibet border. The usual dosage is 125 to 250 mg two times a day. Side effects include frequent urination; tingling in the fingers, toes, or lips; and alteration in the taste of alcohol. Drink plenty of fluids to prevent dehydration while using this drug. Most AMS symptoms resolve with acclimatization. Severe or worsening symptoms may require action similar to treating early HACE, as noted below.

HIGH ALTITUDE CEREBRAL EDEMA (HACE)

HACE is due to swelling in the brain. The symptoms are similar to those in moderate AMS but more severe and less responsive to treatment. The severity of the headache and the presence of vomiting and ataxia (staggering or loss of balance) help differentiate it from AMS. These are important factors, because someone with HACE can deteriorate rapidly, become unconscious, and die.

An easy test for ataxia is to have the individual walk slowly for 10 to 15 feet (3 to 5 m), heel to toe, along a line drawn on the ground (best done without heavy hiking boots). A normal person should easily pass this test; anyone with mild AMS may be slightly off-balance but can complete the test. Suspect HACE if the person steps off the line, staggers, or falls down.

HACE is dangerous and diagnosis can be difficult; treatment is descent. However, descending to a lower elevation in Central Tibet is not always practical. The only choice may be evacuation by plane to the lower elevations of Kathmandu or to Chengdu in Sichuan Province. Vehicle evacuation to Nepal may be the quickest alternative from the Everest and Mount Kailash regions, though this involves crossing high passes to reach the border.

Administering oxygen can be helpful at a flow of 2 liters per minute, though this is not necessarily curative and problems may return once it is discontinued. A new device, the portable hyperbaric pressure chamber (also called a "Gamow" bag after the inventor), mimics descent and can be lifesaving. It is a body-length, inflatable nylon bag with a foot pump that forces air inside, increasing the bag's internal pressure to simulate a lower altitude. Dexamethasone, a potent anti-inflammatory steroid (10 mg injection initially, then 4 to 6 mg every 6 hours) should be used, but is not a substitute for descent.

HIGH ALTITUDE PULMONARY EDEMA (HAPE)

HAPE occurs when the lung tissues become flooded with fluids, and like HACE, may become life-threatening 8 to 12 hours after the onset of initial symptoms. One of the first symptoms of HAPE is a dry, persistent cough that is not associated with a cold or a chest infection and which is present during exercise as well as at rest. Most people experience some shortness of breath at high elevations, but watch for unusually labored breathing compared to others in the group and a long recovery time after exercise. As HAPE progresses, the cough worsens and eventually produces frothy sputum (phlegm) that may have a pinkish color or be streaked with blood. Audible gurgling in the chest suggests serious edema and is a medical emergency.

As with HACE, descent is critical in treating HAPE, and results can be dramatic. A Gamow bag used for 1 or 2 hours may allow an incapacitated person to be carried in a litter or ride on a horse or yak. Oxygen can be helpful for mild cases of HAPE, but is usually not curative without descent. Use an initial flow of 4 to 6 liters per minute for the first 15 minutes, followed by 2 liters per minute. When descent is not possible, the heart drug Nifedipine (10 mg every 8 hours) can be used.

RESPIRATORY AILMENTS

Coughs, colds, and irritated throats are common due to Tibet's dry air. Throat lozenges and hard candies can soothe scratchy throats, while aspirin or acetaminophen with codeine helps control coughs. The viral "common cold" is ever present in Tibet; be alert for signs of more serious infections.

Sinusitis is a bacterial infection of the sinuses causing headache and localized pain at the forehead, beside the nose, or in the upper teeth. Persistent symptoms may require an antibiotic such as tetracycline or Cephalexin.

Persistent cough, often productive of yellow or green phlegm, may indicate a chest infection. Bronchitis is an infection of the larger air passages, which may respond to steam inhalants that can relieve congestion. Antibiotics may be needed depending on the duration and severity of symptoms. Ampicillin, trimethoprim/sulfamethoxazole, or erythromycin are usually prescribed.

Pneumonia is a more serious infection deeper in the lungs, which can be dangerous, particularly in older people. Persistent coughing, chest pain, difficulty breathing, and a fever of more than 102°F (39°C), sometimes accompanied by shaking chills, are the usual symptoms. Ampicillin, penicillin, or Cephalexin are recommended antibiotics for pneumonia.

HYPOTHERMIA

Hypothermia occurs when the body's internal temperature drops to a dangerously low level, often from a combination of being wet, cold, and exhausted. Symptoms can be subtle and difficult to detect. Muscular coordination decreases and simple tasks, especially using the hands, become difficult. Uncontrollable shivering may occur, and if the body temperature continues to fall, shivering can actually stop—a classic sign of hypothermia. Mental confusion, unusual behavior, slurred speech, and ataxia can also occur. If no attempt is made to raise the body temperature, unconsciousness or death may follow, even at temperatures above freezing. A low-reading thermometer is useful for diagnosis; a temperature below 96°F (35.6°C) suggests hypothermia.

Anyone with signs of hypothermia should seek shelter from the conditions causing the problem, particularly the wind. Wet clothes should be removed and the person should drink hot, sweetened liquids; a quick calorie boost is important. If the person cannot be warmed by conventional means, he or she should be stripped to the skin or a layer of underwear and put into a sleeping bag with another person dressed similarly.

Adequate warm clothing, effective waterproof raingear, and clothes that provide protection from the wind are essential for preventing hypothermia. Wool, silk, or synthetics such as polypropylene remain warm even when wet.

FROSTBITE

Frostbite occurs when body tissue freezes; fingers and toes are at the greatest risk. Initially the affected area feels cold, painful, and may be pale. As the tissue freezes, pain subsides to numbness. Prevention is the best way to go; many cases can be avoided by taking adequate protection from the cold.

If frostbite is suspected, try to rewarm that part of the body by placing it under an armpit or on someone's stomach. In minor cases, the color and feeling will eventually return. In more serious situations frozen tissue will feel hard, cold, and be unresponsive to warming. Do not rub the affected area with snow or try to restore circulation by rubbing with your hands. Ideally the frozen area should be thawed and kept thawed, but if walking is necessary, less damage will be done to a frozen foot by walking out on it than by thawing it too soon.

SUN-RELATED PROBLEMS

Tibet's high altitude and thin atmosphere filter out very little ultraviolet light, causing skin to burn more rapidly than at lower elevations. Sunscreens with para-aminobenzoic acid (PABA) are the most effective and longest lasting, but tend to stain light-colored clothes. A sun protection factor (SPF) of 15 or more is best; zinc oxide creams provide 100 percent blockout. In a pinch use toothpaste! Sun hats are essential; broad-brimmed Tibetan felt hats and inexpensive straw hats are sold in the markets. Treat red and painful sunburn like any other burn: Use a soothing cream such as aloe vera and avoid breaking any blisters. For more serious burns, bathe the area gently with cold, clean water and cover with a bandage that won't stick to the burn.

Snowblindness occurs when bright sunlight that is reflected off snow, ice, or water burns the eye's cornea. It can happen after only a few hours of exposure, but is easily prevented. Sunglasses with UV protectant lenses are adequate for most situations, but for winter treks or visits to the mountaineering base camps, glacier glasses with side shades on the stems provide the best protection. Snowblindness is hard to detect because initially there is no indication that the eyes are being burned. Symptoms usually develop in the evening after exposure. The eyes become painful (as if sand is in them), watery, and bloodshot, and the eyelids may swell shut. Cold compresses help ease the discomfort; use an analgesic for pain. An antibiotic ophthalmic ointment or drops help soothe the eyes and may shorten the recovery time.

ANIMAL BITES

Unfortunately for trekkers, dog bites are not uncommon in Tibet. Immediately wash the wound site with soap and water, then rinse for at least 20 minutes, preferably with an iodine disinfectant or with water purified with a double dose of iodine. It is very important to wash out any saliva that might be in the wound. Cover with a sterile bandage and watch for infection.

The presence of rabies in Tibet must be assumed. Because it is transmitted by the saliva of an infected animal, anyone with a bite that has broken the skin should begin the series of rabies immunization shots as soon as possible. A delay of a week to ten days is usually acceptable, but the sooner the series begins the better. The rabies vaccine is available at the Renmin (People's) Hospital in Lhasa and at a number of clinics in Kathmandu.

HOSPITALS AND OTHER HEALTH FACILITIES

The best hospitals and clinics in Tibet and China are located in the provincial capitals (Lhasa, Chengdu, Xining, Kunming, etc.) and in prefecture capitals (Shigatse, Tsethang, Ali, Kangting, etc.). Smaller, more basic hospitals are found in each county seat (Tibetan [Tib.], *dzong*; Chi., *xian;* Gyangtse, Meldrogungkar, Purang, Dege, Rebkong, etc.); district seats (Tib., *chu*, Chi., *qu*) have a small hospital or clinic; and township seats (Tib., *shang*, Chi., *xiang*) at best have poorly stocked health posts. Bring an interpreter with you when visiting these health facilities.

HOSPITALS

In Lhasa, the best hospital and emergency facility is the five-story Emergency Medical Center located just east of the Renmin (People's) Hospital, on Lingkor North Road (Chi., Linguo Bei Lu). The emergency room is on the first floor, and should have one English-speaking staff member on duty.

The Lhasa People's Hospital (City Hospital) is in the east end of Lhasa on Dekyi Shar Lam (Chi., Beijing Dong Lu), not far beyond the Banok Shol Hotel.

The Lhasa Hotel (formerly the Holiday Inn) has a doctor on call for their guests. Fee-based consultations are arranged through the front desk.

The Tibetan Medicine Hospital, called the Menzi Khang, is just west of Barkor Square. It is open Monday through Saturday, 9:30 A.M. to 1:00 P.M., and 3:30 P.M. to 6:00 P.M. on Monday, Wednesday, Friday, and Saturday; the hospital is closed on Sunday. Diagnosis is done by traditional Tibetan medicinal techniques, such as feeling the pulse and examining the urine, and the medicines prescribed are traditional Tibetan herbal preparations. Report to the outpatient section. A beautiful collection of medical-oriented *thangka* paintings is displayed on the hospital's top floor.

In Shigatse, the hospital is a 10-minute walk north of the Shigatse Hotel. If the main entrance is locked, try the emergency room entrance to the right.

In Tsethang, the hospital is located on the north side of the main road to Gongkar Airport, near the traffic circle.

The hospital closest to the Everest region is in Shekar (turnoff at kilometer marker 5133). It has several inpatient wards and a few doctors.

In Western Tibet, the closest hospital is in Purang (facilities are very basic), 100 kilometers to the south of Mount Kailash. The hospital is in the northern part of town, between the main road and the river. The main hospital in Western Tibet is in Ali, the capital of Ngari Prefecture, though it is only marginally better than Purang's hospital and the drive takes up to 10 hours from Mount Kailash.

The best hospital in Eastern Tibet is in Kangting, on the right side of the road leading north out of town. Kanze, Luho, Trewu, Dege and Pelyul have county hospitals. Serious cases should be taken to Chengdu's main hospital.

In Amdo, the provincial capitals of Xining and Lanzhou have the best medical facilities. Labrang (Chi., Xiahe) and Rebkong (Chi., Tongren) have county hospitals.

In Northwest Yunnan Province, Gyelthang (Chi., Zhongdian) and Lijiang have county hospitals. The best medical facilities are in the capital, Kunming.

DENTISTS

The best dental facility (by Western standards) in Tibet is in Lhasa at the Military Hospital Dental Clinic at the end of Nyangre Lam, near Sera monastery. It has modern equipment and accepts foreigners. The only alternative is to use one of the streetside dentists with foot-treadle drills in the city markets.

PHARMACIES

Pharmacies in Tibet and China sell traditional medicines and some western-type medicines (antibiotics, analgesics, and vitamins are the standard), and often serve as outpatient clinics. The signboard typically has a red cross. In smaller cities the hospitals have the best pharmacies. The usual procedure is to meet with a doctor, who then prescribes the medicine. If a doctor is not available, ask the nurse to sell you the medicine you need. It helps to bring a sample of the medicine or the empty container in which it came.

CLINICS IN NEPAL

For serious illness or injury in Central or Western Tibet, consider evacuation to a clinic in Kathmandu. Western doctors see patients at the CIWEC Clinic Travel Medicine Center (tel. 228531) near the Yak and Yeti Hotel, off Durbar Marg. Another reliable clinic with a highly qualified Western-trained doctor is the Nepal International Clinic (tel. 434642), located across from the Royal Palace on a side street near the Jai Nepal Cinema. The Tribuwan University Teaching Hospital in Maharaj Ganj has the best emergency room outpatient service.

4
Traveling in Tibet

The day-to-day basics of traveling in Tibet are often profoundly different from any other adventure destination in Asia. With a bit of patience and understanding, these unusual aspects of Tibet will provide a unique and memorable travel experience.

Accommodations

In Lhasa, most individual travelers choose the cheaper, Tibetan-style accommodations such as the Yak, Banok Shol, Kirey, and Snowlands Hotels near the Barkor. New to Lhasa are a number of medium-priced hotels offering rooms with an attached bath, such as the Kechu (also Kyichu) and Katak Hotels, and the new wings at the Snowlands and Yak Hotels. Upmarket commercial groups generally stay at the larger, more expensive hotels such as the Lhasa Hotel (formerly the Holiday Inn), the Tibet Guesthouse, and the Himalaya Hotel.

Once you venture outside of Lhasa, experiencing the various hotels and guesthouses can be as much of an adventure as trekking. Even after a decade of building hotels across the Tibetan Plateau, the quality of accommodations remains far behind that of mainland China. Cities such as Shigatse, Tsethang, Gyangtse, Xining, and Kangting have passable hotels, but in more remote locations such as Zhangmu, Purang, or Nakchu, the hotels are downright dreadful, yet expensive. Beyond the cities the quality of accommodation is very similar from one town to another: basic. Large towns and some villages along the main roads will have a truck stop with dormitory rooms, which are notorious for having sheets and quilts that haven't been washed in weeks. Just give them a good shake to knock off the dust and sleep in your inner sheet, or use a sleeping bag. The pillows can be real classics—my favorites are the ones filled with sand. For privacy you may want to pay for all the beds in one room to avoid new roommates stumbling in late at night; truck-stop managers try to keep everyone in as few rooms as possible. Boiled, hot drinking water is provided in a thermos, usually in the morning and again at night. Metal wash basins should be under the beds. The manager keeps the keys for your room, which is paid for in the evening, not in the morning. If you plan to return after your trek, it's usually no problem to store gear until you get back.

On overland trips you may find a family willing to take you in. If you stay in a private home, it's appropriate to pay for lodging and any meals provided.

Transportation

Commercial trek and tour groups typically travel overland in Japanese four-wheel-drive Landcruiser-type vehicles or in minibuses. Public transportation in Tibet is usually limited to the regions around the larger cities. In Central Tibet, Lhasa is the transport hub with regular bus service to Tsethang, Shigatse, Kongpo, Nakchu, Golmud, and even Chengdu. Buses leave from the long distance bus station south of the Lhasa Hotel. Destinations to county seats (*xians*) within Lhasa Prefecture such as Meldrogungkar, Phenpo, and Damzhung are served by the Lubuk bus station, just south of Barkor Square. The minibuses in Lhasa ply outlying towns such as Taktse and Tölung Dechen, and the taxis in Central Tibet's cities are a cheap and convenient transportation source to reach nearby trailheads. Pilgrim trucks and buses gather passengers for Ganden, Tsurphu, and Samye monasteries early each morning at Barkor Square, and trucks may be heading to other sites on special festival days. In Shigatse the bus station is a few minutes' walk west of the Shigatse Hotel across from the truck stop, but service is limited to Lhasa, Gyangtse, and Sakya monastery. The bus from Lhasa to the Nepal border (Zhangmu) has been discontinued, and no public transport serves the Mount Kailash area nor Ali, the capital of Ngari Prefecture.

In Eastern Tibet (Kham), public buses serve the road corridor of Chengdu-Kangting-Kandze-Dege-Chamdo, and limited service is available from Kangting, Kandze, and Chamdo to outlying county seats. In Northwest Yunnan, buses operate daily along the corridor of Lijiang-Gyelthang-Dechen. In Amdo, buses serve most of the main towns in Qinghai Province via the capital Xining, and via Lanzhou in Gansu Province. Buses also run between Rebkong and Labrang.

In many regions of Tibet, hitching in trucks is the main transportation source. Prices are comparable to local bus fares. You either ride up front in the two seats beside the driver or sit in back with the load; the fee is the same. Although it is illegal for drivers (particularly Tibetans) to pick up foreigners, many do so anyway to earn extra cash. At checkpoints they'll coach you on how to walk around them and where to meet on the other side.

All flights to Lhasa are currently handled by the regional government airline China Southwest Airlines (CSWA). The main airline office is one block east of the Potala on the road to Sera monastery. A branch office in Lhasa is in the Tibet Hotel and another branch is in Shigatse. In Chengdu, the main CSWA office is across the street from the Jinjiang Hotel.

TRAVEL PERMITS

If you trek in Tibet with a commercial company, all of the necessary travel permits will be arranged by the local Tibetan travel agency. Depending on where you travel, permits are issued by the government, police, and military, but there is no trek permit system. If you plan to trek independently, be prepared for a barrage of misinformation regarding regulations and travel permits; the rules change so much it's hard for anyone to keep track!

As of 1999, Lhasa and anywhere in Lhasa Prefecture is "open" to tourism, and no travel permits are required. Tsethang, in Shannan Prefecture, and Shigatse in Shigatse Prefecture are also "open," but in order to travel elsewhere in these prefectures (or in Ngari, Nakchu, Nyingchi, or Chamdo Prefectures in the TAR) foreigners must have an Aliens Travel Permit (ATP). ATPs are issued by the Foreign Affairs Division of the Public Security Bureau in each prefecture capital, cost 50 *yuan* (about US $6) and list the restricted areas you are allowed to visit and the travel dates. As of 1999, popular destinations such as Gyangtse, Samye, Chongye Valley, and Everest base camp are on the restricted list; the police fine foreigners who visit without an ATP. Certain areas are more tightly controlled (border regions; Southern Shannan Prefecture; and anywhere in Nakchu, Nyingchi, or Chamdo Prefectures) and can only be visited if you have the proper permits, are accompanied by a licensed tour guide, and are using a vehicle and driver arranged through a travel agency.

Travel in Eastern Tibet (Kham) requires no permits if you are in Yunnan, Gansu, or Qinghai Provinces. As of 1999, Sichuan Province opened all of its Tibetan counties to tourism except Ngaba (Chi., Aba) County.

MONEY

The Tibetan monetary system was replaced in the 1950s with the Chinese *renminbi* ("Peoples' Money"), which has units of currency called *yuan*. One *yuan* is divided into tenths, called *jiao* (like a US dime; but in Tibet and Western China people call this denomination a *mao*), and into 100 *fen*. All notes are coded by color and size. The *yuan* note is commonly called a *kwai* in Tibet. As of 1999, 8.26 *yuan* equal US $1.

The old tourist money, called Foreign Exchange Certificates (FEC), was discontinued in 1994, but banks still cash them for *renminbi*.

Before you leave Tibet or China, leftover *renminbi* can be exchanged back to hard currency at the Bank of China if you have bank encashment receipts. Note that the exchange counter at the Lhasa airport is rarely open before the Kathmandu flight, and, except in Hong Kong, *renminbi* is nonconvertible outside China. Plan ahead. Or tip your guide!

TIPPING

Tipping is meant to be an extra "thank you" for exceptional service. While tips are not expected in Tibet's hotels and restaurants, it is appropriate to give 5 *yuan* or so to bell boys handling luggage. At hotel restaurants, tip 5 percent of the bill if you like. For local tour or trek guides, depending on group size and their performance, I often give US $10 to 25 equivalent in *yuan* per week of the trip, about half that for each driver, and something in between for the cook. Don't forget your yak men, porters, and any assistant camp staff.

CULTURAL CONSIDERATIONS

Tourism provides a major source of hard currency for many developing countries, but too often it erodes the very culture and environment that attracts tourists. When you visit Tibet, consider yourself a pioneer of tourism. Your actions and the actions of others in your group, especially while you are trekking in remote areas, will have a bearing upon the way people will react toward other trekkers who visit in later years.

As mentioned in "Hints for Women Trekkers," shorts should never be worn by women or men, even during a trek. Tibetans never show their legs; you should follow their example. Men should wear long pants, though knickers are fine for trekking. Women should wear loose-fitting long pants or a calf-length skirt or dress. Shirts should not be revealing, and a bra should be worn. Sadly, tourists can now be seen parading through Tibetan cities and monasteries wearing shorts and immodest summer attire. Don't be afraid to inform other tourists about the proper dress for monasteries; perhaps they are simply unaware of the etiquette.

BEGGARS

Religious beggars are an accepted part of society in Tibet and most of Asia. Both laypeople and monks may set off across the length of Tibet to Mount Kailash, often on foot, requesting alms to finance pilgrimages that could last months or years. Giving money or food to a pilgrim is considered an act of merit. During large religious festivals, particularly Monlam Chenmo and Saga Dawa, thousands of beggars line the Lingkor and Barkor circuits in Lhasa. The local Tibetans offer each beggar a small note, for an act of merit is said to be multiplied 10 million times on these special occasions. Even when there isn't a festival, religious pilgrims often sit along the Barkor chanting prayers and asking for offerings toward their journey. A typical donation ranges from 1 *jiao* to 1 *yuan*. Have small notes ready when visiting the Barkor. It is also appropriate to give to beggars who are crippled or otherwise unable to work.

Children and some adults have become a nuisance in the Everest region and other popular tourist destinations, especially along the major roads, thrusting their hands out for *ngül* (money) and *jiri* (sweets). Please do not give in to their demands. Complying just makes it more difficult for the next trekkers who come along; besides, sugar is bad for those beautiful teeth.

DALAI LAMA PHOTOGRAPHS

When Tibet first opened to tourists, word spread quickly that Dalai Lama photos were a wonderful gift. As much as this was appreciated, it had the sad effect of encouraging many Tibetans to endlessly hassle foreigners for pictures of their exiled leader. They may have five photographs of him on their altar at home, yet they will still try to secure one more; the pure and unquestioned devotion to this man is unparalleled in our society.

At present photographs of the Dalai Lama are banned in the TAR. Monasteries have been forced to remove his picture from temples, and shops can no longer openly sell them. In 1997 a tour group was expelled from the TAR because one member gave out a Dalai Lama photo and word got to the authorities. Until this situation eases, the best thing is to not bring these photographs to Tibet.

VISITING MONASTERIES

Tibetan Buddhist monasteries typically welcome foreign visitors, though a few rules of conduct should be noted. Central Tibet has no restrictions regarding women entering the monasteries, but a few sites, such as Ganden and Reting, have protector's shrines (*gönkhang*) closed to women. In Kham and Amdo during *yar-ne*, the summer retreat period (about mid-June to early September), most monasteries and hermitages bar visitors (the exceptions are popular tourist destinations such as Labrang monastery). In the Gyelthang and Dechen region of Yunnan Province, monastery kitchens are off limits to women, as they contain a *gönkhang*. Otherwise Tibet's monasteries are very accessible.

Generally Tibetans do not remove their shoes to enter a temple, contrary to the rules in Nepal and India (probably due to the colder climate), but if you notice a pile of shoes at the entrance, take yours off as well. Always remove your hat (Tibetan women loosen their braids). Shorts or revealing clothing are not appropriate, and do not smoke in or near a monastery.

As you enter a temple or shrine, angle to the left in the respectful, clockwise manner. Keep prayer walls and offering cairns to your right, and walk clockwise around pilgrim circuits. If monks are chanting or involved with a religious service, it's not a problem to walk quietly around the room. If they ask you to join them on the rows of cushions where they are sitting, go right ahead. Take your shoes off first, then sit cross-legged. Get into the habit of carrying a cup in your daypack, for you'll undoubtedly be offered butter tea. If you don't like butter tea or have had enough, politely say *me*, which means no, and put your hand over the cup. They will still try hard to serve you more.

Ask permission before taking photographs in a monastery. Besides potentially angering the monks, you might have to pay a stiff photography fee. The monasteries along the main tourist routes tend to be the worst, for the government requires that the monks charge foreigners for photographs, usually a flat fee of 10 to 50 *yuan*. The more remote monasteries rarely ask for money; nevertheless, always inquire before snapping pictures. Regardless of whether you take photographs, the smaller temples appreciate donations of 1 to 10 *yuan* to help finance their reconstruction or pay for butter in the lamps. After placing the money on the altar, you can ask to have a butter lamp lit, a Tibetan Buddhist practice for making an offering.

If you spend the night in a monastery, the monks usually won't ask for money, though a donation of 10 *yuan* or more is appropriate, especially if they provide you with butter tea and *thukpa* stew. Don't, however, treat monasteries as hotels; consider it a privilege to be staying there. If the room where you sleep has an altar, lie so your feet aren't pointing toward any holy images.

There's never a lack of help when you're preparing dinner

VISITING A TIBETAN HOME

As in most places in the world, in Tibet you will be treated with great respect if you are invited into a family's home (or tent). Once you are ushered into the darkened room, you will be directed to a raised platform along the wall padded with carpets or yak-hair blankets. As your eyes adjust, many curious, wind-burned little faces will probably be peering at you. The children are shy but brave, and may cautiously poke at your clothes or pull the hairs on your arm. The mother or daughter will stoke the fire, then pour hot tea from a kettle into a large churn. She'll add a few chunks of yak butter, whoosh the mixture up and down with precise motions, then serve it. Get your cup ready! Despite the popular stories about the horrors of butter tea, it is typically a mild, delicious brew tasting more like a broth than tea. A worn goatskin bag containing *tsampa* may be passed your way. If you like, add a few spoonfuls to your tea, or mix in a few handfuls as the Tibetans do, kneading it to create a ball of dough. "Eat up," they'll insist, and perhaps a leg of dried sheep or yak meat and a knife will be offered. Carve off a slice, then pass it on to the next person.

If you stay the night, you will be shown where to sleep. In general, your belongings will be left alone, but keep valuables in a safe place and don't leave your pack open. Children are sometimes prone to pinching little, easy-to-hide objects. In the Everest region, the old grandmothers are the ones to watch. One octogenarian decided my water bottle was just the container she'd been looking for; it took me half a night of polite negotiation to get it back.

Tibetan homes do not have toilets inside and many don't even have one outside; you just wander off and find a private spot—a difficult task in the daytime. To the west of Shigatse the village toilet is an elevated, mud brick platform with a stairway leading up. Around the squat spot is a low wall 1 to 2 feet high, exposing you to the chilly winds and allowing passersby an opportunity to see who's in town. Take care not to drop anything valuable down the hole; wallets and glasses are the most common casualties!

An invitation to stay in a Tibetan home does not mean you must pay, but you should at least offer. Ten to 20 *yuan* per person per night is an appropriate fee for lodging and meals. Establish the price before you sleep to avoid misunderstandings in the morning. If there is an altar or a holy image in the room where you are staying, sleep with your feet in the opposite direction.

ENVIRONMENTAL AWARENESS

The Sierra Club adage "Take only pictures, leave only footprints" is an appropriate philosophy for preserving Tibet's wilderness. While the vast herds of rangeland animals have been greatly reduced over the last several decades, logging interests continue to pressure the virgin forests, and new mineral deposits are exploited every year, Tibet is probably the least spoiled region along the Himalaya. The low population has much to do with this, but so has the delayed introduction of tourism. The trails in Tibet are surprisingly litter-free, even along the popular routes near Samye monastery and Mount Everest, with the main exception being the Dza Rongphu/Everest base camp area.

It should go without saying that you are not to leave garbage at your campsites. Cigarette butts are as bad as other types of litter once they are on the ground. Put them in your pocket. When you have a bowel movement, dig a shallow hole or scrape away some dirt, then be like a cat and cover up what you deposit. Burn your toilet paper or carry it out; don't just bury or hide it. Unfold the paper before burning; a cigarette lighter works best. Light it from the bottom, allowing the flame to go upwards. If the paper is wadded into a ball it won't burn properly. When the flame is out, step on the ashes to knock them apart. Feminine hygiene products do not burn well. Wrap them in toilet paper and store in a plastic bag until the trek is over.

Commercial trekking companies should provide a toilet tent, which is pitched over a hole in the ground. Make sure your trek staff has a shovel or ice ax, since the ground tends to be hard and rocky. Toilet tents should be 150 feet (45 m) or more from any streams. Don't let the staff dig the hole in the middle of a beautiful meadow; the scar could last for decades. If there is turf, have your staff cut a neat block of sod that can be replaced over the hole. Ideally, collect used toilet paper (each day I hang a new plastic bag inside the toilet tent) and pack it out with other camp garbage. The next best method is to have each person burn toilet paper in the toilet tent. Don't put toilet paper or other trash into the toilet hole—animals and curious herders often dig up these holes, scattering the paper. When you are finished, kick a bit of dirt over your business. Each morning after breaking camp, have someone in your group stay back to check if the toilet hole has been properly filled in, not just partially covered with a big rock. This is a common problem throughout the Himalaya.

Pay attention to how your staff handles the trek garbage. Hiding cans and bottles in the bushes or under rocks is not acceptable, nor is burying the solution. If your pack animals can carry full containers of food in, they can haul empty ones out. Some trek staff may resist this idea, saying the yak or horse men won't agree, but work with your trek guide to make sure your trash is packed out. Food scraps can often be fed to yaks, or else be carried out along with the other garbage, preferably in a plastic-lined sack or duffel bag. On commercial treks, don't have your staff burn any trash. Wet paper, plastic, and foil-lined packets are near impossible to burn, even when doused with fuel, and

Camp at Kong Tsho, below Shishapangma

the resulting burn scar will remain for months, even years. I bring about twenty heavy duty plastic bags to pack everything out. Because small towns have no landfill system or garbage collection service, Lhasa is the best place to dispose of the trek refuse. Or, if your trip ends in Nepal, take it to Kathmandu. Otherwise your trash may end up thrown in a pile behind your hotel or guesthouse.

Children sometimes come to camp or a lunch stop begging for empty containers. While bottles with tops can be used for storage, pop-top soft drink or beer cans will merely be used as playthings until the novelty wears off, then get discarded. Crush all cans after use to prevent this indirect form of littering. Wherever you camp, try to leave the site in better condition than when you arrived. If paper or trash is around, pack it out with the garbage from your trek. If you are camped in an area where bushes or trees grow, encourage your staff to use their kerosene stoves instead of the local wood.

Washing your clothes or body will inevitably introduce soap into the streams. To minimize your impact, use a wash basin 15 feet (5 m) or more from the water's edge. Toss the soapy water away from the stream, then refill with more water. Have your trek staff do the same, and ask them not to wash dishes in streams or lakes. Biodegradable soap is not common in Asia.

DEALING WITH DOGS

Tibetan mastiff guard dogs can be very aggressive, as they are trained to protect livestock and personal possessions from intruders, animal or human. Whenever you approach a herders' camp or a village, keep in mind that a guard dog may be off its chain. Foreigners especially seem to spook Tibetan dogs, perhaps because we smell different. In the cities the dogs are quite relaxed about our presence, but in the countryside they can be ferocious. I always carry a handful of golf ball–sized stones as I enter a settlement or encampment. The dogs are wary of being hit and usually keep their distance if you just raise your arm as if to throw a stone. A sturdy walking stick is also handy for fending off dogs, and loose long trousers may prevent them from biting your leg if they try. If you are bitten, wash the wound with plenty of soap and water for at least 20 minutes; infection is a common problem with any animal bite. The presence of rabies has not been confirmed in Tibet, but you must assume it exists. For more information on treating animal bites, see "Staying Healthy."

SHOPPING FOR FOOD IN TIBET

The trekking company handles all the food purchasing and preparation on a commercial trek; the kitchen staff even does the dishes. On private treks you have the choice of organizing your own food or paying the trekking agent to arrange for it. The latter choice is probably the best, since then all you need to do is spend a few hours in the market before your trek buying fresh vegetables and any special food preferences to supplement what the company provides.

If you have trekked in Nepal, you may be spoiled by the variety of Western food available there. The food in Tibet has improved remarkably over the years, but still pales in comparison with Nepal. Nonetheless, it is possible to find sufficient supplies to outfit your trek. In Lhasa a wide variety of vegetables is grown in hot houses, and some trekking-type foods from Nepal are now available, including porridge, muesli, processed cheese, and packets of soup. For something sweet after the evening meal, bring custard powder, fruit-flavored gelatin, and instant mixes such as pudding, mousse, and cheesecake.

The following foods are available in the city markets, particularly in Lhasa; remember that little is available once you are off the main roads. The Tibetan weight measurement is a *gyama*, which approximately equals the Chinese *jin* (1.1 lbs; 0.5 kg).

Rice. Readily available in the markets.

Noodles. Delicious wheat noodles made locally are sold in packets. Instant noodle soups from China and Nepal are also available.

Tea. Chinese green (jasmine) tea and Tibetan brick tea are the standard, and black tea from Nepal is available. Bring herbal tea from home or Nepal.

Coffee. Chinese-made Nescafe; no filter coffee yet.

Hot chocolate mix. Bring from home or Nepal.

Milk powder. Chinese Nespray is the only brand that is unsweetened.

Sugar. Readily available even in small towns.

Butter. Yak butter is the standard. Try it before buying!

Cooking oil. Low-quality, strong-tasting mustard oil is the standard.

Bread. Baked flat breads are sold every morning in the larger cities, as are twisted fried breads. A few places in Lhasa now have loaf bread and croissants!

Flour. *Tsampa,* roasted barley flour, is the staple food of Tibet and is available everywhere. Use it to make a slightly nutty-tasting porridge. Wheat flour is also available.

Eggs. Mainly available in the cities.

Yogurt. Sold in jars each morning in city markets. It is safe and delicious.

Jam. Sweet fruit jams are available.

Walnuts. Unshelled nuts are abundant during autumn.

Dried fruit. Raisins and apricots from Xinjiang Province. Rinse before eating.

Cheese. Hard, dried types of yak cheese are widely available.

Tinned (canned) meats. Primarily pork products, from pig's feet to quality hams.

Salt. Rock salt is most common, and iodized salt is available.

Spices. Chili peppers are widely available, along with Chinese lemon pepper, cumin, and turmeric. Bring black pepper, cinnamon, basil, oregano, and other favorite spices from home.

Fresh meat. Yak meat and mutton are most common; pork is widely available.

Vegetables. A broad selection is available in Lhasa and larger towns in Eastern Tibet. In remote areas the standards are potatoes, rapeseed greens, and turnips.

Fruit. Apples, apricots, and pears abound in autumn, peaches in summer. Bananas and oranges are brought to Lhasa from Nepal and China.

Preserved fruit. Many different kinds bottled or tinned in syrup.

5
TIBETAN FOR TREKKERS

Every district its own dialect; every lama his own doctrine.

Tibetan proverb (quoted in the 1920 edition of
Charles Bell's *English Tibetan Colloquial Dictionary*)

As the old saying suggests, the spoken word of Tibet is not a single standardized language, but a wide-ranging group of related local dialects that are scattered across the Tibetan Plateau and the northern Himalaya. Since Ü-ke, the "central language" of Lhasa (some scholars prefer to call it Lhasa-ke), is the most widely understood dialect throughout greater Tibet, the following transliterations are based upon the Lhasa pronunciation. In the outer regions of Tibet, particularly in Kham and Amdo, no one except a few monks who have studied in Lhasa, or someone who has been on pilgrimage in Central Tibet, will understand even a few words of Ü-ke; the dialects are so different here that it may be easier to communicate in Chinese! Nevertheless, Ü-ke is the most useful of the Tibetan dialects for travelers, but even near Lhasa you can encounter different pronunciations and vocabularies while on a day hike across the river from the city.

LEARNING TO SPEAK TIBETAN
To get started, first read through the section on pronunciation to learn how the vowels and the consonants are pronounced. Next, practice key phrases with the Tibetan staff at your hotel, or in a restaurant; the people you meet make up one of the best classrooms available. *Tashi de-le* (often spelled *Tashi delek*) can be used in Central Tibet to approximate our "hello," and *ga-le zhu*, one of several ways to say "good-bye," will be quickly understood regardless of your pronunciation. One of the first things a Tibetan will ask you is *khyerang ga-ne yin?*—"Where are you from?" (There are many ways to ask this.) The reply to learn is *Nga . . . Amerika . . . ne yin,* meaning "I am from . . . America." (Sentences in this chapter that have words separated by three dots [. . .] indicate where words can be substituted according to your needs.) Memorize the numbers from one to ten, which will enable you to ask and understand responses to the most common traveler's question, *De gong gatshö re?*—"How much does this cost?" Other helpful sentences are included in the section "Useful Phrases and Conversation." See Appendix B, "Suggested Reading," for a list of Tibetan language books and Chinese phrase books.

To study Tibetan more seriously, contact a Tibetan Buddhist religious center or a university with an Asian Studies or Religious Studies department. At present the only formal language program in Tibet is through Tibet University in Lhasa. There are two semesters: Fall semester starts about the end of August, and spring semester starts in March. Students must live on campus in the dormitories. Write the University at least a year in advance for an application form. Less formal, private tutoring is easy to arrange with freelance Tibetan teachers who frequent the popular travelers' restaurants in Lhasa. Tribuwan University in Kathmandu offers two Tibetan language class sessions each year, starting in February and in July.

Tibet University
Foreign Affairs Office
Lhasa, Tibet, PRC. 850000

Mr. Mohan Sitaula, Director
Tribuwan University, Campus of International Languages
Exhibition Road, Kathmandu, Nepal; Phone: 226713, 255738

PRONUNCIATION

The italicized words in parentheses following the vowel and consonant descriptions are Tibetan words exemplifying each sound.

VOWELS

The five main Tibetan vowel sounds resemble the English vowels **a**, **e**, **i**, **o**, and **u**. Since Tibetan is a tonal language, variations of these vowel sounds occur:

a   Short, like the **a** in **father** (*gompa*; monastery).

aw Like the **aw** in **law** (*yaw-re*; there is).

e   Short, like the **a** in **ate** (*me*; fire).

i   Short, like the **ee** in **feet** (*ri*; mountain).

o   Short, like the **o** in **orange** (*momo*; dumpling).

ö   No equivalent in American English; closest to the **eu** sound in French, e.g., **fleur** (*Bhö*; Tibet).

u   Short, like the **u** in **put** (*thukpa*; Tibetan noodle soup).

ü   No equivalent in English; closest to the **ü** in German, e.g., **füllen** (*ngül*; silver).

CONSONANTS

All Tibetan consonants contain an inherent *a* sound (like the **a** in **father**), so *k*, *kh*, *g*, and *ng* are pronounced *ka*, *kha*, *ga*, and *nga*. Many of these consonants can be pronounced using English phonetic equivalents, though some sounds are not familiar and require further explanation:

ch Much like the **ch** in **cheek**, but unaspirated (*semchen*; animal).

dr Pronounced with the tongue farther back in the mouth than an English **d**, with only a slight **r** sound (*dro-*; to go).

dz Like the **ds** sound in **fads** (*dzong*; fortress).

g   Hard like the **g** in **goat** (*gompa*; monastery); in the Amdo and Kham dialects, when **g** is followed by a **y**, it is soft like the **ju** in **juice** (*Gyagar*; India).

ng Pronounced like the nasalized **ng** in **sing-along** (*Nga*; I).

sz Pronounced halfway between **s** and **z** (*sza-khang*; restaurant)

tr Pronounced with the tongue farther back in the mouth than an English **t**, with only a slight **r** sound (*trimpa*; cloud).

ts Like the **ts** sound in **boots** (*tsampa*; barley flour).

zh Like the **s** in **leisure** (*zhimpo*; delicious).

Some Tibetan consonants are aspirated, which means they are pronounced with a slightly exaggerated puff of air. These consonants are followed by an *h* in this text, with the exception of *ch* (e.g., *kh*, *th*, *ph*, *bh*, *sh*, *zh* and *lh*).

Note:

ph is never like the f sound in photograph (*pha*; father).

th is never like the th in think (*theb-ri*; fresco).

Also note that in different areas people may or may not pronounce the consonants at the end of syllables:

luk (sheep)	May be pronounced *luu*, ending with a long *u* sound.
par (photograph)	May be pronounced *paa*, ending with a long *a* sound.
sarpa (new)	May be pronounced *saapa*.
mik (eye)	May be pronounced *mi*.
phe- (to go [v., hon.])	May be pronounced *pheb*.

GRAMMAR

Since grammar is usually the most complicated aspect of any language, skip this section at first or just have a quick glance through it, then go on to "Useful Phrases and Conversation." Once you're familiar with these sentences, review the grammar for a better idea of how the language works.

PRONOUNS AND POSSESSIVE PRONOUNS

The Tibetan language uses a specialized system of respectful, "honorific" (hon.) words to address elders, government officials, nobility, and high *lamas.* Use informal pronouns only when speaking to close friends, children, when referring to yourself, or to animals.

Person	Pronouns		Possessive	Pronouns	
First	I	*nga*	my	*nge*	
	we	*nga-tsho*	our	*nga-tshö*	
Second	you (hon.)	*khyerang*	your (hon.)	*khyerang-gi*	
	you, plural	*khyörang-tsho*	your, plural	*khyörang-tshö*	
	you, plural (hon.)	*khyerang-tsho*	your, plural (hon.)	*khyerang-tshö*	
Third	he/she	*khorang*	his/hers	*khorang-gi*	
	she	*morang*	her	*morang-gi*	
	he/she (hon.)	*khong*	his/hers (hon.)	*khong-gi*	
	they	*khon-tsho*	their	*khon-tshö*	
	they (hon.)	*khong-tsho*	their (hon.)	*khong-tshö*	

SENTENCE STRUCTURE

The correct structure for a simple Tibetan sentence is subject-object-verb:

Subject	Object	Verb
Nga	*khala*	*sza-gi-yö*
I	food	am eating

VERBS

Tibetan verbs consist of a verb stem and an ending that conjugates according to a specific time reference. Tibetan also has special conjugations for events in the past depending on whether the speaker has first-hand knowledge of an event (attested statement), whether someone informed the speaker (reportative statement), or whether the speaker is making a general statement. The following is a list of verb conjugations using the verb stem *dri-* (**to write**) as an example.

Person	Past	Present	Future
First	*dri-pa-yin*	*dri-gi-yö*	*dri-gi-yin*
	I wrote	I write	I will write
Second and Third (attested statements)			
	dri-song	*dri-gi-du*	*dri-gi-re*
	he/she/they wrote	he/she/they write(s)	he/she/they will write
Second and Third (reportative statements)			
	dri-du	*dri-gi-du*	*dri-gi-re*
	he/she wrote	he/she writes	he/she will write
Second and Third (general statements)			
	dri-pa-re	*dri-gi-du*	*dri-gi-re*
	he/she wrote	he/she writes	he/she will write

The easiest way to conjugate verbs to indicate that you (first person) have felt or done something in the past is to add *pa-yin* to the verb stem. For the second and third persons the verb ending is *song* when the speaker has first-hand knowledge (attested statement) of an event in the past:

I wrote a letter

Nga	*yi-ge*	*dri-pa-yin*
I	letter	wrote

He wrote a letter (attested statement)

khong	*yi-ge*	*dri-song*
he	letter	wrote

When the speaker heard that an event occurred in the past, but did not witness it, the reportative verb ending for the second and third person is *du*. If the speaker is making a general statement about an event in the past, the verb ending for the second and third persons is *pa-re*:

She wrote a letter (reportative statement)

khong	*yi-ge*	*dri-du*
she	letter	wrote

The students wrote letters (general statement)

lobtru	*yi-ge*	*dri-pa-re*
students	letters	wrote

To conjugate verbs to indicate that you (first person) are feeling or doing something at that moment, *gi-yö* is added to the verb stem. For the second and third persons, *gi-du* is the ending added to the verb stem regardless of the speaker's knowledge:

I am writing a letter

Nga	*yi-ge*	*dri-gi-yö*
I	letter	am writing

You are writing a letter

khyerang	*yi-ge*	*dri-gi-du*
you	letter	are writing

To conjugate verbs to indicate that you (first person) will do something in the future, add *gi-yin* to the verb stem. For the second and third persons, add *gi-re* to the verb stem regardless of the speaker's knowledge:

I will write a letter

Nga	*yi-ge*	*dri-gi-yin*
I	letter	will write

He will write a letter

khong	*yi-ge*	*dri-gi-re*
he	letter	will write

Several common verbs, known as time verbs, have their verb stem change when they are conjugated to indicate the past. Some examples are:

dro- (to go) changes to *chin-* (note: Use *chim-* before the endings *pa-yin* and *pa-re*)
sza- (to eat) changes to *sze-*
ta- (to look) changes to *te-*
nyo- (to buy) changes to *nyö-*

THE VERB "TO BE"

The English language utilizes just one form of the verb **to be** (is, am, are, was, were, and so on) in order to identify, qualify, locate, indicate existence, or convey possession, regardless of the subject or pronoun in a sentence. Past, present and future tenses are conveyed depending on the conjugation of this verb. In Tibetan, five different words express the various uses of **to be**. Time references are indicated not by these verbs, but by the sentence context. Like other Tibetan verbs, correct usage sometimes depends on whether the speaker has first-hand or general knowledge of the subject.

The form of **to be** used to identify something in the first person is *yin* (the negative is *men*). For the second and third person the verb used is *re* (the negative is *ma-re*):

I am from America / not from America

Nga	*Amerika*	*ne*	*yin / men*
I	America	from	am / am not

The yak is black / is not black

yak	*nakpo*	*re / ma-re*
yak	black	is / is not

To indicate existence, quality, or possession, or to express location, the form of the verb **to be** used for the first person is *yö* (the negative is *me*). For the second and third person, the verb *du* (the negative is *mindu*) is used when the speaker has first-hand knowledge of the matter being discussed. *Yaw-re* (the negative is *yaw-ma-re*) is the verb used when making a general statement. Note that the postposition *la* needs to be inserted into all sentences expressing possession or location, and it always follows the subject or object being discussed.

I have a camera (possession) / don't have a camera

Nga	*la*	*parche*	*yö / me*
I	to	camera	is / is not

The restaurant is here (location) / is not here

de	*szakhang*	*du / mindu*
in here	restaurant	is / is not

There are many yaks in Tibet (attested statement) / are not many yaks

Bhö	*la*	*yak*	*mangpo*	*du / mindu*
Tibet	in	yaks	many	are / are not

There are many yaks in Tibet (a general statement) / are not many yaks

Bhö	*la*	*yak*	*mangpo*	*yaw-re / yaw-ma-re*
Tibet	in	yaks	many	are / are not

ASKING QUESTIONS

There are two main ways to formulate a question. One is to use an interrogative:

How	*gan-dre*	Where from	*ga-ne*
How much	*gatshö re*	Which	*gagi*
What	*ga-re*	Who	*su*
When	*gadü*	Whose	*sü*
Where	*gapa*	Why	*ga-re je-ne*

Another way to ask a question is to add -ge after the verb du, or add -pe after the verbs yin, yö, re, and yaw-re:

There are hotels in Lhasa / Are there hotels in Lhasa?

Lhasa	la	drön-khang	du / du-ge?
Lhasa	in	hotels	there are / are there?

This is a hotel / Is this a hotel?

di	drön-khang	re / re-pe?
this	hotel	is / is this?

IMPERATIVES

Polite imperatives are created by adding *ronang* to the verb stem. The following examples are for the verb *nang-* (to give):

Please give me tea

Nga	la	ja	nang-	ronang
I	to	tea	give	please

For informal imperatives, add the ending *da* to the verb stem:

Give me tea

Nga	la	ja	nang-da
I	to	tea	give

ADJECTIVES

Adjectives always follow the noun they are describing:

big monastery

gompa	chempo
monastery	big

When the subject is described using an adjective, the *du* form (negative is *mindu*) of the verb *to be* is used when the speaker has first-hand knowledge. If the speaker is making a general statement, the *re* form (negative is *ma-re*) of the verb *to be* is used. The *re* form of the verb **to be** is also used when a color describes the subject.

These *momos* are delicious (attested statement) / are not delicious

momo	dintsho	zhimpo	du / mindu
momos	these	delicious	are / are not

Momos are delicious (general statement) / are not delicious

momo	zhimpo	re / ma-re
momos	delicious	are / are not

The *re* form of **to be** is usually used for colors:

The lake is blue / is not blue

tsho	ngömpo	re / ma-re
lake	blue	is / is not

For superlatives, add -shö to the first syllable or the stem of the adjective:

good	yakpo
best	yakshö

many	mangpo
most	mangshö

One exception is when **big** becomes **biggest**; then the *m* is dropped from the stem of the adjective:

big	chempo
biggest	cheshö

USEFUL PHRASES AND CONVERSATION

In the following sections, some words are translated into both Tibetan (Tib.) and Chinese (Chi.). Nouns are designated by (n.), adjectives by (adj.), and adverbs by (adv.). For verbs (v.), only the stem is given (e.g., *dro-*; to go). In some cases the honorific form (hon.) of a word is given as well as the informal (inf.) form.

USEFUL PHRASES

Hello! Good day! (literally, good luck!)
    tashi de-le!

Where are you going?
(typical greeting)
    gapa   phe-ge?
    where   going (hon.)?

Good-bye (if you are leaving)
    ga-le   zhu
    slowly   stay
                (implying to take care)

Good-bye (if you are staying)
    ga-le   phe
    slowly   go (implying to take care)

Yes
    yin, yö, du, re, or *yaw-re*

No
    men, me, mindu, ma-re, or *yaw-ma-re*

Thank you (hon.)
    thu je che
    thank you

No thank you
    lamen,   thu je che
    oh no,   thank you

OK (don't substitute for thank you)
    drik-gi-   re   (*la so* is also used)
    all right   it is

This is good / not good
    di   yakpo   du / mindu
    this   good   is / is not

I understand   / don't under-
                                stand
    hago-   song / masong
    (I) do understand / don't under-
                                stand

I know   / don't know
    shing-gi-   yö / me
    (I) know   it is / it is not

What is this?
    di   ga-re   re?
    this   what   is?

Excuse me! Pardon me!
    gongdak!
    sorry!

Just a minute
    de-tsa   gu-a
    little   wait

I know a little Tibetan
    Nge   Bhö-ke   de-tsa   shing-gi-
                                                        yö
    By me   Tibetan   little   knowing

Say it again, please (hon.)
    yangkyar   sung   ronang
    again   say   please

CONVERSATIONS AND TYPICAL SITUATIONS

What is your name? (hon.)

khyerang-gi	*tshen la*	*ga-re*	*zhü-gi-yö?*
your	name	what	is called?

My name is ... Tashi

Nga	*ming*	...	*Tashi*	...	*yin*
My	name	...	Tashi	...	is

Pleased to meet you (hon.)

khyerang	*jewa*	*gapo jung*
you	meet	pleased to

How are you? (How is your health?)

khyerang	*kuzu*	*depo*	*yin-pe?*
your	body	healthy	is it?

Where are you from?

khyerang	*ga-ne*	*yin?*
you	where from	is?

Yes, I am fine

la yin,	*szugo depo-*	*yin*
yes	healthy	it is

I am from ... America

Nga	...	*Amerika*	...	*ne*	*yin*
I	...	America	...	from	am

ADDRESSING OTHERS

If you're not sure whether a person is younger or older than yourself, use the honorific pronoun *khong* (Mister / Miss). When addressing a person by his or her given name, it is polite to add the word *la* after the name, especially in Lhasa:

Excuse me, is this the road to Lhasa?

khong,	*di*	*Lhasa*	*gi*	*lamka*	*re-pe?*
Mister / Miss,	this	Lhasa	to	road	is it?

Sonam, are you married?

Sonam la,	*khyerang*	*changsa*	*gyab-pe?*
Sonam,	you	marriage	occurred?

NUMBERS

The counting system in Tibet is similar to ours except for the word connecting the units of ten with the units of one, starting with the twenties; it varies with each set of tens. Simply use *dang* (and) to join numbers (e.g., use *nyi-shu dang chik* instead of trying to memorize *nyi-shu tse-chik*).

1	chik, chi	14	chub-zhi	75	dün-chu dün-nga
2	nyi	15	chö-nga	85	gya-chu gya-nga
3	sum	16	chu-druk	95	gub-chu go-nga
4	zhi	17	chub-dün	100	gya
5	nga	18	chub-gye	200	nyi gya
6	druk	19	chu-gu	1,000	chik tong
7	dün	20	nyi-shu	2,000	nyi tong
8	gye	25	nyi-shu tse-nga	¼	zhicha chik
9	gu	30	sum-chu	½	cheka
10	chu	35	sum-chu so-nga	first	dangpo
11	chuk-chik	45	zhib-chu sha-nga	second	nyipa
12	chung-nyi	55	ngab-chu nge-nga	zero	le-ko
13	chuk-sum	65	druk-chu ra-nga		

TIME

What time is it now?

danta	chu-tshö	gatshö	re?
now	hours	how much	is?

Now it is . . . two o'clock

danta	chu-tshö	. . .	nyipa	. . .	re
now	hours	. . .	second	. . .	is

. . . 2:30

. . .	nyi	dang	cheka	. . .

What time will this restaurant . . . open?

szakhang	di	chu-tshö	gatshö la	. . .	go	che-gi-re?
restaurant	this	hours	what	. . .	door	will open?

. . . close?

. . .	go gyab-gi-re?

DAYS OF THE WEEK

Monday	sza dawa	Friday	sza pasang
Tuesday	sza mingma	Saturday	sza pemba
Wednesday	sza lhakpa	Sunday	sza nyima
Thursday	sza phurbu		

GETTING AROUND/DIRECTIONS

Where is . . . the hotel?

drön-khang	. . .	gapa	yaw-re?
hotel	. . .	where	is?

I want to go to . . . Shigatse

Nga	. . .	Shigatse	. . .	la	dro dö yö
I	. . .	Shigatse	. . .	to	going (desire)

How many hours is it to . . . Lhasa?

Lhasa	. . .	bardu	chu-tshö	gatshö	go-gi-re?
Lhasa	. . .	up to	hours	how many	taking?

Please stop at . . . Dingri

Dingri	. . .	la	kak	ronang
Dingri	. . .	at	stop	please

What time will this . . . bus . . . leave?

motra	. . .	di	chu-tshö	gatshö la	dro-gi-re?
bus	. . .	this	time	what	will be going?

Is this the road to . . . Sera?

di	. . .	Sera	. . .	gi	lamka	re-pe?
this	. . .	Sera	. . .	of	road	is it?

SHOPPING

Although prices in shops and department stores are usually fixed, bargain for all souvenirs, carpets, vegetables, fruit, truck rides, pack animals and porters.

How much does this cost?

de	gong	gatshö	re?
this	cost	how much	is?

Two *yuan* (Chinese dollars)

gormo	nyi	re
dollars	two	it is

This is too expensive!

de	gong	pe	chempo	du!
this	cost	too	big	is!

Is there bargaining?

gong	drikya	yaw-re-pe?
price	adjusting	is there?

How much is one pound (½ kg)?

gyama	chik	gong	gatshö	re?
pound	one	cost	how much	is?

Do you have any . . . matches?

dzaktra	. . .	yö-pe?
Matches	. . .	do you have?

FOOD, EATING, AND RESTAURANTS

Is there any . . . noodle soup?

thukpa	. . .	yaw-re-pe?
noodle soup	. . .	is there?

Please give me . . . a glass of tea

ja chik	. . .	nang	ronang
tea one	. . .	give	please

I don't eat meat

Nga	sha	sza-	gi-me
I	meat	eat	do not

This food is delicious

khala	di	zhimpo	du
food	this	delicious	is

Enough! (thank you)

drik-song	(thu je che)
enough	(thank you)

How much is . . . the total cost?

khyöndom	. . .	gong	gatshö re?
total	. . .	price	how much is it?

ACCOMMODATIONS

I need . . . a place to sleep

Nga	la	. . .	nyesa	. . .	go
I	to	. . .	sleeping place	. . .	need

How much is . . . a room . . . per day?

nyima	chik la	. . .	khangmi	. . .	chik la	gatshö re?
day	each	. . .	room	. . .	one	for how much is?

. . . each bed . . .

. . .	nyetri chik la	. . .

Is there . . . a toilet . . . here?

de	. . .	sangchö	. . .	yaw-re-pe?
here	. . .	toilet	. . .	is there?

Where is . . . the key?

demik	. . .	gapa	yö?
key	. . .	where	is?

Does this dog bite?

khyi	di	so gyeb-	gi-re-pe?
dog	this	bite	will it?

TREKKING

Tomorrow we are going to . . . Dingri

sang-nyin	. . .	*Dingri*	. . .	*la*	*dro-gi-yin*
tomorrow	. . .	Dingri	. . .	to	are going

We need to hire a . . . burro

nga-tshö	. . .	*bung-gu*	*chik*	. . .	*la-*	*gö-yö*
we	. . .	burro	one	. . .	hire	need to

How much is . . . a yak . . . per day?

nyima	*chik la*	. . .	*yak*	*chik la*	. . .	*gong*	*gatshö*	*re?*
day	one	. . .	yak	one	. . .	cost	how much	is?

Where can we buy . . . food?

khala	. . .	*nyosa*	*gapa*	*yaw-re?*
food	. . .	buying place	where	is?

What is the name of that . . . mountain?

gang-ri	. . .	*phagi*	*ming la*	*ga-re*	*re?*
mountain	. . .	over there	name	what	is?

VISITING A MONASTERY

How many monks are in this monastery now?

danta	*gompa*	*de*	*drapa*	*gatshö*	*yaw-re?*
now	monastery	this	monks	how many	is?

I don't have any Dalai Lama photos

Dalai Lama	*gi*	*kupar*	*me*
Dalai Lama	of	religious picture	don't have

Which deity is this?

lha	*di*	*ga-gi*	*re?*
deity	this	which	is?

How old is this . . . monastery?

gompa	. . .	*di*	*nying-lö*	*re?*
monastery	. . .	this	how old	is it?

PHOTOGRAPHY

May I take . . . a photograph?

Nga	. . .	*par*	. . .	*gyebna*	*drik-gi-*	*re-pe?*
I	. . .	photo	. . .	take	all right	is it?

. . . your picture?

. . .	*khyerang-gi*	*par*

Inside the camera is only film. No pictures now.

parche	*nangla*	*pingshok*	*du.*	*danta*	*par*	*mindu.*
camera	inside	film	is.	now	photo	there isn't.

SICKNESS/EMERGENCY

I am sick

Nga	na-gi-	du
I	sick	am

I have . . . diarrhea

Nge	. . .	drokhok she-	. . .	gi-du
I	. . .	diarrhea	. . .	have

It hurts here

de	na-gi-du
here	hurts

Where is . . . a hospital ?

menkhang	. . .	gapa	yaw-re?
hospital	. . .	where	is?

Please help me

Nga	la	rokpa	nang	ronang
I	to	help	give	please

ENGLISH-TIBETAN VOCABULARY LIST

English	Tibetan
a (indefinite article)	zhik, chik
after	jela, jema
afternoon	nyin-gung
ago	gong la, nyela
airplane	namdru
airport	namdru babthang
all	tshangma
alone	chikpo
and then	ani, dang
arm	lakpa
arrive (v.)	leb-
ask (v.)	dri-
at	la
Australia	Astraliya
backpack	tö-pe
barley (toasted flour)	tsampa
barley (uncooked)	dru
beautiful	dzepo
beer, brewed (Chi.)	pijyu
beer (Tib.)	chang
before (time)	ngenla
behind	gyabla
bicycle	kang gari
big	chempo
bird	cha
blanket	kampali, nyezen
boat (ferry)	dru
bowl	phorpa
boy	bu
bread (Tib.)	bak-le
bread, steamed (Chi.)	mon-tou
bread, steamed (Tib.)	tri-momo
break (v.)	chak-
bridge	zampa
brother	pün-kya-bu
brother (sibling)	pün-kya
Buddhist (lit., insider)	nangpa
building	khangpa
bus	motra, bus
bus (Chi.)	gunggung chiche
bus station	motra tisen
butter	mar
butter lamp	chö-me
butter tea	Bhöja
buy (v.)	nyo-
call (v.)	sze-
Canada	Chanada
candle	yangla
candy	jiri
car	motra
carpet	den
cave	phuk
cheap	gong chungchung
cheese, dried	chokom, chura
child / children	phugu
chili pepper	si-pen
China	Gyanak
Chinese (people)	Gyami
chopsticks	khotse
circumambulate (v.)	kora gyab-
clean	tsangma
cold, to feel (v.)	khyak-
cold (adj.)	drangmo
cook (n.)	machen
come (v.)	yong-
cook (v.)	khalak tsö-
coral	jiru
country (birthplace)	kyesa, lungpa
daughter	bumo
day	nyima
day after tomorrow	nang-nyi
day before yesterday	khe-nyima
destroy (v.)	tor-
Dharamsala	Daram

different (other)	*zhempa*	hail (v.)	*sera tang-*
difficult	*ka-le khakpo*	hand	*lakpa*
dirty	*tsokpa*	happy	*kyipo*
dog	*khyi*	hat	*zhamo*
down	*mar*	have (v., first person)	*yö*
down there	*ma-gi*	have (v., second	
dress (Tib.)	*chupa*	and third person)	*du, yaw-re*
drink (v.)	*thung-*	he (inf.)	*khorang*
dust	*thala*	he (hon.)	*khong*
each	*re-re*	head	*go*
early	*ngapo*	headache, to have a (v.)	*go na-*
east	*shar*	hear (v.)	*go-*
easy	*le-lapo*	heavy	*jipo*
egg	*go-nga*	here	*de*
England	*Inji-lungpa*	hermit	*gomchen, tshampa*
glacier (ice)	*khyakpa*	hermitage	*ritrö, tshamkhang*
evening	*gongda*	horse	*ta*
eye	*mik*	hot (water, etc.)	*tshapo*
family	*khim-tsang*	hot springs	*chutshen*
far	*thak-ringpo*	hour	*chu-tshö*
farmer	*zhingpa*	house	*khangpa, nang*
father	*pha*	husband	*khyoga*
ferry boat	*dru*	husband/spouse (hon.)	*kunda*
festival	*düchen*	ice	*khyakpa*
fever, to have a (v.)	*tshewa na-*	incense	*pö*
few	*nyung-nyung*	India	*Gyagar*
field	*zhingkha*	inside	*nangla*
firewood	*me-shing*	Japan	*Ribi*
fish	*nya*	juniper	*shukpa*
flower	*metok*	kerosene	*sanum*
fog	*mukpa*	key	*demik*
food	*khalak, szama*	kilometer (Chi.)	*gung-li*
foot road (trail)	*kang-lam, lamka*	knife	*dri*
for	*la*	lamp, kerosene	*zhuma*
forest	*shing-na*	lantern, tilly	*sa-zhu*
forget (v.)	*je-*	last night	*dang-gong*
fortress	*dzong*	last week	*düntrak nyema*
France	*Pharansi*	last year	*da-nyi*
friend (m.)	*drokpo*	late	*chipo*
friend (f.)	*drokmo*	later	*je-la, je-ma*
from	*ne*	learn (v.)	*lab-, jang-*
front, in	*dünla*	left (direction)	*yön*
fuel (oil)	*num*	leg	*kangpa*
Germany	*Jermani*	light (weight)	*yangpo*
girl	*bumo*	like (v.)	*gapo-*
give (v., hon.)	*nang-*	live (reside, v.)	*de-*
goat	*ra*	lock	*gochak*
good	*yakpo*	look (v.)	*ta-, mikta-/te-*
grandfather	*pola*	lose (v.)	*lak-*
grandmother	*mola*	Madam (respectful)	*genla*
guide	*lamka ten-khen*	Madam (elder sister, title)	*acha-la*

Madam (lit., grandmother)	mola	only	chikpo
make (v.)	szo-/szö-	other	shenda
man	mi	outside	chilok
many	mangpo	over there	pha-ge
many times	theng mangpo	painting (fresco)	theb-ri
map	sabtra	painting (wall hanging)	thangka
market	trom	paper	shugu
maybe	chik-jena	pay (v.)	ngül tre- / tre-
meadow	pang	peak	tse
meat	sha	peas	trema
meditate (v.)	gom-	pen	nyugu
meet (v.; hon.)	thuk- / je-	people	mi
midnight	tshenmo	petrol (Chi.)	chiyo
milk	oma	pilgrim	ne-korwa
minute	karma	place	sacha
Miss	khong	police (Chi.)	gong-an
Mister	khong	police station (Chi.)	gong-an ju
money	ngül	potato	zho-go
monk	drapa	pound (½ kg)	gyama
monk, highly educated	lama	prayer beads	trang-nga
monk, incarnate	trülku	prayer ceremony	cho-ga
month	dawa	prayer flags	lungdar
morning	zho-ke	prayer stones	mani do
(this) morning	darang zho-ke	prayer wheel	mani
mother	ama	quickly	gyokpo
mountain	ri, tse	quilt	po-khe, kampali
mountain, snowy	gang-ri	rain	chapa
mountain pass	la	rain (v.)	chapa tang-
mountaineer	gang-ri dzak-khen	read (v.)	law-
mud	dam	red	marpo
nauseous, to be (v.)	drokhok na-	religion	chö
near	nyepo	religious sect	chöluk
need (v.)	gö-	return (v.)	law-
Nepal	Bel-yül	rice	dre
new	sarpa	rice (Chi.)	mi, mifan
next (later)	jema	ridge	gang
next (immediately)	jela	right (direction)	ye
night	tshen	river (major)	tsangpo, tsangchu
(last) night	dang-gong	river / stream	chu
nomad	drokpa	road (footpath)	lamka
noodles / soup, Tibetan	thukpa	road (for vehicles)	motra lamka
noodles (Chi.)	mien	rock	drak, do
noon	nyin-gung	room	khangmi
north	jang	rope	thakpa
now	danta	ruins	gokpo
nun	ani	salt	tsha
occupation	le-ka	same	chikpa
old (objects)	nyingpa	say (v.) / (hon.)	lab- / sung-
old (people)	lo chempo	school	labdra
onion	tsong	see (v.)	thong-, mi-thong-

sell (v.)	tshong-	there	pha-ge
sheep	luk	thermos	jadam
shop	tshongkhang	these	dintsho
silver	ngül	thief	kuma
sing (v.)	zhe tang-	thirsty, to be (v.)	khakom-
Sir (respectful)	genla	this	di
Sir (grandfather)	pola	those (distant)	phan-tsho
sister	pün-kya bumo	those (nearby)	de-tsho
sister (sibling)	pün-kya	Tibet	Bhö
sister, elder (title)	acha-la	wait (v.)	gu-
sit (v.) / (hon.)	de- / zhu-	Tibetan language	Bhö-ke
sleep (v.) / (hon.)	nye- / szim-	Tibetan people	Bhöpa
sleeping bag	nye-che	ticket	pass-se
small	chungchung	ticket office	pass-se nyosa
smoke	duwa	time	chu-tshö
snow	gang	times (one, two . . .)	theng (dangpo,
snow (v.)	gang tang-		nyipa . . .)
snow mountain	gang-ri	tired, to be (v.)	thang che-
sometimes	tshamtsham-la	today	dering
son	bu	toilet	sangchö
song	lu, zhe	tomorrow	sang-nyin
soon	gyokpo	tonight	dogong
soup (noodle, Tib.)	thukpa	tractor (Chi.)	thola
south	lho	trail / path	lamka,
speak (v.)	kecha she-		kang-lam
spinach	pe-tshe	tree	shingdong
spouse (hon.)	kunda	trek (v.)	rilam gompa gyab-
statue	ku	trek leader	rilam ten-khen
stay (v.)	de-	trekker / traveler	takorwa
steep	szarpo	truck	motra
stone	do	turquoise	yu
store	tshongkhang	wood	shing
stove, fuel	me-thab	until (up to)	bardu
stove, wood	chak-thab	up	ya
strong	shuk-chempo	up there	ya-ge
sugar	jema-kara, chini	up to	bar, bardu
sun	nyima	urinate (v.)	chimpa dang-
take (v.)	len-	valley	lungpa
talk (v.)	kecha lab-	vegetables	tshe
tea / (hon.)	ja / sölja	Venerable (hon. title	
tea, sweet	ja-ngamo	for high lama)	rimpoche
tea, with butter	Bhöja	very	shedra
teach (v.)	lab-	village	drongse, drongtsho
teacher	gegen	walk (v.)	gompa gyab-
teahouse	jakhang	want (v.)	gö-
telephone	khapa	wash (v.)	trü-
temple	lhakhang	wash basin	dungben
tent	gur	watch (n.)	chu-tshö
tent (nomad)	ba	water	chu
that (distant)	phagi	water, boiled	chu köl
that (nearby)	de	weather	namshi

week	*düntrak*	work (v.)	*leka je-*
west	*nub*	wrong	*mindu, ma-re*
wheat	*dro*	yak (female)	*dri*
white	*karpo*	yak (male)	*yak*
wife / (hon.)	*kyimen / kunda*	yak (cattle hybrid, f.)	*dzomo*
wind	*lungbo*	yak (cattle hybrid, m.)	*dzo*
wine (distilled)	*arak*	yak dung (fuel)	*cho*
woman	*kyimen*	year	*lo*
wool	*bel*	yesterday	*khesa*
word	*tshik*	yogurt	*zho*
work	*leka*		

"Om mani padme hum," *the* mantra *of Tibet's patron saint Chenrezik, is the most common of the Buddhist prayers carved into* mani *stones*

THE TREKS
AND TRAILS

The women in Kham often wear elaborate braids of turquoise, coral, and other ornaments in their hair

6
USING THE TREK DESCRIPTIONS

The following trek descriptions, when combined with the relevant maps, should get you to your intended destination with as few difficulties as possible. In the introduction to each description a time frame is noted in bold type (e.g., **3½ to 5 days)** to accommodate both fastpaced trekkers and leisurely walkers. The approximate walking times, which are also in bold type, are based upon the pace set by a pack animal or my own walking pace while carrying a backpack. These figures *do not include any rest stops*, unless the text states otherwise.

In general, 5 to 6 hours of actual walking time per day (not including breaks) is a comfortable trekking pace, depending on the terrain and altitude. Due to the extreme elevations in Tibet, allow about a half an hour of rest stops for every hour of walking detailed in the trek descriptions (i.e., 4 hours of actual walking time takes most people about 6 hours with rest stops. Allow more time if you enjoy photography, wildflowers, bird-watching, or stopping at monasteries and villages. These times are meant only as helpful recommendations). Pace yourself according to your abilities. Don't be discouraged if these times seem too quick (or too slow). If you find that it takes 3 hours to walk a section of trail that is described as taking 2 hours, the chances are you will continue to take an extra hour for every 2 hours described in the text. This difference should be taken into consideration for the remainder of the trek described.

In addition to suggested walking times, the routes are described as heading to the right or to the left, along with the corresponding compass direction. When a trail or route follows a valley, a drainage, or any flowing water, the standard directional terminology from rafting and kayaking is used: Right means the right shore or bank of running water *as you face downstream,* and is symbolized by a capital R in parentheses and usually preceded by a compass direction, "south (R)"; left *as you face downstream* is symbolized "(L)."

If you are not part of an organized group or in the company of a guide with a pack animal, the chances of becoming temporarily "geographically embarrassed" (i.e., lost) are greatly increased. Even if you are using this book, I advise bringing a compass and the best maps you can obtain. Finding someone to ask for directions can be difficult, especially in remote areas. I have had herders run away when they saw me approaching, and as I climbed toward their hiding spot they bolted farther up the ridge, refusing to answer any of my questions.

A number of common Tibetan words have been used throughout the text. Except for proper names, Tibetan words are printed in italics (e.g., *gompa*). If the meaning does not accompany the italicized word, refer to Appendix C, "Glossary of Tibetan and Foreign Words."

The transliteration of Tibetan words and place names is an old problem that has yet to be remedied; place names in this book are based on known Tibetan spellings or phonetic approximations. Many towns and settlements, especially in Kham and Amdo, have both a Tibetan and a Chinese name, particularly if a town is an administrative center, and some places may have older names not commonly used now. The town of Phadruk in the Everest region is known to older Tibetans as Tashi Dzum, while the Chinese call it Paru. Variations can also occur with the common names of important passes, rivers, mountains, and valleys, especially in Eastern Tibet; the people living in one valley often have a different name for a pass crossing than those living on the far side.

All of the trek route maps are based upon the 1:200,000 Russian topographic map series (see "Maps"). The map illustrations have been simplified to detail trekking routes and other necessary geographical information for each area. A key for all the maps follows this section.

The elevations used in the route descriptions are at best approximations, determined by readings from a Swiss-made altimeter and compared against the altitudes on the Russian maps. Lhasa's elevation "officially" ranges from 11,830 feet to 12,087 feet (3607 m to 3684 m). For consistency I set my altimeter in Lhasa at 11,850 ft (3612 m) before departing on a trek. Except for the heights of mountains, which were taken from topographical maps, all of the elevation readings given in this book have been rounded off to the nearest 100 feet (31 m); if a reading was exactly on the 50-foot increment I recorded it as such. The measurements in meters have been rounded off to the nearest 10 meters.

Tibet has no road signs, but most of the main roads have small kilometer marker stones, a reliable means for locating obscure junctions. The kilometer marker readings for important towns and turnoffs in the trek descriptions are usually noted in parentheses (e.g., km marker 5145), and a detailed list of these is included in the "Highway Kilometer Markers" section of this chapter. Note that the odometer in your vehicles may not synchronize exactly with these markers.

KEY TO MAP SYMBOLS

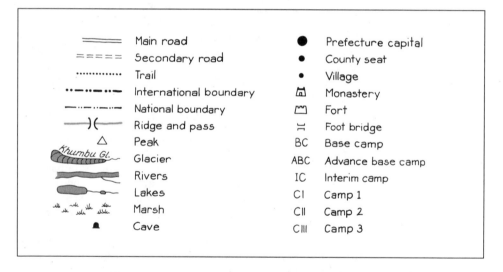

════	Main road	●	Prefecture capital
═ ═ ═ ═ ═	Secondary road	●	County seat
············	Trail	•	Village
•• ••• •••	International boundary	⌂	Monastery
─ ··· ··· ─	National boundary	⌂	Fort
)(	Ridge and pass	⊨	Foot bridge
△	Peak	BC	Base camp
Khumbu Gl.	Glacier	ABC	Advance base camp
	Rivers	IC	Interim camp
	Lakes	CI	Camp 1
	Marsh	CII	Camp 2
▲	Cave	CIII	Camp 3

HIGHWAY KILOMETER MARKERS

Every major road in Tibet (and China) has a series of stone kilometer markers set into its shoulder. The counting systems are rarely contiguous due to differing points of origin, though as Tibet's roads are upgraded new synchronized marker systems are replacing the old, unrelated systems.

The following tables list the kilometer marker systems currently in use in the TAR and in the Kham and Amdo regions of Sichuan and Qinghai Provinces. If a location falls halfway between two markers, both readings are listed, e.g., 54/5 or 89/90. Readings have been approximated where marker stones are missing.

THE FRIENDSHIP HIGHWAY FROM LHASA TO NEPAL

KM MARKER	LOCATION
4638 (marker missing)	Lhasa (long distance station)
4646 (marker missing)	Tölung Dechen/Tibet-Qinghai Highway turnoff
4703	Chaksam bridge/Shigatse turnoff
4758	Nyemo Valley turnoff
4821	Takdruka ferry/Northern Road to Lhasa turnoff
4903	Shigatse (Tashilhumpo monastery front gate)
4917	Narthang monastery
5014	Tsho La; 14,763 ft, 4500 m
5028/9	Sakya monastery turnoff
5040 (marker missing)	Zhichen hot springs turnoff
5051/2	Lhatse
5058	Mount Kailash turnoff
5082	Lakpa La (Jia Tsuo), 17,126 feet (5220m)
5133	Shekar (New Tingri) turnoff
5139	Shekar Checkpoint
5145/6	Dza Rongphu/Everest base camp turnoff
5192	Ra Chu village turnoff
5193/4	Dingri
5206	Tsamda village/Langkor monastery turnoff
5207	Tsamda hot springs
5266	Kyirong/Shishapangma north base camp turnoff
5289	Thong La (Lalung La), 16,580 feet (5050 m)
5318	Ngora village turnoff
5335	Pelgyeling monastery/Milarepa cave
5345/6	Nyelam
5379 (marker missing)	Zhangmu/Khasa/Immigration post
5387 (marker missing)	Friendship Bridge/Nepal border
116 (new system begins)	Friendship Bridge
0	Kathmandu

TIBET-SICHUAN HIGHWAY FROM LHASA TO MELDROGUNGKAR AND KONGPO

KM MARKER	LOCATION
4632 (new system)	Lhasa bridge
4612	Taktse/Dechen Dzong
4611	Shinjang Valley turnoff
4609	Taktse bridge/Phenpo Chu Valley turnoff
4596	Sekhang/Trupshi Valley turnoff
4591	Ganden monastery turnoff
4572/1	Nonda/Gyama Valley turnoff
4564	Meldrogungkar/Drigung monastery turnoff
4509	Rutok village and monastery
4479	Kongpoba La; 16,050 ft, 4890 m
4361	Gyamda
4312	Pasum Tsho turnoff
4232	Bayi

LHASA TO TSETHANG

KM MARKER	LOCATION
4638 (marker missing)	Lhasa (long distance station)
4703	Tsangpo River bridge
66/67 (different system begins)	Tsangpo River bridge
93	Gongkar Airport turnoff
112	Dorje Drak monastery ferry crossing
118	Chedeshöl
147	Mindroling monastery turnoff
155	Samye ferry crossing
190 (marker missing)	Tsethang traffic circle

TIBET-QINGHAI HIGHWAY FROM LHASA TO GOLMUD

KM MARKER	LOCATION
4638 (marker missing)	Lhasa (long distance station)
3879 (new system begins; marker missing)	Tölung Dechen/Tibet-Qinghai Highway turnoff
3853	Tsurphu monastery turnoff
3804/5	Yangpachen
3803	Shigatse Northern Road turnoff
3730/29	Damzhung
3580	Nakchu
2740	Golmud

NORTHERN ROAD FROM LHASA TO SHIGATSE

KM MARKER	LOCATION
4638 (marker missing)	Lhasa (long distance station)
3879 (new system begins; marker missing)	Tölung Dechen/Tibet-Qinghai Highway turnoff
3803	Shigatse Northern Road turnoff
0 (different system begins)	Northern Road turnoff
19 (marker missing)	Yangpachen monastery
20 (marker missing)	Dorjeling monastery turnoff
56	Zhugu La, 17,400 feet (5300 m)
105	Do-ngu La, 15,900 feet (4840 m)
158/9	Takdruka ferry crossing
4821 (new system begins)	Takdruka ferry crossing
4903 (marker missing)	Shigatse (Tashilhumpo monastery front gate)

SOUTHERN ROAD FROM LHASA TO SHIGATSE, VIA GYANGTSE

KM MARKER	LOCATION
4638 (marker missing)	Lhasa (long distance station)
4646 (marker missing)	Tölung Dechen/Tibet-Qinghai Highway turnoff
4703	Tsangpo/Chaksam bridge
59/60 (old system resumes)	Tsangpo/Chaksam bridge
94/5	Kampa La, 15,728 feet (4794 m)
152	Nakartse/Samding monastery turnoff
180	Karo La, 16,437 feet (5010 m)
251	Gyangtse turnoff

The Friendship Highway connects Lhasa and Kathmandu

90 (start of different system)	Gyangtse turnoff
88	Yadong Valley turnoff
20	Zhalu monastery turnoff
0	Shigatse

NORTHERN ROAD FROM LHASA TO MOUNT KAILASH

KM MARKER	LOCATION KM MARKER LOCATION
4638 (marker missing)	Lhasa (long distance station)
4904 (marker missing)	Shigatse (Tashilhumpo monastery front gate)
5058	Mount Kailash turnoff
2140 (new system begins)	Mount Kailash turnoff
2135	Tsangpo River ferry crossing
1906/5 (marker missing)	Raga Junction/Saga turnoff

*No markers beyond this point; the following kilometer readings to Darchen/
Mount Kailash start from zero (0) at Raga Junction.*

0	Raga Junction
20	Tahejia geyser
102	Lagen La, 18,000 feet (5490 m)
228	Tshochen Dzong (Coqen)
396	Amdo turnoff/Tung Tsho
476	Gertse (Gerze or Gerje)
641	Tshakar Qu (Qagcaka)
948	Ali/Shiquanhe/Ngari
1021	Old Töling/Tsaparang turnoff
1079	Baher (Baer)/Töling turnoff
1134	Mon-tser/Tirthapuri turnoff
1189	Darchen turnoff
1195	Darchen/start of Mount Kailash pilgrimage

SOUTHERN ROAD FROM MOUNT KAILASH TO THE FRIENDSHIP HIGHWAY

There are no kilometer markers from Darchen to Old Drongba.

KM MARKER	LOCATION
0	Darchen/Mount Kailash
22	Barka/ Purang turnoff
43	Hor Qu (Hor-re)
138	Mayum (Marium) La, 16,700 feet (5090 m)
278	Paryang
368	Old Drongpa
1703 (new system begins)	Old Drongpa
1846	Saga
1906/5	Raga Junction
2140	Friendship Highway junction

TIBET-SICHUAN HIGHWAY FROM CHENGDU TO CHAMDO

KM MARKER	LOCATION
0	Chengdu
146	Ya'an
2632 (new system begins; marker missing)	Ya'an
2735	Erlang Shan tunnel turnoff
2752/3	Erlang Shan, 9950 feet (3030 m)
2783 (marker missing)	Shimian turnoff
2796 (marker missing)	Luding
2845 (marker missing)	Kangting
2879	Gyetö La (Zheduo Shan), 14,075 feet (4290 m)
2912	Luba (Liuba)/Minyak Gangkar turnoff
2920	Ranaka (Xindu Chau)
2924 (marker missing)	Litang and Batang turnoff
446 (marker missing; old system)	Litang and Batang turnoff
489	pass, 12,850 feet (3920 m)
509	Barme (Chaining, or Taining)
427 (marker missing; different system)	Barme (Chaining, or Taining)
471 (marker missing)	pass, 13,000 feet (3960 m)
505 (marker missing)	Dawu
575 (marker missing)	Luho (Drango)
641	pass, 13,150 feet (4010 m)
672 (marker missing)	Kandze (Ganze)
676 (marker missing)	Pelyul turnoff
721	pass
843 (marker missing)	Manigango/Jyekundo turnoff
865 (marker missing)	Tro La (Chola Shan), 16,128 feet (4916 m)
928/9 (marker missing)	Korlomdo
958 (marker missing)	Dege
979 (marker missing)	Gon-gye-shin turnoff /trailhead to Go-se La
984 (marker missing)	Dri Chu/ Yangtze River/TAR border
1320 (marker missing)	Chamdo

The yak is an important source of dairy products and meat. Its hair is woven into tents and blankets.

7
THE LHASA REGION

Although the high Himalaya is far to the south and west, the mountainous areas near Lhasa offer some of the finest trekking in Central Tibet. The spillover from India's monsoon bathes this region with summer rains, encouraging wildflowers, tall stands of brush, and scattered groves of trees along the streams and lower slopes of the valleys. Families of nomadic herders establish summer camps throughout these drainages, which they share with a variety of wildlife. Although few glaciers lie in these intermediate ranges, the countryside here is as rugged and "Tibetan" as any place near the 26,000-foot (8000-m) peaks.

DAY HIKES NEAR LHASA
MAP NO. 1, PAGE 74

Before starting your trek in Tibet, spend a minimum of two to three days in Lhasa (or Shigatse, Tsethang, Kandze, Labrang, etc.) acclimatizing to the unusually high altitude. To get into shape and reduce the risk of elevation-related problems, base yourself in one location and go on day hikes as often as your time and energy will allow. I need a week or more to feel my best while exercising at these elevations, though commercial

Phurbu Chok monastery, in the Dode Valley

groups typically allow a maximum of three full days. The more time you spend acclimatizing, the more you will be able to enjoy everything around you once the trek begins.

A great way to limber up upon arrival in Lhasa is to walk around the Barkor, the main Tibetan market area and the popular pilgrimage walk circling the seventh-century Jokhang temple. Situated in the heart of the old part of Lhasa, this circuit around the holiest shrine in Tibet takes **about 20 minutes** to complete, not including the inevitable stops for souvenir hunting.

WITHIN LHASA

Many of the larger monasteries in Tibet have a well-traveled *kora* (pilgrimage circuit, which is always walked clockwise) around their perimeters. They are an excellent way to take warm-up walks throughout Tibet. Care must be taken to observe the religious significance of these circuits.

THE LINGKOR

The Lingkor (literally, "around the Lings") is the traditional pilgrim's circuit around the Holy City of Lhasa and three of the four Lings—the Regency Temples of Lhasa. The walk takes **about 1½ hours**. Early each morning steady streams of worshippers complete their rounds with prayer wheels in hand. On certain Tibetan holidays, especially the Saga Dawa Festival in the fourth Tibetan month, an almost endless procession of pilgrims follows this route around the city, adding incense offerings to billowing hearths.

The golden yaks statue to the west of the Potala Palace is an arbitrary place to start the Lingkor. Although this urban setting doesn't look much like a pilgrimage circuit, walk northeast on the right (east) side of North Lingkor Road (Lingkor Nub Lam), past the Bank of China and around to a small lake with a peaked-roof temple in the center, behind the Potala. This is the Lukhang, the temple of the serpent spirits, which was a late-night haunt for the Sixth Dalai Lama and his secret paramours. Continue straight ahead (east) on this road to the second large traffic circle, with statues commemorating the first Chinese ascent of Mount Everest. The Plateau Hotel and a Bank of China are at this intersection.

The Lingkor now turns right (south) onto East Lingkor Road (Lingkor Shar Lam); pilgrims walk on the left side of the street here. The next intersection is Beijing (or Dekyi) Shar Lam (East Beijing Road), the main road through the city. The Banok Shol Hotel is a short walk to the right (west); the first entrance to the Barkor area is several minutes farther. Continue south to the next major intersection with a traffic light, where the Lingkor turns right (west) onto Chingdröl Lam (Liberation Street). Stay on the left side of the street, passing rows of shops until you get to the banks of the Kyi Chu, the Lhasa River.

The Lingkor passes several bridges leading into a resort complex on Thieves Island (Kumalingka), then crosses to the right (north) side of the road toward a huge offering cairn. Do like the pilgrims when they walk around this circuit and toss three stones onto the mound to acknowledge the local spirits, then enter the stone-walled corridor leading north to the base of Chakpori. The side of this hill is covered with a grand display of rock paintings and carvings, including the large blue image of Menlha, the "Medicine Buddha." The *kora* climbs a short distance above this Buddhist art gallery, descends to another walled corridor, then follows a wide path to meet the road connecting the Potala with Norbulingka, the Dalai Lamas' summer palace. To finish the circuit, don't turn here, but continue straight ahead (north) **a few minutes** to return to the golden yaks.

CHAKPORI

The "Iron Hill" of Lhasa, with its tall communication towers rising across from the Potala Palace, was formerly the site of a fifteenth-century nunnery, then later the

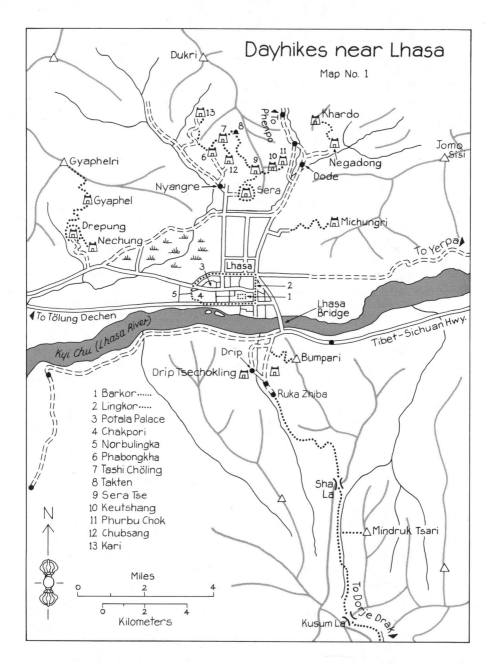

Dayhikes near Lhasa

Map No. 1

1 Barkor......
2 Lingkor.....
3 Potala Palace
4 Chakpori
5 Norbulingka
6 Phabongkha
7 Tashi Chöling
8 Takten
9 Sera Tse
10 Keutshang
11 Phurbu Chok
12 Chubsang
13 Kari

N

Miles
0   2   4

0   2   4
Kilometers

Tibetan Medical College. This famous school of traditional Tibetan medicine was built in the late seventeenth century by Sangye Gyatsho, the regent of Tibet who completed the construction of the Potala while concealing the death of the Fifth Dalai Lama for fifteen years. An entrance *chörten* known as the Western Gate once connected this rocky ridge with the base of the Potala, but that structure and the medical college were destroyed in 1959. Three white *chörtens* have been rebuilt between the hills. Along the cliffs at the east end of Chakpori is one of King Songtsen Gampo's meditation caves, Drakla Luguk, plus several adjacent temples and buildings.

The Potala Palace of the Dalai Lamas, from Chakpori, Lhasa

One of the more direct trails to the top of Chakpori is a **20-minute** ascent that begins at Drakla Luguk. From the upper right temple (dedicated to Tangtong Gyelpo, Tibet's fifteenth-century renaissance man who invented Tibetan opera and built iron link bridges), the trail to Chakpori ascends several steps, passes a derelict building, then goes under an elevated water pipe. Continue about 50 yards (18 m) to where the trail splits, then go left to reach the eastern summit (12,050 ft, 3670 m); photographers prefer the morning and late-afternoon light to capture the Potala's soaring presence.

SERA MONASTERY REGION
Sera monastery is one of the six great Gelukpa sect monasteries in Tibet. This fifteenth-century sprawl of golden roofs and whitewashed walls is just a few miles north of Lhasa at the base of a long, dry ridge called Phurbu Chok. High above the monastery along this ridge are several old hermitages and temples connected by pilgrim trails that are some of the finest day hikes in the Lhasa area.

SERA MONASTERY Kora
A walk around the *kora* is an appropriate way to complete a visit to Sera. Though the actual walking time is **less than 1 hour,** extra time should be allowed for the inevitable encounters with monks and pilgrims. Above this circuit is a short side trip to Chöding Gön, a retreat associated with a famous meditation cave of Tsong Khapa, founder of the Gelukpa sect of Tibetan Buddhism.

Sera is connected to Lhasa by Nyangre Lam, the road leading north from near the Potala. The long, gradual uphill climb takes **about 20 minutes** by bicycle; or take the number 5 minibus to the monastery parking lot, which originates at the bus stand a block west of the Barkor. Some minibuses stop at a tea shop junction just before the gates of the Military Hospital compound, where this road ends. Sera is only a few hundred yards farther to the right (east) on a dirt road. To the left of this same junction is the turnoff to Phabongkha temple (see description below).

A tree-lined road leads from the parking area to Sera's main entrance (12,000 ft, 3660 m), where monks are stationed to collect entrance fees from foreigners, even if you're only doing *kora*. Tour groups are led from here up the main service road bisecting the monastery grounds. Pilgrims usually bypass this main gate, walking past the monastery tea shop to another entrance 150 feet (45 m) farther to the left (west). From here a wide path enters the network of corridors on a prescribed inner pilgrimage circuit that leads to each of the main temples and monastic colleges, starting with the Sera Me Tantric College.

The outer pilgrimage path does not enter the monastery complex. Instead, continue straight ahead (west) for 600 feet (185 m) along the walled-in dirt trail, then turn right around the tall boundary wall. A short switchback trail leads up the granite slopes. To the left (west) across an alluvial outwash is a trail from Sera to Chubsang *ani gompa* and Phabongkha.

The Sera *kora* circles above the golden-roofed Ngakpa Dratsang, a center for Tantric studies, and above Chadral *khangtsen*, a residence building behind Sera Je, the largest of Sera's three colleges. The path descends into a maze of willow trees, boulders with Tibetan *mantras* and a series of trails that seem to lead everywhere except around the monastery. Ask anyone where the *kora lam*, or pilgrimage trail, continues; you will be enthusiastically guided to the right (east) through the trees toward a stone-walled corridor behind Hamdong *khangtsen*, another residence hall for monks. This passage leads to a granite outcrop rising behind the Tsokchen, Sera's grand assembly hall for hundreds of monks. The main route to Chöding Gön (12,200 ft, 3720 m) does not enter this corridor, but ascends the ridge up to the left from the willow grove, reaching this seldom-visited temple in **15 minutes**. This is the same turnoff for the trail to Sera Tse hermitage (see next section).

The *kora* continues behind the Tsokchen along rounded granite outcrops, passing a metal framework where a *köku*, a large silk appliqué *thangka*, is displayed on the first day of Zhotön, the Yogurt Festival. The next part of the route is the most active section of the *kora* for pilgrims, with special rocks that are to be touched or circumambulated, many brightly colored rock paintings, and plenty of dogs who rely upon food offerings from the pilgrims. Some Tibetans believe that these dogs are fallen monks who have been reduced to begging for scraps near monasteries due to misbehavior in their previous lives. If you happen to have a ball of *tsampa* in your pocket, feel free to share it with these fellows.

Although Sera looks impressive from this part of the *kora*, the number of buildings in use is considerably less now than in the 1950s, when more than six thousand monks were in residence. The monastery was hit hard by the Chinese due to its residents' active participation in the 1959 uprising, but now most of the rubble has been cleared away. The *kora* continues through the boulders, then descends steeply to the edge of Sera's eastern boundary wall. Although a larger trail continues straight ahead (south), pilgrims turn right through an opening in the wall. The path from this gap enters a low doorway into the courtyard of an old residence hall, then leads to a white *chörten* beside the tree-lined service road. The main entrance gate is to the left. Tractor taxis, minibuses, and vehicle taxis often wait in the parking area until late afternoon; taxis continue operating on the road to the Potala until dark.

SERA TSE HERMITAGE

The ochre walls of Sera Tse (also Sera Utse; 13,300 ft, 4050 m) cling to the rocky face of Phurbu Chok directly above Sera monastery. Pre-dating Sera, much of the hermitage was destroyed in the 1960s, though several small temples have been rebuilt and a few monks have returned to this lofty retreat. The climb up and back from Sera Tse is a strenuous **half-day** outing; it can also be reached via a high *kora* trail from Phabongkha monastery (see description below). The most direct approach starts from the pilgrimage *kora* around Sera, then climbs to the temples of Chöding Gön (12,200 ft, 3720 m). Before setting off, take a minute at Sera's entrance to locate the hermitage on the ridge face, set in a grove of trees not far above the monastery.

A shortcut to Chöding Gön bypasses the first half of the *kora* by following the willow-lined service road bisecting the monastery. This road ends at the base of the ridge between Sera Je College and Hamdong *khangtsen*. The pilgrim *kora* is only 20 feet (6 m) up this ridge under the canopy of willow trees. The main route up to Sera Tse now climbs above the *kora* and around Gyelchen Kukar, a small residence temple for the *sungma* or guardian protector of Hamdong *khangtsen*. Chöding Gön is a **10-minute** ascent on a trail leading up the granite ridge behind this temple. A faint path is worn into the crumbly rock; the occasional footprint or string of prayer flags in the bushes help verify you are on the right track. A relatively flat, wide trail follows the cliff top to the left (southeast) around the curve of the ridge to several huge trees beside Chöding Gön. The building had been defunct since the 1960s, the temple gutted and the frescoes obliterated with coats of white paint; with the return of several monks, the temple has been renovated and the figures of the *yab-se-sum*, Tsong Khapa and his two main disciples, again grace the central altar downstairs. Directly above this temple is Chöding *drubphuk,* a small shrine over a meditation cave used more than five centuries ago by Tsong Khapa. This great reformer of the Kadampa sect of Tibetan Buddhism composed two of his most famous treatises on Buddhist scriptures and philosophy during the several years he spent here.

Sera Tse is **1 to 1½ hours** above Chöding Gön. The monks reach Sera Tse via a shortcut that climbs straight up behind the cave temple. An easier approach begins at the doorstep of Chöding Gön. Using the trail leading to the left (south) of the temple's entrance, pass a grove of trees and a spring, the last water until Sera Tse. Keep contouring

The ruins of Tashi Chöling gompa, Lhasa

across the ridge for **10 minutes**, past two more small gullies with trees. About 225 feet (70 m) past here the trail switches back up to the left to begin the climb to Sera Tse.

Desert conditions prevail: Lizards laze on hot rocks and fat Himalayan griffin vultures soar on the heated currents rising from these south-facing slopes. The trail enters some switchbacks, then climbs steadily to the ruins at the base of Sera Tse. Zigzag up through the broken walls to a small paved courtyard and a *lhakhang* with commanding views of the Lhasa Valley. This shrine is another Tsong Khapa meditation cave; nearby are the two caves of his main disciples, Khedrub Je and Gyeltsab Je. Farther up the hill is a *gönkhang* with images of the protecting deities Pehar, who possesses the State Oracle during his trances, and the mule-riding protectress of the Gelukpa sect, Pelden Lhamo.

The quickest way back to Sera is to return on the same trail; alternatives include heading west across the ridge for **2 hours or more** to Phabongkha (described in reverse below) or walking east across the ridge face to the Dode Valley (described below).

PHABONGKHA REGION

Phabongkha temple (12,550 ft, 3830 m) is a relatively unknown historical site not far west of Sera on Phurbu Chok ridge. Rivaling the Jokhang in antiquity, this chapel was founded in the seventh century by King Songtsen Gampo. According to tradition, the land near Phabongkha was the residence of a pair of divine tortoises, which were manifested as two granite boulders. The king's wife, the Chinese princess Wencheng, had determined that a huge ogress lay on her back across Tibet, preventing the spread of Buddhism. The protectress Pelden Lhamo recommended that Songtsen Gampo and Wencheng go to Phabongkha to meditate over a solution. The king then built a nine-story temple at this site upon the larger, female tortoise-rock. Four great chains radiating in the four cardinal directions were used to anchor the tower, which was called Phabongkha (On Top of the Big Rock), and another chain connected the male tortoise rock with the female. Upon completion of this temple, the king and Wencheng meditated here for three years, and determined that another temple (the Jokhang) needed to be built over the heart of the demoness, and that a series of twelve geomantically aligned temples should be constructed over her shoulders and hips, elbows and knees, feet and hands. Several of these temples, such as Trandruk temple in Tsethang, are extant today.

Some 200 years after Songtsen Gampo's era the first Buddhist monks in Tibet, seven in all, were ordained at Samye monastery and established their residence at Phabongkha. But persecution of the new religion during the reign of King Langdarma in the ninth century led to the temple's destruction. Phabongkha has been rebuilt and destroyed several times since. The most recently restored temple is still on the tortoise-boulder, but is now only two stories high. Phabongkha is one of Tibet's four main pilgrimage destinations for practitioners of Chakrasamvara Tantricism, a highly developed form of Tibetan Buddhism involving worship of the deity Demchok. Nearby is an important sky-burial site for the Lhasa Valley.

During Drukwa Tsezhi (Fourth of the Sixth Month Festival; also called Chökor Düchen), Phabongkha is the staging point for a pilgrimage procession up to Sera Tse and on to Phurbu Chok monastery, in the Dode Valley. It is also the focal point for several day hikes, an ideal way to get the legs moving and to acclimatize while in Lhasa. The **600-foot (180-m)** climb to Phabongkha follows a well-graded road; most people can manage the elevation gain after three nights in Lhasa. The *kora* ascends from here to Tashi Chöling monastery (13,100 ft, 3990 m) on a nearby ridge spur to the east. Farther up on the cliffs is the cave hermitage of Takten *drakphuk* (13,650 ft, 4160 m). Each of these sites is on a tier where you can rest from the succession of climbs. If you take the route descending from Tashi Chöling to Chubsang nunnery (12,450 ft, 3790 m) and onto the Sera turnoff, the hike up from Phabongkha to the Takten caves is a **half-day** loop walk; continuing beyond Takten to Sera Tse and the Dode Valley is a **full day's** journey.

The walk to Phabongkha takes **1 hour or more** and starts on the opposite side of the main road from the turnoff for Sera monastery. This is a good place to get your bearings. Chubsang *ani gompa* is on the ridge side just above Nyangre village; Phabongkha is farther to the left (west). Tashi Chöling is higher on the ridge between them. From the Sera turnoff, go 200 feet (60 m) beyond a restaurant and shop, then turn left (west) onto a dirt road entering Nyangre. Wind through the lanes of houses to where the road splits on the north side of the village. The right fork leads to Chubsang nunnery, straight ahead (north) on the ridge side. The left fork winds past terraced barley fields and desert scrub toward a cluster of temples on the ridge up to the left (northeast); Phabongkha is in the middle, perched on the boulder. **About 10 minutes** beyond this fork is the pilgrim trail to these temples, well marked by cairns. Or follow the road to reach the lower *lhakhang*. Inside are the *rangjön*, or self-manifested figures of Risum Gompo ("Protectors of the Three Families"), Tibet's three most revered *bodhisattvas*. Songtsen Gampo had visions of this triad during his meditations at Phabongkha; their images then appeared miraculously upon the slab of rock enshrined here.

Beside the temple's entrance are the words *Om mani padme hum* carved into a rock. This is the *mantra* or prayer of Chenrezik, Tibet's *Bodhisattva* of Compassion. It roughly translates as "Hail to the jewel in the lotus," a reference to the Buddhist belief that everyone inherently possesses the wisdom and insight necessary to achieve spiritual enlightenment. According to tradition, this particular inscription was the first example of Tibetan writing presented to Songtsen Gampo by his minister, Tonmi Sambota, who had designed this script for his king during a lengthy period of studies in India.

Just above here are the rounded walls of Phabongkha. Walk clockwise around the large tortoise-boulder to approach the entrance on the far, uphill side. On the left side and set under the base of the boulder is the meditation cave of Songtsen Gampo. The monks usually gather to chant in the morning and early evening in a small assembly hall on the *gompa's* second floor. If a prayer ceremony is in progress, take off your shoes, have a seat, and be prepared for a bowl of Tibetan butter tea. The statues include images of Songtsen Gampo with his Nepalese and Chinese princesses on either side. An ancient *rangjön* stone statue of Jowo Sakyamuni, called Doku Rimpoche, is in an adjacent glass case. A darkened protectors shrine is tucked into a narrow room behind these figures; one of the silk-draped images is Yidrolma, the demoness who reclines across Tibet.

The grounds around Phabongkha have a peaceful desert garden atmosphere, shaded in places by gnarled old willow trees. Adjacent to the *gompa* is the kitchen. Just up the hillside is a meditation cave of Tsong Khapa, and higher up is a third temple with several *lhakhangs*, including one dedicated to Princess Wencheng.

A stunning but difficult walk climbs steeply to the left (northwest) from Phabongkha to Kari *ani gompa* (also called Kargon Samtenling; 13,700 ft, 4180 m), which is situated high on the flanks of Dukri (16,860 ft, 5140 m), the fourth-highest sacred summits around Lhasa. Kari is one of the oldest monastic sites near Lhasa, founded 900 years ago by Padampa Sangye, an Indian ascetic who lived in the Dingri area near Mount Everest. Almost a hundred nuns reside here. The ill-defined route is a surprisingly tough walk over rugged terrain; allow **at least 6 hours** for the round trip. Kari can also be approached by the road up the Nyangre Valley, to the northwest of Phabongkha. On the trail to Kari from Phabongkha is Serphuk, a cave retreat built under a large cliff face.

THE PHABONGKHA-SERA TSE-DODE VALLEY KORA

To begin the pilgrims' circuit to Sera Tse, follow the *kora* trail across from Phabongkha's highest temple and around the male tortoise-boulder, decorated with prayer flags (notched steps lead to the top for making offerings). Just below the boulder the trail leads to the ruined walls of the former residence (*podrang*) of Lhatsun Rimpoche, a *lama* from Sera monastery. The *kora* to Sera Tse follows the path below the walls to the bottom of a dry gully, then ascends the east (L) bank to join a wide trail. Tashi Chöling is **less than 30 minutes** up to the east from the edge of this drainage. Directly below are two white *chörtens*; nearby is a sky-burial site atop a large, flat boulder. (Sky burial is a Western term for the practical Tibetan way to dispose of human corpses. The body is cut into small pieces, then the bones and flesh are mashed into a paste with *tsampa* flour. The mixture is made into offering balls and fed to the flocks of vultures that have gathered. Within an hour nothing remains and the vultures return to the air.)

The trail leads to a stone wall below the monastery and around to a courtyard. Although several buildings above the entrance foyer have been repaired, all of the other structures on the ridge, including the palace of Phabongkha Rimpoche, remain in ruins. Six monks have returned to this retreat of Sera's Ngakpa Dratsang; the small rebuilt *dukhang* and the quarters for Phabongkha Rimpoche (who visited from India in 1994) are located above the monks' residence buildings.

Takten *drakphuk* is **less than an hour** above this hermitage, set into the limestone cliffs on the east (L) side of a deep creek gorge. The trail ascends steeply from the stone courtyard beyond the upper ruins onto the ridge overlooking the monastery, then follows a well-defined trail into the gorge. Takten is **about 10 minutes** up from the creek on the east (L) ridge side. The caves of Takten are on a natural platform under sweeping waves of limestone. Water flows from several springs; sunshine warms the towering, overhanging cliffs; and tangles of shrubs thrive in the protection and moisture of the gully. The views stretch across the valley, from the small mound occupied by the Potala to the rounded shoulders of Gyaphelri, the holy mountain behind Drepung monastery and one of the highest peaks (17,200 ft, 5240 m) around Lhasa.

The higher of the three caves here is a small shrine containing a *rangjön* image on the rock wall of the Tantric deity Demchok's eye. Next to the altar is a small opening at the back of the cave where a spring issues forth water said to be a manifestation of the protectress Dorje Phakmo (this female deity has a human incarnation whose residence is Samding monastery, on the shores of Yamdrok Tsho). The blessing for pilgrims is a handful of this spiritual fluid from a narrow-necked pitcher; cup your right hand, slurp down about half of the water, then run the rest of it back through your hair with the same hand. May the powers of Dorje Phakmo, the "Adamantine Sow," be with you.

By the way, the hermits here aren't as reclusive as the term implies. When they're off on a tea run to the lower temples, the door on the stairway to the Demchok cave is locked.

To return to the road junction near Sera monastery, descend back to Tashi Chöling. The trail can be retraced to Phabongkha, though a more direct route leads steeply from Tashi Chöling for **30 minutes** down to Chubsang *ani gompa* (12,450 ft, 3790 m). Several monks and 130 nuns are in residence. Before the Cultural Revolution, only monks lived here. Be ready for a warm reception and copious cups of butter tea! A dirt access road descends from Chubsang to the Phabongkha Road, or follow the power poles into Nyangre village to return to the tea shops at the Sera monastery turnoff.

The pilgrimage circuit from Phabongkha to the Dode Valley continues up the ridge from the Takten caves, then traverses the flanks of Phurbu Chok to Sera Tse hermitage. From Takten the trail descends briefly, then climbs above the creek gorge to the crest of a ridge spur. The hills here aren't directly exposed to the southern sun, allowing tall grasses, wild iris and other wildflowers to thrive during the summer months; despite the grand views over the Lhasa Valley, it's hard to believe such a remote walk can be so close to the city. Continue the traverse, reaching Sera Tse hermitage (13,300 ft, 4050 m) in **1 to 1½ hours** from Takten. During the Drukwa Tsezhi Festival, many pilgrims descend from here to Sera (**less than 1 hour**; described above in reverse), though others continue on to the Dode Valley.

The longer *kora* trail to the village of Dode traverses east from Sera Tse for **10 minutes** to a saddle on the ridge overlooking the upper Kyi Chu Valley. To the southeast on the opposite ridge is the whitewashed, multistoried Michungri *ani gompa* (13,400 ft, 4080 m); the invigorating walk to this nunnery starts from the terminus of minibus number 6 on Dode Lam, winds through back streets and around a gravel quarry to ascend the ridge. Allow **2 to 2½ hours**. Several small meadows near the stream en route are great picnic spots.

The trail to the Dode Valley now angles left (east) through large boulders, descending in **about 20 minutes** to Rakadrak hermitage (13,100 ft, 3990 m), where Tsong Khapa meditated with his two disciples. (Just above Rakadrak the trail splits; the upper fork bypasses this hermitage and goes directly to Phurbu Chok retreat). Immediately below here are the cliffside ruins of Keutshang *ritrö* (13,000 ft, 3960 m). The new buildings include several temples and an attractive *dukhang*; note the framed painting here of this once grand five-story fortress-hermitage, which previously housed seventy monks.

The next stop is Phurbu Chok (12,500 ft, 3810 m), an impressive hermitage **30 minutes** below Keutshang via a disused service road. Situated on a prominent point overlooking the Dode Valley, this ochre-walled Gelukpa retreat is named for its proximity to the site where a *phurbu*, a ceremonial triple-bladed dagger, supposedly flew from India and landed on this ridge; the dagger is considered one of the most sacred objects at Sera, and is put on display for the public just one day per year, three days before Losar (Tibetan New Year).

The pilgrimage from Phabongkha ends by descending on the service road to the Dode Chu. Some pilgrims turn right (south) here on a trail along the river's west (R) bank to reach Sera's sky-burial site (beware: The police strictly enforce a rule prohibiting foreigners from visiting this burial site or taking photographs) in **20 minutes**. Otherwise, cross the bridge over the river, and soon join the main road of the valley. Dode village is **10 minutes** to the right (north).Turn left (south) toward Lhasa to reach the pavement in **less than 30 minutes**. The number 6 minibus stand is another **30 minutes** farther south on Dode Lam; the terminus is just north of Ramoche temple on North Lingkor Road.

DREPUNG MONASTERY REGION

Five miles (8 km) to the west of Lhasa is Drepung monastery, once the largest and most powerful of the six great Gelukpa religious centers in Tibet. This former Buddhist university lies hidden from most of Lhasa, cradled within the rocky ridges just beyond the city limits. The *kora* at Drepung is a panoramic **1-hour** walk that climbs into the foothills around this fifteenth-century network of stone temples and colleges. The views of the Lhasa Valley and the monastery grounds from these hills are outstanding.

The way to Drepung follows Beijing (or Dekyi) Nub Lam (West Beijing Road) west past the Potala and the Lhasa Hotel. The number 2 minibus serves this route, starting on

Monks enjoying view of the Lhasa Valley from the Drepung pilgrims' kora

Beijing Shar Lam across from the Tashi 1 Restaurant. The terminus is at the bottom of the hill from Drepung, or a bit farther at the Suni-trang cement factory.

Once the largest monastery in the world with upwards of ten thousand monks, Drepung sprawls across the hills like a monastic city. The huge ridge dominating the skyline is the holy mountain Gyaphelri (also known as Gyamphe Utse [see description below]), and Gyaphel *ritrö* is the white hermitage halfway up its flanks. The walk from the main road to the monastery parking lot (12,300 ft, 3750 m) takes **30 minutes**, or catch a ride with one of the tractor taxis plying this route.

Several hundred yards up this service road and to the right is Nechung monastery (11,900 ft, 3630 m), the former seat of Tibet's State Oracle, and the residence of the deity Pehar, who possesses the Oracle during his trances; the murals and temples here shouldn't be missed. Pilgrims usually descend to Nechung on a wide *kora* path after visiting Drepung.

Monks manning a ticket office at Drepung's parking area collect entrance fees from foreigners. The nearby flight of stone stairs up to the left (west) leads to the monastery's entrance gate. This is the start of both the outer *kora* around the complex and the traditional inner circuit used by pilgrims to visit each of the important temples. The first stop is Ganden Podrang, the sixteenth-century quarters that were used by Tibet's spiritual leaders for 150 years, until the Fifth Dalai Lama initiated the construction of the Potala Palace. If you want to visit the temples first, the outer *kora* can be joined by walking **a few minutes** west from the stone courtyard of the Tsokchen, Drepung's main assembly hall.

DREPUNG MONASTERY KORA

To begin the outer circuit, follow the stone stairs from the parking lot up to the entrance gate. The inner circuit is straight ahead up the cobbled path; the outer *kora* turns left up a lane beside a residence hall. The walls soon end in front of a second residence hall. Veer to the right over a water channel, then climb among the rocks, prayer wheels, and bushes between Drepung's western boundary wall and a deep stream gully. The first set of stairs up to the right leads to Ganden Podrang, but it is hidden from view by a stone rampart.

The *kora* continues to ascend beside the stream. Bulbous outcrops of white granite are decorated with paintings, the largest being an image of Tsong Khapa. A little farther up and across the gully is a large metal framework on the hillside where Drepung displays its silk appliqué *köku*, a huge scroll banner portraying religious figures, at the onset of the Zhotön Festival, usually held in August. Continue climbing beside the tall boundary wall, past two more sets of stairs up to the right (both of these lead to the Tsokchen), and onto a trail junction near several large boulders with carvings and painted *mantras* (12,650 ft, 3860 m). The *kora* now turns right (east), away from the stream into a corridor of stone walls overgrown with wild rose bushes. Within the walls to the right is the Tsamkhang, a small meditational retreat associated with Ngakpa Dratsang. An opening in the upper left wall at this junction leads to a clearing dotted with trees. The wide path winding north up this meadow toward the large cleft in the ridge is the pilgrimage route to Gyaphel *ritrö* and the summit of Gyaphelri (see description below).

The *kora* around the monastery continues east from the overgrown walls on a fairly level trail. Immediately below are the devastated buildings of Drepung's eastern limits, as well as the golden roofs of the four colleges and the assembly hall that somehow survived Tibet's recent past. This once vast religious center was founded in 1416 and until the 1950s was the heart of the Gelukpa sect's political power, housing monks from all over Tibet and Asia who came to study the *tantras* and Buddhist philosophy.

The *kora* weaves through more rocks and paintings, then switchbacks down to a wide dirt track which leads to Nechung monastery in **less than 10 minutes**. To return to Drepung's parking area, follow this track for less than 300 feet (90 m), then turn right (west) onto a narrow path along a stone wall. Keep heading west, then turn left at the first opening in the wall. The pilgrim circuit is now outside the monastery walls, passes below the police building and soon leads back to the parking area.

Views of Drepung from the monastery's pilgrimage circuit

GYAPHELRI

Rising above Drepung monastery is Gyaphelri (17,200 ft, 5250 m), one of the highest and most sacred peaks in the Lhasa area; in the past most religious festivals in Lhasa began when the sun's first rays struck the summit. Every year, hours before daybreak on the morning of the Drukwa Tsezhi Festival, hundreds of pilgrims climb from Drepung to the top of Gyaphelri to celebrate Sakyamuni Buddha giving his first teaching at Sarnath, in India, after achieving enlightenment at Bodhgaya. Bundles of incense bush are hauled to the top to be ceremonially lit, sending billowing plumes of fragrant smoke toward the heavens. Traditionally, the Dalai Lama would also go up Gyaphelri, riding a horse in a grand procession on a wide, well-graded trail that ascends nearly 5000 feet (1520 m). Only two other points around the Lhasa Valley are taller (Mindruk Tsari [17,950 ft, 5470 m]) and Jomo Sisi [17,550 ft, 5350 m], but neither is as accessible.

The hike up Gyaphelri is very strenuous, requiring **at least 12 hours** (including breaks and lunch) for the round trip from Drepung, plus the travel time from Lhasa to the monastery and back. As the monastery does not have accommodations, consider hiring a vehicle to assure a predawn start.

A climb of this magnitude flirts with your body's ability to cope with elevation-related problems; pay attention to all members in your party. Only hikers who are well acclimatized should consider doing this walk. Because this summit can become mighty blustery during the summer thunderstorm season, bring a hat, gloves, adequate sun protection, and reliable rain gear.

The route to Gyaphelri follows the pilgrimage *kora* clockwise up the stairs from the far left (northwest) corner of the Drepung parking area (see description above). Climb **about 20 minutes** beside the monastery's west boundary wall until the *kora* turns to the right (east) from the deep stream bed. The trail to Gyaphelri continues straight ahead (north) from here, entering a large clearing through the opening in the upper left wall. Ascend for **20 minutes** beyond the meadows and willow trees into the rocky gully, weaving in and out of boulders above the east (L) bank of the stream. The canyon soon forks and the trail splinters here into a braid of choices climbing up the east (L) ridge. Eventually these small paths merge into a wide, graded trail with reinforced embankments. Climb steadily for **1 to 1½ hours** through a desert of weathered granite to a flat ridge spur (13,900 ft, 4240 m) decorated with prayer flags. Gyaphel *ritrö* (14,800 ft, 4510 m) is **1 to 1½ hours** across the ridge face to the east. This 600-year-old hermitage has been transformed from a goat pen in the late 1980s to a beautiful, functioning retreat with several monks in residence. The views of the Kyi Chu Valley from here are breathtaking and the seldom-visited monks enjoy an opportunity to socialize and share revitalizing cups of butter tea with visitors. The spring for this hermitage is usually the last chance to get water before the summit.

The trail to Gyaphelri climbs north from the retreat for **1½ hours or more** in a series of long switchbacks, passing cushion plants and sprinklings of wildflowers en route to the crest of the main ridge (16,300 ft, 4970 m). If the weather is agreeable, this tundra-covered ridge is a superb lunch spot. The Nyangre Valley falls away to the north, and on clear days the peaks of Bhutan show their snowy faces far to the south beyond the Kyi Chu Valley.

The final **1- to 1½-hour** hike to the summit looks deceptively easy and resembles a path in the land of Oz. Hundreds of cairns piled by pilgrims line the sides of this regal route to the domed crest (17,200 ft, 5250 m). Not far from the top the trail enters a stunning labyrinth of devotional monuments. Thousands of narrow, columnar rock piles (said to be the palaces of *khandroma*, which are a type of female Buddhist spirit) compete for space, complicating attempts to reach the whorl of colorful prayer flags radiating from the main summit cairn. Straw hats, felt hats, fur hats, and baseball caps, as well as shoes, jackets, and gloves are scattered everywhere as special personal offerings to the protecting deities. One of the real treats of this climb, besides the panoramas and the satisfaction of success, is the exhilaration and awe that is generated from being in the presence of such a grand display of devotion and faith.

Although several very steep shortcuts lead down some of the ridges below Gyaphel *ritrö*, the main route up is also the most practical way back down. Allow **4 hours or more** to reach the parking area. When rejoining the Drepung *kora*, remember to descend clockwise around the monastery.

BUMPARI

The ascent of Bumpari (14,100 ft, 4300 m) is a tough but rewarding day hike to a pair of rocky crags towering more than 2000 feet (610 m) above the south (L) banks of the Kyi Chu. Shaped like a pair of offering vases, or *bumpa*, this ridge is another lofty site near Lhasa where incense bush is burned to celebrate special occasions such as Losar and Dzamling Chisang (World Incense Day). A keen eye can spot the streams of prayer flags hung between these rocky points directly above the Lhasa bridge.

The route up Bumpari is a steep climb on a faint but negotiable trail that should be attempted only by people who are accustomed to scrambling over rugged terrain. Allow **5 to 6 hours** for the round trip to the summit, starting from the turnoff at the Lhasa bridge.

From the end of the bridge, turn right along the south (L) bank of the Kyi Chu. The Tibet-Sichuan Highway and the road to Ganden monastery are to the left. Follow the paved road to the right for **10 minutes**, then turn left (south) up the gravel road heading away from the river, beside a walled military compound. Stop here to get your bearings, as the route is obscure in places. The twin crags of Bumpari, festooned with prayer flags, are part of the main rocky ridge up to the left (west). The route to the summit is on the far (south) side of the large ridge spur descending from the Bumpari crags; from this angle the route is hidden, for it follows a smaller, adjacent spur behind this larger ridge.

The gravel road splits at the end of the military compound wall; the right fork winds across a broad plain to Drip village and the Tsechokling Regency temple, one of the four original Ling temples of Lhasa (only three remain). Take the left fork and continue south. In **less than 10 minutes** the route to Bumpari turns left up a faint two-tired tractor track, which ascends the barren slopes. Missing this turnoff will, in **10 minutes**, bring you to the first houses of Drip; this is also the route for approaching Mindruk Tsari, the highest summit around Lhasa (see description below). Nevertheless, the view of Bumpari from these houses provides a good angle for observing the correct route up this ridge, which is the smaller ridge spur leading down from the right (south) half of the twin summits. The trail begins on the lower right (south) side of this spur, then follows the ridge crest until just below the top, where it ascends the gully between the two crags to reach the ridge top.

To ascend Bumpari, follow the tractor track up the left side of a rocky wash. Pass below the end of the large ridge spur descending from the left (north) crag of Bumpari, and continue up a faint track to the base of the smaller spur ridge leading down from the right crag. The best of several routes to the summit initially climbs the right (south) side of this smaller spur on a defined but braided path, then leads onto the nose of the ridge. The trail is very steep and obscure in places, with sections of loose talus and a continuous series of switchbacks crossing slabs of bare rock. Many false turns lead away from the correct route; follow the small rock cairns. Eventually the trail moves into the gully between Bumpari's twin summits to reach the gap in **2 to 2½ hours** from the base of the ridge. Each of the rocky spires has a route leading to the top, though the more southern (right) of the two is slightly higher.

The ashes of burnt incense bush rest silently in small hearths, thick strands of prayer flags flutter their offerings aloft, and the Lhasa Valley is at your feet. Across the river is Gyaphelri, the rounded summit rising behind Drepung monastery. Towering above the east side of the Lhasa Valley is Jomo Sisi, the second-highest peak around Lhasa, and between these two mountains is a low point in the ridgeline where the old trade route from Lhasa crosses Phenpogo La into the Phenpo Valley. The highest peak around Lhasa, Mindruk Tsari, is the immense rocky summit rising directly to the south from the ridge continuing above Bumpari (see description below).

The Lhasa bridge is a descent of **2 hours or more** retracing the same route.

MINDRUK TSARI

Mindruk Tsari (the Gravel Peak of Pleiades; 17,950 ft, 5470 m) is the highest summit around Lhasa, rising above Bumpari and the southern shores of the Kyi Chu. Its name is derived from this mountain's importance regarding Chabshuk, the autumn Bathing Festival; when the Constellation of the Six Brothers (*mindruk*) rises above this peak, all water is said to become *karchu*, or "star water," a life-giving elixir, and the bathing (i.e., splashing) festivities begin.

Unless you are a Heinrich Harrer (he and his partner Peter Aufschnaiter scrambled up to the top in a single day, twice [the locals didn't believe they did it in one day, so they returned and lit a fire on top to prove it!], during their five-year sojourn in Lhasa in the 1940s), this walk requires camping for **at least one night** in the high valley below the summit. Using the route description for Bumpari (see description above), cross the Lhasa bridge to the south (L) side of the Kyi Chu, turn right (west), then turn up the first road to the left (south). Pass the track leading to the base of Bumpari, and reach the first houses of Drip. On the ridge above to the east are two temples. On the left is Dzongtsen Khang, a shrine for the red-faced, horse-riding protector Dzongtsen Tseumar. One of the two "husbands" of the protectress Pelden Lhamo, this figure is taken once a year during Saga Dawa in a procession to Tsal Gungtang monastery, about 7 miles up the Kyi Chu Valley from here, to spend one day with its "wife," the Pelden Lhamo of Tsal. The adjacent temple on this hillside houses a large, three-faced statue of Tamdrin, the "horse-necked" protector. Over to the west in the center of the village is Drip Tsechokling, one of the four Lings, or Regency temples, of Lhasa. This handsome building survived the Cultural Revolution and overlooks a peaceful courtyard.

The route to Mindruk Tsari continues south up the valley for **30 minutes** to the end of the road at Ruka Zhiba (Fourth Commune; 12,250 ft, 3730 m). This is the last chance to hire a pack animal, and a good place to get your bearings; high up on the ridge to the left (southeast) is a wide, obvious trail angling to Sha La (also Tsechokling La), the pass leading into the valley below Mindruk Tsari.

From Ruka Zhiba, the trail follows a rocky streambed past the last barley terraces and across a deep creek gully. After **1 hour** the trail splits. The larger right fork stays along the west (R) side of the streambed. Take the smaller left fork, which leads up a small, steep tributary toward Sha La. Cross another deep gully, then ascend a rutted trail that eventually braids into numerous animal tracks. Choose your own route from here, zigzagging up the hillside to meet the wide track, reaching Sha La (15,250 ft, 4650 m) in **4 to 5 hours** from Ruka Zhiba. After a tough 3000-foot (915-m) climb, take a rest and enjoy the views of Lhasa's highest peak! Continue south on the ridge crest from Sha La, then ascend gradually along the ridge side, reaching a meadow (15,700 ft, 4790 m) by a stream in **75 minutes**.

This spot, directly below Mindruk Tsari, is a perfect base camp. The route to the top is a tricky **3- to 4-hour** ascent through extensive fields of wobbly boulders. The best strategy is to follow the various long fingers of grassy meadows extending through the slopes of shattered granite, then pick your way carefully up to the summit ridge (17,750 ft, 5410 m). The north summit (17,950 ft, 5470 m) is slightly higher than the southern crest. On clear days the snowy massif of the main Nyenchen Thanglha peak rises far to the northwest, in perfect geomantic alignment with the Potala Palace and Mindruk Tsari.

With an early start, strong walkers can summit and return to Lhasa the same day. Or relax and spend two nights here. An alternative exit is to continue south **2 hours** from the base camp, up the valley to Kusum La (also Trango La; 16,200 ft, 4940 m), and on to the Tsangpo Valley. The pass is tucked around Mindruk Tsari to the left (southeast), marked by a huge *la-dze* cairn. Dorje Drak, one of the two main Nyingmapa monasteries in Central Tibet, is a leisurely **2-day** descent to the south from here, situated on the shore of the river. Following the sandy shores of the Tsangpo east for a day will bring you to the Drakyul Valley and a Guru Rimpoche meditation site in the limestone cavern hermitage of Drak Yangdzong.

GANDEN, GYAMA, SAMYE, AND ÖN REGION
MAP NO. 2, PAGE 88

In early 1985 the trek from Ganden monastery to Samye monastery was little more than a rumored alternative to the shorter, more established walk from the county seat (*xian*) of Taktse (also called Dechen Dzong) to Samye over the Gökar La pass. By that summer, the first summer that Tibet was open to individual travelers, news of the ever-changing landscape of mountain passes and alpine lakes between these two historical monasteries quickly changed this walk from an unknown route to the premier trek of the Lhasa region. With minimal backtracking, the shorter trek from Samye to Taktse can be used as the second half of a beautiful loop walk of **8 to 10 days**, which originates in Ganden or in the nearby Trupshi Valley (or in the Gyama Valley, a route described in "The Gyama Valley to Samye Trek"), visits Samye, and finishes at Taktse, 12.5 miles (20 km) east of Lhasa.

Despite its popularity, the Ganden to Samye trek is a tough walk crossing two high passes through a remote region. Ganden (13,700 ft, 4180 m) or the Trupshi Valley (12,800 ft, 3900 m) are the preferred starting points, as they are higher in elevation than Samye (11,600 ft, 3540 m). The walking time in this direction is **4 to 5 days;** strong hikers can complete it in 3½ **days**. The best time for trekking is from late April until late October, though the valleys between these monasteries are bathed by the summer rains from the middle of June until early September—a deterrent for some, but prime wildflower season for others. Winter crossings are possible, but should be attempted only by strong, well-equipped parties.

All food must be brought from Lhasa, and a tent and fuel stove are highly recommended. Beyond Ganden there is only one small village and the occasional *drokpa* camp before reaching the settlements in the Samye Valley. Pack animals are not usually available at Ganden, as there are no villages near the monastery, though it is possible to hire yaks in Hebu or Trupshi villages, located **4 to 5 hours** past Ganden in the next valley south on the trail to Samye.

The nature of the terrain on the trek to Samye can create serious difficulties for anyone suffering from acute mountain sickness (AMS) while crossing Zhukar La (17,050 ft, 5200 m) or Chetur La (16,550 ft, 5040 m) en route to Samye. The valley between these passes is quite high in elevation (16,050 ft, 4890 m) and very remote. The only way to descend to lower ground or seek medical help is to retrace your route back over the previous pass to the nearest roadhead.

A good way to acclimatize for this trek is to spend at least two nights in Ganden before setting off. In addition to exploring the temples, stretch your legs with a day hike in the surrounding hills. A good pre-trek warm-up hike offering panoramas of the

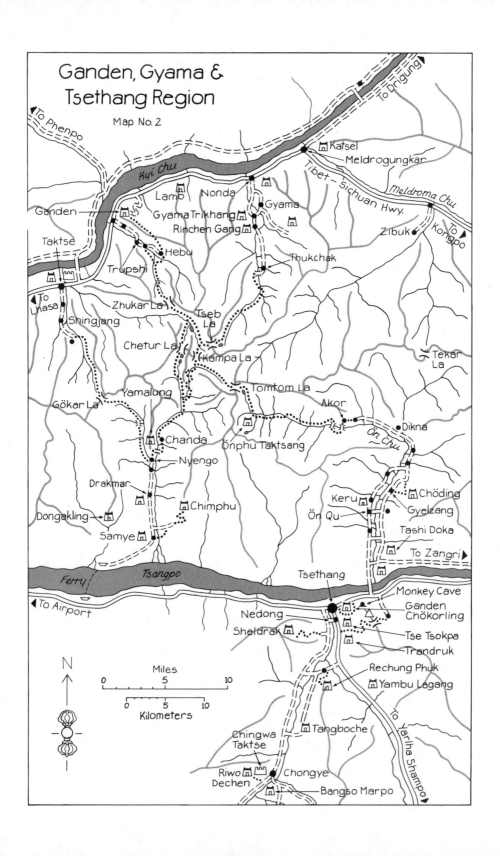

Ganden, Gyama &
Tsethang Region

Map No. 2

To Phenpo

To Drigung

Katsel
Meldrogungkar

Kyi Chu

Tibet - Sichuan Hwy.

Meldroma Chu

Lamo   Nonda

Ganden   Gyama

Gyama Trikhang

Rinchen Gang   Zibuk   To
                                      Kongpo

Taktse   Hebu

Trupshi   Thukchak

To
Lhasa
          Zhukar La   Tseb
                           La
Shingjang
                                              Tekar
           Chetur La   La
                      Kampa La

           Yamalung   Tomtom La
Gökar La   Akor   Dikna

              Chanda   Ön Chu
                       Önphu Taktsang
           Nyengo

Drakmar   Keru   Chöding
                                                 Gyelzang
Dongakling   Ön Qu
            Chimphu   Tashi Doka
Samye
                                              To Zangri

Tsangpo

Ferry   Tsethang   Monkey Cave
                                               Ganden
To Airport   Nedong   Chökorling
                        Sheldrak   Tse Tsokpa
                                              Trandruk

                                          Rechung Phuk
                                          Yambu Lagang

N   To Yarlha Shampo
        Miles
      0   5   10   Tangboche
      0   5   10
        Kilometers   Chingwa
                         Taktse
                      Riwo   Chongye
                      Dechen
                                  Bangso Marpo

monastery and the distant valleys is the high pilgrimage *kora* along the Wangpori ridge top, the southern wall of the Ganden basin. From the west end of this ridge the trail drops down to connect with the main pilgrim circuit around the monastery. Remember to approach either of these walks in the proper, clockwise manner that the pilgrims follow.

GANDEN MONASTERY

Ganden monastery, one of the three great Gelukpa religious centers in the Lhasa area, is cradled in a natural amphitheater high above the Kyi Chu, or Lhasa River, about 32 miles (52 km) by road from Lhasa. Pilgrim buses to Ganden leave Lhasa each morning at 6:30 A.M. from the east end of Barkor Square. The trip takes 2 hours or more. The buses remain at the monastery for the day, returning to Lhasa later in the afternoon. Private transport can be arranged through travel agencies in Lhasa or through your hotel.

Overnight accommodation at Ganden is dormitory-style, located in the large building beside (south of) the monastery parking area. Simple meals of instant noodles and steamed bread are available at the guesthouse restaurant. A shop run by the monks sells few food items other than sweets, brick tea, beer, and yak butter. If you want to camp, the best sites are beside the last bends in the road leading up to the *gompa*.

The monastery was founded as a cave hermitage in 1409 by Tsong Khapa (known as Je Rimpoche), one of the most revered religious figures in Tibet. It was through his teachings and reform efforts that one of the original schools of Buddhism in Tibet, the Kadampa sect, was transformed into the largest, most powerful (and political) religious body in the country, the Gelukpa sect.

The sprawling ruins of Ganden, one of the three major monasteries in the Lhasa region

The rangjön, *or self-manifested image of Tsong Khapa on the wall of his mediation cave, Ganden monastery*

Nearly every temple at Ganden has Tsong Khapa's likeness behind the altar, usually flanked by images of his two disciples, Gyeltsab Je and Khedrub Je. This trio is known as the *yab-se-sum*, the "three fathers" of the Gelukpa sect. One of the most important shrines formerly at Ganden was the Serdung, the gold-covered tomb of Tsong Khapa. This monument, along with the entire monastery, was destroyed in 1966 during the Cultural Revolution. A new *chörten* containing fragments of Tsong Khapa's skull is now housed upstairs in the rebuilt Serdung, the maroon-walled temple with the largest of the golden roofs, in the center of the Ganden complex.

Since 1985 the number of reconstructed temples and residence halls here has been steadily increasing, and the extensive ruins from the 1960s are now mostly gone; nearly 500 monks have returned. Adjacent to the Serdung is the new Tsokchen assembly hall, also painted maroon and housing three huge statues of *yab-se-sum*; unusual copper statues of the Neten Chu-druk (the Sixteen *Arhats*, or Elders, who were contemporaries of Sakyamuni Buddha and achieved spiritual perfection); as well as the Sertri, or Golden Throne, of the *tripa*, the "throne holders" of Ganden's religious lineage. On the right side of the cart track leading up to the Serdung is Ngam Chökhang, a dark but interesting temple with an even darker *gönkhang*. (Women are not allowed into any of Ganden's *gönkhangs*, or protector's temples, a rather unusual rule for Central Tibet). Most of the other buildings are *khangtsen*, and nearly every one contains at least one small temple within its premises.

DAY HIKES NEAR GANDEN

Two pilgrimage circuits lead around the monastery: the high *kora*, which climbs above the monastery onto the ridgeline of Wangpori, and the lower traditional *kora*, which circles the entire complex and leads to Je *drubphuk*, Tsong Khapa's original meditation cave at Ganden.

The higher circuit takes **1½ to 2 hours** and initially follows the trail leading from

Ganden toward Samye monastery. From the parking area beside the guesthouse, take the cart track southwest up the hill for 200 feet (60 m) to where it intersects another cart track. Don't turn here; continue up the hill in the same direction (southwest) along a footpath. Several smaller trails peel off to the right, but continue ascending on the larger trail. In **less than half an hour** the trail forks. The larger left-hand branch leads on to Samye; take the upper right (east) fork for the high *kora* to the Wangpori ridge top. Climb steadily up the dry slopes on this trail, reaching the *la-dze* cairn on the ridge crest in **about an hour** from the monastery. The ridgeline resembles a serpent's backbone, undulating in a series of crests festooned with streamers of colorful prayer flags. Pilgrims plod along the circuit quietly saying *mantras*, burning bundles of juniper or rhododendron incense bush, and adding *tsampa* and *chang* to the fires as offerings to the local deities.

Follow the pilgrims (they're especially abundant on Sundays) and the trail to the right (west) along the ridge top, passing innumerable devotional cairns. Far below is the Kyi Chu, weaving like the tangled roots of an old tree through the vast gravel flats. On clear days the lone snowy summit of the main Nyenchen Thanglha peak (23,330 ft, 7111 m) rises to the northwest beyond Lhasa near Nam Tsho. The *kora* stays atop the ridge of Wangpori, crests at 14,400 ft (4390 m), then descends steeply to rejoin a cart track near the south side of the monastery. You can return to the temples from here or continue to the left (west) to join the lower *kora* route.

The shorter *kora* around Ganden shouldn't be missed. Hardly 5 minutes goes by without groups of Tibetans stopping before a rock, shrine, or crevice in a boulder to perform unusual rituals that "test" their faith and help them earn religious merit, all in a carnival-like atmosphere. This circuit begins at the southwest corner of Ganden. A large rocky cleft draped with prayer flags marks the start of this scenic circuit, which takes **at least 1 hour** to complete.

Right from the start the rocks beside the trail are smudged with yak butter and bushes are decorated with tufts of yak and sheep wool. Throughout the rock fissures are small shrines filled with *tsha-tshas*, small religious offering tablets made of clay and deposited by the pilgrims. Farther along, the pilgrims stop at particular rocks where they pass their hands carefully over a blackened surface, reverently touch their heads, or perhaps rub their backs like a bear with an itch, all the while reciting their prayers. At several locations the pilgrims shout encouragement to one another as they each try to squeeze through the well-worn but narrow gaps between certain boulders. If you're walking alone and want to get in on the action, wait for a party of Tibetans to come along and show you all the intricacies of these rituals.

The trail eventually climbs to a rocky outcrop, then descends past a terrace on the left where sky burials are conducted. Continue around the back of Drok Ri, the northern wall of the Ganden amphitheater. Pass by more shrines and outcrops of well-worn limestone rocks to reach Je *drubphuk*, the meditation cave of Tsong Khapa. Set in a hillside of scrubby juniper bushes, the cave now contains a small *lhakhang* with five self-manifested rock carvings on the wall. Many pilgrimage sites have stones or rock walls with a Tibetan alphabet letter on them, the prayer *Om mani padme hum*, or images of people or deities like the ones here, which are said to be *rangjön*, or self-manifested, because they appeared miraculously on their own. Tsong Khapa is the largest, central image. According to the caretaker, each of these figures is *sung-jolma*, meaning they also possess the power of speech. The caretaker may offer you the blessing from this temple, a handful of water from the long-necked *bumpa* on the altar.

The *kora* now traverses around the ridge to the monastery. When the trail branches near the first buildings, take the left fork to return to the parking area, or the right fork to ascend above the upper limits of the monastery. Another small trail scrambles up to the right from the cave temple to reach several isolated shrines and rock paintings. Farther up on the summit of Drok Ri is a white *chörten* and fine views of the Kyi Chu Valley.

THE TREK TO SAMYE MONASTERY

The trail to Samye monastery climbs south from Ganden up Wangpori, initially following the same route up the ridge as the pilgrims' high *kora* route. From the monastery parking area, reach the saddle (14,650 ft, 4470 m) with a *la-dze* in **1 hour**. The terrain along this ridge is a desert of rocks and lizards, with only a thin covering of vegetation. A peculiar plant growing near the trail is the alpine cushion plant, a dense colony of flowers growing in a humped, spongy green mound that may be from a few inches to several feet in diameter; the compact stems and leaves help the plant reduce water evaporation and protect it against the wind and cold. Tibet has a variety of cushion plants, including several from the carnation and saxifrage families.

Almost due south across the valley from the saddle is a steep drainage leading up to the first pass crossing, Zhukar La (sometimes called Gökar La). The pass is hidden from this vantage point, tucked around to the left (east) behind a ridge. Numerous *ba*, the woven yak-hair tents of the *drokpa*, are scattered across these slopes; the valley bottom is a patchwork of crops. Hebu (13,600 ft, 4150 m; also pronounced "Hewu" or "Lhebu"), the village below this saddle, cannot be seen from here. The route to Samye descends steadily for **2 hours** to Hebu on a well-defined trail, traversing along ridges and crossing several lower saddles. If you had a late start from Ganden, consider camping or spending the night here with a family. This valley is the last place before Samye

The main Utse temple at Samye monastery

where you can hire a pack animal. The villagers here tend herds of yak and grow barley. It could be a day or two before an animal is available for you to hire, as they are usually up on the hills grazing. If necessary, go down the valley **1 hour** to Trupshi village (12,800 ft, 3900 m) to hire yaks. Some trekkers now start their trek in Trupshi due to the lack of pack animals at Ganden. To reach Trupshi, head east from Lhasa past Taktse to Sekhang village (km marker 4596); Trupshi is a 4-mile (7-km) drive east up the valley, or a **2½-hour** walk from the main road. Arranging pack animals is very easy; the villagers actually compete to get your business!

The route from Hebu to Zhukar La crosses to the south (L) side of the creek flowing below Hebu, then parallels the creek for a short distance downstream. A wide trail forms along the base of the ridge and soon enters a tributary valley up to the left (south) draining from Zhukar La. Lumpy campsites can be found in a series of rolling meadows located **1 hour or more** up the valley beyond the creek crossing. A *drokpa* encampment with several tents during the summer months is just above the top of these meadows on both sides of the stream. The mastiff guard dogs may not be chained, so call out before approaching. The total walking time from Ganden to the meadows and the herder camp is **5 to 6 hours**. This area is the last good campsite before reaching the valley beyond Zhukar La.

Finding the correct trail to Zhukar La from the *drokpa* camp can be confusing due to the convergence of three drainage valleys from the left (east), center (southeast), and right (southwest). The central drainage is the correct route. Ascend from the herders' camp on the east (R) side of the main creek. In **10 minutes** cross the stream flowing from the left, then immediately cross to the west (L) side of the central drainage. The trail climbs steeply up the ridge for a short way, but is soon lost in a maze of animal paths through thickets of dwarf rhododendron. The central gully is too rugged to follow at first, so instead find a route that stays high above the west (L) bank of this stream. Climb steeply up to the left (southeast) toward the obvious low point on the ridge, which looks like the pass but is not. The hillside here is dotted with marmot dens, and during the summer the rhododendron bloom in fragrant miniature bouquets of pink, white, and purple flowers. Villagers from Hebu harvest these bushes, carrying them in heavy loads to sell as incense to pilgrims at Ganden.

From the *drokpa* camp to the pass is a long, steep climb. As the ridge becomes more rocky, the route eventually leaves the ridge crest and descends back to the central (southeast) of the three streams. Just before reaching the low point in the ridge, cross to the east (R) side of the stream and continue climbing toward Zhukar La. The terrain begins to level out and soon opens into a broad U-shaped valley littered with boulders and rock debris deposited by an ancient glacier. It takes **2½ to 3½ hours**, not including rest stops, to reach this spot from the herder camp. Unfortunately the ground is much too uneven for camping, for this would be a great place to pitch a tent. Zhukar La is **1 hour or more** from here, without breaks, and is still hidden around to the left until you are almost on top of it. There isn't much of a trail, but keep looking for a series of small stone cairns marking the route to the pass along the east (R) side of the valley. A trail soon materializes near the first cairn, then contours up to the left through a jumble of rocks to reach Zhukar La (17,050 ft, 5200 m), a broad summit clearly marked by a large *la-dze* decorated with prayer flags.

Beyond the pass is a remote valley that must be entered to approach Chetur La. Descend from the pass on a faint path that quickly becomes an easily followed, cairned trail. As you pick your way through a field of broken granite boulders, the upper reaches of this valley and a lake called Palha Tshodü come into view. Like a setting somewhere in Kashmir, the meadows and tall ridges are vibrantly green with lush grasses during the summer. Reach the rushing creek on the valley floor in **less than 2 hours** from the pass. Before the bottom, look up the valley (south) toward a tall ridge covered with shattered rock and gravel. Below this ridge, coming from the right (southwest), is a tributary drainage of the main valley you're about to enter. The direct route to Samye follows this tributary valley up to Chetur La.

The broad, flat meadows where the trail meets the valley floor are good campsites (16,000 ft, 4880 m). From the previous herder camp to this site is **5 to 6 hours**. The route to Chetur La now crosses to the south (L) bank of the stream; shoes and socks may have to come off. Head east up the valley along the base of the south (L) ridge. There is no trail, so aim for the dip in a group of low hills near this ridge. A short climb up through this dip brings you to the top of the hills and to a good vantage point. The mouth of the tributary valley leading to Chetur La is just off to the right (south), below the ridge of shattered rock. Palha Tshodü Lake is to the east; look for formations of bar-headed geese and pairs of Brahminy ducks flying overhead. An alternative route to Samye continues up past this lake to cross Kampa La (16,450 ft, 5010 m), the second pass crossing on the trek from the Gyama Valley to Samye monastery, described in "The Gyama Valley to Samye Trek."

The mouth of the tributary leading to Chetur La is **less than 1 hour** from the meadows below Zhukar La. This is another glacially scoured area, lined with meadows and bursting with wildflowers, including large yellow poppies *(Meconopsis integrifolia)*. This valley swings gently up to the left and soon the rocky cleft of Chetur La can be seen at the far end. The extensive meadows here look ideal for camping from a distance, but pools of water and mounded tundra plates make it almost impossible to pitch a tent. The junction of the valley floor with the slope of the west (L) ridge is one of the drier routes to the pass, which is **2 to 2½ hours** from the valley entrance.

Just before Chetur La (16,700 ft, 5090 m) is a small glacial tarn, and beyond the summit to the south are two larger lakes set in a scoured, barren basin that could be a setting in the Rocky Mountains. Near the top is a flat spot large enough for a tent where you might consider staying the night—if you're like me and enjoy camping on passes. The trail to Samye now follows the drainage from these two lakes south toward the Tsangpo River. A rough track meanders along their west (R) shore and eventually a better trail forms on the west (R) ridge side. About **2 hours** below the pass is a *drokpa* camp. The interior of the *ba* (yak-hair tent) used by the herders typically has the character of a well-established home: Piles of attractive hand-woven blankets and *tsampa* sacks line the edges of the tent, pots and pans and cooking ladles are arranged neatly, and usually there is a wooden prayer altar on which sit the seven offering bowls *(ting)* of water.

Just beyond this camp the trail plunges into a narrow ravine, then the valley opens onto the first of numerous meadows and campsites en route to Samye; dense willow groves and wild rosebushes make it difficult to follow the trail. Fat Prince Henri's laughing thrushes bound through the undergrowth, blue-fronted redstarts perform aerial acrobatics, and colorful Elwes's eared pheasants gobble noisily as they work the ground. You might find yourself in the company of a musk deer; even mosquitoes make an appearance.

One hour or more from the *drokpa* camp a stream enters from the right (west); a large campsite is at the confluence. Cross the main creek here and follow its east (L) side until Chanda, the first village before Samye. **One hour** below the stream confluence, a deep tributary valley enters from the left (east). The path from Khampa La and the Gyama Valley follows the south (L) side of this drainage and joins the trail to Samye here. The stream from this tributary is usually an easy ford, but during heavy rains the crossing may be difficult. On rare occasions even yaks cannot cross, and it may be necessary to wait here for a day or so until the water level drops. The trail to Samye remains on the east (L) side of the main creek. A **few minutes** below the ford is a big meadow camp (14,400 ft, 4390 m) suitable for large groups. **One hour** below here the valley turns sharply to the right (west) as another big tributary enters from the left (east). Sometimes a wooden bridge is built over this creek. Beyond here the valley opens up considerably and the trail is easy to follow.

Chanda (13,200 ft, 4020 m), the first permanent settlement you encounter on this route since Hebu, is **2 hours** farther, with just five or six houses and small plots of barley. **Forty minutes** below here are the Yamalung meadows (13,000 ft, 3960 m), a great place for a rest day. If you're camping here with a commercial trekking company, ask your staff to refrain from digging toilet holes in the meadow, and make sure they pack out all your garbage. Sadly, this beautiful meadow is under threat of becoming a trash pit pocked with old toilet holes.

Across the creek up the west (R) ridge is the trail to Yamalung (13,400 ft, 4080 m; also known as Emmaling), an historical cave hermitage not visible from the meadow camp. To visit this site, cross a small bridge obscured by bushes and go up the trail to the right; the steep climb takes

A high camp on Chetu La, en route from Ganden to Samye monastery

less than 1 hour to this Nyingmapa retreat. Guru Rimpoche, the founder of the Nyingmapa school of thought, and his main disciple, Bairotsana (also Vairocana), meditated here twelve centuries ago. These caves are particularly important because Guru Rimpoche also concealed religious texts here, known as *terma* (hidden treasure), which were discovered hundreds of years later. Several temples have been rebuilt, including a *lhakhang* over the Guru Rimpoche cave. Immediately above is the cave retreat of the Fifth Dalai Lama, and along the cliffs are two caves of Bairotsana and others used by various Buddhist scholars. If you wish to spend the night, inquire with the monk tending the Guru Rimpoche cave; bring your own food and bedding. A small donation is appropriate. A high *kora* route leads to the rocky ridge top (14,000 ft, 4270 m) in **1 hour** of steady climbing from the hermitage, offering distant vistas of the Tsangpo Valley.

About 15 minutes beyond the Yamalung turnoff the trail to Samye crosses a solid wooden bridge to the west (R) bank of the creek. Look back up the ridge from here for a good view of the cave temples. Nyengo village (12,600 ft, 3840 m) is **15 minutes** beyond the bridge, situated at the confluence of a large tributary entering from the right (west). This valley is the old trade route to Lhasa. It crosses Gökar La (17,050 ft, 5200 m) and enters the Lhasa Valley at the county seat (*xian*) of Taktse. (The trek to Taktse takes **2 to 3 days** from here; see "The Samye to Taktse Trek.")

Samye is **3 to 4 hours** away along a hot, sandy track wide enough for animal-drawn carts and rototiller-style tractors. Consider walking this final stretch in early morning or late afternoon during the summer, and carry plenty of water. The track stays on the west

(R) side of the valley most of the way to Samye, passing a series of oasislike settlements. Soon the glittering golden roof of Samye's main temple, known as the Utse or the *tsuk lhakhang,* rises in the distance above stands of willow. The isolated ridge to the left (east) of the monastery is Hepori (considered one of Central Tibet's four main holy peaks), and farther to the south are the sand dunes along the Tsangpo. The Samye Valley would be a desert, like the river shore, were it not for irrigation; barley fields alternating with plots of yellow- and white-blooming rapeseed contrast sharply with the barren hills.

Descend to the temple of Drakmar Drinzang, the birthplace of Trisong Detsen, one of Tibet's revered Three Religious Kings of the Royal Dynasty period. The small shrine, containing the images of the king, Guru Rimpoche and the Indian scholar Shantaraksita (the three founders of Samye monastery, known collectively as Khenlop Chösum) is one of the main stops for prayer wheel–spinning pilgrims as they head up to the Yamalung caves.

Numerous paths along the irrigation ditches beyond Drakmar can make the route confusing. Keep aiming for the golden roofed Utse, which is in the south part of Samye village (11,600 ft, 3540 m). A guesthouse and shops run by the monastery are located in front of the Utse's main entrance, and just outside the monastery boundary wall are several restaurants. The best camping sites are to the south of town in the willow groves.

SAMYE MONASTERY

Samye was the first great Buddhist monastery in Tibet, founded circa 775 A.D. during the reign of King Trisong Detsen. On the advice of Guru Rimpoche and Shantaraksita, the king ordered Samye to be built as a three-dimensional model, or *mandala,* of the Buddhist universe. The original complex contained 108 chapels within a great circular stone wall. In the center of this *mandala* was the Utse, the main temple representing Mount Meru, the central pillar of the Buddhist cosmic universe. Symmetrically positioned around this center were four tall *chörtens,* each painted a different color; twelve temples representing the four major and eight minor continents of Buddhist cosmology; and two temples for the sun and the moon.

Many of these outlying buildings became derelict or were destroyed during the Cultural Revolution, but money from the Chinese government as well as outside sources has helped finance the renovation of the grand Utse, many of the peripheral temples, the four *chörtens* around the Utse (albeit in cement), and the large circular wall surrounding Samye with 1,008 *chörtens.* If you enjoy visiting temples, set aside a full day for visiting the entire complex.

The candlelit interior of the ground-floor *tsuk lhakhang* has an ancient, musty atmosphere befitting its age. The figures within the long, raised cases to either side of the main altar are tributes to the founders of Samye and important Buddhist scholars who visited Samye. In the secondary room behind the altar is an eighth-century stone statue of the Jowo, the Sakyamuni Buddha when he was a young prince. The room adjacent to the chanting hall is a dark *gönkhang* with a towering, shrouded statue of the protector Pehar. To the left of the Utse's entrance is a shrine for Chaktong-chentong, the eleven-headed, thousand-armed, thousand-eyed form of Chenrezik, the *Bodhisattva* of Compassion. The Dalai Lama is the human manifestation of Chenrezik.

Samye monastery is rather unusual in Central Tibet, for it is affiliated with more than one school of Tibetan Buddhism. Originally it was a Nyingmapa monastery, but after centuries of external political and religious influence, Samye is now home to monks from the Sakyapa and Gelukpa sects as well.

Note: Samye is now considered a "closed" area. All visitors must possess an Alien Travel Permit (ATP) or face being fined. ATPs are issued by the Public Security Bureau in Lhasa, Tsethang, or Shigatse. They currently cost 50 yuan (about US $6), and several destinations can be listed on one permit. Police at the Samye ferry crossing regularly inspect these permits, and they occasionally check at the Samye monastery guesthouse. Remember to bargain if you're fined!

DAY HIKES NEAR SAMYE

Although the town of Samye is rather filthy (it's one of the few Tibetan towns where pigs are raised), the nearby hills are worth exploring if you have a few extra days. The solitary, barren ridge just to the east is the sacred Hepori (12,200 ft, 3720 m). A residence palace for Tibet's kings during the Royal Dynasty period once crowned this ridge; now it is topped by a small temple. The hike up Hepori takes **less than 1 hour** along a sandy track, offering commanding views of the monastery and surrounding valleys; fill your water bottles before setting off. The easiest approach from Samye is to head east on the dirt track leading away from the Utse entrance gate. From the base of the ridge, choose any of the numerous routes leading up. One trail leads to an obvious saddle beside a white *chörten*, then continues up the spine of the ridge toward the shrine. Inside are the three images of Khenlop Chösum, the founders of Samye, as well as an image of Tsiumar, the protecting deity of Samye, astride a blue horse.

A more demanding excursion from Samye is the hike up to the Chimphu cave hermitage, taking **4 to 5 hours** each way (to shorten this walk, ask at the Samye guesthouse about hiring a truck to the base of the Chimphu ridge). Set in a densely vegetated amphitheater to the east of the monastery, this retreat is a paradise of birds, flowers, and tumbling streams. Chimphu is also an important pilgrimage site, for this is where Guru Rimpoche meditated and taught his disciples in the eighth century; here he also concealed *terma*, or treasures (usually prayer texts or teachings). Several routes lead to this retreat; one of the most direct heads east from Samye's entrance gate, then skirts the left (north) end of Hepori to enter an adjacent desert valley to the east. A dirt road turns left (north) across the dry plain, leading into the hills toward Chimphu. In 1½ **hours** the track ends at a ghost town of ruined buildings. A trail continues up the valley from here, passing abandoned crop terraces and a small nunnery before ascending into the tangle of rosebushes and barberry engulfing Chimphu.

The hills of this enchanting retreat have dozens of caves under overhanging rocks. Many have been reoccupied by meditating hermits, and at times even a few Western Buddhists have resided here. The white temple that can be seen from a distance is Drakmar Keutshang. A meditation cave of Guru Rimpoche and an associated *lhakhang* are on the lower level. Above it is a smaller building with residences for visiting *lamas* and the meditation cave of Guru Rimpoche's main disciple, Bairotsana.

Directly below Drakmar Keutshang, a solitary, conical outcrop of rock called Zangdok Pelri, the "Glorious Copper-colored Hill," extends from the slopes. A pilgrimage route winds from cave to cave up to its summit. Towering above the entire Chimphu complex is a granite peak, known to some as Gurkartse. A challenging pilgrim's *kora* that takes **8 hours or more** climbs above the Drakmar Keutshang temple onto the ridge top. At the summit is Gurkar *phuk*, the cave where Guru Rimpoche is said to have instructed his 25 disciples. Within the cave is a small shrine with carved stone tablets of this Indian Tantric master and his two consorts. The *kora* then continues down the eastern ridge of this peak on a very faint trail to return to Drakmar Keutshang.

If you plan to spend the night at Chimphu, bring a sleeping bag, sufficient food for your entire stay, and ideally a tent. The monks at Chimphu are in retreat, living on meager food supplies. They have little to spare, and do not have facilities for accommodating foreigners. If you sleep in a temple or in someone's cave, be sure to leave an appropriate donation.

One hour or more to the west of Samye, on the road to the Tsangpo ferry landing, are the five *chörtens* of Zurkardo. Built from the granite boulders on the ridge side, these monuments are said to mark the location where King Trisong Detsen first met Guru Rimpoche. According to tradition, when the two great men initially faced each other, each believed the other should bow down in submission. When the Indian master raised his hand as if to salute, fire sprang out of his fingers, thunder rumbled overhead, and an earthquake shook the ground. Terrorized, the king and his ministers threw themselves in reverence at the guru's feet. As reparation for his error, the king was requested by Guru Rimpoche to build the five "wonderful" *chörtens* from the rock at this site.

Other walks in the Samye area include the **2- to 3-hour** day hike north up the Samye Valley to Drakmar Drinzang, the birthplace of King Trisong Detsen, and the **5-hour** hike to the Yamalung cave hermitage. Both walks are described above, in reverse, in the section "The Ganden to Samye Trek."

LEAVING SAMYE

Samye monastery is a fair distance from the Tsangpo's northern shore, where a ferry crosses the river at Zurkardo to connect with the Lhasa-Tsethang Highway. The ferry departs each day from around 9:30 A.M. to 3:00 P.M. for the one-hour crossing to the highway. Trucks for the ferry leave from the courtyard in front of the Samye Utse's main entrance. The ride takes about half an hour, or it can be walked in **2 to 3 hours**. The ferry lands near the highway at kilometer marker 155, less than an hour's drive west from Tsethang (km marker 190); Gongkar Airport (km marker 93) is about an hour's drive to the west, and Lhasa is another 1½ hours or so beyond the airport.

THE SAMYE TO TAKTSE TREK

The **2½- to 3½-day** trek from Samye monastery to the county seat (*xian*) of Taktse follows an ancient caravan route that connected the Tibetan kings' palaces in the Yarlung Valley with their summer camps in Lhasa. This route is the shortest and most direct of the various trails between Samye and the Lhasa Valley, crossing Gökar La (White Eagle Pass; 17,050 ft, 5200 m), which Guru Rimpoche crossed en route to his first meeting with King Trisong Detsen. It can be combined with either of the treks from Ganden monastery or the Gyama Valley to create a scenic loop walk of **8 to 10 days** that returns to Lhasa.

The route from Samye initially follows the cart track north up the valley to Nyengo village (12,600 ft, 3840 m). This walk is detailed above, in reverse. Nyengo is the last settlement before the pass, situated at the confluence of the Yamalung Valley and a large tributary entering from the left (west). The trail to Gökar La leaves the main valley here, ascending the south (R) bank of this tributary. After weaving through a jungle of wild rosebushes, the trail crosses a bridge to the north (L) bank of the creek, below the junction with a stream entering from the north. A small meadow just above this bridge has room for several tents. Larger campsites are farther up the stream toward the pass.

The old trade route now ascends along the west (R) side of this stream and soon widens into a cobbled path. Apparently each Dalai Lama would pass this way on his once-in-a-lifetime pilgrimage to Lhamo Latsho (see "The Trek to Lhamo Latsho"), an "oracle lake" about a week's journey to the east by horse. After the death of a Dalai Lama, the regents of the Gelukpa hierarchy would also come this way to the lake, seeking insight from the visionary waters to help locate the new, incarnate boy-*lama*. The paving was probably done for one of these occasions, but the stones are so big that everyone opts to walk beside the cobbled path.

The trail to Gökar La remains in this drainage, climbing steadily past several remote *drokpa* camps before reaching the prayer flags and cairns on the summit (17,050 ft, 5200 m). The steep descent from the pass toward Taktse winds down the slopes into a vibrant tributary valley of the Kyi Chu. The pastures of wildflowers yield to barley crops, and the first village, Changsu, is **about 4½ hours** from the pass. The long but relatively flat trail to Taktse broadens into a dirt road near Shingjang village (12,550 ft, 3830 m), where a large tributary valley enters from the left (west). The road intersects the Tibet-Sichuan Highway in Taktse near a shop and a tea house (km marker 4611), in a direct line with the old Dechen Dzong fortress atop the hill looming over Taktse. This *dzong* was the residence of the *depa*, the administrator/tax collector for this area, but is now in ruins. A Gelukpa Tantric college was once on the hillside, but now only the main chanting hall of the monastery is still intact, hidden within a residential area below the hill's west end. Used for storing grain during the Cultural Revolution, this early fifteenth-century building has beautiful old murals. The adjacent Jamkhang temple has a three-story tall statue of Gyelwa Jampa, the "Future Buddha." Minibuses run frequently to Lhasa, 12 miles (20 km) to the west of Taktse.

THE GYAMA VALLEY TO SAMYE TREK

The Gyama Valley is a broad agricultural tributary of the Kyi Chu, 37 miles (60 km) east of Lhasa on the Tibet-Sichuan Highway. Barley fields sprawl across the valley floor, which is speckled with small villages and the sites of several twelfth-century Kadampa sect monasteries. The walk from Gyama to Samye via Tseb La (17,000 ft, 5180 m) and Kampa La (16,450 ft, 5010 m) takes **3½ to 4½ days** and is one of Central Tibet's finest moderate treks. The approach to these passes is considerably easier than the crossings to Samye from either Taktse or Ganden, yet the valleys en route are just as remote and scenic. About the third day of trekking from Gyama this route intersects the trail from Ganden to Samye.

The best time for this trek is generally from late April until the end of October. If you are well equipped it may be possible to cross Tseb La and Kampa La in winter. All food requirements and other supplies should be brought from Lhasa, and tents and fuel stoves are highly recommended, especially during the wet summer months.

To reach the Gyama Valley by public transport, take the Meldrogungkar bus (also spelled Maizhokunggar and Medrokongkar) from Lhasa, which operates daily from the Lubuk bus station, just south of Barkor Square. The driver should know where the Gyama Valley is, but keep an eye on the kilometer stones. Private transport to Gyama can be arranged through your hotel or with any of the travel companies in Lhasa.

The Gyama Valley is south (right) of the highway at Nonda village (12,200 ft, 3720 m; km marker 4572/1). If you are with a commercial trek or have hired a vehicle, you can drive 9 miles (15 km) up the valley to the road end at Thukchak village (13,300 ft, 4050 m), a good place for hiring yaks and a guide. For purposes of acclimatization, consider walking this stretch of the road to Thukchak. Allow **5 to 6 hours**, plus more time for visiting temples and villages en route. Campsites are easy to find, and accommodation can be arranged in local homes.

The trek to Samye heads south along the road from Nonda through extensive fields of barley and rapeseed. **About 30 minutes** from Nonda, perched on the east (R) ridge side above the fields is Gyelpo Gungkar temple (also called Gyelpo Khang), commemorating the birth of King Songtsen Gampo in this valley. Inside are statues of the king flanked by his Nepalese and Chinese wives.

Less than 30 minutes beyond here the road splits. Both forks eventually meet again at Gyama Trikhang village: the left fork leads to the school and the government *shang* offices, crosses the river to the (L) side, and goes to Gyama Trikhang; the right fork continues straight ahead, crosses the river, then goes to Nenakok, where Songtsen Gampo was born. Above this village are three *chörtens* near the ruins of Dumburi, one of the twelfth-century Kadampa monasteries in the Gyama Valley. From Nenakok the road continues a short distance into Gyama Trikhang (ten thousand households of Gyama). The old Kadampa *gompa* here is disappearing as the village builds among the ruins. All that remains is a small temple that survived the 1960s as a grain storage room; the *go-nyer* (doorkeeper) with the keys lives nearby. The central image is a tall thousand-armed Chenrezik, and along the walls are original murals. Monks have yet to be given approval to return to Gyama Trikhang or to the other two monasteries in the Gyama Valley, nor is it possible to rebuild these *gompas*; the only religious site approved by the *shang* officials is a small Gelukpa nunnery across the valley. A *kora* route leads through Gyama Trikhang around the old monastery, passes the ruined house of the Horkhang clan (the noble family that governed over the ten thousand families), then circles the site of three former *chörtens* (only one has been rebuilt) to return to the monastery entrance.

Rinchen Gang, the third Kadampa monastery in this valley, is **30 minutes** beyond Gyama Trikhang. A small temple has been rebuilt in the ruins above the village, which houses a very old stone figure of Sangye Önton, the founder of Gyama Trikhang monastery and the second abbot of Rinchen Gang.

Monks practicing the gya-ling, *a ceremonial horn playing during many tantric Buddhist rituals, Chimphu cave hermitage*

Thukchak (13,300 ft, 4050 m), the last settlement in the Gyama Valley, is **2 hours or more** above Rinchen Gang. The people here are both farmers and herders. Not far up the valley, the last crops give way to grassy hills and yak pastures. The road continues beyond Thukchak, paralleling the tumbling river for **10 minutes** to a wooden bridge. The route to both Samye and the Ön Chu Valley (see "The Gyama Valley to Ön Chu Valley Trek," below) crosses the bridge to the west (L) bank, then proceeds up the valley on a well-marked path. If it's late, consider spending the night near Thukchak. Campsites are hard to find here before the autumn barley harvest, so it may be necessary to stay with a family or continue up the valley for an hour to a campsite.

Less than 1 hour beyond the bridge a tributary enters from the left (east). The first of numerous stream crossings on this trek is nearby. The trail fords the river, now just a creek, to the east (R) bank. Climb steadily for **20 minutes** from the ford through thick brush, then rock hop across a tributary stream. A spacious meadow campsite (14,200 ft, 4330 m) is **a few minutes** up the valley. If you drove to Thukchak and started trekking the same day, these meadows are a good place to stop for the night, even if it's early in the afternoon. The next day's camp could then be in the pastures (15,800 ft, 4820 m) below Tseb La, allowing **2 nights** of acclimatization before you cross the pass. From the meadows continue up the east (R) side of the valley. During autumn dense stands of willow and wild rose are draped in magnificent, feathery white seedpods of *Clematis* vines, which drift in the wind like giant dandelion seeds.

Two hours or more beyond the meadow camp the trail fords the creek to the west (L) bank. The valley opens out and the vegetation is noticeably thinner and more stunted. A rugged, rocky ridge dominates the head of the valley, but Tseb La remains out of sight, hidden by the ridges up to the right (west). The trail rambles over hills of moraine to the first of a series of gently sloping meadow camps (15,800 ft, 4820 m). The last of these yak pastures is beside several crumbling stone corrals (16,400 ft, 5000 m) near the base of the west (L) ridge, **1½ hours** above the last creek ford. Beyond this camp a faint trail angles up the ridge to the right (southeast) toward Tseb La. Don't head south along the valley floor toward the basin below the rocky ridge. Several trails in this area lead toward other passes, away from Tseb La and into tributaries of the Ön Chu Valley on routes too rugged for pack animals.

Sidle up the ridge from the corral camp for **about half an hour** to an obvious dip in the ridge. The terrain now opens onto an elevated plateau of grass hummocks and rolling hills. Tseb La is the gap in the rocky ridge straight ahead (west) with a well-defined trail leading up to it. Angle toward this summit trail, keeping a good distance to the right (north) of Tsebla Tsho, a deep blue glacial lake. Reach the top of the pass (17,000 ft, 5180 m) and the *la-dze* in **1½ hours** from the stone corrals. Descend steeply from Tseb La into a broad, open basin dotted with grazing yaks in summer. **Thirty minutes** below the pass cross to the west (L) side of a small stream (16,300 ft, 4970 m), then continue straight ahead (southwest) up the sloping pastures. The route to Samye and the Ön Chu Valley is not well marked here, but as you follow the curve of the main valley up to the left (south), a trail forms along the base of the left ridge. Don't go down the main valley (north), which leads to Palha Tshodü, a lake near the trekking route from Ganden monastery to Samye.

After 40 minutes of easy climbing above the creek crossing, a cairn comes into view on a nearby hill sandwiched between two ridges. Kampa La (16,450 ft, 5010 m) is the boulder-strewn cleft with three *la-dze* to the left of this hill. The horizon beyond this summit is etched with jagged ridges, and below is a deep, canyon-like tributary of the upper Samye Valley. The trail from the pass drops steeply for a **few minutes** then forks. The smaller route to the left (southeast) stays high along the ridge side toward the

Ön Chu Valley, a fertile agricultural area across the Tsangpo from Tsethang (see route description below). Continue descending toward Samye via the right fork. In **30 minutes** pass a large *drokpa* encampment near the valley bottom (15,650 ft, 4770 m), where a family with two *ba* spends the summer months. Campsites are in the meadows nearby. Ask the herders if they have milk or yogurt to sell. Keep an eye out for their mastiffs.

The route to Samye crosses to the south (L) side of the creek near this camp. A vague trail descends through dwarf rhododendrons. The valley quickly narrows from here, with towering rocky outcrops forcing the trail across the creek a number of times. These fords can get rather tricky during July and August; ask the herders about a high trail on the (L) ridge side that avoids most of these crossings. Descend through this lovely canyon for **2 hours** to the confluence of the main Samye Valley with the tributary from Chetur La, on the trekking route from Ganden. Continue descending for **a few minutes** below this junction to a sprawling meadow campsite (14,400 ft, 4390 m). Samye monastery (11,600 ft, 3540 m) is still **8 hours or more** from here, not including rest stops. Although the monastery could be reached in a long day of walking, the journey through this valley is worth an extra day. Nyengo village (12,600 ft, 3840 m) is **about 4½ hours** downstream. The remainder of the trek to Samye is detailed above in "The Ganden to Samye Trek."

THE GYAMA VALLEY TO ÖN CHU VALLEY TREK

This walk from the Gyama Valley is a longer alternative to the trek from the Gyama Valley to Samye monastery, requiring **7 to 9 days** to reach the Ön (also spelled Yon) Chu Valley, a broad, fertile tributary of the Tsangpo just a few miles east of the city of Tsethang. En route are two eighth-century sites: Önphu Taktsang, a meditation cave of Guru Rimpoche, and Keru *lhakhang*, a temple founded during the reign of King Tride Tsukden.

Using the trail description "The Gyama Valley to Samye Trek," trek south from Nonda up the Gyama Valley, crossing Tseb La and Kampa La. **A few minutes** below Kampa La, the route forks. The left (southeast) branch is the trail to the Ön Chu Valley. Turn here, then sidle across the ridge on a rocky trail for **less than an hour** to a large meadow (16,200 ft, 4940 m) beside the creek in the valley. Consider spending the night here before crossing Tomtom La, the final pass before the Ön Chu Valley. A trail initially ascends the valley from this meadow, weaving around hills of moraine. As the trail disappears, stay on the far north (R) side of the valley to avoid wet, uneven tundra and rocks; the footing may be difficult. This is prime marmot country; these husky critters are everywhere, screeching at intruders from their rock perches.

As the valley swings to the right (south), don't cross the obvious pass at the head (south) of the valley, for this leads to Samye. Tomtom La (17,050 ft, 5200 m) is **2 hours or more** from the meadow camp, tucked around to the left (east), out of sight until you're almost on top of it. Valleys lead in all directions from the pass, making routefinding to Ön confusing. Straight ahead (east) from Tomtom La is a rocky, conical peak. The wide valley on the left (northeast) of this summit leads to Zibuk village and the Tibet-Sichuan Highway; the trail to Ön stays to the right (south) of it. In **30 minutes** pass to the left (north) side of a glacial tarn and stay on the (L) side of the outlet stream. The trail soon swings toward the south into a deep gorge. Although a rough trail does lead all the way through, the route for pack animals goes up along the east (L) ridge, then descends along the nose of the ridge to the valley bottom; it is not marked well. Either way, descend **2½ to 3 hours** to a meadow camp (15,400 ft, 4690 m) at the junction with the upper Ön Chu Valley.

This is a good place for a rest day, since the Önphu Taktsang (Tiger nest retreat of the upper Ön Chu Valley), one of the three main Guru Rimpoche *taktsangs* in the

Interior of Keru lhakhang *in the Ön Chu Valley*

Himalaya (the others are Bhutan's famous Paro Taktsang and the Rongme Karmo Taktsang in Kham), is **about 30 minutes** west up the main valley from the meadow camp. A trail follows the north (L) side of the creek past the former site of the Kargyüpa sect Taktsang *gompa*. The remains of the Önphu Taktsang hermitages are within a large group of boulders on the south (R) side of the creek; unlike the other two *taktsangs*, this one is not in use at present. The main cave is located under a large boulder, near a network of ruined walls overgrown with stinging nettles. A simple stone altar, an old sword, and some blackened butter lamps are all that remain in this famous hermitage where Guru Rimpoche imparted Buddhist teachings to his consort, Yeshe Tshogyel, and where Orgyen Lingpa, a Nyingmapa sect scholar–treasure finder discovered *terma*, religious texts hidden by the Great Guru.

The trail to the lower Ön Chu Valley crosses to the south (R) of the main creek below the meadow camp, then in **a few minutes** crosses a tributary stream from Taktsang Latsho, the "life-spirit lake" for Önphu Taktsang. The autumn colors are spectacular as the trail winds east through long meadows with herder camps and thick stands of dwarf rhododendron, willow, wild rose, and barberry bushes. **About 2 hours** below the meadow camp near the *taktsang*, rock hop to the north (L) side of the creek. The first cultivated fields (13,900 ft, 4240 m) are 1½ to 2½ hours farther down the valley. Nearby are the ruins of Ganden Lhatse nunnery, and below is another ruin beside large juniper trees. The trail now crosses a bridge to the south (R) side of the creek, and in **less than half an hour** crosses again to the north (L) side at Akor (13,400 ft, 4080 m), an attractive, compact village of about twenty houses. **Thirty minutes** farther is Tramdo village and its terraced potato fields. The trail is now wide enough for tractor carts, and more settlements are passed en route to Dikna (12,600 ft, 3840 m), **2½ hours** below Tramdo. This is the first large village (there's electricity!) of the Ön Chu Valley, with over fifty families.

Less than 10 minutes below Dikna cross a bridge to the east (L) side of a large tributary from the north. A route up this valley leads to Tekar La and beyond to Zibuk village and the Tibet-Sichuan Highway. The cart track to the mouth of the Ön Chu Valley now turns south into a wide plain of extensive fields dotted with settlements. **About 2½ hours** below the Dikna bridge the cart track makes a sharp right-hand (west) bend.

Stay on this track to reach Keru *lhakhang*, which is **2 hours or more** down the valley on the west (R) side. Or you can take the small trail that continues straight ahead (south) when the road angles to the right; this leads toward the massive ruins of Chöding *gompa* (13,600 ft, 4150 m).

The side trip to Chöding is **almost a full day's** excursion; if you camp somewhere near the sharp right-hand bend in the road, both Chöding and Keru *lhakhang* can be visited on the same day. To reach the monastery, take the trail south from the sharp bend, pass several houses, then follow the trail up the ridge to the left (southeast; aim for the scar of a long water channel). **Two and a half hours** farther up this ridge is Chöding, a Gelukpa monastery originally founded about the twelfth century and formerly the largest religious complex in the Ön Chu Valley. Nearby was Samtenling nunnery and the *podrang*, or living quarters of Chöding's head *lama*, the Gyese Rimpoche (the fourteenth incarnation of this *lama* became the Regent of Tibet for nearly ten years while the Seventh Dalai Lama was in exile). The extent of the destruction here is a sobering display of the fury that gripped Tibet and China during the Cultural Revolution. A direct route down from the monastery leads to Gyelzang village, on the valley floor.

Otherwise, from the sharp bend in the road, continue following the road down the valley. In **less than an hour** pass Gyelzang village, below Chöding *gompa*. In **another hour** the cart track comes to a junction at the settlement of Ruka Sumba (Third Commune). The road due south leads to Tashi Doka hermitage and the Tsangpo. The road to the right (west) crosses a bridge to the (R) bank of the river. Ön Qu (11,800 ft, 3600 m), the administrative *shang* for the valley, is **5 minutes** west of the bridge; several small shops are at the junction of the bridge road and the main north-south road running through town. **Twenty minutes** south of Ön Qu is a large meadow beside the road, perfect for camping and a good rendezvous point if you plan to have vehicles meet you at the trek's end. If you are walking, allow **3½ hours** to reach the Tsangpo bridge and the main road (km marker 5). Tsethang is a **1½-hour** walk to the right (west).

Keru *lhakhang* (also called Kachu) is **20 minutes** north from Ön Qu along the main road, set back in to the left (west) behind several houses in Ruka Dangpo (First Commune). This temple is one of only a handful still standing from the "first diffusion" of Buddhism in Tibet, founded during the Yarlung Dynasty in the eighth century by King Tride Tsukden and his Chinese princess Kongjo. According to the noted historian Roberto Vitali (see his definitive work, *Early Temples of Central Tibet*), the inner temple at Keru, behind the *dukhang*, is the original eighth-century structure and the grand 15-foot (4.5-m) tall Buddha statue housed inside is of a similar age. Vitali also believes the eight standing *bodhisattva* figures, the two statues of the founding king and princess, and the two protecting deities guarding the entryway are the originals, but perhaps a century older and constructed during renovation in the ninth century by King Ralpachen. If this is true, the Keru statues may well be the oldest extant in Tibet. According to the locals, the temple and its statues were spared in the 1960s when Khampa salt traders filled the ancient *lhakhang* to the ceiling with salt, preventing the Red Guards from entering. The *dukhang* is a more recent structure, with beautiful but disintegrating wall murals. The caretaker monks are from Dorje Drak, a Nyingmapa *gompa* on the Tsangpo, upstream from Samye. The monks' residences, a *gönkhang*, and a temple honoring the Indian scholar Atisha's visit here are entered from the courtyard.

The Tsangpo bridge can be approached on the less-traveled east (L) side of the Ön Chu Valley. Cross over the bridge again from Ön Qu, then turn right (south) at Ruka Sumba. Follow the cart track for 2½ **hours or more** to reach Tashi Doka hermitage, an oasis of greenery tucked up into the barren hills on the left (east). In 1415 the founder of the Gelukpa sect, Tsong Khapa, stayed here in retreat for over two months and met a new disciple, Gendun Drub, who went on to be honored as the First Dalai Lama. The monks are from Ngari Tratsang, a destroyed Gelukpa college 1½ **hours** farther south along the cart track, on a hillock in the middle of the valley. Nearby is a dirt road along the north (L) shore of the Tsangpo, connecting Tsethang to the town of Zangri and its copper mines, 28 miles (45 km) to the east. The Tsangpo bridge is a **1-hour** hike to the west.

DAY HIKES NEAR TSETHANG

Tsethang (km marker 190; 11,500 ft, 3510 m), Central Tibet's third-largest city and capital of Shannan Prefecture, is situated on the broad river plains at the junction of the Yarlung Valley and the Tsangpo's southern banks. If you are flying into Tibet, the city is 60 miles (97 km) east of Gongkar Airport in a district of Southern Tibet known as Lhoka. Due to the relatively low elevation of the Yarlung Valley—350 feet (100 m) lower than the Lhasa Valley—Tsethang is an alternative location to spend the first several days acclimatizing to the high altitude and getting in shape for a trek.

Few places in Tibet have as diverse a history as the Tsethang area, particularly the Yarlung Valley and its tributary, the Chongye Valley. According to tradition the Tibetan race originated in Yarlung, and the first king of Tibet, who is said to have descended from heaven, came here to rule from Yumbu Lagang, a medieval-looking castle reputed to be the oldest building in Tibet. Descendants of this king ruled Tibet from this fertile region until the tenth century; their burial tombs are in the Chongye Valley, Tibet's "Valley of the Kings," and more tombs are in other valleys of Yarlung. Notable religious personalities came to meditate in the caves tucked into the mountainsides here, and during the fourteenth and fifteenth centuries the Yarlung Valley was again the power base for the rulers of Tibet, this time the Phakmodru family, who governed from their palace in Nedong, a few miles south of Tsethang.

Many of the historical sites and monasteries near Tsethang are mostly in ruins or have disappeared. Still, there are numerous opportunities for day hikes in the surrounding hills and valleys, ranging from easy strolls to serious full-day efforts. A good warm-up walk near the city's main commercial area is the inner *kora* leading from Ngachö monastery to Ganden Chökorling, the largest *gompa* remaining in this part of the valley. A much longer outer *kora* circles Zodang Gangpori, the long, barren ridge towering above the eastern flanks of Tsethang. It is one of the four most sacred peaks of Central Tibet, for near its summit is the Monkey Cave, where the *bodhisattva* Chenrezik, in the form of a monkey king, mated with an ogress to create the first Tibetan people. The name Tsethang means the "playground" of their offspring.

The inner pilgrimage *kora* takes **1 hour,** not including breaks or visits to the different monasteries en route. From the Tsethang traffic circle, turn right (east) and follow this road out of town for **10 minutes**. The tall, maroon-walled Ganden Chökorling monastery rises above the other buildings up to the right, though the pilgrim's circuit starts a little farther along the road, up an alley to the right leading into a residential area. If you pass kilometer marker 1, you've walked a couple of minutes beyond this junction. After turning up the alley, proceed about 100 feet (30 m), then take the second passageway on the left. The *kora* circuit is confusing for the next few minutes as it enters a labyrinth of Tibetan homes. Keep asking for Ngachö, the first monastery on the *kora*. It is **less than 10 minutes** from the road. About thirty monks are in residence at this renovated Gelukpa *gompa*. The temple behind the assembly hall contains three striking statues of Dusum Sangye, the Buddhas of the Three Times. An adjacent *gönkhang* houses a powerful, multiheaded figure of Dorje Jikjye, the bull-headed *yidam*, or tutelary deity, of the Gelukpa sect.

The *kora* does not drop down to Ganden Chökorling, but circles behind (south of) Ngachö *gompa* on a path between several houses to approach the base of the ridge. A well-marked trail winds up a rocky gully to a sacred spring where pilgrims drink and bathe with the medicinal water. The *kora* now leads to an overlook with several large *ladze* cairns and a tall pole topped by a banner. Pilgrims circle these piles twice, then continue across the ridge face to Sang-ngak Simjin *ani gompa*. This compact, well-cared-for nunnery has a small but fascinating *lhakhang* off the main courtyard, and two hidden chapels tucked into another building below the courtyard entrance. Nearly seventy nuns and a *trülku* are in residence here. The site dates from the seventeenth century; this was one of the first Gelukpa nunneries established. Climbing above it is the trail to the Monkey Cave and to the summit of Zodang Gangpori (see description below).

The *kora* now follows small offering cairns down to a road between several houses to Ganden Chökorling *gompa*, a beautiful seventeenth-century building with detailed woodworking on the structural beams. The building was used for salt storage in the 1960s and thus was spared from destruction. Original murals can still be seen on the ground floor along the ceiling, and in back of this assembly hall are three huge statues of the *yab-se-sum*. Fewer than ten monks reside in this Gelukpa monastery; 130 were here before 1959. The last leg of this pilgrimage walk descends west beyond more houses and a cinema to end at Tsethang's main street, just left (south) of the traffic circle.

―――――――

The pilgrimage to the Monkey Cave of Chenrezik (there are two caves) and to the summit of Zodang Gangpori (marked by a peak symbol on Map No. 2) starts behind the Sang-ngak Simjin nunnery; allow **7 hours or more** for the round trip up to the caves and to the summit. In **less than 10 minutes** from the *ani gompa* (11,650 ft, 3550 m) reach the ruined walls of Samtenling, an old Sakyapa sect monastery. The trail continues ascending, enters a rocky gully then leads up onto grassy slopes. Aim for a cairn on the ridge crest (13,050 ft, 3980 m), **1½ to 2 hours** above the nunnery. The cave where Chenrezik mated with the ogress and produced the first Tibetan people is **less than 10 minutes** down a trail to the left, festooned with many prayer flags high above the Tsangpo.

To continue onto the second cave and the summit, retrace your steps back to the cairn, then follow the trail up the ridgeline on a steep **20-minute** climb to the next cave (13,300 ft, 4050 m), which is much smaller but also draped with prayer flags. Several nuns I met here told me this was where Chenrezik lived before he agreed to take the ogress as his wife. *Tsha-tshas* lie in piles on the floor. The trail to Zodang Gangpori continues up to a false summit with prayer flags (13,600 ft, 4150 m), then leads east from here, curving along the spine of the ridge to the main summit (14,300 ft, 4360 m) in **1½ hours or more** from the second cave. Have a seat and enjoy the views of other holy peaks from this holy peak! Almost due east (L) is the snow-capped Odegungyel, residence of the father of Nyenchen Thanglha, the Western King of the mountain gods; to the south is Yarlha Shampo, residence of the Southern King of the mountain gods; and far to the west are the sacred snowy Jomo Karak peaks, which rise beside the Tsangpo between the Chushul bridge and Shigatse.

―――――――

The outer pilgrimage *kora* circumambulating Zodang Gangpori takes **10 to 12 hours**. During the Saga Dawa Festival, hundreds of pilgrims set off on this meritorious journey, for on this special day throughout Tibet the effects of positive (or negative) actions are said to be multiplied 10 million times. To ensure an early start, many pilgrims come on foot or by vehicle the day before the festival to camp at the base of the mountain. Others ascend the pass in the evening, celebrating the arrival of the Saga Dawa full moon at midnight by drinking copious quantities of *chang*. The *kora* starts from Tsethang and heads east past the traffic circle on the road along the Tsangpo to kilometer marker 6. Just past the Ön Chu Valley bridge at the end of Zodang Gangpori's northernmost ridge, turn right (south) from the main road (near a smoke-spewing cement factory) up a broad, barren plain. The trail soon meets a dirt road which leads to Luchung village (12,150 ft, 3700 m), **1 hour or more** from the main road. The wide *kora* trail climbs steeply from here for **2 to 2½ hours**, first through terraced fields, past the ruins of Tongdröl *ani gompa* and up the desert slopes to reach the ridge crest (13,300 ft, 4050 ft) cairns and prayer flags. During the Saga Dawa festivities, singing and making offerings—and not sobriety—are

Interior of Ganden Chökorling monastery, Tsethang

the foremost concerns with the large crowds gathered here.

The descent to the Yarlung Valley drops south through eroded gullies, past the ruins of Chasa *gompa* to the valley floor, where the trail splits. The left fork leads pilgrims to the rambling, seventh-century Trandruk *lhakhang*, one of four "inner" temples founded by King Songtsen Gampo to pin down a demoness obstructing the spread of Buddhism in Tibet. To return to Tsethang, take the right fork, which leads around a compound to the main Tsethang road. Turn right (north) and soon pass below Nedong Tse Tsokpa, a Gelukpa monastery beside the former site of Nedong *dzong*, the old palace of the Phakmodru family. A short *kora* trail leads into the hills around this *gompa*. To reach the commercial end of town, return to the main road and turn right (north). The Tsethang Hotel is about **15 minutes** away, and the traffic circle about **10 minutes** farther.

Another ambitious day hike is the **full-day**, round-trip journey up to Sheldrak (also called Yarlung Sheldrak), the Crystal Rock cave of Guru Rimpoche. Nestled high into the craggy summits on the west side of the Yarlung Valley, Sheldrak is one of the most sacred Nyingmapa pilgrimage sites in Tibet. Guru Rimpoche had been invited to Tibet in the eighth century by King Trisong Detsen to subdue the evil spirits plaguing the country, and it was here that he retreated to conjure up the terrific powers necessary to bring these beings under his control. In the Pema Shelphuk cave the "treasure finder" Orgyen Lingpa discovered this Tantric master's biography, the *Pema Katang*, an important Nyingmapa text that had been concealed some 600 years earlier by Yeshe

Tshogyel, the Guru's consort. The main cave is enclosed by a shrine, and below in a dip in the ridge is a two-story whitewashed residence-cum-retreat for several monks.

The trailhead for Sheldrak is about 2.5 miles (4 km) west of Tsethang. It is near Tsechu Bumpa (Vessel of Long-life Water), a crumbling white *chörten* at the base of the Yarlung Valley's western hills. Dating from the eighth century, it once contained a rock crystal image that had been presented to Trisong Detsen. Legends claim "long-life" water issues from this *chörten* on the full moon. The **4- to 5-hour** route to Sheldrak initially ascends the wide, dry valley west of Tsechu Bumpa on a cart track ending at a small settlement. A trail then climbs west up the ridge to Sheldrak (14,750 ft, 4500 m). The first temple in the cliffside building is the Guru Tsengye *lhakhang*, a tribute to the eight manifestations of Guru Rimpoche. Directly above is the revered Guru Rimpoche *drubphuk*, containing his image flanked by his two consorts, and a number of *rangjön* figures along the left wall. The "crystal" of this site is the highly polished blackish green rock on the cave floor. The Pema Shelphuk cave, where the life story of Guru Rimpoche—the *Pema Katang*—was discovered, is farther around the mountain overlooking the Tsangpo. Bring a guide along, as it's difficult to find.

High on a ridge spur separating the Chongye and Yarlung Valleys is Rechung Phuk monastery. This prominently situated Kargyü/Nyingmapa sect *gompa* was built around the meditation cave of Rechungpa, a disciple of the ascetic Milarepa. Several temples have been rebuilt adjacent to the original cave, where Rechungpa spent three years, three months, and three days in retreat. His figure, along with those of his spiritual masters Milarepa and Marpa, are honored in the shrine built over the cave. The monastery is best approached from the village of Rechung at the base of the ridge. Several different trails lead up the ridge, taking **less than 1 hour** to reach the cave temple. Continue up the ridge to the massive stone walls of the former monastery for outstanding valley views.

The Chongye Valley is where most of Tibet's kings were buried until the Royal Dynasty collapsed in the ninth century. The main group of tombs is near the town of Chongye, 17 miles (28 km) south of Tsethang. The most prominent is Bangso Marpo (Red Tomb), a large earthen mound in the middle of the valley containing the remains of Songtsen Gampo. It is the only tomb with a temple crowning the summit. Across from here on the ridge to the north is Riwo Dechen *gompa* and the ruins of Chingwa Taktse, the "Tiger Peak" castle.

Riwo Dechen is **less than 1 hour** from Chongye village. A road leads toward it between the rows of whitewashed houses, then a trail ascends from the base of the hill to an entrance on the left side of the monastery compound. This fifteenth-century Gelukpa *gompa*, now a fraction of its former size, was designed after the great Ganden monastery near Lhasa. When the Italian scholar Guiseppe Tucci visited here in 1948, he noted that "the temples and chapels were nearly drowned among the houses accommodating the monks." The monastery was completely destroyed in the 1960s; one main building with two temples and a *gönkhang* have been rebuilt above an enclosed courtyard.

A **20-minute** walk along the ridge brings you to the ruins of the old assembly hall. Its magnificent cobbled courtyard is inlaid with a large white swastika, an ancient symbol favored by both the Bönpo and Buddhists in Tibet. Farther up the slopes are the ramparts of Chingwa Taktse, a palace of the early Tibetan kings until Songtsen Gampo shifted his residence to the Lhasa Valley. In later years the castle became the home of the Chongye princes, the feudal landlords who ruled over this valley. In the early seventeenth century one of their sons was recognized as the Fifth Dalai Lama. Lower on the

Yumbu Lagang, the palace of Tibet's first king and the oldest building in Tibet, near Tsethang

ridge, below an ill-placed cement pagoda, are the ruins of the old Chongye *dzong*.

Other excursions around the Chongye region include visiting the various burial mounds of the kings, or hiking 1½ **hours** farther up the main valley to Pelri *gompa*. The monks are caretakers for the Bangso Marpo temple on Songtsen Gampo's tumulus. Pelri's rebuilt *lhakhang* overlooks the upper Chongye Valley, where a pass leads west to the Drachi Valley and on to Mindroling *gompa*, one of the main Nyingmapa sect monasteries in Central Tibet.

LHAMO LATSHO REGION
MAP NO. 3, PAGE 111

Tucked into a remote eastern corner of the Lhasa-Tsethang region is Lhamo Latsho, the "life-spirit" and "oracle" lake sacred to Gyelmo Makzorma, the wrathful aspect of Tibet's protectress, Pelden Lhamo. Each Dalai Lama was to visit this lake at least once in his life, arriving here in a great procession to make offerings to Makzorma, and to contemplate the visionary water for insight into his future. After the death of a Dalai Lama, the Regent of the Gelukpa sect and an entourage of *lamas* would journey to Lhamo Latsho seeking clues from the oracle lake for finding the boy who was the new Dalai Lama. In an adjacent valley to the lake is Chökhorgyel monastery, founded in the early sixteenth century by the Second Dalai Lama.

Lhamo Latsho and Chökhorgyel monastery can be approached via a remote **6- to 8-day** trek starting from Rutok (14,150 ft, 4310 m; km marker 4509), 76 miles (123 km) east of Lhasa on the Tibet-Sichuan Highway. En route are two moderate pass crossings, Magong La (15,800 ft, 4820 m) and Gyelung La (17,000 ft, 5180 m). The trek can be shortened to **3 to 5 days**, crossing only Gyelung La, by driving about 37 miles (60 km) east of Tsethang and starting the walk from the town of Olka Taktse. There's even a road to Chökhorgyel, a long day's drive east of Tsethang via the county seat (*xian*) of Gyatsa.

The best time for trekking to Lhamo Latsho is generally from mid-May to mid-October, though snow can fall on the passes any of these months. The summer rains affect this area more than other valleys in Central Tibet; the wildflowers are outstanding in July and August, but bring good rain gear! A fuel stove and tent are highly recommended for this trek, though numerous herder camps and several settlements are found throughout the walk.

Packhorses can be arranged at the trailheads of Rutok or Olka Taktse. Start asking as soon as you arrive, and with luck you'll be off the next morning. Make sure your guide has a tarp to sleep under, and negotiate for his return journey. From Rutok it may be necessary to first hire horses for two days to the town of Dzingchi, then get a different guide and horses on to Chökhorgyel.

Purchase all food requirements in Lhasa, or in Tsethang if you're starting from Olka Taktse. Noodles, potatoes, and perhaps some greens are usually available at the restaurants in Rutok, a sprawling truck stop below Rutok monastery; over 150 log trucks rumble through here daily on their two-day journey to Lhasa from Kongpo, hauling out trees from Central Tibet's largest stand of virgin forest. The guesthouses in Rutok are rather basic and dormitory-style; pay for all the beds in your room to avoid having company stumble in at midnight.

It may also be possible to stay at Rutok monastery, a steep **30-minute** ascent north of the truck stop. This compact but beautifully situated Gelukpa *gompa* has about ten monks, a small *dukhang*, and two protector chapels. Since the monks are all from local herder families, they may be able to help arrange packhorses.

The only public transport to Rutok from Lhasa is via the bus to Bayi, the Nyingchi district seat (*xian*) in Kongpo. Buses depart daily from the long distance bus station south

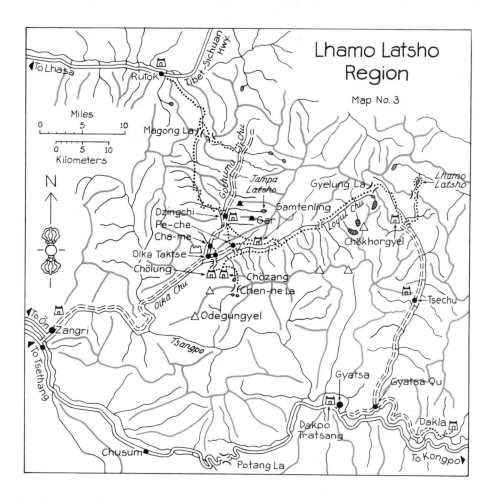

of the Lhasa Hotel. It may also be possible to hitch with the empty log trucks returning to Kongpo from Lhasa.

THE TREK TO LHAMO LATSHO

The route to Magong La and Lhamo Latsho initially heads east from Rutok following the Tibet-Sichuan Highway. In less than **15 minutes** cross a bridge spanning a tributary flowing in from the south. Just past here a rock outcrop comes down to the road on the right (south); the trail to Magong La turns off the highway to the right just past these rocks, **about 10 minutes** beyond the bridge. A well-marked path climbs steadily up the ridge side through tall potentilla bushes and soon enters a scenic valley of green meadows, grazing yaks, and a meandering creek with winding oxbows. The route now heads south, following this valley all the way up to the pass. At times the trail is a bit hard to follow, but generally stays above the west (L) side of the creek. Other than a few houses, the valley is mainly inhabited by yaks and frisky golden marmots.

Pass several spacious meadow camps with large pika colonies. About **5 hours** from the highway, cross the creek to the east (R) side. To acclimatize properly before crossing Magong La, consider camping in one of the meadows (15,000 ft, 4570 m) here, as the valley now narrows and starts to ascend more steeply. Cross a stream entering from the left

Lhamo Latsho is the "life-spirit" lake of the Dalai Lamas

(east), then climb for **45 minutes** beside the tumbling creek, passing stands of potentilla bushes to reach a large *la-dze* cairn, then another. At the second cairn, cross the creek to the west (L) bank. The valley now starts to level and open out into a vast grassy basin dotted with black yak-hair *drokpa* tents. A wide, flat tributary comes in from the left (east); a pass hidden from view up this valley to the southeast also leads to Chökhorgyel (and may also be called Magong or Machen La). Although both routes will work, continue straight ahead (south), following a wide trail up the ridge side for **1 hour or more** to reach the large *la-dze* at Magong La (15,800 ft, 4820 m).

Like a scene from Amdo, the rolling hills and meadows extend in all directions; it is certainly one of the largest grassland areas in all of Central Tibet. The village of Dzingchi is **7 hours or more** from here, with plenty of places for camping the entire way. Continue south from Magong La, passing herder camps fortified with walls of woven branches. The trail rollercoasters in and out of small tributary drainages, staying on the west (R) side of the main valley, which I dubbed the Pika Plains; these little critters are everywhere! If the weather is clear, the sacred summit of Odegungyel (18,766 ft, 5720 m) soars to the south, and the snowy peaks farther off to the left (southeast) form the southern boundary of the valley leading to Gyelung La.

Some **2 hours** beyond Magong La the trail passes a *sung khang*, a protector shrine for the Eleventh Dalai Lama, who was born in Dzingchi. Cross the stream here then climb between thousands of cushion plants to a nearby ridge summit with grand views. Below is a large wet plain with several ponds. The route to Dzingchi heads straight (south) across it on a faint path; don't take the larger trail to the right (west), which stays along the edge of the plain. **About one hour** past the *sung khang* the plain ends and the trail drops to a wide basin. Beyond here the valley narrows into a delightful chasm lush with tall yellow *Primula sikkimensis*, blue poppies, edelweiss, yellow buttercups, pink geraniums, willow, wild rose, barberry, and potentilla bushes. White-capped river chats dart near the creek, and Tibetan partridge mothers and their babies scurry into the undergrowth. The trail swings back and forth across the creek a half-dozen times and eventually passes barley fields and the skeleton of a large stone house (13,500 ft, 4110 m), probably a former estate of the Eleventh Dalai Lama's family.

Dzingchi (13,200 ft, 4020 m) is **1 hour** past this old manor, on the west (L) side of the Gochumu Chu. Cross the wooden bridge and follow the wide track up to the village. The golden roof of the monastery rises above the cluster of whitewashed houses; three hundred families reside in this area. The large three-story ruins at the south end of town are the former house of the Eleventh Dalai Lama's family. There are no shops in Dzingchi, nor a guesthouse. Accommodation can be arranged with a family, or perhaps in the local government (*shang*) compound. Campsites are difficult to find if the crops have not been harvested.

DZINGCHI MONASTERY

The glory of Dzingchi was lost with the Cultural Revolution, and all that remains is the shell of the old Gyelwa Jampa ("Future Buddha") *lhakhang*. Where five hundred monks once resided, now there are but twelve. Dzingchi was founded in the tenth century by Garmi Önten Yungdrung, a disciple of Lachen Gonga Rabsel, who helped initiate the second diffusion of Buddhism in Central Tibet after the collapse of the Royal Dynasty. The monastery was renowned for its ancient Gyelwa Jampa statue, which Tsong Khapa restored in the late fourteenth century during his long sojourn in the Olka region. One of his main disciples, Gyeltsab Dharma Rinchen, became the first throne holder at Ganden monastery, and Dzingchi became the seat of his lineage of *trülkus*. His *labrang*, or residence, was torn down along with the old chanting hall, to be replaced by a cavernous, unused public meeting hall.

Now the community is struggling to raise funds to restore the gutted Jampa *lhakhang*. The beautiful old frescoes, including the self-manifested mural of the thirty-five Confessional Buddhas on the left wall as you enter, are damaged but still visible. A large, seated Jampa statue flanked by the Eight Great *Bodhisattvas* has replaced the original in the back temple. On the roof is a *gönkhang* and a good overview of the area, which has a wealth of religious sites.

At the mouth of a side valley just northwest of the monastery is a small nunnery, and above in the cliffs is the meditation cave of Gyelwa Jampa and two other caves. Following this drainage west for **7 hours or more** leads to Jampa Latsho (16,450 ft, 5010 m), the life-spirit lake of the Future Buddha. About 2½ **hours** up an adjacent tributary to the southeast from Dzingchi is Garphuk cave hermitage (marked as Gar on the map), where the Indian master Guru Rimpoche hid religious texts and assumed the form of a dancing *khandroma* during his meditations. Tsong Khapa and Gampopa, one of Milarepa's main disciples, spent time meditating here. Monks of the Kargyüpa sect now come here to spend three years and three months in retreat, a prerequisite for their spiritual training. **One and a half hours** beyond Garphuk is Samtenling, another cave hermitage of Tsong Khapa's, on the route to Chökhorgyel. The direct route to Samtenling from Dzingchi initially enters the valley leading to Garphuk, then turns right (southeast) on a wide trail over the hills, reaching this hermitage in **about 3 hours**.

TO CHÖLUNG AND CHÖZANG HERMITAGES

Although the direct route to Lhamo Latsho heads southwest from Dzingchi toward Samtenling, the diversion to the Chölung and Chözang hermitages in the Olka Valley is worth the few extra hours of walking—or a few days if you have the time. From Dzingchi, follow the road south toward Olka Taktse, the former administrative center and fortress (*dzong*) for this region. In **20 minutes** the road splits; the fork to the left leads up to Garphuk cave hermitage. The route to Chölung and Chözang continues straight ahead on the right fork, winding through barley fields for 1½ **hours** to Cha-me, a small town of about thirty families. The valley now opens out and the ruined *dzong* above Olka Taktse is visible to the southwest. **Fifteen minutes** beyond Cha-me is a large tree on the left side of the road, associated with Tsong Khapa. About 600 feet (180 m) past the tree a stream crosses the road, and just beyond here the trail to Chölung and Chözang turns left (south) off the road through the barley fields. Follow this trail above the terraces, which are overseen by cleverly attired scarecrows. Reach the crest of a hill, offering panoramic views of the Olka Valley. Due south on the flanks of the Odegungyel Range is a white *chörten* near Chölung, though the hermitage itself is hidden. Chözang is along the ridge in a grove of trees to the left (east) of the *chörten*, and the tributary valley a bit farther east leads up to Chen-ne La, the gateway to the pilgrim's *kora* around Odegungyel.

Chölung (13,520 ft, 4120 m) is **1½ hours** from the hilltop. Descend to a road running through Khani, the settlement below. Cross the bridge (12,700 ft, 3870 m) to the south (L) side of the Derimu Chu (the lower stretch of the Loyul Chu), and follow the service road up to the *chörten*. This delightful retreat is where Tsong Khapa spent five years at the end of the fourteenth century with his Eight Disciples of Olka, and where he performed 350,000 prostrations. His meditation cave, Öser *phuk,* and three other caves are on the hill above the *gompa.* An ornate *dukhang* has been rebuilt, with statues of Tsong Khapa and his Olka disciples; in the back left corner is the horse-riding statue of Odegungyel, the mountain god who is father of Nyenchen Thanglha, the king of Tibet's mountain gods.

For those planning to spend the night, a simple guesthouse with wooden bed platforms is available for pilgrims.

If you will be starting the trek to Lhamo Latsho from Olka Taktse, turn right from the government *shang* compound entrance and follow a dirt road that swings east toward the north (R) bank of the Derimu Chu. The road to Dzingchi does not go this way, but heads northeast from Olka Taktse, a **2- to 2½-hour** walk from here. For Lhamo Latsho and Chölung, continue east. In **less than 15 minutes** the road forks. Turn right and soon reach the houses of Khani. Just beyond is the bridge over the Derimu Chu and the service road to Chölung. The direct route to Lhamo Latsho continues straight ahead (east) on the road paralleling the north (R) bank of the river, reaching the town of Pe-che in **about 1½ hours**. The main route to Lhamo Latsho crosses a bridge near this small administrative *shang* to the south (L) side of the Derimu Chu, then continues east up the valley on a wide trail. Gyelung La is **2½ days** from Olka Taktse, and at least one other day should be spent acclimatizing before crossing the pass.

From Chölung, the trail to Chözang (13,450 ft, 4100 m) hermitage turns east at the white *chörten.* Sidle across slopes of pink and white-blooming dwarf rhododendron for **30 minutes** to yet another idyllic retreat of Tsong Khapa's. In the lower temple is a rock *zhabje* of this Gelukpa master's footprint, and on the wall are 999 *tsha-tshas* of Tsepame ("Buddha of Long Life") made by Tsong Khapa, along with the main statue of Tsepame on the altar. Two other temples are above here.

Two trails depart from Chözang to the east; the lower is the shortcut to meet the main trail to Lhamo Latsho, at the bridge crossing near Pe-che. The upper trail ascends the ridge for about **4 hours** to Chen-ne La (16,100 ft, 4910 m), the pass on the pilgrim's circuit around the holy mountain Odegungyel. It's a spectacular crossing, with five

Trekking to Lhamo Latsho

lakes and towering snowy peaks nearby. A few cave retreats and small hermitages are several hours farther down the south side of the pass toward the Tsangpo. The *kora* takes **2 to 3 days** for the locals, but they say the trail along the river is not in good condition.

To Gyelung La and Chökhorgyel Monastery

From Chözang hermitage, the most direct route toward Gyelung La angles east across the ridge toward the valley floor. The trail gets faint at times, so just stay above the barley fields and follow a stone wall, meeting the bridge and the main trail from Pe-che in **2 to 2½ hours**. To visit Samtenling hermitage, cross the bridge at Pe-che to the north (R) bank and head upstream for **1½ hours** to this secluded cave retreat. Much of the former hermitage and the four-story chanting hall remain in ruins, but the main cave temple is up on the forested slopes.

The route to Lhamo Latsho stays along the south (L) bank of the Derimu Chu from Pe-che, following the wide path east toward the pass. The valley begins to narrow and soon the first of nearly a dozen large tributaries spills in from the snowy peaks of the Odegungyel Range. **One and a half hours** past Pe-che is another bridge, which can also be used to reach Samtenling. Continue toward Gyelung La on the south side of the river, which is now called the Loyul Chu, after the name of this region. Large meadows and herder camps line the valley floor all the way to the pass, making it easy to choose campsites.

The trail stays on the south side of this lush valley for **5½ hours** to reach the junction of two large tributaries. The route to Lhamo Latsho crosses at the confluence on a long pile of stones, then continues upstream along the north (R) side of the smaller tributary from the left. Three large herder settlements, Rama, Ome, and Emando (15,800 ft, 4820 m), are spread across the valley below the pass; the last of these is about **2½ hours** above the creek crossing. Consider spending two nights here to acclimatize before going over Gyelung La; your extra day can be spent exploring the big glaciated valleys to the south. For mountaineers, this chain of rugged peaks is a paradise of virgin summits just under 6000 meters (19,700 ft). The herders told me the impressive peak to the south is called Sang Gangri (19,586 ft, 5970 m; marked on Map No. 3 with a peak symbol).

Gyelung La (17,000 ft, 5180 m) is the obvious dip in the ridge to the east, **2 hours** from Emando along the north (R) side of the creek. A huge glacier spills in from the south, yellow poppies (*Meconopsis integrifolia*) and delicate pink and white *Pedicularis* dot the meadows, and a large aqua glacial lake sprawls below the glacier and the pass. Circle the *la-dze* cairn at the summit three times, toss three rocks onto the pile as an offering to the deities, then have a seat and enjoy this incredible scene.

Chökhorgyel monastery is **4 hours** below the pass in another deep glacial valley enclosed by rocky peaks. Campsites can be found along the entire route, as well as just above (north of) the monastery. If you do camp near the *gompa*, keep an eye on your gear. A compound built beside the monastery by the Gyatsa Qu *shang* officials has a couple of funky guesthouse rooms, and a school has been built nearby for the herder children of this area.

CHÖKHORGYEL MONASTERY

Founded in the early sixteenth century by Gendun Gyatsho, the Second Dalai Lama, the once-grand complex of Chökhorgyel monastery (14,750 ft, 4500 m) is now a jumble of overgrown crumbling temples, very reminiscent of how Ganden monastery looked in the 1980s. All that has been rebuilt is a chanting hall for the fifteen monks who have returned; 500 were here before 1959. The central figure in the *dukhang*, seated on a high throne, is the Second Dalai Lama. A large Future Buddha sits in the *lhakhang* behind the altar area. The *gönkhang* has an outstanding statue of Dorje Jikjye, the bull-faced guardian of the Gelukpa sect, and hidden behind silk *kataks* is Gyelmo Makzorma.

The triangular monastery grounds are situated at the junction of three large valleys in the appropriately named region of Metokthang—the Flower Meadow. The stone masonry of the old walls is outstanding, and the ruins are definitely worth a wander. The large red-walled temple was formerly the Jampa Lhakhang, a chanting hall which once had 60 pillars supporting the roof over the Future Buddha statue. At the base of the hill just north of the monastery are the tall ruined walls of Tiktse Podrang, the former residence of the Second Dalai Lama, which was built over his original cave retreat. On the ridge to the east are the tri-colored ruins of Gyangtse Karmar. When the Dalai Lamas came here on pilgrimage, they often stayed in the central white building, known as the Potala. The adjacent red- and blue-walled ruins were colleges for visiting monks from the Sakyapa and Nyingmapa sects.

Note: Chökhorgyel and the Olka-Zangri-Gyatsa region to the south of Magong La are in Shannan Prefecture. Unlike in the Lhasa Prefecture, foreigners are required to obtain an Aliens Travel Permit to legally visit these areas. The police in Zangri and Gyatsa will turn back all travelers without permits, and may impose a fine. They occasionally check permits at Chökhorgyel as well.

TO LHAMO LATSHO FROM CHÖKHORGYEL

To go all the way to the shore of Lhamo Latsho from Chökhorgyel and return is a full **11- to 12-hour** day of walking. To reach the pass (17,050 ft, 5200 m) overlooking the lake involves a **4-hour** walk, one way, on a tough 2300-foot (700-m) climb; to reach the lake (15,700 ft, 4790 m) is an additional **3- to 4-hour** round trip; allow **another hour** to walk the *kora* around the lake. If you drive to Chökhorgyel, spend at least two nights here to acclimatize before attempting this walk. Even then the altitude will slow you down.

The trail to Lhamo Latsho heads up the tributary to the east from Chökhorgyel. To start, cross to the east (L) side of the main creek; the bridge is about halfway along the monastery wall. Follow the trail up the ridge below the ruins of Gyangtse Karmar, then ascend into the valley leading to the east. Stay above the south (L) side of the creek for **1 hour**, then cross on rock platforms to the right side. The trail to Lhamo Latsho now heads up the east (L) side of the stream tumbling from the tributary drainage to the north. Climb through stands of willow and potentilla bushes to enter a hanging glacial valley. The pass for viewing Lhamo Latsho is straight ahead to the north, just left of a large, obvious rock outcrop along the ridgeline. The trail stays on the east (L) side of the stream until just below the pass. It's still 1300 feet (400 m) from here to the top; pace yourself. The rocky summit is strewn with thick strands of prayer flags, and far below is the phallus-shaped Lhamo Latsho. Find a secluded spot and join the pilgrims as they recite *mantras* and gaze upon the lake.

The trail to the lake descends from the east end of the ridge crest in a series of steep switchbacks. As the valley levels out the trail gets hard to follow. Stay above the east (R) side of the stream to avoid wet ground. To circumambulate the lake, cross to the stream's west (L) side a few hundred yards before the shoreline. At the far end of the lake are prayer flags and a simple shrine built from the ruins of the Gyelmo Makzorma temple. It was here in 1935 that Reting Regent rode a yak down from the pass to make his offering to the *latsho* of this protectress. During three visits to the lake he had a vision of a one-story house with a blue roof situated on a hill near a monastery. He also saw the Tibetan letters *ah*, *ka*, and *ma*. The interpretation of these letter visions was that *ah* stood for Amdo. The Regent's search for the incarnation of the Thirteenth Dalai Lama, who had died two years earlier, was then directed to Amdo, in the Northern Plains of Tibet. The young boy the Regent recognized as the Fourteenth Dalai Lama was discovered in a blue-roofed house similar to that in his vision, near Kumbum monastery in Amdo (one of the six main Gelukpa monasteries in Tibet).

Pilgrims toss offerings of silk *kataks*, with a small amount of money rolled inside, into the lake. It is considered very auspicious if this "spiritual pollution" sinks quickly. And if you have a vision, it is not meant to be told to others.

Allow **2 hours or more** to climb back up to the ridge top, and **3 to 4 hours** to return to Chökhorgyel.

LEAVING CHÖKHORGYEL

If you haven't arranged transport to meet you at the monastery, it's often possible to catch a lift with pilgrim trucks returning to Tsethang. Otherwise plan on a spectacular **2- to 2½-day** walk south down the Gyatsa canyon to cover the 26 miles (42 km) to Gyatsa. The only village in the valley is Tsechu (13,350 ft, 4070 m), **about 5 hours** below Chökhorgyel if you're carrying a pack. A small hermitage on the mountain side here is beside a prominent rock outcrop shaped like a *bumpa*, a vessel used for holding *tsechu*, "long-life" water. The village of Gyatsa Qu (10,600 ft, 3230 m) is **6 hours or so** farther, at the junction with the Tsangpo Valley. The small shops here sell the most delicious walnuts in Tibet! Gyatsa and the highway to Tsethang are still **4 hours or more** upstream (west) along the Tsangpo.

There is no public transport linking Gyatsa (10,650 ft, 3250 m) with Tsethang, 93 miles (150 km) to the west via Potang La (15,800 ft, 4820 m). The guesthouse in Gyatsa is located in a compound to the south off the main street; nearby are several Chinese restaurants. Just west of town is Dakpo Tratsang, the largest *gompa* in this region. Originally a Zhamar Kargyüpa monastery, it was taken over by the all-powerful Gelukpa sect and the Great Fifth Dalai Lama in the mid-seventeenth century, to became closely affiliated with Chökhorgyel monastery. Several of the buildings, including the *dukhang*, survived the 1960s.

To the north of Lhasa, beyond the wall of ridges rising behind Sera monastery, are the large parallel valleys of the Phenpo Chu and the Kyi Chu. Before 1959 some fifty monasteries were located in these two major agricultural areas. Most were completely razed in the 1960s. The Phenpo Chu Valley is where the second diffusion of Buddhism spread in earnest during the eleventh century, following the arrival of the Indian master Atisha in Central Tibet. His foremost disciple, Dromtön Gyelwai Jungne, founded Reting monastery in the Reting Tsangpo Valley (the upper stretch of the Kyi Chu) in 1056, where he established a new school of Buddhism called the Kadampa (Spiritual Advice) sect, based on Atisha's teachings and emphasizing scholarship and monastic discipline. Over the next fifty years about a half-dozen large Kadampa monasteries, many with a thousand monks or more, sprung up in the Phenpo Chu Valley (and others were built nearby, such as in the Gyama Valley and along the lower Kyi Chu above Lhasa), founded by Dromtön's contemporaries and their disciples. Although several of these sites disappeared so many years ago that their exact location is now unknown, others were appropriated by the Gelukpa, Sakyapa, or Kargyüpa sects and continue functioning today, albeit in a much reduced state from their eleventh-century glory.

A second wave of monasticism came to these valleys in the late twelfth century with the arrival of another new branch of Tibetan Buddhism, the Kargyüpa (Oral Tradition) sect. Based on the teachings of the poet-saint Milarepa, this school emphasizes contemplative studies and a strong teacher-student relationship. Through two disciples of the Kargyüpa master Phakmodru, Drigung Til monastery was founded in 1179 up a tributary of the Kyi Chu to the west of Lhasa, and the next year Taklung monastery was established in another tributary of the Kyi Chu, north of Lhasa closer to Reting. Both monasteries grew rapidly, and today two major subsects of the Kargyüpa lineage of teachings, the Taklung Kargyüpa and the Drigung Kargyüpa, bear their names.

Despite this area's proximity to Lhasa, trekking has yet to become popular. Complicating the situation is that the people here are farmers; unlike herders living in the high valleys, they are reluctant to hire out their pack animals or leave their fields for more than a day or two before the autumn harvest. Still, it is possible to trek in this area if you don't mind hiring a new guide and pack animals almost everyday. To trek from Lhasa to Drigung via Reting monastery takes **2 to 2½ weeks**, not including layover days; I felt four weeks wasn't enough time for this route, which I found myself calling "Le Grande *Kora*." For those traveling by vehicle, the various monasteries can be used as a base for hiking to the many religious and historic sites north of Lhasa.

THE TREK FROM LHASA TO THE PHENPO CHU VALLEY

The Phenpo Chu Valley is a **2- to 3-day** trek from Lhasa via Phenpogo La (The Door to Phenpo), plus another day for acclimatization before the pass. The trek route initially follows a little-used road up the Dode Valley, the first large drainage to the east of Sera monastery. The road goes to Ling Dzong, the last settlement before the pass, then continues along an unused section over Phenpogo La to the Phenpo Chu Valley. A four-wheel-drive vehicle can usually reach Ling Dzong, and the small taxis in Lhasa can get within a few miles if you want to shorten the walking time.

Starting from Lhasa, head north on Dode Lam (the north end of East Lingkor Road), toward the mountains from the traffic circle at the northeast corner of the Lingkor pilgrim circuit. About 2 miles (3 km) past this roundabout the paved road changes to dirt. The small temple off to the left (west) across the valley is a sky-burial site, but it is off limits to foreigners. Up on the cliffs is the fortresslike Keutshang monastery, and beside it to the left is Rakadrak hermitage. Up on the ridge to the right (east) is the

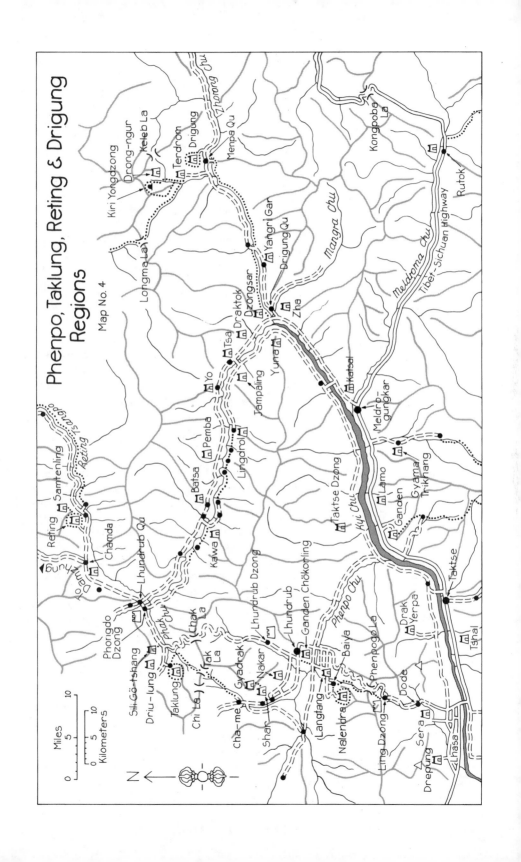

Phenpo, Taklung, Reting & Drigung Regions

Map No. 4

large, white-walled Michungri nunnery (for more detail of the location of these temples, see Map No. 1).

The road splits about a mile (1 km) past the pavement's end; the left fork leads to a bridge over the Dode Chu, below the ochre-colored, hilltop citadel of Phurbu Chok *gompa* (a walk from Sera Tse hermitage to Phurbu Chok is described in "The Phabongkha-Sera Tse-Dode Valley *Kora*"). Stay on the right fork, which continues up the valley on a tree-lined road, past barley fields and houses to the Dode *shang* compound (12,200 ft, 3720 m).

One hour or more up the tributary to the right (east) from Dode is Negadong (12,650 ft, 3860 m; see Map No. 1), a small Gelukpa *ani gompa* with about forty nuns. Above it on the rocky ridge to the north are the ruins of Khardo *ritrö*, founded by Sera monastery's Khardo Rimpoche in the eighteenth century. The Third Khardo *lama* had his retreat in a cave beyond Negadong, which is acclaimed as a Guru Rimpoche meditation site. Other trails up this valley lead to Yi La, another access to the Phenpo Chu Valley; to Sinmo La, leading to Drak Yerpa hermitage; and up Jomo Sisi, a holy peak and Lhasa's second-highest summit.

The village of Ling Dzong (13,800 ft, 4210 m) is a **3½- to 4-hour trek** from the Dode *shang*. The road continues north from here and soon crosses a bridge to the Dode Chu's west (R) bank. Climb steadily up the narrow rock canyon, passing small agricultural settlements and the shrine for the valley's protector. **About 1½ hours** before Ling Dzong, the road crosses back to the east (L) side of the creek (12,800 ft, 3900 m). Campsites are rather limited below this point, but above here are several good meadows between the road and the creek. If you stay two nights in the Ling Dzong area to acclimatize, the nearby tributary valleys are scenic day hikes.

Phenpogo La (16,200 ft, 5030 m) is a steep 2400-foot (730-m) climb from the nine houses of Ling Dzong. It should be possible to hire a burro to carry gear up to the pass, which is the obvious low point in the ridge to the north, with a large *la-dze* cairn. The old motor road over Phenpogo La now turns up a side valley to the east from Ling Dzong. The walking route climbs north beside the houses, below the ruins of the old *dzong* and up the ridge, shortcutting large bends in the road to reach the pass in **3½ to 4½ hours**. Many a pilgrim and trader has reached this summit after months or years of traveling and hardships, to gaze south for their first view of the Lhasa Valley; this is the last pass on the old caravan route to Lhasa from China and Eastern Tibet. The huge cairn has been formed by centuries of visitors, who would toss a stone or three onto the pile as an offering of thanks to the protecting deities for their safe passage to the Holy City.

Below to the north is the Phenpo Chu Valley, an extensive agricultural region with numerous towns and some of the largest fields of barley and wheat anywhere in Central Tibet. The road turns east from the pass, following the ridge side to eventually descend in a long series of switchbacks down to the county seat *(xian)* of Lhundrub. The walking route descends north into the valley forming below the pass. The trail is well graded, passing numerous devotional cairns and several good camping meadows before reaching the town of Baiya (12,550 ft, 3830 m) in **4 hours**, just above the junction with the Phenpo Chu Valley. As you approach this settlement, several golden-roofed and red-walled monasteries and nunneries are visible in the valley and on the far ridges. The closest is Langtang monastery, **30 minutes** to the east of Baiya on the valley floor. **About 1½ hours** farther is Ganden Chökorling *gompa*, in the heart of Lhundrub. Along the ridges on the north side of the Phenpo Chu is Nakar *ani gompa*, and a bit farther west is another nunnery, Shar *ani gompa*. **One hour** from Baiya in an adjacent valley to the west is Nalendra monastery.

NALENDRA MONASTERY

To visit Nalendra (13,050 ft, 3980 m) monastery from Baiya, angle to the left (west) on a trail through the barley fields, toward the base of the striking magenta-colored hills. The trail climbs around the end of the ridge to a *chörten* and an overlook of Phenpo. The trail then angles to the left (southwest), meeting the service road leading up to the monastery.

Nalendra was founded in the mid-fifteenth century by Rongtongpa, a legendary Kadampa sect scholar and a contemporary of Tsong Khapa. The monastery flourished under his guidance, but within fifty years of his death the Sakyapa sect had appropriated the site and Nalendra became one of the larger and more important Sakyapa monasteries in Tibet. In 1966 the huge Tsokchen chanting hall, several colleges, and five monk residence halls were torn down by the Red Guards. A mural of the former monastery, which had 600 monks before 1959, has been painted inside the new Tsokchen immediately on the left as you enter. Fewer than a hundred monks are currently in residence. The main figure in the chanting hall behind the rows of cushions is a large Sakyamuni Buddha, flanked by Nye-we Sechen Gye, the Eight Great *Bodhisattvas*. A figure of Rongtongpa flanked by two of his Sakyapa successors (known as *yab-se-sum*, the "three fathers") is below the Buddha. The *gönkhang* has a huge figure of Gompo Gur, a form of the deity Mahakala and a protector of the Sakyapa sect.

A **1-hour** pilgrim's *kora* circles the large stone wall around the Nalendra complex. Other trails lead up the hill to the ruins of Ri-ding nunnery and Drakar hermitage, offering grand views of Nalendra and the Phenpo Chu Valley.

To trek north from Nalendra to Taklung and Reting monasteries, it is necessary to cross to the north (L) side of the Phenpo Chu. The nearest bridge is near Langtang monastery (12,200 ft, 3720 m), **75 minutes** northeast of Nalendra.

LANGTANG MONASTERY

All that remains of this once grand Kadampa sect monastery are two 500-year-old buildings: a protector's chapel and a former *lama's* residence; the latter has two chapels, including a chanting hall. Langtang was founded by the Buddhist scholar Langtangpa in 1093 during the rapid rise of the Kadampa sect in the eleventh century; he is said to have had two thousand disciples based here with him. The large former assembly hall is now a skeleton of walls nearby within the village. Today, the monastery, like Nalendra, belongs to the Sakyapa sect, and has about thirty-five monks. The new chanting hall has a tall Gyelwa Jampa (Future Buddha) statue overlooking four rows of cushions for the monks; a small *sung-jolma*, or "talking" statue of Drolma (Tara) is in the cabinet to the right, and several statues of the Sakyapa hierarchy are to the left. The adjacent *gönkhang* has black walls with murals of wrathful deities highlighted in gold paint. The central, red-hatted figure is Langtangpa.

THE TREK TO TAKLUNG MONASTERY

Taklung monastery is a **2½- to 3-day** trek north from the Phenpo Chu Valley over the mountains via Tak La (16,250 ft, 4950 m). To the east of this pass is Chak La (15,400 ft, 4690 m), the road crossing from Phenpo into the Reting Tsangpo Valley. From Langtang monastery, walk north past the village along a tree-lined dirt road, through the barley and wheat fields for **30 minutes** to a bridge over the Phenpo Chu. Turn right (east) over the bridge. This road continues east, paralleling the Phenpo Chu to it's junction with the Kyi Chu. About 300 feet (90 m) after the bridge the route to Taklung turns left (north) from the road. Follow this trail for a few hundred yards and meet another east-west road at the base of a rocky ridge. The commercial area of Lhundrub (formerly called Ganden Chökor) is an hour or more from here to the right (east). Here you will find several small restaurants, well-stocked shops, a market selling fresh meat and vegetables, a hospital, and a rather basic guesthouse. Several buses make the three- to four-hour journey to Lhasa in the mornings. South of the market area is Ganden Chökorling, a fairly large Gelukpa monastery with a hundred monks. The *gönkhang* is the original, with fine old murals.

The route to Taklung turns left (west) at the junction with the east-west road. Follow this road for a few hundred yards until it makes a sharp right-hand bend to the north, toward Lhundrub Dzong and Chak La. The trekking route to Taklung continues straight ahead (west) on a smaller road, toward Nakar and Shar nunneries. A confusing patchwork of trails, tracks, and dirt roads cross the plain beyond here (and throughout the Phenpo Chu Valley, far too many to detail on Map No. 4). Nakar *ani gompa* is **about 2 hours** from here, readily visible in the hills to the northwest; ask the locals for the best trail choices. Nakar is associated with Taklung monastery, and is the home of close to a hundred nuns. A road winds up to this compact clutter of cliffside residences packed around the maroon-walled chanting hall.

SHAR ANI GOMPA

Shar *ani gompa* (12,550 ft, 3830 m) is **1½ hours** northwest of Nakar, tucked into a fold of the hills; these barren slopes are a striking contrast to the lush environs across the valley at Nalendra. Founded in the eleventh century by yet another Kadampa master, Sharapa Önten Drak, Shar was originally used by monks; sometime this century it became a Gelukpa nunnery. Just below it is perhaps the most elegant gathering of *chörtens* anywhere in Tibet; the squat, round structure known as Shar Bumpa is attributed to Sharapa, and others have been built around it. A popular *kora* route circles around all of them, and a **1-hour** circuit also surrounds the nunnery and the nearby hills. The ornate chanting hall is reverently maintained, with a statue of Sharapa on the altar. The holiest relic is an impressive rock with a *rangjön*, or self-manifested Tibetan letter *ah*.

Less than 2 hours north of Shar is Gyadrak (13,850 ft, 4220 m), a large nunnery associated with Taklung. In the cliffs above it are hermitages and the meditation cave of Padampa Sangye, an eleventh-century ascetic from India who spent time in the Dingri and Phenpo regions. His mummified remains were formerly entombed at Langtang monastery.

TO TAKLUNG MONASTERY

From Shar *ani gompa* to Taklung monastery is a **2-day** trek; allow another day below Tak La if you need to acclimatize. The route heads northwest from Shar for **2½ hours** to the town of Cha-me. Follow the road down from the monastery for **10 minutes** to a fork, then turn right toward a small settlement. Head northwest past these houses across dry ground to pick up a trail beside the barley fields. This trail meets a road just before another settlement. Turn right, then head into the rocky Taiga Chu Valley to Cha-me. All around high on the granite walls are prayer flags, cave sites, temples, a nunnery, and an old fortress. Cha-me sits at the junction of two valleys. A route to Damzhung follows the valley to the left; Tak La is up to the right (northeast).

At a T-junction by the Cha-me *shang* compound, turn right up the road, which soon narrows to a trail along the west (R) side of the creek. **One hour or more** above Cha-me the trail splits; the route up to the left (north) is a longer route to Taklung over Chi La;

the lower path to the right (northeast) leads to Tak La in **5 to 6 hours** up a lush, sparsely inhabited valley. En route are numerous flat meadows and herder settlements. The last camp (15,000 ft, 4570 m) is about **1½ hours** below the pass. The trail is poorly marked above here and the pass stays hidden from view for most of the way; if you don't have a guide, have a herder show you the way.

The valley splits **15 minutes** above this final *drokpa* encampment. Take the left (north) branch here and pick up a trail along the east (L) side of this drainage. At a meadow where several small streams converge, follow the one on the far right (south) up the ridge, then angle left (north) away from the stream, up to the large *la-dze* cairn atop Tak La (16,250 ft, 4950 m). Chak La is about 5 miles (8 km) to the east; the road can be seen below in the adjacent valley.

Taklung is a **4-hour** descent from Tak La down a delightfully green valley with numerous potential campsites; it's worth spending a night (or two) at one of these secluded camps with the local marmots. About **3 hours** below the pass, this tributary joins the valley with the road from Chak La. The trail to Taklung doesn't meet this road. Instead, cross to the creek's (L) side on a truck-frame bridge, then angle up the west (L) ridge on rock stairs to the crest. As you descend, the cliffside Sili Gö-tshang hermitage can be seen across the valley to the northeast, and soon Taklung comes into view, surrounded by a mosaic of green barley and yellow rapeseed fields above the Phak Chu.

Shar ani gompa *in the Phenpo Chu Valley*

TAKLUNG MONASTERY

The enormous ruined walls of the former three-story Lhakhang Chempo (Great Temple) tower over the rebuilt chanting hall and temples of Taklung monastery (13,600 ft, 4150 m). Taklung Tashi, a Buddhist scholar whose teachings combined practices from the Kadampa and the Kargyüpa sects, established this site in 1180. He resided here for thirty years and gathered three thousand disciples around him by the time he died; his teachings form the basis of the Taklung Kargyüpa subsect. In 1959 there were over 500 monks and three incarnate lines of *trülkus*; today about a hundred monks are in residence here. Below in the village of Koru are the former *podrangs*, or residences, for two of Taklung's incarnate *lamas*. A pilgrimage route circles around both the monastery and the village; this *kora* takes **about 1 hour**. Driu-lung hermitage (14,550 ft, 4430 m) is just visible in the hills north of Taklung, a pleasant **2-hour** journey one way. Above this *ritrö* is a Guru Rimpoche cave and an adventurous pilgrim's *kora*; bring a guide.

Lhasa is a 74-mile (120-km) journey from Taklung heading east and then south via Chak La and the Phenpo Chu Valley. Reting monastery is 24 miles (39 km) to the north, via the village of Phongdo Dzong. If you don't have transport, it's a scenic **4- to 5-hour** walk to Phongdo Dzong, and another **7 hours or more** to Reting.

TO RETING AND DRIGUNG MONASTERIES

The road from Taklung to Phongdo Dzong follows the north (L) side of the Phak Chu the entire way. About 4 miles (7 km) past Taklung the road passes a large *chörten* situated below Sili Gö-tshang (14,200 ft, 4330 m; the Eagle Nest of Sili), an imposing fortresslike edifice clinging to the mountainside. The third abbot of Taklung, Sangye Yarjon, founded this cave hermitage in the thirteenth century. Monks from Taklung come here to perform three-year, three-month retreats. A trail leads up from the road, climbing steeply for **almost 1 hour** through thick wild rose and barberry bushes to reach the cave and temples.

Phongdo Dzong (13,000 ft, 3960 m) is another 4 miles (7 km) north of Sili Gö-tshang at the junction of three rivers: the Phak Chu; the Phongdolha Chu flowing in from the Damzhung area; and the larger Reting (or Miggi) Tsangpo from beyond Reting monastery. These three drainages meet to form the Kyi Chu, or Lhasa River. Phongdo Dzong village is perched on a plain between the Phongdolha Chu and the Phak Chu. The destroyed old *dzong* sits above it. A large cement bridge spans the Phongdolha Chu, and beside it are the chains from an old iron link bridge attributed to Tibet's famous bridge-building ascetic, Tangtong Gyelpo. Up on the north (L) bank is the former government compound for Lhundrub Qu, but the county offices have been moved to the new county seat of Lhundrub in the Phenpo Chu Valley. Several shops here sell instant noodles, beer, clothes, and candy at the intersection with the road running west along the Kyi Chu's north (L) bank. A large metal suspension bridge crosses the Reting Tsangpo just above the junction with the other rivers. Bus service from Lhasa is meant to come several times a week along this road; the 100-mile (160-km) journey via Meldrogungkar takes at least 8 hours. Drigung monastery is 65 miles (105 km) east from Phongdo Dzong up the Zhorong Chu, a tributary of the Kyi Chu.

A third bridge near Phongdo Dzong crosses to the south (R) bank of the Phak Chu, allowing access to the seldom-traveled southern (R) side of the Reting Tsangpo. Drigung monastery is a **5- to 6-day** trek from Phongdo Dzong following either side of this river, then heading up the Zhorong Chu.

Reting monastery is 15 miles (25 km) north of Phongdo Dzong along the Reting Tsangpo. Many large meadows for camping are on embankments above the river. About 9 miles (14 km) beyond Phongdo Dzong is Chamda *lhakhang*, a small temple beside the road with a statue of a wild-looking local protector riding a black, Tasmanian

The assembly hall at Reting monastery

devil–type animal. Just past here near Chamda village the road crosses a bridge over a creek entering the Reting Tsangpo; a road follows this tributary up to the west and over a pair of passes for 47 miles (76 km) to Damzhung, and the turnoff for Nam Tsho. To reach Reting, cross the bridge over this tributary and continue north for 5 miles (11 km). The road splits by a long prayer wall; the left fork leads up the ridge into a juniper forest to the monastery; the right branch leads to the local *shang* compound below Reting and continues up the Reting Tsangpo.

RETING MONASTERY

Few places in Central Tibet can rival the serenity of Reting monastery (13,350 ft, 4070 m). His Holiness the Fourteenth Dalai Lama has said if he returns to Tibet, he would choose to reside at Reting, not Lhasa or the Potala. Completely destroyed in the 1960s, the ruins of this once grand monastic complex and its rebuilt temples are surrounded by a hobbit-forest of gnarly, stout old juniper trees. Circling above the forest are dozens of hawklike dark kites, and within the trees are bounding parties of giant babaxes, cheeky magpies, and the occasional Elwes's eared pheasant. These magnificent trees are said to have sprung from the hairs of Dromtön Gyelwai Jungne, the chief disciple of the Indian Buddhist master Atisha, and founder of Reting in 1056. With this monastery as a base, Dromtön managed to unite the different disciples of Atisha and established the Kadampa sect of Tibetan Buddhism, a school of thought that spread quickly in Central Tibet.

In 1240 the Mongol general Dorta invaded Tibet, sacking Reting and killing some 500 people. The *gompa* was rebuilt, but like all the Kadampa sect monasteries, Reting was eventually absorbed by another school of Tibetan Buddhism, in this case the Gelukpa sect. In the eighteenth century the Seventh Dalai Lama appointed his tutor as the abbot of Reting; from that time onward the incarnate lineage of the Reting Rimpoche became eligible for selection as Regent of Tibet during the minority of a Dalai Lama. Three times the Reting *trülku* was Regent, a powerful appointment that brought great wealth and prosperity to the monastery and the Regent's family. Before 1966 the *labrang*, or residence, for Reting Rimpoche, was a grand building beside the old Tsokchen chanting hall. During the minority of the current (Fourteenth) Dalai Lama, the Fifth Reting Rimpoche was Regent; he died in prison, probably from poisoning, following his abdication of the Regency and his aborted coup attempt to forcefully regain the position from his successor. The Sixth Reting incarnation passed away in 1997.

The main building at Reting is the rebuilt Tsokchen hall, about half the size of the former four-story structure it replaced. In the center of the hall, behind the rows of cushions for the monks, is a small, dark protector's shrine containing the treasures of the monastery: a small solid gold image of Jampeyang (the *Bodhisattva* of Knowledge), Jowo Jampai Dorje; a small gilded "talking" *thangka* of the protectress Drolma; and four blackened *thangkas* said to be nine-hundred years old, which survived a great fire. Note that women are not allowed to enter. Around this chapel is a circuit for pilgrims, and at the back of the chanting hall is another temple with a thousand figures of Sakyamuni Buddha. The colorful masks on display here are worn by monks during *cham*, the religious dances that are held twice a year at Reting, on the 15th day of both the first and the fourth Tibetan months. Two outer temples are on either side of the Tsokchen.

A peaceful **1-hour** pilgrim's *kora* around Reting ascends into the forest. The circuit starts near the elevated Tsokchen courtyard, following the service road briefly before climbing around the various ruined buildings and *chörtens*. Near the top of the *kora* is a retreat called Gompa Kong, with several temples, monk's residences, and a *gönkhang*. Like many pilgrimage circuits around large Gelukpa monasteries, the pilgrims are busy making offerings at specific sites, even hopping on one foot around one of the *chörtens*; let the pilgrims be your guide to these special places.

From the high point of the *kora* is an indistinct route leading north up the forested ridge side for about **45 minutes** to the ruins of Önkhang (14,100 ft, 4300 m), formerly the main retreat for monks at Reting and where Dromtön preferred to reside. This hermitage is also renowned as the site where Tsong Khapa composed his famous treatise on Buddhism, the Lamrin Chenmo (The Graduated Path to Enlightenment), after meditating here and having a vision of the master Atisha. A smaller former hermitage is just above, and another retreat is in the adjacent valley to the west.

The *kora* gradually descends through the junipers, past a shrine with *tsha-tshas* and carved yak skulls, to a row of crumbling *chörtens*. Just beyond here a small trail leads off to the left (east) from the main circuit. Samtenling *ani gompa* is **1 hour** away along this damp, forest path. Built over a meditation cave of Tsong Khapa, this tangle of temples and little residence huts is home to 108 nuns. The *kora* continues down past this turnoff for the nunnery and around the former debating yard to return to the Tsokchen hall.

Below the monastery by the river are several small farming villages and the *shang* compound, which occupies the site of a former summer palace for the *lamas* at Reting. The beautiful old buildings here are boarded up and the shady garden is overgrown.

If you camp near Reting, be kind to this forest sanctuary. Leave your camp cleaner than you found it, and if you are with a commercial group, make sure your camp staff covers your toilet hole properly. Better yet, cover it yourselves!

TO DRIGUNG MONASTERY

The direct route to Drigung monastery from Reting takes **6 to 7 days** following the Kyi Chu downstream from Phongdo Dzong. Another route heads upstream (east) along the Reting Tsangpo for **about 3 days**, then turns south for **4 days** over Longma La, past

Cham *practice at Drigung monastery*

Terdrom nunnery to reach Drigung. As mentioned earlier, hiring pack animals in this region may be impossible. I once spent four days at Reting unsuccessfully trying to hire animals for the route along the upper Reting Tsangpo. This led to my first walk along the upper Kyi Chu and the Zhorong Chu to Drigung monastery.

Along the route to Drigung monastery below Phongdo Dzong are a dozen or more small monasteries perched above the Kyi Chu and the Zhorong Chu; a *gompa*-stomper's paradise! Numerous small towns and meadows for camping are on both sides of the river. The mouth of the Zhorong Chu is about 40 miles (64 km) below Phongdo Dzong. Drigung Dzongsar *gompa* (marked Dzongsar on Map No. 4) is high above this junction on one ridge, and Yuna monastery is across the Kyi Chu on the opposite ridge. A fifteenth-century Tangtong Gyelpo iron link bridge once spanned the river here, and Zha *lhakhang*, which dates from the time of King Trisong Detsen, is not far to the southeast on a plain of the Mangra Chu.

Drigung Qu (formerly Nyima Changra) is just up from the confluence. The administrative center here is now a *shang*, with the first shops of any kind since Phongdo Dzong for resupplying a few basics. Drigung monastery is 25 miles (40 km) up the Zhorong Cu. (If you prefer not to walk on dirt roads, use the secluded trail that runs along the opposite side of this sparkling blue river.) Yangri Gar monastery is 6 miles (10 km) past Drigung Qhu along the road, with an associated hermitage in the hills above. The road crosses to the north (R) side and climbs to the junction for Terdrom *ani gompa* and Drigung monastery. The nunnery is 8 miles (13 km) up the side valley to the left (north), and Drigung is just 4 miles (6 km) up the main valley.

DRIGUNG MONASTERY

Drigung monastery (14,050 ft, 4280 m) is built like a fortress 600 feet (180 m) above the valley floor. The road passes the *shang* compound at Menpa Qu, then a service road turns off to the left to ascend steeply to the main courtyard of the Tsokchen assembly hall. The monastery was founded in the late twelfth century by Rinchen Pel, who is reverently known as Kyowa Jigten Sumgon, the first Drigung Rimpoche. A statue of him is found in almost every temple; in the chanting hall his image is beside the large Guru Rimpoche figure in the back corner, and there is a reliquary *chörten* here with his remains. His original meditation cave is above the Tsokchen. Like other great teachers, Jigten Sumgon quickly attracted a large following. The monastery continued to grow after his death, and soon Drigung was a political and religious rival to the Sakyapa sect rulers of Tibet. During the thirteenth-century Drigung *lamas* traveled across Tibet, establishing meditation "colonies" at famous pilgrimage sites, particularly at Mount Kailash, the Lapchi caves on the frontier with Nepal, and Tsari, a sacred mountain to the east of Tsethang. After Dorta's Mongol armies sacked Reting in 1240, Drigung managed to ward off the invaders. But it was the challenge of Drigung's political power which brought another Mongol army, led by the Sakyapa general Aklen, to march on Drigung in 1290 and destroy it. This effectively ended Drigung's political influence, but the monastery continued to be a center for contemplative teachings and home of the Drigung Kargyüpa subsect.

Several temples are upstairs from the main chanting hall. A small building above the Tsokchen is the *gönkhang* for Apchi, the protectress of Drigung, where she is portrayed in her wrathful, horse-riding manifestation, and in her peaceful aspect. Across the hillside are small residence huts for Drigung's two hundred monks.

A pilgrimage *kora*, taking **less than 1 hour** to complete, circles the monastery. It begins from the courtyard, descending below the chanting hall then climbing up the slopes to reach the ridge crest and the monastery's famous sky-burial site (14,300 ft, 4360 m). The trail continues around *chörtens* and small offering shrines before descending past monk's residences to the chanting hall.

There are no guesthouses near Drigung, though large meadows for camping are along the embankment above the Zhorong Chu. Terdrom nunnery has a guesthouse beside its hot springs.

The Potala Palace, Lhasa

"Modern" boats used to ferry across a broad stretch of the Tsangpo (Brahmaputra) River

Preceding pages: Mount Kailash is revered
ground for Tibetan Buddhists, Hindus, Jains,
and Bön practitioners.
Inset photos: (above) The ritual drum and bell
are used in Tantric Buddhist ceremonies.
(below) A pilgrim at Mount Kailash bows
before a stone wrapped with prayer flags.

*Stuck in
the mud on
the road
to Lhasa*

*The kitchen of
a monastery
in Lhasa*

Offering pile of yak horns along the shore of the holy lake, Manasarovar, near Mount Kailash

Monks during a debate session at Monlam Chenmo, the Great Prayer Festival, Lhasa

Three Tibetan friends

A monk strolling along the kora, *or pilgrimage circuit, encircling Reting monastery.*

Mount Everest and Dza Rongphu monastery

*Minyak Gangkar, a holy mountain in
East Tibet* (Photo by Jon Meisler)

*Camp II on East
Rongphu Glacier,
Mount Everest*

*Gyama
Valley camp*

Rakshas Tal and Gurla Mandata, Western Tibet

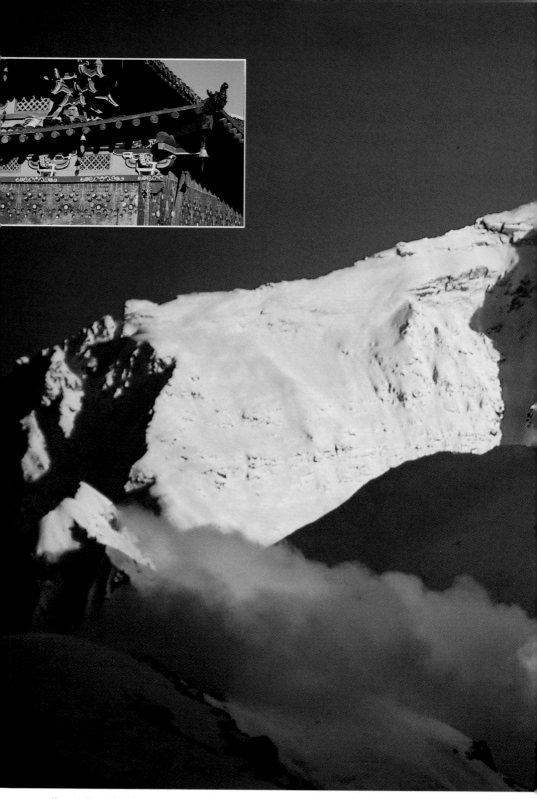

(Inset) Detail of woodworking at Zhalu monastery, Central Tibet

The North Face of Mount Everest

Pilgrim with prayer beads before the Jokhang, Tibet's most sacred temple, located in the center of Lhasa

On any given day trucks arrive at Drigung with corpses swathed in white cloth, to be disposed according to the traditional Tibetan practice of sky burial. Each afternoon the monks gather in the courtyard around the deceased and perform a ceremony; the following morning the bodies are carried to the burial site. Two small temples, several *chörtens,* and thick strings of prayer flags surround a circular gathering of dark rocks (representing the *mandala* of the Tantric deity Demchok), where the corpses are placed. If you happen to be present, put your cameras away and sit discreetly off to the side. This is truly a sobering experience; at one point in his or her life every Tibetan must observe a sky burial (tradition dictates that one does not watch the sky burial of a relative) as a lesson in the impermanence of a human's physical body. Just the sight of some hundred or so huge Himalayan griffin vultures gathering all around, cackling and fighting before the bodies are dismembered, is an extraordinary event. And that's just the beginning. When it's all over, the trilling horns of the monks stop, the vultures take off on long wings, and nothing remains of the bodies. Ashes to ashes, dust to dust.

TERDROM NUNNERY

In a limestone canyon about 12 miles (19 km) from Drigung is Terdrom (Treasure Box; 14,300 ft, 4360 m) *ani gompa.* Situated at the junction of two valleys, the nunnery is renowned as a Guru Rimpoche meditation site, and for its medicinal hot springs. To the west of Terdrom is the rigorous pilgrimage to Kiri Yongdzong, a cavern temple inside the mountain where Guru Rimpoche fled with his consort Yeshe Tshogyel after being banished from Samye by his opponents. On the hill above the nunnery is another Guru Rimpoche cave, and beside it is the residence of Khandro-la, the female incarnation of Yeshe Tshogyel. Across the hills below her quarters are dozens of small houses where Terdrom's 130 nuns live. To the north up the narrow Drong Chu (Wild Yak Creek) gorge from the nunnery is Drong-ngur (Wild Yak Grunt) *gompa.* A simple guesthouse has been built beside the hot springs, and several shops sell instant noodles and beer. Campsites are almost nonexistent, except along the river about halfway back to the road junction near Drigung monastery. If you do decide to soak in the hot springs, the men's pool is on the right, the women's to the left. Unlike elsewhere in Tibet, nudity is acceptable, though a bathing suit helps prevent curious fellow bathers from staring and comparing. Soap and shampoo are used in the pools, though clothes are washed in smaller hot pools by the river.

The *dukhang* at Terdrom is above the hot springs, near the confluence of the two valleys. Each morning the nuns gather in this hall after being called to order by the blowing of a conch shell. A great pile of shoes accumulates before the entrance way, and inside colorful silk banners hang everywhere from the pillars and the ceiling, above the rows of cushions where Terdrom's *anis* are seated. The ethereal sound of their chanting voices shouldn't be missed. Statues of Guru Tsengye, the eight manifestations of Guru Rimpoche, and Drigung's founder Jigten Sumgon grace the altar behind the nuns' cushions.

THE KIRI YONGDZONG KORA

One of the classic—and most challenging—pilgrimages in Central Tibet is the Nangkor, a **10- to 12-hour** *kora* from Terdrom nunnery to the Kiri Yongdzong cave retreat. The trail is difficult to locate without a guide; the route to the cave is off the main circuit and not well marked; and Chebchuk La (17,100 ft, 5210 m), the high point on the *kora,* is a 2800-foot (850-m) ascent that should only be attempted if you are well acclimatized. Otherwise, it's a great walk!

The trail initially leads up the Drong Chu Valley from the chanting hall through tall stands of wild rose and willow bushes. About 150 yards (140 m) past the *dukhang*, cross the creek on a bridge to the west (R) bank. The trail forks here. To the right, up along the creek is the route to Drong-ngur monastery, a **2-hour** walk one way. The trail to Kiri Yongdzong is the left fork, which leads up the slope through the bushes to a ridge crest. Off to the right below cliffs are several retreats and Cha-khyung (Garuda) *drubphuk*. The pilgrim circuit heads left (southwest) across a meadow and continues climbing up another ridge. Numerous cairns and prayer flags mark the correct route to this second summit. Beyond here the trail is rather obscure and generally heads west along waves of ridges to a rebuilt *lhakhang* at the site of Tingye nunnery (15,500 ft, 4720 m). The route to Kiri Yongdzong now heads due north up the steep rocky slopes to the prayer flags of the first pass, Norbu La (17,000 ft, 5180 m). Huge scree slopes of red and gray rock cascade into a jumble of limestone pillars, and all around are panoramic vistas. The high point, Chebchuk La, is nearby along the rim of this rocky basin, about **3½ to 4 hours** from Terdrom.

The pilgrim's circuit now plunges steeply down a gravel slope to enter the next valley. About **40 minutes** below the pass the valley begins to swing right (east). The main pilgrimage path continues down the valley for **1 hour or more** to reach Drong-ngur *gompa*. The route to Kiri Yongdzong leaves the main trail here, but there is no real path. Look up to the right (southeast) for prayer flags and a higher trail leading up through limestone towers. Reach the ridge crest (16,600 ft, 5060 m) in **about 45 minutes**; Kiri Yongdzong is **20 minutes** away along a precipitous trail to the right (east).

Prayer flags are strung everywhere, and within the yawning cavern mouth are several dilapidated buildings and shrines. Two sets of wooden ladders with yak hide lashings lead 50 feet (15 m) above the cavern floor to the Guru Rimpoche cave, where he stayed in exile with his consort Yeshe Tshogyel; bring a flashlight. Thick sheets of clear crystal ice line the upper walls and ceiling of this secluded cave; imagine spending years here, as Yeshe Tshogyel did after her Guru returned to India, meditating in the dark and cold. A statue of Guru Rimpoche is in a glass case above a simple altar for butter lamps.

To return to the main pilgrim route, retrace your steps from the cave back to the valley floor; or your guide may show you a steep shortcut down a scree slope. Both routes lead to Drong-ngur (15,150 ft, 4620 m), an isolated monastery built over the meditation cave of Rinchen Phuntsok, a great sixteenth-century Drigung *lama,* and the founder of Terdrom. The valley up to the northeast from here leading to Keleb La is the route for the Chikor, the longer, outer pilgrimage circuit around Drigung and Terdrom performed in the Monkey Year (the next one will be in 2004). The Nangkor circuit continues downstream to the nunnery in about **1½ hours**. The hot springs are the perfect way to end a long day of pilgrimage!

TSURPHU AND THE YANGPACHEN VALLEY REGION
MAP NO. 5, PAGE 131

Tsurphu monastery (14,400 ft, 4390 m) is located high in a tributary of the Tölung Valley, 40 miles (64 km) by road from Lhasa. A wild and scenic trek of **3 to 4 days** originates from the monastery, crosses Lasar La (17,300 ft, 5270 m), then winds through a series of remote valleys to the seldom-visited Dorjeling nunnery. The trek ends at Yangpachen monastery, set in the vast Yangpachen Valley at the foot of the Nyenchen Thanglha mountains.

ARRIVING IN TSURPHU

Minibuses leave every morning from Lhasa to Tsurphu at 7:30 A.M. from the parking area at Barkor Square's west end. Tickets are sold on board. Arrive early to reserve a seat! The ride takes 2½ hours, initially following the Tibet-Qinghai Highway to a steel girder bridge (km marker 3583) at the mouth of the Tsurphu Valley, then turns west for the 17-mile (27 km) ascent to the monastery.

The trekking season in the Tsurphu area is generally from April through October, though the summer rains can cause the rivers and creeks to run high in July and August. Winter treks are also possible, for the snow seems to skirt this region. On my first trip over this route in early 1986, all of the creeks were frozen, making the crossings quite easy compared to my next visit, which was a wet mid-September trek several years later.

All food for your trek should be purchased in Lhasa. The only shops en route are at Tsurphu, which sell little more than religious items, candy, soft drinks, beer, and instant noodles. During the summer several tea shops offer *momos* and *thukpa*. A guesthouse has been built adjacent to the monastery, and meadows near the monastery provide good campsites. Due to the remote nature of the trek, tents and fuel stoves are recommended, though it's usually possible to obtain lodging at the monasteries and the few isolated herders' settlements along the way.

Tsurphu monastery is a **2-day** walk along the Tsurphu Phuchu River from the bridge

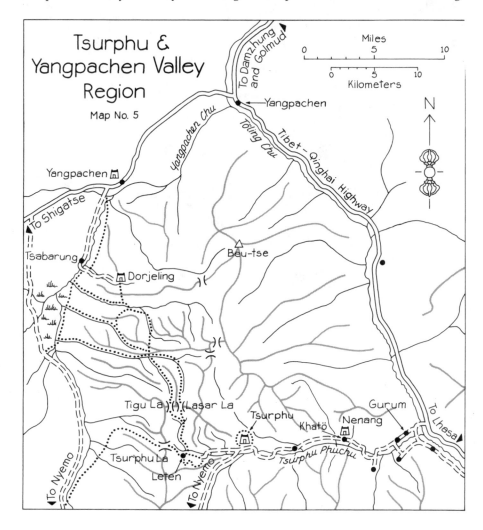

Nuns sharing a quiet moment at Tsurphu monastery

at the valley mouth. Even though this walk follows the road, there's great scenery the entire way. If you want to hire a pack animal to carry your gear, ask at Gurum shang, a **30-minute** walk past the bridge. Accommodation is usually no problem, for there are settlements most of the way up the valley.

The town of Khatö is **3 to 4 hours** (7 miles, 11 km) up from the bridge, on the north (L) side of the Tsurphu Valley. In the hills above is Nenang *gompa*, a Kargyüpa monastery dating back to the fourteenth century. Nenang was the original seat of power for the Zhamarpa *trülkus*, who were known as the "Red Hat" *lamas* because of the ceremonial red crowns that they wore. The *gompa* began as a small meditation retreat and has always had a close affiliation with nearby Tsurphu, also a Kargyüpa monastery. The Fourth Zhamarpa shifted his seat to the Yangpachen *gompa* in the late fifteenth century, and Nenang then became the seat for the lineage of Pawo Rimpoches. The current (eleventh) Pawo *trülku*, a young boy who was recognized by the Karmapa in 1996, greets visitors in a reception room above the chanting hall. Bring a *katak*, a ceremonial scarf, as an offering. The protocol is to hold the scarf in both hands with palms up, then bend forward and extend your arms toward the *lama* as you present the scarf.

Beyond Khatö the valley narrows and steepens. About 1 mile (1.6 km) below Tsurphu is Yarke Podrang, the monastery's summer palace, a high-walled compound with a dish antenna, several temples, a receiving room for the Karmapa, and a peaceful wooded park. Upstream from the summer palace the road crosses a bridge to the north (L) bank of the river. It then climbs a short way to reach the walls and main entrance gate of Tsurphu.

TSURPHU MONASTERY

The huge temples and chanting halls of Tsurphu monastery have been rebuilt from the rubble of the Cultural Revolution, and once again it is the seat of the Karmapa, the incarnate spiritual head of the Zhanakpa, or "Black Hat" Karma Kargyüpa sect of Tibetan Buddhism. (The name is derived from the legendary black crown worn by the Karmapa, said to be made from the hairs of a million *khandroma* and to possess magical powers.) In 1991 a *drokpa* boy from the Chamdo region in Kham was recognized as the seventeenth incarnation of the Karmapa lineage. A grand procession wound its way across Central Tibet to deliver this young *lama* to his residence here.

Tsurphu was founded as a meditational retreat circa 1187 by Dusum Khyenpa, a *lama* from Kham who received his teachings from a disciple of the ascetic Milarepa. Dusum Khyenpa is now regarded as the First Karmapa, beginning a lineage of *trülkus* that continues to this day. During the next five centuries Tsurphu grew into a great religious center. Like most of Tibet's large monasteries, it was eventually drawn into the political arena, leading to its destruction by a Mongol army in 1642 during a lengthy power struggle with the Gelukpa sect, led by the Fifth Dalai Lama. Tsurphu slowly rebuilt and gradually restored its status as an important Kargyüpa center; nearly a thousand monks were in residence when the Chinese army arrived in the 1950s. Foreseeing the plight of Tibet, the Sixteenth Karmapa fled to Sikkim's Rumtek monastery in 1958 with a large retinue of disciples and many of the monastery's most important treasures. He never returned to Tibet before his death in 1981.

According to a former monk from Tsurphu, a Chinese artillery unit came up the valley in 1966 at the onset of the Cultural Revolution with intentions of destroying the monastery. But the thick temple walls were so solidly built that they withstood the cannon fire. The soldiers went back down the valley, but later a demolition team returned with explosives. For one week they drilled holes in the walls and planted charges, systematically working their way from one end of the complex to the other until all the buildings were razed.

Today Tsurphu is one of the largest monasteries in Central Tibet; six major temples and many monks' residences have been rebuilt since the mid-1980s. In the center of the complex is the Karmapa Labrang. The main chanting hall for Tsurphu, the Tsokchen, is on the ground floor and upstairs is the residence of the Karmapa. Each day at 1:00 P.M. he receives throngs of pilgrims in a special room above the Tsokchen. Again, bring a *katak* scarf as an offering; most pilgrims place a small sum of money in the *katak*, but this is optional.

The pilgrim's circuit to each temple leads to the left (west) from the Labrang to an adjacent building with five small *gönkhangs* above the courtyard (note the stuffed yak and other animals hanging from the balcony, which act as protectors). The circuit then continues west around clusters of residence buildings and up past a white *chörten* to the Gyeltsab Podrang, the residence of Gyeltsab Rimpoche, one of the three regents of the Karma Kargyüpa sect. Immediately below the Podrang is the new Lhakhang Chenmo, replacing the dynamited enormous red-walled chanting hall which once housed one of the largest cast-metal statues in Tibet. The new temple, though smaller, houses a 60-foot (18-m) tall copper statue of Sakyamuni Buddha flanked by Nye-we Sechen Gye, the Eight Great *Bodhisattvas*. The pilgrims then wind their way down between the Labrang and an ochre-walled college to finish the circuit.

Perched high on the cliffs above the monastery is the Pema Khyung Dzong hermitage. A breath-grabbing pilgrimage *kora* climbs 700 feet (210 m) to this retreat and to several meditation caves. The unusual terraced area built into the south (R) ridge side across from the monastery is used for laying out a large silk appliqué *köku* during religious festivals.

THE TSURPHU KORA

Before starting the trek to the Yangpachen Valley, consider spending at least two nights at Tsurphu to acclimatize, particularly if you arrive by vehicle rather than on foot. The pilgrimage *kora* up to Pema Khyung Dzong takes **2 to 3 hours** including rest stops, picture taking, and encounters with pilgrims and monks. The *kora* follows the road west past the monastery for **15 minutes,** past an extensive succession of *mani* walls piled high with beautifully crafted prayer stones. The enclosure to the left is the Karmapa *lingka,* another parklike area associated with Tsurphu. Just past the *lingka* the road splits. Follow the smaller fork to the right for **about 5 minutes**, then turn north (R) up a narrow trail that ascends a low, flat-topped hill; look for the small rock cairns leading up the hillside. At the crest of this flat hill and about 300 feet (90 m) to the right is Tsurphu's sky-burial site. Bone chips and knives can be found scattered among the rocks.

The pilgrim circuit continues north up the hill. The trail soon becomes well defined, climbing past rose bushes decorated with fluffs of yak wool to a saddle draped with prayer flags. The circuit now weaves along the rocky ridge, passing several small retreats and Mayum (Mother's) *drubphuk,* an isolated house under the cliffs enclosing the cave retreat of Dusum Khyenpa and his mother. About 300 feet (90 m) beyond here the *kora* splits. Some pilgrims continue straight (east) on the lower trail; the upper left fork climbs in **a few minutes** to Samtenling *ritrö* (visible on the ridge above Tsurphu), where monks perform the traditional Kargyüpa retreat of three years, three months, and three days. Tucked behind here is Pema Khyung Dzong hermitage (Lotus Garuda Fortress; 15,100 ft, 4600 m) built over the meditation cave of Karma Pakshi, the Second Karmapa.

The *kora* now traverses east from the hermitage into a creek gully, then descends to rejoin the lower path. Several shortcuts plunge down the ridge side here, though the main route continues to a small, red temple before dropping steeply to meet the road beside the monastery's eastern wall. The main entrance is **a few minutes** to the west (R).

THE TSURPHU TO YANGPACHEN VALLEY TREK

If you want to hire a guide and pack animals, ask the monks and wait for word to get out, since there are no villages close to the monastery. If this doesn't work, the alternative is to hire a guide and pack animal at the village of Leten (16,400 ft, 5000 m), a small herders' settlement 2½ hours above (west of) Tsurphu. When negotiating with the guide, remember he will probably want compensation for his return journey.

The trek to Yangpachen initially follows the road west up the valley from Tsurphu. Not far past the Karmapa *lingka* the main valley splits. Don't take the turnoff to the left; stay on the road paralleling the north (L) creek bank. **Less than 1½ hours** above the

The spectacular setting of Dorjeling ani gompa, *en route from Tsurphu monastery to the Yangpachen Valley*

monastery a tributary enters from the right (northwest). Several *drokpa* tents are situated above the road. Cross this stream, then ford the main creek to the south (R) bank. Watch for slippery rocks.

The valley levels out and the road follows the south (R) side of the creek. **Thirty minutes** beyond the ford is a trail junction. The wide path branching up to the left (south) leaves the road here toward Leten village. Leten can also be approached by staying along the creek and skirting the cliff (if the water is not too high), but the village is hidden from the creek and easy to miss. Otherwise, take the left fork and climb steeply to the top of the ridge (16,600 ft, 5060 m) in **40 minutes**. The scattered houses of Leten lie just below on an elevated plateau. This is a good place to get your bearings. The broad trail continuing west along the ridge side is the route to Tsurphu La. The Tsangpo is **3 days** south from this pass via the Nyemo Valley. Lasar La, one of several passes on the way to Yangpachen, is approached by the wide braid of animal tracks ascending above the main drainage into a tributary valley to the right (northwest).

Leten must be one of the highest "permanent" settlements in the world. It is inhabited by families who, during the summer months, live in yak-hair tents throughout the adjacent valleys to graze their herds of yak, goats, and sheep. They return to the shelter of their rock-walled homes in the winter. Consider spending the night here, for it is the last settlement before Lasar La and is well positioned to help the acclimatization process. Reaching Lasar La requires **3 hours or more** of walking through undulating hills, and the next camps are **more than 1 hour** beyond the pass. One bonus of staying in Leten is the opportunity to consume huge quantities of fresh milk, cheese, and yogurt.

I recommend that individual trekkers hire a guide for the walk up to Lasar La, because the terrain beyond Leten is confusing. Although this pass is rather high in elevation, it is a broad, unmarked summit that can easily be confused with other crossings. The herders are often reluctant to go much beyond Lasar La, since they prefer to return home on the same day.

Looking north from Leten, the route to Yangpachen stays to the left (west) of a prominent, domed mountain rising to the north, then crosses the low ridge behind it. Descend from Leten, crossing the creek to the north (L) bank, then climb the ridge on one of the many animal trails leading to the top. The tracks beyond the last house lead into a shallow drainage basin, but soon become obscure near the base of the domed peak. Look for a *la-dze* cairn up to the right (north) on the low ridge that extends behind this peak. The trail leading up to this *la-dze* is the route to Lasar La. Reach the cairn in **30 minutes or more** from the creek crossing and continue to the top of the ridge spur (17,000 ft, 5180 m) **a few minutes** beyond. Mountainous ridges and ranges now come into view but Lasar La is still **2 hours** away and out of sight.

The route to Lasar La descends briefly from the top of the ridge spur then ascends along a creek gully to the right (east) of an obvious, deep red ridge. Use whichever side of the creek is more suitable for walking as it winds along an S-shaped course into the barren hills. Jagged peaks emerge on the horizon and the terrain begins to open out. Wherever water flows, the ground is covered in plates of thick tundra; some of the large meadows near the stream would make fine campsites. Chubby little pikas race about on the drier patches of ground, but keep your eye up on the ridges. The steep, rocky hills are perfect habitat for the herds of blue sheep that roam this area.

About 1½ hours from the ridge spur a small stream sweeps in from the right (east). Just beyond here the main stream angles sharply to the left, but the route to Lasar La continues straight ahead (north). Climb for **a few minutes** toward a cairn of rocks (17,000 ft, 5180 m) atop a low moraine. Lasar La is **30 minutes** farther to the north across a flat, wet plateau of uneven tundra. Another pass to the Yangpachen Valley, Tigu La (17,200 ft, 5240 m), is about **30 minutes** farther to the left (northwest) and marked by a tall, narrow cairn. Either pass can be used; the drainages descending from them eventually merge farther north.

The actual summit of Lasar La is not easy to pinpoint, though a pond and a small pile of rocks are near what appears to be the highest point. Keep heading north. The plateau eventually drops into a U-shaped, glacially carved valley. The large range of snowy peaks in the distance (north) are the Nyenchen Thanglha mountains, which separate the Yangpachen Valley from Nam Tsho. Eventually a trail forms on the west (L) side

Pilgrims awaiting an audience with the Karmapa, at Tsurphu monastery

of the main creek, near the base of the ridge, avoiding meadows of deep hummocks on the valley floor. Pass a herders' camp then reach a stone goat corral (16,100 ft, 4910 m) **1½ hours** below the summit. The valley now enters a long, almost 90-degree bend to the left (west) as a large tributary spills in from the right.

Descend **another 30 minutes**. Before reaching the confluence, ford the main creek to the north (R) bank, then cross to the north (R) side of the tributary. Follow one of the many animal tracks for **30 minutes or more** to several stone *drokpa* houses (15,600 ft, 4750 m). If you are on your own, consider hiring a guide for this portion of the trek to Dorjeling *ani gompa*, as the route is obscure and there are few people around to ask directions.

The nunnery can be approached from several directions, though the most direct and scenic is a high route that climbs out of the valley below this settlement. Continue descending on the north (R) side of the valley. Following the trail soon becomes a battle with the grass hummocks; stay along the base of the ridge. As the valley starts bending to the right, more peaks come into view. The locals call the most prominent of these summits Da-tse (Horse Peak; 20,180 ft, 6150 m). A small stream enters from the right **30 minutes or more** below the *drokpa* houses. Just beyond this crossing a heavily braided track climbs for **10 minutes** up the dry north (R) ridge to a low saddle (15,550 ft, 4740 m). This is the high route to Dorjeling nunnery.

Although another ridge must still be climbed, this saddle offers a grand panorama of mountains: toward the south is a tall peak known as Ra-tse (Goat Peak), and Da-tse peak dominates to the west. The meadows near the saddle, clipped short like putting greens by livestock, are remote, scenic campsites; drinking water (be sure to boil or purify) can be found in small pools between the grass hummocks.

The high route to Dorjeling ascends without a trail onto the ridge rising straight ahead (north) from the saddle. An alternative, lower route to Dorjeling descends via the drainage which forms to the left (northwest) beyond the saddle (it's easier to approach this lower route via a second saddle, **10 minutes** farther left (west). After **1 hour or more** this lower route turns right (north) near the first settlements in the valley below. It then leads into a series of rolling hills to reach Dorjeling in **about 3 more hours**. A guide is also recommended for this route.

If the weather is good, consider taking the high route for the outstanding views from the top. From the saddle, pick your way north across the eroded tundra. Stay to the right of a ruined hut and keep aiming for the obvious low point in the ridge. There's no trail, but as you ascend keep to the right of a deep gully in the slope. Reach a false summit in **less than an hour** from the previous saddle, then head north for **5 minutes** to a *la-dze* and the scenic ridge summit (16,100 ft, 4910 m). The large peak to the right (northeast) with the impressive glacial icefall is Beu-tse (Calf Peak; 19,000 ft, 5800 m). The rugged summits and deep valleys of the Nyenchen Thanglha Range stretch majestically from north to south across the entire horizon. Da-tse is to the left (west), and the huge massif of the main Nyenchen Thanglha peak (23,330 ft, 7111 m) looms in the distance to the north. Try to be here early in the morning for the sunrise.

The route to Dorjeling descends to the right (northeast) from the *la-dze;* use Beu-tse as your bearing. A braided animal track forms, leading off the tundra plates to the east (R) side of a drainage gully. The bottom of the next valley (15,100 ft, 4600 m) is **40 minutes** from the ridge crest.

Don't cross the main creek draining this valley. Instead, stay high on the trail along the south (L) bank, then walk cross-country, still heading downstream, for **40 minutes** to a lone herder's house. Descend from this house to a broad trail alongside the creek. A *mani* wall sits within the entrance to a small gorge. Once the valley opens out again, cross to the north (R) side of the creek (shoes and socks may have to come off), **30 minutes** beyond the herder's house. Several *drokpa* families live here during the summer months, and near the creek are a few good meadows for camping or picnics. The elevation is noticeably lower; the scrub juniper bushes on the ridges are the tallest vegetation since Tsurphu.

A wide track now descends the valley on the north (R) side of the creek, but the most direct route to Dorjeling leaves the valley from here on a trail climbing up the north (R) ridge. Reach the saddle (14,700 ft, 4480 m) in **30 minutes** from the stream crossing. The *ani gompa* is **less than an hour** to the north across a dry plateau wrought with mine fields of pika burrows. Aim for the group of rounded hills that end with deep, vertical clefts of exposed rock.

Dorjeling nunnery (14,300 ft, 4360 m) is at the base of these weathered cliffs, geomantically in alignment with the twin sentinels of Beu-tse and Da-tse. Locations such as this deserve being called a *nechen,* or "power place," by the Tibetans. The central building of this Kargyüpa *ani gompa*, with its stone stairway and covered porch, is the *lhakhang.* It is decorated simply but reverently. Visitors are warmly greeted with copious cups of butter tea and accommodation is usually easy to arrange. Donations are very much appreciated. Note: Dorjeling is incorrectly marked on the NH 46-9 JOG maps. The correct position is about 2 inches (5 cm) to the northeast, at approximately 29° 53'N, 90° 26'E.

The walk to Yangpachen *gompa* initially follows the access road along a creek draining west from Dorjeling. Pass several houses near the first cultivated fields since below Tsurphu, then cross to the south (L) side of the creek **40 minutes** below the monastery. The valley soon swings to the right and opens out onto the huge expanse of the Yangpachen Valley and the Nyenchen Thanglha Range. In **15 minutes** a trail crosses to the (R) side of the creek over a small cement bridge. The road continues down the valley for **less than half an hour** to Tsabarung (14,200 ft, 4330 m), the main trading center in this region. If you're walking in the opposite direction from Yangpachen to Tsurphu, this is a good place to hire a guide and a pack animal (expect a horse or a burro). Accommodation can often be arranged with one of the families here.

The most direct route to Yangpachen *gompa* is the trail leading north across the small cement bridge. In **2½ hours** arrive at the bridge over the Yangpachen Chu. The northern road to Shigatse is **5 minutes** beyond (km marker 20). Shigatse is 137 miles (221 km) to the left (southwest), and Yangpachen *gompa* (marked Angchen Gompa on the NH 46-9 JOG map) and the junction with the Tibet-Qinghai Highway are to the right. The white-walled *gompa* (km marker 19) is perched in the hills up to the left. A steep trail leads directly up to the monastery, and a cart track winds up from the village.

YANGPACHEN MONASTERY

This Zhamar Kargyü monastery (13,900 ft, 4324m) overlooks the northern half of the Yangpachen Valley. The Nyenchen Thanglha mountains march into the distance and another range of peaks, including Ber-tse, forms the impressive eastern rim of the valley. Yangpachen was quickly transformed into one of Tibet's major political centers when the fourth Zhamarpa moved here from Nenang *gompa*. Destroyed during the Cultural Revolution, the *gompa* now consists of a rebuilt *lhakhang* and courtyard overshadowed by the immense walls and ruins of the former complex. The seat of the present Zhamar *trülku*, the thirteenth, is the Buddhist monastery beside the Swayambhu *chörten* in Kathmandu.

No public buses serve this part of the valley. If you have not arranged transport, walk or hitch to the Tibet-Qinghai Highway, 12 miles (19 km) to the west. Along the way you will pass a commercial hot spring, as well as steam release towers and many other modern-looking buildings, which are part of a large geothermal project that supplied Lhasa with all of its electricity prior to construction of the controversial Yamdrok Tsho hydropower plant. The town of Yangpachen (km marker 3804/5), less than a mile (1 km) south of the highway junction, has a hotel and several eating establishments. Public minibuses operate frequently from here to Lhasa, 52 miles (83 km) to the southeast.

THE NYENCHEN THANGLHA AND NAM TSHO REGION
MAP NO. 6, PAGE 140

The loop walk across the Nyenchen Thanglha mountains to the pebbled shores of the holy Nam Tsho (Sky Lake; also known as Tengri Nor, the "Heaven Lake") takes **6 to 7 days**. The trail for this circuit begins and ends at Damzhung (13,550 ft, 4130 m; km marker 3730/29), a roadside town 99 miles (160 km) north of Lhasa on the Tibet-Qinghai Highway. This spectacular trek climbs out of the Damzhung Valley via Largen La (16,300 ft, 4970 m), then descends to the mystical environs of Tashi Do hermitage and the vast Nam Tsho, the second-largest salt lake in Tibet. The final leg of the loop enters a remote region of the Nyenchen Thanglha Range, crosses Kong La (16,900 ft, 5150 m), then winds through deep glaciated valleys back to Damzhung.

Damzhung (also called Dam) is a windblown gathering of *chang* halls, shops, and restaurants. The largest building in town is a multistoried hotel with few amenities. **Forty minutes** to the south of Damzhung is Ngang-tsendo, a small town of herders where horses or yaks can be hired to carry gear to Nam Tsho.

The best season for trekking in this area is late May to mid-October, though you must be prepared at all times for wet weather, snow, and cold winds. Nam Tsho is a very high lake (15,060 ft, 4590 m) situated at the edge of the Chang Thang, Tibet's vast Northern Plateau. During July and August the summer rains can be quite persistent; snows of up to a foot or more can fall during these months, blocking the road over Largen La for days at a time.

Tents and fuel stoves are a must for this trek, and most provisions should be purchased before arriving in Damzhung, or in Nam Tsho Qu, the government *shang* near the lake. Noodles, powdered milk, meat, and a few other basics are usually available, but don't count on much more. The Chinese restaurants in Damzhung will sell fresh vegetables if you ask, but bargain!

Damzhung is a beautiful 5-hour drive from Lhasa through the Yangpachen Valley and along the Nyenchen Thanglha Range. Public buses depart from Lhasa several times

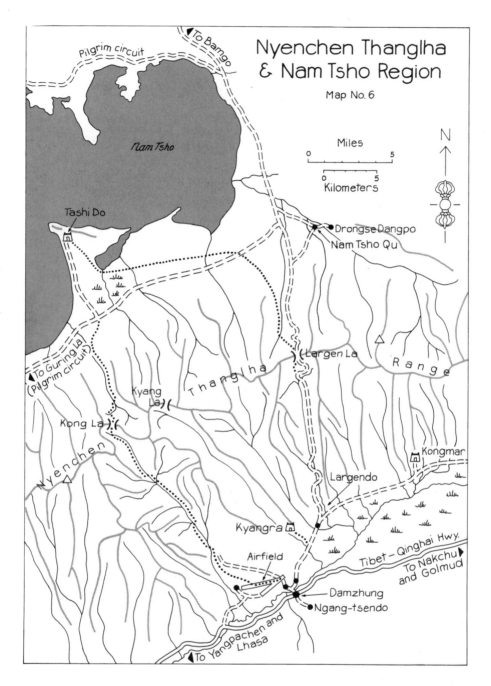

Nyenchen Thanglha & Nam Tsho Region

Map No. 6

daily from the long distance bus station south of Norbulingka. Private transport to Nam Tsho and Tashi Do can be arranged through your hotel or a travel agency in Lhasa. If you are in Damzhung, trucks and tractor carts sometimes cross Largen La to Nam Tsho Qu; they stop to gather passengers in front of the shops along the highway.

For day hikes near Damzhung, consider the **2-hour** walk to Kyangra *gompa,* a small Gelukpa hermitage near the road to Nam Tsho; or the **5- to 6-hour** hike to Kongmar *gompa*, the largest monastery in the Damzhung Valley. Details of these hikes are in the trek description below.

THE DAMZHUNG TO NAM TSHO LOOP TREK

Tashi Do hermitage and Nam Tsho are 43 miles (70 km) north of Damzhung via a dirt road crossing Largen La. Trekkers should allow **2 to 3 days** to reach the lake, and **another long day** of walking to arrive at Tashi Do. Hiking along roads is usually unpleasant, but this track is an exception: most of the traffic consists of yak herders and people on horseback. Years ago this was the caravan route for the salt traders of the Chang Thang. From May until July it is still possible to see yaks setting off on the forty-day journey across this plateau, taking tea and other goods to remote herding settlements and returning laden with salt.

From Damzhung, the road to Largen La leaves the Tibet-Qinghai Highway about 300 feet (90 m) to the west of the Damzhung Hotel (the main tourist hotel in Damzhung) and crosses a bridge (near km marker 3730) to the north (R) side of the river. Before leaving the highway, take a few minutes to get your bearings. The highest peak in the Nyenchen Thanglha Range (23,330 ft, 7111 m), which is the abode of Nyenchen Thanglha, the Western King of the mountain gods of Tibet, looms in the distance to the left (west). Four deep valleys drain from these mountains into the Damzhung area. The one farthest to the left (northwest) and beyond the airfield is the drainage from Kong La. Almost due north is the next valley to the right, with Kyangra *gompa* perched on the barren (L) ridge, and two more valleys farther to the right (north-northeast) is the route to Largen La.

About 1500 feet (460 m) beyond the river bridge a paved road leads up to the left into the walled compound of the Damzhung County seat (*xian*), beyond an entrance way. The road to Nam Tsho does not enter this compound. Instead, turn right (north) onto the dirt road just before the compound. This road leads across the Damzhung Valley, past Gungtang village and a two-story school. **About 1½ hours** beyond the river bridge the dirt road crosses a creek draining from the valley to the left. Kyangra *gompa* is **less than 1 hour** up to the left (north), built on an eroding ridge dotted with cave hermitages. Though a cart track leads near this retreat, the quickest approach from Damzhung is to cut across the flat plain from the road once you see the monastery.

Forty minutes from here cross another creek and pass the striped houses of Lando village. **Twenty minutes** farther the road forks. Kongmar, a large Gelukpa *gompa*, is about **3 hours** to the right (northeast) tucked in a side valley. The left fork leads to Largen La and soon passes a vehicle check point. Just beyond here the road turns left (north) up a tributary valley to the spacious meadow camps of Largendo. The road now winds up the Largen Valley, climbing under scrubby hillsides of barberry and juniper. **About 1½ to 2 hours** beyond Largendo the valley narrows into a gorge where the road crosses a bridge (14,300 ft, 4360 m) to the east (L) side of the creek. White-breasted dippers dive for insects here, then bob up and down on the rocks beside the water. The high, steep slopes enclosing this gorge are ideal terrain for the noisy Tibetan snow cocks. These giant partridges glide in tight, fixed-wing formations like squadrons of fighter jets, filling the air with their unusual high-pitched gobbles.

High above along the rock clefts is the domain of the lammergeier, the monstrous but elegant bearded vulture of Tibet and the Himalaya. Its abdomen and head are a beautiful golden color; a streak of dark brown feathers extends down from the eye to form a beard under its beak. These birds glide noisily on enormous wings that can reach 9 feet (2.8 m) or more in length. No other bird in Tibet has such a wingspan, though another vulture, the Himalayan griffin, actually stands taller. The griffin's white head, neck, abdomen, and the white leading half of its underwing help to distinguish this bird in flight from the lammergeier.

The road crosses the creek several more times but stays mainly on the east (L) side of the valley. Campsites are limited to small meadows until Largen La. **Five to 6 hours** above Largendo the road crosses the final bridge (15,900 ft, 4850 m) before the pass, to the west (R) side of the creek. A large valley enters from the left (west); Largen La is straight ahead to the north. While the road swings off to the right in long switchbacks to reach the summit, a wide animal track continues straight up the gravel slopes toward a large outcrop of red rock. Largen La (16,300 ft, 4970 m) is a **40-minute or more** climb from the bridge.

The blue waters of Nam Tsho lie to the north of Largen La; only the easternmost end of this inland sea is visible through the rounded hills. The town of Nam Tsho Qu is on the plains to the right (east) of the lake, but cannot be seen from here. The caravan route skirts this end of the lake, entering the low hills beyond for the journey across the Northern Plateau.

From Largen La the road weaves down onto the lakeside plains. To avoid the long bends in the road, drop down the side of the ridge to the left (northwest) from the huge summit *la-dze* and prayer flags. Descend the slope in an arc along the ridge side to a creek bed. Cross to the west (L) bank, then descend on braided animal trails to a series of large meadows on the valley floor. These are excellent campsites, well protected from the winds that can buffet the Nam Tsho basin. *Drokpa* families erect tents here in the summer.

The road to Nam Tsho Qu (15,200 ft, 4630 m) branches off beyond here to the northeast. This small settlement, **2 hours** away, consists of a few poorly stocked shops, a guesthouse, residences, and a bizarre "planned community" of several identical cement houses, all white, all rectangular. Trucks and tractors going to Damzhung usually park in front of the shops to take on paying passengers. If you need to hire yaks, ask here or inquire at Drongse Dangpo (First Village), where the *drokpa* live, a **40-minute** walk to the southeast of Nam Tsho Qu. Tashi Do hermitage is **1 long day** due west from Nam Tsho Qu, at the far end of a long, humped hill that looks like the Ayers Rock of Tibet.

If you don't choose to visit Nam Tsho Qu, the most direct route to Tashi Do follows a trail on the creek's west (L) bank that leads north from the large meadow camps. In a **few minutes** the trail skirts the base of a rocky ridge. Beyond these cliffs the stream turns away to the right, but the route to the lake continues straight ahead (north), without a trail, along the base of these hills; the best terrain for walking is along the junction of the plains and the hills. **About 1½ to 2 hours** beyond the meadow camps the hills start fading into the plains and Nam Tsho comes into view. Nam Tsho Qu, Drongse Dangpo, and several other clusters of houses can be seen across the plains to the right (northeast). Two prominent snowy peaks in the Nyenchen Thanglha Range jut high above the other mountains beyond these settlements. The locals call the taller, more pointed summit Samten Gangzang (20,505 ft, 6250 m). The large mountain to the right (south) is known as Harku Lhargö (19,740 ft, 6016 m).

Continue walking along the base of the ridge. Instead of aiming for the lake, angle across the flat expanse toward Tashi Do, the lone humped hill to the left (west). Although you might want to walk along the lakeshore, a long, narrow bay must be skirted before you reach the cave hermitages. **Four hours** past the meadow camps the plains end abruptly, dropping about 6 feet (1.8 m) over a steep embankment stretching for miles. A jeep track to Tashi Do parallels this shelf, a former shoreline of Nam Tsho. All of the lakes in North Tibet are ringed by similar embankments, some as much as 660 feet (200 m) higher than their present level. Apparently the lakes here were considerably larger 2 to 3 million years ago, but changes in the climate, probably due to the rain shadow effect caused by the uplifting of the Himalaya, have made the region more arid.

The jeep track to Tashi Do can also be reached by following the road north from the meadow camps. The turnoff for Nam Tsho Qu is just beyond the foothills to the right (east). Don't turn here, but continue straight ahead on the main road, which gradually angles away from the hills that lie to the left. **About 3 hours** beyond the meadow camps the road passes to the right of the only houses along this entire stretch. The jeep track heading west to Tashi Do runs between the main road and this scattered settlement, though the turnoff is farther ahead (north). Once you are near these houses, leave the main road and angle left (west) across the plain for **a few minutes**. The jeep track is at the base of the old shoreline. Follow it west for **1 to 1½ hours** from the last houses until the embankment and the jeep track start angling away from the lake to the left. This is approximately where the cross-country route from the meadow camps intersects with the track.

Although the jeep track leads to the cave hermitages, this is a roundabout route if you are on foot. Instead, head across the plains toward Tashi Do, aiming a bit to the left (south) of the domed hill where the caves are located to avoid a long detour around the bay. If the ground becomes too wet or uneven, adjust your course toward the mountains and higher ground. These plains are the home of vast numbers of pikas; some colonies are so huge you might not be able to find an area 10 feet (3 m) across without at least a few burrow holes, and some tracts are perforated with hundreds of holes.

Large flocks of migratory birds—including bar-headed geese, mallards, Brahminy ducks, brown- and black-headed gulls, black-necked cranes, terns, and several types of pochard—congregate along the shores of the bay, resting during their long journeys across Asia, especially from April until November. The Chinese government has declared this area a bird sanctuary. Perhaps the most interesting terrestrial birds in these parts are the sand grouses. They fly in swift, acrobatic formations, swooping noisily over the plains with their long, pointed tails trailing behind. Sand grouse are pale tan and gray, with very fine black stripes on the head, neck, and across the breast. They act

The twin limestone sentinels at the Tashi Do hermitage, Nam Tsho

much like quail when feeding and can be surprisingly fearless if you pass nearby.

Once you find a route around the bay, angle toward Tashi Do. Eventually it's possible to distinguish that this humped outcrop consists of two separate hills. The larger, Tashi Do Chen (Auspicious Great Rock), is to the right (east); Tashi Do Chung (Auspicious Small Rock) is to the left. Both hills have caves, though the main hermitage site is at Tashi Do Chung. The jeep track approaches from the south, paralleling the lakeshore and leading directly to a pair of immense limestone monoliths at the entrance to Tashi Do Chung (15,150 ft, 4620 m).

TASHI DO HERMITAGE

Few hermitage sites can rival the power and grandeur surrounding Tashi Do. The unusual twin pillars of rock are the watchtowers for a myriad of cave temples and grottos dotting the red limestone cliffs. Though most of the caves' façades were destroyed in the Cultural Revolution, monks and nuns have been returning to this hermitage; a large cave temple and several residences have been rebuilt. The main summit of the Nyenchen Thanglha Range dominates the southwestern horizon of peaks. Nam Tsho's 50-mile (80 km) length can now be appreciated, although the far end is still lost from sight. Nam Tsho is considered a saltwater lake, but on each visit I have found its water deliciously free of a saline taste. The fish here are high-altitude scaleless carp.

The main campsites are on the south side of Tashi Do Chung near the caves, though a fair amount of trash and broken beer bottles have been scattered around. One of the nicest campsites, beside the long *mani* wall stretching between the Tashi Do hills, is reasonably protected from the wind. Please keep it clean! A small, very basic guesthouse is located near the rock towers, and a pilgrims' resthouse has been built farther west along the base of the hill.

The *kora* around Tashi Do Chung is a leisurely **1½-hour** lakeside walk under sculpted limestone cliffs; allow more time to visit the different caves. The climb to the summit (15,500 ft, 4720 m) takes **30 minutes or more** and is best approached from the east side near the *mani* wall. Piles of carved prayer stones decorate the summit and the views are outstanding. Almost due south from Tashi Do is the broad-mouthed valley that leads to Kong La (16,900 ft, 5150 m). The third valley to the left (east) of the Kong La route leads to Kyang La, which descends to Kyangra *gompa*; and far to the west beyond the massive Nyenchen Thanglha peak is a higher crossing over Guring La (19,590 ft, 5970 m). The trek from Tashi Do over Guring La to the Yangpachen Valley is a difficult trek of **7 to 8 days** that involves crossing a glacier. The Austrian climbers Heinrich Harrer and Peter Aufschneiter crossed here in 1945 during their daring two-year escape to Lhasa from a British POW camp in India.

The Tashi Do Chen circuit is not as popular with pilgrims, but is nonetheless spectacular. Allow **2 to 3 hours**. The easiest access to the cairns and prayer flags on top of this hill (15,650 ft, 4770 m) takes **1 hour** or more from the far west side, near the long *mani* wall. The summit vistas include the best view of the bay to the east of the Tashi Do peninsula.

TASHI DO KORA

A logical place to start the *kora* around Tashi Do Chung is the limestone towers, which some say represent the *yab-yum* (male and female energy) of Tamdrin, the "horse-necked" Tantric protector (most easily recognized by a horse head atop his crown of flames). Another legend says the smaller, southern tower is a manifestation of the male and female protectors Trowo-Tromo, and the larger, northern tower (closest to Tashi Do) represents Zangdok Pelri, the mythical abode of Guru Rimpoche. Exquisitely carved *mani* stones surround the base of these crags.

The shore of Nam Tsho, at Tashi Do hermitage

The main cave temple, Shabdrung Phukpa, is opposite (north of) the rock pillars. This small, restored Nyingmapa chapel has a large figure of Guru Rimpoche in the form of Guru Tshogye Dorje, flanked by his two consorts; an image of the horse-riding "King of the Mountain" gods, Nyenchen Thanglha, is in the wooden cabinet to the right; and on the left is the *shuktri* of the Tashi Do *lama*, Dotrül Rimpoche, who resides in Damzhung.

The circuit continues clockwise around Tashi Do Chung, past the guesthouse and beyond a tall, crescent-shaped cave. Beyond the cement pilgrim's resthouse is a large limestone outcrop with prayer flags and *mani* stones, the Deshek-gyekyi Podrang or Palace of the Eight Medicine Buddhas. The rock corridor on the right leads to the Cave of Menlha, the Medicine Buddha. The *kora* now turns the corner around Tashi Do, providing views across the western expanse of the lake. At the end of the peninsula is a large pole of prayer flags at Trugo Shar, the "eastern head-washing site," one of four places around Nam Tsho (similar to Manasarovar, the holy lake in Western Tibet) where pilgrims receive the *chinlap*, or blessing, of this lake by slurping from a handful of water, then running the remainder through their hair. There are also four *gompas*, including Tashi Do, on the two-week circumambulation of Nam Tsho's perimeter (prostrating around the lake takes four months or more). Pilgrimage is usually performed in winter so rivers can be crossed; the holy sites on the lake's four main islands are also accessed in winter, when the lake's surface is frozen.

From the southeast corner of Tashi Do, the *kora* passes two Guru Rimpoche caves, one with a large ice mound inside, then skirts a rock face with two white *chörtens* and a sky-burial site for young children. The twin rock towers just to the north are called the Demchok *yab-yum*, yet another Tantric union of male and female energy; Mount Kailash is the primary abode of Demchok. A small flat area at the northwest corner of Tashi Do is the *chaktsal gang-shar*, the eastern of four prostration sites around Nam Tsho. Beyond here the *kora* turns west, passing a series of deep rock fissures in the limestone walls where pilgrims perform various tasks, such as crawling through narrow rock passageways to determine if they are free of sin. If you are on your own, wait for pilgrims to show you the intricacies of their activities here. Beyond here the circuit stays high above the cobbled shoreline to the caves at the east end of Tashi Do Chung, where red-ochre rock paintings of wild yak, deer, and a man on a horse decorate the cliff walls amidst more recent Buddhist art with the same ochre. The *kora* now turns away from the hill to circle one of the longest *mani* walls in Tibet, stretching between the two Tashi Do hills. Along the wall is a *chörten* with a stone *chakje*, or handprint, at its base. This handprint was made by the Third Karmapa, Rangchung Dorje, who is credited with "opening"

Hip yak herders approaching Largen La, near Nam Tsho

Tashi Do to Buddhists; his meditation cave is on the south side of Tashi Do Chen. On the rock walls of this hill, just beyond the end of the *mani* wall, are the largest galleries of rock paintings in this area. The *kora* finishes by angling across the plain to the rock towers at the entrance to Tashi Do Chung.

To DAMZHUNG VIA KONG LA

The return to Damzhung over Kong La can be trekked in **2 long days**. The route begins along the lakeshore on the jeep track leading south from Tashi Do. In **2 hours or more** the track meets a T-intersection. The road to Nam Tsho Qu leads to the left (east); the west end of Nam Tsho and the approach to Guring La follows the track to the right (west). The valley opening onto the plain due south from this junction is *not* the way to Kong La. The correct route is up the next major valley to the right. The west (L) ridge of this drainage from Kong La is a steep, sweeping wall that curves back into the mountains, with a tall, pyramid-shaped peak looming behind.

From the intersection, angle to the right (southwest) across the plain toward the mouth of this valley. The old lakeshore ledge is **15 minutes** away. Continue climbing, staying to the right (southwest) over the grassy alluvial plain. There is no real trail to follow, but as you enter the valley keep to its east (R) side. **Two hours** beyond the jeep track, cross a large gravel wash spilling from the talus slopes of the east (R) ridge. Near the creek draining this valley is a plateau of narrow meadows where *drokpa* may be camped.

Not far from here the valley bends to the left and the meadows are interrupted by large, rolling moraines. To avoid climbing each hill, stay close to the base of the east (R) ridge. As the hills smooth out, the valley turns back toward the right, widening into a broad basin of red mountains and green meadows with several herders' camps. Reach the largest of these camps (15,700 ft, 4790 m) **3 hours** after leaving the jeep track. Kong La is a long climb of **2 to 3 hours** from this basin; there are no suitable campsites for **another 2 hours** after crossing the pass. If it is getting late, camp here for the night.

The route to Kong La remains on the east (R) side of the valley for **40 minutes** past the last *drokpa* camps, then crosses to the west (L) bank to avoid a steep slope of moraine.

The vegetation is now very sparse and the valley quickly assumes a high alpine feel as it turns sharply to the right (southwest). Follow the livestock tracks near the creek for **15 minutes** until the creek forks. Cross to the south (R) bank above this confluence, then ascend the left fork into a narrow red rock gully. Climb for **another 15 minutes,** then cross to the east (R) side of this small streambed. The gully soon opens into a steep catchment area with several small tributaries spilling through the red crags. If the route becomes obscure, yak droppings are as good as cairns for relocating the trail.

Kong La (16,900 ft, 5150 m) is **30 minutes or more** above the last stream crossing, with *la-dze* marking the broad summit at either end. The descent follows a stunning valley system that has been scoured by repeated glacial advances and retreats. Initially a trail leads down from the summit, though it is not easy to follow as the valley widens. Stay to the west (R) side of the stream which forms to drain this area. The main valley becomes noticeably U-shaped and littered with pieces of rock torn from the ridges by glaciers. Continue descending, choosing the path of least resistance around morainal hills and boulders. When convenient, cross to the east (L) side of the stream. Soon it becomes obvious that this large drainage is merely a tributary for a much greater valley coming in from the right (west). The easiest route down hugs the base of the east (L) ridge. Descend steeply along a trough between the ridge and the hills of moraine. Where a tumbling stream from the left cuts across this trough, veer right and follow this stream down the steep embankment, reaching the broad valley floor in **2 hours** from the pass. A herders' camp (16,000 ft, 4880 m) and stone corrals are above the junction of this stream with the creek draining the larger, main valley.

These isolated meadows are superb campsites, but most impressive is the vast grandeur of this location. Four gigantic glacial valleys converge here to form a fifth, a geological rarity made even more unusual by the extreme elevation. The western glacier was the main ice floe, for the mouths of the other drainages have been left hanging with great vertical walls of moraine spilling from them. For those who are walking this route in the opposite direction, the second valley on the right from this camp, up to the northwest, leads to Kong La.

Damzhung is only **6 hours or more** of steady walking away, but the terrain below this camp is rather demanding. Stay to the east (L) side of the main valley, for soon another large tributary enters from the right with a towering moraine sweeping from its mouth. The descent is more a route than a trail. At times a good path follows the base of the east (L) ridge, but as the valley narrows hummock fields must be conquered and piles of rock rubble are everywhere. **Two hours** beyond the herders' camp a long, unstable rockslide spills from the east (L) ridge. Don't try to negotiate the thin trail winding through it. Instead, rock hop to the west (R) bank of the creek; during the summer this crossing can be quite difficult. The trail on this side is much easier to follow, though the valley remains quite rugged. This area becomes noticeably more green and alive as you descend; dwarf rhododendron and barberry bushes start cluttering the slopes, brilliantly colored rose finches sing from the bush tops, and brown dippers bob beside the stream. The Damzhung area soon comes into view, enclosed by a parade of rocky peaks.

Less than an hour below the rockslide the trail climbs out of the valley to a viewpoint (14,400 ft, 4390 m) overlooking the Damzhung region. An airfield (marked LA SA on the NH 46-5 JOG map and the ONC aeronautical maps) stretches in two oblique swaths across this end of the valley. A campsite in the meadows below this viewing spot is the first decent flat area for camping since the high herders' camp, though the only source of water is a long walk back to the creek. On the opposite ridge across the creek are several ruined walls, possibly an old fortress or a well-chosen hermitage site.

The route to Damzhung angles down to the right from the meadows and through a network of scrubby trails to reach the creek gully. Several potential campsites are along

About a quarter of Tibet's population consists of drokpa, *nomadic herders living in woven yak-hair tents*

here as well. Descend on the west (R) bank for **about 10 minutes,** then cross to the east (L) side below a powerhouse. Damzhung is **3 hours or more** across the valley floor. Aim for the tall white Damzhung Hotel rising above all the other buildings, though a fenced area causes a detour near the airfield.

Ascend the embankment on the east (L) side of the stream to reach the outflow from the powerhouse. Beyond here the valley has a gentle downward slope, making it easy to walk cross-country without a trail. Cross a jeep road **about 30 minutes** beyond the outflow. This road eventually leads into Damzhung, but it is a circuitous journey; instead, continue toward the town to a fenced enclosure. Walk to the right (south) along the fenceline to meet the abandoned runways of Central Tibet's first airfield. To avoid marshy ground and another fenced area, follow the runway to the left (east). When it ends, turn left onto the second runway. At the end of the fence paralleling this runway a dirt road leads off to the right (south) toward the first houses of Damzhung. Turn here and continue straight ahead to eventually meet the cement-paved avenue running through Damzhung's government compound. Beyond the gate at the end of the pavement is the bridge crossing to the Tibet-Qinghai Highway and the hotel.

If you have not made arrangements for a vehicle to meet you in Damzhung, look for the minibuses to Lhasa that solicit passengers along the commercial strip. Also, the buses from Golmud and Nakchu usually stop here before continuing on to Lhasa.

8
THE SHIGATSE REGION

MAP NO. 7, PAGE 149

Shigatse (12,650 ft, 3860 m; km marker 0/4903) is Central Tibet's second-largest city and the capital of Shigatse Prefecture; before 1950 it was the capital of the old Tibetan province of Tsang. Situated near the confluence of the Nyang Chu and the Tsangpo, about 160 miles (265 km) west of Lhasa, the city is a standard stop for groups touring Tibet. The main attraction in this sprawling market town of tree-lined avenues is the monastic complex of Tashilhumpo, the seat of the Panchen Lamas and one of the six great Gelukpa monasteries in Tibet.

In former times Shigatse was called Sam-drubtse. In the late sixteenth and early seventeenth centuries the Tsang kings ruled Tibet from the *dzong* on the hill above the city. Their reign came to an abrupt end in 1642 when Mongol armies fighting for the Fifth Dalai Lama and his Gelukpa sect invaded Sam-drubtse, capturing the king and killing him. The fortress, which pre-dates the Potala Palace in Lhasa, was converted to a military garrison by the Chinese in the first half of the eighteenth century; then it became the residence for the governor of Western Tibet in the twentieth century. It was

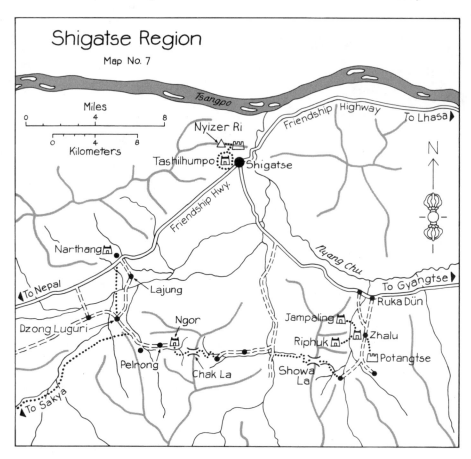

reduced to its present condition after the 1959 Lhasa Uprising. A mural in the Shigatse Hotel's dining room portrays this Potala-style *dzong* in its former grandeur.

TASHILHUMPO MONASTERY

Tashilhumpo is an impressive city of temples and monks' residences sprawling across the foot of Nyizer Ri. The main entrance gate is along the lower south wall, beside the Friendship Highway (km marker 4903) to Lhatse and Nepal. The entrance is a **20-minute** walk from the market area, a bit longer if you're starting from the Shigatse Hotel. Tashilhumpo was founded by one of Tsong Khapa's main disciples, Gendun Drub, in the mid-fifteenth century. He was the first abbot here, and his tomb is a major shrine in the Kelzang *lhakhang*. Gendun Drub is now revered as the First Dalai Lama, though the original person to actually receive this title, Sonam Gyatsho, is regarded as the Third Dalai Lama.

Tashilhumpo's role in the Gelukpa hierarchy changed dramatically in the seventeenth century when its abbot, Losang Chökyi Gyeltsen, was recognized by the Fifth Dalai Lama as an incarnation of Öpame (Amitabha), the Dhyani Buddha of Infinite Light and the spiritual teacher

Young monks at Tashilhumpo monastery

of Chenrezik, the patron saint of Tibet. Along with this recognition came the title Panchen Lama: Panchen is the shortened form of Pandita Chempo, meaning "Great Scholar." Like the title of Dalai Lama, the honorific title of Panchen Lama was retroactively given to the three previous abbots of Tashilhumpo, making Losang Chökyi Gyeltsen the fourth *trülku* in this lineage. His burial *chörten* is in the Labrang temple, beside the tall red building containing the 85-foot (26-m) statue of Gyelwa Jampa, the "Future Buddha." The Tenth Panchen Lama died at the beginning of 1989; a dispute between the current Dalai Lama and the Chinese government over the selection process for the eleventh incarnation has led to a situation where there are now two Panchen Lamas.

DAY HIKES IN AND NEAR SHIGATSE

If you plan to trek in the Shigatse region or in any of the mountainous regions farther west in Tibet, consider spending a few extra days in Shigatse en route to your trailhead. Since the altitude here is 800 feet (240 m) higher that Lhasa, walks in this area will provide an additional period of acclimatization before the trek begins.

TASHILHUMPO KORA

The *kora* around Tashilhumpo takes **less than 1 hour** to complete, not including breaks, though more time should be allowed to enjoy the views and all the pilgrim

Pilgrim stopping before one of the many special rocks and shrines on the Tashilhumpo kora

activities along the way. Heading clockwise from the monastery entrance, follow the main boundary wall away from the gates and turn right (west) onto the main road. Continue alongside this wall for 300 feet (90 m), then turn up the first alley on the right (north) where the prayer wheels end. The *kora* now ascends toward the hills between the boundary wall and rows of houses. The trail soon opens out at another row of prayer wheels; an enormous *chörten* and the maroon Gyelwa Jampa temple are to the right. The Tenth Panchen Lama helped spare Tashilhumpo from total destruction during the Cultural Revolution; the ruined mud walls here are one of the last reminders of the monastery's former size.

The *kora* now climbs above the northern boundary wall to an avenue of merit-earning sites where pilgrims rub parts of their bodies against certain rocks and place offerings of incense bush, *tsampa*, or *chang* onto smoldering hearths. At one spot the pilgrims line up to watch each other test their skill at directing a finger into a small hole in a rock, which is done blindfolded. If no one happens to be present while you're walking this portion of the trail, find a seat and enjoy the scenery until it's possible to join some pilgrims.

The circuit crests behind a tall, windowless stone edifice resembling a drive-in movie screen where a giant *köku* is displayed on special occasions. During Tashilhumpo's biggest annual festival, in the middle of the fifth Tibetan month (usually in late June or July), three different *kökus* portraying Dusum Sangye are hung on three consecutive days before huge crowds.

On the far side of the *köku* wall the trail forks; the upper route traverses to the Shigatse fortress, **15 minutes** away. Locals living in the town below the *dzong* finish their circuit along this trail. The lower route, the traditional *kora*, descends steeply from this junction, following the eastern boundary wall before intersecting a dirt road leading from the market area. The *kora* jogs right (south) past a *mani* temple, then left (east) along the boundary wall to the paved road. Turn right (south) to complete the circuit at Tashilhumpo's entrance; a left turn leads past the police station to the Samdrubtse Hotel, a block west of the Tibetan market.

Shigatse Dzong

The immense ruins of the old Shigatse fortress dominate the skyline of the city. Although nothing remains of this sixteenth-century structure but crumbling stone walls, the *dzong* is worth a visit for its commanding views of the valley and Tashilhumpo. If you're planning to walk the *kora*, the fortress is an easy side trip from the *köku* hanging wall. Head east across the ridge side to several houses, then go up to the saddle with a *la-dze* cairn, just below (west of) the ruins.

Nyizer Ri

Nyizer Ri is located along the highest ridge rising above Shigatse, running west from the fortress behind the monastery. The ridge is crowned by a square shrine with prayer flags for the *yul-lha*, the local protector of Tashilhumpo; incense offerings are made here on the third day of Tibetan New Year. The most direct approach up this ridge is from the saddle below the *dzong*. The offering shrine on Nyizer Ri (13,550 ft, 4130 m) is a steep climb taking **about 1 hour** from the saddle below the fortress, though the highest point along the ridge (13,950 ft, 4250 m) is **30 minutes** or more farther west. Bring plenty of water, as this is a dry ridge.

Yungdrungling Monastery

The most accessible Bön monastery in Central Tibet is Yungdrungling, a few hours' drive east from Shigatse toward Lhasa on the Friendship Highway. At the Takdruka ferry (km marker 4821), cross to the Tsangpo's north (L) bank then go north about 1 mile

(1.6 km) to where a dirt road turns off to the right (east). Descend to the creek and cross to the east (L) side. The monastery is perched on a plateau overlooking the Tsangpo. Several temples and a chanting hall have been rebuilt at this 160-year-old site, which housed several hundred monks in the 1950s.

THE ZHALU, NGOR, AND NARTHANG REGION

The **2- to 3-day** walk from Zhalu monastery to Narthang monastery is a good choice if you want a taste of trekking without the commitment of a long or difficult route; the two pass crossings along the way are not particularly high compared to most other walks in Tibet. The route travels through the hills to the south of Shigatse; Zhalu monastery is only 15 miles (24 km) from Shigatse on the way to Gyangtse, while Narthang monastery is about 9 miles (14 km) west of the city on the Friendship Highway to Nepal. Ngor monastery is in the hills between them.

Although this walk can be completed in **2 long days**, **4 days** are recommended if you wish to spend time at the monasteries and day hike into the hills above Zhalu. This trek is best accomplished between March and November, though late May and June can be hot, with dust storms blowing most afternoons. The Shigatse region generally receives less precipitation than Lhasa, though enough rain falls in July and August to turn the hills a pastel green. Winter treks are also possible, since snow is not usually a problem here. Overnight accommodation can be arranged in the monasteries and the settlements along the trekking route; a tent is not a necessity. The small shops at the entrance to Zhalu sell the usual basics: instant noodles, cigarettes, and beer. Purchase all of your trekking food requirements in Shigatse or Lhasa. If you are camping, bring a fuel stove. Wood is almost nonexistent in this region. This circuit was suggested to me by Keith Dowman, author of numerous works on Tibet and Buddhism.

The wall murals at Zhalu monastery are some of the oldest extant in Tibet

SHIGATSE TO ZHALU

Zhalu monastery is situated in a tributary valley of the Nyang Chu, 2.5 miles (4 km) south of the highway between Shigatse and Gyangtse. The turnoff is just past kilometer marker 20 at a small village called Ruka Dün (Seventh Commune). The peaked roofs of Zhalu can be seen rising above the flat plain from the highway.

If you are trekking as an individual, note that minibuses leave Shigatse for Gyangtse each morning starting about 8:00 A.M. in front of the bus station (officially tourists are not allowed to ride these buses for "safety" reasons, but most drivers will accept you). Tickets are sold on board. Pay attention to the kilometer markers or you could end up having lunch in Gyangtse (km marker 90).

Zhalu is a **1-hour** walk south from Ruka Dün. To the right (west) of the road heading south amid the barley fields, **about 20 minutes** before reaching the village of Zhalu, is a small rebuilt tenth-century shrine for Dorje Rabtenma, a form of the protectress Pelden Lhamo. In the thirteenth century the great abbot of Sakyapa monastery, the Sakya Pandita, was ordained here. Within the small courtyard is the stone basin used for cutting his hair during the ordination. Up in the hills to the west of this temple are the ruins of Jampaling *ani gompa*. The road to Zhalu leads into the village. The monastery's entrance gate is on the right (west).

ZHALU MONASTERY

The courtyard of Zhalu (also Shalu; 12,750 ft, 3890 m) is a dazzling display of color amidst this valley's naked red-brown hills. The site was established in the eleventh century, though the main temple in the courtyard, all that remains of the original complex, was renovated and enlarged in the early fourteenth century by Buton Rimpoche, Zhalu's most illustrious abbot and one of the greatest Tibetan Buddhist scholars. The tiled, peaked roof lines and interlocking beams of Zhalu are not typical of Central Tibetan architecture and reflect the influence of the Mongol Yuan dynasty who ruled Tibet and China during Buton's time. Facing into the courtyard is a darkened *gönkhang* with wall murals believed to date from the original eleventh-century temple. The main trove of artwork, however, is in the *dukhang* behind the *gönkhang*; in the pilgrim's circuit (*korsa*) around the *dukhang*; and the *mandala* paintings in the temples upstairs. These murals are the best preserved examples of fourteenth-century art in Central Tibet, plus there's an impressive array of ancient statues. Bring a flashlight. For a detailed account of the history and art of Shalu, see Roberto Vitali's *Early Temples of Central Tibet*, listed in Appendix B, "Suggested Reading."

The central figure in the two *lhakhangs* facing each other across the upstairs courtyard is Buton Rimpoche. Among his many achievements, he edited a vast, authoritative collection of Tibet's Buddhist and Tantric texts, known as the *Tengyur* (Translation of the Treatises), and helped compile an important set of doctrinal texts called the *Kangyur* (Translation of the Buddha's Words). These massive volumes form the backbone of Tibetan Buddhist thought. The monks at Zhalu say they are Bu-luk, the "Buton sect," which is closely associated with the Sakyapa sect. In later centuries, Zhalu and the nearby Riphuk hermitage (where Buton mostly stayed, in the hills to the southwest) were recognized as a center for mystical and psychic training, particularly for *lung-gom* (wind-walking) and *tummo* (generating body heat). Around the village are the ruined walls of the former monastery, which in the 1950s consisted of eleven *lhakhangs* and several chanting halls. According to the monks, Zhalu and Riphuk were like twin monastic cities during Buton's time, with thousands of monks studying under this great master.

Overnight accommodation can usually be arranged with villagers.

DAY HIKES NEAR ZHALU

Riphuk hermitage (13,150 ft, 4010 m) is well hidden by the rolling, naked ridges above Zhalu. If you walk to the far west side of the village, the wide trail to the hermitage can be seen snaking up an alluvial fan spilling from the hills to the southwest. The Tibetan letters *Om mani padme hum* are written on a nearby hill. There doesn't seem to be a specific trail starting from the village toward Riphuk. Choose a path between the barley plots, then go up the alluvial fan to the whitewashed walls of the rebuilt *dukhang*, **1 hour** above Zhalu.

In the 1950s there were seven *lhakhangs*, two main chanting halls, and more than 300 monks; a small chanting hall and a few temples have been rebuilt. Springs flow through the ghostly reddish brown ruins, nourishing willow trees, bushes, and wildflowers. One spring under a rock overhang is the *drubchu*, or "attainment-water," of Atisha, the great Indian scholar who stopped here for several months on his journey from Sakya monastery to Samye in the eleventh century; the blessing for pilgrims is three pitchers of chilly water poured over their head. (A similar blessing is given at the Jampa *lhakhang* behind the Jokhang, in Lhasa). A *kora* climbs into the hills around Riphuk, taking **1 hour or more** to complete. The *go-nyer* will point out the route and may even join you. Two smaller retreats for nuns, Chuk *ritrö* and Galung *ritrö*, stood nearby in the hills north of Riphuk.

The remains of Jampaling *ani gompa* (13,150 ft, 4010 m) are **1 hour or more** from Zhalu in a drainage gully to the northwest. Starting from the north side of Zhalu village, follow a cart track through the barley fields toward the base of the ridge. Jampaling is above the broad gravel wash dumping out of the hills to the left (west). It once had six or seven buildings with twenty nuns in residence, but is presently uninhabited. The tall, red stone walls were the main assembly hall. Climb **another hour** above Jampaling for panoramic views overlooking Zhalu monastery and the upper Nyang Chu Valley. The highest point on the main ridge (14,606 ft, 4452 m) is **about an hour** farther up to the west.

The ruins of Potangtse *dzong* (13,050 ft, 3980 m) are **1½ hours** from Zhalu, perched upon a solitary hill across the valley (southeast). The most direct approach is to walk cross-country over the plains. A more roundabout route follows the road up the valley (south) to the base of Potangtse hill, past the turnoff for the cart track leading to Showa La on the trek to Ngor (see description below). The easiest way to the summit is along the ridge spur leading up the far (east) side. This is a great picnic spot, set high above the geometrical configurations of barley fields.

THE ZHALU-NGOR-NARTHANG TREK

The walk from Zhalu to Ngor monastery takes **10 to 12 hours**. Although this can be completed in one long, hard day, I recommend staying somewhere in the valley between the two passes, then continuing on to Ngor the following day. To hire a burro or horse, inquire at Zhalu village (or Narthang if you start there).

To start, follow the dirt road up the valley (south) from Zhalu past small settlements and extensive fields alive with busy villagers, whistling and singing, but always quick to note a visitor. After **45 minutes** is a junction where the main road angles southeast across the valley to the base of Potangtse *dzong*. The route to Ngor continues straight ahead (south) on a smaller cart track, paralleling the east (R) side of the riverbed. **Two hours** past Zhalu reach two small groups of houses at the base of a tall rocky prominence topped by ruins.

The trail to Ngor now leaves the cart track and turns right (northwest) toward Showa La (also Shok La; 13,450 ft, 4100 m), the first and lower pass; little water is available until the next valley. Showa La cannot be seen from these settlements, but the route toward the pass climbs the gravel wash spilling from the hills to the right (west). Walk along the edges of the barley fields, staying toward the south (R) side of the drainage where a path eventually forms. After **1½ hours** the gravel wash narrows into a deep gully. The trail generally follows this ravine of red volcanic mud imbedded with river rocks, but near the pass the trail can be tricky to find; goat droppings are good route markers. If the gully begins branching and you need to scale small rock ledges to continue, you've gone too far up the streambed and have missed the easier path along the north (L) side. The summit of Showa La is **2 hours or more** from the last settlements, marked with a small pile of white *la-dze* rocks and carved *mani* stones. The Indian master Atisha crossed this pass on his way to Zhalu, which had been founded just a few years prior to his arrival.

Chak La (14,650 ft, 4470 m), the last pass before Ngor monastery, is the obvious cleft in the ridge directly across (west of) the Chaklung Valley. Several settlements and a braided trail can be seen on the broad alluvial fan leading toward this summit, but the actual pass is out of sight behind several ridges. The road on the valley floor meets the highway connecting Shigatse and Gyangtse near kilometer marker 9.

The descent to the road takes **1½ hours or more**. Stay on the south (L) side of the main gully forming below the pass, winding down through a world of eroded hills. Despite the bleakness, brilliant wildflowers such as the crimson Younghusband's lily (*Incarvillea younghusbandii*) thrive on this rocky ground. As you near the bottom, the trail from Showa La jogs left over a small rocky outcrop marked by cairns. The route to Ngor does not go over this low hill. Instead, continue walking straight ahead (west) without a trail for **5 minutes** to reach the road. If you want to return to Shigatse, the highway is **3 to 4 hours** to the right (north). The stony desert of the Chaklung Valley is a remarkable contrast to the fertile expanses near Zhalu monastery.

The route to Ngor follows the road to the right (north) for **less than 10 minutes,** then turns left onto a smaller cart track leading up a broad alluvial fan. Reach the first of two settlements in **1 hour** from the road. This is the group of houses that could be seen from Showa La. **An hour or more** higher is the last settlement before Chak La. The cart track initially stays on the north (L) side of the valley, then crosses to the south (R) side. Just below the village is a welcome picnic spot/campsite in a row of poplars near an irrigation pond. These last houses are **7 hours or more** from Zhalu; Ngor is at least **4 to 5 hours** farther.

As you approach the settlement, the cart track passes to the left of a walled poplar grove. The trail to Chak La turns off to the right here, away from the houses on a narrow footpath which soon drops steeply into a gravel streambed. Beyond here the route to the pass is not always obvious. Cross to the north (L) side and continue upstream to the mouth of a narrow gorge, then go up the north (L) embankment. Follow the network of animal trails to a stone-reinforced pond. This is the last potential campsite before the pass, with room for only a few tents. The trail now drops back into the gully, crosses over to the south (R) side and ascends a series of switchbacks. When the trail levels out, Chak La comes into view. Look for several small cairns beside a flat-topped rock outcrop on the ridgeline. Cross a small drainage coming in from the left, then ascend steeply to the pass. The route is often obscure where it crosses stretches of barren rock, but with

Woodworking repairs at Ngor monastery, near Shigatse

a little scouting the large cairn of stones on Chak La can be reached in **3 to 4 hours** from the last settlement.

The pass is a delightful surprise. Barren red hills etched with numerous ravines are speckled with stands of willow and poplar. In the middle of these badlands is Ngor monastery. Descend to the *gompa* in **1 hour**, following the trail along the south (L) side of the gully forming below the pass.

NGOR MONASTERY

Ngor (13,900 ft, 4240 m) was founded in 1429 by Ngorchen Kunga Zangpo, a prolific writer and Buddhist scholar who was educated at Sakyapa monastery. The tenets of the Ngorpa subsect of the Sakyapa tradition are based upon Ngorchen Kunga Zangpo's teachings, in particular his voluminous commentary on Tantric practice called Lamdre. Before 1959, Ngor boasted five *labrangs*, eleven residence halls, two large chanting halls for its six hundred monks and seven lineages of incarnate *trölkus*. The monastery was also famous for a style of mural painting that developed here. Unfortunately the entire complex and its outstanding frescoes were destroyed in the Cultural Revolution, but an enthusiastic renovation project has brought the *gompa* back to life again; Ngor is now one of the largest monasteries near Shigatse. Two beautifully crafted *dukhangs* have been rebuilt, side-by-side, in the center of the grounds. The Wangkhang, on the right, is currently the main chanting hall for the forty monks allowed to reside at Ngor (the *gompa* actually had up to two hundred monks until the late 1990s, but a government policy has reduced the number of active monks and nuns allowed in monasteries and nunneries throughout the TAR). The throne in the center of this hall is for Ngor's head *lama*, Lubding Khempo, who currently resides in Nepal and is one of Ngor's four remaining *trülkus*. Upstairs are two *gönkhangs* flanking the Lamdre Lama *lhakhang*, which celebrates Ngorchen Kunga Zangpo, the red-hatted figure in the center behind the metal grillwork. The *dukhang* on the left is called the Tsamdru Tondrö Chempo.

The tall building on the hillside above the chanting halls is Tartse Labrang, the residence for two of Ngor's *lamas* (one is in India; the other is in the United States), and below the *dukhangs* to the left is the *labrang* for Lubding Khempo. Immediately below here is the rebuilt Shedra, or "college," for Ngor. The only *trülku* currently in residence at Ngor is Khangsar Shabdrung, a young man being trained in the Lamdre tradition. He lives in the Namgyel Podrang, below the *dukhangs* to the right. A rough pilgrim's *kora*, taking **less than 1 hour**, ascends from the eleven *chörtens* at the base of the monastery to climb above Tartse Labrang and encircle the grounds.

Accommodation can be arranged at the monastery or in the settlement of Pelrong, **20 minutes** down the hill from Ngor.

TO NARTHANG

The walk to Narthang monastery takes **5 to 6 hours**. Descend to Pelrong along the service road, or by the trail shortcutting the curves. The whitewashed houses here are decorated with thick maroon and gray stripes, much like those on homes in the Sakya monastery and Dingri regions. From Pelrong the road winds down onto a broad gravel plain, past a steep-sided tributary entering from the left. As the valley starts bending to the north, the road angles left across the river plain toward a hill of multicolored rock. The old pilgrim and caravan route from Ngor to Sakya monastery, a **5- to 6-day** trek, ascends the ridge here.

Stay on the valley floor, and in **2 hours or more** reach a solitary three-humped hill in the valley mouth. The village along its base is Dzong Luguri (or Dzong), named for an ancient fortress. In the distance to the north are the square-walled ruins of Narthang monastery, **2 to 3 hours** from here across the flat plain. Fill your water bottles and enjoy some butter tea with the locals before resuming your walk. The most direct route to Narthang leads north, though the trail can become obscure in the maze of barley and mustard plots; just keep heading north. A less direct but more obvious route follows the dirt road northeast from Dzong Luguri, crosses the dry river bed (except in the rainy season) to Lajung to reach the Friendship Highway, Narthang village and the monastery.

NARTHANG MONASTERY

Narthang monastery (12,800 ft, 3900 m; km marker 4917) is 9 miles (14 km) west of Shigatse within the village of Narthang. The monastery's lifeless moonscape of immense mud-walled ruins creates an eerie atmosphere, so removed from the vitality and beauty at Ngor. Narthang belonged to the Kadampa school of Tibetan Buddhism, founded in the mid-twelfth century by a disciple of Atisha. This sect was one of the first organized schools of Buddhism to evolve in the eleventh century during *chidar*, the second diffusion of Buddhism to the Tibetan Plateau.

Narthang was once renowned for its religious printing, particularly for producing the voluminous copies of the Tibetan Buddhist Canon—the *Kangyur* and the *Tengyur*. One hundred and twenty-five thousand oblong hand-carved wooden printing blocks were used to print these texts, but most of them were destroyed along with the monastery in 1966. By the mid-1980s a *lama* from Narthang had built a small residence building-cum-temple within the ruins, then a *lhakhang* dedicated to Neten Chu-druk was built nearby; the old painted rock carvings of these sixteen Buddhist elders along the back wall are from the original temple. In 1993 enough funds were raised to rebuild a small but ornately decorated chanting hall for the twenty-five resident monks. Like many Kadampa monasteries, Narthang is now Gelukpa. It is closely associated with the Ngakpa College at Tashilhumpo.

There are no shops nor eateries in this town, but the hotels and restaurants of Shigatse are not far. If you haven't arranged for transport to meet you in Narthang, late afternoon is a good time to try hitching, for most vehicles will be heading to Shigatse for the night.

9
THE EVEREST REGION

MAP NO. 8, PAGES 160-161

Nowhere in the Himalaya can the immense height of Mount Everest (29,028 ft, 8848 m), the highest point on earth, be appreciated as it can be in Tibet. The northern flanks of this grand massif are unobstructed by neighboring peaks or ridges, allowing excellent views of the entire mountain from both the Rongphu (typically misspelled Rongbuk) and Kangshung Face base camps. A good portion of the summit is even visible from several points along the Friendship Highway, particularly from the Dingri (or Tingri) plains.

The Tibetan name for Mount Everest is Chomolangma (Chi., Qomolangma), also spelled Jomolangma and Chomolungma. The mountain was first recognized as the world's tallest in 1840, when it was labeled Peak XV during the Great Trigonometrical Survey of India and the Himalaya. In 1865, after attempts failed to discover a local name, the survey named it Mount Everest in honor of the genius behind this huge project, Sir George Everest. A great debate has raged for decades over the correct local name and its meaning. "The Abode of the Mother Goddess of the Universe" is a common interpretation; "Mother Goddess of the Wind" is another. A more accurate literal translation is "Lady Cow," as *chomo* (also *jomo*) means lady or princess, and *langma* is a cow or female ox. Noted Tibetan scholar Edwin Bernbaum has informed me that the full name for Chomolangma is *Chomo migyo langzangma*, which translates as "Lady Immovable Good Cow."

The Kangshung (East) Face of Mount Everest is arguably its most spectacular side, a sheer wall of rock and ice rising 2.5 vertical miles (almost 5 km) above the Rongphu base camp and the picturesque environs of Dza Rongphu monastery. This isolated retreat in the upper reaches of the Dzakar Chu Valley is said to be the highest monastery in the world (16,150 ft, 4920 m). An interesting topographical feature on the Tibet side of Mount Everest is the unusually gentle slope of the valleys descending from this mountain. The glaciers that fill these drainages are not wrought with impassable crevasses, nor do they tumble in steeply broken icefalls. Well-prepared and well-acclimatized trekkers can continue beyond the Rongphu base camp without ice axes or crampons and reach the higher advance camps used by the climbing expeditions.

The Kangshung (East) Face of Mount Everest, considered one of mountaineering's great challenges, is approached via the Kangshung Valley, a tributary of the Phung Chu (which becomes the Arun River when it crosses into Nepal). The trailhead for this classic **10- to 12-day** trek to the Kangshung base camp is Kharta Qu, a small town 40 miles (64 km) southeast of Tashi Dzom, the main administrative *shang* in the Everest region.

Also spectacular but relatively unknown is the walk up the Menlung Valley, a remote tributary of the Rongshar Tsangpo (a major tributary of Nepal's Tamba Kosi River) to the west of Mount Cho Oyu. It was here in 1951 that British mountaineer Eric Shipton snapped the celebrated yeti footprint photographs during an expedition exploring the valleys west of Mount Everest.

The best time for trekking to Mount Everest is generally between May and October, though in the Rongphu area it is possible to trek throughout most of the year. The wall of peaks stretching from Makalu to Everest and across to Cho Oyu creates a particularly effective rain shadow over this region, blocking most of the moisture that would

Everest Region

Map No. 8

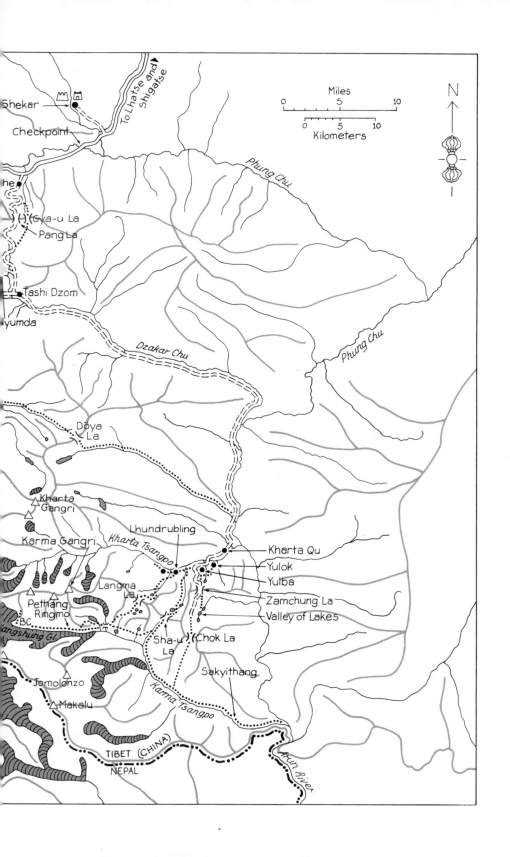

Shekar

Checkpoint

To Lhatse and Shigatse

Phung Chu

he

( ) (Gya-u La
Pang La

Tashi Dzom

yumda

Dzakar Chu

Phung Chu

Doya
La

Kharta
Gangri

Lhundrubling

Kharta Tsangpo

Kharta Qu

Yulok

Yulba

Karma Gangri

Langma
La

Zamchung La

Valley of Lakes

Pethang
Ringmo

BC

angshung Gl

Sha-u
La

Chok La

Sakyithang

Jomolonzo

Karma Tsangpo

Makalu

TIBET (CHINA)

Arun River

NEPAL

Miles

0   5   10

0   5   10

Kilometers

N

otherwise cause snow in the winter and heavy rains in the summer. The temperatures from May to October are fairly mild and at times surprisingly hot. Between July and early September the monsoon still manages to push over the mountain barrier, draping Everest in clouds and occasionally dropping snow on the high ridges. The lower valleys receive rain, and at times the road from Tashi Dzom to Dza Rongphu monastery is a quagmire of muddy ruts deep enough to swallow a four-wheel-drive vehicle up to its frame.

During the winter months the weather pattern over Tibet is often very stable with clear, brisk days and little snowfall. Although storms sometimes dump a foot or more of snow, the biggest obstacle to trekking this time of year is the incessant, numbing afternoon wind. Night temperatures drop well below freezing, but are tolerable with the proper gear. On my first visit here, in midwinter, the food on our plates kept freezing before we could finish eating.

The trekking season for the East Everest base camp/Kangshung Valley area and the Menlungtse Valley is of much shorter duration than for the Rongphu region. The Himalayan rain barrier, which keeps the Dzakar Chu Valley and the Dingri plains so dry is severed to the east of Makalu by the Arun River Valley, one of the deepest canyons in the world. The monsoon is channeled past the Himalaya to the Kangshung Face. The Menlungtse Valley experiences a similar effect due to the Tamba Kosi Valley. Pre-monsoon (mid-May until late June) and post-monsoon (September until mid-October) are generally the best seasons. Trekking during July and August is also possible—but be prepared for an unforgettable wilderness experience of misty glacial valleys, brilliant wildflowers, and very soggy hiking boots. By late October winter weather usually returns to the high ridges. Sha-u La and Langma La, the two main accesses into the Kangshung region, become so choked with snow that the locals don't attempt to cross again until the following May. Pozer La, the pass into the Rongshar/Menlungtse area, closes to vehicles much of the winter, but locals continue to cross on foot.

The town of Dingri (km marker 5193/4) and the turnoff for Everest base camp near kilometer marker 5145/6, located about 350 miles (570 km) by road to the west of Lhasa, are the main trailheads for treks into the Everest region. The journey is a stunning two-day drive over rugged, dusty, occasionally paved roads. For treks into the Kangshung or Menlungtse Valleys, plan on an extra day's drive to reach the trailheads at Kharta Qu and Rongshar Qu, respectively.

Unless the public bus service from Lhasa to Khasa/Nepal border resumes, individual trekkers going to the Everest region must either hire a private vehicle from Lhasa or Shigatse (travelers regularly place notices on the budget hotel bulletin boards advertising rides to share to destinations all over Tibet) or hitchhike to the trailheads.

If you are coming from Nepal, Dingri is less than a day's drive from the border. However, the rapid ascent by road from Zhangmu (7300 ft, 2230 m) to Dingri (14,150 ft, 4360 m), followed by a trek that quickly crosses one of the high passes into the Rongphu or Kangshung area, is not recommended unless you have recently been to high elevations. To properly acclimatize, stop in Nyelam (12,200 ft, 3720 m) for a minimum of two nights, then spend another two nights when you arrive at Dingri. Or else continue on to Shigatse or Lhasa and base yourself there for three days or more, then return to the Everest region for your trek. To stay in shape, go on warm-up hikes around these areas to prepare for your trek.

The Everest region is a long day's drive to the nearest major medical facility in Shigatse. Shekar (turnoff at km marker 5133) has a small hospital with a few doctors, and Kharta Qu has a small health post. In a life-threatening situation, consider evacuation to Kathmandu, also a day's drive away, as the medical facilities (and if necessary, airline connections) are much better than in Tibet.

CHOMOLANGMA NATURE PRESERVE

The entire Tibetan side of Mount Everest is part of the Chomolangma (also Qomolangma) Nature Preserve, a large protected area covering approximately 13,000 square miles (34,000 km²; about the size of Massachusetts) along the north slope of the Himalaya. It is the first nature preserve in Tibet or China to include people and their cultural heritage in its preservation agenda, and the first to accept international collaboration in its planning and management.

The boundaries extend west to the headwaters of the Kyirong Tsangpo (Nepal's Trisuli River) to include the whole Shishapangma-Pelku Tsho region. The northern boundary lies to the north of the Friendship Highway to include the headwaters of the Phung Chu (the main tributary of Nepal's Arun River). The eastern limits encompass the southward sweep of the Phung Chu toward Nepal, but not it's easternmost tributaries. The southern boundary is the Tibet-Nepal border, linking the preserve with the Langtang and Sagarmatha National Parks, and the Makalu-Barun Conservation Project in Nepal. Within the perimeters of the preserve are five of the world's 8000-meter peaks.

The Chomolangma Nature Preserve encompasses four counties and is administered by the Shigatse Prefecture. A branch office is in Shekar and a preserve officer/warden is stationed in Dingri. An ambitious master plan includes development of educational, cultural, and public health services to raise the local people's quality of life; protection and rehabilitation of the unique mountain, forest, and grassland ecosystems; protection of wildlife, including a ban on hunting; protection of the area's cultural heritage, including financial aid for the reconstruction of Dza Rongphu monastery; and environmental cleanups in places such as Everest base camp.

Tibetan women in the Everest region

THE DINGRI TO EVEREST BASE CAMP LOOP TREK

The town of Dingri (14,150 ft, 4310m) is the trekkers' gateway to Mount Everest. It is also the turnoff for treks in the Rongshar and Menlungtse area. This former staging point on the Lhasa-Kathmandu caravan route, situated within sight of Everest's northern slopes, is in the middle of an expansive plain not far west of the Dzakar Chu Valley and Dza Rongphu monastery. Between these two drainages is a long dividing ridge with four main passes, all about 16,000 feet (4880 m) or higher. The highest and most southern of these crossings is called Pang La (16,900 ft, 5150 m)—not to be confused with the Pang La along the vehicle road to Everest base camp (see "The Trek to Everest Base Camp via Pang La"). About 1 mile (1.5 km) to the northeast is Lamna La (16,600 ft, 5060 m), a more traveled and slightly lower pass that has become the standard trekking route to approach the Everest region. There are no shops nor lodges in the few villages beyond Dingri, so it's advisable to carry tents, stoves, and all your food requirements.

An old trade route from Dingri to the town of Tashi Dzom crosses Dingri Lamar La (15,800 ft, 4820 m), the lowest and the northernmost of the passes into the Rongphu region. The trek from Tashi Dzom to Dza Rongphu up the Dzakar Chu Valley takes **2 to 3 days**. Walked in the opposite direction (from Dza Rongphu to Tashi Dzom and up the Gara Chu Valley to Dingri), this route can be combined with the trek over Lamna La to create a scenic loop of **8 to 10 days** that requires only a half day of backtracking. When you start in Dingri and walk this loop counterclockwise, you will have access to the few amenities available in Tashi Dzom at the end of the trek rather than at the beginning.

The least known of these four passes is Ding La (16,200 ft, 4940 m), a remote approach to Everest via a tributary valley rising to the east behind the town of Lungjang. Several infrequently traveled high passes also connect the Ding Chu Valley with the Gara Chu and Zomphu Valleys.

DINGRI

Dingri is a windblown government *shang* with a hundred houses or more bunched along the base of an isolated hill. Its true name is Ganggar, but people from outside the region know it as Dingri. Despite the large army camp and the sprawl of guesthouses and shops along the Friendship Highway, the actual town and the surrounding area offer a fascinating glimpse of Tibetan village life. The area earned its name when the Indian Tantric master Padampa Sangye came to these plains near the end of the eleventh century on his search for a special black rock. A manifestation of the Buddha, Sakyamuni had used his great powers to throw this rock all the way from India to Tibet. The rock first landed on a frozen body of water, near the present site of Dingri. It struck the ice with a loud "ding," said to be like the sound of a hammer hitting steel. Since that time this region has been called Dingri, the "Hill of Ding." After bouncing off the ice, the magically lofted stone settled upon a spot at the far western edge of the Dingri plain, where Padampa Sangye recovered the rock and established Langkor *gompa*. All that is left of this famed monastery is a small *lhakhang* within the village of Langkor, a **5-hour** walk west of Dingri.

The crumbling walls on Ganggar Ri, the hill above Dingri, are the remains of a garrison. This Chinese-built fortress was erected as a line of defense after the Nepalese army captured the area in the late eighteenth century. Many of the dissolving mud-walled ruins along the highway in this region are testimony to several attacks by the Gurkha armies. A small temple once stood beside the garrison.

The top of Ganggar Ri is also one of the finest places for watching the sunset on Mount Everest, the huge massif of Cho Oyu (Tib., Jobo Oyuk; 26,748 ft, 8153 m; the world's sixth-highest peak), and Lapchi Gang (23,092 ft, 7038 m), the highest summit in the snow-covered range to the southwest.

A yak caravan returning from Nepal to Dingri after crossing Nangpa La

Staying in Dingri is no longer the dreaded experience it once was: The earthen-floored hovels with wobbly wooden sleeping platforms have given way to new, relatively clean guesthouses. If you want to hire pack animals and a guide, the guesthouse managers can make arrangements with someone from the village. Saddle horses are available for day hire around the Dingri area, plus they can outfit groups for **7- to 8-day** round-trip horseback trips to Everest base camp.

Although there are a number of small shops, the shelves stock mostly an odd assortment of canned fruit, noodles, candies, soft drinks, beer, and army sneakers. Purchase all of your food requirements in Shigatse, Lhasa, or Nepal.

If you spend a day or two in Dingri acclimatizing before your trek, a good warm-up walk follows a cart track south to the town of Gönphuk. Set below a low hill with a ruined *gompa* atop the crest, this settlement is **about 2 hours** from Dingri across the flat plain. The new *lhakhang* on the slopes above town is all that remains of this monastery, once the largest in the Dingri area.

If you have a full day free, a long but flat loop walk continues southeast from Gönphuk for **2 hours or more** to the town of Chölung, situated at the base of a tall, narrow, and rocky ridge. The ridge, a good bearing to aim for, can be recognized by the extensive ruins of Chölung *gompa* crowning its top. A *lhakhang* has been built among the crumbling walls. The return walk to Dingri takes about 3½ **hours** along a cart track leading north from Chölung.

DINGRI TO CHO OYU BASE CAMP

An alternative trek from Dingri is the walk south to Cho Oyu base camp (15,800 ft, 4820 m), located at the foot of high gravel moraines below the Kyetrak Glacier, in the upper Ra Chu Valley. A dirt road threads for 25 miles (40 km) across the expansive Dingri plains to the base camp, a **2-day or more** walk from Dingri, then continues another 28 miles (46 km) to the southwest over Pozer La (17,400 ft, 5300 m) to the Rongshar and Menlungtse Valleys. Not far north of the base camp on the east (R) side of the Ra Chu Valley are the ruined buildings of Kyetrak, a former salt depot on the Nepal caravan route that crosses glaciated Nangpa La (18,753 ft, 5716 m). The trail to Cho Oyu's advance base camp follows this trade route up the east (R) side of the glacier.

———————————

A beautiful day hike from the base camp, with panoramic views of Cho Oyu, Jobo Rabtsang (21,870 ft, 6666 m; it's the impressive snowy peak due south of the base camp), and towering overviews of the Kyetrak Glacier and its huge lake, follows the road south from the base camp toward Pozer La for **1 hour or more**. When the road swings to the right (west) to start the steep ascent to the pass, continue straight ahead (south) up the trough along the west (L) side of the glacier. Ascend onto the high lateral moraine whenever convenient. Follow the crest until it joins the side of the mountain (17,200 ft, 5240 m) below the icefalls of Jobo Rabtsang, **3 hours** from base camp.

The Everest-Rongphu base camp can be reached in **2½ days** from Cho Oyu base camp via a trail that climbs out of the Ra Chu Valley, then turns east across the hills to join the cart track crossing Lamna La. The route over this pass, starting from Dingri, is detailed below.

THE TREK FROM DINGRI TO DZA RONGPHU MONASTERY

The first half of this loop trek to Dza Rongphu monastery takes **3 to 4 days**. The route begins at the bridge on the southeast edge of town and follows a well-graded cart track for most of the way to Lamna La. Cross the wooden bridge to the east (R) bank of the Ra Chu and follow the track across the plains. (**A few minutes** beyond the bridge are several good camping areas, but they are rather exposed to the wind.) The track soon angles toward the south, with Cho Oyu looming straight ahead. Several trails shortcut some of the long bends in this road. The plains here are a strange mixture of silence and activity: The wind rustles the grasses, young boys whistle at their herds of miniature goats, and groups of women bent over from the waist chat and sing as they tend the barley.

One hour or more from Dingri the track passes the settlement of Ra Chu, a distant cluster of white buildings along the hills rising to the east. As the road continues south, the grasses gradually yield to sparsely vegetated gravel expanses. Somehow barley can be coaxed to grow in these conditions. **One hour** beyond Ra Chu the line of hills edging the plains is interrupted by a broad valley mouth. The route over Dingri Lamar La to Tashi Dzom follows this wide tributary up to the left (east). Finding the proper approach to this pass can be somewhat confusing from this direction, for there are actually three different drainages converging here through the jumble of dry hills. The correct route leads up the valley to the far right (southeast), reaching the village of Nelung (14,700 ft, 4480 m) in **2 hours**. Another graded cart track originates near Lungjang, a settlement farther to the south, and ascends the south (L) side of the Nelung Valley to Dingri Lamar La and over to Tashi Dzom. This route is described below in reverse.

The cart track from Dingri to Lamna La continues south toward Cho Oyu. **Two hours** beyond the valley entrance to Nelung, a prominent rocky ridge erupts from the plains along the west (L) bank of the Ra Chu. Chölung village is situated at the base of this outcrop; scattered across the ridge crest are the extensive ruins of Chölung *gompa*. A small temple has been rebuilt amidst the rubble.

The open plains are eventually squeezed between this ridge and the hills to the left (east). **Forty-five minutes** past the end of the Chölung ridge, the wide trail from the

Nelung Valley comes in from the left to join the cart track from Dingri to Lamna La. In **another 45 minutes** the track enters Lungjang (14,600 ft, 4450 m), the last settlement in this part of the Dingri plains. A wind-generator farm in Lungjang could supply half of Western Tibet with electricity. It is a bleak region surrounded by barren gravel flats, yet the people manage to harvest barley. Most of the villagers are also herders. If you are coming from Dingri with pack animals and a guide, this is probably where you will stop for the night. A small guesthouse–cum–*chang* hall in Lungjhang will put up travelers, or friends of your guide may have you stay with them. Unless you have a tent for your guide, the next available shelter where he would be able to sleep is at a *drokpa* camp **about 3 hours** farther south. Inquire in Lungjang regarding the whereabouts of these herders.

Unfortunately, hospitality in this town is a bit lacking. Beware of greedy hosts, keep your belongings close at hand, and make sure prices are established before you consume any food or drink.

The cart track continues south from town beyond a huge circular stack of *mani* stones. A **few minutes** from this prayer wall the track forks, the left half angling into a large tributary valley. This is the route to Ding La (16,200 ft, 5940 m), the most remote of the crossings into the Dzakar Chu Valley. The journey over this pass to Dza Rongphu monastery takes **3 long days**, but it is a beautiful walk.

The right fork stays on course with Cho Oyu's diminishing summit. In **30 minutes** pass to the right of a rocky crag topped with ruins, which may be an old *dzong*. The high ridge extending along the Ra Chu's west (L) bank now closes in on the river to form a gorge. **One and a half hours** past Lungjang the gorge forces the track to turn left into the scrubby hills. In **30 minutes more** climb to a ridge summit with panoramic views looking across the gorge to the Himalayan peaks.

Descend from here onto an unusually straight section of the track neatly bordered by white river rocks. **One hour** from the ridge top the road begins climbing into the hills again. To the right at the base of these hills is a *drokpa* camp with stone corrals. If you don't mind sleeping beside a few hundred sneezing goats, this is one of the more sheltered campsites before the pass. The track ascends past this camp and over the eastern hills that guard the entrance to a tributary valley. Cho Oyu, massively close, soon disappears behind its foothills. To the west is an endless succession of morainal ridges dumped by the glaciers of past ice ages. A bit of geological history lies scattered on the gravel slopes near the track: The shell fossils are remnants from the ancient Tethys Sea that once covered Tibet.

One and a half hours from the *drokpa* camp the track descends into the tributary drainage, passing a stone corral and several meadows. As the valley veers left (east) the road crosses the creek to the north (L) bank. Just beyond this ford is a large corral and herder camp (15,400 ft, 4690 m) to the right. Used almost year-round, this is often the last inhabited camp and one of the better places to stop before the pass. The next settlement is Zomphu, **4 hours** away, including the crossing of Lamna La. The corral walls provide a welcome break from the wind.

Not far from this camp the valley opens out, but quickly divides into two separate drainages. The cart track hugs the base of the far south (L) ridge and ascends the larger valley to the right (southeast) toward both Lamna La (also known as Zomphu La) and Pang La. If you plan to cross the more remote and somewhat higher Pang La (16,900 ft, 5150 m), stay on the cart track for **1½ hours** past the *drokpa* camp. When the track starts angling to the left (northeast) toward Lamna La and the Zomphu Valley, a cross-country route to Pang La leaves the road and continues right (southeast) toward a network of high, gravel-covered ridges. Although this is the shortest approach to Dza Rongphu monastery, it is a steep ascent and the area is mostly uninhabited. This terrain is too rugged for crossing with pack animals, and herders rarely graze livestock here.

If you remain on the cart track, Lamna La is a **2-hour** climb to the left (northeast). When the locals travel between Dingri and Zomphu, they typically use a shortcut that also goes over Lamna La, though at a slightly higher point on the ridge than where the cart track passes over. This shorter route follows the road for **about 20 minutes** past the last *drokpa* camp. It then leaves the track where the valley divides and follows the smaller drainage up to the left (northeast). There isn't a trail at first, so choose a convenient cross-country route over the wet tundra and grass hummocks. Aim for the hills on the south (L) side of this drainage. Not long after you enter the mouth of this side valley the walking becomes much easier and a trail forms along the base of the south (L) ridge. The terrain beside this ridge is very dry and supports large colonies of pikas. They're everywhere, scurrying into their burrows and quickly reappearing to inspect whoever is approaching. Several small piles of *mani* stones grace the trail along here. **One hour** beyond the last herders' camp is a stone corral (15,700 ft, 4790 m) at the base of the ridge. The area around this enclosure is the last good campsite before Lamna La. Grazing grass and water are found nearby.

Just beyond this camp the valley floor turns into a stony desert plain. The trail is easy to follow at first and stays near the south (L) ridge. The actual pass crossing is not visible from here, though a saddle in the ridge marked by a rock cairn can be seen to the southwest near the summit. Occasionally a lone *kiang*, the wild ass of Tibet, can be spotted in this region. It looks like a small horse from a distance, with a reddish brown coat and black markings.

As the valley turns to the right (south) the trail leaves the base of the ridge. The path becomes faint but continues to the southeast across rocky flats and into a group of low hills, then descends steeply into a narrow creek bed. Cross to the east (L) bank of the creek and up the embankment to the last stone corral before the pass. The cairn on the saddle is directly above on the ridge, though the trail is quite faint until just below the top of the saddle; aim for the cairn. During summer the high-altitude blue poppy *(Meconopsis horridula)* dots these rocky slopes, and *gowa*, the Tibetan gazelle, may be grazing along the ridges near the pass. The cairn is a breath-grabbing **1-hour or more** climb, without rest stops, from the creek crossing. Lamna La (16,600 ft, 5060 m) is **less than 10 minutes** farther, marked by a *la-dze*. The cart track is out of sight and crosses a few hundred feet below this point. The snowy peaks off to the south are the lower flanks of Gyachung Gang (25,990 ft, 7922) and Cho Oyu. Pang La crosses the large ridge system in front of them.

The trail swings gently to the left (east) before starting its steep descent, intersecting the cart track **20 minutes** below the summit. The track stays on the north (L) side of the valley for much of the journey to Zomphu, though the locals follow a more direct route down the south (R) side of this drainage. The vegetation here is considerably more lush than on the Dingri side of the pass, capable of supporting a half-dozen *drokpa* families and hundreds of yaks.

Where the trail from the pass meets the cart track, cross the track and continue descending without a trail toward the valley floor. The hummocks can make walking difficult, though eventually a trail materializes at the base of the south (R) ridge. The cart track winds down into the valley, staying near the base of the north (L) ridge. **One hour** below the pass the valley narrows and the trail swings over to the left near two *drokpa* camps. The road from the pass is also forced near these two camps. Cross the cart track, then cross to the north (L) bank of the main creek.

The trail climbs for **a few minutes** from the creek to the top of a boulder-strewn ridge. The white walls of Zomphu village (15,500 ft, 4720 m), probably the highest permanent settlement in the Everest region, are only **30 minutes** away to the left (northeast). The trail descends from this ridge crest to a wooden bridge, then climbs above a rushing stream to the town. The best sites for camping are a few minutes downstream from the bridge, away from the houses.

Zomphu is set high above the valley in a moonscape of barren hills with views of Mount Everest and Gyachung Gang. Because crops cannot survive at this elevation, the forty families residing here rely upon animal husbandry. Every morning and evening, in a large pasture above the town, dozens of *dri*, the female yak, are tethered for milking. During the summer the villagers supply yak to haul gear for Everest treks and expeditions.

If you are trekking with pack animals, Zomphu is the last place where your guide can find shelter before continuing on to Dza Rongphu monastery. As in other towns near Everest, choose your host carefully and watch your belongings.

The drainage north of Zomphu is Changku Lung, "Wolf Valley." A **45-minute** walk in this direction above the village provides grand views of Gyachung Gang's massif. **One hour** farther is an unnamed pass (16,300 ft, 4970 m) into the Ding Chu Valley. This beautiful alternative route to Dingri takes **2 long days** of walking. Ding La (16,200 ft, 4940 m) must be crossed as well. Routefinding is not always easy—consider hiring a guide from here.

Dza Rongphu monastery is only **1 day** south from Zomphu. The route descends from Zomphu to the Dzakar Chu, the main river draining the Rongphu area and one of the Phung Chu's tributaries. The trail initially remains high on the ridge side, then drops near the creek to join the cart track. The confluence with the Dzakar Chu is a **2-hour** descent from Zomphu. The desert environment and gravel wastelands along the river are a dramatic change from the green meadows of the Zomphu Valley. Find a suitable ford before the confluence and cross to the south (R) bank of the creek. The route to Dza Rongphu now follows a trail on the west (L) bank of the Dzakar Chu for **2 hours** to a wooden bridge, past the ruins of Chöphuk, a Nyingmapa cave hermitage built into limestone cliffs. This was once the seat of Lama Sangwa Dorje, who in the seventeenth century founded Pangboche, the first monastery in Nepal's Khumbu region near Mount Everest. The fifth incarnation of this *lama* was Ngawang Tenzing Norbu, who founded Dza Rongphu and was instrumental in the founding of Thangboche and several other monasteries in the Khumbu. Despite Chöphuk's sad condition, ten monks presently associated with this retreat now conduct ceremonies in Chödzom (also Chözang) village, an hour downstream, although they do not reside here. The caves are worth investigating, though these days birds are the main inhabitants, not meditating monks.

Continue along the Dzakar Chu to the wooden bridge and cross to the east (R) bank. The road to Dza Rongphu monastery from the Friendship Highway and Tashi Dzom runs along the top of the embankment. The walk to the monastery is **3 hours or more** up the valley.

A short distance upstream from the wood bridge a large tributary descends from the glaciers of Gyachung Gang, a massive peak along the ridge running east from Cho Oyu. As you continue ascending along the road, the large snow peak dominating the head of the valley is Nuptse, Everest's West Peak (25,790 ft, 7861 m), which is completely within Nepal. **A half hour** above the wood bridge a spring emerges from a grassy knoll to the left of the road. Except during the rainy season, this is often the only fresh water available other than the river until reaching the monastery. **Thirty minutes** farther, high in a side valley up to the left (northeast) is Kyelung, a former retreat for Dza Rongphu's senior monks and the seat, or *podrang*, of Trülzhik Rimpoche, the current Dza Rongphu *lama* and the senior *lama* in the Nyingmapa sect hierarchy. He fled to Nepal's Solu region in 1959 and established Tubten Chöling *ani gompa*, which has grown into the largest nunnery in Nepal. The castlelike Kyelung was destroyed during the Cultural Revolution. The meadows near here provide one of the few good campsites in this area, though it takes **nearly 1 hour** of climbing along a steep side trail to reach them.

The main road continues its ascent, twisting away from the river through arid hills and rocky plains to pass beside a large stone *chörten*. Trülzhik Rimpoche says this monument was probably built around two centuries ago when the Sherpa people from Nepal used Lho La (19,700 ft, 6006 m) instead of Nangpa La (also known as Khumbu La) as their trade route between the Khumbu Valley and Tibet. It is known locally as the Khumbu or Belyül (Nepal) *chörten*. Mountaineers familiar with the sheer 1500-foot (460-m) cliffs on the Nepal side of Lho La find it hard to believe that a glacier large enough to cross on foot could have existed there only 200 years ago.

Throughout this area are hundreds of small rock piles erected by devout Tibetans who have made the journey to Dza Rongphu and the sacred cave retreat of Guru Rimpoche farther up the valley. **About 30 minutes** past the Belyül *chörten*, Everest finally comes into view. Numerous trails now shortcut the long bends in the road along this final stretch to the monastery. In **another 30 minutes** the road descends into a deep creek bed. The Chu Ara *ani gompa* (also called Samten Chöphuk) once stood at the base of the cliffs where this creek emerges from the cleft in the ridge; it is now mostly obliterated.

Ascend from the creek gully, then follow the road for **30 minutes** into a series of morainal hills. Soon the road arcs around a rocky ridge spur and Dza Rongphu monastery explodes into full view, with the massive North Face of Mount Everest dominating the entire head of the valley.

DZA RONGPHU MONASTERY

Situated at 16,150 feet (4920 m) elevation, the monastery at Dza Rongphu (often misspelled "Rongbuk") and its accompanying hermitage retreats were introduced to the world in the 1920s through the accounts of the British mountaineering teams climbing Everest. Their descriptions of this secluded monastic hideaway, where "every animal that we saw in the valley was extraordinarily tame," could have been the inspiration for the lamasery of Shangri-La in James Hilton's well-known novel *Lost Horizon*.

Today the retreat cells are abandoned and only one of the seven monasteries and nunneries that once thrived in this remote valley is now functioning. According to Trülzhik Rimpoche, the Rongphu area was first established as a religious site 250 to 350 years ago. The first *gompa*, a Buddhist nunnery, was established about 200 years ago. By the 1950s there were nearly 250 residents, most of them nuns. The two largest *ani gompas*, Changchub Tarling and Rongchung, are now in ruins along the ridge side past Dza Rongphu. Most of the nuns fled to Nepal in 1959 with Trülzhik Rimpoche.

The present Dza Rongphu monastery is on the site where the *lama* Ngawang Tenzing Norbu originally founded the Nyingmapa *gompa*, Do-ngak Chöling, in 1901 to 1902. (This is the real name of the monastery; Dza Rongphu is actually the cave retreat farther up the valley where Guru Rimpoche meditated.) Like a phoenix, this monastery has risen from the ashes of the Cultural Revolution. About thirty monks and nuns now reside here, and a large *dukhang* has been built. At the center of this chanting hall is the raised *shuktri* of Trülzhik Rimpoche; murals of Guru Rimpoche and numerous protectors of the Nyingmapa sect adorn the walls. An adjacent temple houses a set of the *Kangyur* texts. The old photograph on this *shuktri* is of the founder, Ngawang Tenzing Norbu.

The Karma Tsangpo Valley, en route to Everest's Kangshung Face base camp

The first temple rebuilt here, Shetro *lhakhang*, is part of the nunnery and overlooks the *dukhang*. The central figure is an image of the founder.

A new guesthouse with rooms facing Mount Everest has been built near the nuns' residences at the base of the monastery. The area below the large *chörten* has been walled in and can accommodate half a dozen tents. The water source is a spring **a few minutes** to the south of the monastery along the ridge. Several small tent sites can be found on the grassy patches below the spring. A shop and restaurant are beside the parking area, although it's best to bring all the food you'll need rather than rely on this meagerly stocked establishment.

From Dza Rongphu to Everest Base Camp

Everest base camp (16,700 ft, 5090 m) and the Rongphu Glacier are a **2- to 3- hour** walk above the monastery. The road to the base camp (which takes 40 minutes by vehicle), can be bypassed for the first **30 minutes** of the hike by taking a path that stays high along the east (R) ridge side. From the entrance gate of Dza Rongphu, follow the trail north toward the freshwater spring. Continue past the pipe and traverse along the ridge. In **about 10 minutes** the path forks; the right branch descends to the base camp road in **20 minutes**. The left fork continues along the ridge, leading to the ruins of Changchub Tarling *ani gompa*. Most of the buildings were residences for the nuns; the larger structure with red walls was once the chanting hall. A little farther along the ridge are the ruins of Rongchung *ani gompa*. Below the crumbling walls are the remains of an unusual gathering of small, crudely built stone huts. The Dza Rongphu region was once a well-known meditational retreat where Buddhist hermits would have themselves sealed into one of these huts for a year, three years, or even a lifetime. Food and water were passed to them daily through an opening in the wall by an unseen servant.

The trail descends to the road below the nunneries. Initially the road parallels a tumbling but much smaller Dzakar Chu, and as the valley opens out, the road and the river diverge to opposite sides of a broad gravel plain. Before reaching the low morainal hills separating this part of the valley from the end of the glacier, the road swings around a tremendous rockfall from the east (R) ridge. At the base of this slide is a square mud-and-stone monument called a *tsha khang*, a reliquary for clay *tsha-tsha* offerings. This is a particularly good location for viewing Everest. The mountain is very close, and the broad yellow band of rock across its North Face glows with geologic antiquity. These colorful layers of compressed clay, silt, and limestone near the summit, which were once sediments at the bottom of an ancient ocean, are evidence of the cataclysmic forces that shaped the Himalaya Range.

Along the top of the rockslide between the gigantic boulders are numerous square monuments and prayer flags. A trail marked by cairns leads up through the rocks to Dza Rongphu, the Guru Rimpoche cave retreat. If you want to visit the *drubphuk*, request at Do-ngak Chöling to have the *go-nyer* accompany you with the keys. Be prepared for an incredible tour of the holy sites here! Hidden from the road are the ruins of Sherabling, a former nunnery, and the red-walled *podrang* of Ngawang Tenzing Norbu. The cave temple is enclosed by a low building; a hatch in the floor allows access into the Great Guru's soot-blackened enclave.

A pilgrim's circuit leads around the entire complex, past the *zhabje* of Lama Sangwa Dorje and several *rangjön* images in the rocks to one of the more amazing pilgrimage "sin tests" (*dikpa*) I have experienced in Tibet. A side trail from the *kora* leads up to the base of a large boulder below the cliffs, then descends into a narrow, challenging subterranean labyrinth to a chamber where no light penetrates. The *go-nyer* has all flashlights turned off, waits, then asks everyone, "Are you afraid?" Those who can truthfully say "no" are said to be free of sin. Regardless of your karma, bring a jacket—it's chilly down there, even in midsummer. After you've scrambled back up to daylight, continue in a clockwise direction on the *kora* leading back to the cave temple building.

Beyond the rockslide, the road enters a series of gravel hills that mark the advance and retreat of the Rongphu Glacier. At the far side of these deposits, below (north of) the final gravel hill before the glacier's terminus, is Everest base camp. This is the most popular site used by expeditions, as it is protected from the wind and supplied with fresh water from a natural spring. It was the base camp used by the 1924 British Everest expedition.

Rongphu Glacier Day Hike Options

Many base camp sites are scattered between the old British location and the Rongphu Glacier, including the 1960 Chinese base camp near the glacier on the far west (L) side of the valley. The Tibet Mountaineering Association (TMA) has constructed a building atop the moraine above the British camp. Besides having a small shop (alcohol and cigarettes dominate the list of goods) and several empty rooms that can be hired for the night, it features a TMA liaison officer who is stationed there during tourist season. In addition to assisting climbing expeditions, he is also here to enforce a new rule requiring all tourists hiking above 18,000 feet (5500 m) to pay a fee of US $100 *per day*. Unfortunately, the liaison officer will try to insist that all tourists on a day hike above base camp must also pay this fee, which is incorrect, and no official receipt will be issued. Bargain hard, and report the name of the errant officer to the TMA. Liaison officers are also now based at the Cho Oyu and North Shishapangma base camps. Some groups have been refused permission to hike past these base camps, while others paid a "fee" to do so.

Mount Everest and the North Face base camp

The terminal moraine of the glacier is **less than 30 minutes** across the gravel flats from the British campsite. Follow the road past base camp for **about 10 minutes** to a stream crossing. Early in the morning this ford is typically just a rock hop; by evening, especially during the summer months, the current quickens and the water level can be well above the knees in many places. If this is the case, remember that the widest part of the stream is usually the shallowest. The road continues beyond this crossing to the left (east) side of the terminal moraine.

The Rongphu Glacier is an impressive frozen river of ice waves and should not be missed if you take the effort to reach base camp. The views of the glacier and the Himalayan peaks are some of the most dramatic in Tibet. Running along the east (R) side of the glacier is the trail that expeditions use to begin their climbs. The terrain is rocky but easy enough to negotiate, as this track follows a relatively flat, natural trough between the glacier's lateral moraine and the side of the ridge. **Two hours** above the glacial terminus is a trail junction at a small, flat area (17,300 ft, 5270 m) overlooking the gully of a rushing creek. The right fork is the trail to the North Face advance base camp (ABC). To reach ABC, you must descend to the creek, but this is often a dangerous crossing. If it's possible to rock hop here, ABC is **2 to 3 hours** to the south along a hilly route on the east (R) side of the glacier. Old tin cans indicate you're getting close to ABC (also called Tilman's Camp, and Lake Camp; 17,900 ft, 5460 m), which is an oasis of green meadows, flowing water, and shallow ponds set in a world of shattered rock slopes. A rock enclosure has been built for containing expedition garbage. If possible, continue a little farther and higher along the ridge past this camp for views of Everest peaking around Changtse (24,780 ft, 7553 m; the North Peak of Everest) and a chance to look down on the thousands of jagged ice seracs thrusting from the Dza Rongphu Glacier. Continuing up the valley toward Lho La (19,704 ft, 6006 m) requires crossing the glacier. Although ice axes and crampons are not necessary, only experienced and well-equipped parties should attempt this route.

If the creek is too high to cross, expeditions are forced to detour up the left fork from the flat area above the creek gully. The trail climbs steeply, passing Camp I (17,700 ft, 5400 m) for the North Col route up Everest, then onto the terminus of the East Rongphu Glacier. A cairned route leads over hills of moraine to the south (L) ridge above the glacier and the creek. The route to the North Face ABC then descends left (west) back down to the main valley. The route to the advance base camp at Camp III (20,600 ft, 6280 m) for expeditions climbing the North Col or Everest's Northeast Ridge continues east along a cairned route on the East Rongphu Glacier. This trek, which should be attempted only by extremely fit and thoroughly acclimatized parties, is described in "Beyond Everest Base Camp."

LEAVING DZA RONGPHU

If you trekked to the Rongphu area from Dingri and plan to walk back, at least three different routes loop back to Dingri and the Friendship Highway. The trek from Dza Rongphu to Dingri takes **3 to 4 days** regardless of which pass you cross. If food supplies need replenishing, the routes going through Pasum or Tashi Dzom and then crossing Ding La or Dingri Lamar La are the best choices. If you trekked along the road over Pang La from the turnoff on the Friendship Highway at kilometer marker 5145/6 (see "The Trek to Everest Base Camp via Pang La," below), there are four passes to choose from to complete the loop trek from Dza Rongphu to the Dingri plains.

Transportation from the Dzakar Chu Valley to the highway and Shekar typically originates in Tashi Dzom, which is a **1½- to 2-day** walk from the monastery, or a 2-hour drive. The highway junction at kilometer marker 5145/6 is at least another 2-hour drive away. With an early start and optimum road conditions, a vehicle can reach Nyelam (km marker 5345/6), and sometimes even Zhangmu (km marker 5379), from Dza Rongphu in one day. Occasionally a truck or a tractor-pulled cart will take passengers from the monastery to Tashi Dzom and Shekar, although the travel time will be considerably slower. A tractor heading to Shekar from Dza Rongphu will often take two days, including an overnight at Tashi Dzom. Most vehicles that come to the monastery or base camp have been hired by tour groups or climbing expeditions. If you need a ride, asking the driver is as important as asking the group.

THE RETURN TO DINGRI VIA DINGRI LAMAR LA

The **4- to 5-day** trek from Dza Rongphu monastery to Dingri over Dingri Lamar La (15,800 ft, 4820 m) is the easiest of the four different routes crossing from the Dzakar Chu Valley to the Dingri plains. It is also the final leg of an **8- to 10-day** loop walk to Everest base camp that begins in Dingri and crosses Lamna La (the first half of this loop is described above).

The route to Dingri Lamar La from Dza Rongphu initially descends north along the road to the village of Tashi Dzom. If you don't plan to camp, note that Chödzom (also Chözang; 14,550 ft, 4430 m) is the first possible place to spend the night, **5 to 7 hours**

Dingri village and Cho Oyu peak

below the monastery. A tea shop and guesthouse are next to the school compound, and nearby there are two small shops selling a variety of noodles, candy, and beer. In town are the remains of a crumbling monastery now used as a goat pen. A *lhakhang* associated with Chöphuk *gompa* has been built above the town on its southern outskirts. The residents in this town and other settlements along the Dzakar Chu are not as friendly or as helpful as people elsewhere in Tibet. You might think that their attitudes have been influenced by the great influx of tourists and climbing expeditions over the past decade— until you consider the Sherpas, who have had even greater exposure to trekkers and climbers for a longer period of time, yet remain warm and receptive. How can there be such a difference between these neighboring people? A fellow from India once told me that people are like the soil they live on; when the soil is hard, so are the people. The ground here is definitely hard.

Below Chödzom the valley opens out and the gradient is much less steep. **One and a half hours** down the valley the road crosses to the west (L) side of the Dzakar Chu on a cement bridge. This structure was built in 1988 to facilitate the Tri-nation (Japan, China, and Nepal) Everest expedition, which placed climbers starting from different sides of the mountain on the summit at the same time. **A few minutes** past the bridge is the settlement of Dza-phün, which is split into two small clusters of houses. The second group of houses is **another 10 minutes** farther along. Across from Dza-phün a large tributary enters the Dzakar Chu on the east (R) side of the valley. In 1921 the Everest Reconnaissance team followed this drainage on the approach to Kharta Qu from Dingri during their survey of Mount Everest. This trek to Kharta Qu and to the upper stretches of the Arun River crosses Döya La (16,810 ft, 5124 m) and takes **4 days**.

The settlements and topography along this stretch of the river have an uncanny resemblance to the scenery of the Southwestern United States. You'll see flat-roofed, white adobe houses; people with dark, braided hair wearing turquoise jewelry; and grand ridges of swirling rock formations. You'll also breathe in clear, dry desert air. The swirling flocks of gray-and-white hill pigeons fluttering across the fields seem almost out of place here.

Eventually the road crosses a smaller cement bridge over a creek from the left (west) draining the Ding Valley. Dingri, via Ding La (16,200 ft, 4940 m), is a **long 2 days** away.

A series of lush meadows at the upper end of this valley offers some of the nicest wilderness camps in the Everest region. The meadows beside this bridge are perfect for a picnic lunch, offereing one of the best views of Everest in the Dzakar Chu Valley.

Pasum is **a half hour** below the Ding Chu. Up on the ridge to the left (west) before you reach the town is Zaphu *gompa*, an affiliate of Dza Rongphu monastery and one of the only active *gompas* in this lower part of the Dzakar Chu. A handful of monks have returned here, and several buildings have been rebuilt, including a rustic *lhakhang*. The raised platform presiding over the floor cushions is reserved for Trülzhik Rimpoche, the head *lama* for Dza Rongphu. Beside the rows of cushions is a colorful rack of prayer texts with twelve volumes of the Yum, a metaphysical text of Indian origin that is an important part of the Nyingmapa religious tradition.

Pasum (13,800 ft, 4210 m) is the largest settlement above Tashi Dzom. A local resident has established a guesthouse/tea shop in the middle of town. It has a few beds and the kitchen serves sweet or salted tea, *thukpa*, and *momos*. Watch out for the kids in Pasum; they sometimes chuck rocks at trekkers passing through who don't yield a pocketload of *jiri*, or sweets. Don't encourage this bad habit by complying with their requests. **Less than an hour** beyond Pasum the road squeezes between the river and a prominent rocky outcrop capped by Tretong Dzong. Throughout the mud-walled ruins are hundreds of stone offering piles erected by visiting pilgrims. Fading frescoes can still be seen on a few inner walls.

The valley opens out and is remarkably fertile compared to the dry desert environs of the upper valley. With the help of irrigation, the predominant crops are barley, wheat, peas, and rapeseed. Because the road tends to wander between numerous small settlements, you can save considerable time by following the shortcuts, which bypass the wide bends in the road.

Tashi Dzom (13,500 ft, 4110 m), the *shang* for the Everest region, is **2½ to 3 hours** below Pasum. (Tashi Dzom is also called Phadruk Qu, and is known as Paru to the Chinese. On some maps it is spelled Pa-drug or Pharuk.) At Tashi Dzom the road splits after a small bridge crossing. The right fork leads east to Kharta Qu, the starting point for the Kangshung base camp trek. The road to the left continues up the tributary valley to the north toward the Gara Chu Valley and to Pang La and the Friendship Highway. At this junction are two small but tidy guesthouses with restaurants; stock up on fresh vegetables, meat, eggs, kerosene and other supplies, for there is little available anywhere else except in Dingri or Shekar. Several general stores are also at this junction.

If you spend a day in Tashi Dzom, it is worth climbing up to the ruined walls decorated with prayer flags on the ridge directly above (south of) the town. West of town and hidden high on the ridge across from these ruins is Gyedong *gompa*, an isolated hermitage that has yet to be repaired. The easiest approach is to walk **15 minutes** north up the valley toward Pang La, but on the west (R) side of the creek, not along the road. The *gompa* is set into a cleft in the twisted rock formations towering over Tashi Dzom. An obscure trail leads to the ruins starting from the base of the ridge.

Since it is located at a major crossroads, Tashi Dzom is the main transportation junction for this area. Intermittent trucks and tractor-pulled carts carry passengers to Kharta Qu, Dza Rongphu, and Shekar. Burros and horses can usually be hired here to carry gear. Bargain hard and watch for hidden charges such as the guide's food, lodging, or animal feed.

The route to Dingri Lamar La from Tashi Dzom initially heads north on the road toward Pang La. **In less than an hour** a smaller road into the Gara Chu Valley veers off to the left (northwest). Turn here and follow this track across the barren plain, reaching the quiet, whitewashed settlement of Nyumda in **20 minutes**. The desert has been brought to life here with irrigation; shimmering fields of barley and rapeseed cover the valley floor during the summer.

Ruins lie scattered throughout this region atop high embankments and craggy ridges. **About one hour** past Nyumda the ruins of Seyum *gompa* are perched above the rocky mouth of a tributary entering from the right (north). Across the main valley are the remains of an old *dzong*. The road remains on the north (L) side of the valley for most of the way to the pass. Few vehicles ever come this way, making it seem more like a wide country path than a motor road. Small settlements dot the valley floor, and wherever water flows there are barley fields. **Two hours** from Nyumda the track passes the ruins of a former noble family's residence. **Fifteen minutes** farther is the village of Trongpa. At the base of a cliff above this town is Kare *gompa*, a functioning monastery with several monks in residence.

From Trongpa the valley starts edging around to the left (west). The ridges become more rocky and close in on the broad valley plain. Across the river along the south (R) bank are an extensive series of ruins that may have been a fortified town. The ruins of Rejung, a fortress/monastery destroyed during the Cultural Revolution, sit on a hillside above the road **40 minutes** beyond Trongpa. The monks affiliated with this temple reside in Gara, a village **10 minutes** up the road.

Gara (14,600 ft, 4450 m), the largest settlement in this valley, is divided into two main groups of houses located **a few minutes** apart. Many of the buildings are beautiful three-storied residences with inward-sloping fortresslike walls. The painted stripes on these houses consist of three colors; most other homes in the Dingri and Rongphu areas have only two. The interiors of these buildings are a maze of rooms leading in different directions, all connected by a network of zigzagging staircases.

If you are walking with a guide, this is one of the last places to spend the night before ascending Dingri Lamar La; only a few small clusters of houses lie beyond Gara. The pass is still a **5-hour** climb up the valley from this town. If you stay in Gara for the night, it is possible to reach Dingri the next day with an early start and **a long, steady day** of walking. Burros and horses can be hired in Gara.

The terrain in this area is noticeably wilder, with picturesque rock formations bursting from the ridge tops like rows of flatirons. Large tributaries enter from both sides of the main valley, and each of these leads up to a high pass crossing into one of the adjacent valleys. **One hour or more** beyond Gara the cart track passes below the ruins of Nyasa *gompa*. A small *lhakhang* here has been rebuilt by the local monks. In **10 minutes** the road climbs onto a rocky outcrop above the river, overlooking the arid pasturelands that have replaced the cultivated fields. The meadows provide numerous potential campsites beside the river, which is now just a stream.

In **1 hour or more** the road crosses to the south (R) bank of this drainage. Continue up the valley for **1½ hours** to where an obvious shortcut climbs up the south (R) ridge to bypass several large switchbacks in the road. Dingri Lamar La (15,800 ft, 4820 m) is a **1-hour** climb, not including rest stops, from the base of this ridge. The pass is a broad, gentle summit marked with *la-dze* and prayer flags. Good pasturing grass covers the nearby ridges, but below to the west the Dingri plains and the surrounding hills are dry and barren.

Descend from the pass into a long, winding valley, reaching another large *la-dze* beside the track in **1½ hours**. **Ten minutes** beyond here the road continues left (west) toward Lungjang, following the stream through a rocky cleft between the ridges. A wide trail leaves the road at this turn and continues straight ahead (northwest) to Nelung, the only village before Dingri. **Twenty minutes** beyond this junction the trail passes a long *mani* wall, then ascends a low, rocky saddle in the ridge. Descend to Nelung (14,700 ft, 4480 m) in **40 minutes** from the saddle, passing the ruins of Tsaribuk *gompa* on the hill to the left (south).

Dingri is **4 to 5 hours** beyond Nelung. If it is late, consider staying here for the night. The route to Dingri descends from Nelung for **30 minutes,** then fords the main stream of this drainage. The cart track from Dingri Lamar La runs along its south (L) embankment. The terrain becomes very arid as the valley turns right to meet the plains. The track eventually extends beyond the last ridges, then swings right (north) onto the Dingri plains. Dingri is easily recognized by its large cluster of white buildings at the foot of a large, lone hill to the right (northwest).

THE TREK TO EVEREST BASE CAMP VIA PANG LA

When Tibet opened to tourism in 1984, Everest base camp quickly became the most popular trekking destination. Because there were few vehicles in the country at that time, the road over Pang La, constructed for the 1960 Chinese Everest expedition, was the preferred walking route. Traffic was almost nonexistent, and, despite being on a road, one had a feeling of remoteness in grand scenery, making this route an outstanding trek. Although vehicles are far more common these days, it is worth considering doing the journey on foot.

This trek of **3 to 4 days** begins in a desert valley to the south of the highway between kilometer markers 5145 and 5146, about 4 miles (7 km) west of the Shekar Checkpoint (km marker 5139). Food and shelter are available for the entire journey up to Dza Rongphu monastery, and the monks there hire out basic but fairly comfortable rooms. There's even a small restaurant in operation during the summer months. A tent and a stove are not necessary, but they do provide freedom from constantly relying upon villagers for food and lodging.

The turnoff for Pang La is a minor junction that can easily be overlooked; a small sign for the Chomolangma Nature Preserve marks the turnoff. If you are coming from the Shekar Checkpoint, look for a small bridge after kilometer marker 5145. A few hundred yards farther to the west the road to Everest turns south into a dry tributary valley, following the base of a sweeping rocky ridge. Che (14,400 ft, 4390 m), the only village before the pass, is **1 hour or more** from the turnoff. This town of forty houses ringed by concentric circles of terraced barley fields is situated above a deep stream channel near the junction of two large valleys. Pang La is a climb of **4 hours or more** from Che into the barren hills to the south. Unless you get an early start, consider spending the night here with a family or camping above the town near the stream. Camping lower in the valley can be a problem, because the stream tends to disappear into the sand and rocks. Unless it has rained heavily, the only available water is near Che. One of the pleasures of this town's hospitality is the chance to sample the local *chang*. The brew here is served by pouring hot water over fermented barley berries. It is drunk with a wooden straw in much the same way as millet *tongba* is consumed in eastern Nepal and Sikkim.

Burros can usually be hired in Che to carry gear to Pang La. For a burro and guide to continue beyond the pass to Tashi Dzom, the next major village, you might have to pay at least an extra day's wages for their return journey. The folks in Che may not be enthusiastic about taking their pack animals all the way to Dza Rongphu; plan on hiring another animal and guide in Tashi Dzom for the rest of the journey.

Che is one of the entrance points to the Chomolangma Nature Preserve. As of 1999, the entry fee for foreigners was 65 *yuan* (about US $8). Stiff vehicle tariffs (400 *yuan* per car, 600 *yuan* per supply truck) are collected from groups to cover road maintenance. Your Alien Travel Permit for Everest base camp will be checked here. Shigatse is the nearest Public Security Bureau (PSB) office where these can be issued.

Pang La (16,700 ft, 5090 m) is a **4- to 5-hour** walk following the road south up the valley past the last houses of Che. In **10 minutes** the road veers left (east) to begin a long series of switchbacks up a wide alluvial fan. The first of several shortcuts leaves this route to avoid the bends in the road.

When locals travel in this area they often use an adjacent pass called Gya-u La (16,600 ft, 5060 m), located farther to the left (east) of the road. This is a much better walking route, with good, remote campsites along the way. This alternative rejoins the road a few hours above Tashi Dzom. If you're trekking on your own, it's worth hiring a guide and a pack animal to take you to the top of the pass, as the approach is obscure in places. From the summit the route down is easy to follow.

When the road leaves the valley floor to begin a series of long switchbacks up to the Pang La used by vehicles, the foot trail over Gya-u La continues up to the south toward the stream flowing along the far left (east) side of the valley. The trail to Gya-u La crosses to its east (R) bank and ascends the ridge beside a narrow creek gully. Climb **15 minutes** above the stream ford to a long switchback in the road cutting across the ridge. Don't turn onto this road, but cross it and continue climbing steeply beside the small gully to the rounded top of this ridge (16,300 ft, 5970 m). Take a break here to enjoy the fabulous scenery. The snowcapped peaks far to the north are part of the Nyenchen Thanglha Range. Gya-u La is still **45 minutes** away on the trail leading around the ridge to the right (south).

Follow the flat ridge top, then traverse south across the slope of the ridge to reach the cairns on the Gya-u La summit (16,600 ft, 5060 m). The pass for vehicles is farther to the right (west) and hidden by the ridge. If the weather is clear, the giants of the Himalaya Range can be seen marching majestically across the southern horizon. The large, pale, snowy peak looming to the south is Makalu (27,805 ft, 8475 m). After a few intermediate mountains, the next large peak to the right is the massive triangular summit of Everest (29,028 ft, 8848 m). Farther to the right is a huge, snowy massif that includes Gyachung Gang (25,990 ft, 7922 m) and Cho Oyu (26,748 ft, 8153 m). Several breaks in the ridges below the pass yield views of the Dzakar Chu and its broad, flat valley.

Only **10 minutes** below the pass is a grassy campsite (16,400 ft, 5000 m) beside a freshwater spring. Although this site is only big enough for a couple of tents and offers limited protection from the wind, it's a great location for viewing the mountains. In summer look for the obvious flat patches of green vegetation to the right (west) of the main trail. The nearest settlement is **2 hours** below Gya-u La. The town of Tashi Dzom, which has several guesthouses and restaurants, is **about 5 hours** from the pass.

The trail from Gya-u La descends along the east (L) side of a gently curving valley to reach the road in **1 hour or more**. The route to Dza Rongphu monastery and Everest base camp now follows the road to Tashi Dzom and the Dzakar Chu Valley. Many trails shortcut the longer switchbacks. Descend steeply beside a rushing torrent that crashes through a narrow gorge of upended rock. **About an hour** after meeting the road, pass a small cluster of houses tucked into a bend on the east (L) bank. Despite the parched hillsides, the irrigated barley crop is vibrantly green here during the summer.

About 2 hours beyond this small settlement, a road turns off to the right (west) into a broad valley. This is the old trade route up the Gara Chu Valley to Dingri Lamar La (15,800 ft, 4820 m). The trek over this pass from Tashi Dzom to the Dingri plains is described above (see "The Return to Dingri via Dingri Lamar La") as an alternative exit from the Dzakar Chu Valley. Tashi Dzom (13,500 ft, 4110 m) is **45 minutes** farther down the road.

Dza Rongphu monastery is **2 days** to the south following the Dzakar Chu to its source at the Rongphu Glacier. The last place where you will find accommodations is Chödzom, a **1-day** walk above Tashi Dzom. Dza Rongphu is **another long day's** walk; consider breaking up this stretch over **3 days**. This walk is described above, in reverse.

Beyond Everest Base Camp

Note: Trekking beyond Everest base camp (16,700 ft, 5090 m) should not be attempted unless you are prepared to take the time to acclimatize properly while ascending to the higher camps. Acute mountain sickness (AMS) is a serious environment-related illness that can strike anyone, especially at these extreme elevations. You should be well acquainted with the symptoms of AMS and be capable of monitoring yourself and others in your group for the adverse affects that can occur on a trek such as this (see "Staying Healthy").

This adventure, which I have named the World's Highest Trek, is an incredible journey to advance base camp at Camp III (20,500 ft, 6250 m) and the base of the North Col via the East Rongphu Glacier (also called Rongphu Shar Glacier). Nowhere else on this planet can you hike on a trail to such elevations without needing crampons, ice axes, or mountaineering skills. This tributary of the main Rongphu Glacier flows through a remarkably flat valley in a great arc around the Changtse massif (24,878 ft, 7583 m; marked by a triangular peak symbol on Map No. 8), Everest's North Peak. Along the central crest of this glacier a corridor of flat moraine, known to climbers as the Serac Highway, winds safely between the towering ice pinnacles all the way up to Camp III.

The East Rongphu Glacier is relatively free of crevasses and other hazards on its surface, but you should know that ice conditions and the location of the trail vary from year to year as well as during a single summer. Caution should always be used when traveling on a glacier. Climbing gear may not be necessary, but common sense definitely is. If the weather deteriorates or trail conditions become unsafe, turn back and be satisfied with where you stopped. Or try again in another day or two.

A trek of this nature is best left for a professional trekking company to organize: The food and equipment requirements are more than most people want to carry at these elevations, and arranging yaks to haul gear beyond base camp is not possible unless you can supply tents and warm clothing for the yak herders.

The best months for good glacial conditions are June to August, although this is also when monsoon clouds can obscure Everest's summit for days at a time. The route up the East Rongphu Glacier is not particularly difficult to follow, with the exception of the rough terrain between Camp I and the Interim Camp below Camp II. To ensure proper acclimatization, I highly recommend trekking up to the Rongphu base camp rather than driving. After reaching base camp, allow **6 to 8 additional days,** including rest days, to safely complete the round-trip journey to Camp III and back. **At least 1 night** should be spent at Dza Rongphu monastery, and **at least 2 nights** should be spent acclimatizing at base camp. Don't just laze around during these rest days: A day hike to higher elevations is one of the best ways to help your body adjust to the altitude. Allow **a minimum of 5 days** to reach Camp III from the base camp, plus **1 or 2 more days** for the return trek.

Daytime temperatures on the glacier during the summer are quite mild despite the elevation, but that doesn't mean it can't get cold. Light snowfalls are not uncommon; at times it may rain. Apply sunblock frequently and wear dark glacier glasses. A broad-brimmed felt hat like those worn by Tibetans is a good pre-trek investment.

Camp I is **2½ hours** from Everest base camp. Initially the trail follows the east (L) side of the main Rongphu Glacier (the beginning of this walk is described in "Rongphu Glacier Day Hike Options"). **One and a half hours** south from the glacial terminus is a flat area (17,300 ft, 5270 m) along the lateral moraine, above a steep creek gully. The trail forks here; the smaller track to the left (east) climbs up to Camp I in **less than 1 hour**.

During rest stops enjoy the views of the Himalaya and the Rongphu Glacier's frozen waves of blue ice. The graceful, bullet-shaped summit across the glacier to the southwest

Ice seracs on the East Rongphu Glacier

is Pumori (23,441 ft, 7145 m); behind this peak is Kala Pattar, a popular trekking destination for viewing Mount Everest on the Nepal side.

Camp I (17,700 ft, 5400 m) is set in a barren world of morainal hills under beautifully sculpted, yellow-orange granite cliffs. It is easy to spot, as dozens of tent sites have been leveled throughout the rocks and boulders. The next camp is too far to reach in a single day, so stop here for the night. To help yourself acclimatize spend the remainder of the afternoon exploring the gravelly snout of the East Rongphu Glacier, only **20 minutes** beyond this camp. The glacial terminus resembles the tailings of a huge gravel quarry, with great mounds of crushed rock and sand filling the valley floor. The outlet creek emerges from the base of these hills, although little ice is visible until farther up the valley.

Camp II is a long way off and 1500 feet (460 m) higher. Rather than go that far in one day, most expeditions walk **3 hours or more** and stop at the Interim Camp (18,800 ft, 5730 m). From Camp I the route to Camp III crosses to the end of the East Rongphu Glacier. The trail descends to the edge of the outlet creek, then angles south over the gravel hills along a cairned route to the south (L) side of the glacier.

The trail descends from the gravel mounds onto a mud plain, then climbs into a jumble of rocky moraine. The route is generally well marked, although it is easy to stray onto dead ends. The trail climbs and descends over the gravel hills, always staying above the (L) edge of the ice. There is one particularly unstable section where small rock and gravel slides often obliterate the trail, making progress slow, especially for loaded yaks. **Two to 3 hours** above the glacial terminus the trail climbs high onto the hills above the west (L) flank of the glacier. The large tributary ice floe tumbling down across the valley (east) is the Far East Rongphu Glacier. Directly across from it and in the middle of the main glacier is where the Interim Camp (18,800 ft, 5730 m) is typically located. This is a good place to spend **2 nights** acclimatizing before advancing to Camp II. Nearby, the first ice seracs, or *nieve penitentes*, resemble dozens of Sydney Opera Houses sailing on a choppy gray sea. (*Nieve penitentes*, a Spanish term meaning "snow nuns," is used in the Andes to describe the peaks of ice rising from the surface of glaciers, which resemble the white-robed attire of many South American Catholic nuns.)

Sometimes the Interim Camp is established in the hills along the west (L) side of the glacier, while other years it has been located near the base of the long gravel-covered moraine running along the center of the glacier. The moraine is a good landmark, for the route to Camps II and III follows this central spine of ice and talus. If there are no tents at this Interim Camp, look for flattened tent sites with beds of straw laid over the rocks. A creek flows below the camp along the base of the glacier's central ridge, although early in the season it is usually hidden by a thick snow bridge. For trekkers who have climbed 2000 feet (610 m) in two days, this Interim Camp is a well-placed rest stop. Not far from camp are views of Everest emerging above the smooth white wall of Changtse.

Camp II is **3½ hours** above this Interim Camp. When the snow bridge spanning the creek is intact, the most direct route climbs onto the central ridge behind this camp. By mid- to late August this bridge has often melted, exposing short but slippery inclines of ice that can be a problem to get past, especially for loaded yaks. Hunt around for an alternative access. It may be necessary to cut a few steps in the icy slopes and pile up small rock platforms to help the yaks through.

The scenery from this central ridge is stunning. Huge seracs soar as high as 50 feet (15 m) above the glacier's surface along both sides of this rocky spine. The trail remains a safe distance from these icy turrets as it rollercoasters over the great heaps of gravel. At times the path becomes rather faint, but the route used by the expeditions typically follows the ridge crest and is usually marked with rock cairns. Unfortunately, candy wrappers are as good as cairns for identifying the way.

Two to 3 hours above the Interim Camp the central ridgeline leads into a confusion of ice where the Changtse Glacier enters from the right (west). Camp II (19,500 ft, 5940 m) is only **15 minutes** from here, but the correct route can be difficult to find. This camp is typically located along the south (L) side of the glacier, below a large cliff at the eastern end of the Changtse Glacier junction. The abundance of rusty tin cans is a sad tribute to the many expeditions that have camped here. The most historic bit of refuse in

The Serac Highway on the World's Highest Trek

this area is an old cloth-and-rubber insulated wire that pops up now and again among the rocks and gravel. This is the original telephone line laid between base camp and the North Col in 1924 to keep the British climbers informed about the advance of the monsoon from India. It's not unusual to see the herders using lengths of it to tie down loads on their yaks.

Glaciers large and small spill into the valley from every direction around Camp II; the appropriately named Serac Highway continues to extend its unusual gravel arm through the center of the ice formations. The third camp is another 1200 feet (370 m) higher. If anyone has a rough time at Camp II trying to sleep or wakes up with a headache in the morning, consider visiting the higher camp on a day hike and return to spend a second night here. If you're with a commercial trek, often it's the Nepalese staff who have the worst problems with the altitude, not the group.

The route to Camp III takes **4 hours or more** and returns to the center of the seracs from the second camp. The glacier now bends to the right (southeast) around the eastern flank of Changtse, and the trail soon ascends the largest series of hills on this part of the trek. This is a hard way to start the morning, but soon the morainal spine mellows into a gentle incline that is sometimes no more than 30 feet (9 m) wide between the icy walls. The infamous "Unclimbed Ridge," the Northeast Ridge of Mount Everest, can be seen at the end of the valley; it was finally climbed by Russell Brice (New Zealand) and Harry Taylor (United Kingdom) in 1988.

As the glacier turns sharply to the right, the seracs quickly disappear. The trail along the moraine now follows a series of low gravel humps on the west (L) edge of the glacier. As if a magic spell has been cast, the rough, broken surface of the glacier transforms into a smooth, vast plain of snowy ice fields lapping onto the ridge sides and spilling over the passes in great white sheets. Nowhere else is there an area so large and flat at this height. Follow the cairns (and the candy wrappers) along the gravel slopes to the top of a ridge. There are a few cleared tent sites here—and probably several discarded oxygen bottles. The main camp is **15 minutes** farther up the valley, depending on how well your lungs are handling this climb.

Camp III (20,500 ft, 6250 m), the advance base camp for the North Col route up Mount Everest, is situated within a group of gravel mounds beside the glacier. The Pinnacles, the fearsome group of rock palisades that kept the Northeast Ridge unclimbed for so long, rise nearly 1 mile (1480 m) straight up (south) from this camp. Toward the west is the North Col (23,182 ft, 7066 m), a snow-choked dip in the mountains connecting Everest's Northeast Ridge and Changtse. Most amazing of all is the ridge extending above the Pinnacles to the southwest: the striated rock summit of Everest. The top of this mountain appears phenomenally close, as it is little more than 8000 feet (2400 m) higher than Camp III. This is the closest nonclimbers can get to the top. With a pair of binoculars, you're almost there.

The gravel hills can be followed beside the glacier for **about 1 hour** beyond Camp III, passing more littered campsites along the way. The elevation is around 21,000 feet (6400 m) where the moraine ends at the snowfields extending from the foot of the North Col. You've completed the World's Highest Trek! But don't attempt to walk across the glacier unless a route has been previously established.

The journey from Camp III back to Camp II takes **2 hours**; base camp is a **long 1-day** walk. If you have the time (and enough food), spend **2 days** walking out so you can enjoy the scenery and get your eyes off the toe of your boots.

THE KANGSHUNG FACE BASE CAMP TREK

The **9- to 10-day** loop walk to the secluded Kangshung Face base camp of Mount Everest begins at Kharta Qu (12,100 ft, 3690 m), a small administrative town (*shang*) above the Phung Chu, just north of the Nepal border. Unlike the arid environs found a few ridges over in the Dzakar Chu Valley, this region is affected by India's summer monsoon. Forests of scrub juniper, dwarf rhododendron, and birch cover the higher ridges, and dense thickets of willows edge the creeks in the lower valleys. Farther to the south, in the Karma Tsangpo Valley, the monsoon is virtually unimpeded, supporting a lush coniferous forest.

Kharta Qu is 40 miles (64 km) southeast of Tashi Dzom on a road descending the lower stretches of the Dzakar Chu. If you need transportation, you'll find trucks and tractor carts gathering paying passengers in Tashi Dzom for this half-day journey.

The road to Kharta Qu branches east from Tashi Dzom at the junction in the center of town. The broad, green Dzakar Chu Valley soon narrows into a spectacular rocky gorge then opens out again into a deep desert canyon. About halfway to Kharta Qu the Phung Chu (the main tributary of Nepal's Arun River) enters from the left (northeast), punching through a wild range of rugged peaks to meet the Dzakar Chu. The road climbs above this confluence and remains high on a plateau of silt and rock debris all the way to Kharta Qu, a gathering of walled administrative compounds that includes a boarding school for Tibetan children, several shops, a small health post, a few residences, and a very basic guesthouse. Trek groups usually continue 2 miles (3 km) past Kharta Qu to a large meadow camp beside the Kharta Tsangpo, just below the town of Yulok. Individual trekkers heading to the Kangshung base camp can arrange for yaks and a guide in the *shang*, or in the towns of Yulok or Yulba, where the herders live. Tents and stoves are necessary due to the remote nature of this walk. All food should be purchased before arriving in Kharta Qu.

The most direct route used by climbing expeditions to reach the Kangshung Face base camp takes **4 to 5 days** via Langma La (17,200 ft, 5240 m), a spectacular pass and, if weather allows, some of the grandest Himalayan scenery to be found. A slightly longer, alternative trek to the base camp crosses Sha-u La (15,700 ft, 4790 m), a lower pass to the southeast of Langma La that approaches the base camp via the Karma Tsangpo Valley. This route, which is popular with commercial trekking agencies, requires **5 to 6 days** (depending on the pace of your yak men) to reach the base camp. It then takes **4 days** to loop back to Kharta Qu via Langma La.

Since it often takes a day to arrange for yaks before the trek can begin, consider going on a day hike to acclimatize and stretch your legs. Visit the towns of Yulok and Yulba, stroll along the Kharta Tsangpo, or do the **4-hour** hike up to Zamchung La (14,300 ft, 4360 m). The latter is an opportunity to gain some altitude and have views into the

Valley of Lakes, a remote glacial basin with a dozen or so lakes, named during the 1921 British Reconnaissance of Mount Everest.

An easy but roundabout route from the meadow camp near Kharta Qu to Zamchung La follows a derelict logging road to the west of Yulba. The most direct way follows the river upstream for **20 minutes**, then crosses a bridge to the south (R) side. A trail leaves the road and ascends up to the left (south) in **less than 10 minutes** to Yulok, an attractive town of twenty-five houses. Beyond here trail finding is not always easy; consider hiring a guide.

Walk through the village, then head south on a trail up through terraced barley fields. At the top of the fields the trail splits. Go right and ascend the scrub-covered hill. A good trail leads west from the crest down through hills of moraine, into the creek draining the series of glacial lakes below Zamchung La. Rock hop to the west (L) side, then follow the trail up the ridge to meet the logging road. In May and June the ridges in this area are abloom with rhododendrons—white, purple, and pink-flowering bushes grace the lower slopes, while higher up they're mostly yellow.

Several trails shortcut bends in the road, then meet up at Zamchung La. From the pass, the Valley of Lakes falls away at your feet. A steep trail zigzags down to the valley floor. The road continues south to where construction was halted. A trail continues along the upper ridges to Chok La, then descends into the forests of the Karma Tsangpo Valley. There's a good chance you'll meet yak caravans or locals carrying sawed boards to Kharta Qu; the timber industry here, though small, is an important aspect of the local economy. Allow **2½ hours or more** for the return to Yulok from Zamchung La.

TO THE KANGSHUNG FACE BASE CAMP

The route to both Langma La and Sha-u La follows the road west from the meadow camp along the milky glacial waters of the Kharta Tsangpo. Fortified by this flowing water, the nearby desert terrain supports thickets of wild rose and barberry. You might also see brilliant white-capped river chats flashing red tails as they wing above the water, or small parties of Prince Henri's laughing thrushes stealing through the undergrowth. As the road winds upstream the valley walls open up, revealing distant views of great forested ridges. Langma La is at the head of a large tributary entering from the left (southwest). The route over Sha-u La also ascends to the south via the adjacent valley to the east.

Follow the road past the bridge crossing to Yulok. In **less than 1 hour** the road crosses to the south (R) side of the river on a wooden bridge, then continues upstream. About 600 feet (180 m) farther along the road is a side trail up the embankment to Yulba, the largest town in this area. The rock walls of these houses are not painted white as in other areas in Central Tibet, creating the feeling that they are fortifications. Stacks of firewood are piled neatly atop the flat roofs of each home, providing an orange-brown ring of color above the somber gray walls.

Not far past the trail to Yulba, the road, which has fallen into disrepair and is now just a wide track, climbs away from the river toward Zamchung La. The trail to the base camps, though, continues west following the river. In **15 minutes** the trail forks above a stream.

The larger path down to the right is the direct route to Langma La and the Kangshung Valley. It crosses the stream gully and leads farther up the river to the settlements of Raphuk and Lhundrubling (13,100 ft, 3990 m). Although Langma La can be reached in **1½ days**, you should keep in mind that it is 4100 feet (1250 m) above Lhundrubling. In order to acclimatize properly, consider resting two nights en route to the pass, with a final camp at Lhatse meadows (15,700 ft, 4790 m). From here Langma La is **2½ to 3½ hours** away; the Pethang Ringmo camp in the Kangshung Valley can be reached in **2½ days** (see below for the trek description, in reverse).

The route to Sha-u La follows the smaller left fork from the junction at the stream. Cross the stream and climb up the west (L) ridge. The trail soon follows the right side of an irrigation ditch, past stands of dwarf rhododendron and a large meadow. The yak men in this area are notoriously difficult. If you have hired yaks and they haven't caught up to you yet, wait, as you may be camping here if they get their usual late start. From this meadow the trail now crosses to the left side of the irrigation channel and ascends to the top of a large moraine ridge, marked by a *la-dze* and prayer flags. Across the Kharta Tsangpo Valley and high above the barley fields, tucked in a stand of stunted junipers, is a small white *lhakhang* called Tarpaling. Lower on the ridge are the ruined walls of Ganden Chöpel *gompa*, which was visited when the Everest Reconnaissance team explored this valley in 1921.

The trail now angles up the moraine to the south, toward the mountains and Sha-u La. In **30 minutes or more**, reach a large meadow camp (13,650 ft, 4160 m) above the Dambuk Chu, which drains from Sha-u La. If you have yaks, the herders will probably call it a day once they reach here. The next good camp is **2 to 3 hours** farther up the creek, but it is 1300 feet (400 m) higher, situated by a group of lakes at the base of Sha-u La. In order to acclimatize before crossing the pass, stop here for the night. The yak herders typically stop here as the first of five to six stages to the Pethang Ringmo camp below base camp. While this means each trekking day only lasts 2 to 4 hours, it allows time for exploration of nearby ridges for the incredible Himalayan vistas.

Ten minutes from the meadow camp the trail crosses the Dambuk Chu to the west (L) side. Willow bushes line the creek here, although in general the vegetation is more sparse than in the valleys farther east. The trail is very rocky as it ascends beside the Dambuk Chu, taking **2 to 3 hours** to reach the next camp (14,950 ft, 4560 m) at the north end of a pair of lakes known as Tsho Sha-u. If the weather is clear, this is a superb campsite. Makalu (27,805 ft, 8475 m), the world's fifth-highest peak, looms impressively to the south, and to the right (west) is Jomolonzo (25,557 ft, 7790 m). Hidden from view below them is the deep course cut by the Karma Tsangpo. If you camp at this lake or beside any body of water, be sure that your kitchen crew washes and rinses the cooking gear a good distance from the water.

Sha-u La is **1½ hours** farther up the valley to the southwest. This trail follows the west (L) side of the first lake, but before the second lake the trail splits. Yaks are taken on a longer route along the west (L) side of the second lake. The shorter walking route angles to the left (east) to ascend the hills above the east side of this lake. This trail then climbs onto the top of a morainal ridge. Sha-u La is the obvious dip in the ridge up to the southwest. Stay to the right of a small tarn and reach the pass *la-dze* (15,700 ft, 4790 m) for more outstanding panoramas of Makalu, Jomolonzo, and other peaks.

The route from Sha-u La into the Karma Valley heads southwest across high meadows, passing to the right of a series of four small lakes. The trail then starts to switchback down through rough, rocky terrain. Eventually the slope is less steep and the trail follows the east (L) side of a tumbling stream. Huge boulder erratics sit by the stream, dumped off here by glacial retreats. The valley narrows into a lush canyon with soaring granite walls. Moss covers the rocks, primulas are particularly plentiful, and the slopes are thick with juniper and yellow-blooming rhododendrons. As the canyon opens out the stream begins meandering across wide meadows. **Three hours or more** below the pass the trail crosses a bridge to the west (R) side of the stream. **A few minutes** later is a broad meadow camp (13,100 ft, 3990 m), dotted with the dens of golden-colored marmots and a lot of yak chips. Either this camp or a meadow **15 minutes** downstream is stage three to Pethang Ringmo for the yak herders. Firewood is available, but encourage your kitchen staff to cook with their fuel stoves rather than using the local wood. The route to Sakyithang continues south from here. This abandoned salt depot and frontier trading post is **1 to 1½ days** down into the forests of the Karma Tsangpo, not far above (northwest of) the junction with the Phung Chu. The mountaineers with the Everest Reconnaissance team described this area as one of the most beautiful valleys in the world. Logging is still allowed, even with the inauguration of the Chomolangma Nature Preserve. Luckily the trees are being felled with handsaws and hauled out by porters or on yak, a slow process that should contain major deforestation.

Woodcutter in the Kharta region

The trail to base camp turns west from the meadow camp, leaving the valley floor and angling up the ridge side into a forest of juniper, birch and rhododendron. Green, wispy strands of *Usnea* lichen dangle from the branches, a sight more typical of the cloud forests in Nepal than Tibet. Far below the Karma Tsangpo winds through broad gravel flats, and not far upstream is a glacier flowing off the snowy flanks of Makalu. The walking is brilliant as the trail meanders through high meadows and rolling hills of dwarf rhododendron. Keep looking up to the west for glimpses of two snowy peaks at the head of the valley. Everest is on the right, separated by a dip in the ridge (called the South Col) from Lhotse (27,890 ft, 8501 m), the tall peak to the left and the world's fourth-highest summit.

The trail crests at a stunning overlook, then descends to the lower end of Tsho Nak, the Black Lake. Cross the outlet and climb to a series of flat meadows (14,300 ft, 4360 m), **2½ to 3 hours** past the meadow camps below Sha-u La. Continue climbing, then sidle across the ridge for **1½ hours** to a large side valley. Pass several herder camps to reach Shalung Tsho. The trail skirts the right (north) side of the lake, and a good meadow for camping (14,500 ft, 4420 m) is just below the lake. This is stage four. Climb high on the nearby ridges for views of Everest and Lhotse.

Thirty minutes or more farther up the trail are the first views of Lhotse Shar (27,503 ft, 8383 m; marked by a triangular peak symbol beside Lhotse on Map No. 8), the East Peak of Lhotse. The great jumble of rock and rubble in the main valley is the Kangshung Glacier. Below its terminus the Kangdoshung Glacier spills from the north side of Jomolonzo into the lower Kangshung Valley. Sweeping in from the right (north) off the snowy Karma Gangri peak (20,560 ft, 6745 m; marked on Map No. 8 by a triangular peak symbol to the north of Pethang Ringmo) is the huge, glaciated tributary valley of

A working girl, from Kharta

the Rabka Chu. The junction of these valleys is the headwaters of the Karma Tsangpo. Below in the main valley, the parallel rippling hills of moraine tell tales of advancing and retreating glaciers in former times.

The trail soon comes to Thangsham (14,700 ft, 4480 m), a beautifully situated herder camp on a narrow sloping pasture, but the nearest water is too far away to make this a practical camp. This odd piece of land, suspended on the edge of a very steep drop-off, was the gap between the ridge and the lateral moraine of a tremendous glacier that once flowed from Karma Gangri. The glacier has retreated considerably, but it must have been at least 1000 feet (300 m) thick to deposit a moraine of this height. Several other troughlike depressions located farther up the ridge from this plateau suggest that previous glacial advances were even larger.

One hour past Shalung Tsho, the trail from Langma La intersects the route from Sha-u La just below a large glacial erratic boulder with a rock enclosure along the base. The trail to base camp now plunges steeply down the ridge through scrub juniper and dwarf rhododendron, reaching the valley floor (13,800 ft, 4210 m) in **20 minutes**.

Good campsites straddle both sides of the Rabka Chu between the meadow edges and the willow groves. The next camp of any size is **more than 2 hours** away, including a rugged 1200-foot (370-m) ascent alongside the Kangshung Glacier. A wooden bridge spans the stream between two low hills of moraine bordering the lower end of the meadow campsites. At one time these hills were a continuous ridge of deposits, probably left by an advance of the Kangdoshung Glacier. The flow of the Rabka Chu would have been blocked by the intruding wall, causing a small lake to form. Eventually the water sliced an exit low enough to drain the lake, leaving these flat meadows and willow groves in its place.

The route up the Kangshung Valley crosses the bridge to the west (R) bank of the stream, following the base of the hillside briefly before reentering the dense scrub. Some of the rhododendrons in this area are at least 6 feet (1.8 m) high, remarkably tall for this elevation. Beyond here the trail enters the succession of rolling morainal hills. **Twenty minutes** past the bridge is a creek crossing that can be troublesome during heavy rains. Otherwise the trail remains easy to follow and soon descends to the meadows of Bathang (13,900 ft, 4240 m), another favorite haunt for marmots. In 1921 George Mallory of the Everest Reconnaissance team used a base camp farther up the valley, which he called Pethang Ringmo. A trail leading up into the hills to the right (north) leads to Tsechu (Long-life Water), a *beyul*, or "hidden valley," with a holy lake and a Guru Rimpoche cave temple.

The Kangshung Valley, which I nicknamed Thunder Valley on my first visit here one August, absolutely roars during the summer monsoon with the sound of rushing water, rockfalls, and avalanches. Snow that accumulates daily on the surrounding peaks starts rumbling about noon and continues falling noisily throughout most nights. Another interesting feature of this area and the Karma Tsangpo Valley is the giant wild rhubarb (*Rheum sp.*), with great leaves several feet long and thick, tasty-looking stalks. Watch out. I stewed a batch one morning to complement our breakfast. The yak man declined his share with apprehension, but we thought it was great. When it came time to load the yaks we were so nauseated we had to unpack our gear and lay over an extra day to recover. The wild mint that grows in this region is much safer and makes a nice tea.

From Bathang continue ascending along the north (L) side of the valley through the dense scrub. The trail soon reaches a steep slope where the hills of moraine suddenly fall away to the river. When the 1921 Everest Reconnaissance team came up this valley, the Kangdoshung Glacier reached all the way across to this point, nearly sealing off the valley. The glacier is now considerably smaller, leaving this giant scar. The trail traverses these rocky slopes to the base of a large rockslide, which is relatively stable but should be crossed with caution. The route is cairned and usually easy to follow.

From the end of the slide the trail traverses high above the rushing river along scrub-covered slopes. Mount Everest and Lhotse come into view, and **30 minutes** beyond the slide the trail descends into Oka (also Opka), an active herder camp (15,000 ft, 4570 m) **4 to 5 hours** from Shalung Tsho. Jomolonzo's massive triple summits and Lhotse are visible from here, but only the tip of Everest shows. Depending on the pace of your yak men, this large grazing area is often stage five; or it may be at one of the previous meadows. However, Pethang Ringmo, the base camp of the 1921 Everest Reconnaissance team, is more spectacular than here and only **another hour** up the valley. Cross the main stream draining Oka and ascend the moraine hills to the northwest. Another trail leads up into the hills to the right (northeast), leading to the Tsechu hidden valley in **about 3 hours** via Latsho La (15,900 ft, 4850 m). Keep an eye on the upper slopes for blue sheep, which are common in this area. The trail to base camp follows a small stream, then crosses to the north (R) side. Continue ascending on braided trails leading into a series of morainal hills, then emerge onto the large meadow of lush grass (15,800 ft, 4820 m) of Pethang Ringmo. The area is graced with several unusual domed storage shelters.

During monsoon this lovely plateau is ablaze with a thick carpet of yellow wildflowers. All around are huge snowy white ice floes pouring from the peaks into the Kangshung Glacier. Mount Everest, Lhotse, and Lhotse Shar dominate the west end of the valley; the Jomolonzo massif provides endless excitement with its booming avalanches. Although this view of Everest cannot rival the grandeur of its North Face, the gentleness of so many flowers in such rugged alpine terrain makes this a memorable camp.

Most expeditions establish their base camp 2½ **to 3 hours** farther up the valley (16,700 ft, 5090 m) at a rather insignificant meadow with numerous stone fire rings and the usual scattered garbage typical of climbing camps. It is also the last point that yaks can carry loads up the valley. Beyond here climbers must either use porters or carry the gear themselves across the glacier to begin their assault on the East Face. Because the Pethang Ringmo meadows are so delightful, the base camp could be saved for a day hike. However, one advantage of sleeping at the base camp is the opportunity to hike onto the high ridge (18,300 ft, 5580 m) to the north of this camp, which overlooks the Kangshung Valley. In 1921 Lieutenant Colonel Charles K. Howard-Bury ascended this spectacular vantage point. Looking to the left of Everest he could see "a huge amphitheater of mighty peaks culminating in a new and unsurveyed peak, 28,100 feet in height, to which we gave the name Lhotse, which in Tibetan means the 'South Peak.'" The massive, Matterhorn-like peak looming above the base camp to the left (east) of Lhotse Shar is Pethangtse (22,014 ft, 6710 m), and poking up behind Jomolonzo is Makalu. En route to this ridge-top viewpoint are two glacial lakes nestled between the rocky, barren slopes.

It is possible to continue west past base camp for **about 45 minutes**, following the crest of a long moraine to its end (17,050 ft, 5200 m). Below is a large glacial lake, and across the valley is one of the great views of the Himalaya, with three of the world's five highest mountains towering so close. If you have the time and the energy, head north from this moraine for **1 to 2 hours** up to the crest of the main ridge for even grander views on Howard-Bury's ridge.

THE RETURN TO KHARTA QU VIA LANGMA LA

The return trip to Kharta Qu can be completed in just **3 or 4 days** by crossing Langma La (17,200 ft, 5240m). The route initially backtracks to the Rabka Chu meadow camp, only **2 hours or less** below Pethang Ringmo. From here begin the big climb back up to the Thangsham meadows to Langma La. From the junction with the route to Sha-u La, continue up the ridge for **a few minutes** past the big boulder to the top of the moraine ridge (14,550 ft, 4430 m). The trail first leads north, then northeast up to the pass; it can be obscure in places and difficult to follow, particularly if clouds reduce visibility.

From Thangsham, head north up the meadow between hills of moraine. After **30 minutes** the trail begins angling right (northeast) into the hills along a gully between ridges. At the crest of the ridge, the trail divides into many braided tracks. Keep angling to the right, taking the largest of these braids to a stream crossing below a small pond. The grassy slopes are like the Scottish moors, especially when misty waves of fog pour over the hilltops. Climb more braided trails up to the left (northwest) to the ridge crest above the pond. The trail now becomes more defined. Keep heading up along the top of the ridge, then cross to the north (R) side of the stream draining Tsho Melongme, the smaller of two lakes along the trail to the pass. The scenic meadows (15,900 ft, 4850 m) near this lake are 2½ **hours** or more above the Rabka Chu, and one of the last good camps before Langma La. Off to the west, icy fingers of the upper Rabka Glacier dramatically collide in great frozen rivers; the contact point is marked by a pile of gray moraine heaped in the middle. Makalu is just south across the valley and now reigns over its larger cousins to the west. The tundra is lush, considering the elevation, attracting a *drokpa* family each summer. If you camp here, keep an eye on your gear. The children of these nomads know that unwatched backpacks and tents are a treasure trove of food and useful items, all of which will be sorely missed in the middle of a remote trek.

Langma La is located near the dip in the rocky ridges up to the northeast, but the actual pass is hidden by a rock outcrop. The route to the pass continues up to the northeast from the lake to the top of a moraine, then passes a ruined hut to reach the shore of Tsho Zhukri-me (also Zhukrim and Zhumori; 16,200 ft, 4940 m) in **20 minutes**. The trail now ascends the ridge above the north (R) shore of this deep, aqua blue lake. Bare rock makes it hard to follow the route at times; look for cairns. Reach the summit prayer flags (17,200 ft, 5240 m) in 1½ **hours** from Tsho Melungme.

On clear days the view to the south is outstanding. Makalu is the impressive peak to the southwest dwarfing all of the other summits from this angle, including Everest. Jomolonzo is the closer, North Peak of Makalu; Pethangtse is the lone bullet-shaped summit a little farther to the right (west); and the big trio at the far west end of the Kangshung Valley, from left to right, are Lhotse Shar, Lhotse, and Mount Everest.

The trail from Langma La now descends into a jumbled world of rocky moraine and cliffs to Tsho Dramnyen (Guitar Lake; 16,300 ft, 4970 m), a lake shaped like a long-necked Tibetan guitar. Despite this austere environment, patches of grass and delicately petaled blue poppies manage to find a foothold between the rocks. **Less than 2 hours** below the pass is Lhatse (15,600 ft, 4750 m), a beautifully stark, high mountain camp at the base of a crumbling cliff, and the first meadows on this side. Stone shelters have been constructed under the ledges of several large boulders.

Just below Lhatse the first rhododendrons make an appearance and soon cover the hillsides. Descend for **1 hour** into a steep, glacially carved valley to reach Tröse meadow camp (14,500 ft, 4420 m), **about 10 minutes** below the trail by the large creek. **Less than an hour** below here, through juniper and dwarf rhododendron, is a sprawling meadow camp, Shomale (13,650 ft, 4160 m). Deep marmot holes puncture the grassy flats, and tall willows and wild rosebushes nearby act as a sanctuary for redstarts, rose finches, and little warblers.

Soon terraced fields can be seen below in the Kharta Tsangpo. The next tributary to the right (east) is the Dambuk Chu, which drains from Sha-u La. The trail now switchbacks steeply through juniper and rose bushes, then down barren slopes to reach the town of Lhundrubling (13,100 ft, 3990 m), a medieval-looking collection of stone houses and muddy alleyways. Just above town the yak trail splits off to the right to stay high above the barley fields. There are no shops here, but families often have milk, yogurt, *chang, arak,* and vegetables, and perhaps some yak meat for sale. Judging from the mud-encrusted pigs roaming around, there's a good chance a side of pork may be procured as well.

The route to Kharta Qu leads east through barley fields, past stands of wild rose and barberry, and over several stone fences to a pleasant tree-lined path. In **less than 30**

minutes pass a mill house on the Dambuk Chu. Continue east, climbing high above the river and behind the settlement of Raphuk to a stone house with several large, old birch trees. **Ten minutes** farther is the turnoff for Sha-u La, and in **15 minutes** meet the road leading up the mountain to Zamchung La. Pass several mill houses and the trail up to Yulba village to reach the bridge over the Kharta Tsangpo and the meadow camps along the river. If you haven't arranged for transportation to meet you, walk for **about 1 hour** to Kharta Qu; with luck a truck or tractor might be gathering passengers for Tashi Dzom and Shekar.

THE MENLUNGTSE BASE CAMP TREK

To the south of Dingri but hidden from view by the Lapchi Himal is the little-known holy peak of Menlungtse (Tib., Jobo Garu, the "Venerable Saddle"; 23,560 ft, 7181 m). Towering nearby is another 7000-meter holy peak, Gauri Shankar (Tib., Jomo Tseringma; 23,405 ft, 7134 m). Separating these summits is the sacred valley of Menlung (Medicine Valley). Geographically in Nepal but politically in Tibet, this remote corner of the Himalaya has rarely been visited by anyone other than local yak herders and a few climbing expeditions, yet it has acquired a unique fame in the West. The first photographs of what are believed to be yeti footprints were taken in the upper reaches of the Menlung Valley in 1951 by British mountaineer Eric Shipton. The area is also renowned as a haunt of Jetsun Milarepa, Tibet's most famous ascetic, and it was at the mouth of the Menlung Valley, in a cave at Chubar, where this great yogi passed away.

Access to the Menlung area is via the Rongshar Valley, one of the upper tributaries of Nepal's Tamba Kosi River. The **6- to 8-day** round-trip trek to Menlungtse base camp begins at Rongshar Qu, the administrative *shang* for the region, 52 miles (85 km) from Dingri. The road from Dingri turns south across the Dingri plains past Cho Oyu base camp, climbing over Pozer La (17,400 ft, 5300 m) before plunging 6400 feet (1950 m) to the lush environs of Rongshar Qu (11,100 ft, 3380 m). The small shops in the *shang* have little to offer, if they are ever open; purchase all supplies ahead of time. A fuel stove and tent are necessary. Transportation to Rongshar, which originates at Dingri, is sporadic at best. If the pass is closed from snow or the road is washed out, allow **4 to 5 days** to walk to Rongshar Qu.

Yaks can be hired through the *shang* leader. Or you can go directly to Tsamboche, the town where the herders live, which is a **15-minute** walk past the government compound. If the trail to base camp is in bad shape (a common problem after monsoon), yaks cannot make the journey and porters must be used. But they carry half as much and cost more than yaks. Accommodation here is very basic, with just a few spare rooms near the *shang* offices. Another option is to stay with a local family. About the only campsite is an embankment between the road and the river about a mile (1 km) upstream from here.

TO MENLUNGTSE BASE CAMP

The trek to the Menlungtse base camp begins at the *shang* compound, where the road dead-ends. Although it's only 1½ **hours** away, Chubar *gompa* (Isthmus monastery; pronounced "Chuwar"; 10,650 ft, 3250 m) is a logical place to stop for the night. If you have yaks or porters they may decide this for you! So enjoy a leisurely descent beside the churning Rongshar Tsangpo. This jungley canyon is a wild departure from the moonscapes near Dingri. Thick stands of flowering wild roses, rhododendron, barberry, *Caragana*, cotoneaster, and spiraea tower beside the trails. The damp undergrowth supports asters, forget-me-nots, anemone, wild thyme, *Senecio*, *Ligularia*, iris, ephedra, dock, and even jack-in-the-pulpits.

Tsamboche (11,050 ft, 3370 m), **less than 10 minutes** below Rongshar Qu, is situated

Afternoon thermal clouds rising around Gauri Shankar

beneath striated cliffs. As in towns in Kongpo or Nepal, the thirty-five homes here have peaked, wood shake roofs typical of regions experiencing high rainfall. The trail winds between the houses and rock-walled alleys, then past terraced barley and potato fields. Again the river narrows, at one point disappearing under a tremendous rockslide. **About 1 hour** below Tsamboche the path crosses a stream meandering out of a slot in the cliffs. Not far inside is a 50-foot (15-m) waterfall.

Continue descending to Chörten Karchung, a small shrine in the center of the trail featuring a painted stone tablet of Milarepa. He is typically portrayed in the meditational pose of holding his right hand up to his ear and wearing white cotton robes. His name means "Mila the Cotton-clad," a title given only to masters of *tummo*, a meditational technique whereby unusually high levels of body heat are generated. The red sash across his shoulder is a strap used to support one's back and knees during extended periods of deep meditation. Legends claim that when Milarepa died at Chubar, his disciple Rechungpa, who was far away in Southern Tibet, rushed to be at his master's side and rode the first sunbeam of the morning to land on Pozer La (Sunbeam on the Summit), the pass between Dingri and Chubar. As Rechungpa was nearing Chubar, the deceased Milarepa performed his final miracle by manifesting himself at this spot, allowing the two ascetics to have their last conversation before the cremation.

Soon the valley yields the first views of Chubar *gompa*'s red-walled, two-story ruins. Cross a wooden cantilever bridge to the south (L) bank of the Rongshar Tsangpo. Just before the monastery, the trail forks. The right (west) half leads down the canyon to the villages of Drobde and Drin and beyond to Nepal. The left fork continues up the hill to several large apricot trees and a *mani* wall above the monastery. The Menlung Valley enters from the left (south).

Chubar *gompa* is perched on an isthmus of land suspended above the confluence of the Tashi Oma Chu (Auspicious Milk River; marked "Oma Chu" on Map No. 8), which flows from Menlungtse, and the Rongshar Tsangpo. Perched above on the nearby cliffs is Driche *phuk* (*Dri* [Female Yak] Tongue cave; also known as Dreche *phuk,* Demon's Tongue cave), where Milarepa died. This revered twelfth-century poet-saint renounced worldly pursuits and spent most of his life meditating in caves. His displeasure with the rich monastic establishments and their worldly approach to Buddhism often put him at odds with the *lamas* and famous teachers of his era. One such conflict developed with Geshe Tsakpukwa (*geshe* is a title, similar to a doctorate in Buddhist philosophy) after Milarepa embarrassed him in a public debate. Incensed, the Geshe bribed his female companion with offers of marriage and wealth if she delivered a bowl of poisoned yogurt to Milarepa, who was residing in Drin village. Fully aware of his fate, the enlightened 84-year-old yogi accepted the curds out of compassion for the woman, allowing her to fulfill her agreement with the Geshe. Knowing he was to die, Milarepa moved to Chubar, where he gathered all his disciples for a final teaching.

Driche *phuk* is named after a bulge of rock inside the cave resembling a *dri's* tongue. The interior is very simple, with a wooden sleeping platform on one side and a small altar area. The moss-covered rock walls nearby were once a meditation retreat. The two square monuments with prayer flags on the ledge in front of the cave are the residences of Chubar Gyelpo, the *sungma,* or protector for the Menlung area, and for Tseringma, the powerful *khandroma* who resides on Jomo Tseringma (Gauri Shankar). The latter often obstructed Milarepa's meditations until he subdued her, converting her and her retinue of four "long-life" sisters to become protectors of Buddhism. Just past the ruined walls are two small *chörtens* at the site where Milarepa was cremated.

Chubar monastery, a more recent addition here, was founded by the Tenth Karmapa, Chöying Dorje, around the 1630s. Within a decade the Fifth Dalai Lama had consolidated his political control over Tibet, and Chubar was taken over and converted to the Gelukpa sect, which affiliation it retains today. The monks and the head *lama,* the First Yangzi Rimpoche, fled to Nepal after 1959 and established Tshosham monastery in Lamabagar, a town two to three days downstream. The People's Liberation Army arrived in 1972 and moved into the abandoned monastery. After several years the roof of the chanting hall collapsed, forcing the soldiers to relocate to the meadows above the *gompa.* Their barracks were the rows of parallel stone walls now in ruins; there was even a basketball court.

The old chanting hall of Chubar is now an overgrown maze of collapsed roof beams and stinging nettle. The remaining two-story structure was the back temple, which once housed a large Sakyamuni Buddha statue. Flanking the empty central pedestal are the remains of his two attendants. Along the wall are two rows of seated figures—probably Nye-we Sechen Gye, the Eight Great *Bodhisattvas*—which now tilt at angles, limbs torn off, straw stuffing bundles spilling out, but with many faces relatively intact. The receiving room for Yangzi Rimpoche was upstairs on the second level; the ruins behind this temple were his residence. The current, Second Yangzi Rimpoche is studying at Sera monastery in India.

The route to Menlungtse base camp turns south from Chubar up the forested Menlung Valley. In **10 minutes** the trail forks; take the lower path to the right. The trail stays high above the east (R) side of the Tashi Oma Chu's deep ravine, weaving between stream gullies. Birch, fir, several species of rhododendron (including *R. arboreum,* Nepal's national flower), bamboo, and a riot of wildflowers thrive in these damp environs. *Angelica cyclocarpa,* perhaps the tallest member of the carrot family, grows like a miniature tree with a huge head of white flowers; this species is particularly common near Chubar *gompa.* Waterfalls cascade off the canyon walls, and snowfields peek through the clouds that often shroud Gauri Shankar. Warm, moist air from the Bay of Bengal is funneled up the Rongshar Tsangpo, creating this lush environment. You really feel like you're in Nepal!

Climb 2½ **to 3 hours** up the narrow valley and eventually meet the river at a large landslide area called Zhabje (Footprint; 11,700 ft, 3570 m). The trail formerly crossed a bridge above here, but the trail now stays on the northeast (R) side. Ascend through a field of boulders coated in red lichen, then scramble over a series of landslides. **One hour** above Zhabje is a small cliffside camp called Yarle (Summer Place, 12,500 ft, 3810 m). A dense, dark rhododendron forest covers the surrounding slopes; up the valley looms the sheer pyramid of Menlungtse's Northwest Face. **Ten minutes** farther is a larger meadow that's not so close to the canyon's edge. If you have yak men or porters, they will probably want to camp here. The herders typically stop rather early each day, which is good for acclimatization in such a steep valley.

From Yarle the trail now ascends steadily for **2½ hours** through tall willow and rhododendron onto the top of a large glacial moraine with meadows and large erratics. At the high end of the moraine is Domphuk (Bear Cave; 13,650 ft, 4160 m; marked as Dom on Map No. 8), a huge boulder with a cave beneath it. According to one legend, Milarepa changed himself into a bear and stayed here several months. The small potato fields nearby are the only cultivation in Menlung. Domphuk was the base camp for the first official mountaineering expedition to attempt Menlungtse, led by British climber Chris Bonington. It took him a second try in 1988 to place two climbers on the West Summit, but they couldn't complete the long traverse to the higher East Summit. American John Roskelley and three other climbers attempted Menlungtse's East Summit in 1990 via the eastern ridge, but dangerous snow conditions turned them back. The main East Summit was finally climbed in 1992 by two Slovenians, Marko Prezelj and Andrej Stremfelj. Apparently no one has climbed Gauri Shankar from the Tibet side. Roskelley and Sherpa climbing companion Dorje made the first ascent in 1979 via Nepal.

Twenty minutes below Domphuk the route to base camp crosses a rocky creek from the glacier flowing off Menlungtse's northern flanks. Look for a log spanning the banks, or find a safe place to ford. About **3 hours or more** up this tributary is Shing Kyong Namtsho, a lake that is the residence for the *sungma* of Chubar monastery. One of five "visible" holy lakes within the Menlung Valley (a sixth, invisible "yellow lake" can only be seen by enlightened beings; the other four lakes, plus the yellow lake, are associated with Tsering Che-nga, the Five Long-life Sisters), this "black lake" is the most powerful; any improper actions such as shouting near the lake are said to have a bad affect upon Chubar.

A few minutes past this crossing is Garu (13,700 ft, 4180 m), a stunning meadow camp directly below Menlungtse and Gauri Shankar. The yak men and porters will probably want to camp near here; consider spending a second night to acclimatize properly. The trail now climbs steeply through hills of moraine covered in dwarf rhododendron. Baphuk (pronounced "Bawu"; 15,000 ft, 4570 m), Bonington's 1988 base camp, is a broad, flat plain **2 hours** or more above Garu. Families from Tsamboche spend the summer season tending horses and herds of yak here, directly below Menlungtse's impressive Southwest Face. If the *dri* are being milked, be prepared to sample some of the world's most delicious yogurt.

The return to Rongshar Qu retraces the route to base camp and takes **2 days**.

DAY HIKES ABOVE BASE CAMP

The vast basin above Menlungtse base camp is a jumble of glaciers and moraine hills ringed by a barrier of 6000-meter (19,700-ft) peaks. It's easy to spend at least two or three days here exploring the region. Four holy lakes associated with the Tsering Che-nga Sisters are scattered about this sacred valley. A wild and unbelievable pilgrim circuit connects three of them, and the other is directly above base camp. The route to Roskelley's advance base camp follows the eastern flanks of Menlungtse and provides superb views of the East Summit and the upper Menlung Valley.

The closest lake to base camp is the abode of Tekar Drönzangma, the "green" long-life sister who rides a dragon. It's up the ridge to the south, cradled in a basin of moraine. Find a wide point in the Tashi Oma Chu and wade across to the south (L) bank. Walk for **5 minutes** downstream and cross two small streams. The first drains from the lake, the second flows from a ridge below Gauri Shankar. A series of animal trails ascends above the west (L) side of this second drainage. Eventually the trail becomes better, crosses this stream back to the (R) side then angles up the ridge. Reach a rocky ridge crest (15,600 ft, 4750 ft) overlooking the lake in **about 1 hour**. A smaller tarn (16,000 ft, 4880 m) is **30 minutes** higher.

The pilgrim's *kora* to the other three lakes is not a journey for inexperienced walkers. You'll also need a guide; this route clambers over steep, crumbly hills of moraine with few trails and only occasional cairns marking the way. The circuit initially follows a trail hugging the far north (R) side of the valley, then crosses a clear running stream. **About 1½ hours** above base camp the valley bends to the right (north) around the base of Menlungtse. The pilgrim trail continues straight ahead (east), across a narrow rocky draw, then up a moraine. A trail marked with bamboo poles climbs above the north (R) side of a crashing glacial creek, reaching the crest (16,000 ft, 4880 m) in **40 minutes**.

This is a good place to get your bearings. Due east is a bullet-shaped peak (marked 6301 m on the 1:50,000 Rolwaling Himal map by Schneider), which Bonington almost climbed in 1988; the Slovenians Prezelj and Stremfelj succeeded in 1992. To the north is a large glacier flowing in icy fingers off distant craggy peaks; the lower end of this great ice floe is covered by several large lakes. When Eric Shipton entered this valley from the Khumbu in 1951, he probably crossed Dingjang La, the 5877-meter pass on the Schneider map (Shipton erroneously called it Menlung La, which is farther south). His yeti footprint photos were taken somewhere in the upper Menlung Valley.

Along the west (R) side of the upper main glacier is a long lateral moraine leading north. This can be followed for about **2 hours** to reach the junction (16,800 ft, 5120 m) with Menlungtse's sheer eastern flanks. The route to Roskelley's advance base camp followed this moraine, crossed the glacier, then ascended the far wall of glacial rubble. The camp was situated just past this moraine in the meadows at the base of the northeast ridge. As I sat on the moraine contemplating his route over the glacier and up to the advance camp, I heard a noise to my left. Six blue sheep were 30 feet away, all staring at me. They had just come straight up the steep moraine from the glacier; eighteen more followed in single file. Each one of them stopped, looked at me, gave a sneezy snort, then darted past. Eventually they regrouped below and wandered off toward the upper ridges.

The circuit to the three other holy lakes of the Long-life Sisters begins with the "white lake" of the snow lion–riding Tashi Tseringma. It is the most important and largest of these lakes, about **1½ hours** or more southeast from the viewpoint across a rollercoaster of moraine hills. You'll find few trail markers; definitely bring a guide. Up to the south from here is Menlung La, the obvious low point in the ridge forming the border with Nepal. This glaciated pass leads into the Rolwaling Valley, a Sherpa region adjacent to the Khumbu. The folks from Tsamboche make the journey in two days. The trail to the pass leads up from the valley floor on the large moraine immediately below the pass and the glacier. The "red lake" of the wild ass–riding Miyul Lozangma is at the base of this moraine on the left (east) side; the "blue lake" of Ting-ge Zhalzangma, whose mount is a horse, is below on the right side. Allow a total of **4 more hours**, not including breaks, to reach these two lakes from the first lake and to then return to base camp.

DAY HIKE TO DRIN FROM CHUBAR MONASTERY

Drin village, where Milarepa lived when he was given the poisoned yogurt, is **a half day's hike** up to the northwest from Chubar monastery. From the trail junction just below the *gompa*, turn left and descend for **a few minutes** alongside the Rongshar Tsangpo. Cross a bridge over the Tashi Oma Chu, then cross another to the north (R) bank of the Rongshar Tsangpo. Pass a mill house, then climb through wild rose and barberry bushes, reaching the village of Drobde (10,750 ft, 3280 m) in about **2 hours** from Chubar. Two Milarepa caves, Kyiphuk Nyima Dzong and Shelphuk, are located here. Ask in the village for the *go-nyer* and the keys.

Steep switchbacks begin the **1½-hour** climb up the ridge to Drin (also Drinthang; 11,900 ft, 3630 m). As you ascend, Gauri Shankar's summit appears above the ridges to the west; the Rongshar Tsangpo is swallowed by a deep canyon on its journey to Nepal. As the trail begins to level, you pass a few ancient-looking *mani* walls and a small pond. The villagers of Drin (which means "Grateful," as the locals felt very privileged to have Milarepa living nearby), built Milarepa a stone shelter atop the large boulder with a prayer flag beside this pool; it was here that he ate the yogurt.

Drin is nearby, up past fields of barley. The homes are bunched together in the middle of an elevated plain beside a large boulder on top of which sits Drakar Lhakhang (White Rock Temple), an old Nyingmapa temple. At the base is an old *mani khang*. This big rock is a Guru Rimpoche meditation site and represents Zangdok Pelri, the mythical abode of the Great Guru. These structures are the only religious buildings in the entire Rongshar area to have survived the Cultural Revolution; all statues are new except for one of Guru Rimpoche in the center. The white female figure to the far right, riding a white snow lion, is Tashi Tseringma, whose residence is on Gauri Shankar. Flanking her are the four other Long-life Sisters, each one astride her different colored mount.

The cave of Geshe Tsakpukwa, who was behind the plot to kill Milarepa, is due south from the *gompa*; it's under the highest boulder along the ridge top. Other Milarepa hermitage sites nearby include Sengye *phuk*, **less than 1 hour** above Drin, and Khyunglung, a holy valley **about 1 day** away. The trail to Lapchi monastery and cave hermitages, another meditation site of Milarepa's, follows the walled path up to the north from Drin and takes **2 to 3 days**. Yaks can be hired here; Nyelam (km marker 5345/6) is **3 days** farther. If you try to trek this route without a military permit (which must be obtained through a commercial trekking agency), you will probably be stopped by the *shang* officials in Rongshar Qu.

10
THE SHISHAPANGMA REGION

MAP NO. 9, PAGE 199

Despite being only 50 miles (80 km) northeast of Kathmandu, Shishapangma (26,397 ft, 8046 m) was for a long time one of the least well known of the world's fourteen highest peaks. The mountain is mostly hidden from Nepal, tucked behind the Jugal Himal near the frontier with Tibet and Nepal. Shishapangma was the last 8000-meter (26,246-ft) peak to be climbed, and is the only one entirely within Tibet.

Shishapangma (Chi., Xixabangma) is known to the Nepalese as Gosainthan, a sacred abode of the god Shiva. The first group of mountaineers to attempt its summit was a huge Chinese expedition in 1964; they also built a road to what is now the north base camp. The first expedition to attempt the mountain from the south was a British team in 1982 that made its way up Shishapangma via the immense 6500-foot (2000-m) Southwest Face. With the opening of Tibet to tourism in the early 1980s, Shishapangma suddenly became one of the most visible and easily visited 8000-meter peaks; it towers impressively near Thong La pass on the Friendship Highway. Tour groups can now drive to the north base camp, and the mountain has become one of the most popular 8000-meter peaks for commercial climbing expeditions.

On the opposite side of Shishapangma, where yak trails are the only access, the round-trip journey from Nyelam to the south base camp, taking **4 to 5 days**, is one of Tibet's best-kept trekking secrets. An alternative exit from the southern base camp is the high route over Kong Tsho La (17,000 ft, 5180 m), which skirts Shishapangma's eastern flanks to finish at Ngora village, north of Nyelam.

The trailhead is at Nyelam (Hell Road; also Nyalam Nyanang and Tshongdü; Nepalese name is Kuti; km marker 5345/6; 12,200 ft, 3720 m), an old trading post on the Lhasa-Kathmandu caravan route. The access for the southern base camp is the Tshongdü Chu Valley, a tributary of the wild Phu Chu, headwaters of Nepal's Sunkosi River. Not far upstream from Nyelam the Tshongdü Chu Valley opens into a spectacular arena of snow peaks and tumbling glaciers. In addition to hosting the Shishapangma massif, the area's western flanks are buttressed by the Jugal Himal, a rugged range with about ten summits over 21,000 feet (6500 m).

When traveling overland from Nepal to Lhasa, Nyelam is the logical place to spend a night acclimatizing before crossing Thong La (also Lalung La; 16,568 ft, 5050 m), the first high pass en route. Nyelam is only 21 miles (34 km) up the Phu Chu canyon from the border town of Zhangmu (Tib., Dram; Nepali, Khasa; km marker 5379), yet the elevation gained is 6400 feet (1950 m); Thong La is over 4000 feet (1200 m) higher again. The town of Nyelam is of little interest, but nearby are several fine day hikes. The Snowland Hotel is by far the most comfortable accommodation in town and the owner can help arrange yaks or porters for the trek to the south Shishapanga base camp.

DAY HIKES NEAR NYELAM

A well-known historical site near Nyelam is Pelgyeling (km marker 5335), a simple, attractive monastery built over the meditation cave of the twelfth-century poet-ascetic Milarepa. The hike to this cave hermitage takes **2½ hours** and is a scenic walk along the Phu Chu canyon, following the Friendship Highway the entire way. Pelgyeling is 6 miles (10 km) north of Nyelam, below the road on a steep slope overlooking the river.

The beautiful frescoes in the assembly hall are the work of a Nepalese artist; a large figure of Sakyamuni is behind the altar, and on the right-hand wall is a portrait of

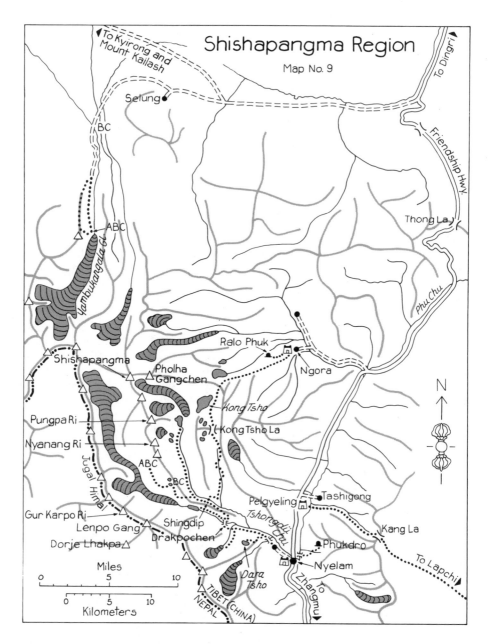

To Kyirong and Mount Kailash

To Dingri

Selung

BC

Friendship Hwy.

ABC

Thong La

Phu Chu

Yambukangala Gl.

Ralo Phuk

Shishapangma

Pholha Gangchen

Ngora

Pungpa Ri

Kong Tsho

Nyanang Ri

Kong Tsho La

ABC

N

Jugal Himal

BC

Gur Karpo Ri

Pelgyeling

Tashigong

Lenpo Gang

Shingdip

Tshong chu

Kang La

Dorje Lhakpa

Drakpochen

Phukdro

Miles

0   5   10

Dara Tsho

Nyelam

To Lapchi

0   5   10

Kilometers

TIBET (CHINA)

NEPAL

To Zhangmu

Milarepa in the classical pose with his hand held to his ear. The white cotton dress he wears is the special garb of Tantric practitioners who have mastered *tummo*, the art of spiritually generating unusually high body temperatures. On the opposite wall is a painting of Marpa the Translator, Milarepa's beloved teacher.

To the left of the assembly hall is the Stomach cave, where Milarepa spent time meditating clad only in thin cotton. The low opening leads into a rock overhang, the ceiling blackened from fires and speckled with dabs of *tsampa* offerings like stars on a dark sky. A large boulder rests inside the cave, suspended by a rock support in a peculiar manner. Milarepa is said to have lifted this boulder using his powers of concentration during a debate with several scholarly monks from a monastery in Nyelam. The caretaker will show you the imprint of Milarepa's fingers where he held the rock. The cave of Rechungpa, one of Milarepa's main disciples, is on the ridge above the main temple.

In the next major valley to the east from Pelgyeling is Lapchi *gompa*, one of the most sacred pilgrimages in Tibet and another of Milarepa's meditation sites. Unfortunately the trek from Pelgyeling over Kang La, which takes **2 to 3 days,** enters an area closed to foreigners; the nineteenth-century monastery at Lapchi and its nearby cave hermitages straddle the Nepal-Tibet border. The trail to Lapchi from Pelgyeling crosses the Phu Chu to Tashigong village, where the Chinese border patrol are stationed. Kang La is up to the east from here following the south (L) side of the valley. Lapchi can also be approached from the Rongshar Valley, south of Dingri (see "The Menlungtse Base Camp Trek").

Close to Nyelam is Phukdro *ritrö,* a small cave hermitage up a tributary of the Phu Chu, to the northeast of Nyelam. This old Kargyüpa retreat, **2 to 3 hours** away, is hidden high up above the barley terraces. The foot bridge crossing to the east (L) side of the Phu Chu is **15 minutes** above Nyelam, at the first bend in the highway. The trail ascends the nose of the steep ridge above the bridge, then enters the valley off to the left (northeast), crossing to the north (R) side of the stream. Look for prayer flags to locate the hermitage (12,800 ft, 3900 m). It is unoccupied, but the views from here back toward the Jugal Himal are worth the climb.

If you have an entire day free at Nyelam, the hike up to the Drakpochen *drokpa* camp (13,300 ft, 4050 m) takes **3 to 4 hours** and is an outstanding glacial valley walk. Depending on how early you start, it may be possible to reach the terminus of the main glacier and a large lake, located **1½ hours** above Drakpochen. About the only way to glimpse Shishapangma's southern flanks on a day hike from Nyelam is to tackle the **4-hour** ascent to Dara Tsho (14,000 ft, 4270 m), an unusual holy lake trapped high in a ridge of glacial moraine above the valley. Both of these walks are detailed below.

DAY HIKES FROM THE NORTH SHISHAPANGMA BASE CAMP

The north Shishapangma base camp (15,900 ft, 4850 m) is 28 miles (46 km) west of the Friendship Highway. The access road leaves the highway at kilometer marker 5266 to enter a broad desert valley. Some 18 miles (29 km) from the turnoff the road fords a deep creek, then immediately divides on the west (L) side. The larger, right-hand fork leads to one of Tibet's immense lakes, Pelku Tsho, then continues west toward the Kyirong Valley and onto Mount Kailash. The left-hand turn leads to the northern base camp. A few kilometers beyond this junction is Selung (15,200 ft, 4630 m), the largest village in this region and the only permanent settlement en route to the base camp. All fifty families here are herders; expeditions climbing Shishapangma hire yaks from them. Note: A toll gate close by has been charging stiff road use fees for each vehicle (US $50 to 75) as well as entry fees for each tourist going to the north base camp.

The base camp is 10 miles (15 km) past Selung around a ridge of barren hills. The lone but massive summit looming beyond Selung is not Shishapangma, but Gangbenchen (23,658 ft, 7211 m), the tallest of the peaks forming the watershed between the headwaters of Nepal's Trisuli and Arun Rivers. As the road swings around to the south, both Shishapangma and its pointy neighbor Pholha Gangchen (Chi., Molamenchen; 25,269 ft, 7702 m) finally come into view. The base camp is an elongated series of meadows wedged between the ridge and the river draining from Shishapangma's Yambukangala glacier, the main ice floe on this side of the mountain. The summit route established by the 1964 Chinese expedition (now the "standard" climbing route) ascends the west (L) side of this glacier, then traverses its upper flanks to approach the mountain.

A long but rewarding outing from base camp is the hike to advance base camp and the snout of this glacier's jumbled surface of frozen ice waves. Another good hike fol-

Shishapangma rises straight up from Kong Tsho, a lake sacred to Guru Rimpoche

lows the crest of the ridge directly across (south of) the river from the base camp, providing outstanding views of the entire Shishapangma–Pelku Tsho region. The base camp is so far from the glacier that most people cannot walk to the advance camp and return in a single day. However, a jeep track crosses to the river's south (L) side at the base camp and continues 5 miles (8 km) south to a flat plateau above the river (16,700 ft, 5090 m); if you have a vehicle, try to cajole your driver into taking you the extra distance and picking you up later in the day. The walk from here to advance base camp takes **about 4 hours** and follows the west (L) bank most of the way. The advance camps (17,300 ft, 5270 m) are usually established above a small lake near the terminus of the Yambukangala glacier or a little farther up in the trough between the glacier and the west (L) ridge. Climb up the side of the ridge or up the moraine for views of the ice floe; a spectacular display of icy white pinnacles extends up its entire length.

For the best views of Shishapangma, don't follow the river from the end of the jeep track. Instead, climb up the ridge and head south along its crest. Aim for the obvious summit (19,100 ft, 5820 m) of these gently sloping hills, but you need not be on top to enjoy the panoramas. The walk is a deceptively long, breath-consuming journey, so allow **at least 4 to 5 hours** to reach the top from the end of the jeep track. Bring plenty of water, as this is a dry ridge, and carry extra clothing for afternoon winds. These two walks can be combined by descending from the ridge crest to the glacier and the advance camps, then returning via the river to the end of the jeep track. Note: The Tibet Mountaineering Association (TMA) has begun stationing a liaison officer at the north base camp during the pre- and post-monsoon seasons. Besides overseeing the expeditions, the officer enforces a new rule preventing tourists from traveling beyond base camp if they don't have a climbing permit allowing them to ascend above 18,000 feet (5500 m). If you're stopped, ask if there is a "fee" for going past base camp similar to that imposed by the TMA at Everest base camp. Fees are negotiable.

THE SOUTH SHISHAPANGMA BASE CAMP TREK

The round-trip trek from Nyelam to the south Shishapangma base camp takes **4 to 5 days**. This high alpine walk does not involve a pass crossing, plus the pace is leisurely enough to allow day hikes into remote side valleys where blue sheep and even snow leopard are known to live. The best time is generally from mid-May through October, but snowstorms may occur any month of the year. The rain shadow created by the Shishapangma massif blocks most of India's monsoon, bringing only sporadic summer showers to the barren northern slopes. On the southern side the climate is remarkably different. Here the monsoon funnels up the Phu Chu canyon, bringing rain most nights (and some days) from June until early September, nourishing lush meadows and fields of wildflowers high into the mountains. Tents and fuel stoves are necessary.

Nyelam has a number of shops selling basics such as rice, noodles, flatbreads, vegetables, and meat. Kerosene is usually available; ask around. Hiring pack animals at Nyelam is often a problem in the summer. All of the horses and yak are pastured high in the hills, a half-day walk above the town at the herding camp of Drakpochen. Commercial trek companies will send someone to arrange pack animals in advance. Otherwise, your only choices are to send word up to the herders and hope that someone arrives the following day, or to hire porters to carry your gear to the camp; ask the owner of the Snowland Hotel to help make these arrangements. If you do use porters, watch your gear. Porters in the Zhangmu-Nyelam-Dingri area are notorious for being troublesome, sometimes removing things from unlocked packs and side pockets. Try not to let your porters stray behind or get too far ahead on the trail.

To the South Base Camp

The route to Drakpochen and the south Shishapaugma base camp starts at Tshongdü *gompa*, in the upper part of Nyelam. A dirt road leads around the temple's right side, then down along the south (R) bank of the Tshongdü Chu, passing a hydroelectric plant on the far bank. Springs tumble everywhere from the hills of glacial rubble, nourishing a delightful array of greenery and color: Flowering barberry, spiraea, and wild rosebushes crowd beside the trail; yellow primulas (*Primula sikkimensis*) stretch upward on

Dri *(female yak) milking time in the pastures above Nyelam*

stems almost 2 feet tall; and deep purple mountain irises rise majestically between the rocks. As the valley broadens, cultivated fields line both sides of the trail. At the head of these terraces, **1 hour** from the temple, is Phulok, a small settlement with a stone hut and a larger ruined house (12,650 ft, 3860 m). The first snowy peaks of the Jugal Himal poke above the ridges to the left (west). **Twenty minutes** farther the trail crosses a small bridge over a creek. The route to base camp continues up the main valley.

The smaller trail to the left up this creek's west (L) ridge is the steep pilgrimage trail to Dara Tsho (*dara* is a watery type of buttermilk). Allow **2½ to 3 hours** to reach this holy lake, which remains hidden until you're fairly close. The shoreline (14,000 ft, 4270 m) is speckled with hundreds of small stone offering piles and larger cairns with prayer flags. Dara Tsho has no inlet nor outlet, and is said to be around 130 feet (40 m) deep. According to local legends, the lake manifested from a piece of ice brought here by a *lama* (or Milarepa) returning from Mount Kailash. My guess is that the lake actually did originate from a piece of ice, but due to a huge chunk left by the glacier that once filled the valley. The lake sits in a broad plateau of glacial debris that must have been deposited by an enormous ice floe. As the glacier retreated, a section of ice could have been stranded in the huge moraine. Seepage from rain and melted snow, and perhaps an underground stream, must help maintain the lake's water level. The Jugal Himal rises impressively to the left (west); Nyanang Ri is the huge summit across the valley; the Shishapangma massif rises in the distance (north); and Pholha Gangchen is the tall pointed peak to the right of it.

The pilgrims complete up to three circumambulations of the lake, then return to Nyelam the same way they arrived. If you're continuing up the valley to the herders' camp at Drakpochen, you can descend directly from the lake to this camp. There's no trail; just pick a route down to the valley floor. From the far (north) end of the lake, climb to the ridge top (14,600 ft, 4450 m), then continue north. As you descend, aim for the big boulder in the Drakpochen meadows.

The trail to the south base camp bypasses Dara Tsho, continuing up the valley from the bridge. As the terrain opens out the meadows are surrounded by thickets of white and purple rhododendron, which bloom in June. **About 1½ hours** above the bridge, cross another creek; sometimes a simple plank bridge is set up. The giant boulder in the nearby meadows is Drakpochen, the "Big Rock." A small stone herders' hut (13,300 ft, 4050 m) is nearby. Although these meadows are only **3 to 4 hours** from Nyelam, stop for the night in this picturesque valley to acclimatize. Campsites are everywhere, but ask the herders before setting up tents. The next camps en route to the base camp are beyond the top of the huge moraine ridge to the north, nearly 1500 feet (450 m) higher than here.

If you arrive early in the afternoon, you can hike farther up the main valley for **1½ hours or more** to a large milky lake that sits precariously behind a wall of glacial debris. Other walks from Drakpochen include the hard **2- to 3- hour** ascent to Dara Tsho up the south (R) ridge spur to the southeast, or the hike up the sweeping side valley to the south below this same ridge. Following this valley, in **1 hour** you'll reach a sprawling meadow beneath a basin of glaciers and peaks. The locals call the main summit of this group Jhakhyung, the "Garuda Peak"; in Nepal it is known as Phurbi Chachu. Blue sheep descend from the ridges to graze on the meadow here. While I was staying at the south base camp one year, the herders found one of their baby yaks had been attacked by a snow leopard. I cannot help but feel an energizing sense of awe knowing that somewhere high among the ridges here, one of these magnificent cats might be peering down at me, silently watching my every move.

The route to the south base camp leaves the valley floor at Drakpochen, crossing the river on a wooden bridge near the big rock. Before setting off, look across the valley for the stone cairns atop the north (L) wall of glacial moraine. The main trail swings far to the left from the bridge before it turns back toward these cairns. Dozens of interweaving yak tracks make it easy to lose the way through the boulders and thick bushes. Reach the cairns on the ridge top (14,400 ft, 4390 m) in **1½ hours** from Drakpochen. From the summit the trail angles left and parallels the ridge crest, sometimes becoming faint but staying above the plateaulike trough that separates the hills of moraine from the true northern (L) ridges. In **less than 1 hour** pass the mouth of a broad tributary valley entering from the right. A route up this drainage crosses Kong Tsho La to the village of Ngora, **2 days** away from here (see trek description below).

Continue straight ahead (northwest) along hills thick with dwarf rhododendrons. If the weather is clear, the snowy flanks of Nyanang Ri (23,199 ft, 7071 m) are dead ahead, and farther back to the right (north) is Pholha Gangchen (25,269 ft, 7702 m); looming behind them is the first view of Shishapangma's summit. **One hour or more** beyond the valley to Kong Tsho La is Shingdip (14,700 ft, 4480 m), a beautiful meadow camp with a large boulder near the junction of converging morainal valleys. Several herder families spend the summer here grazing yak. The south base camp is **3 hours or more** beyond this meadow following the main valley west, but it is nearly 1500 feet (450 m) higher in elevation; camp here for the night, or perhaps two nights, to acclimatize.

If you take a rest day, consider doing the **3-hour** day hike up the valley to the right (north) to a large turquoise lake at the base of the glaciers flowing from Nyanang Ri, Pungpa Ri (24,426 ft, 7445 m), Pholha Gangchen, and Shishapangma. A trail follows the west (R) side of the stream draining this tributary up to two smaller lakes in a flat basin. The large lake is **less than 1 hour** farther up the valley near the base of the mountains on the left (northwest).

From Shingdip, a cross-country route continues west toward the base camp. I recommend hiring one of the herders as a guide, because the base camp is not easy to locate. As you ascend the main valley, angle left (west) toward the hills until you reach the crest of the main ridge. The edge of this moraine falls steeply to the glacier below, and the peaks of the Jugal Himal tower across the valley. Stay atop the ridge for **1 hour or more** until it ends at a deep circular basin. Drop to a small saddle (15,600 ft, 4750 m), then angle into the hills on the right. As you ascend, look farther up to the right (north) for a craggy, pyramid-shaped peak of dark gray rock. Using this summit as a bearing, chose a route a little to its left; the base camp (16,150 ft, 4920 m) is just below it by a glacial lake.

Shishapangma is out of view from base camp, but the Jugal Himal is a worthy stand-in. Directly across the valley is the star in this cast of snowy rock faces, Lenpo Gang (23,238 ft, 7083 m), the highest peak in the range. To its left is Gur Karpo Ri (22,552 ft, 6874 m), and behind them but hidden is Dorje Lhakpa (22,938 ft, 6990 m), a prominent double summit visible from Kathmandu. On a higher ledge above the base camp is another glacial lake.

Shishapangma can first be seen from a boulder-studded plateau 1½ **hours or more** above the base camp. Walk around the south side of the lower lake, then ascend the steep ridge behind it, angling up to the left (west) as you go. High-altitude rhododendrons (*R. nivale*) just inches tall cover the hillside. Continue climbing over rolling hills, then angle up to the right (north) toward an obvious boulder with cairns stacked on top. The Jugal Himal towers over this part of the valley; farther up to the right (north) is the steep Southwest Face of Shishapangma. The closest mountain up to the northeast was appropriately dubbed the "Ice Tooth" (marked by a peak symbol on map just south of Nyang Ri) by the 1982 Southwest Face expedition, and what appears to be the tallest summit from this angle is Nyanang Ri. Looking back southeast down the valley is the Lapchi Himal marching ruggedly across the distant skyline.

The advance base camp (16,900 ft, 5150 m) is **about 2 hours** farther north beyond a flat, stony ridge extending from the Ice Tooth. The top of this ridge (17,700 ft, 5400 m) looks directly onto an unusually thick mass of white ice oozing down the face of this peak. The route to the advance base camp area crosses a low point at the far left end of the ridge. From this narrow saddle (17,300 ft, 5270 m) descend to a paisley-shaped lake in the valley draining the Ice Tooth. The advance camp used by the 1982 British expedition was a "friendly place in a little hollow amongst grass and boulders" a short distance above the top end of the lake. Higher in the ravine below Ice Tooth is a cobalt blue glacial lake.

The return to Nyelam from base camp can be completed in **1 long day,** but if you have hired pack animals, the guide will probably want to stop for the night in Drakpochen. With an early start from this herders' camp it is possible to reach Zhangmu, complete the China-Nepal border crossing formalities, and drive to Kathmandu in a single day.

THE TREK TO NGORA

The trek from the Tshongdü Chu Valley to Ngora village, via Kong Tsho La, takes only **2 days** starting from the herder camp at Shingdip. It's a long **6- to 8-hour** day to cross the pass and reach campsites beside the lake, so get an early start. Ford the creek at Shingdip to the north (L) side, then descend east down the valley, staying along the far left side to avoid grass hummocks. A large moraine sits at the mouth of the tributary valley leading to Kong Tsho La. Angle up to the left, reaching the top of this moraine in **about 1 hour**. The arid terrain is much in contrast to the lush environs below at Drakpochen; stunted juniper bushes dot the slopes, and during summer the gossamer-thin petals of blue poppies (*Meconopsis horridula*) poke up between the rocks.

Kong Tsho La is **4 to 5 hours** to the north up this valley. Sidle along the west (R) ridge side above this clear-running stream. The valley becomes very rocky and barren with few decent places for camping. Remind yourself to turn around occasionally for views of the Jugal Himal. Initially it's easier walking on the west (R) side of the stream, but as you get higher the east side is best to avoid the rocky valley floor. Eventually an obvious dip in the ridge, Kong Tsho La (17,000 ft, 5180 m), can be seen at the head of the valley adjacent to a pointed peak. To the left (west) from the pass are two glacial lakes, and beyond are two others. Kong Tsho remains hidden from here, but soon this large blue lake comes into view below the pass. As you descend, stay to the east (R) of the stream flowing on to the gravel plain. Kong Tsho (16,500 ft, 5030 m) is **1 hour** below the pass. In July and August, thousands of yellow daisies (*Cremanthodium sp.*) carpet the ground as you approach the lake. Good, flat campsites line the eastern shore.

Shishapangma and Pholha Gangchen rise straight up from the lake, spilling monstrous icefalls from their flanks, nourishing this holy lake associated with Guru Rimpoche. Cairns have been erected near the shore, and a rough pilgrimage circuit leads around the perimeter. Kong Tsho is a *latsho*, a life-power lake for the Nyelam region.

The waters are said to freeze on the same day each year, then thaw every spring on the same day. Any differences from these dates are believed to have a negative effect upon the upcoming year.

Ngora is **5 to 6 hours** from Kong Tsho. The route from the lake is not obvious, and does not follow the lakeshore. Instead, angle northeast up the large moraine paralleling the right (east) side of the lake. Aim for a tall rock cairn (16,800 ft, 5120 m) on the ridge crest, reaching this scenic ridge crest in **1 hour** from the lake. Keep heading northeast, sidling along the ridge on a series of braided animal tracks. Not far past Kong Tsho is a second large glacial lake. The trail has turned almost east now, but eventually it disappears; look for rock cairns marking the route, which lead to a ridge crest overlooking the valley below. Descend to a series of meadows and continue down the valley. Keep looking up to the left (north) for a large, lone glacial boulder stuck high in the side of the moraine ridge. Tucked beneath this erratic boulder is Ralo *phuk*, the cave hermitage of Ra Lotsawa, a renowned eleventh-century Buddhist scholar and translator of Tantric texts who was born in Nyelam. Prayer flags and a walled-in entrance at the base of the rock help identify the site. The cave can also be reached in **about 30 minutes** by a trail leading west above Ngora.

Ngora remains hidden behind a large domed hill to the left. Stay to the right (east) of this barren ridge, descending past terraces of barley to reach this village (14,250 ft, 4340 m) of thirty houses. The red-walled Nyingmapa *gompa* is simple inside and only used when the local *ngakpas* meet for offering ceremonies and prayer text readings. Ask around for the *go-nyer* to get the key. Before the crops are harvested, the rock-walled animal pens are the best campsites. There are no shops here, and little is available for purchase besides butter, *tsampa,* and perhaps some potatoes. The Friendship Highway (km marker 5318) is about 7 miles (11 km) east of Ngora on a dirt road. Allow **3 to 4 hours** if you're on foot. Nyelam is 17 miles (27 km) south of this junction along the Phu Chu.

Would you hire a horse from these guys? I did!

11
THE MOUNT KAILASH REGION

*In a hundred ages of the gods I could not tell thee the glories of [the Himalaya] . . .
there is no mountain like [the Himalaya] for in it are Kailash and Manasarovar.*

From the Hindu epic *Ramayana*

MAP NO. 10, PAGE 211

Few mountains in the world rival the grandeur of Mount Kailash (22,028 ft, 6714 m), the famed holy peak in Western Tibet. Situated to the north of the Himalayan barrier, this legendary snow-shrouded rock dome is revered by four different religions as one of the most sacred pilgrimage destinations in Asia. The sources for four of South Asia's greatest rivers are nearby, and at the base of the mountain are two vast lakes, Manasarovar (Tib., Mapham Yumtsho, the Unconquerable Turquoise Lake; also called Madrö Tsho, the Cool Lake) and Rakshas Tal (Demon Lake; also Rakkas Tal; Tib., La-ngak or Langka Tsho).

Hindus regard Mount Kailash (lit., Silver Mountain) as the earthly manifestation of Mount Meru, their spiritual center of the universe, described in ancient texts as a fantastic "world pillar" 84,000 miles high, around which all else revolves, its roots in the lowest hell and its summit kissing the heavens. On top is the abode of their god Shiva, Lord of the Mountains, who shares this lofty peak with his consort, Parvati. Sprawling below is the sacred Manasarovar, where a ritual bath will deliver a pilgrim to Brahma's paradise and a drink of its waters relinquishes the sins of a hundred lifetimes. For the Jains, a religious sect holding many beliefs similar to those of Buddhists, Kailash is acclaimed as the site where their first prophet achieved enlightenment. Although they look much like Hindu pilgrims, Jains can often be identified by the small cloth bag containing prayer beads clutched in their right hands.

Mount Kailash is known to the Tibetans as Gang Rimpoche (Precious Jewel of Snow) or by its aboriginal name, Ti-se (also Gang Ti-se). Tibetan Buddhists, like Hindus, recognize Kailash as the manifestation of Mount Meru, the "navel of the world" rising "like the handle of a mill stone" into the heavens. From the slopes of Mount Meru a stream is said to pour into Mapham Yumtsho, and from this lake flow four rivers in the four cardinal directions toward the oceans: the Senge Khabab (also Khambab; River from the Lion Mouth) to the north; the Tamchok Khabab (River from the Horse Mouth) to the east; the Mapcha Khabab (River from the Peacock Mouth) to the south; and the Langchen Khabab (River from the Elephant Mouth) to the west. These mythical rivers are now associated with the four major rivers originating near Mount Kailash: the Indus, the Tsangpo (Brahmaputra), the Karnali, and the Sutlej, respectively. Kailash is also regarded as the residence of Demchok, a multi-armed, wrathful deity worshipped in the Chakrasamvara Tantric cycle of Tibetan Buddhism, and his consort, Dorje Phakmo. The mountain also has a special association with the poet-saint Milarepa, who spent several years here meditating in caves.

Mount Kailash is sacred to the Bön religion as well, as it is the site where its founder, Tönpa Shenrab, is said to have descended from heaven, and formerly it was the spiritual center of Zhang Zhung, the ancient Bönpo empire that once extended from Persia across through Western Tibet. The Bönpo circumambulate the mountain in their traditional counterclockwise manner, in the opposite direction of Buddhist and Hindu pilgrims.

Mount Kailash from the hills above Darchen

The pilgrimage to Mount Kailash and Manasarovar has always been one of the most difficult in Asia, if not the world. The distances were tremendous, weather particularly harsh, supplies almost nonexistent, and bandit attacks a constant worry. Nevertheless pilgrims came from the far corners of the continent, defying hardships to walk the 32-mile (52-km) circuit around Kailash and to bathe in or circumambulate the sacred waters of Manasarovar.

Even with the convenience of roads and four-wheel-drive vehicles, the shorter southern route from Lhasa following the Tsangpo is an arduous adventure requiring **5 days or more** to drive the 900 miles (1450 km) to Mount Kailash. The spectacular 1140-mile (1850-km) northern route from Lhasa across the Southern Chang Thang via Ali (also called Shiquanhe) takes **6 to 7 days** in good conditions, while a third road from Kashgar, in far western China, is popular with tour groups coming from Pakistan over Khunjerab Pass on the Karakoram Highway. There is currently no public transportation to anywhere in Ngari Prefecture.

If you're like me and prefer walking to bouncing in a vehicle for a week, a **4½- to 5½-day** trek route has been opened to commercial trekking groups starting from Purang, in Western Tibet, crossing the Tibet/Nepal border to finish at the airfield in Simikot, in the Humla district of West Nepal (see "The Purang to Simikot [Nepal] Trek," below). A potential trek route yet to open to foreigners is the pilgrimage and trade route between India and Purang, over Lipu Lekh pass.

Mount Kailash is located in the southwest corner of Ngari (formerly known as Ngari-korsum), the TAR's westernmost prefecture. Its lone, conical summit rises magnificently above all the neighboring peaks, the highest point at the west end of the Gangtise–Nyenchen Thanglha Range. Across the broad Barka plains to the south, beyond the waters of Manasarovar and Rakshas Tal, towers another impressive mountain, Gurla Mandata (Tib., Menmo Nanyi; 25,242 ft, 7694 m). The inhabitants of this region are primarily *drokpa*, the sturdy nomadic herders, since at this end of the Tibetan Plateau the land is so high and barren that there is little farming; fields of barley are a rare sight.

Darchen (Great Flag; 15,150 ft, 4620 m) is the pilgrim's gateway to Mount Kailash. This windblown settlement is 3 miles (5 km) north of the main road between Ali and Purang, about 15 miles (24 km) west of the Barka Qu road junction. Darchen is a small community with only about a dozen permanent buildings, but during summer it swells into a teeming tent city from the influx of pilgrims. The largest structure is the decaying Darchen *gompa*, a two-story stone building that formerly housed a monk-officer from Bhutan's Drukpa Kargyüpa sect; now it is the residence for the *lama* and *trülku* of Gyangdrak monastery, which is located in the hills above Darchen.

Over the past decade the growing popularity of Mount Kailash as a tourist and pilgrimage destination has seen Darchen transform into a pit of garbage and broken glass, barking dogs, loud Chinese disco music, and revving truck engines. It is also, sadly, a haunt for prostitutes. Two rather basic guesthouses have both dormitory and private rooms (a tourist hotel is planned), and several seasonal restaurants offer Tibetan and Chinese food. Also, a small police office inspects tourists' Alien Travel Permits. If you want to camp, stay away from Darchen; the local regulations require foreigners to set up tents only at the "designated campsite," a series of cement pads beside the guesthouse compound surrounded by trash and glass, costing as much per person as the guesthouses. Some commercial groups now bypass Darchen and drive west to the flat plains along the Lha Chu to camp near Darpoche, where the Saga Dawa Festival is held.

If you come to Kailash from Lhasa or Kashgar, stock up on supplies in the provincial capital, Ali, 150 miles (250 km) northwest of Darchen. Fresh fruit and vegetables, rice, meat, kerosene, and so on are usually available. Or try the bazaar (June to October) at Purang (also known as Taklakot), the Indian/Nepali border town 70 miles (112 km) south from Darchen. In Darchen several small shops sell noodles, instant soup, *tsampa,* yak butter, brick tea, and beer. During summer entrepreneurs living in canvas tents (many of them Khampas, from Eastern Tibet) sell canned meats, kerosene, apples, a few fresh vegetables, and religious items.

The best time of year to trek in Western Tibet is between mid-May and mid-October. During the first and last months of this season the weather is generally stable and clear, with cool temperatures during the day and nights below freezing. July and August are usually warmer, but this is when the monsoon pushes beyond the Himalaya, swelling the creeks and coating the valleys with greenery and wildflowers. Be prepared with cold-weather gear, as storms occasionally dump snow on the circuit, particularly near the pass. Fuel stoves are necessary unless you plan to cook over a yak dung fire with the pilgrims, and tents are highly recommended.

The main hospital in Western Tibet is in Ali, but its facilities do not meet the standards of those in Lhasa or Shigatse. The county hospitals in both Purang and Töling (also called Trada and on some maps Zanda; near Tsaparang, the old kingdom of Guge) have little more than beds, a few medical supplies, and a poorly trained staff. For altitude-related problems, Purang is the lowest elevation of any place near Mount Kailash. Helicopter evacuation from Nepal is almost impossible to arrange, and evacuation by vehicle to the Zhangmu/Nepal border can take up to three days, driving day and night.

Consider spending at least two nights in the Darchen or Manasarovar area to acclimatize before your trek, or layover in Purang if you trek there from Simikot.

DAY HIKES NEAR MOUNT KAILASH

The summit of Mount Kailash is visible from Darchen, but the best views of the mountain are a climb of **1 hour or more** up the ridge directly behind (north of) the town. From the guesthouses, walk up the west (R) side of the Darchen Chu, past the pilgrim camps to the base of the ridge. A faint trail leads from the camping area to a small rocky draw, then continues up through the rocks for **about 10 minutes** to an overlook with prayer flags and stone cairns (15,500 ft, 4720 m). Continue climbing up to the left (northwest) along the spine of the ridge to a huge prayer wall. The views extend in all directions, but the panorama from the ridge top (16,500 ft, 5030 m) is worth the additional **1 hour** climb.

The southern "sapphire" face of Kailash is stunning from this summit, its symmetrical white slopes and brownish red base halved by a vertical slash known to Hindus as the "Stairway to Heaven." According to Buddhist legend, this large cleft in the mountain occurred during a contest between Milarepa and Naro Bönchung, a resident Bönpo priest who challenged the presence of Buddhists at Kailash. To decide which was the deserving religion of the area, the two men engaged in a test of magical strength. The last of several competitions was a race to the summit of the holy peak. Naro Bönchung set off first early in the morning, flying toward the mountain upon his magical *damaru* drum. Milarepa remained in bed until the Bönpo priest was nearly at the summit, then "snapped his fingers, donned a cloak for wings," and in a second arrived on top before his rival. Naro Bönchung fell down in defeat, his drum slicing a deep groove as it tumbled down the southern face. Naro Bönchung begged permission to continue circumambulating the mountain in the counterclockwise Bön manner, then asked for a place to stay where he could see the mountain. The victorious Milarepa agreed. Tossing a handful of Kailash's snow onto a nearby peak to the east, he offered it as a dwelling place to the priest. This summit is now called Bönri, the Bön Mountain, and on the lower flanks are the ruins of Bönri *gompa.*

The two drainages flowing from Kailash's South Face are the Selung Chu and Gyangdrak Chu drainages. To the south across the Barka plains are the blue waters of

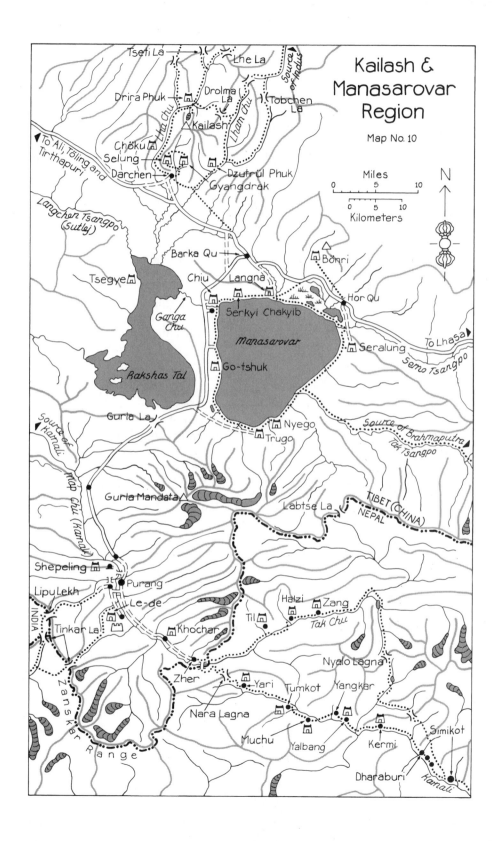

Kailash &
Manasarovar
Region

Map No. 10

Miles

0   5   10

0   5   10
Kilometers

N

Tseti La

Lhe La

Source of Indus

Drira Phuk

Drolma La

Tobchen La

Kailash

Lha Chu

Lham Chu

Chöku

Selung

Darchen

To Ali, Töling and Tirthapuri

Dzutrül Phuk
Gyangdrak

Langchen Tsangpo
(Sutlej)

Barka Qu

Bönri

Tsegye

Chiu

Langna

Hor Qu

Ganga Chu

Serkyi Chakyib

Manasarovar

Seralung

To Lhasa

Semo Tsangpo

Rakshas Tal

Go-tshuk

Gurla La

Nyego

Trugo

Source of Brahmaputra
Tak Tsangpo

Source of Karnali

Map Chu (Karnali)

Gurla Mandata

Labtse La

TIBET (CHINA)
NEPAL

Shepeling

Purang

Lipu Lekh

Le-de

INDIA

Tinkar La

Khochar

Halzi

Zang

Til

Tak Chu

Nyalo Lagna

Zher

Yari

Tumkot

Yangkar

Nara Lagna

Zanskar Range

Muchu

Yalbang

Kermi

Simikot

Dharaburi

Karnali

Rakshas Tal. A small portion of Manasarovar can be seen farther to the east, below Gurla Mandata's snowy massif.

―――――――――

A moderate hike from Darchen is the **2½-hour** walk north into the foothills to Gyangdrak (also spelled Gengta on maps) *gompa*, the first monastery founded in the Mount Kailash region. To start, cross the Darchen Chu to the east (L) side on the wooden bridge just above the guesthouse compounds. Go upstream along the embankment past the trader's tents. At the far end of a long prayer wall, an obvious track leads steeply up the east (L) ridge. As the trail levels out, Gyangdrak can be seen ahead, perched on a hillock; to the south are outstanding views of Gurla Mandata and Rakshas Tal. The valley soon divides, with the left branch leading in **1 hour or more** to Selung *gompa* (16,200 ft, 4940 m), a small retreat associated with Gyangdrak. The trail to Gyangdrak follows the right branch into a high, dry amphitheater guarded by whistling marmots. Cross to the north (R) side of the Gyangdrak Chu, then ascend past hundreds of small devotional cairns and a group of *chörtens* to reach the monastery (16,450 ft, 5010 m).

Gyangdrak was founded in the thirteenth century by the Drigung Kargyüpa sect. It became the administrative center for overseeing the legions of meditators sent to the Mount Kailash area by Drigung monastery's founder, Kyowa Jigten Sumgon. Following a vision in which he was beckoned by the protecting deities from Kailash, Lapchi, and Tsari (three of Milarepa's most important meditation sites), Jigten Sumgon initiated three expeditions of meditators to each site. Monasteries and hermitages were established to accommodate the ascetics, particularly at Kailash. Gyangdrak was the personal residence of Guya Gangpa, the first Drigungpa administrator, who was responsible for governing the estates donated to the Drigungpa by the King of Guge to support the Kailash monks. During a period of decline for the Drigungpa in the fifteenth century, most of their *gompas* around Kailash and elsewhere in Western Tibet were "leased" to the Drukpa Kargyüpa sect of Bhutan, and these temples remain under their control today.

Like all religious structures around Mount Kailash, Gyangdrak was destroyed during the Cultural Revolution; the *lhakhang* on the hilltop was the first to be rebuilt, in 1983. A new chanting hall for the ten monks based here stands beside the sleeping quarters for both the young *trülku* and the *lama* of Gyangdrak, who reside in Darchen at the old *gompa*. One of the four *zhabjes*, the stone footprints of Buddha around Mount Kailash, was once here, but it disappeared in the 1960s.

―――――――――

Selung (Gray Valley; also Serlung) *gompa,* the only other retreat at Mount Kailash that is not on the main pilgrimage *kora*, is **about 2 hours** west of Gyangdrak. The trail starts near the *chörtens* behind the monks' residences, climbs the far west (R) ridge (16,950 ft, 5170 m), then descends to the Selung Chu. The *gompa* is on the west (R) bank. A small temple is upstairs, and residence rooms for monks and nuns are on both levels. Up the valley from Selung is the route to Sheldra, site of the inner pilgrimage circuit of Mount Kailash. Near the base of the mountain was Serdung Chuk-sum (Thirteen Reliquary *Chörtens*), where relics of the former Gyangdrak administrators where enshrined. Many meditation caves are found here as well. The inner *kora* follows the base of the mountain east to Tsho Kapala, neighboring glacial lakes said to have black water in one, white in the other. According to tradition, only those having completed thirteen circuits around Kailash are meant to perform the inner circuit and visit these sacred lakes.

Some pilgrims continue west for **2 hours or more** from Selung *gompa*, crossing a pass (16,550 ft, 5040 m) on the west (R) ridge to enter the Lha Chu Valley at Darpoche, where the Saga Dawa festivities are held each year. To return to Darchen from Selung,

Pilgrim circumambulating Mount Kailash, Lha Chu Valley

follow the trail downstream along the Selung Chu to meet the track between Gyangdrak and Darchen.

THE MOUNT KAILASH CIRCUIT TREK

The pilgrim's *kora* around Mount Kailash starts and finishes at Darchen. The clockwise circuit initially enters the Lha Chu (Divine River) Valley, swings behind Kailash's sheer northern face to Drolma La (18,200 ft, 5550 m), the highest point en route, then descends into the Lham Chu Valley and onto Darchen. The hearty Tibetan pilgrims usually take one long day to complete the *kora*, starting about 4:00 A.M. and returning late in the afternoon or evening; they believe that walking three or thirteen circuits is particularly auspicious. Some pilgrims complete the *kora* doing full-body prostrations along the ground, a slow journey that can take two weeks. For Tibetans, walking around this holy mountain is more than an act of merit: One circuit is said to purify all the sins of a lifetime; 108 circuits will bring enlightenment during this lifetime. In *ta lo,* the "Year of the Horse" in the twelve-year Tibetan calendar (1990 was a "Horse" year; 2002 will be the next), walking the *kora* is equal to thirteen circuits completed during other years. Commercial trek groups and Indian pilgrims generally spend **2½ days** on the circuit, camping one night near Drira Phuk *gompa* and a second night at Dzutrül Phuk *gompa* before returning to Darchen.

If you have the time, spend at least **4 days** on the Kailash circuit. A leisurely pace allows time to visit all three of the monasteries en route and a chance to explore the Gangjam Glacier below Kailash's sheer northern face. Hiring pack animals (usually yaks) at Darchen is generally not a problem, although it can take a day or more for them to arrive. The guesthouse managers can help with the arrangements. If Drolma La has too much snow, it may be necessary to hire pilgrims as porters!

The circuit around Mount Kailash is a wide, obvious trail starting near the old Darchen monastery. Lined with rocks and devotional cairns, the *kora* undulates over a desert of scrub and sandy soil, following the seam where the Barka plains lap against the foothills. Gurla Mandata rises unchallenged, a massive block of tilted rock and ice dwarfing the distant spires of the Zanskar Range off to the right (west), which delineate the Nepal-India-Tibet border. **One hour** from Darchen the trail ascends a low ridge of moraine topped with prayer flags, where Kailash's North Face reemerges above the hills. Heaped beside the trail are stone cairns and offerings of clothing, an act considered auspicious at the most holy of pilgrimage sites. On this ridge is the first of four *chaktsal gang,* or prostration sites, found around the *kora.* Pilgrims perform full-body prostrations here, first touching their joined hands to the head, the mouth, and the heart, in

Festival at Kailash

quick succession before reclining on the ground, face down with arms extended over the head in an act of complete devotion.

Beyond the ridge opens the magnificent desert valley of the Lha Chu, where immense eroded walls of purple sandstone and conglomerate rock sweep into craggy pinnacles, and the towers of mythical castles loom above the river plain. Descend into the valley for **45 minutes** to the grazing area of Serzhong (Golden Basin). Above the trail to the right is Darpoche (Great Flagpole; 15,300 ft, 4660 m), the site of an annual religious festival held on the full moon of Saga Dawa, the fourth Tibetan month (usually between late May to mid-June). Each year the tall pole here is taken down, redecorated with prayer flags, then raised before a great crowd on this day to celebrate the enlightenment of Buddha. A route crossing over from Selung *gompa* enters the valley here. Just north of the pole is Kyilkhor Teng (Mandala Terrace), a rocky plateau with an important sky-burial site in the center. Nearby is a rock enclosure protecting the first of the Buddha footprints on the Kailash *kora,* created when the Buddha Chomdende ("The Victorious One") flew here with a retinue of 500 *arhats* (spiritual elders). He landed at this spot first, then at three other places around the mountain, which "nailed down" Mount Kailash just as the demon Gompo Beng was about to carry it away on his back to his home in a land called Langka. Pilgrims leave a piece of clothing here as an offering.

Near Serzhong the *kora* route comes to a long *mani* wall and Chörten Kangnyi (Two-legged *Chörten*), where pilgrims earn merit by walking through this gate to the Lha Chu Valley. Many paths traverse the gravel flood plain below here, but the main trail stays near the hills, reaching several crumbling *chörtens* and a prayer wall in **30 minutes**. About 150 feet (45 m) up the ridge to the right is Naro Bönchung's cave; look for prayer flags. The bridge to Chöku *gompa*, the first temple on the Kailash circuit, is **10 minutes** from here. Several large meadows are in the gravel expanse near the river. Stop here for the night if you're spending four days on the circuit; Drira Phuk is **about 4 hours** farther.

Chöku *gompa* (also called Nyenri and Nyenpo *ri dzong*; 15,650 ft, 4770 m) clings to an immense rock face, a steep **25-minute** climb above the Lha Chu. Established by the Drigungpa in the thirteenth century, this retreat houses the self-manifested image of

Chöku Rimpoche—a squat, white marble statue of Öpame, the "Buddha of Boundless Light," enshrined in the central glass case. Two other objects of interest to pilgrims are a silver-lined conch shell that belonged to the Indian master Naropa, which Milarepa is said to have recovered from the depths of Manasarovar, and Naropa's large copper tea cauldron. In the seventeenth century an invading army stole the Chöku statue, which they said belonged to the Guge kingdom. They also took Naropa's conch and teapot. The local deities used their powers to make the Chöku statue so heavy that the soldiers had to abandon it by the river. Next the conch magically flew back to the *gompa*. When they brewed tea in the stolen pot, the tea turned to blood. The invaders promptly retreated from the valley empty handed. Later an old man saw the statue, and finding it "light as a feather," returned it to the *gompa*. The statue, conch, and cauldron were spared from the Red Guards at the request of the Bhutanese government, and were kept in Barka until the 1980s when the temple was rebuilt.

The separate, smaller building overlooking the cliff is a *gönkhang* dedicated to Gangri Lhatsen, the protecting deity residing in Nyenri, the high ridge rising behind Chöku. Several retreat caves are located near the *gompa,* including Langchen Bephuk, the "Secret Elephant Cave" where Guru Rimpoche concealed religious texts. A rough trail leads up the gully above Chöku to Rechung *phuk,* one of Milarepa's caves.

A trail continues on the Lha Chu's west (R) bank, but most pilgrims cross the bridge to rejoin the main circuit. The route now waltzes under huge ramparts of weathered rock towering thousands of feet high. The valley's unusual natural formations have been interwoven with myths of the area, particularly with Gesar of Ling, the hero-king of Tibet's great epic story. A long, trailing waterfall spilling off the west (R) side of the canyon is known as the tail of Lhata Kyang-lu, Gesar's horse, and the large rock ridge nearby is said to be Gesar's saddle. A prominent, conical peak on the east (L) side is known as the *torma,* or offering cake, of Guru Rimpoche. A waterfall separates it from a lofty rock palace where Gompo Beng is said to reside after having been converted into a protector of Buddhism by the Buddha Chomdende.

Two hours beyond the Chöku bridge crossing, the trail passes the second *zhabje* of Chomdende, a large, well-defined footprint imbedded in a rock on the ground; it's on the right side of the trail. Sometimes a local *drokpa* family sets up a tent nearby, selling tea and biscuits. The Lha Chu soon swings right (east) as two large tributaries enter from the north. The second of these valleys, the Dronglung (Wild Yak) Valley, is one of several routes that leads to Senge Khabab, the source of the Indus River. The second *chaktsal gang* of the circuit is along here as well, marked by a large cairn beside the trail. The meadows below are popular picnic spots for pilgrims. Fat marmots race between burrows screaming at these intruders, the smell of yak chip fires permeates the air, and the first view of Kailash's "golden" North Face appears above the hills. On the north (R) bank farther up the valley is a campsite established for Indian pilgrims. These lucky folks are among several hundred each year selected by means of a lottery system to enter Tibet and perform *parikrama,* the circumambulation around Kailash. Commercial trekking groups walking the *kora* in three days often camp here as well, though less congested sites can be found upstream.

The main pilgrimage trail stays above the Lha Chu's south (L) bank, crossing the Gangjam Chu, then leads to a stone hut. Drira Phuk *gompa* is across the river on the north (R) ridge. The sheer icy North Face of Mount Kailash is now unveiled. It is framed perfectly by rounded, symmetrical hills—"like a huge silver dome placed on a pedestal with two guards on either side" according to Swami Pranavananda, an Indian holy man who spent many years in this area and wrote an informative pilgrim's guide, *Kailas Manasarovar.* To Buddhists these hills are the thrones of the Risum Gompo *bodhisattvas* Chanak Dorje and Chenrezik, while a third hill farther east is the residence of Jampeyang.

If time permits, the **half-day** hike up the Gangjam Chu Valley provides excellent views of the Kailash massif and the Gangjam Glacier. From the hut, head south up the ridge toward a row of stone *chörtens*. The best route up to the glacier is in the center of the valley, along the east (R) side of the Gangjam Chu, where a faint trail winds through the rocks. Reach the base of the glacier (17,300 ft, 5270 m) after **about 2 hours** of steady climbing. Pilgrims continue onto the glacier's surface to make offerings and prostrate before Gang Rimpoche.

The main pilgrim trail to Drolma La continues straight ahead (east) from the stone hut and crosses to the north (R) bank of the Drolma Chu, a tributary of the Lha Chu. The *kora* continues up this side valley and soon ascends steeply above the creek. To visit Drira Phuk, follow the Drolma Chu downstream and cross the bridge over the Lha Chu. Below the *gompa* is a "sleeping house" with six empty dirt-floored rooms for hire. A short distance up the hill is Drira Phuk (16,450 ft, 5010 m), the "Female Yak Horn Cave." This was the meditation cave of Gyelwa Götsangpa, a Drukpa Kargyüpa monk credited with discovering the route around Mount Kailash. According to the story (there are numerous versions), Götsangpa followed a *dri,* or female yak, up the Lha Chu Valley. The *dri* led him into this cave, where he realized that it was really an emanation of Khandro Senge Dongma, the lion-faced *khandroma*, a female guardian spirit of these upper valleys. The site is now enclosed by a shrine and tended by a *go-nyer*, who has the keys. Ask him to point out the horn marks and indentations from Götsangpa's hat on the cave ceiling. Outside the cave are images of Milarepa, Götsangpa, and Senge Dongma. Drira Phuk is affiliated with the Drukpa Kargyüpa sect.

Beyond Drira Phuk the Lha Chu turns toward the north. The route used by Swami Pranavananda to reach Senge Khabab, the source of the Indus, follows this valley up to its headwaters and crosses Lhe La. The Swedish explorer Sven Hedin also ascended the Lha Chu, though his route was over two adjacent passes, Tseti La (18,465 ft, 5628 m) and Tseti Lachen La (17,933 ft, 5466 m). Hedin was the first Westerner to venture around the Kailash *kora*, which he completed by riding a yak. Senge Khabab is **2½ to 3 days** away from Drira Phuk.

The final ascent from Drira Phuk to Drolma La takes **3½ to 4 hours**; Dzutrül phuk, the next temple on the circuit, is **3 to 4 hours** beyond the pass. From the monastery the *kora* climbs east above the Drolma Chu on a steep moraine of white granite rocks. Reach the second of two high points in **1 hour**. The meadow below here is the last campsite (17,050 ft, 5200 m) of any sort before the pass. Directly across the valley is Pölung (Incense Valley), a large basin cradled by Kailash's rocky eastern arm. This entire region is a geology lesson on glaciation: All of the valleys are broad, U-shaped, and scoured by ancient ice floes; the granite they scraped away was cast aside in tremendous moraine piles. The trail climbs less dramatically above the meadows for **20 minutes** to Silwa-tsel (Cool Grove) cemetery. The site is littered with piles of clothing and surrounded by small stone cairns. Pilgrims make offerings here to ensure the smooth passage of their spirit into the Bardo, an interim period that Tibetan Buddhists believe follows death. Just above the trail is a rock where pilgrims sometimes leave one of their teeth or draw blood from their gums or a small cut to appease Shinje, the "Lord of Death." Those who die while on *kora* are given a sky burial here; it is considered a very meritorious way to end one's life.

Family of pilgrims brewing tea while on pilgrimage around Mount Kailash

Across the valley (south) another tributary opens to reveal the snow-choked approach to Khandro Sanglam (Secret Path of the *Khandroma*) pass. This alternative route around Kailash bypasses Drolma La, which tradition says can be crossed only if you have completed twelve previous circuits around the mountain. With binoculars, a cairn can be seen on the snowy summit.

The trail to Drolma La now levels out briefly, weaving between the chunks of granite on the valley floor. Three large rocks stacked on top of each other beside the path are said to be the result of a contest between Milarepa and Naro Bönchung; Milarepa won by placing the last one on top. A bit farther is a large "sin-testing" boulder with a narrow passage underneath. Pilgrims watch intently as each member in their party attempts to slither through to prove that he or she is free of sin. Soon the rocky path swings up from the valley onto a ridge of glacial rubble for the final 600-foot (180-m) climb to the pass; the top is **1 hour** away. Kailash's North Face peers over neighboring ridges for the last time. About halfway along is a small stream crossing the trail; pilgrims wash their hands in it to cleanse away their sins, then rub a smoothed rock where Gesar of Ling's butcher left his handprint after washing away his sin of killing animals. Beside the route are mounds of rock, devotional cairns, and stones etched with prayers. Nature also plays at decorating the trail, spraying the rocks with brilliant orange patches of lichen. The incessant mumbling of prayers by the pilgrims turns to hushed pants as they labor up the steep switchbacks.

Even without the glimmering white cap of Mount Kailash in view, Drolma La (18,200 ft, 5490 m) is a stunning spectacle. Stretching 150 feet across the summit are thick garlands of colorful prayer flags dancing in the wind. The large boulder among all this festivity is Drolma Do, the Rock of Drolma (Tara). When the monk Götsangpa was first trying to find his way around Mount Kailash, he wandered into the valley of the lion-faced *khandroma*, where a pack of twenty-one blue wolves led him to this boulder. The wolves were actually the twenty-one emanations of Drolma, the protectress who resides here. Once on the summit, the wolves magically merged into one wolf, which dissolved into the boulder and disappeared. Pilgrims prostrate themselves before this revered throne of Drolma, some climb on top to attach more prayer flags, and others struggle through the tangle of flags to complete the traditional three circuits around the rock. On the far side of Drolma Do the atmosphere is festive, as this is both the physical and the spiritual pinnacle of the Kailash pilgrimage. Groups and families settle down among the rocks, huddling around yak dung fires as they prepare kettles of tea. Leather bags of *tsampa* are opened, small wooden bowls are produced from their sheepskin coats, tea is poured, and the feast begins.

The pilgrim trail now descends east from the summit. Gaurikund Lake (Tib., Tuje Dzingbu, the Bathing Pool of Compassion) quickly comes into view, a milky green glacial tarn about 200 feet (60 m) below the main trail. Hindu pilgrims are supposed to take a ritual bath here, but the surface ice is often too thick to actually do so. Buddhist pilgrims receive their blessing by slurping from a handful of water, then running the remainder through their hair. Beyond the lake the *kora* descends steeply through an eerie world of shattered granite. Gurla Mandata can soon be seen to the south, and below is the welcome greenery of the Lham Chu Valley. The bottom is a knee-cracking **1-hour** descent, 1300 feet (400 m) below Drolma La. The Tibetan picnics that started on the pass continue here on the grassy meadows, where both water and warmth are in abundance. To the right of the trail beside a stone hut is the third of Buddha Chomdende's footprints, imbedded on top of the large boulder. The pilgrimage route now divides on the valley floor. The main trail stays on the creek's west (R) bank, but the ground can be very wet in places. A drier path follows the east (L) bank and offers the best views of Kailash's East Face, but there are no bridges.

Except for the marshy patches, the walking is easy along the broad meadows of the Lham Chu Valley. The hills here are more rounded and not rocky like the Lha Chu canyon. More than once along this stretch of the trail a sudden rush of air swooshed above my head: lammergeiers! The area seems to be a haven for these graceful bearded vultures; I find myself referring to this region as Lammergeier Valley.

Thirty minutes after reaching the valley floor a tributary enters from the west, where the third of the prostration *chaktsal gangs* is located. The ever-changing Kailash now presents the only view of its "crystal" East Face. The "secret" route over Khandro Sanglam La descends here to rejoin the main *kora*.

About 2 hours farther down, the Tobchen Chu (Powerful River) comes in from the east. A three-day route to the source of the Indus leads up this drainage and over Tobchen La. Below this confluence the river assumes a new name, the Dzong Chu (Fortress River). Dzutrül Phuk is **30 minutes** farther. Many rows of *mani* walls line the trail near the *gompa*. Like the other temples around the circuit, Dzutrül Phuk (Cave of Miracles; 15,700 lt, 4790 m) is an earth-colored structure built into the mountain above the trail. The cave's name comes from another event in the legendary contest between Milarepa and Naro Bönchung. At one point during the competition it started to rain, so they stopped to build themselves a rock shelter. Milarepa used his powers to set a great roof stone in place, but once inside they discovered the ceiling was too low. The poet-saint pushed the stone upward, but the shelter became too drafty, causing him to go outside to push the stone back down with his foot. The caretaker will point out Milarepa's handprints and finger marks on the black ceiling; his footprint on top of this great stone is enshrined at the base of a boulder. A *kora* route leads to it and around the temple. A figure of Milarepa is inside the cave, set on a self-manifested golden base. The rectangular piece of stone beside the cave entrance is the remaining half of a 7-foot (2-m) column said to be Milarepa's walking stick. Pilgrims used to try to lift this pillar as a test of strength, but it was damaged by the Red Guards. I was told that after they destroyed the building, the rock overhang was dynamited five times, but the Cave of Miracles remained intact. This *gompa* dates back to the 1220s, although the building you see here was rebuilt in 1983; it is affiliated with the Drukpa Kargyüpa sect. On the hill above is a sky-burial site and a number of meditation caves including Ah-phuk, where Milarepa etched the Tibetan letter *ah* into the rock. The meadows below Dzutrül Phuk are used as the second campsite along the Kailash circuit for Indian pilgrims and commercial trekking groups. Below the *gompa* is another sleeping house with six rooms.

Darchen is only **3 hours** from Dzutrül Phuk. Initially the trail is a wide, delightful stroll under weathered, mesalike hills reminiscent of the Southwestern United States. Several tributaries enter from the right (west); the largest is spanned by a bridge. A shortcut leads over these hills to Gyangdrak *gompa* via Darchung La (also called Zhabje La), but the trail is not very good.

The Dzong Chu narrows into a gorge and the surrounding hills swirl into a kaleidoscope of colors. Shrubs reappear near the trail, and Rakshas Tal comes into view. Pass numerous *zhabje* rocks, then come to the final *chaktsal gang* and a nearby cairn at the end of the gorge. The Barka plains are straight ahead, edged in the distance by the white teeth of the Zanskar Range.

The trail now leaves the Dzong Chu and returns to the desert. The route for the pilgrimage around Manasarovar leads off to the left (southeast) near a group of *mani* walls; the traditional start of the lake circuit is at the town of Hor Qu, a **2-day** walk from here. The Kailash *kora* now turns right (west), following the base of the foothills. The pilgrimage circuit ends with the return to Darchen, **1 hour** past these prayer walls. *Om mani padme hum!*

Other trekking possibilities in the Kailash region include the **4- to 5-day** circumambulation around Manasarovar (see "The Trek around Manasarovar," below) and the more difficult trip to Tamchok Khabab, the source of the Tsangpo. Its headwaters are approached by trekking to the south of Seralung *gompa*, on the east shore of Manasarovar, then up the Tak Tsangpo Valley and over Tak La (17,400 ft, 5300 m) to the glacial origin.

TIRTHAPURI

After Kailash and Manasarovar, the third most important pilgrimage site in Western Tibet is Tirthapuri (14,200 ft, 4330 m), renowned for its sacred hot springs and a Guru Rimpoche cave. From Darchen, drive 38 miles (60 km) west on the Ali road to the turnoff at Mon-tser. Tirthapuri is another 7 miles (11 km) to the south, on the banks of the Sutlej River. The Guru Rimpoche cave is enshrined in this Drukpa Kargyüpa temple. A **1-hour** outer pilgrimage *kora* circles the temple, with its striking backdrop of colorfully eroded badlands, natural formations, and famous meditation caves.

Another cave temple in this area is Gurujam (13,900 ft, 4240 m), a Bönpo site located a **3- to 4-hour** walk west of Tirthapuri along a dirt road on the north (R) bank of the Sutlej. This spectacular cliffside cave is said to be three thousand years old, and contains the reliquary shrines of the eight Tsawai Rimpoches of Gurujam. The current, Ninth Tsawai Lama has re-established this ornate cave and rebuilt the monastery below. The hills on both sides of the river are perforated with ancient cave sites. A day's walk or more farther down the Sutlej are the remains of Khyunglung, the cave-city capital of the ancient Zhang Zhung empire, which was conquered in the seventh century by Songtsen Gampo's armies.

TÖLING AND TSAPARANG

Tsaparang, capital of the former Guge kingdom in Western Tibet, is 163 miles (232 km) northwest from Darchen. The turnoff is at Baher (Baer), an army camp another 34 miles beyond the Tirthapuri turnoff at Mon-tser. It's a long, hard day of driving from either Darchen or Ali to reach the Grand Canyon of the Sutlej (Langchen Tsangpo) and Töling (Chi., Trada; 12,400 ft, 3780 m), the last town before Tsaparang. The kingdom was founded in the early tenth century by a great grandson of Langdarma, the king whose assassination led to the collapse of the Tibetan Royal Dynasty. Guge is well known in the history of Tibet, not for its strength or conquests, but as a focal point for the resurgence of Buddhism in Tibet following its persecution by Langdarma. The monastery at Töling was one of the first temples built in Tibet at the onset of the "second diffusion" of Buddhism. It was established in 996 by the renowned King Yeshe Ö, when Töling was the capital of Guge. Two other temples founded at that time, Khochar (south of Purang) and Tabo (in Spiti, now a part of Northern India), are still extant today. Yeshe Ö also sponsored the acclaimed translator Rinchen Zangpo to spend seventeen years studying and translating texts in Kashmir and India, and the king played a role in inviting the Indian master Atisha to Guge in 1042. Later in the eleventh century the Guge king Tselde sponsored a great Buddhist conference at Töling. Gyatsa *lhakhang* (also called the Yeshe Ö temple), an original tenth-century temple, is now in ruins, but two fifteenth-century chapels used for grain storage during the Cultural Revolution have survived; both have exquisite murals, but Lhakhang Karpo's are particularly fine. The other temple is the ornately decorated *dukhang,* a frilly show for this monastery of just a few Gelukpa monks and a *lama.* Entry permits must be purchased from the local Cultural Affairs office to visit the Töling or Tsaparang temples, regardless of any permits you've obtained elsewhere.

By the early seventeenth century the capital of Guge had shifted to Tsaparang, 12 miles (19 km) west of Töling along the Sutlej River. The old city is a fairytale castle of caves and passageways honeycombed in a tall ridge of ancient ocean deposits. In the upper portion of the mountain was the king's palace, a network of interconnecting chambers with a balcony and windows overlooking the valley. Unfortunately the castle, the adjacent city, and most of the monastic buildings have fallen into decay since the Guge kingdom was conquered by Ladakh in 1630, but several fifteenth-century temples have survived along the lower flanks of the ridge. Like Töling, their walls are a museum of superb mural art. Bring a flashlight to inspect the incredibly ornate patterns in the clothing, the historical accounts, the wonderful mythical animals, and the floral designs surrounding the main images. The *go-nyer* with the keys to Tsaparang lives in the village below the ruins. Be sure to have him take you above the lower four temples to the Demchok shrine and the old palace on top; access to the inner passageways is also from the summit.

There are no facilities to spend the night at Tsaparang, but it may be possible to stay with a family in the village. Several guesthouses are in Töling, along with a few Chinese restaurants and small shops. The best campsites are in the meadows of the two tributary valleys south of Töling. The Trada County (*xian*) hospital is to the east of town, and the post office has a satellite telephone.

THE TREK AROUND MANASAROVAR

Even if you don't have time to hike the **4- to 6-day** pilgrimage circuit around the sacred Manasarovar, set aside at least a few days to walk or camp along the shores of this magnificent lake. The trail is almost flat for the entire journey, the water is crystal clear, and the views are befitting the most famous lake in Tibet. From the southern shores sweep in the icy flanks of Gurla Mandata (25,242 ft, 7694 m), the highest peak in Western

Mani *wall and a* tsha khang, *where* tsha tshas *are offered, near Manasarovar*

Tibet. Visible to the north from many points on the lake is the white, rounded pyramid of Mount Kailash, and around the shores are six active temples.

Tibetan pilgrims take **3 days** to complete the circuit and usually start at Hor Qu (also called Hor-re and Le-gya; 14,950 ft, 4560 m), 28 miles (46 km) from Darchen at the northeast corner of the lake. Their first stop is Trugo *gompa* at the southeast end of the lake, and the second night is at Chiu *gompa*, on the northwest shore, before returning to Hor Qu. To complete the circuit at this pace requires **10 to 12 hours** of steady walking each day, leaving little time for exploring the temples or enjoying the scenery. The circuit can be shortened by **4 to 5 hours** if you finish at Langna monastery, on the north end of the lake. Except in winter when the water level is down, the *kora* has to leave the lakeshore here to avoid marshy ground and deep water. The pilgrims head northeast from Langna across the plains around three smaller lakes, then follow the road back to Hor Qu. Taking **4 days** from Hor Qu around the lake to Langna is a much better pace, but I found **6 days** to be just perfect. If you have transportation, an alternative to walking the entire *kora* is to hike the eastern shore for **2 days** and camp one night en route from Hor Qu to Trugo *gompa*. Your vehicles can then drive around to Trugo to meet you.

Hor Qu is a windblown scattering of mud brick homes and *shang* compounds along the southern road to Lhasa. The army has a checkpoint here, and Mayum La (17,000 ft, 5180 m) is 62 miles (100 km) to the east. There is a very basic guesthouse (a nicer "nonpublic" one for officials is behind it) and a couple of small shops. If you need to hire packhorses, the guesthouse manager is a good person to ask. Don't expect to leave the next day, as the horses are usually pastured away from Hor Qu.

If you spend an extra day waiting for horses, the ruins of Bönri monastery (15,700 ft, 4790 m) are **3 hours or more** to the northwest of Hor Qu. Bönri is the higher, western summit of two snowy mountains to the north. The *gompa* is along a deep gully below the left (west) side of the main peak. Despite its name and location, this monastery was a Gelukpa meditational retreat associated with Sera Je college in Lhasa. Although nothing has been rebuilt, the ruins are fascinating and the higher ground offers a fine overview of the lake and Gurla Mandata. With binoculars it is possible to sight several temples around the *kora*.

THE MANASAROVAR KORA

Pilgrims begin the Manasarovar circuit from Hor Qu by first walking clockwise around a group of *chörtens* southwest of town, then turning south toward the lakeshore.

Seralung, the first temple on the *kora*, is **3 hours** from Hor Qu. A faint trail leads past the *chörtens* and eventually meets a dirt road heading to the *gompa*. After crossing the Semo Tsangpo, which has a large camping meadow on the south (L) bank, the road angles left (east) into the hills. The pilgrim's path leads south into the sand dunes toward the lake. The lakeshore is a bit tricky to walk on, but eventually you get the knack of following the edge of the high waterline, where the sand and gravel are most firm. Unusual egg-shaped balls of vegetation float onto the shore, which pilgrims collect as *chinlap* (blessing). They also collect the brilliantly multicolored sand here, which is called *chema ne-nga*, "five-colored sand." The wide strips of maroon sand along the shore are the dust of pulverized red garnets. Bobbing on the deep blue waters are large mixed flocks of bar-headed geese, crested grebes, mergansers, coots, gulls, Brahminy ducks, and a variety of other ducks. Along the shoreline race shy sandpipers and red-legged redshanks, their piercing warnings often causing the waterbirds to take flight. Gurla Mandata looms to the southwest, and the white pyramid of Kailash rises to the northwest; a more amazing sacred place would be hard to find.

The road eventually comes to the shore, then climbs briefly into the sand hills to Seralung (Hailstorm Valley) monastery, which is well hidden from the shore. This Drigungpa hermitage was founded in the seventeenth century farther up in the hills, but has been rebuilt closer to the lake. The *lhakhang* and a protector's shrine overlook a small courtyard, with residences on each side for the monks.

Trugo *gompa*, the next temple on the circuit (Nyego *gompa* remains in ruins), is **6½ hours** to the south. The first campsite beyond Seralung and away from the windy shore is a **1½-hour** hike. It is located a short distance up the first stream entering from the left (east). Just beyond here the *kora* leaves the lake and heads cross-country to avoid a promontory jutting into the lake. The trail disappears in the sand and bushes, but you should stay inland and somewhat parallel with the shore for **2 hours** to meet the Tak Tsangpo, the largest drainage entering the lake. The *kora* crosses the river (shoes must come off if there's no bridge), climbs a hill and returns to the shoreline. The Tak Tsangpo is considered by some to be the Langchen Khabab, the source of the Sutlej River; others believe Rakshas Tal is the source. The Tamchok Khabab, the source of the Tsangpo, is reached by heading east up the Tak Tsangpo and over Tak La. The plains along the Tak Tsangpo, which I call the Valley of Kiangs (the Tibetan wild ass), are a haven for wildlife. I counted 201 *kiang* one evening, and saw several gazelle and a sand fox as well. **About 2 hours** up the river is a series of hot springs, including a wild, boiling creek sending up great clouds of steam.

The Manasarovar circuit now stays along the shore most of the way to Trugo *gompa*. It soon passes one of the lake's four prostration *chaktsal gangs*. **Two hours** beyond the Tak Tsangpo are the ruins of Nyego *gompa*, a former Sakyapa retreat built on the site where the Indian master Atisha was so overcome with the beauty of this area he stayed for several days making clay offering *tsha-tshas*.

Trugo *gompa*, the largest of the monastic sites around Manasarovar, is **less than 1 hour** from Nyego. Originally founded as a site for Drukpa Kargyüpa meditators, it was later handed over to Shepeling, the large Gelukpa monastery in ruins high on the ridge north of Purang. The central three figures in the ornate *dukhang* are Dusum Sangye, the "Buddhas of the Three Times." Many of the small statues here were originally at Shepeling.

Trugo and Chiu *gompas* are the most active pilgrimage sites on the lake, since they are the traditional overnight stops on the circuit. Many pilgrims now travel by vehicle to the Kailash region. While they walk the lake *kora*, the drivers deliver their belongings to Trugo and Chiu, where they camp in large groups often for days at a time. (Trugo is 10 miles [17 km] from the road connecting Darchen and Purang). Two buildings adjacent to the monastery are very basic pilgrim guesthouses. Before 1959 Trugo *gompa* was the traditional bathing place for Nepalese Hindu pilgrims, as this was where they would first arrive at Manasarovar on their pilgrimage, via Labtse La pass from the Limi region.

Depending on the season, the *kora* initially stays inland beyond Trugo to avoid a marshy region by the lake, then returns to the shore after crossing several streams flowing from Gurla Mandata. The chilly lake water is clear and blue; the gravel shore makes it a perfect place for a ritual bath. The pilgrim route now arcs from the southern to the western shore. Numerous *mani* stones, along with pieces of clothing, wooden *tsampa* bowls, and locks of hair strewn about as offerings help identify another of the lake's four prostration sites, strategically placed at a point just before Kailash slips out of view behind the western hills.

Go-tshuk (Starting Point) *gompa* is in these hills, **4 to 5 hours** past Trugo. Several caves below it are dug into a cliff of conglomerate deposits beside the trail, including Drön-khang *phuk*, the two-roomed "guesthouse cave" where Atisha stayed for a week. Just beyond these caves is the trail up to Go-tshuk. This delightful little temple is built over the *drubphuk* where the *lama* Gyelwa Götsangpa first meditated in the Kailash and Manasarovar area. From here he went north and pioneered the Kailash circuit, making this spot the "starting point" for the spread of the Kargyüpa sect in Western Tibet. A statue of the Buddha Chomdende graces the altar in the *lhakhang*, and upstairs is a room with a hundred carved and painted *mani* stones of Buddhist deities. When leaving Go-tshuk, a panoramic *kora* route climbs above the temple, then returns to the lakeshore.

The second camp for pilgrims on the Manasarovar circuit is Chiu (Little Bird) *gompa*, **3½ hours** past Go-tshuk. **About 2 hours** en route is the Tseti Guesthouse, a popular stop for Indian pilgrims between Purang and Mount Kailash. Small dormitory rooms are available, and the manager runs a tea shop and sells a few basic food items such as instant noodles.

Chiu monastery is built over the cave where Guru Rimpoche spent his last seven days on earth. It is spectacularly situated on a red, craggy outcrop that represents Zangdok Pelri, the Great Guru's mythical abode, with Mount Kailash as a backdrop. Six Drukpa Kargyüpa monks now reside here; the Guru's cave is on the lower level, below a *lhakhang* with his image and a statue of Buddha Chomdende. Upstairs is a *gönkhang* of fierce protector statues. A **30-minute** pilgrim *kora* circles the temple. The Ganga Chu, an intermittent river connecting Manasarovar with Rakshas Tal, exits the lake here, with hot springs bubbling along its bank. Nearby is Chiu village, with a tidy guesthouse and a shop. The caravans of pilgrim trucks camp on the broad sand flats near the lake.

The Manasarovar circuit turns east from Chiu *gompa* along the lake's northern shore, following a long series of hills and cliffs. (If the water level is too high, an alternative trail to Langna *gompa* ascends the hills to the east of Chiu.) The lake water along here is crystal clear, the cliffs reflect the sun's warmth, Gurla Mandata is again in view, and the pebbled shores are a rock collector's fantasy. The cliffside cave retreats of Serkyi Chakyib (Golden Bird Shelter) are **less than 2 hours** beyond Chiu. Mostly abandoned now, this site is renowned as the location where the Buddha Chomdende and his accompanying 500 *arhats* first landed after they flew here to save Mount Kailash from the demon Gompo Beng. Several meditational communities were established in these extensive cave colonies over the last 700 years, but recently only a lone Gelukpa nun has been in residence, in Marpo Phuk (Red Cave), where Chomdende is said to have stayed.

Langna (Elephant Trunk) *gompa*, the final temple on the circuit, is **2 hours or more** beyond Serkyi Chakyib in the hills north of the lake. The *kora* follows the shore for **about 1½ hours**, then turns inland at a large white boulder, traversing the slopes of the "elephant trunk" hill to the *gompa*. Originally founded as a Drigungpa meditation center, the monastery eventually passed into Drukpa Kargyüpa hands, but since being rebuilt in the 1980s, it is now a Nyingmapa retreat for a half-dozen monks. The chief sacred object of Langna was a Buddha Chomdende statue, with a small *rangjön* image of the protectress Dorje Pakmo recessed in its chest. It was destroyed in the 1960s, but the smaller figure was hidden, and today it is proudly displayed in the chest of the new Buddha statue. Campsites can be found by the creek below the *gompa*.

The final **4- to 5-hour** leg of the Manasarovar *kora* to Hor Qu crosses the creek on a bridge to the east of the monastery. In winter the pilgrims can return to the lakeshore, but in other seasons the route angles northeast across a grassy, desert plain to skirt the north shore of Gurgyel Tshomgo, a small lake where *khandroma* bathe, but humans are not to enter. Try to join up with pilgrims, as there is no real trail until you meet the road between Barka Qu and Hor Qu.

If you have transportation, it's possible to end the Manasarovar circuit at Langna and have your vehicle meet you here. A service road leads northwest to the main road. Barka Qu, a government *shang* compound with a small guesthouse, is about 6 miles (10 km) from the *gompa*, situated at the major road junction of this region. Darchen is 14 miles (22 km) northwest along the road to Ali; Hor Qu is 15 miles (24 km) to the east; and Purang, the largest town in this corner of Western Tibet, is 56 miles (90 km) southwest via Gurla La (15,350 ft, 4680 m).

THE PURANG TO SIMIKOT (NEPAL) TREK

The **4½- to 5½-day** trek from Purang to Simikot, in the Humla region of West Nepal, is a welcome alternative to exiting Western Tibet by vehicle. At this time only bona fide commercial trek groups with proper permits, a guide and trek staff, and a Nepalese government liaison officer (for the Nepal portion) are allowed to walk this route or cross the China-Nepal border at Zher (also spelled Sher; 12,400 ft, 3780 m). The route is currently not open to individual travelers, nor can the trek be organized in Purang. Nepalese visas and restricted area trekking permits for Humla must be pre-arranged by a trekking agency in Tibet or Nepal before you arrive in Purang, and the liaison officer must accompany the group from Zher (or Yari, in Nepal) to Simikot, as this part of Nepal is otherwise not open to foreigners. At Zher a small army of Nepalese porters will have been hired to carry food, kerosene (no wood burning allowed), and equipment for the trekking group and staff in this remote area. Camping sites can be found near Zher and also at Hilsa, just across the river in Nepal.

PURANG

Half military garrison and half tri-nation summer bazaar, Purang (Nepalese and Indians know it as Talkakot; 12,800 ft, 3900 m) is the administrative center (*xian*) for Bulan (Purang) County, situated on the Map Chu (Karnali) River. Accommodation for tourists is in the Indian Pilgrim Guesthouse, at the south end of town. A number of Chinese restaurants operate along the road, and in the market areas on both sides of the river are a few Nepalese and Muslim restaurants. Farther east from Purang is Peli Thangka, the Nepalese and Indian bazaar above the north (R) bank of the Takla Chu, a tributary of the Map Chu. The Purang County hospital is between the road and the river, in the middle of town, and the satellite telephone is in the telecommunications building at the south end of town.

Along the cliffs on the west (R) bank of the Map Chu is Gungpur (Fly to Heaven) cave temple, a fascinating thirteenth-century *gompa* consisting of three caves connected by ladders and balconies. On the main ridge north of Purang, above Gungpur, are the maroon-walled ruins of Shepeling (Simbiling on old maps; 13,650 ft, 4160 m), formerly the largest monastery in Western Tibet. Allow **about 1½ hours** to hike there from town. The most direct route passes under the Gungpur caves, then climbs steeply up a ridge toward the Peli Thangka bazaar. The trail levels out on a plateau, and a side trail climbs up to the right (north) up the ridge. The ruins are enormous considering only about sixty monks lived here (although another hundred monks resided in affiliated temples throughout Western Tibet, such as Trugo *gompa* at Manasarovar). The three Shepeling *lamas* are now in India, Nepal, and Lhasa. At the far end of the hill are the thick walls of the former five-story *dzong* for the *pönpo*, or "Lord of Purang." The ridge side below the ruins and the adjacent ridge to the north are riddled with old meditation caves. Off to the northeast are the furrowed slopes of Gurla Mandata. The impressive group of snowy peaks to the southwest is known to the locals collectively as Tshering Che-nga, the "Five Long-life Sisters." They are part of the Zanskar Range of the Himalaya, forming Tibet's border with Nepal and India. A glaciated pass crossing over these mountains via Tinkar La leads directly to Nepal, but the route over Lipu Lekh into India is much easier. Nepalese pilgrims and traders prefer to use the latter, then cross a second pass, also known as Tinkar La, to enter Nepal and descend to the town of Darchula. These passes are not currently open to foreigners.

Another monastery in the region is Le-de (13,400 ft, 4080 m), a **2½-hour** walk south of Purang, high above the west (R) bank of the Map Chu. The *gompa* has fifteen monks and is unusual in that they are from two sects, Sakyapa and Drigung Kargyüpa. Before the Cultural Revolution there were three monasteries on this plateau; Le-de has been rebuilt on site of the original Sakyapa sect *gompa*. Also here are the ruins of a multistoried *chörten*, called Kumbum Chempo, and beside Le-de are the massive walls of an ancient castle called Zhidekar. Before 1959 the *dzong* for the Tibetan governor of Ngari Province was located here as well.

Khochar (Khojarnath on many maps) *gompa* is 11 miles (18 km) south of Purang along the Map Chu's east (L) bank, on the road to the border town of Zher. Khochar and Töling are two of the oldest monasteries extant in Western Tibet. According to historian Roberto Vitali, Khochar was founded in 996 by King Khor-re of the Guge kingdom, and construction was completed by his son. A famous self-manifested, talking silver statue of the Jowo Jampel (Jampeyang, the *Bodhisattva* of Knowledge) from this era was housed here, and in about the twelfth century the king of Purang added two other silver statues of Chenrezik and Chakna Dorje to complete the Risum Gompo triad. Khochar is also

The ruins of Shepeling monastery, overlooking Purang

sacred to Hindus, who believe the three statues represent Rama, Lakshmana, and Sita. According to Swami Pranavananda, the Jowo Jampel has spoken seven times, and when it speaks six more times, the world will be resurrected.

This Sakyapa sect monastery currently has fifteen monks and consists of two main buildings around a small courtyard; the structures were spared in the Cultural Revolution so they could be used to store grain. The dark and atmospheric Jowo Lhakhang, the older of the two temples, houses the famous Jowo Jampel. The three standing silver figures draped in silk are replacements, although parts of the original statues have been used to construct the replicas; the *rangjön* stone base, for example, is original. Ask the *go-nyer* to show you. The adjacent building is the chanting hall, with stuffed animals hanging in the entrance foyer as protectors.

If you are trekking to Nepal, the border town of Zher is 6 miles (10 km) southeast of Khochar.

THE TREK TO SIMIKOT

After passports are checked by the Chinese border officials in Zher, follow the route to Simikot over a bridge to the south (R) bank of the Map Chu (called the Karnali River in Nepal), to the barley fields of Hilsa in Nepal. An alternative trail to Simikot climbs from Zher above the north (L) side of the Karnali toward the Limi Valley and the villages of Til, Halzi, and Zang. This more difficult route to Simikot takes **about 7 to 8 days**, but this area is currently closed to foreigners.

The "open" route to Simikot crosses Nara Lagna (also Nara La; in Humla, the word for pass is *lagna*) to avoid the gorges of the Limi Valley, then rejoins the Karnali on the far southern side. From Hilsa the trail climbs very steeply to this pass (15,000 ft, 4570 m), then drops into the greenery of Nepal. The change is remarkable as grasses, wildflowers, and flowering bushes spring up beside the trail as you descend. To the south and east are the snowy summits of the Saipal Himal, while off to the west are peaks in the Api Himal. Several good meadows for camping are above the first town along this route, Yari (12,050 ft, 3670 m), which has a checkpoint where police inspect passports and trek permits. If your Nepalese liaison officer didn't come to Zher, he will be waiting here to meet your group. Two rather new Nyingmapa monasteries, Chökatok and Yangzi, are on the ridge above town. The trail continues descending to the compact town of Tumkot (10,200 ft, 3110 m), where you can see the beautiful but neglected Dungkar Chözang, a 350-year-old *gompa* on the ridge above town, and a cave hermitage for the local *lama*.

From Tumkot the trail descends into a tributary of the Karnali, then climbs to the Nepal Immigration Checkpoint (10,050 ft, 3060 ft) near Muchu, where passports, trek permits, and luggage are inspected. Nepal entry (and exit) stamps are issued here. The actual town of Muchu is above the trail, along with Kharsapani *gompa*, another lovely but neglected temple; inside is a standing figure of Chenrezik represented as the Jowo Kharsapani, which is flanked on either side by three-dimensional dragons. The sacred footprint (*zhabje*) of this *bodhisattva* is enshrined by the *chörten* near the immigration post. The trail now descends to the Karnali River Valley, crossing a suspension bridge (9400 ft, 2870 m) to the north (L) bank. Spacious campsites are on both sides of the bridge. The river soon enters another gorge. The trail climbs along steep rock faces, then drops to the river several times to reach the covered alleyways of Yangkar (9500 ft, 2900 m), a compact, fortresslike town similar to those farther east in Nepal's Mustang region. Sidle across scrubby slopes of wild rose and juniper to Yalbang (9600 ft, 2930 m), where the large monastic school and Nyingmapa monastery of Namka Khyungdzong (9900 ft, 3020 m) is overseen by Pema Rimpoche, one of the three *lamas* of Shepeling monastery in Purang. Good camps can be found below here, near the school.

The trail enters forests of Himalayan blue pine and spruce as it descends back to the banks of the Karnali and a spacious meadow camp (9200 ft, 2800 ft). Cross the Sali Khola on a log bridge, then climb steeply through a lush forest with ferns and maples to reach a ridge crest called Sali Lagna (10,000 ft, 3050 m). A smaller trail leads up the ridge here to the Limi Valley. The main trail drops down to the terraces of Kermi (9150 ft, 2790 m), the last Buddhist town en route to Simikot; a small *gompa* is above the school near a bubbling sulfur hot springs. The trail now undulates high above the churning blue-green waters of the Karnali to a police checkpoint at Dharaburi (7700 ft, 2350 m). The people here are Thakuri, a Hindu ethnic group of the lower Humla region. Many women wear necklaces of silver coins, and sometimes braid coins and small cowry shells into their hair. Pass through two more Thakuri villages, Tuling and Majgaon, then begin the final ascent to a ridge crest (10,300 ft, 3140 m) before finishing at Simikot (9400 ft, 2870 m). Campsites can be found in the terraces below the airfield. The bazaar area, with shops, restaurants, guesthouses, and airline offices, is at the northeast end of the runway. The police checkpoint and other government buildings are on the opposite side of the airstrip to the south. Reconfirm your air tickets at least one day in advance. Simikot has daily flights to Nepalganj, in Southern Nepal, where there are regular connections to Kathmandu and Pokhara. The weekly direct flight from Simikot to Kathmandu is convenient, but if it is canceled due to clouds or bad weather, the next direct flight may not be scheduled for a week.

Trugo gompa *has a commanding view over Manasarovar*

12
THE MINYAK GANGKAR REGION

. . . there is no more beautiful spot on earth than Minya Konka. One night spent on the mountain is equivalent to sitting ten years in meditation in one's house and praying constantly; one offering of burning juniper boughs is equivalent to hundreds of thousands of prayers.

Tibetan saying (Translated by Joseph Rock, in *The Glories of Minya Konka, National Geographic*, October, 1930)

MAP NO. 11, PAGE 230

Situated on the eastern edge of the Tibetan Plateau, Minyak Gangkar (White Snow of Minyak; also Minya Konka; Chi., Gongga Shan; 24,790 ft, 7556 m) is Asia's highest summit east of the Himalaya, with the world's largest glaciers for this latitude (about 30°N). To the Tibetans, Minyak Gangkar is the sacred abode of the protector Dorje Lutru. Along with Amnye Machen and Khawa Karpo, it is one of the three main holy mountains in the Kham and Amdo regions of Eastern Tibet. The peak gained notoriety among geographers and mountaineers in 1930 following a cable message to the National Geographic Society from botanist/explorer Joseph Rock, in which he claimed Minyak Gangkar was 30,250 feet (9220 m) in elevation, over 1000 feet taller than Mount Everest! Two years later an American team journeyed overland across China to survey the peak and attempt the summit. They determined the height was actually closer to 24,900 feet (7590 m). In October 1932, two of the party, Terris Moore and Richard Burdsall, successfully climbed what they called "one of the great mountain giants of our planet." At that time it was the highest peak that had ever been summited, and no other American was to climb higher until 1958, when a U.S. team reached the top of Gasherbrum I (26,469 ft, 8068 m) in the Karakorum Range.

Minyak Gangkar is most easily approached from Kangting (km marker 2819), capital of the Kandze (Chi., Ganze) Tibetan Autonomous Prefecture and a former tea caravan staging point, 158 miles (256 km) west of Chengdu in Sichuan Province. While it is possible to reach Kangting in one long day of driving on the Tibet-Sichuan Highway from Chengdu, the journey is best broken into two days with an overnight in Ya'an (km marker 146), 90 miles (146 km) west of Chengdu. This allows an early start the next day for crossing Erlang Shan (9950 ft, 3030 m; km marker 2752/3), the main pass en route to Kangting. (Note that a new tunnel will soon bypass Erlang Shan.) Daily buses to Kangting depart from the Xin Nan Men (New South Gate) bus station in Chengdu, located next to the Traffic Hotel, a popular traveler's stop.

The best season for trekking in the Minyak Gangkar region is from late April to October, but be aware that snow can fall on the passes at any time. The rainy season is generally from mid-June to mid-September. The best visibility is often in late April and early May, and from late September to late October. A tent and fuel stove are necessary. The premier trek of this region is the **12- to 15-day** loop walk to Gangkar *gompa*, at the base of Minyak Gangkar's western flanks, which starts near Kangting at Laoyulin. This route crosses three moderate passes (the highest is Bu Chu La, 16,200 ft, 4940 m), approaching the mountain via the rarely visited Bu Chu Valley, then returning up the Yilong Chu Valley (also Yulong and Yulongshi), the route Joseph Rock took on his 1929

Gangkar monastery, on the flanks of the holy mountain Minyak Gangkar

expedition sponsored by National Geographic. An alternative **6- to 7-day** round-trip trek to Gangkar *gompa* starts at Luba (Chi., Liuba), to the west of the mountain. Daily bus service connects Luba with Kangting via Laoyulin.

The Minyak Gangkar region is open to tourism, so no permits are required for foreigners. Packhorses can be hired at Laoyulin, and horses or yak can be hired in the Luba region. If your trek does not return to where it started, it is necessary to pay for the guide's return journey. Though Kangting is a much smaller city than Chengdu, it's possible to outfit a trek here, as most basic food items, kerosene and other camping needs are available. Purchase all food requirements before the start of the trek. The only provision shops en route are near Luba, but you may be able to get meat, butter, potatoes, radishes, and some greens from the locals along the way.

KANGTING

Kangting (Tib., Dartsedo; formerly called Tatsienlu; 8450 ft, 2580 m) is the gateway to Minyak Gangkar and the Eastern Tibetan Plateau. Until the early twentieth century, this town was the capital of the Tibetan kingdom of Chakla, as well as the ethnic boundary between China and Tibet. As a tea trading center, this town saw a constant influx of opium-smoking coolies hauling heavy bundles of tea here from Ya'an, a town in the Sichuan lowlands southwest of Chengdu. The tea was stored in large warehouses, then loaded onto yak caravans to be sold to Tibetans across the Plateau. Until the 1990s, Kangting city was still quite small and retained some of its "wild west" character. However, a flood in 1995 damaged many of the old two-story wooden houses along the river, as well as a church established by Western missionaries who were based here in the late nineteenth and early twentieth century. The old structures were replaced by more modern, multistoried buildings.

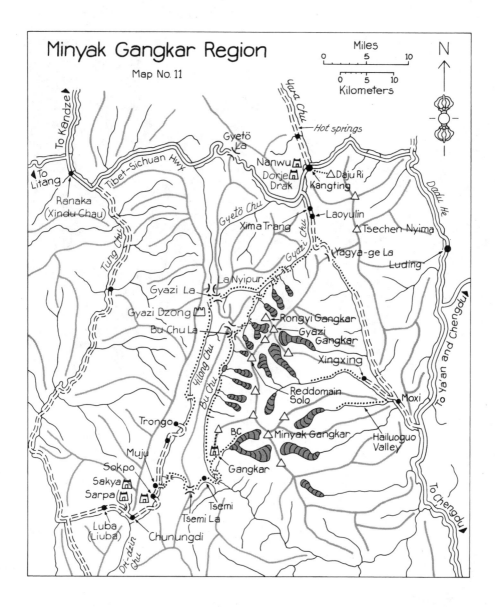

The city is built along the junction of two rivers, the Gyetö Chu and the Yara Chu. The Kangting Hotel (Chi., Kangting *Binguan*) where some tour groups stay is in the upper, south part of town beside Ngachö monastery, above the west (L) bank of the Gyetö Chu. Currently, the best hotel in town is the new Paoma Shan *Binguan*, a few hundred yards north of the Kangting Hotel on the same side of the street. A small guesthouse is above a popular tea shop adjacent to the monastery, and other more typical Chinese hotels and guesthouses are at the north end of town, near the long distance bus station. Buses depart daily for Chengdu and for towns throughout the Kandze Prefecture. Minibuses to Laoyulin and other nearby destinations wait to gather passengers on a street one block east of the river, below the Kangting Hotel.

The main bazaar for vegetables, fruit, spices, and meat is at the north end of town, near the junction of the two rivers. The Prefecture hospital is not far north from this market along the Yara Chu. An enjoyable soda hot springs with clean, private pools is a **1-hour** walk farther north on the road along the river. Another commercial hot springs is on the road to Laoyulin.

Before setting off on a trek, spend a day or two hiking into the hills around Kangting to acclimatize for your trek.

DAY HIKES NEAR KANGTING

The Kangting area has numerous monasteries in town and on the surrounding hills. While most of the peripheral buildings were destroyed in 1959, each site has at least one original building that has been restored. Ngachö *gompa* is a seventeenth-century Gelukpa monastery next to the Kangting Hotel. Just to the south of the city on the hillside is Nanwu *gompa*, a wonderful 400-year-old Gelukpa monastery, and a few hundred yards farther along the hillside is Dorje Drak *gompa*. Its grand old chanting hall houses a large Guru Rimpoche statue. Both temples are approached by walking **20 minutes or more** south past the Kangting Hotel, following the road toward Gyetö La (Chi., Zheduo Shan), the pass to Kandze. Cross the river, and about 300 feet (90 m) beyond the bridge is an alley up to the right (west) leading to Nanwu *gompa*. Another 300 feet up the road is an alley leading up to the right to Dorje Drak.

The wooded ridge rising to the southeast of Kangting is Daju Ri (Chi., Paoma Shan). Each spring Ache Lhamo, a Tibetan opera festival, is held in a cement amphitheater midway to the summit. On the slopes facing town, located along the various routes up to the amphitheater, are several large pavilions with peaked orange-tiled roofs. At the lower east end of the hill is an old Kuan Yin (a female manifestation of Chenrezik) temple, where Chinese worshippers burn incense, offer small Kuan Yin statues, and prostrate three times before the main image. An adjacent temple has Droljang (the "Green Tara") and her twenty manifestations, and the lower temple has a standing Sakyamuni. A cement staircase leads steeply up from the temple for **about 1 hour** through scrub and pine forest to the amphitheater (9000 ft, 2740 m) and a large white *chörten*. Nearby on the hillside is Denthong, a Gelukpa *gompa* with a *go-nyer* but no monks. The standing Sakyamuni figure is flanked by Neten Chu-druk, the Sixteen *Arhats*. A trail continues up through the forest to an unusual Baby Buddha Bathing Pavilion (9250 ft, 2820 m), and on to the summit where peaks of the Minyak Gangkar Range are visible but the main peak is too far south to be seen. Several trails lead back down to the center of Kangting.

The ridge to the northwest of Kangting has yak pastures offering good overviews of the Kangting Valley and, if the weather is clear, the snowy peaks in the Minyak Gangkar Range. The best access is a trail along the nose of the ridge, starting from a Chinese community on the hillside to the west of the Prefecture hospital. A service road leads to a communication building, then a trail continues up the ridge crest, past terraces of wheat and into pine forest to a large meadow (10,650 ft, 3250 m) where yak and horses graze. In early June bushes of pink and white azaleas and white rhododendrons bloom. You can either retrace your steps back down the ridge, or follow a trail angling to the left (south) across the slopes, which eventually descends into the Gyetö Chu Valley to the south of Kangting.

THE MINYAK GANGKAR LOOP TREK

The **12- to 15-day** loop trek to Gangkar monastery, on the western slopes of Minyak Gangkar, begins at Laoyulin (also called Luning Gao and Laoyuning; 10,200 ft, 3110 m), a small community about 9 miles (14 km) south of Kangting in the Gyazi Chu Valley, a tributary of the Gyetö Chu. If you are trekking as an individual, note that public mini-buses make the 45-minute run once or twice a day to Xima Trang (9700 ft, 2960 m), a Chinese administrative *shang* of cement roads and buildings; Laoyulin, the original Tibetan village in this part of the valley, is a **1-hour** walk up a rough dirt road past the *shang*.

If you want to hire packhorses, inquire with the families in Laoyulin. Since the horses are pastured up in the hills, plan on spending a day in this attractive village. The houses are solidly built with thick stone walls and timber beams. They have pitched roofs covered with curved, clay tiles and large rooms with plenty of windows. In the center of a home's main living area, surrounded by benches, is a low table with a round, recessed area where coals are placed to keep tea warm and food is cooked using a wok. The diet here and in the Minyak area is an interesting combination of Tibetan staples (butter tea and *tsampa*) and Chinese food (rice with side dishes of stir-fried meat and vegetables).

THE TREK TO GANGKAR MONASTERY

Bu Chu La, the first pass en route to Gangkar monastery, is a **3-day** trek up the Gyazi Chu Valley. From Laoyulin, head south on a wide cart track, past terraced fields above the east (R) bank of the river. Looming above the ridges up to the east are large 20,000-foot (6000-m) peaks forming the north end of the Minyak Gangkar mountains, and at the head of the valley to the south are more snowy peaks in this range, the majority of them unclimbed. Just beyond one of the last houses, a wide trail leaves the track to ascend the ridge to the left (southeast). This is the approach to Yagya-ge La (13,100 ft, 3990 m), the first pass on the traditional two-week pilgrimage *kora* around Minyak Gangkar. Nearby to the east is an impressive snow peak, Tsechen Nyima (19,977 ft, 6089 m). The circuit then follows the large valley below the eastern flanks of Minyak Gangkar (an area designated as a nature preserve, yet the forests are being clear-cut) past Moxi to the Dadu He River, then turns west up the lower Bu Chu toward Gangkar monastery. To avoid high water and snow-choked passes, the preferred season for this circuit is late autumn. However, few pilgrims ply the *kora* at all these days.

The route to Bu Chu La continues south up the valley on the cart track for **about 1½ hours**, at which point it turns left up the ridge side toward Yagya-ge La. Although construction has stopped short of the pass, this road was originally supposed to access the forests above Moxi. Don't follow the road. Instead, continue south on a wide, well-used path enclosed by tall stands of white-blooming wild rose, spiraea, and willow bushes. During summer, the lush undergrowth offers a spectrum of wildflower colors: Primulas, geraniums, peonies, irises, anemone, jack-in-the-pulpits, clematis, and at least seven species of rhododendron grow here. The area looks like it has been logged, but as you ascend the first trees appear: birch, larch, fir, and spruce. There are even wild onions. **About 2½ hours** beyond the road's end is a huge meadow (12,170 ft, 3710 m) called Gesar Tsera, where the warrior-king Gesar of Ling is said to have camped. If you had a late start from Laoyulin, stop here for the night.

The trail continues ascending this impressive glacial valley beside the crashing, milky blue Gyazi Chu, crossing a log bridge (12,250 ft, 3730 m) to the west (L) side **30 minutes** past the big meadow. The craggy peaks here reminded me of formations in Patagonia: Waterfalls spill from hanging valleys, and the valley floor is littered with glacial erratics and alluvial debris. In **about 2 hours** the route to Bu Chu La crosses a log bridge back to the east (R) bank. The trail continuing up the river's west (L) side leads to Gyazi La and the Yilong Chu Valley, which is the second half of the loop trek back to Laoyulin from Gangkar *gompa*.

The main valley soon splits above the bridge. The access to Gyazi La ascends the high, hanging valley up to the right (west), where the cascading Gyazi Chu tumbles over the cliffs. The route to Bu Chu La stays on the valley floor, following the larger drainage up to the left (south). Continue up the valley for 1½ **hours** past several large meadows to reach a spacious herder's camp with a few *ba*, the yak-hair tents of the *drokpa*. Up to the southeast the rocky, conical summit of Rongyi Gangkar (18,635 ft, 5680 m) dominates the head of the valley. Ten minutes beyond the herder's camp, cross a bridge to the west (L) side of the main creek. The trail climbs steadily from here for **3 hours** past more meadows and herder camps, fords the creek back to the east (R) side, then ascends to the crest of a terminal moraine (14,400 ft, 4390 m).

The valley now opens into a broad glacial basin (14,300 ft, 4360 m) with flat meadows, a perfect place to lay over for **2 nights** to acclimatize before crossing the pass. The large peak up to the east is Gyazi Gangkar (22,312 ft, 6801 m), the highest peak at this end of the Minyak Gangkar Range. The next large peak to the right (south) was named Mount Grosvenor (21,653 ft, 6600 m; marked on Map No. 11 with a triangular peak symbol between Gyazi Gangkar and Reddomain Solo) in 1929 by Joseph Rock, after the president of the National Geographic Society (which funded his expedition). Day hike possibilities include hiking east beside the moraine toward the glaciers and high peaks, or south up the main valley to a large glacial lake.

Bu Chu La is a minor dip in the rocky ridge up to the southwest, **2½ to 3 hours** from the glacial basin. If you do not have a guide, consider hiring one from the herder camps lower in the valley, as the route is not obvious. Ford the various branches of the main creek to the west (L) side of the valley floor, then walk upstream. A braided trail soon forms and leads to the right (west) up the ridge side, which is speckled with yellow and blue poppies in summer. In **less than 1 hour**, cross a crashing stream to the west (R) side. The route to Bu Chu La now ascends the crest of a moraine hill up to the left (west), paralleling the stream for **15 minutes or more.** The trail soon disappears, but keep climbing to a point across from (south of) the confluence of the stream and a smaller tributary from the right (northwest). Now head cross-country up to the left (south) toward the pass, which is **less than 2 hours** from here. From the tops of moraines, look for a long, low rock wall along the rocky ridge, the best landmark for the pass. The route winds up and around hills, scree slopes, and small streams, then climbs steeply for the last 100 feet to Bu Chu La (16,200 ft, 4940 m). (If the snow is too deep on Bu Chu La, use an alternative, unnamed pass not far to the west, which is marked by cairns on the ridge crest, to cross into the Yilong Chu Valley.)

In clear weather the rugged, snow-capped Minyak Gangkar Range stretches dramatically from north to south; the large snow peak now visible to the southeast was identified as Reddomain Solo (19,754 ft, 6021 m) by Joseph Rock, although my horseman was not familiar with this name. Just below to the south are the headwaters of the Bu Chu. The trail to Gangkar *gompa* now follows this valley for **2½ days**. Descend steeply from the pass on scree slopes for **30 minutes** to a stream, then cross to the southwest (R) side. The valley floor is marshy, so stay up on the ridge side where a trail soon forms. If you're trekking up the Bu Chu Valley from Gangkar *gompa*, the pass is almost impossible to locate without a guide; look for a slight dip in the ridge with several long, narrow pinnacles of rock just to the left.

The route to Gangkar *gompa* waltzes down this remote alpine valley, passing numerous meadows and potential campsites. Dwarf rhododendron, potentilla, barberry, and juniper bushes cover the hillside, along with poppies and small red *Pedicularis* flowers. The peaks and jumbled glaciers of the Minyak Gangkar Range loom beyond the ridges to the left (east). After **5½ hours** the trail leads to a herder camp (12,100 ft, 3690 m) with huts constructed from woven branches. The trail is not obvious, but descends from here to the

Trekking in the forests of Minyak Gangkar

gravel bed of the Bu Chu and crosses to the east (L) side. Look for a log spanning a narrow section, or find a wide, shallow place to wade across. The trail now ascends the ridge side, again passing a number of meadows. The tributary creeks from the mountains are quite large in this region, and the Bu Chu soon swells into a rushing river. In 1½ **hours or more** reach the last good camp before Gangkar *gompa*, a large meadow (12,750 ft, 3890 m) with a stone-and-wood herder hut.

The monastery is **about 7 hours** beyond here. The slopes are now more steep and become forested with juniper, fir, rhododendron, oak, bamboo, and birch. Damp gullies harbor fern gardens, and long strands of green *Usnea* lichen dangle from the trees. White-eared pheasants gobble in the undergrowth, and parties of Elliot's laughing thrushes bound across the trail. You may encounter a few wild pigs, which will have dug up many sections of the forest floor. Far below is the Bu Chu, cutting through a deep canyon. Piles of *mani* stones indicate the monastery is not far. The trail eventually comes to a junction with a wide path, marked by a 4-foot-high pile of prayer stones in the center of a clearing (12,450 ft, 3790 m). This is the main pilgrimage trail leading up from Tsemi village. Gangkar *gompa* is a delightful **30-minute** stroll through the forest to the left (north) up a huge tributary valley. The majestic Minyak Gangkar, which has remained out of sight until now, rises straight ahead, and the milky Gangkar Chu thunders below from the base of its glaciers.

GANGKAR MONASTERY

The whitewashed walls of Gangkar *gompa* (12,550 ft, 3830 m) are dwarfed by the soaring icy flanks of Minyak Gangkar. The monastery was founded about six hundred years ago, leveled by the Red Guards, and rebuilt in the 1980s. Twenty monks and a *lama* are again associated with this remote Karma Kargyüpa retreat, which is closely related to Sakya and Sarpa *gompas* in the Yilong Chu Valley. The main building here is a rambling, two-storied structure with a temple at one end overlooking a courtyard surrounded on three sides by monks' residences with wooden balconies. The chanting hall is on the ground floor, with several rows of cushions and a large wooden cabinet set along the back wall. In the center stand a Drolkar (White Tara) statue and figures of Marpa, Milarepa, and Gampopa. A large photograph of Tai Situ Rimpoche, a Regent of the Karma Kargyüpa sect who raised funds to help rebuild Gangkar, is beside the statues. The Sixth Gangkar Rimpoche is in India studying at Tai Situ's monastery.

A short *kora* circles the *gompa*, the adjacent buildings, canopied *chörtens*, and a shrine dedicated to Dusum Khyenpa, the First Karmapa. Tent sites can be found in the vicinity of the monastery; if you are with a commercial group, make sure your staff keeps a clean camp and respects this area as a religious site.

The best views of Minyak Gangkar are from the ridge crest above the *gompa*. Strong walkers can try to reach a site now known as Rock's Ridge (17,200 ft, 5240 m; marked on Map No. 11 with a triangular peak symbol), where Joseph Rock photographed the mountain for his National Geographic article. The trail ascends the ridge behind the monastery at the water source, and soon enters a forest of oak and rhododendron inhabited by white-eared pheasants. **In less than 1 hour** the trail climbs up to the ruins of a stone-walled meditation cell (13,140 ft, 4010 m) at the edge of the forest. The route to Rock's Ridge now heads north up the scrubby ridge crest on a small trail, which soon braids into many animal tracks. Minyak Gangkar is superb from here, and the views improve as you climb higher. Allow **5 hours** or more to reach the rocky cleft where Rock captured some of his finest pictures of Minyak Gangkar.

The route to the base camp of the 1932 American expedition is a difficult journey involving bush bashing without a trail to the river bottom. Stay on the west (R) side of the glacier, ascending in the natural trough beside the lateral moraine, reaching a small grassy meadow (14,400 ft, 4390 m) in **4 to 5 hours** at the foot of the mountain's southwest ridge.

THE RETURN TREK TO LAOYULIN

The second half of the loop trek from Gangkar Monastery to Laoyulin takes **4½ to 5 days** and crosses two passes en route, Tsemi La and Gyazi La. If you have time, consider the **2½- to 3-day** side trip down the Yilong Chu (or Yilongshi) Valley to Sakya and Sarpa monasteries in the Luba region.

TO THE YILONG CHU VALLEY

The route from Gangkar monastery to the Yilong Chu Valley takes **2 days** and crosses Tsemi La (15,300 ft, 4660 m). Retrace the trail from the *gompa* to the round *mani* wall at the junction from Bu Chu La. Don't turn here, but continue straight ahead (south) and descend on a wide, forested pilgrim's path lined with *mani* stones and offering cairns. In **1½ hours or more**, cross a wooden cantilever bridge (11,400 ft, 3470 m) to the east (L) side of the Gangkar Chu. **A few minutes** later is the first house and barley fields in the lower half of Tsemi village. The people here are from Minyak, an old region of Eastern Tibet that extends west and north from Minyak Gangkar. Their dialect is different from the Tibetan spoken on the north side of Bu Chu La, and their dress is different, as are their hair styles, jewelry, and even their facial features. The houses are stout, two-story fortresslike stone structures with decorative wooden windows. Like many areas of Tibet, animals are kept on the ground floor and the living area is upstairs. These friendly folks are quick to invite visitors inside. Have your cup ready for hot salted tea!

In **less than 10 minutes** pass a few more houses, then come to a trail junction (11,150 ft, 3400 m) at a bridge over the Bu Chu. The trail that stays along the north (L) side of the river follows the Bu Chu east to its confluence with the Dadu He River, and it is the pilgrims' *kora* used to circumambulate Minyak Gangkar. The route to the Yilong Chu Valley crosses the bridge to the south (R) side of the Bu Chu, skirts the edge of a barley field then climbs the south (R) ridge on a wide trail. The four houses in the upper part of Tsemi (11,800 ft, 3600 m) are **less than 1 hour** above the bridge, in a small tributary of the Bu Chu. The trail continues up to the west along the north (L) side of a stream, and soon climbs steeply through rhododendron and oak forest toward Tsemi La. **Two hours** past the last houses of Tsemi is a large, sloping meadow (13,400 ft, 4080 m), the last campsite before the pass. **A few minutes** later the trail forks; take the right branch, which climbs up the ridge. The vegetation soon becomes stunted as the trail begins a long series of switchbacks up rocky slopes, reaching Tsemi La in **about 2½ hours** from the meadow camp. If you're lucky enough to have good weather, the views of Minyak Gangkar and its snowy neighbors are outstanding.

The *la-dze* cairn on the summit has prayer flags as well as several large offering arrows, which are common on passes or at shrines for local protectors throughout Kham and Amdo. Place three stones on the *la-dze* as an offering for your safe passage (and clear weather!), then begin the decent into the Yilong Chu Valley. The trail stays on the north (R) side of the creek for **2 hours**, then crosses to the south (L) side on a log bridge (13,600 ft, 4150 m). Just beyond here is the first large camping meadow. The trail follows the creek, then turns left (south) above the confluence with the Yilong Chu. Follow the east (L) side of the river for **less than 30 minutes**, then cross to the west (R) bank on a cantilever bridge to Muju *shang* (12,600 ft, 3840 m). The Minyak Gangkar loop trek now turns right (north) on a dirt road up the Yilong Chu Valley toward the last pass, Gyazi La. Laoyulin is a **3½ to 4-day** walk from here.

Luba (Place of the Serpent; Chi., Liuba; 11,950 ft, 3640 m), the main administrative *shang* for this region, is **4½ hours** down the forested Yilong Chu Valley, following the road to the left (south) from Muju. The trek from Laoyulin can be shortened by several days by having your vehicles meet you in Luba (or at Muju, if the road is passable). Or the trek can be reduced to a **6- to 7-day** round-trip journey to Gangkar *gompa*, not including rest days, starting from Luba or Muju and crossing Tsemi La. If you haven't arranged for transportation, note that public buses depart each morning from Luba to both Litang and Kangting; purchase tickets a day in advance. The town has a guesthouse and a shop with a few food items.

Along the road to Luba are several temples and monasteries. The village *gompa* in Sokpo, **45 minutes** south of Muju, is a grand stone building by the road. It was used for grain storage during the Cultural Revolution, and more recently as the *shang* offices. The new central figure is a 10-foot (3-m) tall statue of the white haired, top-knotted bridge builder, Tangtong Gyelpo. Many of the murals are water damaged. The paintings on the back wall portraying Dusum Sangye, Neten Chu-druk, and the Karma Kargyüpa lineage are in the best condition.

About 2½ hours past Sokpo is the settlement of Chunungdi (12,200 ft, 3720 m), where the Dri-dzin Chu meets the Yilong Chu. It's a rather industrial place, with a power-house, a lumber mill, a small guesthouse, and a couple of shops. **Thirty minutes** farther down the river is a side road turning up to the right (north). Ascend here for **45 minutes or more** to reach Sarpa and Sakya monasteries. Sarpa *gompa* (New monastery; also called Khamsu Drak; 12,800 ft, 3900 m) was founded about 600 years ago, and is associated with Tai Situ Rimpoche and the Karma Kargyüpa sect. Monks from here spend three years in retreat at Gangkar *gompa*. The glass-enclosed reliquary *chörten* contains the previous, Fifth Gangkar Rimpoche, who died in the 1960s. The face you see is his!

The stone-walled fortress about 100 yards farther up the ridge is actually Sakya *gompa*, which is named after its sect affiliation. One hundred monks were previously here before the monastery was destroyed; thirty-five monks are presently associated with the *gompa*, living in rooms behind the immense wall seen from below. The main figure in the chanting hall with the red hat is Sakya Pandita, one of the great Sakyapa scholars.

TO GYAZI LA AND LAOYULIN

The route to Gyazi La initially follows the dirt road north up the Yilong Chu Valley. In 1½ hours pass a two-storied, L-shaped house up to the left (west) made from brown stones; other homes in the area are built with a dark rock. This was the site of the king of Chakla's summer palace, where Joseph Rock based himself in 1929 during his explorations of the Minyak Gangkar area. The house was destroyed by the Red Guards and rebuilt in 1991 by the former king's grandson; his elder brother is the heir to the deposed royal lineage.

The road meanders along this broad valley for **1 hour or more**, passes a school, then crosses a bridge (13,100 ft, 3990 m) to the east (L) side of the Yilong Chu. In **15 minutes** the road turns down to the left, back to the river and over a bridge to Trongo, the last settlement in the valley. The route to Gyazi La doesn't turn off here but continues straight ahead (north) on a wide, braided animal trail (this is yak-herding country). As the valley narrows, the trail winds through hillsides of purple-blooming dwarf rhododendron, spiraea, barberry, willow, and yellow potentilla bushes. In **less than 2 hours** the trail forks. Take the lower left branch and soon cross a bridge (13,400 ft, 4080 m) back to the west (R) banks of the Yilong Chu. The route to Gyazi La now stays on this side of the valley for **4 to 5 hours** until just below the pass. During summer, the extensive meadows in these upper reaches are covered in oceans of yellow buttercups. Families from the lower villages move their yak herds here in late June, living in woven yak-hair tents for the summer rainy season.

The trail to Gyazi La crosses the Yilong Chu, now just a creek, near the rock-walled ruins of Gyazi *dzong*. Rock hop to the east (L) side (14,300 ft, 4360 m), then sidle along the ridge side. In **about 30 minutes** the trail splits. The lower route to the left stays closer to the valley floor and heads north to cross La Nyipur, a pass crossed by the American missionary Marion Duncan, when he traveled through this valley in 1935. The upper right trail now climbs up to the northeast for **45 minutes** to the large cairn at Gyazi La (Chi., Pan Pan Shan; 15,350 ft, 4680 m), which Rock crossed in 1929.

The last view of Minyak Gangkar is off to the southeast, poking above the closer peaks in the range. Directly across from (east of) the pass is the pointy summit of Rongyi Gangkar. The snowy massifs to the right are Gyazi Gangkar, Mount Grosvenor, and (closest to the pass) Rock's Reddomain Solo. In the distance to the northeast is Tsechen Nyima, the peak above Laoyulin. For even better views, scramble up the hill (15,750 ft, 4800 m) to the right (south) for **20 minutes or more**.

Descend from the pass and soon cross a small stream, one of the upper tributaries of the Gyazi Chu, to the north (L) side. The trail now plunges into a deep glacial valley, staying high above the Gyazi Chu for **1 hour or more** until meeting the first of several large meadow camps (14,200 ft, 4330 m). Continue descending to the edge of this hanging valley, where the rushing creek drops off in a great cascade. The lower canyon of the Gyazi Chu Valley falls away at your feet. The trail switchbacks steeply for the final 600 feet (180 m), meeting the west (L) bank (13,100 ft, 3990 m) of the creek draining from Bu Chu La in **about 2 hours** from the first meadow camp. The route to Laoyulin descends beside the river. In **about 30 minutes** pass the first bridge (12,700 ft, 3870 m), which is the way to Bu Chu La. Continue downstream for **1 hour or more** and cross the second bridge (12,200 ft, 3720 m) to the east (R) side of the river. The large meadow at Gesar Tsera is **less than 2 hours** down the valley. If it's late in the afternoon, stop here for the night and walk the final **3 hours** to Laoyulin the following day.

If you haven't arranged transportation to meet you, continue **40 minutes** past Laoyulin to the *shang* at Xima Trang. Public minibuses depart about 1 P.M. for Kangting, and there may be a second bus leaving late in the afternoon.

A popular trek with Chinese tourists is the **6 to 7 day** round-trip journey to the eastern glaciers of Minyak Gangkar, in the Hailuoguo (Conch) Valley. The trailhead is at Moxi, 32 miles (52 km) southwest of Luding (km marker 2796). Accommodation huts are situated at each of the three camps en route. Guides can be hired for walking onto the snout of the glacier, which is said to be the lowest in Asia (9510 ft, 2900 m). The adjacent valley north of Hailuoguo, starting from Xinxing, approaches a different glacier. Buses operate between Luding and Moxi.

The fertile Meshö Valley, from Dzongsar monastery

13
THE DEGE REGION

MAP NO. 12, PAGE 240

Until the early twentieth century, Dege was the largest, wealthiest, and most important of the former Tibetan kingdoms in Eastern Tibet. Claiming descent from the family of Gar, who was Songtsen Gampo's main minister and army commander, the 1300-year-old lineage of Dege kings was based in what is now the town of Dege. Under these rulers, the kingdom evolved into one of the great religious, political, and industria l centers in this half of the Tibetan Plateau and became the cultural heart of Kham, the home of Tibet's famous Khampas. The realm of the Dege kings stretched from west of the Dri Chu (Chi., Jinsha Jiang, or upper Yangtze River) to the river plains of Kandze in the east across the mountains, and from the vast grasslands in the north to the hill regions south of Pelyul. Some eight thousand families and 170 monasteries with ten thousand monks were under their jurisdiction, including the great religious centers of Palpung, Dzongsar, Kathok, Pelyul, Dzokchen, and Zhechen monasteries. The kingdom effectively came to an end in 1910 when the Chinese general Chao Erh Feng invaded Dege. He captured the king and queen and had them sent off to Chengdu, where they died in prison. The last male descendant of this king passed away in the early 1990s.

Today, Dege (also spelled Derge; km marker 958) is the county seat (*xian*) of Dege County, in the Shi Chu Valley, a tributary of the Dri Chu. This corner of Eastern Tibet is particularly rugged and includes the Trola mountains, a glaciated range with several peaks over 19,700 feet (6000 m) forming the watershed between the Dri Chu and one of its main tributaries, the Dza Chu (Chi., Yalong Jiang). The lower valleys in the southern part of the Dege region are rich agricultural areas, while the northern highlands are mainly grasslands and rolling hills inhabited by nomadic herders.

Trekking is quite new to this area, as is the concept of hiring out pack animals to strangers. Complicating this problem has been the attitude of local officials, who are reluctant to allow trekking even if the proper permits have been issued in Chengdu. But as of 1999, Sichuan Province announced that Dege County and most of the other Tibetan counties in Sichuan are now open to tourism, and foreigners are no longer required to have permits to visit these areas.

The Dege region is laced with ancient pilgrimage and caravan routes, connecting the major monasteries and trading centers with the surrounding regions. A classic 8½- to 10-day trek from Dege to the Dzin Chu Valley follows one of these traditional routes, winding over spur ridges of the Trola Range and across tributaries of the Dri Chu to Palpung and Dzongsar monasteries. A less traveled but scenic alternative is the 4-day trek approaching Dzongsar from the north, which crosses the Trola Range via Dzen La. A third trek option is the 7- to 9-day loop trek to Dzokchen monastery starting north of Dege from Khorlomdo, in the upper Shi Chu Valley.

The best time for trekking in the Dege region is generally from May until October, with a rainy season that can extend from June to September. The most stable weather is in winter; snow closes the passes over the Trola Range, but treks in the lower elevation areas are possible. Tents and fuel stoves are highly recommended. Most basic food needs and trek supplies such as kerosene are available in Dege, Manigango (km marker 843), Kandze (km marker 672), and Pelyul. Purchase all of your food requirements before the trek begins. On the trek routes, the main supplies available are meat, butter, *tsampa*, rice, potatoes, turnips, spinachlike greens, and—of course—dairy products. The small shops near the larger monasteries usually sell rice, noodles, flour, vegetables, and apples.

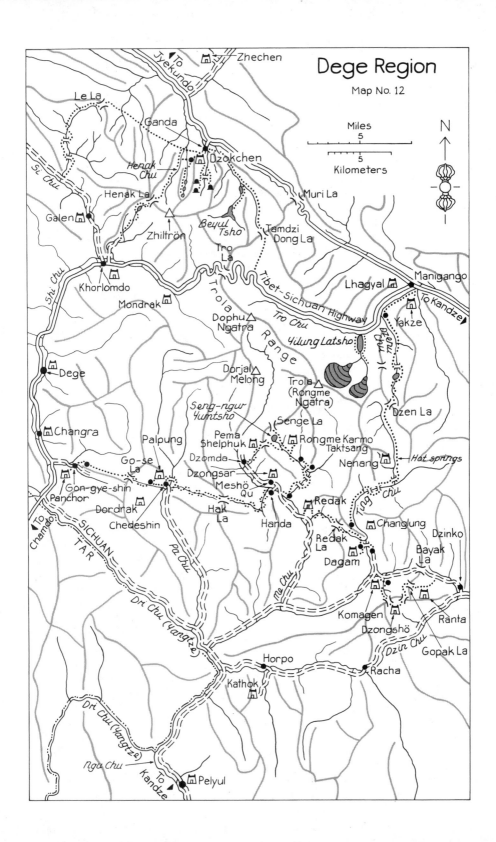

Dege Region

Map No. 12

Miles
5

Kilometers
5

N

To Jyekundo
Zhechen
Le La
Ganda
Henak Chu
Dzokchen
Muri La
Si Chu
Henak La
Galen
Beyul Tsho
Tamdzi Dong La
Zhiltrön
Tro La
Khorlomdo
Tibet-Sichuan Highway
Lhagyal
Manigango
To Kandze
Shi Chu
Mondrak
Trola Range
Tro Chu
Yakze
Dophu Ngatra
Yilung Latsho
Dzen La
Dege
Dorjal Melong
Trola (Rongme Ngatra)
Seng-ngur Yumtsho
Changra
Senge La
Rongme Karmo Taktsang
Palpung
Pema Shelphuk
Go-se La
Dzomda
Nehang
Hot springs
Gon-gye-shin
Dzongsar
Meshö Qu
Redak
Changlung
Dzinko
Panchor
Dordrak
Hak La
Redak La
Bayak La
To Chamdo
Chedeshin
Handa
Dagam
SICHUAN TAR
Pa Chu
Ngu Chu
Komagen
Ranta
Dri Chu (Yangtze)
Ne Chu
Dzongshö
Gopak La
Dzir Chu
Horpo
Racha
Kathok
Dri Chu (Yangtze)
Ngu Chu
To Kandze
Pelyul

DEGE

Dege (11,100 ft, 3380 m) is 637 miles (1032 km) northwest of Chengdu via the Tibet-Sichuan Highway. The long journey crosses seven passes and can be completed in four to five days, driving 10 hours or more per day; add a few extra days for acclimatization and visiting monasteries along the way. Public buses operate daily from Chengdu to Kandze, via Kangting, and less frequent bus service continues from Kandze on to Dege. See the section "Highway Kilometer Markers" for a list of the main towns and passes en route between Chengdu and Dege.

An alternative to driving is the Tuesday, Wednesday, Friday, or Saturday flight from Chengdu to Chamdo, the capital of Chamdo Prefecture in the TAR, which is 207 miles (336 km) west of Dege. The Bangda airport is about 3 hours from Chamdo, then it's another one and a half to two days of driving to reach Dege. Permits and an official tour guide are required to visit Chamdo and the Eastern TAR.

Dege is situated in a narrow section of the Shi Chu Valley, at the junction with a small tributary just 16 miles (26 km) north of the Dri Chu. The newer Chinese section is in the lower part of town near the river, where you will find the Dege Hotel (Chi., *Binguan*), several small guesthouses, the police station, and a number of shops and restaurants. A bit higher in the side valley is the older Tibetan section of Dege, with impressive two-story homes made from rammed earth walls. The windows are decoratively carved and painted, and the upper floors have walls of interlocking logs very similar to North American log cabins.

Adjacent to these homes is the Dege Parkhang, Tibet's most famous printworks for religious texts, and Dege Gönchen monastery. Within the village is Tang-gyel *lhakhang*, a temple dedicated to the bridge builder Tangtong Gyelpo.

DEGE PARKHANG

Although the kingdom of Dege no longer exists and the former palace has been converted to a school, the Parkhang (Storehouse of Printing Blocks) has managed to survive Dege's turbulent history (with the help of China's Premier Chou Enlai, who stepped in to prevent its destruction by the Red Guards in the 1960s). Established in 1729 by Dege's King Tenpa Tsering, this handsome three-story building is Tibet's largest center for producing and storing religious texts. Over 200,000 hand-carved wooden blocks, arranged in extensive rows of shelves, are used to print encyclopedic works such as the *Kangyur* and the *Tengyur*, as well as texts on Tibetan medicine, mathematics, logic, music, astrology, painting, and a broad range of religious subjects from all the main schools of Buddhism. The printworks on the second floor bustles, as energetic monks make the paper, carve Tibetan characters backwards into the boards, prepare the ink, and roll the paper over the inked boards. The ground floor *dukhang* has beautiful old murals painted with gold ink, and an adjacent temple has an eclectic array of important religious figures and deities, as well as a statue of King Tenpa Tsering.

DEGE GÖNCHEN

The chanting hall for Dege Gönchen is all that remains of this Ngorpa/Sakyapa sect monastery, located a short distance above the printworks and the former king's palace. Tangtong Gyelpo originally consecrated the Dege area in the mid-fifteenth century at the invitation of the King of Dege. A local legend tells how this valley was once filled with a poisonous lake inhabited by demons, which the famous ascetic subdued by covering these evil waters with his cloak. His meditation cave is high up in the cliffs across the valley to the west of Dege (prayer flags mark the site), and a red-walled temple on the hillside above the town is all that remains of Lhundrubteng, the Nyingmapa college he founded. In the mid-seventeenth century Lhundrubteng was taken over by the Ngorpa sect, and Dege Gönchen was established on the valley floor. The *gompa* was razed in the Cultural Revolution; the large *dukhang* was rebuilt in the 1980s using the original rammed earth walls. The main hall has a musty, unused feel, but the statues and new wall murals are outstanding works of art. The murals are actually huge *thangkas* attached to the walls, a new tradition being used in Eastern Tibet for replacing damaged frescoes. In the center of the assembly hall is the *shuktri* for Sakya Trizin, the throne holder of the Sakyapa sect, who resides in India. Temples dedicated to Guru Rimpoche and Sakyamuni are at the back of the hall.

PALPUNG, DZONGSAR, KATHOK, AND PELYUL REGION

Five adjacent tributaries of the Dri Chu drain the rugged Trola foothills to the east of Dege: the Pa Chu, Me Chu, Ting Chu, Dzin Chu, and Ngu Chu. Each of these valleys has regions where the fertile river plains support fields of barley, wheat, and potatoes; the hillsides are covered in spruce forest; and the upper slopes are home to *drokpa* families with large herds of yak and horses. It is within these prosperous valleys that the four great monasteries of Palpung, Dzongsar, Kathok, and Pelyul were founded.

Although roads now reach each of these monasteries, the 8½- **to 10-day** trek along the old caravan route from Dege to Dzinko, in the upper Dzin Chu Valley, is an excellent introduction to the Kham region of Eastern Tibet. This trek crosses five moderate passes; the highest is Go-se La (15,150 ft, 4620 m). Although the route involves a few hours of walking along roads, these tracks rarely see vehicles. They are more like wide paths and allow the option of walking short portions of this trek rather than the entire route. Kathok monastery is tucked up a tributary at the southern end of the Dzin Chu, about 7 miles (11 km) from Horpo, the center for making the famous Khampa knives. Pelyul is in the next tributary to the south, in the Ngu Chu Valley on a hill above the town of Pelyul (Chi., Baiyu), the administrative center (*xian*) of Baiyu County.

THE TREK TO PALPUNG AND DZONGSAR

The 3½- **to 4-day** walk to Palpung and Dzongsar monasteries starts at Gon-gye-shin (pronounced "Gyan-che-shin"; 10,850 ft, 3310 m), an administrative *shang* 15 miles (25 km) south of Dege in a tributary of the Shi Chu. The turnoff is at kilometer marker 979, and is readily identified by a white *chörten* at the junction. Gon-gye-shin is 2½ miles (4 km) from here up the valley to the left (east). The town is a small cluster of six log and mud-plastered houses beside a school, surrounded by barley fields at the junction of two wooded valleys. The trail to Palpung and Go-se La, the first pass of the trek, heads east up the nose of the ridge separating the two valleys. On the opposite ridge up to the south and hidden in the forest is Panchor, a branch monastery of Palpung with about a hundred monks; the trail starts near the school, taking **about 3 hours**. If you need to hire pack animals (horses or yaks), Gon-gye-shin is a good place to start asking. Consider coming here several days before your trek to give the villagers time to bring their animals down from the high pastures.

The trail to Go-se La (Gray Head Pass) is a stiff 4300-foot (1310-m) climb up the scrub-covered ridge from Gon-gye-shin following an old telephone line most of the way to Dzongsar. **Less than 2 hours** up the ridge you will see a log cabin–style *chörten* (12,000 ft, 3660 m) and the first fields of Shigar, an extended village of stately flat-roofed homes. It's big country here, with deep valleys, high ridges, and paisley-patterned terraces cut into the steep slopes, reminiscent of the Annapurna foothills in Nepal. I had great crowds of children come to greet me as I trekked past. But unlike Nepal, none of them had their hands out begging. Let's keep it this way. Please don't give away pens, candy, balloons, or other "unsolicited" gifts to these kids (or adults).

Pass the last fields of Shigar after **another hour** and continue ascending toward the pass; it's the obvious dip in the ridge to the southeast. Sidle through scrubby spruce forest for **less than an hour** to a sloping meadow (13,200 ft, 4020 ft) below the trail to the left. Though it's not a great camp, it's the last large meadow with water nearby before reaching the pass; consider spending two nights here to acclimatize. The trail now climbs less steeply through scrubby rhododendron, willow and spruce bushes. Reach the prayer flags and *la-dze* at Go-se La (15,150 ft, 4620 m) in **about 3 hours** from the meadow camp. The highest of the snow peaks off to the left (northeast) is Trola (Chi., Que-er Shan; also Chola Shan; 20,236 ft, 6168 m), the main summit in the Trola Range; in the Meshö area it's called Rongme Ngatra, and the other tall peak just to the left is locally known as Dophu Ngatra (20,078 ft, 6120 m), the protector, or "landlord" of Dophu. Directly across (east of) the valley is Hak La, the pass between Palpung and Dzongsar monasteries.

Palpung remains out of sight, a knee-cracking **3½-hour** decent from Go-se La. Two trails lead down from the pass; they connect below, though the right fork is the larger, more used route. Meander along the ridges, passing several good meadows for camping. A large cairn marks Domo La (13,850 ft, 4220 m), where the trail drops off steeply from the ridge; Palpung is directly below, a soaring, red-walled castle commanding a world of green hills and thick spruce forest. Partially hidden behind a craggy rock pyramid off to the right (south) is Dordrak, a Nyingmapa *gompa*. The trail to Palpung soon forks, though both choices meet at the small village of Rashenda (12,500 ft, 3810 m), below the monastery; the route straight ahead (right) is less steep and a bit longer. Cross the bridge by the village to the north (L) side of the creek. The trail splits here; the right fork by the creek leads to Chedeshin, at the confluence with the Pa Chu. Palpung (12,900 ft, 3930 m) is **20 minutes** up the trail to the left through Rashenda.

PALPUNG MONASTERY

The enormous chanting hall of this eighteenth-century *gompa* was not destroyed in the 1960s, and is said to be the second-largest of the old buildings still standing on the Tibetan Plateau, rivaled only by the Potala Palace. It has more than a hundred rooms and is about 300 feet (90 m) in length. A major renovation is underway to restore this magnificent, five-story complex. Palpung is the seat of Tai Situ Rimpoche, one of the four main regents for the Karma Kargyüpa sect of Tibetan Buddhism. The current, Twelfth Tai Situ resides in India. In the nineteenth century Palpung was also the home of Jamgon Kongtrül. A great scholar and philosopher, he was one of the three main architects of the *ri-me* movement, a nonsectarian school of thought that originated in Kham emphasizing tolerance and patronage to all the main sects of Buddhist teaching. The current, Fourth *trülku* of Jamgon Kongtrül, who is one of the four main regents for the Karma Kargyüpa sect, is a young boy whose seat is in a new monastery above Boudha, in Kathmandu.

Palpung's huge *dukhang* overlooks a large courtyard, and a smaller reliquary temple for the Tai Situ Rimpoches stands in front of the entrance. The roof for the chanting hall is supported by eight colossal wooden pillars. A large copper statue of Gyelwa Jampa, the "Future Buddha," is the central figure. It is flanked by Guru Rimpoche and Drolma. The *shuktri* for Tai Situ is in the center of the hall. Surrounding the complex is an array of residence buildings fashioned of logs and mud walls in which the monks live. On the hill above the monastery is a new *drubkhang*, or meditation center, and **1½ hours or more** up the Pa Chu Valley is Tsandra, the *ritrö* of Jamgon Kongtrül. *Cham* dances are held on the 10th day of the 6th Tibetan month (about the end of August or early September) marking the end of the seventy-five-day *yar-ne* summer retreat, when most of the monks throughout Kham and Amdo either return home for the harvest or stay within the *gompa* for intensive studies. Outsiders, particularly women, are not meant to visit the monasteries during these retreats.

A road built to facilitate harvesting this valley's timber has now reached the Palpung area. The 1998 ban by the Chinese government on all logging within the watersheds of the Yangtze River will hopefully be enforced and spare this pristine forest. No regular transportation serves this valley. If you have hired a vehicle, it is possible to start or finish your trek at Palpung.

TO DZONGSAR

Dzongsar monastery can be reached in **1 long day** of walking from Palpung via Hak La (pronounced "Ha La"; 14,850 ft, 4530 m). A steep trail descends from Palpung for **20 minutes** to the Pa Chu and Chedeshin (12,400 ft, 3780 m), the *shang* for the valley. Cross the river on a bridge to the east (L) bank, then angle up the tributary to the left (east), which is the valley leading to Hak La. The trail soon crosses the creek on a bridge to the south (L) side, the first of a half-dozen or so crossings before the pass. Climb through patches of spruce forest, passing several good camping meadows and following the omnipresent telephone poles to reach Hak La in **4½ to 5 hours**.

The trail from the pass descends to Dzongsar in **3½ hours**. Initially the route swings to the north (L) side of the valley on a rocky path, then crosses a log bridge to the south (R) side of the creek. The ground is quite boggy in places, and this is prime habitat for the *tremong*, the huge Tibetan brown bear. It's not uncommon to see droppings along the trail. Willow and spruce line the creek bed as the valley narrows. A large meadow camp (12,550 ft, 3830 m) is at the big bend where the drainage angles north. Below here the trail descends through a delightful spruce-clad gorge, crossing eight log bridges to reach the Meshö Valley and Handa, an attractive village with handsome, multistoried houses typical of this region. Dzongsar monastery is straight ahead (north), sprawling across the ridge side. Pass through the village and cross the bridge (11,700 ft, 3570 m) to the Me Chu's north (L) bank. The road to Meshö from the Dri Chu runs past the bridge. The large gray building with orange and white stripes across the road near the bridge is the Shedra, a monastic college associated with Dzongsar. Nearby is the Meshö Qu government *shang* compound.

DZONGSAR MONASTERY

Several trails climb steeply up the hillside to the Dzongsar complex (12,100 ft, 3690 m), **20 minutes** above the valley floor. The monastery occupies a commanding position over this rich agricultural valley, its central red-walled temples stacked close together, surrounded by dozens of gaily striped residences for 180 monks. The site is said to date back to at least the eighth century, when it was a sacred place of the Bönpo. In the thirteenth century the head *lama* of the Sakyapa sect, Phakpa, came here en route to meet Kublai Khan, who had become emperor of China. Since that time Dzongsar has been the largest center of Sakyapa teachings in Kham, and the seat of Jamyang Khyentse Wangpo, one of the original proponents of the nonsectarian *ri-me* movement. Five hundred monks were associated with the monastery before 1958, and another three hundred monks studied at the Shedra, which Jamyang Khyentse Wangpo founded in the nineteenth century.

The entire monastery was destroyed when the Chinese army arrived in 1958; large mud-walled ruins are still scattered along the ridge side. The main building is the new *dukhang*, a large hall utilizing the original earthen walls with thirty-six main pillars supporting the raised ceiling. The well-crafted wall *thangkas* depict the life of Jamyang Khyentse Wangpo, and true to the *ri-me* tradition, the lineages of the various schools of

A nomad family in Kham about to set off on pilgrimage

Tibetan Buddhism are portrayed. The large central throne is for Dzongsar Khyentse
Rimpoche, the third *trülku* of Jamyang Khyentse. He now lives in India. Upstairs is the
Rimpoche's residence, where there is a shrine dedicated to his two previous incarnations. Also here are treasures that the First Khyentse discovered in Seng-ngur Yumtsho,
a nearby sacred lake in the Rongme Valley.

THE MESHÖ AREA

Meshö is the chief agricultural area of the Dege region, with a population of about
five thousand people. There are eight government primary schools within the valley.
The *qu* compound across the road from the Shedra has a police post and a small health
center with a doctor. Nearby are rows of log cabins with shops and several small restaurants. Rice, noodles, flour, meat, and vegetables are generally available, but kerosene
can be hard to find. The Dri Chu is 25 miles (40 km) from the monastery along the road
following the Me Chu; Dege is another 41 miles (66 km) to the northwest. The Meshö
road continues up past Dzongsar to the last settlements; beyond the barley fields are the
yak pastures of Dophu, at the base of the snowy peak Dophu Ngatra in the Trola Range.

In a tributary valley to the west of Dzongsar is Pema Shelphuk (14,800 ft, 4510 m), a
Guru Rimpoche cave and hermitage. Jamyang Khyentse Wangpo and another *ri-me*
scholar, Chögyur Lingpa, meditated here and discovered *terma*, hidden religious texts.
Kongtrül Rimpoche of Palpung monastery also used this retreat, which is considered
one of the twenty-five most important *nechen*—Buddhist "power places"—of Kham and
Amdo. This famous pilgrimage site is **4 to 5 hours** from Dzongsar, at the base of two
limestone towers. The turnoff from the Meshö Valley is at the town of Dzomda.

RONGME KARMO TAKTSANG

To the north of Dzongsar in an adjacent valley is Rongme Karmo Taktsang, one of the three main "tiger liar" caves of Guru Rimpoche; the other two are Önphu Taktsang in Central Tibet (see "The Gyama Valley to Ön Chu Valley Trek") and Paro Taktsang, Bhutan's most famous temple. Although several steep paths go directly north over the ridge, the standard approach to this retreat follows the Rongme Valley, taking **6 hours or more** from Dzongsar. The Rongme Valley turns north from the Me Chu near the road bridge at kilometer marker 36, about a **75-minute** walk downstream from the Shedra at Dzongsar. The trail climbs to a *chörten* and a house on a low ridge crest, then descends through houses of Dama *shang* to the Rongme Chu. The ruins up on the ridge were a *podrang* of the Dege kings. The route to the Taktsang initially stays along the west (L) side of the creek up this lush valley. Secluded meadows are found all along the route. **About 2½ hours** beyond the road is a *chörten* (12,300 ft, 3750 m) where the valley forks. The Rongme Chu is the valley up to the left (northwest); to the right is the Danda Chu, which drains from Rongme Ngatra, the main Trola peak.

Walk through barley fields and past the first of three settlements in the valley, collectively known as Rongme. At the second group of houses the trail splits. Go left (northwest) up the smaller valley, which soon opens out into a forested basin to reach the third settlement (13,700 ft, 4180 m), a group of herder huts made of logs and woven mats. I call this area the Valley of Friendly People. Every family here came out to greet us, cheerfully offering *tsampa* and dairy products for our stay at the Taktsang. Continue climbing along forested slopes. High on the ridge side is the hermitage, and below is a large flat meadow (14,250 ft, 4340 m) where pilgrims camp. The hermitage trail is a steep ascent through the trees.

From a distance Rongme Karmo Taktsang (14,500 ft, 4420 m) looks like a tower rising up through the forest. The Guru Rimpoche cave may be closed to visitors, since monks from Dzongsar stay here for three- and five-year retreats. A second cave, Mipham *drubphuk*, is usually open to the public. It is named after Mipham Rimpoche, the great *lama* of the *ri-me* movement in the late nineteenth century who spent thirteen years here in retreat. The three founders of the nonsectarian teachings all spent time meditating here as well.

Farther up the Rongme Valley is Seng-ngur Yumtsho (Lion's Roar Turquoise Lake), the sacred lake where Jamyang Khyentse Wangpo recovered prayer texts and gold. The trail leads north from the meadow below the Taktsang. Sidle along the ridge for **15 minutes** to a herders camp of woven huts (14,400 ft, 4390 m). The valley splits here; the lake (15,500 ft, 4720 m) is a steep 1½-**hour** climb up the drainage to the left (north). The blue-green waters of this small glacial tarn are wrapped in an eerie, barren world of shattered slate ridges. **About 1 hour** beyond the lake is Senge La (16,000 ft, 4880 m), a pass leading into the Dophu region of upper Meshö. The prominent rocky pyramid rising to the north is called Dorjal Melong.

Most pilgrims and locals return to Meshö down the Rongme Valley. An alternative 6½- **to 7-hour** trek to the Meshö Valley via Pema Shelphuk crosses two passes (note that only one "pass" symbol is used on Map No. 12 for these two passes), Hachung La (15,550 ft, 4740 m) and Dzonka La (15,700 ft, 4790 m), starting from the herder huts en route to Seng-ngur Yumtsho. A braided trail leads up the ridge to the west. Hire one of the herders here as a guide, as the trail is often obscure. Allow 1½ **hours or more** to reach the first summit, and **less than an hour** to the second. The trail disappears as the route descends to Pema Shelphuk. Dzongsar monastery is **3½ hours** down the valley via Dzomda.

THE TREK TO THE DZIN CHU VALLEY

The Dzin Chu Valley is a **2½- to 3-day** trek from the Meshö Valley. Starting from the Shedra at Dzongsar, follow the road downstream along the Me Chu. After **1 hour or more** the road crosses to the river's south (R) side, then after **another hour**, not far past kilometer marker 31, the road crosses back to the north (L) bank. About 150 feet (45 m) beyond the second bridge (11,500 ft, 3510 m) a trail leads up the ridge to the left (north). Redak La, the first pass to the Dzin Valley, is **4½ hours** up this path. Turn here and ascend toward the lofty ruins of a *dzong*, reaching Redak *gompa* (11,800 ft, 3600 m) in **less than 30 minutes**. This small Bönpo monastery is being renovated, and is only opened for special prayer ceremonies. Larger Bönpo *gompas* are farther east in the Terlung and Dzinko areas.

The trail now turns into the Yang Chu Valley, descending to the creek and soon crossing a log bridge to the east (L) side. The valley now splits, with the trail angling up to the right (east) into a spruce forest. Pass a *mani* wall at another creek junction. The large meadow here (12,400 ft, 3780 m) is suitable for a large group to camp. Continue up the valley through patchy forest, cross the creek to the north (R) bank then ascend steeply to Redak La (13,700 ft, 4180 m). The passes are getting lower, but it's still big country here. The Terlung Valley and the Ting Chu are **2 hours** below the pass. The trail initially descends to the east, staying on the south (R) side of the stream that forms. A short way below the pass is a trail off to the left, which stays high along the ridge side. This is the route from Manigango to Dzongsar that crosses Dzen La over the Trola Range (see "The Trek from Manigango to Dzongsar," below). The trail toward the Dzin Chu continues down the valley, crossing the stream twice before coming into the town of Dronton (12,250 ft, 3730 m) at the confluence with the Ting Chu. The route now turns south through the barley fields for **10 minutes** to a log bridge. Cross to the east (L) bank, then head downstream along the river.

High on the ridge back to the north is Changlung, the main Bönpo *gompa* for the Terlung Valley. It has about seventy married monks, or *ngakpas*, and two incarnate *lamas*. Across the valley to the west are the whitewashed walls of Dagam Wangphuk (Semi-circle Power Cave), a small *ritrö* with two monks in residence. This is another important retreat of Jamgon Kongtrül and the *ri-me* movement, where *terma* texts were discovered. This valley is also the birthplace of Jamyang Khyentse Wangpo. The track along the river is very wide, and eventually becomes big enough for vehicles. Continue downstream for **1 hour** to a road junction, passing several small agricultural settlements. Where the valley narrows a small temple sits against the cliff; it has unusual rock carvings inside. Just beyond is a large meadow (11,950 ft, 3640 m) and a road junction at the confluence with the Jowang Chu, a tributary from the east. Pass a large, square *chörten*, then a come to a second one with a rounded dome and a spire, similar to *chörtens* found in Central Tibet. This is a great place to camp.

About 20 minutes above this junction and hidden around the ridge to the left (south) is Komagen monastery (12,300 ft, 3750 m). This Nyingmapa *gompa* is built around a Guru Rimpoche cave called Dawa Phuk (Moon Cave); the Indian master and his consort Yeshe Tshogyel are said to have spent a month here meditating together. The monastery currently has sixty-five monks. Their residences are an attractive jumble of balconied log cabins stacked around the chanting hall and the courtyard. The cave temple is above on the ridge, enclosed by a huge façade. The simple grotto inside has a large statue of the Great Guru with his two main consorts: Yeshe Tshogyel from Tibet, and Madarava from Nepal.

The Ting Chu now turns west, joining the lower Me Chu Valley in about 12 miles (20 km). The route to the Dzin Chu Valley heads east from the large meadow along the road up the Jowang Chu. Bayak La (13,000 ft, 3960 m) is **3 hours or more** from here. The road soon crosses the Jowang Chu to the south (R) side, passing extensive gold diggings, the bane of Kham's rivers. **About 1 hour** upstream is the village of Jowangpa (12,300 ft, 3750 m), built on a ridge between two valleys.

A trail up the tributary to the right (south) past Jowangpa leads to Dzongshö hermitage (14,000 ft, 4270 m), a **4½-hour** walk from here. The trail crosses to the west (L) side of the creek below the village, then ascends to a ridge crest (14,600 ft, 4450 m) in about **3 hours**, passing several good meadow camps along the way. Descend south from this summit to reach Dzongshö in **1½ hours**. Set among craggy limestone towers, the hermitage has a commanding view across the forested Dzin Chu Valley. It is one of the twenty-five power places of Kham and Amdo, and an important meditation site of Jamgon Kongtrül. The monks here are associated with Palpung's Tsandra hermitage. Eight main caves are scattered through the cliffs and outcrops, and on a slope below the largest towers is a *dukhang* and residences for forty monks. A pilgrim's *kora* leads around to the various caves and temples.

Several trails lead off from Dzongshö into the Dzin Chu canyon. To reach Dzinko, climb north along the crest of a ridge for **1 hour** to a summit called Sashak La (14,600 ft, 4450 m; marked with a pass symbol on Map No. 12), then sidle north along the ridge top to Gopak La (14,350 ft, 4370 m). The Trola Range spans across the distance, and below to the east are the extensive sloping barley fields of Dzinko. The road crossing over Bayak La is not far to the north. Descend right (east) from Gopak La on a steep trail. **Thirty minutes** below the summit is the turnoff for Ranta (13,000 ft, 3960 m), a Sakyapa sect *gompa* tucked into a fold of the ridge, off the main trail **30 minutes** to the right (east). The main trail continues down a rocky gully, meeting the road (12,100 ft, 3690 m) from Bayak La in **1 hour** near the upper houses of Dzinko. The lower reaches of Dzinko are **2 hours** farther downstream past barley, wheat, and potato fields and numerous small settlements.

Bayak La is **2 hours or more** above Jowangpa village following the road. The lower Dzin Chu Valley is **3 hours or more** beyond the pass. During autumn harvest the fields of Dzinko are bustling with the villagers cutting, hauling, and threshing barley. The men in this area are quite swashbuckling—as Khampas often are—with long knives on their belts (undoubtedly made in Horpo, at the mouth of the Dzin Chu), tall boots, and long coats. The women have strands of turquoise braided into their hair. It is also common for a woman to wear a very large piece of amber or turquoise on the crown of her forehead. Anyone who has been to Lhasa will surely have encountered the "you-how-much" girls in the Barkor, with all the jewelry in their hair, hounding tourists to buy Buddhist trinkets and necklaces. Well, almost everyone of them is from the Dzin Chu Valley. When you meet these folks (here or in Lhasa), ask them *"ka-a-ti?"* which is the Khampa greeting (lit., are you tired?). The reply is *"ka-ma-ti"* (I'm not tired); you'll get a great reaction!

Several caravan and herding routes cross the Trola Range to the north from Dzinko to the Aser grasslands, taking **4 to 6 days** to reach the great river plains of Rongbatsa and Kandze. Due to high water caused by the summer rains, these trails are usually only used in winter and early spring. The main year-round access to Dzinko is the road along the Dzin Chu from Horpo, 23 miles (43 km) to the west. Dege is another 44 miles (71 km) to the northwest up the road along the Dri Chu, and Pelyul is 24 miles (39 km) to the southwest.

KATHOK MONASTERY AREA

Kathok monastery (13,200 ft, 4020 m) is situated high up a side valley about 7 miles (11 km) south of Horpo (10,300 ft, 3140 m). It was the first major Nyingmapa *gompa* in Tibet, and is one of the four main Nyingmapa monasteries in Kham (along with Pelyul, Dzokchen, and Zhechen). Kathok was established in the mid-twelfth century by the renowned teacher Kathokpa Dampa Deshek, who emphasized scholarship and the propagation of the Nyingmapa *tantras*. The monastery later fell into decay during the fifteenth and sixteenth centuries, then was revitalized in the seventeenth century, during the era of the Fifth Dalai Lama when the great Nyingmapa *gompas* in Central Tibet flourished. About eight hundred monks and seven lineages of incarnate *trülkus* resided at Kathok in the 1950s before the Chinese army arrived. A large chanting hall and a beautifully crafted four-tiered Zangdok Pelri temple (the latter represents the mythical copper-roofed mountain paradise of Guru Rimpoche) have been rebuilt. In the hills above the monastery is a pilgrim's *kora* and several hermitages.

Horpo has several shops, a few restaurants, and a small guesthouse. A good camping area is across from the town on the south (R) bank of the Dzin Chu, along the road to Kathok. Be sure to visit the large, three-story homes around the edge of town. In each one is a foundry for making the famous Horpo knives, which are used by Tibetans throughout the Plateau.

PELYUL MONASTERY

The seventeenth-century Pelyul monastery (10,700 ft, 3260 m) sprawls across the hills above the Ngu Chu, the next major tributary of the Dri Chu to the south of Horpo and the Dzin Chu. One of the four main Nyingmapa monasteries of Kham, Pelyul had six hundred monks and seven lineages of incarnate *lamas* before the 1950s. In 1935 the American missionary Marion Duncan stayed three nights near the monastery, which at that time consisted of " . . . 120 highly colored monastic buildings of the Red Cap sect ranged in parallel lines upon the mountain spur create(ing) one of the most spectacular lamasery cities I have ever seen." Completely destroyed after 1958, the parallel rows of maroon and white monks' residences once again surround the main chanting hall and the three large white temples beside it. On the slopes above is the Shedra associated with Pelyul, and on a prominent hilltop is a three-tiered Zangdok Pelri *lhakhang*. Several hundred monks are now associated with the monastery, and a hundred study at the Shedra. Penor Rimpoche, the main *lama* of Pelyul, resides in India. He is currently one of the head *lamas* of the Nyingmapa sect, along with Trülzhik Rimpoche of Dza Rongphu monastery. A precipitous *kora* route clinging to the ridge side encircles the complex.

Pelyul *gompa* is directly above the town of Pelyul (Chi., Baiyu; 10,350 ft, 3150 m). Gold mining and the timber industry have attracted a thriving Chinese community, one of the biggest in Kham. The service road to the monastery leads up from the center of town beside the cinema. Numerous restaurants and the best-stocked shops since Kangting line the main street. The hotel for tourists is across the Ngu Chu in a compound, and small guesthouses line the commercial strip. No public bus service operates to Dege at this time, but buses run every other day for the 222-mile (360-km) journey to Kandze.

THE TREK FROM MANIGANGO TO DZONGSAR

The **4-day** trek to Dzongsar *gompa* in the Meshö Valley is a wild and remote journey starting between Manigango and the sacred waters of Yilung Latsho. This walk initially goes up the Dzenu Chu Valley to cross Dzen La (16,400 ft, 5000 m), one of the higher passes in this region over the Trola mountains. The route descends into the granite canyon of the Ting Chu, a tributary of the Me Chu, then turns west to cross Redak La to reach the Meshö Valley and Dzongsar.

THE MANIGANGO AREA

Manigango (13,000 ft, 3960 m; km marker 843) is a "wild west" truck stop stretching along an important road junction in Northern Kham. The road leading west through town is the Tibet-Sichuan Highway from Kandze (km marker 672), which crosses Tro La pass (16,128 ft, 4916 m; km marker 865) en route to Dege (km marker 958) and on to Chamdo in the TAR. The road to the south leads to Kandze, and the northern road goes past Dzokchen monastery to Jyekundo and the grasslands of Amdo, in Qinghai Province. Log cabin restaurants, shops, and small guesthouses line the road to serve truckers and rugged-looking Tibetans wearing large felt cowboy hats, their long knives tucked in wide belts. Though the town offers little more than a place to resupply, it's situated in a beautiful alpine area with snow peaks of the Trola Range nearby, Yilung Latsho at their base, and two monasteries in the nearby hills. Along the river is a pilgrim's *kora*, starting from a *mani khang* in the center of the commercial area.

In the hills **less than 1 hour** above the town to the south is Yakze *gompa* (pronounced "Yazer"; 13,400 ft, 4080 m). Founded in the late eighteenth century and affiliated with Dzokchen monastery, this Nyingmapa *gompa* has over a hundred monks and a Shedra for training monks to become abbots. The monastery has been closed to visitors for a number of years, as its monks are in a lengthy retreat.

About **45 minutes** in the hills to the northwest of Manigango is the Sakyapa monastery of Lhagyal. Like Yakze *gompa* it cannot be seen from the town; a wide trail leads up a small side valley just beyond the west end of the commercial strip. A large triangular array of orange prayer flags are on the grassy slopes near the monastery, which stays hidden until you're almost there. Dozens of monk's residences with the Sakyapa tri-color stripes surround the chanting hall. The courtyard in front of the *dukhang* is enclosed on three sides by balconied residences, a kitchen, and store rooms. The interior of this chanting hall, though small, is beautifully decorated with silk banners hanging from every possible pillar and beam. Some 200 monks have returned to this recently rebuilt monastery, which had been leveled after 1958.

The "soul lake" of Yilung Latsho (13,500 ft, 4110 m) is 7 miles (12 km) west of Manigango, at the foot of the Trola Range. This is truly an amazing setting, with two large glaciers spilling off these mountains into the forests above the lake. A pilgrims' *kora* circumambulates the shore, but can only be walked before or after the summer rains. If you have the time, hike up the valley to the upper yak pastures, following the east (R) side of the lake. Beware of mosquitoes! A high pass leads into the Dzenu Chu Valley, where a route heads to Dzongsar *gompa*.

TO DZONGSAR MONASTERY

The **4-day** trek to Dzongsar monastery can begin at Manigango, or from Yilung Latsho. If you need to hire pack animals, the best place to inquire is with the herder families living near Yakze or Lhagyal *gompas*, above Manigango. If they only want to go for one day, the *drokpa* in the upper Dzenu Chu Valley can be hired to haul gear on their horses to at least Dzongsar. If your walk ends at Dzongsar, you will need to pay for your guide's return journey to the Dzenu area.

Starting from Manigango, cross one of the bridges near town and follow the south (R) side of the Tro Chu upstream, reaching the mouth of the Dzenu Chu Valley in 2½ **hours or more**. In summer the wildflowers along here—including edelweiss, red *Pedicularis*, white *Bistorta macrophylla,* and white umbels of the carrot family—are knee deep. Allow **about 1½ hours** to reach here if you're starting from Yilung Latsho. From the mouth of the Dzenu Chu Valley, pass Trogyama (13,400 ft, 4080 m), a small settle-ment of herder huts and the only buildings in the valley. The trail climbs gently up the east (R) side of the creek for **2 hours or more**, reaching a herder's camp (13,800 ft, 4210 m) with several large *ba*. The woven yak-hair tents of Kham and Amdo are huge com-pared to their Central Tibetan counterparts—I call them double-wides. Have a cup of butter tea, then rock hop across the creek here to the west (L) side. Up to the west is Shön La (marked on Map No. 12 with a pass symbol), a pass over the ridge to Yilung Latsho. **Thirty minutes** farther is the last *drokpa* camp in the valley (14,000 ft, 4270 m), and the last large camp before the pass. If you need to get different packhorses, it should be possible to hire some from these herders. To acclimatize properly, consider staying two nights here before climbing higher.

From these *drokpa* tents, cross the creek to the east (R) side on a log bridge and begin the steep **4-hour** ascent to Dzen La (16,400 ft, 5000 m). The last small meadow camp (15,350 ft, 4680 m) is 2½ **hours** up. Beyond here the path switchbacks over scree slopes to the summit *la-dze* cairn, where many sticks are left as offerings, a few of them carved like spears. The granite spires of the Trola mountains tower to the west, gouged by an-cient glaciers that have left deep U-shaped tributaries hanging high above the valley floor. The trail now plunges into the canyon of the upper Ting Chu, reaching the bottom (14,100 ft, 4230 m) in **1 hour**. The first possible camp (15,500 ft, 4720 m) is **less than 30 minutes** below Dzen La, and a larger camp is **10 minutes** farther.

The Ting Chu canyon is national park material. The soaring granite cliffs with water-falls spilling off the hanging valleys could be somewhere in Northern Yosemite. The trail follows the east (L) side of the Ting Chu, which is already a river, winding through wil-low and potentilla bushes. Soon the valley is filled with vast flat meadows of white-bloom-ing *Bistorta macrophylla*; campsites can be almost anywhere. Pass the first herder huts (13,900 ft, 4240 m) in **1 hour**, then come to a second group (13,750 ft, 4190 m) after **another 1½ hours**. Just below these huts is a shallow hot springs. Get your boxing gloves out for the mosquitoes! Across the valley in a tributary is Nenang *ritrö*, a small Bönpo retreat center with many orange prayer flags.

One hour below the hot springs the trail crosses a log bridge (13,400 ft, 4080 ft) to the river's west (R) side. As the valley enters a big bend to the west, the slopes become forested with spruce and juniper. The route to Dzongsar stays in this spectacular valley for **another 3 hours**, crossing the river twice before reaching the first barley fields (12,750 ft, 3890 m) below the village of Chisha. The trail now ascends steeply for **1 hour or more** up from the Ting Chu to avoid a gorge, climbing past the six houses of this settlement to the top of a ridge crest (13,600 ft, 4180 m). High across the valley to the east is Changlung, a Bönpo monastery. To the south is a trail leading down a side valley of the Ting Chu to Terlung and onto Dzinko (see "The Trek to the Dzin Chu Valley," above). Redak La (sometimes called Yangam La in this area; 13,700 ft, 4180 m) is **1 hour** up to the right (west) from this ridge, and Dzongsar monastery is **3 to 4 hours** beyond the pass. The route to Dzongsar is described, in reverse, above.

DZOKCHEN MONASTERY LOOP TREK

Dzokchen monastery (13,000 ft, 3960 m) is in the grasslands of the northern Dege region, 32 miles (52 km) north of Manigango via Muri La (14,850 ft, 4530 m). One of the great Nyingmapa *gompas* of Kham and Eastern Tibet, it was founded in the late seventeenth century by the accomplished Buddhist master Pema Rigdzin, who was sent to Kham by the Fifth Dalai Lama to encourage the propagation of Nyingmapa teachings. The monastery is situated at an important junction of the old caravan routes to Jyekundo and Amdo to the north, and on the direct route to Central Tibet via Le La pass to Dege and Chamdo.

The **7- to 9-day** loop trek from Dzokchen to the town of Khorlomdo (11,750 ft, 3580 m) initially ascends a remote alpine valley, crossing the Trola Range via Henak La (16,250 ft, 4950 m). It then follows the old Dege caravan route from Khorlomdo over Le La (14,400 ft, 4390 m) to return to the monastery. The trek can also begin at Khorlomdo, though it may be difficult to hire pack animals there.

DZOKCHEN MONASTERY

"Never have I seen, anywhere in the world, a place apter for the life of contemplation . . . dominated by tremendous snow covered peaks which towered in unchallenged mastery over the whole valley," French adventurer André Migot, in his book *Tibetan Marches*, wrote describing Dzokchen monastery in the 1940s. Built on the side of a great glacial moraine at the foot of Zhiltrön (the residence of this area's *yul-lha*, or protector, Zhiltrön Dorje Yungdrung; 19,645 ft, 5988 m), the third-highest peak in the Trola Range, Dzokchen is indeed in a remarkable setting. Like most of the monasteries in Kham, it was totally destroyed after the Chinese armies arrived in 1958. It rivaled Kathok as the largest Nyingmapa monastery in this region, with upwards of eight hundred monks and eleven incarnate *trülkus*. The head *rimpoche* is the lineage of Pema Rigdzin; the current Seventh Dzokchen Rimpoche lives in India.

Dzokchen is hidden from the main road behind a great wall of moraine. Below the road is the administrative *shang* for this region and the village of Ganda (12,750 ft, 3890 m),

Friendly monk at Galen gompa

where a half-dozen shops sell rice, meat, vegetables, apples, kerosene and other basics. A service road climbs west from this settlement up the ridge to Dzokchen monastery. Nearly fifty log cabins (monks' residences) are spread across the grassy slopes above the complex, which includes the Lhasa (also Lhakhang Sarpa, the New Temple) Assembly Hall and the *podrang* for Dzokchen Rimpoche. Beside them are the huge mud walls of the former *dukhang*. The impressive new chanting hall has large images of Khenlop Chösum, the three founders of Samye. Upstairs is a shrine with the golden reliquary *chörten* of the Sixth Dzokchen Rimpoche, who died the night the monastery was sacked, at the age of 25.

The Shedra, or college, for Dzokchen is **20 minutes** farther up the valley above the river plain. Several hundred students engage in various programs of study here, including a twelve-year course to become a *khempo*, a position in a monastery similar to an abbot. The building adjacent to the Shedra is the residence of *trülku* Kalzang, the *lama* who has overseen the extensive rebuilding of Dzokchen since the early 1980s.

In the past the hillsides from the Shedra to the spruce forest of the upper valley were dotted with hermitages and cave retreats, for Dzokchen was a center for meditation and philosophy. Even though all of the buildings were destroyed, the sites have retained their powerful feeling of serenity that originally attracted many great Buddhist teachers to reside here. One small hermitage has been re-established, and several of the caves are pilgrimage sites.

Currently there is no guesthouse at Dzokchen, but the valley is an ideal setting for camping. Pack animals are not easy to arrange. Try asking both at the monastery and in Ganda. It may take a day or more to get the animals ready, a perfect excuse for hiking into these outstanding mountains.

Day Hikes near Dzokchen

A delightful **3- to 4-hour** round-trip warm-up walk heads south from the Shedra to the cave retreats, following a cart track along the north (L) side of the Dzokchen Chu. In **25 minutes** ford the icy, milky waters of the river to the east (R) side, reaching the ruins of Pemathang hermitage in **another 25 minutes**. A narrow trail leads up through the forest (look for cairns) for **less than 1 hour** into a glacial basin of rock cliffs and waterfalls to Shinje *drubphuk*, the Cave of the Lord of Death (13,500 ft, 4110 m). The cave is enclosed under the overhang of a large boulder, at a clearing surrounded by spruce and rhododendrons. Two interconnecting caves are **a few minutes** above here, under another large rock, with broken but expertly carved marble tablets inside. The top of this upper boulder has prayer flags and an outstanding overview of the Dzokchen area.

A trail from here leads down to the river in **about 10 minutes**, where several logs span the Dzokchen Chu before it plunges over a cascade. On an embankment above the west (L) side are many orange prayer flags at Tsering Jong hermitage (13,250 ft, 4040 m), where monks have built several log cabins as retreat residences. A trail leads above here into the forest for less than **10 minutes** to Tsering *phuk*, which is walled in with a door. One of the most famous caves, Peltrül *drubphuk*, is reached by a smaller trail from the water source below Tsering *phuk*. It's a steep, muddy path through damp forest for **30 minutes** to the simple cave retreat (13,750 ft, 4190 m) of Peltrül Rimpoche, a great nineteenth-century proponent of the *ri-me* tradition. A trail returns from Tsering Jong to Dzokchen along the west (L) side of the river.

In an adjacent valley high to the west of Dzokchen are three holy lakes known collectively as Shama-kama-parma. The trail to the lakes is not very clear, so bring a guide. This long **1-day** walk starts on the wide trail up the moraine from the southwest corner of the Shedra, passing several hermitages en route. The first lake is Tsho Shama (14,400 ft, 4390 m), **2½ hours** above the monastery. **About 1½ hours** higher is Tsho Kama (15,100 ft, 4600 m), a milky blue lake sacred to Guru Rimpoche; his meditation cave is under a large glacial erratic boulder above the shore. A **1-hour** *kora* circumambulates the lake. **Two hours more** up the valley is Tsho Parma (16,000 ft, 4880 m), set in a stunning Yosemite-esque granite amphitheater. Get an early start for this walk.

Another lake sacred to Guru Rimpoche is Beyul (pronounced "Bi-re") Tsho, in the next main valley to the east of Dzokchen. Allow **5 to 6 hours** one way from Ganda, the village below (north of) the monastery. A wide trail crosses the Dzokchen Chu on a bridge near the town, then angles east into the hills to a low saddle. Descend to a large creek, which drains Tamdzi Tsho, the lake below Beyul Tsho. Wade across the creek to the east (R) side, then follow the wide path up the valley. When the valley splits, turn right (south) for the lakes. The trail to the left (southeast) leads to Tamdzi Dong La, a pass crossing to the Yilung Tsho region.

Zhechen monastery (12,400 ft, 3780 m) is 11 miles (18 km) northeast of Dzokchen. It is one of Kham's four main Nyingmapa monasteries, founded in the mid-eighteenth century by a student of Pema Rigdzin. The turnoff is about 6 miles (10 km) north of Dzokchen on the road to Jyekundo, and the monastery is another 5 miles (8 km) up a side valley. A large, red chanting hall and a white *podrang* have been rebuilt, and several hermitages are on the upper slopes.

THE TREK OVER HENAK LA TO KHORLOMDO

The trek from Dzokchen to Khorlomdo via Henak La takes **2½ days**. Allow **another day** for acclimatization before reaching the pass. The route leads west past the drainage for the Shama-kama-parma Lakes, then ascends the adjacent valley of the Henak Chu to cross the Trola Range. Follow the wide trail west up the moraine behind the Shedra, reaching a cairn on the ridge crest in **30 minutes**. The path leading up to the left (south) is the route to the three lakes. The trail to Henak La continues straight ahead (west) along rolling ridges for **30 minutes** to Yojeden, a settlement of fifteen herder houses. If pack animals can't be arranged at Ganda, near Dzokchen, try asking here. Take the wide path leading west up the moraine from the village for **45 minutes** to reach the valley floor (13,150 ft, 4010 m) of the Henak Chu. The large snowy peak to the south is Zhiltrön, which cannot be seen from Dzokchen. Henak La crosses its rugged west shoulder.

The trail leads through the willow and potentilla bushes of this broad U-shaped valley, then fords the Henak Chu to the west (L) bank near a *drokpa* camp. Henak La is **8 hours** from here. Follow this side of the creek the entire way to the pass. As I hiked along this flat valley a stocky, brown, white-maned animal bounded like a deer through the brush and up the slopes. This was my first encounter with a serow, a species of goat-antelope found in the forested regions of the Tibetan Plateau.

A good camp to aim for is **5 hours** up the valley from the creek crossing, in a large meadow (14,650 ft, 4470 m) with several erratic boulders. Beyond this point are only small meadows. A good trail leads steeply up the ridge from here, entering a Patagonia-like world of craggy granite towers and jumbled glaciers, then switchbacks over scree to Henak La. Add a few stones to the *la-dze* cairn!

Zhiltrön's snowy massif looms just to the left (east), and down to the south is the deep canyon leading to the Shi Chu. The rock crags around the pass are the haunt of blue sheep—many hoofprints can be seen in the soft soil at this summit. Khorlomdo

Chörtens *and* mani *stones in Kham*

(11,750 ft, 3580 m) is a steep **5-hour** plunge into a verdant land of yak pastures and forest. In **less than 1 hour** pass a pea green lake (15,100 ft, 4600 m), then descend into a sweeping glacial valley flanked by two large lateral moraines. After **1½ hours** come to a herder camp with a mud-daubed woven hut (14,050 ft, 4280 m), the first large area for camping. Just below here the trail crosses the creek to the west (R) side, then angles into an adjacent spruce-draped drainage with wooden huts in Switzerland-green meadows. Reach the junction of two valleys and the first houses (12,900 ft, 3930 m) in **1 hour**. The route to Khorlomdo now swings right (west) along the valley floor, passing a few more houses and the first barley fields. The valley soon narrows and the trail meets a road, criss-crossing the creek several times past logging and gold mining sites to reach the Shi Chu and the Tibet-Sichuan Highway (11,800 ft, 3600 m) in **2 hours**. Khorlomdo *gompa* is **30 minutes** to the right (west), toward Dege, and the village of Khorlomdo is **20 minutes farther**.

KHORLOMDO

The small roadside stop of Khorlomdo (km marker 929) is on the west side of Tro La pass, 17 miles (28 km) northeast of Dege on the Shi Chu. A few small shops here sell instant noodles, candy, and beer. Picturesquely perched on a hill above the town is Khorlomdo *gompa*, a 100–year-old Sakyapa sect monastery with about fifty monks. A large stuffed yak hangs in the entrance way. The chanting hall, which is the original building, has ornate woodworking around the doors. A fine old copper statue of the Jowo Sakyamuni is the central figure. Women are not even allowed to enter the courtyard during the *yar-ne* summer retreat.

THE RETURN TO DZOKCHEN VIA LE LA

The **3- to 3½- day** return walk for the Dzokchen loop trek turns north from Khorlomdo just **a few minutes** downstream from the shops. Cross the bridge over the Shi Chu and enter the Si Chu Valley. The road here is the old caravan route between Lhasa and Chengdu, and the way from Dege to Jyekundo. The dirt road winds past meadows of wildflowers, following the east (L) side of this beautiful, clear green river. Like most of Kham and Amdo, this is horse country; the only people on foot are typically monks or pilgrims, and us trekkers. Cross to the west (R) side of the Si Chu in **1½**

hours; Galen *gompa* (pronounced "Ga-le"; 12,150 ft, 3700 m) is **another 30 minutes** up the road. This Sakyapa monastery has thirty-five monks; the central *dukhang* is surrounded by several dozen log cabin–style houses with lovely wood-latticed windows. No one is allowed to visit during the *yar-ne* retreat. The head *rimpoche*, Namkai Norbu, lives in India.

The road crosses the Si Chu to the east (L) bank just above the monastery, and stays on this side for **3½ to 4 hours** to a large meadow (12,450 ft, 3790 m) and *drokpa* camp at the turnoff for Dzokchen. Marmots and meadows are everywhere along this valley, making camping easy and entertaining. In mid-July the baby marmots are scampering about, their curiosity almost winning over their fear of new neighbors. If it's late in the afternoon, stop at this junction for the night.

The road continues up the main valley along the Si Chu from this junction. The trail to Le La leads off to the right (northeast) into a steep-walled side valley; the pass is **about 6 hours** away. Willow and buckthorn bushes line the route, with laughing thrushes bounding through the undergrowth. When the trail is by the creek, watch for brown dippers diving from the rocks. Cross the creek twice on wood bridges, then come to where the valley splits (12,700 ft, 3870 m). The main trail stays on the right side of the right (northeast) branch. The path starts climbing more steeply; the ridges up ahead are rounded, with grassy slopes instead of forest. Pass a small bubbling hot springs, then rock hop across the creek (13,300 ft, 4050 ft) to the west (R) bank. The route to Dzokchen now stays on this side of the creek up to the pass, which is **2½ hours** away.

Ascend past numerous meadows and herder camps. Notice the great double-wide black tents hanging from cat's cradles of support rope. If you're invited in, have a rest and enjoy a cup of salted tea, and perhaps a round of delicious flatbread, a specialty of the *drokpa* in Kham and Amdo. Herds of yak speckle the green hillsides below Le La (14,550 ft, 4430 m). To the east from the summit is an endless succession of grassy treeless hills stretching across the horizon. The pass is actually a double summit; below the second crest the trail swings right (east) across the ridges. Dzokchen is **7 to 8 hours** from Le La. Wind in and out of the scrubby hills, passing several herder camps and meadow areas. The road to Jyekundo is at the far east end of the valley, and the turnoff for Zhechen monastery is at the confluence of two rivers. Zhiltrön holy peak comes into view up to the southeast, and **6 to 7 hours** beyond the pass is a spacious meadow (12,800 ft, 3900 m) with a huge erratic boulder. On top is a log cabin *chörten;* this rock is the residence of a local protector. The rushing stream here is the Henak Chu, draining from Henak La.

A wide track continues east toward Ganda, the village below Dzokchen. In **30 minutes** a shortcut to the monastery forks to the right from the main path to climb the high ridge of moraine. The main chanting hall and residence buildings (13,000 ft, 3960 m) are **about 1 hour** up from this junction; Ganda (12,750 ft, 3890 m) is **30 minutes or more** straight ahead (east).

If you haven't arranged transportation to meet you at Dzokchen, go to the main road above Ganda. Pilgrims, monks, locals, and not-so-locals gather at the roadside, having picnics and snoozing while waiting for a vehicle to come along. Tell the others where you're headed and they'll help you get a ride.

14
THE LABRANG REGION

MAP NO. 13, PAGE 259

Labrang (also Labrang Tashikyil; 9500 ft, 2900 m) is one of the six great Gelukpa sect monasteries of the Tibetan Plateau. With some fifteen hundred monks, it is currently the largest of this select group. The *gompa* sprawls like a monastic city along the river plain of the Sang Chu (Chi., Daxia He), a tributary of the Ma Chu, or Yellow River (Chi., Huang He). Nearby is the county seat (*xian*) of Xiahe, 136 miles (220 km) south of Lanzhou, in Gansu Province. The next major river to the west of Labrang is the Gu Chu, in the Rebkong Valley. Also a tributary of the Ma Chu, this valley system is a lower, drier and more rugged region, yet it hosts perhaps fifty monasteries. The largest is Rongwo Gönchen (marked as Rongwo on Map No. 13), another major Gelukpa establishment located in the county seat of Rebkong (Chi., Tongren), 117 miles (190 km) south of Xining, in Qinghai Province.

The **5-day** trek from Labrang to Rebkong is a beautiful journey through Serchen Thang, one of Amdo region's more important grazing areas. What a sight it is to see hundreds of *drokpa* tents and their vast herds inhabiting one great plain. Although the tall, glaciated peaks are much farther south in the Amnye Machen Range, this region of grasslands and remote alpine valleys is one of Amdo's finest moderate treks. Three passes are crossed en route, though the highest, Chadang Ka, is just 13,150 feet (4010 m) high. (In the Amdo dialect, *ka* is the word for pass.) As in Kham, the practice of hiring packhorses to trekkers is not really established yet in Amdo. If you're trekking with a commercial company, they can send a representative ahead of the group to arrange horses through a government official or some other connection. If you're trekking independently, try asking monks at Labrang who have families in this area. Or visit Sakar village, just **20 minutes** west of Labrang's main entrance gate, where the families are *samadro*, both farmers and herders.

The best season for trekking is generally from May to October, with a rainy period lasting from late June to early or mid-September. The lower altitudes of Amdo mean the climate is more temperate compared to Central Tibet and Kham, but when there's a heat wave, it's hot, with temperatures pushing 90°F (32°C).

Xiahe and Rebkong are both medium-sized county towns (Xiahe is larger), so basic food needs such as rice, meat, vegetables, flour, and fruit are readily available, as are trek supplies such as kerosene and strong trash bags. Purchase all of your food requirements before the trek, as there are no shops en route. Dairy products, *tsampa* and perhaps some meat can be purchased from the herders, and it may be possible to have a family bake a few rounds of their delicious Amdo flatbread. A tent and a fuel stove are recommended, but it's possible to stay in herder tents for the entire journey. Bring along a small musical instrument if you play, such as a harmonica or a tin whistle, for the Amdo people love to sing and play music; many *drokpa* families have a guitar or mandolin-type instrument in their tents. Even the children can usually pluck a few songs.

The two towns are 62 miles (100 km) apart by road and connected by a daily public bus. Both also have regularly scheduled buses to their respective provincial capitals. More locally, minibuses, pickup trucks, and rototiller-style tractor taxis serving the outlying country can be hired for personal use at reasonable rates to reach areas where public transportation is not available.

Before your trek begins, spend a day or more walking in the surrounding countryside. Labrang and Rongwo Gönchen have pilgrimage *koras* around their perimeters, and both areas have a large network of valleys nearby with seldom-visited villages and remote monasteries and hermitages.

To the north of Labrang is Gan-gya Drakar (marked as Drakar on Map No. 13), a Gelukpa hermitage at the base of an extensive range of limestone cliffs. A challenging *kora* circles these towering outcrops, and an adventurous journey into a cavern leads to a pair of sacred underground lakes.

LABRANG MONASTERY

Despite being extensively damaged during the 1950s and 60s, Labrang monastery has one of the largest gatherings of original, old temples on the Tibetan Plateau. Founded in the early eighteenth century by the renowned Jamyang Zhepa, this Gelukpa *gompa* quickly grew into the greatest monastery in Amdo, as well as one of the main religious institutions in all of Tibet. The current, Sixth Jamyang Zhepa Rimpoche resides in Lanzhou, along with two of the four throne holder *trülkus* of Labrang. At the center of the complex is the Tsokchen, a vast, decorative chanting hall with ten rows of fourteen pillars supporting the raised ceiling. This was the first building constructed by Jamyang Zhepa. Unfortunately it was gutted by a fire in the 1980s. The rebuilt structure shouldn't be missed, especially when throngs of monks gather for ceremonies, but the "official" monks in charge of ticket collecting and crowd control here (Labrang is very popular with Chinese tour groups; one Saturday we saw twenty large bus loads arrive!) create an unwelcoming atmosphere. But don't be deterred, for the rest of the temples, colleges, and *nangchens*, or lamas' residences, are tended by friendly monks who delight in having visitors.

Many of the other large structures at Labrang are beautiful old buildings with outstanding stone work, expertly carved wood beams and doorways, and old murals of the Four Guardian Kings in the entry foyers. A few of the temples have original copper statues. The monastery is so large it is overwhelming; rather than try to see everything in one day, choose to visit just a few temples so you can enjoy the peaceful settings in each of the courtyards, the fine art and statues, and the lovely monks and pilgrims at each site. Some of my favorite temples are the Serkhang Chenmo, with its blackened old murals; Deyang Podrang, which is the residence of the Jamyang Zhepa Rimpoches; the Jokhang; the atmospheric Tuje Chempo Lhakhang; the Sangye Naro Lhakhang; the Drolma Lhakhang, with a superb 25-foot (8-m) tall copper image of this protectress; and the new Kungthang Chörten.

DAY HIKES NEAR LABRANG

A great way to limber up near Labrang is to walk the three different pilgrimage *koras* that circumambulate the monastery. The inner *nangkor* is within the boundary walls and winds clockwise from the Tsokchen around to the various temples; allow **30 minutes or more**, not including visits to the temples. The intermediate *barkor* takes **1 hour or more** and follows the great rows of prayer wheels along the Sang Chu, starting from the southeast corner of the monastery boundary wall, closest to Xiahe. The circuit passes the impressive Kungthang Chörten, then climbs beside the west boundary wall onto the ridge immediately behind the *gompa*, passing several upper temples to finish at the long rows of prayer wheels along the eastern wall.

The longer, outer *chikor* is a more strenuous **1½-hour** circuit that circles the entire Labrang complex. This route initially follows the *barkor* past the prayer wheels along the Sang Chu. Just after the Kungthang Chörten, the *chikor* turns west at the main road and leads into Sakar village. When the road splits, turn right. About 100 feet (30 m) beyond this junction, the *chikor* angles to the right up an alley, toward a nunnery appropriately called Ani Gompa. Before the convent the trail forks. The right branch visits the nuns,

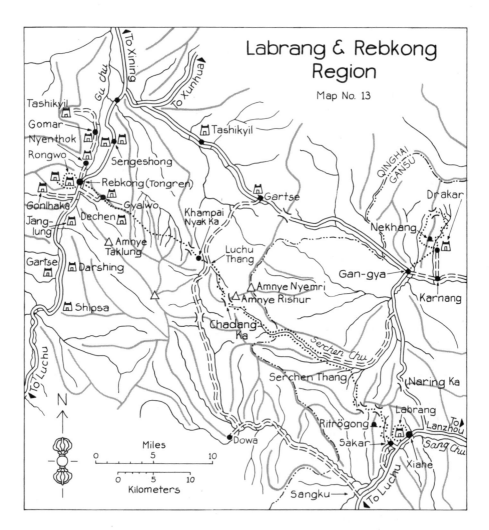

the left one is the *chikor*. Follow this past the last houses to a trail leading onto the ridge side. Zigzag up this dry ridge, aiming toward a cairn and a prayer flag pole at the ruins of Gyabri-tse *ritrö* (10,000 ft, 3050 m), a former hermitage associated with Labrang. The trail then traverses north across the ridges and soon splits. Both these trails return to the east boundary wall of the monastery; the right fork, a popular picnic spot, provides wonderful overviews of Labrang's monastic maze. The left fork is the cairned pilgrim's route, leading down a rocky gully, past a sky-burial site with offerings of clothes scattered about, to reach the valley floor. Nearby is the confluence with a larger valley. Labrang is several hundred yards down to the right (south). **About 20 minutes** up to the left are the ruins of a hermitage, Phuyi Gönthang, and higher on the ridge above is another former retreat, Lamo *gompa*.

Another good warm-up is the **30-minute** hike to the top of the Köku Thang, the stone terraced area on the south (R) bank of the Sang Chu. Every year just after Losar, the Tibetan New Year, Labrang conducts Monlam Chenmo, one of the great religious festivals of the year. Elaborate ceremonies and *cham* mask-dances are performed, and a large *köku* silk appliqué banner is unfurled on this hillside. For a grand panorama of the entire monastery, follow one of the trails up the left side to the top of the display area.

Trails climb higher into the spruce forest, which is said to have sprung from the hairs of the first Jamyang Zhepa. The tributary below leads past small settlements to hilly pastures of wildflowers.

RITRÖGONG HERMITAGE

A pleasant **half-day** outing is the walk to Ritrögong, a cave hermitage with a sacred spring. The direct route follows the road west from Labrang's main entrance gate (or along the *chikor*; see description above) for **20 minutes** to the village of Sakar. After the first fork in the road, don't turn up the alley for the *chikor*, but keep following the road. About 300 feet (90 m) on the right is Ngokwa Tratsang, a *gompa* for married Nyingmapa *ngakpas*. The residents wear white-and-red robes and have great lengths of braided hair coiled atop their heads. This sect is quite widespread in the villages of Amdo, particularly in the Rebkong Valley. This old, ornately decorated temple features a statue of Guru Rimpoche.

A few minutes past Ngokwa Tratsang the road forks again. The left choice leads across a bridge for **20 minutes or more** to the *binguan*, the Labuleng Hotel for tour groups in the Labrang/Xiahe area. The hotel utilizes the old summer palace of Jamyang Zhepa for guest rooms, and has a new building as well. The route to Ritrögong follows the upper left fork and soon leads past the last houses of Sakar into terraced barley and mustard fields. The wide cart track initially continues up the east (L) side of this verdant valley, then becomes a wide trail lined with devotional cairns. Cross the streambed twice. **About 1 hour** past Sakar the trail forks (10,300 ft, 3140 m). The ruins of the Ritrögong *lhakhang* are on a ridge spur up to the left (west), and the cave hermitage is higher on the cliffs. The trail continuing up the main valley is the route to Serchen Thang and the Rebkong Valley (see "The Trek from Labrang to Rebkong," below).

The sacred spring (10,700 ft, 3260 m), or *drubchu*, is a steep **30-minute** climb through spruce and juniper trees. The blessing is three pitchers of this clear, icy water over one's head and back. **A few minutes** higher is the meditation cave of Jamyang Zhepa, and a bit farther up are the ruined walls of a hermitage (10,800 ft, 3290 m) that had been built at the cave of Kalden Gyatsho, the founder of Rongwo Gönchen monastery in Rebkong. This is a great place for a picnic lunch, and not a bad choice for contemplating enlightenment.

GAN-GYA DRAKAR

About 25 miles (40 km) north of Labrang in the grasslands is Gan-gya Drakar (White Rock of Gan-gya), a hermitage associated with the Kungthang *lama* of Labrang. The 6-mile long (10 km) limestone cliffs of Drakar rise 2000 feet (600 m) from the plains to the north of Gan-gya (9700 ft, 2960 m; km marker 28), the administrative *shang* for this area. Shops and restaurants extend along this sharp bend in the road between Labrang and Rebkong.

Drakar is about 7 miles (11 km) northeast of Gan-gya, via a dirt track leading east to the walled city of Karnang, an ancient fortification that shouldn't be missed. Its massive, 25-foot (8-m) tall earthen ramparts are laid out in a twelve-sided cross-pattern stretching 400 yards (365 m) between the far walls; the entire complex is surrounded by a double moat. A Tibetan and a Muslim village are situated inside, with room to grow crops as well. I was told that this was the castle (*kar*) of the Minyak Gyelpo, or King of Minyak (the Minyak kingdom flourished from the ninth to thirteenth centuries in the Gansu/Qinghai area, until it was conquered by Genghis Khan), although it may predate the Minyak era. The Chinese built a series of fortified towns about two thousand years ago along this frontier after failing to contain their Tibetan rivals through engagement and trade agreements.

Many villages in Amdo have married Buddhist practitioners, called ngokwas, *who wear flowing white-and-red robes, and tie their long, braided hair atop their heads*

If you're on foot, take the braided animal path that leads cross-county from Gangya in about **2½ hours** to the *gompa* (10,450 ft, 3190 m). Aim for the obvious cleft in the wall of cliffs; the monastery is in the foothills just to the right (east), and the village of Drakar Tawa is below. The 300-year-old hermitage was completely destroyed after 1959, and is still in the process of being rebuilt. A Jampa *lhakhang* dedicated to the Future

Buddha and a chanting hall are the two main structures. Next to them are the white-washed monk's residences and the ruins of the former abbot's quarters. Above on the hill is the *nangchen*, or residence of the Kungru Khandroma, a lineage of female incarnations. The current *trülku* of the *nangchen* is married with children, and lives in Xiahe. The *labrang*, or palace for the Kungthang *lama*, which is in ruins by the village, was founded by the second *trülku*. The current incarnation is the fifth, and, like the Jamyang Zhepa, he resides in Lanzhou rather than here in his *nangchen* or at Labrang.

The main pilgrimage site is Nekhang, a cavern **30 minutes** from the *gompa*. The entrance is a gaping hole in the rock tower guarding the left (west) side of the limestone gorge. Be prepared for a deep, steep, slippery excursion of ladders, ropes, and cables, through the bowels of this mountain to the *yab-yum* sacred pools of the Tantric deity Demchok and his consort Dorje Pakmo. Numerous rock formations here represent various Buddhist deities. The most fascinating feature of this cave is its *chinlap*, or blessing. On a recent trip, one of my monk guides (you'll never find your way without one) lowered himself through a hole in the cave floor near the pools, then came back up with a handful of white clay. He told me that this is the *chura*, or cheese, of Drukmo, the wife of King Gesar of Ling. "Eat up!" he urged. I tentatively took a little taste. Darned if it's not similar to the soft, sweet cheese made by herders from *dri* milk! Bring good batteries for your flashlight. The journey takes **nearly 1 hour**.

As with many pilgrimage sites in Kham and Amdo, three *kora* routes circle Drakar. The *nangkor* is a **20-minute** circuit around the *gompa*. The *chikor* is a **6- to 8-hour** excursion that climbs up past the white *chörten* on the moraine to the west (R) of the limestone gorge. This unmarked, uncairned route then goes up to the top of the cliffs to a pass (12,700 ft, 3870 m) before descending steeply through verdant limestone gullies of up-ended rock pinnacles on the return to the monastery. A longer *barkor* circuit initially follows the *nangkor* route over the same pass to the main gorge, then continues east up onto the ridges to circumambulate the entire 6 miles of cliffs before returning to the *gompa*. Allow **14 hours or more**, or bring camping equipment and stay the night by one of the alpine lakes on the second half of the circuit. Saga Dawa is the main month for this pilgrimage. Again, bring someone along as your guide.

THE TREK FROM LABRANG TO REBKONG

The **5-day** trek from Labrang monastery to the Rebkong Valley begins at the village of Sakar, to the west of Labrang's main entrance gate. Following the trail to Ritrögong hermitage (see description above), walk through Sakar and then head north up the valley for **about 1 hour**. Just beyond the turnoff for the hermitage (10,300 ft, 3140 m), cross the stream to the west (R) side. Continue up the main drainage for **less than 1 hour** to a meadow at the confluence of two valleys (10,950 ft 3340 m). This flat area is the last camp with water until the next valley.

The trail up the draw to the right leads to Gan-gya. The route to Rebkong goes left (northwest), following a narrow, flower-speckled gully for **1 hour** to a huge pasture (11,450 ft, 3490 m) of rolling hills. The mounds of earth everywhere are due to gophers (Tib., *shilong*), a common "mole-rat" in Amdo somewhat similar to a pocket gopher, but larger. A distinct path now wades west through the wildflowers to a nearby ridge top. The first pass is **1 hour** from here; it's the obvious dip in the ridge at the far west side of the next valley. Descend to a *drokpa* camp, then climb gradually through lush pastures to the summit of the second pass (11,600 ft, 3540 m). When I crossed here in July, the wide valley below, called the Serchen Thang (Great Golden Plain), completely caught me off guard. Above this great basin were three separate lightning storms joining together to boom with thunder, uninterrupted, for 30 minutes. Below on the grassland were nearly a hundred herder tents, and I guessed there must have been tens of thousands of yak, *dri*, sheep, goats, and horses. Nowhere else in my Tibetan travels had I seen such a large gathering of *drokpa* and animals. (I later met a family who told me there were three hundred families camped in the Serchen Thang area, including in the side valleys. They personally owned 600 animals, and said many other families had the same. If each family averaged 400 livestock, then more than 100,000 animals are being herded in this basin.)

In the distance to the northwest of Serchen Thang is a flat-topped peak with a tall, pointed *la-dze* cairn. This is Amnye Nyemri (14,101 ft, 4298 m), the residence of the main *yul-lha*, a type of "country-protector," for this region. The border for Gansu and Qinghai Provinces runs through this summit. Amnye Rishur, the domed "wife" of Amnye Nyemri (which also has a tall *la-dze*) rises to the left (west), and Chadang Ka, the main pass en route to Rebkong, crosses the west shoulder of Amnye Rishur.

Initially an animal trail drops to the right (north) from the pass, but soon braids and disappears into the rocky slopes. Keep angling right, down toward the base of a large spur ridge coming into the valley off the main ridge. Eventually a trail forms near this spur and leads to the first *drokpa* tents in **1 hour or more**. In this part of Amdo, many of the herder tents are made from cotton, rather than wool, with only a center strip of wool sewn in. The herders also prefer cooking on metal stoves rather than over open fires; stove pipes poke through the tops of nearly every tent in this region. Pick up a few small rocks before you approach, and as you pass check to see if the guard dogs are on their leashes. Use the Amdo greeting, *Cho demo!* (lit., are you well?) when you meet someone. If you are invited into someone's tent, and chances are you will be, put your pack down and enjoy some Amdo hospitality. If the Rongme Valley in Kham is the Valley of Friendly People, then Amdo is the Land of Friendly People. Rarely have I met such outgoing, welcoming folks who were so genuinely concerned about whether we'd had enough to eat, or if we wanted them to load our packs onto their horses.

The route to Rebkong heads cross-country (north) for **1 hour** to the Serchen Chu, on the far side of the grassy plain. Use two tall, pointed *la-dze* cairns on the far ridge as your beacon; beyond this ridge to the right (northeast) are the white cliffs of Gan-gya Drakar. The meadows along the Serchen Chu make fine campsites (10,500 ft, 3200 m), and the way to Chadang Ka follows this tumbling creek upstream (west) to Gyawo Luchu, the last main herding area before this pass. Either stay on the south (R) side of the creek (it's more fun), or follow the dirt road running along the base of the ridge. The road leads past Gan-gya Ka-gya, a summer community of tents where goods are sold to the herders. There's even a tea shop tent. **About 1 hour** up the creek is the confluence with a large tributary from the left (west). A trail up this drainage crosses several passes to eventually reach Janglung *gompa*, in the upper Rebkong Valley about 7 miles (12 km) to the south of Rebkong (Chi., Tongren), the county seat (*xian*).

Continue up the main valley to the right (northwest). Both sides of the creek are lined with a succession of white *drokpa* tents. The embankment along the southwest (R) side is somewhat more flat, though the main trail is on the northeast (L) side. The route to Chadang Ka is **about 5 hours** from here following this big grassy valley full of white tents, wildflowers, green hills, and *yin-yang* herds of yak and sheep. Amnye Rishur, the conical "wife" peak with a large *la-dze*, comes into view several times. The border for Qinghai crosses the valley just before it makes a sharp swing to the right. Cross the creek twice and pass below an embankment with the first herder tents of Gyawo Luchu (pronounced "Lichi"; 11,500 ft, 3500 m). Amnye Nymeri looms up to the north; it's now possible to see that the large *la-dze* cairn is surrounded by thirteen smaller ones, a common tradition on holy mountains and passes throughout Amdo. At many sites the poles in the cairns are protection offerings of giant arrows, called *dashang*.

Pilgrims on the kora *around Labrang monastery*

The Gyawo Luchu herders are in two groups; the second camp (12,100 ft, 3690 m) is **1 hour** before the pass. If it's late, stay here for the night with these amiable folks. If you're a small group, try camping at one of several remote meadows lining the stream near the pass. The valley now splits at this last herder camp. The route to the pass follows the drainage up to the left (west), climbing steeply into a vibrantly green hanging valley, then up scree slopes to the summit of Chadang Ka (also called Chubzang La; 13,150 ft, 4010 m). The 360-degree panorama from the top of Amnye Rishur (13,500 ft, 4110 m) is worth the **25-minute** side trip from the pass. The herders climb here to burn offering fires, and once each year a procession goes up Amnye Nyemri to offer incense, new *dashang,* and wood poles. The next peak to the north with a *la-dze* is called Chadang Ra. The route to Rebkong descends into the valley below, called Luchu Thang, and beyond to the northwest on a ridge top is the row of fourteen *la-dze* cairns on Khampai Nyak Ka, the next pass.

Tighten your bootlaces for the steep talus slopes below Chadang Ka. As the stream beside the trail increases in size, cross to the east (R) side to avoid wet ground. Pass the first small meadow for camping (12,250 ft, 3730 m) in **30 minutes**, then soon come to a herder camp with a half-dozen tents. Below here a braided track weaves through hilly meadows of purple gentians, yellow *Pedicularis*, purple asters, pink geraniums, and 2-foot-tall edelweiss. To avoid marshy areas, angle over a low ridge into the tributary drainage entering from the right (east). Several herder huts are along the base of the far ridge; the route to Rebkong crosses this tributary stream to the north (R) side below the huts. The ground is quite wet in summer, requiring a lot of rock hopping. The valley soon narrows, then spills out onto Luchu Thang, a great plain of grass and flowers, reaching the road in **2 hours or more** from Chadang Ka.

The town of Gartse is about 9 miles (14 km) to the right (northeast), along the road between Labrang and the Rebkong Valley. The trek route follows the road to the left for **20 minutes**, then turns right up a cart track to a group of herder houses (10,900 ft, 3320 m). The fences in this valley are new to Amdo, and are part of a government program to create winter grazing areas. Where the road passes through a gate, the trail to Khampai Nyak Ka leads between two houses up the grassy ridge to the left (northwest), staying to the left of a large moraine of boulders. A good trail winds across the hills for **1 hour or more**, over a fence and up to the long row of *la-dze* cairns and poles with prayer flags at the pass (also called Khampa La; 11,600 ft, 3540 m). Back to the southeast are views of Amnye Nyemri and Amnye Rishur.

The trail to the Rebkong Valley now heads northwest for **3 hours or more**, crossing a series of thirteen rolling hills and ridges that lead down from the main ridge to the south. Just below the pass the trail forks; go right, descend to a ridge crest, then head down to a beautiful rocky creek surrounded by meadows. In early August, marmots gallop playfully here among the deep grass and wildflowers, their babies racing in and out of the burrows, too curious to stay underground as you walk past. Each of the small valleys between the ridges are excellent campsites, and most have streams. The ridges become lower and more rolling as the trail gets closer to Rebkong, and several herder camps take advantage of the rich grass meadows.

The final ridge crest (10,700 ft, 3260 m) offers the first views of the deep Rebkong Valley. The dry, red earth–colored hills are heavily terraced, with many villages dotting the slopes. Below to the left is the golden roof of Dechen *gompa*. The prominent ridge high above (south of) it with a tall *la-dze* cairn is Amnye Taklung, the residence of the *yul-lha* for this part of the Rebkong area. The next high crest to the southeast along the ridge is Amnye Taklung's "wife," Amnye Jomo. The mountain residence for the main *yul-lha* for this entire region is Amnye Shakhyung (the Garuda), the highest rocky peak in the distance to the west.

Many trails now lead to Rebkong. One of the more direct routes does not descend to Dechen *gompa*. Instead, sidle along the ridge sides to the right (north) on a braided trail; aim for a distant *la-dze* on the left (south) side of a domed hill. When the trail forks at the first barley terraces, go up to the right. Reach the *la-dze* (10,400 ft, 3170 m) in **1 hour**, then descend for **30 minutes** to the village of Gyalwo (9800 ft, 2990 m), which is the administrative *shang* for this area. The houses are built along the top of the ridge, as are other settlements on adjacent ridges. When the trail meets the road, keep heading straight (northwest) toward the houses. On the right is a small, ornate *gönkhang* ("mok hun" in the local dialect) with silk-covered figures of all the main *yul-lha* for this region. (On a ridge top to the west of Gyalwo is a 10-foot-tall (3-m) effigy made from woven sticks; I was told this is a figure of Amnye Rishur, constructed by the local *ngokwas* to ensure a good harvest. A figure of Amnye Rishur is also in this temple.) Not far from the *gönkhang* is the assembly hall (*digung*) for Gyalwo's fifty long-haired *ngokwas*. This beautiful temple was used in the Cultural Revolution for storing grain; the support pillars still have notches from the bins. The gilded clay statue in the center is Guru Rimpoche.

If you haven't organized transportation to meet you at Gyalwo, you can walk to the central commercial area of Rebkong, a steep **2-hour or more** descent from here. Follow the road out of the village to the west for **30 minutes** to the first big turn. A shortcut continues straight (west) through the wheat fields, then plunges into a labyrinth of earthen-walled corridors. Or follow the road. Both routes meet at the bridge (8350 ft, 2550 m) over the Gu Chu, the river draining the Rebkong Valley. Just beyond the bridge the road forks. Both paths join up in **30 minutes** at Rebkong's (Chi., Tongren; 8500 ft, 2590 m) main traffic circle, which has a statue of a white horse in the center. The left branch ascends to the main road through Rebkong, passing the main entry gates for

Rongwo Gönchen monastery in **less than 10 minutes**. The main tourist hotel (*binguan*) in Rebkong is **5 minutes** to the left (west) of the traffic circle. The bus station is along the main road leading south from town, a few hundred yards down to the right from the circle.

RONGWO GÖNCHEN MONASTERY

Resembling a miniature version of Labrang, the monastic complex of Rongwo Gönchen sprawls along a hillside, its great golden-roofed temples enclosed by a tall boundary wall. The monastery, founded in the sixteenth century by the Gelukpa master Kalden Gyatsho, pre-dates Labrang. It was ransacked by the Chinese in 1958. The rebuilding, which started in the 1980s, was still in full swing in the late 1990s, with construction projects involving a half-dozen large buildings. I was told nearly five hundred monks are associated with Rongwo Gönchen.

The 400-year-old central building, the Tsokchen chanting hall, which was not destroyed, was one of the first structures to be refurbished. The clay statues and the wall murals here are outstanding; the Rebkong style of statuary and mural painting is famous throughout Amdo and Tibet. Unlike those in Central Tibet, these statues are not covered in robes. The figure's clothing is elaborately styled into the clay, then the entire statue is gilded and usually displayed uncovered. The temples and monasteries throughout the Rebkong Valley have beautiful new (and a few old) statues, murals and *thangkas*. (Two monasteries renowned as the home of this art style are found in the town of Sengeshong, 5 miles [8 km] south of Rebkong on the main road. Yango *gompa* is on the right [east] side of the road, and Mago *gompa* is set back in the village to the left [west] side.) An impressive array of statues lines the back wall of the Tsokchen, including the *yab-se-sum*, featuring a large figure of Tsong Khapa in the center.

An inner *nangkor* pilgrim's circuit leads clockwise within the *gompa's* boundary walls to each of the temples. The *barkor* path circumambulates the monastery outside the walls, taking about **1 hour**. Temples that shouldn't be missed include the Tamdrin *lhakhang*, with a towering statue of this protector; the Je Yab-se-sum *lhakhang*, which has very nice word carvings; and the large, new Jowo Khang above the Tsokchen hall.

DAY HIKES NEAR REBKONG

One could spend a couple of weeks based in Rebkong and visit a different site nearly every day. The inhabited part of the valley stretches for about 30 miles (50 km), with numerous villages scattered the entire way. Many of the settlements have a *digung*, or assembly hall, for their *ngokwas*, and there are nearly a dozen monasteries for the celibate sects.

A good hike to help get your bearings for the valley leads up from Rongwo Gönchen to Drakar Shar (Eastern White Rock) hermitage (9400 ft, 2865 m; marked with a monastery symbol on Map No. 13). This steep **1- to 2-hour** climb starts from the *barkor* pilgrim's circuit around the monastery. Follow the outer boundary wall clockwise up the south side, to a group of monk's residences. The *kora* climbs above them, angles to the right of the *köku* banner display area, then heads above the temples. A smaller trail zigzags up the nose of the ridge here, eventually leading into the next valley to the west. This is also the approach for Drakar Shar. The path climbs steeply through terraces, staying beside a large gully. In **30 minutes** or more the route starts angling to the left to cross the ridge crest. Drakar is set among a grove of trees above the trail, at the base of the large cliffs. The trail leading up from here isn't very defined; look for cairns marking the way. The *tsamkhang*, or "meditation retreat," sits on a grassy, wooded plain overlooking the valley. Reconstructed sleeping rooms and a temple lie within the crumbling walls of the former retreat.

The high ridge across the valley to the southeast from Drakar Shar is Amnye Taklung, the residence for one of the main *yul-lhas* for the Rebkong area. The "wife" of this protector, Amnye Jomo, is behind it to the left. A wide trail leads up the ridge crest to the main summit starting from the village of Gyalwu Gang, which is on its lower flanks. A festival takes place each summer, during which locals climb the peak to offer new prayer flags and *dashang*. It's a big climb; allow **5 to 6 hours** one way.

To the north of Rebkong are several less-visited villages along the west (L) bank of the Gu Chu. **Forty minutes** from the center of town is Nyenthok, which has ruins of an ancient castle and a monastery with several original temple buildings. Adjacent to the *gompa's* chanting hall is the Jampa *lhakhang*, which has a new, beautifully crafted 40-foot-tall Future Buddha statue; the wall murals here are some of the finest older paintings extant in the area.

Another hour south along the road on the Gu Chu's west bank is the village of Gomar. A new multistoried *chörten* lies below the town, and up among the houses is a trail to the monastery. The two main buildings are about 300 years old; the Jampa *lhakhang* also has a huge, gilded Gyelwa Jampa statue.

One of the Four Guardian Kings; an example of the famous Rebkong-style of painting

15

BICYCLING IN TIBET

BY TIM YOUNG

Travelling by bicycle offers a challenging way to see Tibet, and a cycling excursion here requires more planning than most other destinations in Asia. If you go to Tibet with a commercial bicycling trip, the travel company and the group leader will be responsible for handling all the permits and logistics. Also, your group will be accompanied by a "sag wagon," a vehicle that carries the group's personal gear, camping equipment, and food; you can also catch a ride if you're tired!

If you're riding on your own, ask other travelers or cyclists for the current information regarding travel permits. As of 1999, independent cyclists riding from Lhasa to Nepal were not required to have any special permits other than the standard Aliens Travel Permit to travel from Shigatse to the Nepal border, and for Everest base camp. However, be forewarned that the rules can change from one year to the next; several cyclists were fined and sent back to Lhasa by a police checkpoint on the Southern Road to Gyangtse, while another group on the Friendship Highway from Lhasa to Shigatse had no problems.

Another concern regarding bicycling in Tibet is your fitness for a journey of this nature. This is the highest mountain biking in the world. The demands of big climbs, rough roads, remote surroundings, and extremely high elevations must all be taken into consideration.

PREPARATIONS

Tibet is worth the difficulties that traveling by bicycle entails. I have listed a few issues for you to consider before you set off.

BICYCLE EQUIPMENT

Your bike should be of good quality, dependable, and in first-class mechanical shape. Riders must be capable of handling a multitude of repairs on their own, carrying the necessary tools and spare parts in case of breakdowns. On my last trip in Tibet we had the tools for a complete overhaul. Each cyclist carried one spare tube (we also had one spare tire for every two bikes); extra cables; an extra rear derailleur, chain, and freewheel; extra spokes; a sewing kit; and a small, basic repair kit. This was a vehicle-supported trip, so we also had tools for other repairs. If you choose to travel self-contained in Tibet, you will need to carry a complete repair kit and the necessary spare parts. If this is the case, one way around excessive weight is to have the group use the same bike components, allowing tools and spares to be shared.

OTHER SUPPLIES

Whether you travel with a support truck or self-contained, you will need a sturdy waterproof tent, a sleeping bag, a first-aid kit, and sufficient quantities of food and water. Resupplying on the road can be quite difficult at times; the smaller villages may have only *tsampa*, yak butter, meat, and Tibetan brick tea. Some truck stops sell only instant noodles or simple rice dishes. Many villages do not even have a store. One alternative is to ask the locals if they have any vegetables, noodles, or meat for sale; they are generally very helpful.

Maps are important and so is the ability to ask questions, such as "Is there a shop in the next town?" and "How far is the next village?" Most maps still have some inaccuracies,

Bicycling along the Ra Chu near Dingri (photo by Tim Young)

which are not such a big deal if you're in a vehicle. However, a 20-mile correction at the end of a long day on a bicycle could be impossible. Carry an emergency supply of food just in case you don't quite make your destination.

WEATHER AND CLOTHING

Summers mean cool nights and warm days. It can rain for days at a time in July and August, and frost in September is common. Strong winds and sandstorms are not unusual, nor is snow on the passes. At higher elevations, freezing temperatures are common throughout the year. During September at 17,000 feet (5180 m), the nights are usually in the low teens to single figures. In January nighttime temperatures can drop to -33°F (-27°C), and daytime temperatures often hover just below freezing.

Bring enough clothing to meet the coldest expected temperatures. For spring, summer, or autumn cycling, light cycling pants and a short-sleeved shirt usually will be sufficient. If you add a pair of warm-up pants, a long-sleeved jersey, a wind shell, and gloves, you can handle most conditions in good weather. For poor weather you should also have a fleece or down jacket, an extra layer of synthetic long underwear, a rain jacket, wind or rain pants, warm shoes, and a hat. If you are camping, remember that you will require extra clothing to stay comfortable while sitting still in the cold night air.

PHYSICAL PREPARATION

It is wise to arrive in Tibet in good physical condition. Cyclists should train to build up their cardiovascular systems, for nowhere will they be put to the test as in Tibet. Hill training that gets the heart rate up and keeps it up for an hour at a time is highly recommended. The higher the elevation you train at while at home the better, even though Tibet will be higher yet. A well-designed strength training program two or three times a week to build overall power and condition the upper body is an excellent supplement. While physical fitness does not prevent altitude sickness, it does help the body deal with all the other physical demands of rough, remote travel.

Standard cycle touring advice applies: Arrive at a good weight, in healthy condition, and well rested. Eat well (always a challenge in Tibet), and consider taking a vitamin and mineral supplement. Drink plenty of water to remain properly hydrated. Be sure to acclimatize properly before your cycling tour begins. You might need up to a week or more to get used to the change in elevation. Once you're in Tibet, relax. Don't push it. Go on some walks around town, then after several days of taking it easy try a few short rides around Lhasa. Use your bike to shop for yogurt at the Barkor or cruise the streets with the locals on their Chinese one-speeds. In the vicinity of Lhasa, work out in the hills; the rides to the nearby monasteries of Sera and Drepung are great for cycle training.

The historical sites of Samye monastery and the Yarlung Valley, near Tsethang, are just **a few days** to the south. This route follows the river valley at elevations below 12,000 feet, so a relatively easy round trip could be completed in **7 days or so**. Another possibility from Lhasa is a visit to Ganden monastery, which is a pleasant 25-mile (41-km) ride to the east up the Kyi Chu, followed by a steep 1500-foot (460-m) climb above the valley. The round trip could be done in **2 days** of riding, and allow an extra day for visiting the monastery.

CLASSIC BICYCLE ROUTES

The journey from Lhasa to Kathmandu is the most popular bicycling route in Tibet, and with good reason. In just under 600 miles (1000 km) and **13 to 16 days**, this journey crosses six major passes, traverses the backbone of the Himalaya, offers a look at the North Face of Mount Everest, and visits two of Asia's most interesting cities. The reverse of this ride, from Kathmandu to Lhasa, can also be done. A challenging **4- to 6-day** side trip is the ride to Mount Everest base camp.

LHASA TO KATHMANDU

Plan on **at least 3 weeks** to do the trip justice and not hurt yourself. A month is even better, since you should spend about a week in Lhasa acclimatizing. It takes **5 days** to reach Gyangtse (km marker 251); consider taking a day off in this interesting town.

Shigatse (km marker 0/4903) is **a long day's** ride from Gyangtse. A worthwhile side trip en route is to Zhalu monastery, about 3 miles (4 km) south of the main road from kilometer marker 20, at the town of Ruka Dün. Once in Shigatse, set aside a day to stock up on supplies, as this is the last large market before Nepal.

Three or 4 days of cycling are required to reach Shekar (turnoff at km marker 5133) from Shigatse, during which you must cross Lakpa La (17,126 ft, 5220 m), the highest pass on the route. The trip to Dingri (km marker 5193/4) from Shekar takes **1 day**, then it's **another day** of riding to Thong La (km marker 5289; 16,580 ft, 5050 m), the second-highest pass on this route. From there the road makes the greatest downhill plummet in the world, a 14,000-foot (4300 m) vertical drop from the Plateau to the Sunkosi River in Nepal. Plan on **1 day** to reach the border and an hour or so for customs formalities before crossing into Nepal. Kathmandu is 72 miles (116 km) from the border, though frequent landslides in the steep-walled canyon can change a trip of **1 day** into several. If you are on your own, ask about the roads ahead so you can plan properly.

Suggested Itinerary from Lhasa to Kathmandu

ROUTE	DISTANCE	PASSES	TIME
Lhasa to Gyangtse	155 mi (251 km)	Kampa La	5 days
Gyangtse to Shigatse	56 mi (90 km)	None	1 day
Shigatse to Shekar	144 mi (232 km)	Tsho La	3 to 4 days
		Lakpa La	
Shekar to Nepal border	158 mi (256 km)	Thong La	3 to 4 days
Border to Kathmandu	72 mi (116 km)	Banepa Pass	1 to 2 days
Totals:	585 mi (945 km)		13 to 16 days

Mount Everest Base Camp

For an extra 104 miles (169 km) and several giant climbs, the adventure cyclist can actually ride a mountain bike all the way to the Rongphu/Mount Everest base camp. It starts from the Friendship Highway at kilometer marker 5145/6, then shoots up a long set of seventeen switchbacks to Pang La (16,700 ft, 5090 m), with its stunning views of Mount Everest, the Himalaya, and the Dzakar Chu Valley. It is a push to reach Dza Rongphu monastery in **2 days** from the highway; count on **3 days** if you're carrying full panniers of gear. The road was originally built by the Chinese for their 1960 climb of Mount Everest. Several small villages are on the way: Tashi Dzom, Pasum, Chödzom, and Dza Rongphu monastery have guesthouses and shops. The smaller settlements have little food available, although a resourceful cyclist can round up some eggs, a few vegetables, *tsampa*, and yak butter.

From Dza Rongphu monastery, Mount Everest looms at the valley's head; it's a great place to spend a night on the way up. Base camp (16,700 ft, 5090 m) is **less than a half-day's** ride, situated at the base of the Rongphu Glacier.

The Rongphu region can be exited by two routes, both taking **2 to 3 days** for the return to the highway. You can either retrace your steps along the road or cross one of the trekking passes into the Dingri Valley (see "Dingri to Everest Base Camp Loop Trek"). These passes are considerably more remote and difficult, and should be attempted only by skilled and well-equipped riders.

Other Options

Tibet offers an almost endless choice of bicycling opportunities. Eastern Tibet is traversed by reasonable road networks supported by thousands of miles of yak trails. Because the river valleys are low with the mountains rising to tremendous heights, hill climbing by bicycle in this region can be fierce. Adventurous cyclists might consider tackling the "wild west" of Tibet, journeying to Mount Kailash and on to China's Xinjiang Province.

No matter where you decide to cycle in Tibet, adequate advance planning is essential for the success of your journey. Good luck!

Tim Young spent six and a half years on the "Too Tyred Tour," an around-the-world bicycle expedition, and has traveled by bicycle in over fifty countries. Tim currently lives in Jackson Hole, Wyoming, where he designs bicycling equipment and works with the city government designing public bicycle paths.

The Jokhang in Lhasa, during the Monlam Chenmo festival

SECTION III

THE COUNTRY AND ITS PEOPLE

16
THE NATURAL HISTORY OF TIBET

According to Tibetan Buddhist tradition, Tibet lay under a great ocean of water after the universe was first created. Then, by the blessing of Chenrezik, the *Bodhisattva* of Compassion, the waters slowly receded and from the depths rose Tibet, a land surrounded by vast chains of mountains, within a world comprised of four major and eight minor continents.

GEOLOGY

The geologic history of Tibet and the Himalaya presently being pieced together by geologists has fascinating similarities to the ancient account. The Tibetan Plateau is actually an accretion of separate continental fragments that collided with the Asian continent over a period of some 200 million years. A succession of large and small seas, collectively known as the Tethys Sea, was created and eventually drained as each fragment merged with the mainland. The most recent of these bodies of water existed until about 50 million years ago and extended from the Atlantic to the Pacific, between Africa and Europe and between India and the rest of Asia. In the hills to the south of Dingri, near Mount Everest, it is possible to find shell fossils from this ancient ocean alongside the trails. Even the rock on the summit of Mount Everest was once submerged, although that body of water pre-dates the formation of these Tethys Seas; climbers have found fossils of small marine animals called crinoids imbedded in the layers of limestone near the top.

Tsamda hot springs near Dingri

How is it that some of the highest landmasses on earth were once submerged under oceans? Using fossil evidence, the dating of rocks, and clues from the magnetic alignment of rock crystals, most Western geologists now believe that this fantastic upheaval of the earth's surface resulted from the forces of plate tectonics. According to this theory, the continents and the ocean floors do not form a continuous, static surface enveloping the earth like an eggshell, but instead are divided into a giant mosaic of rigid yet movable shell pieces, or tectonic plates, which overlie the planet's hotter, softer interior.

At present the continents and ocean floors consist of ten major plates and several smaller plates. Geologists believe there was a time, however, when the earth's landmasses were all bunched together into one huge "super continent," called Pangaea. About 250 million to 200 million years ago (the Triassic period, when the first reptiles and the earliest dinosaurs appeared), this great continent started to break apart, initially creating two distinct land areas. To the north was Laurasia, a landmass that consisted of present-day North America, most of Asia, and all of Europe. The great southern continent of Gondwanaland was made up of what is now Australia, Antarctica, Africa, South America, and India.

Over the next 100 million years, Laurasia and Gondwanaland continued to break up, their various pieces drifting across the globe toward their present locations. It was during this period that numerous smaller fragments of Gondwanaland, including segments of Southern Tibet and the Indian subcontinent, broke away and started their amazing northward journeys toward the Asian mainland. The rocks that are now part of India and the Himalaya originally lay 5000 miles (8000 km) farther to the south, near present-day Antarctica.

The collision of the Indian subcontinent with the Asian plate was one of the most dramatic geological events of the last 150 million years. India's persistent northward movement caused massive changes in both landmasses, uplifting the Tibetan Plateau and the Himalayan Range to their extraordinary heights. Tibet is the largest and highest plateau in the world, averaging over 15,000 feet (4500 m) in elevation. Even more spectacular was this collision's role in the creation of the 1900-mile-long (3100-km) chain of Himalayan peaks that span south and central Asia, boasting ten of the world's fourteen highest summits, and the emergence of a dozen or more related mountain ranges. When this great uplift of the Himalaya and the Tibetan Plateau occurred is still subject to much debate. The inaccessibility of these areas and the complex nature of their rock structures have prevented geologists from accurately detailing the sequence of events. Some regions of the Himalaya seem to have been uplifted at different times, but there is no conclusive evidence indicating whether portions of Southern Tibet were elevated before the collision with India, whether the two regions were elevated at the same time, or whether the uplift of the Himalaya and Tibet was rapid and relatively recent.

Regardless, geologists believe that the Indian subcontinent is still pushing into Asia. And the great upheaval of the Himalaya seems far from over. Evidence of this is the frequency of large slips along major faults underneath the mountains, which have caused several big earthquakes over the last 100 years. One particularly severe earthquake, in 1934, was estimated at 8.4 on the Richter scale (the 1906 San Francisco earthquake was probably 8.3); it knocked down buildings in Calcutta and Kathmandu and destroyed Thangboche monastery near Mount Everest. In 1988 a less severe earthquake of more than 6 on the Richter scale left 25,000 people homeless around its epicenter near the Nepal-India border. More welcome indications that the Himalaya is still geologically active are the many hot springs and large thermal sites found near the mountains. Nepal claims more than 600 hot springs, while Tibet has a significant geothermal area in the Yangpachen Valley, where steam-driven generators provide electricity for Lhasa.

PHYSICAL GEOGRAPHY

Tibet is the largest and highest plateau on earth, averaging nearly 15,000 feet (4570 m) in elevation. Buttressing its southern flanks is the Great Himalaya Range, stretching 1900 miles long from Pakistan's Nanga Parbat (26,657 ft, 8125 m) in the west to the cloud-hidden Namche Barwa (25,446 ft, 7756 m) in Eastern Tibet. Along its length are ten of the highest points on our planet, including the "third pole," Mount Everest (29,028 ft, 8848 m).

This vast plateau of Tibet sprawls across 830,000 square miles (2.2 million km²), an area about 30 percent greater than Alaska and 20 percent of the landmass of modern-day China. Springing forth from these extensive highlands are the sources for ten of Asia's major rivers, a gigantic watershed complex supplying nearly half of the earth's population with fresh water. Though large tracts of Tibet are uninhabited and sparsely vegetated, the lower eastern end of the plateau is heavily forested, providing China with its greatest source of timber.

Tibet can be subdivided into three natural regions according to its primary water-sheds: the Northern Plateau, the Outer Plateau, and the Southeastern Plateau. The largest of these is the Northern Plateau, a harsh, arid 400,000-square-mile (1 million km²) tract of high basins, huge lakes, and extensive ridge systems. It is bounded to the north by the Astin Tagh and the Altin Tagh mountains and along its southern edge by the 1500-mile-long (2500-km) Gangtise–Nyenchen Thanglha Range, which includes the sa-cred Mount Kailash (22,028 ft, 6714 m) in the west and the main Nyenchen Thanglha summit (23,330 ft, 7111 m) north of Lhasa.

The principal feature of the Northern Plateau is the Chang Thang, a mostly unin-habited expanse of windswept alpine plains and internal drainage systems ending in large brackish lakes. It is the world's largest roadless area and the largest intact ecosys-tem outside of the polar regions. Averaging 16,400 feet (5000 m) in elevation, the Chang Thang is dotted with hundreds of lakes and intersected by heavily eroded ridges and mountains, the largest being the Kun Lun Ranges. There are no trees and few bushes due to an annual precipitation of just 4 to 10 inches (100 to 250 mm). Until the 1950s no roads nor trails crossed the Chang Thang, though several caravan routes rimmed its fringes. This remote part of the Northern Plateau provides a totally unspoiled environ-ment for its endemic wildlife, particularly Tibetan antelope, wild yak, and Tibetan wild asses. To protect this unique ecosystem, the Tibet Forest Bureau, with the assistance of wildlife biologist George B. Schaller, established the Chang Thang Nature Preserve, the second-largest protected area in the world. It encompasses an area of about 100,000 square miles (385,000 km²), which is roughly the size of Colorado.

The two other regions of the Northern Plateau are the Tshadam (Salt Marsh; Chi., Qaidam) basin and the basin of Tsho Ngompo (Blue Lake; Chi., Qinghai Hu; also called Kokonor), the largest lake in Tibet. If you are traveling to Lhasa from China via Golmud, the train across Qinghai Province passes the lake's northern shore.

The Outer Plateau is a relatively thin but lengthy strip of land to the south of the Gangtise–Nyenchen Thanglha mountain belt, stretching from Ladakh in the west to the source of the Yellow River in the east. It parallels the northern side of the Himalaya and follows the watersheds of two major South Asian rivers, the Indus and the Tsangpo (Brahmaputra). The western end of this plateau is the narrowest and has a cold, arid climate. It also provides the sources for the Karnali and Sutlej Rivers, two other major drainages descending through South Asia. Correctly identifying the sources of these four rivers proved to be one of the last great challenges for geographers, as all originate in this remote corner of Tibet near Mount Kailash.

The central part of the Outer Plateau is bisected by the broad, fertile river valleys of the former Ü and Tsang Provinces. The biggest population centers of Central Tibet

(Lhasa, Shigatse, and Tsethang), as well as many of Tibet's largest religious institutions, are located here, the country's agricultural heartland. The climate is considerably more temperate than the Northern Plateau, and the summer monsoon from India is not entirely blocked by the Himalaya. The Lhasa Valley (11,850 ft, 3610 m) is at about the same latitude as New Orleans and annually receives 10 to 20 inches (250 to 500 mm) of precipitation. The hills and high valleys are covered with grassy steppe vegetation that supports nomadic families and their herds, and along the southern frontier with Nepal and India are found extensive conifer forests. Farther east the Outer Plateau broadens considerably and includes the part of Tibet known as Amdo. The large tracts of grasslands and alpine steppe here are the source for all of the main rivers of China and Southeast Asia, supporting a large population of *drokpa*, the nomadic herders, as well as boasting the largest monasteries outside Central Tibet. The most significant feature of the Eastern Outer Plateau is the Yellow River, which cuts an immense, S-shaped desert canyon around the holy summit of Amnye Machen (20,610 ft, 6282 m).

The Southeastern Plateau is very different from the typical image of Tibet. Bathed by the southern monsoon, it is a rugged, heavily forested area intersected by high mountain ridges and river gorges. It is the smallest and the lowest in altitude of the three main plateaus, encompassing the Southern Amdo, Kham, Kongpo, and Pemako regions of Eastern Tibet. This plateau's southern boundary dips below the main Himalaya chain and includes the great 180-degree bend of the Tsangpo around Namche Barwa, the end of the Himalaya. The far eastern limits of this plateau are formed by a series of north-south ranges (collectively called the Hengduan Shan by the Chinese), which include the holy mountains of Minyak Gangkar (24,790 ft, 7556 m) and Khawa Karpo (22,113 ft, 6740 m). Draining these mountains are the deep, parallel valleys of the Yangtze, Mekong, and Salween Rivers, which at one point bottleneck into an area only 43 miles (70 km) across as they descend south from their sources in the steppe of the Outer Plateau. The population centers of Chamdo, Jyekundo, Kandze, and Kangting are in this region.

VEGETATION

The geologic events that led to the extraordinary rise of the Himalaya and the Tibetan Plateau have created not only a geography of superlatives, but also a diverse flora and fauna that had to adapt to this swiftly changing landscape. Chinese scientists have recorded over 12,000 species and 1,500 genera of vascular plants on the Tibetan Plateau and its eastern and southeastern fringes, as well as 5,000 species of fungi, 210 species of mammals, 532 species of birds, and 115 species of fish.

The distribution of these species, however, is far from even due to the effects of India's monsoon, the varying altitudes, and the wide range of mean annual temperatures found in Tibet. In the Southeastern Plateau, the north-south trending canyons of the Brahmaputra, Salween, Mekong, and Yangtze Rivers act like huge funnels, directing the monsoon from the Bay of Bengal to about 30°N latitude in Eastern Tibet, its most northern penetration anywhere in Asia.

As result, the heavily forested Three Rivers area of the Southeastern Plateau, where the political borders of Burma, Yunnan, Sichuan, and the TAR converge, is the most biodiverse region of the Tibetan Plateau. The average annual rainfall exceeds 8 feet (2.5 m) in some regions, with annual mean temperatures exceeding 64°F (18°C). Some scientists have estimated that the Tibetan Plateau has no less than 2,000 endemic plant species representing 50 genera; 90 percent of these occur in the monsoon-affected southeastern and eastern fringes of the Plateau. The Tibetan Plateau is also recognized as the differentiation center for a number of plant genera, particularly *Rhododendron*, *Primula*, *Saussurea*, *Pedicularis*, *Picea* (spruce), and *Abies* (fir). Of the world's 850 rhododendron species, 60 percent are found on the Plateau, especially in the east and southeast;

one species recorded by noted explorer and plant hunter Joseph Rock grows to over 100 feet (30 m) tall.

Due to the slope of the Tibetan Plateau from the southeast to the northwest, the influence of India's monsoon is greatly reduced in the Northern Plateau and negligible in the far northwest corner of the Chang Thang, where rainfall is reduced to as little as 0.6 inches (25 mm) per year. With an average mean temperature in some areas of only 18°F (-8°C), this high-altitude region is a stony desert almost void of vegetation (a similar situation occurs in Tibet just north of Bhutan, where the monsoon is blocked by the Himalaya). Because these are the two main regions where explorers traveled in the late nineteenth and early twentieth centuries, the outside world is still convinced that Tibet is primarily a barren land.

The extensive spruce, fir, and hemlock forests of the East and Southeast Tibetan Plateau start in the south in the Gyelthang-Dechen area (Southern Kham, now in Northwest Yunnan Province), where the Salween, Mekong, and Yangtze Rivers converge, and continue up north through Kham along the Yangtze and Yalong Jiang River's watersheds (now in Western Sichuan Province and the Eastern TAR) into Eastern Amdo (now in Western Qinghai and Eastern Gansu Provinces). Going west, the forest extends into the Pemako and Kongpo regions of Central Tibet; a one-day drive east of Lhasa on the Tibet-Sichuan Highway, over Kongpoba La, brings one into forested valleys where some trees are 5 feet or more in diameter at the base.

Farther north, the eastern end of the Outer Plateau (Western and Southern Amdo) is home to hundreds of thousands of nomadic herders and millions of yak, domestic goats, sheep, and horses; over 50 percent of Tibet is covered in grasslands. This vast grazing region, considered the finest in Asia, is composed primarily of sedges (*Kobresia spp.*) and grasses (*Stipa spp.*), which are also the main forage for Tibet's unique plateau wildlife, including wild yak, Tibetan antelope, Tibetan wild ass, and gazelle.

In Central Tibet, the annual rainfall is just 12 inches (0.3 m) and occurs mostly between June and September. Thunderstorms boom most every night, swollen rivers frequently wash out the roads, and the hills are vibrantly green. The lower valleys are not forested (except a remnant juniper forest at Reting monastery, north of Lhasa), but typically support thick stands of flowering shrubs, such as barberry (*Berberis spp.*), wild rose (*Rosa spp.*), spiraea (*Spiraea spp.*), and willow (*Salix spp.*). At the upper end of the valleys these shrubs are replaced by yellow and white-blooming cinquefoil (*Potentilla spp.*) bushes and a number of white, purple, pink, and yellow-blooming dwarf *Rhododendron spp.*

The wildflowers all across Tibet are spectacular, particularly in the more moist environs of the eastern half of the Plateau. But even in the desert of the Chang Thang, vast blooms of the maroon Younghusband's lily (*Incarvillea younghusbandii*) and the sweet-scented pink and white jasmine (*Stellera chamaejasme*) blanket the plains in color.

In Central and Eastern Tibet, the more common wildflowers tend to be from the daisy (*Compositae*), pea (*Leguminosae*), mint (*Labiateae*), buttercup (*Ranunculaceae*), carrot (*Umbelliferae*), figwort (*Scophulariaceae*) and rose families. In the lower valleys, common wildflowers include iris, primrose, lousewort, anemone, monkshood, delphinium, buttercup, potentilla, daisy, aster, and even jack-in-the-pulpits. Higher up in the valleys are gentians, edelweiss, giant wild rhubarb, and a number of poppies, including the delicate blue poppy (*Meconopsis horridula*) and the elegant yellow poppy (*M. integrifolia*). In the alpine regions above 14,000 feet (4300 m) are found many types of cushion plants, particularly *Androsace spp.* and *Saxifrage spp.*; this is also the home of many *Saussurea spp.*, probably Tibet's most unusual looking group of wildflowers. Many of this genera are used in the preparation of traditional Tibetan medicine; some 2,000 species of plants on the Tibetan Plateau have been identified by the Dalai Lama's personal physician as having medicinal qualities.

Though technically not a plant, perhaps the most unique medicinal substance harvested in Tibet is Yartsha Gunbu (Summer Grass, Winter Worm; *Cordyceps sinensis*). Also known as caterpillar fungus, it occurs when this species of caterpillar burrows into the ground to create a cocoon, but succumbs to a fungus. A brown stem several inches long then grows above ground from the deceased caterpillar, which is what collectors look for when harvesting it. Yartsha Gunbu is used as an ingredient in general health tonics, and is particularly beneficial for the kidneys and sexual organs.

MAMMALS

Less than 100 years ago explorers and mountaineers marveled at the abundance of wildlife on the Tibetan Plateau. "As far as the eye could see, the whole country seemed covered with [Tibetan antelope] does and their young [with] 15,000 to 20,000 visible at one time." So wrote Captain C. G. Rawling in his 1905 publication *The Great Plateau*, after exploring trade route possibilities for Britain in Western Tibet. Sadly, it is no longer possible to encounter wildlife in numbers similar to those reported a century ago. Despite this bleak situation, a variety of wildlife can still be observed on the Tibetan Plateau once the roads are left behind for the trails.

Over 200 species of mammals have been recorded on the Tibetan Plateau. The emphasis in the pages that follow is on the larger and more unique wildlife of the central, western, and northern sections of the Plateau, where most visitors travel, though mention is given to some of the more common or unusual species to the northeast, east, and southeast of the Plateau. Several large families of smaller mammals found on the Plateau that tend to be nocturnal, or which are difficult to differentiate from other species have been omitted from this section due to space constraints. These include bats, shrews, moles, flying squirrels, squirrels, mice, rats, and a few other rodents.

In the following descriptions, the common name is followed by the Latin name in parentheses. An italicized Tibetan name (which often varies with the region) may then be given. An asterisk indicates an animal has fully protected Class I status in China; the sale of skins, horns, or any other products from these animals is illegal. If a shop or vendor is selling such goods, you can do your part by informing local government officials, particularly the Forestry Department in Lhasa, or the Forest Bureau in other cities and towns.

PRIMATES

*Common Langur or Hanuman (*Presbytis entellus*). A striking, long-tailed, black-faced monkey with a white ruff, found in forests along Tibet's southern border with Nepal. The yellow to dark brown *Assamese macaque (*Macaca assamensis*) is also found in the southern forests, and in East and Southeast Tibet. Its range overlaps with that of the rather similar-looking Rhesus monkey (*M. mulatta*) found in forested areas of the Tibetan Plateau; its coat is brown with a lighter underside, and adults have a distinguishing red face and red rump. On the eastern edge of the Plateau is the gray-brown Tibetan macaque (*M. thibetana*), the monkey commonly seen at Mount Omei Shan and once thought to be the same species as *M. assamensis*. On the Plateau's eastern edge in giant panda country is found the beautiful *golden snub-nosed monkey (*Rhinopithecus roxellana*). Its cousin, the *black snub-nosed monkey (*R. bieti*), is seen in the far southeast corner of Tibet and the adjacent northwest corner of Yunnan.

CARNIVORES

Wolf (*Canis lupus*), *changku*. Resembles the Alaskan wolf, with a long coat and thick bushy tail often tipped with white. Footprints can measure 5 inches (13 cm) from heel to toe. Color of coat ranges from black to silver gray, though brownish gray is most common. Usually avoids forests and rugged mountain terrain. Uses caves, holes and overhanging rocks for shelter and dens. Widespread across plains and rolling uplands of the Tibetan Plateau, but becoming locally scarce in some areas.

Red fox and Tibetan sand fox *(Vulpes vulpes* and *Vulpes ferrilata), wa* or *wama.* The larger red fox is nearly 3½ feet (1 m) from head to tail. Coat is usually red and luxurious with a very full, bushy tail often tipped with white. Tibetans use the pelts as wraparound hats. Found in forest, scrub, and nearby plains and alpine areas of the Tibetan Plateau. The sand fox has a short, grayish coat with a shorter tail and smaller ears. Prefers open plains and rolling hills, though the habitats of both foxes overlap. Look for black hair behind the red fox's ears to help identify in the field.

Cuon, or wild dog *(Cuon alpinus), pharwa.* Very similar to a domestic dog, but with a distinctive red coat and bushy tail. Hunts by day, often in a pack, in open country and forests of the Eastern Tibetan Plateau.

Tibetan brown bear *(Ursus arctos pruinosus), tremong.* One of the more endangered species on the Tibetan Plateau, yet omitted from the list of protected animals in China. Habitat is now mostly reduced to the Chang Thang, and scattered very thinly throughout the Eastern Tibetan Plateau. A large bear standing almost 6 feet (1.8 m) tall on its hind legs, with a heavy neck ruff and hairy ears. Has a broader build and a lighter coat than the Himalayan (Asiatic) black bear *(U. thibetanus;* Tib., *dom),* found in forests of the Southern and Eastern Plateau.

*Red panda *(Ailurus fulgens).* A rarely seen, raccoonlike chestnut-colored "cat-bear" about 2 feet (60 cm) long with a ringed, bushy tail about half that length. Its home is in the Plateau's southern and eastern forests where bamboo grows. DNA tests suggest it is a distant relative of the raccoon family, but was long thought to be related to the critically endangered *giant panda *(Ailuropoda melanoleuca),* found in forests along the eastern fringe of the Tibetan Plateau.

Stone or beech marten *(Martes foina), semong.* A brown minklike animal with a large white patch under the chin and throat extending to the forelegs. Body can be 2 feet (60 cm) or longer, the tail at least half that length. Sometimes seen scavenging near human settlements, even near Lhasa. Widespread across the Tibetan Plateau. The larger yellow-throated or forest marten *(M. flavigula)* lives in the Southern and Eastern Plateau.

Weasel *(Mustela sibirica* Pallas and *Mustela altaica* Pallas). Typically seen bounding between rocks above treeline, but also found living in the walls and roofs of homes. Much smaller than the marten, similarly built, but with a light throat patch. Widespread across Tibetan Plateau. *M. sibirica* can be upwards of 2 feet (60 cm) long, with a tail half that length. Coat varies, though is often a golden fawn shade. *M. altaica,* the pale weasel, is about 5 inches (13 cm) smaller, with a grayish brown coat, white paws, and a creamy white throat patch.

Ferret or Eversmann's polecat *(Mustela eversmanni).* A large weasel nearly 2 feet (60 cm) long with a relatively short tail. Closely resembles the critically endangered black-footed ferret of North America, with a dark brown coat, black feet, and a distinctive raccoonlike black mask. Feeds primarily on pikas on the steppes of the Plateau.

Eurasian badger *(Meles meles).* A rare relative of the weasel, similar to the North American badger. Burrows in grassy plains near pika colonies, in the eastern part of the Plateau. The smaller hog-badger *(Arctonyx collaris),* distinguished by its pale throat and dark cheek stripe, is found in forested areas.

Common otter *(Lutra lutra).* Little is known about the range or abundance of this gray, thick-furred otter. A graceful swimmer, found in rivers and lakes of the Central, Southern, and Eastern Tibetan Plateau. The smaller, brown clawless otter *(Aonyx cinerea)* is mainly in the southeastern section of the Plateau.

Large and small civet (*Viverra zibetha* and *Viverricula indica*). A seldom-seen, mostly nocturnal, catlike omnivore of Southeast Tibet with a pointy snout, bushy tail, and a pale throat with wide dark stripes. When threatened it sprays an offensive fluid from a scent gland. *V. zibetha* is over 2½ feet long (80 cm), with mottled gray-brown fur and a zebra-striped tail half again as long. *V. indica* is about a third smaller, its coat tawny gray with long stripes along the back and spots on the flanks. The masked palm civet (*Paguma larvata*) of the Southern and Southeastern Plateau is uniform gray or brown with no body marks. The spotted linsang (*Prionodon pardicolor*) is distinguished by its lack of a scent gland and its spotted, golden coat and is seen in forests of the Southeastern Tibetan Plateau.

Pallas's or Manul cat (*Felis manul* Pallas), *ri-zhum*. This unusual, beautiful feline is the only small cat in the open plains and hills of Tibet. Similar in size to a small domestic cat, it has distinctive black marks on its face, stripes on its lower back, and a long, thick, striped tail that ends in a black tip.

Jungle cat (*Felis chaus*). A small sandy to yellowish gray feline, larger than a domestic cat, with few body marks and a dark-tipped striped tail. Prefers lower-elevation scrub and forest in Southern Tibet. The golden cat (*F. temmincki*) of the Plateau's southern and eastern forests is about a third larger. Coat is quite variable, from rust to almost black. It may be spotted, or have few or no body marks nor tail marks. Has distinctive black and white stripes across the cheek. The Chinese mountain cat (*F. bieti*) is gray with nondescript stripes on the legs; it is found in the Northeastern Tibetan Plateau.

Lynx (*Lynx lynx*), *yi*. Similar to the North American lynx, with long tufts on the ears and a short, stubby tail. Coat is plain sandy gray to tawny; may have white spots on legs. Found throughout the Tibetan Plateau from plains to forests.

*Forest or spotted leopard (*Panthera pardus*), *zik*. Similar to a large dog, with a long, spotted tail. Coat is soft, yellowish tan, with distinctive rosette markings. Found in forests of Eastern and Southeastern Tibetan Plateau. The smaller *clouded leopard (*Neofelis nebulosa*) has a patterned coat with large, dark, irregular spots. Seen in dense evergreen forests, mainly in the Southeastern Plateau. The leopard cat (*Felis bengalensis*) resembles a miniature leopard about the size of a domestic cat, and is found in forests of the Southern and Eastern Plateau.

*Bengal tiger (*Panthera tigris tigris*), *tak*. Limited to the jungles of Pemako, just east of the big bend in the Tsangpo (Brahmaputra). Little is known about the abundance of the Tibetan Plateau's largest feline, although attacks on livestock here are on the rise due to overhunting of it's prey, particularly the takin.

*Snow leopard (*Panthera uncia*), *saa*. This magnificent high-altitude cat of Asia's mountain ranges can still be found in low numbers where blue sheep are common. Mostly a nocturnal hunter, it covers a large range while searching for prey. About the size of a large dog, with a wide, bushy tail nearly 3 feet (90 cm) long. Coat is a soft, pale gray, with distinctive markings like broad, pale rosettes.

Yeti or Abominable snowman, *migö*. Periodic claims of sightings in Tibet by local inhabitants and mountaineers continue to fuel the controversy of whether this apelike creature of the high Himalaya does or does not exist.

HOOFED ANIMALS

*Tibetan wild ass or kiang (*Equus kiang*), *kyang*. The largest of the Asiatic wild asses, standing 4 feet (1.2 m) at the shoulder. Once found in abundance on the plains and hills across the Plateau, its domain is now mostly limited to the Northern Plains. Avoids rugged terrain and forests. The upper half of its body is a fawn rust color; the throat, chest, and abdomen are white. A distinctive line of black hairs extends from the head along the back.

Wild pig (*Sus scrofa*), *phakgö*. Males can be 3 feet (90 cm) at the shoulder, weighing over 200 pounds (90 kg). Has a mane of black bristles from the nape to the back. Prefers forests of the Southern and Southeastern Tibetan Plateau.

Alpine musk deer *(Moschus sifanicus)*, *la* or *lawa*. A small, stocky deer with no antlers standing less than 2½ feet (75 cm) at the shoulder. Often seen alone or in small groups on steep terrain and near cliffs, preferring thickets of brush and generally higher country than other musk deer. Found in the eastern half of the Tibetan Plateau. Coat is gray-brown with some white markings. Hind legs are heavy and elongated, causing it to bound like a large rabbit. Has 2-inch-long (5 cm) fanglike upper canine teeth, most prominent in males. Almost indistinguishable from three other species on the Plateau, and taxonomy is

Tibetan antelope (Pantholops hodgsoni) (photo by George B. Schaller)

uncertain: Himalayan musk deer (*M. chrysogaster*), considered by some to be same species as *M. sifanicus*, is found in the Central Himalaya, its range farther east is uncertain; black musk deer (*M. fuscus*) is seen mainly in Southeast Tibet; and forest musk deer (*M. berezovskii*) is found in forests across the Plateau. Musk obtained from a gland in the male's belly is so highly prized in Asia for its medicinal qualities that musk deer are now rare on the Plateau due to overhunting.

Barking deer or red muntjac (*Muntiacus muntjak*). A favorite prey of leopards, this rust red deer is 20 to 30 inches (50 to 75 cm) tall at the shoulder and weighs about 55 pounds (25 kg). Males have two-pronged, 5-inch (13-cm) antlers. Often seen singly or in pairs in wooded hills and forest edges of the Southern and Southeastern Tibetan Plateau. Call is like the bark of a dog. The much smaller Reeves muntjac (*M. reevesi*) weighs 22 to 33 pounds (10 to 15 kg), has a grizzly gray-brown coat, and is found along the eastern edge of the Plateau. The tufted deer (*Elaphodus cephalophus*) of the Southeastern Plateau and the Eastern Plateau fringes is not truly a muntjac, but is related. Distinguished by a tuft of head hair that hides its small antlers. Coat is gray to almost black, underparts are white, and it weighs 33 to 55 pounds (15 to 25 kg).

*White-lipped deer (*Cervus albirostris*), *shawa*. A large, elklike deer with long, branched antlers, brown coat, cream-colored belly, and a characteristic white chin and muzzle. Males weigh 400 to 500 pounds (180 to 230 kg). Prefers forested hills and plains as well as treeless hills, from about the Tibet-Qinghai Highway eastward. The Tibetan red deer, or Sikkim stag (*Cervus elaphus wallichi*; Tib., *sho*) , is also elklike with a large rack, but is gray-brown with reddish tinges, a whitish or pale belly, and a white rump. Very limited numbers are found southeast of Lhasa. Is much lighter colored than the dark brown McNeill's, or Sichuan, red deer (*C. e. macneilli*) found scattered through East Tibet, especially near Chamdo, and in Sichuan.

*Wild yak (*Bos grunniens*), *drong* or *yak*. A large, black (very occasionally amber or golden in Northwest Chang Thang), shaggy species of wild cattle. Males are usually a third larger than females, weigh up to 1750 pounds (800 kg), and stand up to 6½ feet (2 m) at the shoulder. Once found in abundance on the Tibetan plains, they are now rare and seen mainly in the Northern Chang Thang of Northwest Tibet and Southwest

Qinghai west of the Tibet-Qinghai Highway, though a few remain in Northeast Qinghai. Prefers open terrain. Most yaks seen in Tibet are either domestic or hybrid yak-cattle crosses. If a yak has any white markings, it is domestic or a crossbreed.

Tibetan gazelle *(Procapra picticaudata), gowa.* The most widespread ungulate on the Tibetan plains. Similar to Thomson's gazelle of East Africa, weighing about 33 pounds (15 kg), with a tan or fawn coat, a conspicuous white heart-shaped rump patch, and a small black tail. Male has closely ringed, 12- to 14-inch (30- to 35-cm) thin black horns curving up, back, and up again. Female has no horns. The larger *Przewalski's gazelle (P. przewalskii)*, found only near Tsho Ngompo (Qinghai Lake), is the most endangered species on the Tibetan Plateau; only about 200 are known to exist. Unlike *P. picticaudata*, its horns bend sharply inward at the top. The goitered gazelle *(Gazella subgutturosa)* is found in the Tshadam (Qaidam) basin on the northeast edge of the Tibetan Plateau.

*Tibetan antelope or chiru *(Pantholops hodgsoni), tsöd* or *tsö.* Was once the most abundant hoofed animal on the Tibetan Plateau, but is heavily hunted for its prized wool, *shatoosh.* Now primarily seen in the Northern Chang Thang, preferring dry plains and rolling hills. A medium-sized antelope with long, light gray fawn hair. Male is about a third larger than the female, weighing 80 to 90 pounds (35 to 40 kg), and is readily identified by its 20- to 24-inch-long (50- to 60-cm), ridged, lyre-shaped horns. Female has no horns.

Takin *(Budorcas taxicolor), bamen.* A stocky, shaggy, cowlike animal, 3½ to 4½ feet (110 to 130 cm) at the shoulder with a distinctive broad face, bulging convex muzzle, and short thick horns sweeping out and back. Generally seen on forested mountain slopes. Once gathered in groups of up to 300 in summer, now mostly in herds of fewer than fifty. Found in the Southern Tibetan Plateau, south and east of the Tsangpo, and on the far eastern edge of the Plateau.

Serow *(Nemorhaedus sumatraensis).* This sturdy goat-antelope has a large head, thick neck, and ears like that of a mule; both sexes have 9-inch (23-cm) conical horns. Males can weigh up to 300 pounds (135 kg). Coat varies from blackish gray to red brown, with a mane ranging from white to black. Found in forested areas throughout the Plateau. Makes a whistling snort when disturbed.

Gray goral *(Nemorhaedus goral).* A smaller version of the serow, resembling a stocky domestic goat with a longer tail. Coat is yellowish gray, often with a dark spinal stripe. Chin, upper lip and throat patch are white, horns are spiky, short and ridged. Generally seen in rocky forested areas up to 13,000 feet (4000 m) in the Southern and Eastern Tibetan Plateau. The rust-colored *red goral (N. baileyi)* is found in Southeast Tibet.

*Himalayan tahr *(Hermitragus jemlahicus).* A handsome wild goat with short horns and long flowing hair covering the body; older males have an impressive mane extending from the neck and shoulders to the knee. Color varies from dark brown to reddish brown. Habitat is precipitous, rocky terrain and wooded mountain slopes. Probably only found in the Nyelam-Zhangmu area of Tibet near the Nepal border.

Blue sheep or bharal *(Pseudois nayaur), na, nawa,* or *naya.* Widely distributed throughout the Tibetan Plateau. A stocky, gray-brown animal with a white belly and white rump patch, black tail, and black markings on the front of each leg. Male has thick horns, up to 28 inches (70 cm) long, that sweep up, out, and back. Female has thin, short horns 4 to 8 inches (10 to 20 cm) long. Prefers rugged cliffs above treeline. Has certain behavioral patterns more typical of wild goats. Commonly seen near Dza Rongphu monastery and Everest base camp.

Tibetan argali sheep *(Ovis ammon hodgsoni), nyen.* This cousin of the Marco Polo sheep is the Tibetan Plateau's largest wild sheep. Endangered, yet omitted from the list of fully protected species in China. Males are enormous, weighing up to 230 pounds (105 kg), standing nearly 4 feet (1.2 m) at the shoulder, with massive curling horns up to

43 inches (110 cm) long. Female is about a third smaller, with thin, upright horns up to 18 inches (45 cm) long. Coat is buff brown. Stomach, belly, and rump are white. Males have a prominent short, white ruff on the chest in winter. Distribution is patchy, with populations small and declining. Prefers open rolling hills, from Aksai Chin across to Western Sichuan, and from the Himalaya north to the Kun Lun–Arjin Shan region.

PANGOLINS
Scaly pangolin (*Manis pentadactyla*). Covered with thick, overlapping horny scales, including on the legs and tail. When threatened, curls into a ball. Measures 27 to 38 inches (80 to 95 cm) from head to tail. Inhabits open country and forests of Eastern Tibet, feeding on ants, termites, and other insects. Is heavily hunted for its scales, which are prized for their medicinal value.

HARES AND RABBITS
Pika or Himalayan mouse-hare or rock hare *(Ochotona spp.), abra* or *pu-se.* This small, playfully cute, tail-less relative of the rabbit is the most frequently seen mammal on the Tibetan Plateau. Has light brown fur and resembles a guinea pig, weighing 3½ to 5½ ounces (100 to 150 g). The black-lipped pika *(O. curzoniae),* the most common species in Tibet, is found in large colonies on the plains and in valleys. A large-eared species *(O. macrotis)* more similar to the North American pika lives among rocks and talus. Several other species are found across the Tibetan Plateau.

Tibetan woolly or gray-rumped hare *(Lepus oiostolus), rigong.* Endemic to the Tibetan Plateau. A brownish hare about the size of a North American jack rabbit, with a large patch of gray fur over the rump. Prefers rocky and shrub-covered plains or hillsides that provide cover.

RODENTS
Himalayan marmot *(Marmota himalayana), jibi.* A large burrowing member of the squirrel family. Found throughout the Tibetan Plateau in colonies on the plains and in grassy mountain valleys. A close cousin of the North America marmot, with beautiful golden brown fur and a short, black tail.

Porcupine *(Hystrix hodgsoni).* A large nocturnal rodent with a bristly mantle of black and white quills up to 6 inches (15 cm) long. Found mainly in Southeastern Tibet, where it is scarce.

Hamster *(Cricetulus longicaudatus).* A sandy-colored mouselike animal resembling the domestic pet hamster, found on grassy or vegetated plains. Usually smaller than a pika and with a short tail. Lives in communal burrows with openings smaller than a pika's burrow.

Vole *(Alticola stoliczkanus* and *Pitymys leucurus).* Lives higher in elevation (up to 18,000 ft, 5490 m) than any other mammal. Related to the lemming, the mountain vole *(A. stoliczkanus)* is a pleasant-looking rodent 3 to 4 inches (8 to 10 cm) long with gray fur, white belly, small ears, and a short, hairy tail. *P. leucurus* is similar in size, resembles the North American pine vole, and looks more like a mouse. Fur is brown to dark brown and the tail is very short with little hair. Voles live in burrows and do not hibernate. A number of other species are found across the Tibetan Plateau.

FISH
The two main types of fish in Tibet are carp and scaleless loaches. Tibetan carp are schizothoracines, a subfamily of Cyprinidae, the carp family. They are the predominant freshwater fish in Tibet, growing to 2 feet (60 cm) or more in length and having a mottled greenish brown color. Carp living at lower elevations typically have scales and two pairs

of fleshy "whiskers," called barbels, protruding near the mouth; these are used as an aid for finding algae or vegetable matter along river and lake bottoms. At higher elevations these fish become more omnivorous and have less need for barbels. Between 9000 to 12,300 feet in elevation (2750 to 3750 m), these carp have only one set of barbels. From 12,300 to 15,600 feet (3750 to 4750 m), the diet is so specialized that the carp no longer have barbels, nor do they have scales.

Scaleless loaches (subfamily Nemachilinae, family Cobitidae) are carplike fish resembling a whiskered trout with a carp's mouth. More slender and elongated than the Tibetan carp, they are most easily recognized by three pairs of barbels near the mouth. As the name implies, they have no scales. Scaleless loaches live only in open-valley rivers and can be found at elevations up to 17,000 feet (5200 m); they are the highest-dwelling Tibetan fish. Dozens of different species, measuring from 4 to 21 inches (10 to 55 cm) long, are found on the Tibetan Plateau and adjacent areas.

BIRDS

Despite extreme elevations and relatively low rainfall, a remarkable variety of resident and migratory birds can be found in the fertile river valleys as well as in the hills and higher alpine regions of Tibet. Over 500 species of birds have been recorded across the Tibetan Plateau; in just Central Tibet nearly 200 species of birds are known. Surely others will be found as more information is collected on the avifauna of this area. The best season for bird-watching is generally from March until October. The spring migration starts around late February or early March with the arrival of ducks and graylag geese, and finishes about May with the arrival of wading birds. Tibet's summer residents leave about late September or early October. The autumn migration occurs between October and mid-November. Cranes pass through during the first two weeks of October and eagles from about mid-October to mid-November. If you want to see waterfowl, head for Tibet's large lakes such as Tsho Ngompo (Qinghai Lake) and Nam Tsho, where large mixed flocks commonly congregate along the shores until the waters freeze in winter. The towering black-necked crane (*Grus nigricollis*) is endemic to Tibet and has received much attention since being placed on the Endangered Species list. Standing 5 feet (1.5 m) high, it is the tallest of Tibet's birds. It can sometimes be seen near the shores of Nam Tsho, along the Phung Chu near Dingri, and in the Tsangpo Valley near Samye monastery.

The following is a checklist of species recorded across the Tibetan Plateau. Latin names are in italics; the notation LV indicates it is found in the Lhasa Valley. See Appendix B, "Suggested Reading," for titles concerning birds in Tibet.

BIRD CHECKLIST

Grebes (*Podicipedidae*)
❑ Great crested grebe (*Podiceps cristatus*, LV)
❑ Black-necked grebe (*Podiceps nigricollis*)
❑ Little grebe (*Podiceps ruficollis*, LV)
Cormorants (*Phalacrocoracidae*)
❑ Great cormorant (*Phalacrocorax carbo*, LV)
Bitterns, Egrets, and Herons (*Ardeidae*)
❑ Bittern (*Botaurus stellaris*)
❑ Chinese pond heron (*Ardeola bacchus*)
❑ Cattle egret (*Bubulcus ibis*)
❑ Great egret (*Egretta alba*, LV)
❑ Grey heron (*Ardea cinerca*)
Ibises (*Threskiornithidae*)
❑ Crested ibis (*Nipponia nippon*)

Storks (*Ciconiidae*)
❑ White stork (*Ciconia ciconia*)
❑ Black stork (*Ciconia nigra*)
❑ Painted stork (*Ibis leucocephalus*, LV)
Swans, Geese, and Ducks (*Anatidae*)
❑ Graylag goose (*Anser anser*)
❑ White-fronted goose (*Anser albifrons*, LV)
❑ Bean goose (*Anser fabilis*)
❑ Bar-headed goose (*Anser indicus*, LV)
❑ Swan goose (*Anser cygnoides*)
❑ Mute swan (*Cygnus olor*)
❑ Whooper swan (*Cygnus cygnus*)
❑ Bewick's swan (*Cygnus columbianus bewickii*)
❑ Brahminy or Ruddy shell duck (*Tadorna ferruginea*, LV)

- ❏ Common shelduck (*Tadorna tadorna*)
- ❏ Mallard (*Anas platyrhynchos*, LV)
- ❏ Spotbill duck (*Anas poecilorhyncha*, LV)
- ❏ Green-winged teal (*Anas crecca*, LV)
- ❏ Falcated teal (*Anas falcata*)
- ❏ Gadwell (*Anas strepera*, LV)
- ❏ Wigeon (*Anas penelope*, LV)
- ❏ Pintail (*Anas acuta*, LV)
- ❏ Garganey (*Anas querquedula*, LV)
- ❏ Shoveler (*Anas clypeata*, LV)
- ❏ Red-crested pochard (*Netta rufina*)
- ❏ Common pochard (*Aythya ferina*)
- ❏ White-eyed pochard (*Aythya nyroca*, LV)
- ❏ Tufted duck (*Aythya fuligula*, LV)
- ❏ Common goldeneye (*Bucephala clangula*, LV)
- ❏ Smew (*Mergus albellus*)
- ❏ Red-breasted merganser (*Mergus serrator*)
- ❏ Merganser, or Goosander (*Mergus merganser*, LV)

Ospreys (*Padionidae*)
- ❏ Osprey (*Pandion haliaetus*, LV)

Kites, Hawks, Eagles, Harriers, and Vultures (*Accipitridae*)
- ❏ Dark or Black kite (*Milvus migrans*, LV)
- ❏ Brahminy kite (*Haliastur indus*, LV)
- ❏ Pallas's fishing eagle (*Haliaeetus leucoryphus*, LV)
- ❏ White-tailed eagle (*Haliaeetus albicilla*)
- ❏ Goshawk (*Accipter gentilis*, LV)
- ❏ Northern sparrow hawk (*Accipter nisus*, LV)
- ❏ Upland buzzard (*Buteo hemilasius*)
- ❏ Long-legged buzzard (*Buteo rufinus*)
- ❏ Common buzzard (*Buteo buteo*)
- ❏ White-eyed buzzard (*Butastur teesa*)
- ❏ Booted eagle (*Hieraaetus pennatus*)
- ❏ Twany eagle (*Aquila rapax*)
- ❏ Spotted eagle (*Aquila clanga*)
- ❏ Imperial eagle (*Aquila heliaca*)
- ❏ Golden eagle (*Aquila chrysaetos*)
- ❏ Lammergeier, or Bearded Vulture (*Gypaetus barbatus*, LV)
- ❏ Black or Cinereous vulture (*Aegypius monachus*)
- ❏ Himalayan griffon (*Gyps himalayensis*, LV)
- ❏ Northern or Hen harrier (*Circus cyaneus*)
- ❏ Pale harrier (*Circus macrourus*)
- ❏ Marsh harrier (*Circus aeruginosus*)

Falcons (*Falconidae*)
- ❏ Altai falcon (*Falco altaicus*)
- ❏ Saker falcon (*Falco cherrug*, LV)
- ❏ Peregrine, or Shaheen falcon (*Falco peregrinus*)
- ❏ Eurasian or Northern hobby (*Falco subbuteo*, LV)
- ❏ Merlin (*Falco columbarius*)
- ❏ Eurasian or Northern kestral (*Falco tinnunculus*, LV)

Grouse (*Tetraoninae*)
- ❏ Severtzov's grouse (*Tetrastes sewerzowi*)

Pheasants, Partridges, and Quails (*Phasianinae*)
- ❏ Snow partridge (*Lerwa lerwa*)
- ❏ Verreaux's pheasant partridge (*Tetraophasis obscurus*)

- ❏ Szechenyi's pheasant partridge (*Tetraophasis szechenyii*)
- ❏ Himalayan snowcock (*Tetraogallus himalayensis*)
- ❏ Tibetan snowcock (*Tetraogallus tibetanus*, LV)
- ❏ Przevalski's partridge (*Alectoris magna*)
- ❏ Daurian partridge (*Perdix dauuricae*)
- ❏ Tibetan partridge (*Perdix hodgsoniae*, LV)
- ❏ Common quail (*Coturnix coturnix*)
- ❏ Japanese quail (*Coturnix japonica*)
- ❏ Common hill partridge (*Arborophila torqueola*)
- ❏ Red-breasted hill partridge (*Arborophila mandellii*)
- ❏ Blood pheasant (*Ithaginis cruentus*)
- ❏ Western tragopan (*Tragopan melanocephalus*)
- ❏ Crimson tragopan (*Tragopan satyra*)
- ❏ Temminck's tragopan (*Tragopan temminckii*)
- ❏ Gray-belled tragopan (*Tragopan blythii*)
- ❏ Koklass pheasant (*Pucrasia macrolopha*)
- ❏ Impeyan, or Monal pheasant (*Lophophorus impejanus*)
- ❏ Sclater's monal pheasant (*Lophophorus sclateri*)
- ❏ Kalij pheasant (*Lophophorus leucomelana*)
- ❏ White-eared pheasant (*Crossoptilon crossoptilon*)
- ❏ Elwes's or Harman's eared pheasant (*Crossoptilon harmani*)
- ❏ Blue-eared pheasant (*Crossoptilon auritum*)
- ❏ Common pheasant (*Phasianus colchicus*)
- ❏ Lady Amherst's pheasant (*Chrysolophus amherstiae*)

Button Quails (*Turnicidae*)
- ❏ Yellow-legged button quail (*Turnix tanki*)

Cranes (*Gruidae*)
- ❏ Common crane (*Grus grus*)
- ❏ Black-necked crane (*Grus nigricollis*, LV)
- ❏ Siberian crane (*Grus leucogeranus*)
- ❏ Demoiselle crane (*Anthropoides virgo*)

Rails, Gallinules, and Coots (*Rallidae*)
- ❏ Water rail (*Rallus aquaticus*)
- ❏ Baillon's crake (*Porzana pusilla*)
- ❏ Common moorhen, or Indian gallinule (*Gallinula chloropus*, LV)
- ❏ Coot (*Fulica atra*, LV)

Oystercatchers (*Haematopodidae*)
- ❏ Oystercatcher (*Haematopus ostralegus*)

Painted Snipes (*Rostratulidae*)
- ❏ Painted snipe (*Rostratula benghalensis*)

Lapwings and Plovers (*Charadriidae*)
- ❏ Northern or Eurasian lapwing (*Vanellus vanellus*, LV)
- ❏ Asiatic or Eastern golden plover (*Pluvialis dominica*, LV)
- ❏ Gray plover (*Pluvialis squatarola*)
- ❏ Little ringed plover (*Charadrius dubuis*)
- ❏ Long-billed plover (*Charadrius placidus*)
- ❏ Kentish plover (*Charadrius alexandrinus*)
- ❏ Mongolian plover (*Charadrius mongolus*)
- ❏ Geoffrey's or Greater sand plover (*Charadrius leschenaultii*)

❑ Turnstone (*Arenaria interpres*)

Sandpipers, Curlews, and Snipes (*Scolopacidae*)
❑ Little stint (*Calidris minuta*)
❑ Red-necked stint (*Calidris ruficollis*)
❑ Long-toed stint (*Calidris subminuta*)
❑ Temminck's stint (*Calidris temminckii*)
❑ Sharp-tailed sandpiper (*Calidris acuminata*)
❑ Dunlin (*Calidris alpina*)
❑ Curlew sandpiper (*Calidris ferruginea*)
❑ Red knot (*Calidris canutus*)
❑ Ruff and Reeve (*Philomachus pugnax*, LV)
❑ Spotted redshank (*Tringa erythropus*)
❑ Redshank (*Tringa totanus*, LV)
❑ Greenshank (*Tringa nebularia*)
❑ Green sandpiper (*Tringa ochropus*, LV)
❑ Common sandpiper (*Tringa hypoleucos*, LV)
❑ Wood sandpiper (*Tringa glareola*)
❑ Wandering tattler (*Heteroscelus incanus*)
❑ Terek sandpiper (*Xenus cinereus*)
❑ Black-tailed godwit (*Limosa limosa*)
❑ Common or Eurasian curlew (*Numenius arquata*)
❑ Whimbrel (*Numenius phaeopus*)
❑ Eurasian woodcock (*Scolopax rusticola*, LV)
❑ Common or Fantail snipe (*Gallinago gallinago*, LV)
❑ Pintail snipe (*Gallinago stenura*, LV)
❑ Swinhoe's snipe (*Gallinago megala*)
❑ Solitary snipe (*Gallinago solitaria*, LV)
❑ Wood snipe (*Gallinago nemoricola*)

Stilts, Avocets, and Ibisbills (*Recurvirostrae*)
❑ Black-winged stilt (*Himantopus himantopus*)
❑ Avocet (*Recurvirostra avosetta*)
❑ Ibisbill (*Ibidorhyncha struthersii*, LV)

Phalaropes (*Phalaropodidae*)
❑ Red-necked phalarope (*Phalaropus lobatus*)

Prantincoles (*Glareolidae*)
❑ Oriental or Eastern collared pratincole (*Glareola maldivarum*)

Gulls and Terns (*Laridae*)
❑ Great black-headed gull (*Larus ichthyaetus*, LV)
❑ Little gull (*Larus minutus*)
❑ Common black-headed gull (*Larus ridibundus*)
❑ Brown-headed gull (*Larus brunnicephalus*, LV)
❑ Black tern (*Chlidonias niger*)
❑ Whiskered tern (*Chlidonias hybrida*)
❑ Common or Tibetan tern (*Sterna hirundo*, LV)

Sandgrouse (*Pteroclidae*)
❑ Pallas' sandgrouse (*Syrrhaptes paradoxus*)
❑ Sandgrouse (*Syrrhaptes tibetanus*)

Pigeons and Doves (*Columbidae*)
❑ Eastern stock dove (*Columba eversmanni*)
❑ Snow pigeon (*Columba leuconota*)
❑ Blue rock or "City" pigeon (*Columba livia*, LV)
❑ Blue hill pigeon (*Columba rupestris*, LV)
❑ Speckled wood pigeon (*Columba hodgsonii*)
❑ Ashy wood pigeon (*Columba pulchricollis*)
❑ Pale-capped pigeon (*Columba punicea*)

❑ Oriental or Rufous turtle dove (*Streptopelia orientalis*, LV)
❑ Collared turtle dove (*Streptopelia decaocto*)
❑ Red turtle dove (*Streptopelia tranquebarica*)

Parrots and Parakeets (*Psittacidae*)
❑ Lord Derby's Parakeet (*Psittacula derbiana*)

Cuckoos (*Cuculidae*)
❑ Common or Eurasian cuckoo (*Cuculus canorus*, LV)
❑ Lesser cuckoo (*Cuculus poliocephalus*)
❑ Pied cuckoo (*Clamator jacobinus*)

Owls (*Strigidae*)
❑ Great horned or Eagle owl (*Bubo bubo*, LV)
❑ Little owl (*Athene noctua*, LV)
❑ Tawny owl (*Strix aluco*)
❑ Long-eared owl (*Asio otus*)
❑ Short-eared owl (*Asio flammeus*)
❑ Tengmalm's owl (*Aegolius funereus*)

Nightjars (*Caprimulgidae*)
❑ Jungle nightjar (*Caprimulgus indicus*)

Swifts (*Apodidae*)
❑ Himalayan swift (*Aerodramus brevirostris*)
❑ Black nest swiftlet (*Aerodramus maximus*)
❑ Black or Eurasian swift (*Apus apus*, LV)
❑ White-rumped swift (*Apus pacificus*, LV)

Rollers (*Coraciidae*)
❑ Blue foller (*Coracias garrulus*)

Kingfishers (*Alcedinidae*)
❑ Eurasian or Common kingfisher (*Alcedo atthis*)

Hoopoes (*Upupidae*)
❑ Hoopoe (*Upupa epops*, LV)

Woodpeckers (*Picidae*)
❑ Wryneck (*Jynx torquilla*, LV)
❑ Scaly-bellied green woodpecker (*Picus squamatus*)
❑ Gray-headed woodpecker (*Picus canus*)
❑ Large yellow-naped woodpecker (*Picus flavinucha*)
❑ Lesser yellow-naped woodpecker (*Pica chlorophus*)
❑ Great spotted woodpecker (*Picoides major*)
❑ Darjeeling pied woodpecker (*Picoides darjellensis*)
❑ Crimson-breasted pied woodpecker (*Picoides cathpharius*)
❑ Rufous-bellied pied woodpecker (*Picoides hyperythrus*)
❑ Three-toed woodpecker (*Picoides tridactylus*)
❑ Great black woodpecker (*Dryocopus martius*)

Swallows and Martins (*Hirundinidae*)
❑ Collared sand martin (*Riparia riparia*, LV)
❑ Mountain crag martin (*Hirundo rupestris*, LV)
❑ Barn swallow (*Hirundo rustica*)
❑ Striated or red-rumped swallow (*Hirundo daurica*, LV)
❑ House martin (*Delichon urbica*)
❑ Asian house martin (*Delichon dasypus*, LV)

Larks (*Alaudidae*)
❑ Short-toed lark (*Calandrella cinerea*)

- ❑ Hume's short-toed lark (*Calandrella acutirostris*)
- ❑ Asian short-toed lark (*Calandrella cheleensis*)
- ❑ Long-billed Calandra lark (*Melanocorypha maxima*)
- ❑ Mongolian lark (*Melanocorypha mongolica*)
- ❑ Horned lark (*Eremophila alpestris*, LV)
- ❑ Crested lark (*Galerida cristata*)
- ❑ Common skylark (*Alauda arvensis*)
- ❑ Little or Oriental skylark (*Alauda gulgula*, LV)

Pipits and Wagtails (*Motacillidae*)
- ❑ Richard's pipit (*Anthus novaeseelandiae*)
- ❑ Blyth's or Godlewski's pipit (*Anthus godlewskii*)
- ❑ Tree pipit (*Anthus trivialis*)
- ❑ Hodgson's or Olive tree pipit (*Anthus hodgsoni*, LV)
- ❑ Hodgson's or Rose-breasted pipit (*Anthus roseatus*)
- ❑ Water pipit (*Anthus spinoletta*)
- ❑ Upland pipit (*Anthus sylvanus*)
- ❑ Yellow wagtail (*Motacilla flava*, LV)
- ❑ Yellow-headed wagtail (*Motacilla citreola*, LV)
- ❑ Gray wagtail (*Motacilla cinerea*)
- ❑ Pied or White wagtail (*Motacilla alba* spp., LV)

Shrikes (*Laniidae*)
- ❑ Red-backed shrike (*Lanius collurio*)
- ❑ Gray-backed shrike (*Lanius tephronotus*, LV)
- ❑ Black-headed or Long-tailed shrike (*Lanius schach*)
- ❑ Great gray shrike (*Lanius excubitor*)
- ❑ Chinese gray shrike (*Lanius sphenocercus*)

Old World Orioles (*Oriolidae*)
- ❑ Golden oriole (*Oriolus oriolus*)

Starlings and Mynas (*Sturnidae*)
- ❑ Common starling (*Sturnus vulgaris*)
- ❑ Rose-colored starling (*Sturnus roseus*, LV)
- ❑ White-cheeked or Gray starling (*Sturnus cineraceus*)

Magpies, Jays, Crows, and Allies (*Corvidae*)
- ❑ Eurasian jay (*Garrulus glandarius*)
- ❑ Azure-winged magpie (*Cyanopica cyanus*)
- ❑ Magpie (*Pica pica*, LV)
- ❑ Yellow-billed blue magpie (*Urocissa flavirostris*)
- ❑ Henderson's ground jay (*Podoces hendersoni*)
- ❑ Hume's ground jay (*Pseudopodoces humilis*, LV)
- ❑ Nutcracker (*Nucifraga caryocatactes*)
- ❑ Red-billed chough (*Pyrrhocorax pyrrhocorax*, LV)
- ❑ Yellow-billed chough (*Pyrrhocorax graculus*, LV)
- ❑ Jackdaw (*Corvus monedula*)
- ❑ Daurian jackdaw (*Corvus dauuricus*)
- ❑ Rook (*Corvus frugilegus*)
- ❑ Jungle crow (*Corvus macrorhynchos*)
- ❑ Carrion crow (*Corvus corone*)
- ❑ Raven (*Corvus corax*, LV)

Minivets (*Campephagidae*)
- ❑ Long-tailed minivet (*Pericrocotus ethologus*, LV)
- ❑ *Leafbirds (Irenidae)*
- ❑ Orange-bellied leafbird (*Chloropsis hardwickii*)

Bulbuls (*Pycnonotidae*)
- ❑ Black or Gray bulbul (*Hypsipetes madagascariensis*)
- ❑ Brown-breasted bulbul (*Pycnonotus xanthorrhous*)

Waxwings (*Bombycillidae*)
- ❑ Bohemian waxwing (*Bombycilla garrulus*)

Dippers (*Cinclidae*)
- ❑ Brown dipper (*Cinclus pallasii*, LV)
- ❑ White-breasted dipper (*Cinclus cinclus*, LV)

Wrens (*Troglodytidae*)
- ❑ Wren (*Troglodytes troglodytes*, LV)

Accentors (*Prunellidae*)
- ❑ Alpine accentor (*Prunella collaris*, LV)
- ❑ Himalayan or Altai accentor (*Prunella himalayana*)
- ❑ Robin accentor (*Prunella rubeculoides*, LV)
- ❑ Rufous-breasted accentor (*Prunella strophiata*)
- ❑ Brown accentor (*Prunella fulvescens*, LV)
- ❑ Black-throated accentor (*Prunella atrogularis*)
- ❑ Maroon-backed accentor (*Prunella immaculata*)

Thrushes, Chats, Redstarts, and Allies (*Turdidae*)
- ❑ Gould's or Chestnut shortwing (*Brachypteryx stellata*)
- ❑ Blue or White-browed shortwing (*Brachypteryx montana*)
- ❑ Siberian or Eurasian rubythroat (*Erithacus calliope*)
- ❑ Himalayan or White-tailed rubythroat (*Erithacus pectoralis*)
- ❑ Bluethroat (*Erithacus svecicus*, LV)
- ❑ Fire throat, or Pere David's orangethroat (*Erithacus pectardens*)
- ❑ Indian blue robin, or Blue chat (*Erithacus brunneus*)
- ❑ Orange-flanked bush robin (*Erithacus cyanurus*)
- ❑ Rufous-breasted bush robin (*Erithacus hyperythrus*)
- ❑ White-browed bush robin (*Erithacus indicus*)
- ❑ Golden bush robin (*Erithacus chrysaeus*)
- ❑ Przevalski's redstart (*Phoenicurus alaschanicus*)
- ❑ Blue-headed redstart (*Phoenicurus caeruleocephalus*)
- ❑ Black redstart (*Phoenicurus ochruros*, LV)
- ❑ Hodgson's redstart (*Phoenicurus hodgsoni*, LV)
- ❑ Blue-fronted redstart (*Phoenicurus frontalis*, LV)
- ❑ White-throated redstart (*Phoenicurus schisticeps*, LV)
- ❑ Daurian redstart (*Phoenicurus auroreus*)
- ❑ Guldenstadt's or White-winged redstart (*Phoenicurus erythrogaster*, LV)
- ❑ White-capped river chat, or redstart (*Chaimarrornis leucocephalus*, LV)
- ❑ Plumbeous redstart (*Rhyacornis fuliginosus*, LV)
- ❑ White-bellied redstart, or Hodgson's shortwing (*Hodgsonius phoenicuroides*)
- ❑ Grandala (*Grandala coelicolor*)
- ❑ Little forktail (*Enicurus scouleri*)
- ❑ Spotted forktail (*Enicurus maculatus*)
- ❑ Collared bush or Stone chat (*Saxicola torquata*, LV)
- ❑ Hodgson's stone chat (*Saxicola insignis*)

- Gray bush chat (*Saxicola ferrea*)
- Pied or Pleschanka's wheatear (*Oenanthe pleschanka*)
- Eastern pied wheatear (*Oenanthe picata*)
- Desert wheatear (*Oenanthe deserti*, LV)
- Isabelline wheatear (*Oenanthe isabellina*)
- Chestnut-tailed rock thrush (*Monticola saxatilis*)
- Rock thrush (*Monticola solitarius*)
- Chestnut-bellied rock thrush (*Monticola rufiventris*)
- Scaly or Golden mountain thrush (*Zoothera dauma*)
- Plain-backed mountain thrush (*Zoothera mollissima*)
- Long-tailed mountain thrush (*Zoothera dixoni*)
- Blue whistling thrush (*Myophonus caeruleus*)
- Black/Red-throated thrush (*Turdus ruficollis*, LV)
- Naumann's thrush (*Turdus naumanni*, LV)
- Fieldfare (*Turdus pilaris*)
- White-collared blackbird (*Turdus albocinctus*)
- Common or Eurasian blackbird (*Turdus merula*, LV)
- Chestnut or Gray-headed thrush (*Turdus rubrocanus*)
- Kessler's thrush (*Turdus kessleri*)
- Chinese or Verreaux's song thrush (*Turdus mupinensis*)

Babblers, Laughing Thrushes, and Allies (Timaliidae)
- Rufous-necked scimitar babbler (*Pomatorhinus ruficollis*)
- Rusty-cheeked scimitar babbler (*Pomatorhinus eyrthrocnemis*)
- Red-headed babbler (*Stachyris ruficeps*)
- Scaly-breasted wren babbler (*Pnoepyga albiventer*)
- Lesser scaly wren babbler (*Pnoegyga pussila*)
- Bar-winged wren babbler (*Spelaeornis troglodytoides*)
- Chinese babax (*Babax lanceolatus*)
- Giant babax (*Babax waddelli*, LV)
- Kozlov's babax (*Babax koslowi*)
- White-throated laughing thrush (*Garrulax albogularis*)
- Straited laughing thrush (*Garrulax striatus*)
- Pere David's laughing thrush (*Garrulax davidii*)
- Giant laughing thrush (*Garrulax maximus*)
- Spotted laughing thrush (*Garrulax ocellatus*)
- Gray-sided laughing thrush (*Garrulax caerulatus*)
- Streaked laughing thrush (*Garrulax lineatus*)
- Scaled or Plain-colored laughing thrush (*Garrulax subunicolor*)
- Elliot's laughing thrush (*Garrulax elliotii*)
- Prince Henri's laughing thrush (*Garrulax henrici*, LV)
- Black-faced laughing thrush (*Garrulax affinis*)
- Red-headed laughing thrush (*Garrulax erythrocephalus*)
- Red-billed leiothrix, or Peking robin (*Leiothrix lutea*)
- Fire-tailed myzornis (*Myzornis purrhoura*)
- Nepal cutia (*Cutia nipalensis*)
- Red-winged shrike babbler (*Pteruthius flaviscapis*)
- Green shrike babbler (*Pteruthius xanthochloris*)
- Hoary barwing (*Actinodura nipalensis*)
- Red-tailed minla, or siva (*Minla ignotincta*)
- Bar-throated minla, or siva (*Minla strigula*)
- Whiskered or Yellow-naped yuhina (*Yuhina flavicollis*)
- Stripe-throated yuhina (*Yuhina gularis*)
- Rufous-vented yuhina (*Yuhina occipitalis*)
- Dusky green tit babbler, or fulvetta (*Alcippe cinera*)
- Chestnut-headed tit babbler, or fulvetta (*Alcippe castaneceps*)
- White-browed tit babbler, or fulvetta (*Alcippe vinipectus*)
- Mountain tit babbler, or Chinese fulvetta (*Alcippe striaticollis*)
- Spectacled tit babbler, or fulvetta (*Alcippe ruficapilla*)
- Gray-headed tit babbler, or fulvetta (*Alcippe cinereiceps*)
- Black-capped sibia (*Heterophasia pulchella*)

Parrotbills (Paradoxornithidae)
- Bearded tit, or Reedling (*Panurus biarmicus*)
- Great parrotbill (*Conostoma oemodium*)
- Brown parrotbill (*Paradoxornis unicolor*)
- Spectacled parrotbill (*Paradoxornis conspicillatus*)
- Fulvous parrotbill (*Paradoxornis fulvifrons*)
- Nepal or Black-throated parrotbill (*Paradoxornis nipalensis*)
- Greater rufous-headed parrotbill (*Paradoxornis ruficeps*)

Warblers (Sylviidae)
- Chestnut-headed ground warbler (*Tesia castaneocoronata*)
- Mountain bush warbler (*Cettia montanus*)
- Large or Chestnut-crowned bush warbler (*Cettia major*)
- Aberrant bush warbler (*Cettia flavolivaceus*)
- Hume's or Yellow-bellied bush warbler (*Cettia acanthizoides*)
- Rufous-capped bush warbler (*Cettia brunnifrons*)
- Spotted bush warbler (*Bradypterus thoracicus*)
- Large-billed bush warbler (*Bradypterus major*)
- Chinese bush warbler (*Bradypterus tacsanowskius*)
- Pallas's grasshopper warbler (*Locustella certhiola*)
- Grasshopper warbler (*Locustella naevia*)
- Paddyfield warbler (*Acrocephalus agricola*)
- Blyth's reed warbler (*Acrocephalus dumetorum*)
- Reed warbler (*Acrocephalus scirpaceus*)
- Great reed warbler (*Acrocephalus arundinaceus*)

❑ Booted warbler (*Hippolais caligata*)
❑ Barred warbler (*Sylvia nisoria*)
❑ Whitethroat (*Sylvia communis*)
❑ Lesser whitethroat (*Sylvia curruca*)
❑ Desert lesser whitethroat (*Sylvia minula*)
❑ Hume's lesser whitethroat (*Sylvia althaea*)
❑ Desert warbler (*Sylvia nana*)
❑ Chiffchaff, or Brown leaf warbler (*Phylloscopus collybita*)
❑ Plain willow warbler (*Phylloscopus neglactus*)
❑ Tytler's willow warbler (*Phylloscopus tytleri*)
❑ Tickell's leaf warbler (*Phylloscopus affinis*, LV)
❑ Buff-throated warbler (*Phylloscopus subafffinis*)
❑ Olivaceous willow warbler (*Phylloscopus griseolis*)
❑ Dusky warbler (*Phylloscopus fuscatus*)
❑ Yellow-streaked or Milne-Edward's warbler (*Phylloscopus armandii*)
❑ Orange-barred leaf warbler (*Phylloscopus pulcher*)
❑ Plain or Yellow-browed leaf warbler (*Phylloscopus inornatus*)
❑ Pallas's or Yellow-rumped leaf warbler (*Phylloscopus proregulus*)
❑ Gray-faced leaf warbler (*Phylloscopus maculipennis*)
❑ Arctic warbler (*Phylloscopus borealis*)
❑ Large-billed leaf warbler (*Phylloscopus magnirostris*)
❑ Greenish warbler (*Phylloscopus trochiloides*, LV)
❑ Large-crowned leaf warbler (*Phylloscopus occipitalis*)
❑ Blyth's crowned leaf warbler (*Phylloscopus reguloides*)
❑ White-tailed leaf warbler (*Phylloscopus davisoni*)
❑ Yellow-eyed warbler (*Seicercus burkii*)
❑ Gray-headed warbler (*Seicercus xanthoschistos*)
❑ Chestnut-crowned warbler (*Seicercus castaneiceps*)
❑ Black-faced warbler (*Abroscopus schisticeps*)
❑ Goldcrest (*Regulus regulus*)
❑ Crested tit warbler (*Leptopoecile elegans*)
❑ Severtzov's or Stoliczka's tit warbler (*Leptopoecile sophiae*)
❑ Chinese hill warbler (*Rhopophilus pekinensis*)
❑ Black-throated hill prinia (*Prinia atrogularis*)

Flycatchers (*Muscicapidae*)
❑ Red-breasted flycatcher (*Ficedula parva*)
❑ Orange-gorgeted flycatcher (*Ficedula strophiata*)
❑ Rufous-breasted blue flycatcher (*Ficedula hyperythra*)
❑ Rusty-breasted blue flycatcher (*Ficedula hodgsonii*)
❑ White-browed blue flycatcher (*Ficedula superciliaris*)
❑ Slaty-blue flycatcher (*Ficedula tricolor*)
❑ Sapphire flycatcher (*Ficedula sapphira*)
❑ Large niltava (*Niltava grandis*)

❑ Small or Rufous-bellied niltava (*Niltava sundara*)
❑ Vivid niltava (*Niltava vivida*)
❑ Spotted flycatcher (*Muscicapa striata*)
❑ Sooty or Dark-sided flycatcher (*Muscicapa sibirica*)
❑ Brown flycatcher (*Muscicapa latriostris*)
❑ Gray-headed flycatcher (*Culicicapa ceylonensis*)
❑ Yellow-bellied fantail flycatcher (*Chelidorhynx hypoxantha*)
❑ White-throated fantail flycatcher (*Rhipidure albicollis*)

Long-tailed Tits (*Aegithalidae*)
❑ Long-tailed tit (*Aegithalos caudatus*)
❑ Black-browed or Rufous-fronted tit (*Aegithalos iouschistos*)
❑ Red-headed or Black-throated tit (*Aegithalos concinnus*)

Penduline Tits (*Remizidae*)
❑ Penduline tit (*Remiz pendulinus*)
❑ Fire-capped tit (*Cephalopyrus flammiceps*)

Titmice (*Paridae*)
❑ Marsh tit (*Parus palustris*)
❑ Willow tit (*Parus montanus*)
❑ White-browed tit (*Parus superciliosus*)
❑ Gray-crested tit (*Parus dichrous*)
❑ Coal tit (*Parus ater*)
❑ Rufous-vented tit (*Parus rubidiventris*)
❑ Gray or Great tit (*Parus major*, LV)
❑ Green-backed tit (*Parus monticolus*)
❑ Yellow-cheeked tit (*Parus spilonotus*)
❑ Yellow-breasted tit (*Parus flavipectus*)
❑ Yellow-browed tit (*Sylviparus modestus*)

Nuthatches (*Sittidae*)
❑ Eurasian nuthatch (*Sitta europaea*)
❑ Naga nuthatch (*Sitta nagaensis*)
❑ White-tailed nuthatch (*Sitta himalayensis*)
❑ Prezevalski's or White-cheeked nuthatch (*Sitta leucopsis*)
❑ Chinese nuthatch (*Sitta villosa*)
❑ Beautiful nuthatch (*Sitta formosa*)
❑ Wall creeper (*Trichodroma muraria*, LV)

Tree Creepers (*Certhiidae*)
❑ Northern or Common tree creeper (*Certhia familiaris*)
❑ Himalayan or Bar-tailed tree creeper (*Certhia himalayana*)
❑ Nepal or Rusty-flanked tree creeper (*Certhia nipalensis*)

Flower peckers (*Dicaeidae*)
❑ Yellow-bellied flowerpecker (*Dicaeum melanoxanthum*)
❑ Fire-breasted flowerpecker (*Dicaeum ignipectus*)

Sunbirds (*Nectariniidae*)
❑ Mrs. Gould's sunbird (*Aethopyga gouldiae*)
❑ Nepal or Green-tailed sunbird (*Aethopyga nipalensis*)
❑ Black-breasted sunbird (*Aethopyga saturata*)

- ❏ Fire-tailed sunbird (*Aethopyga ignicauda*)

White-eyes (*Zosteropidae*)
- ❏ White-eye (*Zosterops palpebrosa*)

Sparrows and Snow Finches (*Ploceidae*)
- ❏ House sparrow (*Passer domesticus*)
- ❏ Tree sparrow (*Passer montanus*, LV)
- ❏ Cinnamon sparrow (*Passer rutilans*, LV)
- ❏ Rock sparrow (*Petronia petronia*)
- ❏ Eurasian snow finch (*Montifringilla nivalis*)
- ❏ Adam's or Tibetan snow finch (*Montifringilla adamsi*, LV)
- ❏ Mandelli's or White-rumped snow finch (*Montifringilla taczanowskii*)
- ❏ Pere David's snow finch (*Montifringilla davidiana*)
- ❏ Red-necked snow finch (*Montifringilla ruficollis*)
- ❏ Blanford's snow finch (*Montifringilla blanfordi*)

Finches (*Fringillidae*)
- ❏ Brambling (*Fringilla montifringilla*)
- ❏ Gold-fronted serin, or finch (*Serinus pusillus*)
- ❏ Tibetan siskin (*Serinus thibetanus*)
- ❏ Oriental or Gray-capped green finch (*Carduelis sinica*)
- ❏ Black-headed green finch (*Carduelis ambigua*)
- ❏ Himalayan gold finch, or green finch (*Carduelis spinoides*)
- ❏ Eastern or Eurasian gold finch (*Carduelis carduelis*)
- ❏ Tibetan twite (*Acanthis flavirostris*, LV)
- ❏ Redpoll (*Acanthis flammea*)
- ❏ Hodgson's or plain mountain finch (*Leucosticte nemoricola*)
- ❏ Brandt's mountain finch (*Leucosticte brandti*)
- ❏ Mongolian desert finch (*Rhodopechys mongolica*)
- ❏ Desert finch (*Rhodopechys obsoleta*)
- ❏ Long-tailed rose finch (*Uragus sibiricus*)
- ❏ Przevalski's rose finch (*Urocynchramus pylzowi*)
- ❏ Crimson or Blanford's rose finch (*Carpodacus rubescens*)
- ❏ Nepal or Dark rose finch (*Carpodacus nipalensis*)
- ❏ Common rose finch (*Carpodacus erythrinus*, LV)
- ❏ Beautiful rose finch (*Carpodacus pulcherrimus*, LV)
- ❏ Pink-rumped or Stresemann's rose finch (*Carpodacus eos*)
- ❏ Pink-browed rose finch (*Carpodacus rhodochrous*)
- ❏ Vinaceous rose finch (*Carpodacus vinaceous*)
- ❏ Large or Dark-rumped rose finch (*Carpodacus edwardsii*)
- ❏ Sinai rose finch (*Carpodacus synoicus*)
- ❏ Three-banded rose finch (*Carpodacus trifasciatus*)
- ❏ White-browed rose finch (*Carpodacus thura*)
- ❏ Red-mantled rose finch (*Carpodacus rhodochlamys*)
- ❏ Eastern great rose finch (*Carpodacus rubicilloides*, LV)
- ❏ Great rose finch (*Carpodacus rubicilla*, LV)
- ❏ Red-breasted rose finch (*Carpodacus puniceus*)
- ❏ Roborovski's rose finch (*Kozlowia roborowskii*)
- ❏ Crossbill (*Loxia curvirostra*)
- ❏ Crimson-browed or Juniper finch (*Propyrrhula subhimalacha*, LV)
- ❏ Gold-headed finch (*Pyrrhoplectes epauletta*)
- ❏ Brown bullfinch (*Pyrrhula nipalensis*)
- ❏ Red-headed bullfinch (*Pyrrhula erythrocephala*)
- ❏ Beavan's or Gray-headed bullfinch (*Pyrrhula erythaca*)
- ❏ Allied or Collared grosbeak (*Mycerobas affinis*)
- ❏ Spot-winged grosbeak (*Mycerobas melanozanthos*)
- ❏ White-winged grosbeak (*Mycerobas carnipes*)

Buntings (*Emberizidae*)
- ❏ Crested bunting (*Melophus lathami*)
- ❏ Pine bunting (*Emberiza leucocephala*)
- ❏ Rock bunting (*Emberiza cia*, LV)
- ❏ Long-tailed or Meadow bunting (*Emberiza ciodes*)
- ❏ Gray-necked bunting (*Emberiza buchanani*)
- ❏ White-capped bunting (*Emberiza stewarti*)
- ❏ Ortolan bunting (*Emberiza hortulana*)
- ❏ Rustic bunting (*Emberiza rustica*)
- ❏ Yellow-breasted bunting (*Emberiza aureola*)
- ❏ Kozlov's bunting (*Emberiza koslowi*)
- ❏ Red-headed bunting (*Emberiza bruniceps*)
- ❏ Black-faced bunting (*Emberiza spodocephala*)
- ❏ Pallas's reed bunting (*Emberiza pallasi*)
- ❏ Common reed bunting (*Emberiza schoeniclus*)

17
THE PEOPLE AND THEIR CULTURE

Although the Tibetan civilization is far younger than the both the Hindu society flanking its southern tier and the Chinese empire along its eastern periphery, the noble Tibetans have developed one of the most diverse and fascinating cultures on the planet. Few other world religions can rival the mental complexity or visual pageantry of the Tibetan Buddhists or their brethren on the Plateau, the Bön. The twentieth century has delivered a cruel fate to these remarkable people who shunned modern technology and weaponry, but their tenacity and courageous belief in what is Tibetan will hopefully be the catalyst to carry them through one of the greatest challenges their unique civilization has faced.

THE PEOPLE OF TIBET
BY CHARLES RAMBLE

Tibetans are the descendants of a number of nomadic peoples who apparently migrated southward and westward from the Central Asian steppes and the Chinese borderlands before settling down to cultivate the fertile Tsangpo Valley. The development of a fixed, agriculture-based civilization provided a nucleus for the new Tibetan empire when, in the sixth and seventh centuries, one noble family in Yarlung managed to unite the warring chiefs around it; but it was surely their nomadic heritage, the hardiness it engendered, and a willingness to live in the saddle that enabled these warriors to push the frontiers of their empire to the west of Mount Kailash, north of the Kun Lun Mountains, and even as far as the gates of Chang'an (now Xian), the capital of T'ang China.

Settled agriculture permitted the development of the extraordinarily rich Buddhist civilization, channeling much of the Tibetans' martial ferocity into religious zeal. About a quarter of Tibet's population continues to pursue a nomadic lifestyle, while the farming majority still exhibits remarkable mobility for an agrarian society. Tibetans think nothing of trading expeditions and pilgrimages lasting many months, or even years. The nomadic life was always considered more prestigious than that of the farmer. The chief reason for this attitude is that those working the land were not usually free to move around, since tax obligations compelled them to remain and farm their hereditary plots. Revenue on land and livestock was not the only form of tax farmers were required to pay. These varied from one region to another, but might include supplying pack animals for visiting of officials, free labor, the provision of a soldier to the army, and even a "monk tax," which required that one son be sent to the regionally dominant monastery. While agriculture might not have provided much scope for profit, even the peasantry could amass considerable wealth through trade as long as they could ensure there was someone to take care of their land and meet the necessary tax obligations.

Parallel to the economic hierarchy in Tibet was a system of social stratification based principally on descent through the male line. The political relevance of this situation has largely been replaced by the new order of the Communist meritocracy, but it is clear that certain aspects survive into the present. There were four main ranks in the hierarchy, the two highest being the nobles and the priests. Unlike the Indian caste model, in which the priests (Brahmans) always occupy the highest position, the relative status of priests and nobles in Tibet was never so clearly defined. As a general rule the nobility probably ranked higher. In the Dingri area the priests came first, but this may have been because the local aristocracy belonged to a lower category: The Tibetan nobility was itself subdivided

Family portrait

into four grades. We should be careful not to confuse these priests with the monastic community, who could be recruited from all but the lowest stratum of society. The idea that priestly qualities are transmitted from father to son is probably a Buddhist adoption of an ancient Tibetan tradition. The priests in question must marry and consequently belong to the older lamaist sects, the Nyingmapa and the Bön, for whom celibacy is not always obligatory. The great majority of Tibetans belonged to the commoner rank, which formed the bulk of the taxpaying farmers and nomads. Last came the outcastes. These people were usually landless, and included artisans such as blacksmiths who survived on the patronage of the farming communities in which they lived and vagrants who earned a living in exchange for their labor or for slaughtering livestock.

Marriage between members of different ranks was unusual and generally prohibited. In a few regions it was customary for priests and nobles, or for priests and commoners, to intermarry, but intermarriage with outcastes was far more unusual; this remains the case up to the present day. Commoners claim that outcastes "do not have the same mouth" as they do, and will not share a cup with them. A number of priestly lineages survive, and reverence for their hereditary sanctity has again become overt. Noble families are also represented, but of course are no longer part of the Tibetan political machinery. Those who remained in Tibet after 1959 predictably did not thrive in the new climate, and most were astute enough to leave. Many of the large ruins one sees in villages in Central Tibet are the shells of abandoned noble houses, stripped of their timbers and other usable building materials and left to decay.

The nobility formed an integral part of the Tibetan administrative system. The ruling classes of Tibet fell into two principal divisions: the monastic hierarchy and the various ranks of the laity, almost all of noble status. In all parts of Tibet, land was considered to belong to the ruler, and in Tibet the absolute ruler was the Dalai Lama. The taxpaying peasantry merely leased land from the government. In addition, some land was under the direct control of the Dalai Lama or his district commissioners (the *dzongpon*), and the entire produce of this went to the state. This land, having no tenants, was worked by conscripted labor provided by the peasants as part of their tax requirements. Only three entities in Tibet could hold revenue-yielding estates: the church (who held about 42 percent), the government (37 percent), and the nobility (21 percent).

DOMESTIC LIFE

With the exception of a disastrous experiment in the 1960s to introduce winter wheat, barley has always been the principal crop of the Tibetan Plateau. In lower areas it is just possible to follow a spring crop of barley with one of buckwheat, but in most places a single annual harvest in August and September is generally the limit. In this case subsidiary crops such as buckwheat, rapeseed (grown for its oil), peas, turnips, and potatoes are relegated to a few minor plots.

The staple food throughout Tibet is *tsampa*, which is made by roasting barley in heated sand, separating it out again by means of a sieve, and grinding the grain to flour in a water mill or household quern. *Tsampa* made from dried peas is sometimes added to the roasted barley flour to produce an especially nutritious mixture. *Tsampa* is mixed in a cup or a little goatskin bag with tea or the whey from yogurt and eaten as a dough called *pak*. Fresh vegetables do not figure prominently in Tibetan cuisine, and night blindness, resulting from a deficiency of vitamin A, is common in many areas.

Tibetans also use barley to produce beer, known as *chang*, which is made by adding yeast to boiled and cooled grain and storing the mixture in earthenware fermenting jars. A potent form of beer, called *nyingkhu*, is made by allowing the barley to ferment in a large volume of water, which is drawn off after a couple of weeks and drunk. A milder, thicker drink is produced by pouring water through a sieve containing fermented grain and squeezing the alcoholic content out of it. The residue is dried for animal feed. The fermented mash can also be used as the basis of a distilled alcohol called *arak*.

Agricultural produce is supplemented by pastoralism. Most households keep sheep and goats, plus at least a few cattle, yaks, or *dzo*, the crossbreeds of these animals. Most of the large yak herds in Tibet are under the care of the nomadic and seminomadic population. The herds move with the seasons, ascending to the high pastures in spring and summer, then returning to the lower settlements with the onset of colder weather.

Nomads, of course, cover a considerably larger area than do farmers; they also embark on long trading expeditions from the lakes and plains regions of the high Northern Plateau, loading bags of salt and animal products onto yaks and sheep alike, then heading for the areas of settled cultivation in the south, even as far as Nepal, to trade their goods for grain.

Milk and its derivatives are the chief product from livestock. Butter is used principally in salted Tibetan tea, as an oil for the hair and face, and for a range of ceremonial purposes such as fueling ritual lamps. A dried cheese called *churpi* is made from buttermilk; it will keep indefinitely.

Yaks are the source of many important materials, and little of the animal goes to waste. The meat is eaten raw and fresh while the animal is being butchered and for a few days thereafter, or raw and dried in the following months. The blood, which in some areas is drunk fresh and warm by young men as an aphrodisiac and general tonic, is the major ingredient in sausages, as are the lungs, spleen, and stomach. The stomach is also used as a receptacle for fat and butter. Horned animal skulls often adorn rooftops and lintels as a deterrent to potentially harmful spirits, while the horns themselves have a number of other, chiefly magical, functions. Yak hides are sometimes dried as floor coverings or, with the hair removed, cut into long spirals for use as rope. Wood is scarce on most of the Plateau, making dried yak dung an important source of fuel. The ash from the burned dung is spread on the fields as a meager fertilizer. The long, coarse hair that grows as a skirt on the flanks and legs of the yak is woven into ropes, sacks, blankets, and, most important for the nomads, warm and durable tents. The finer wool beneath is spun into yarn for clothing or compressed into felt to make large-brimmed hats and the soft, rope-soled boots worn by both sexes. Both men and women spin the wool, though only women weave, using either backstrap looms or more sophisticated devices with treadles. Sewing is considered to be men's work, and leather-sheathed needle cases are among the numerous objects that might hang from a man's belt beside his flint and striker and his silver knife sheath.

The division of labor between the sexes is generally not as clearly defined in Tibet as in many other Asian societies. Both men and women fetch water, for example, and men often perform tasks such as milking animals, cooking, and taking care of children. Women generally have nothing to do with butchering animals or handling and cooking fresh meat (although dried meat is acceptable), and nowhere do women plow the fields. Other agricultural chores such as weeding, irrigating, harvesting, and threshing are usually performed by both sexes.

The usual form of marriage in Tibet is fraternal polyandry, according to which a woman marries all the brothers in a household except, of course, the family monk, traditionally the second brother. The brothers' status in the house and their sexual rights to their wife were normally determined by seniority, and the youngest of several brothers might opt out of the marriage, forfeiting his rights to the inheritance and finding a wife of his own. The chief reason for the prevalence of polyandry seems to have lain precisely in this matter of inheritance: With only one childbearing woman in each generation of a household there could be only one line of succession (in many areas all the brothers are addressed indiscriminately as "Father" by the children), and the landholding, which in many cases could barely support a family, did not need to be subdivided among heirs. Polyandrous marriages are still widespread in Tibet, but monogamy is increasingly common, with young couples building new houses for themselves away from the rest of the family.

As for the houses themselves, architectural styles vary from one place to another, with climate being a major design factor. In the monsoon-washed southeastern region, for example, all houses have pitched roofs, and the abundance of forests makes it possible

The yak is the most common domestic animal on the Tibetan Plateau

to use large quantities of wood in the construction. The ground floor often serves as an animal shelter, with the family living on the first floor, while the attic, generally open-sided to allow air to circulate, is used for drying fodder. Flat roofs are the rule in Central Tibet, and only wealthy houses have two stories. Walls are made of sun-dried mud bricks covered in mud plaster and painted with a wash of white lime. Livestock is kept in a courtyard, which may contain a roofed stable to protect weaker animals in the winter months.

FROM COLLECTIVIZATION TO THE PRESENT

The collectivization of agriculture and pastoralism during the 1960s was not popular with most Tibetans, and the reintroduction two decades later of the private sector in the form of the "responsibility system" was a welcome move. Animals and fields were redistributed equally to individuals, entirely irrespective of age and sex. This was clearly the fairest way to go about the division, but since it was the household that had been, and had again become, the basic economic unit, larger families obviously did better. Predictably enough, the economic parity with which the responsibility system began has not lasted: some people flourished in the new environment of commercial freedom while others failed disastrously. Interestingly, it seems that among both farmers and nomads there is a trend for families to return to the economic niche they occupied before collectivization. The Tibetans' business acumen is apparently as hard to kill as their religious faith.

Religious freedoms began to reappear in the early 1980s, and with them, religious practice has come into the open. The government has provided limited funding for the restoration of certain monasteries, and the public is supplementing this with voluntary donations. Restoration, of course, can never be synonymous with replacement, and the relationship between the government and the reestablished monasticism remains tenuous at best.

The resurgence of popular religion is evident from a glance at the appearance of villages. Hilltop cairns devoted to territorial divinities and shrines to household gods that stand at rooftop corners have a cared-for look about them. They are often decorated with red clay and surmounted by little flags of many colors. The tradition of prayer-flags probably has its origin in the ancient custom (which still survives) of hanging black and white wool in trees; flags printed with appropriate prayers are the more respectable Buddhist version of the practice. The bamboo stems that support the flags on the shrines do not grow on the dry Plateau but are brought from the cloud forests of the Nepalese borderland. The white swastikas painted over doorways are an ancient symbol of good fortune that found their way into Tibet from India. Traditionally, the feet of Buddhist swastikas point clockwise, while the direction is reversed among the Bönpos. The abundance of counterclockwise swastikas in Central Tibet does not indicate a large Bönpo population; they are slips of the artists' brushes occasioned by decades of unfamiliarity with the convention.

Another favorite doorway design is a round sun sitting in the shallow cup of the moon, often with a squiggle appearing from the top of the sun. As far as most villagers are concerned, the emblem is some sort of protective sign, but it originates from a fundamental Tantric idea. The moon is the masculine principle and represents Means, while the sun represents Wisdom, the passive feminine principle (the gender attributed to the sun and moon actually varies in certain contexts). The squiggle at the top is the "drop," the "thought of enlightenment," which arises from the union of Wisdom and Means.

Theocratic societies are rarely characterized by good government, and in Tibet the introspective conservatism of the former monastic establishment left the country without any effective foreign policy, and consequently with no diplomatic defense against the disastrous events of the 1950s. But Tibetans, to their credit, never seem to have confused church politics for religious matters. Buddhism flourished in Tibet long before there was a theocracy. It has survived it by four decades, and may well outlive another regime.

Charles Ramble is an anthropologist who has carried out research in Tibetan communities in both Nepal and Tibet. He has lived in Nepal and India for twenty years and is currently associated with the Universities of Hamburg and Vienna.

HISTORY AND RELIGION

It is difficult to differentiate Tibet's history from the growth of its religions, as the religious aspirations of the great monastic orders were often intertwined with politics and intrigue; as the wealth and landholdings of the monasteries increased, so did their ability to exert temporal power over Tibet. Modern Tibetan history dates back to the seventh century AD, when a standard written language was introduced. The traditional accounts of history before this time are based on both fact and legend. A mythical king is said to have descended from heaven onto a mountain in Southern Tibet, and the royal line later established their palace at Yumbu Lagang, a structure believed to be the oldest in Tibet. His descendants are the line of kings that included King Songtsen Gampo, the skillful seventh-century administrator and commander who led his armies from their small kingdom in the Yarlung Valley, conquering a huge area that sprawled across Central Asia to China and included almost all of the Himalaya. The great Tibetan empire lasted about 250 years, until the Royal Dynasty collapsed in the ninth century, not from external pressures but from internal strife centered around religion. From that time onward Tibet's political and religious history are almost inseparable.

BUDDHISM IN TIBET

Tibetan Buddhism is by far the predominant religion in Tibet and the entire Himalayan region. Although its roots can be traced back to the teachings of Sakyamuni, the historical Buddha, the highly ritualized Tantric form practiced in Tibet bears little resemblance to Theravada Buddhism as practiced in Sri Lanka, Thailand, and Burma. Buddhism was slow to find Tibet relative to its appearance throughout the rest of Asia. The first Tibetan Buddhist temples, including the well-known Jokhang in Lhasa, were built in the seventh century during the reign of King Songtsen Gampo, some 1300 years after the death of Sakyamuni Buddha. Although this king is traditionally acknowledged as one of the great Buddhist kings in Tibet, he apparently followed the pre-Buddhist practices of his ancestors, followers of the Bön religion. King Trisong Detsen was even more sympathetic to the new religion, helping to found Samye, Tibet's first Buddhist monastery, in the eighth century. He also invited several Indian Buddhist scholars to teach in Tibet. This included Guru Rimpoche (his Sanskrit name is Padmasambhava, the "Lotus Born"), a Tantric master/sorcerer who is now revered as the founder of the Nyingmapa Buddhist tradition in Tibet.

Adherents of the Bön religion, however, resisted this growth of Buddhism. The clash between the two groups over political influence ultimately caused the Royal Dynasty to collapse in the ninth century following the murder of King Langdarma, who is infamously remembered in Tibet as the great persecutor of Buddhism. Although organized religion languished due to a lack of wealthy patrons, both the Buddhists and the Bön priests continued their teachings on smaller grassroots levels without temples or shrines.

Some 100 years after Langdarma's death, monastic Buddhism started reestablishing itself. Religious scholars returned, temples were built, and the Indian Tantric texts were translated and brought to Tibet. In the eleventh century the Indian Buddhist master Atisha was invited to Western Tibet by descendants of the old royal dynasty. His teachings emphasized monastic discipline and the tradition of direct instruction from teacher to student, laying the foundation for Tibet's first great school of Buddhism, the Kadampa sect. Later that century disciples of Atisha founded two important monasteries in Central Tibet, Reting and Narthang.

This second diffusion of Buddhism spread quickly in Tibet, encouraging more Buddhist scholars and ascetics to venture north of the Himalaya. The form of Buddhism that particularly interested Tibetans was Tantricism, a school of thought that emphasizes highly ritualized worship of deities and the use of specialized meditational and yogic techniques to achieve spiritual enlightenment, even in one lifetime. This tradition is called Vajrayana Buddhism, the "Diamond Path."

Some Tibetans traveled to India to study Sanskrit Tantric texts. Most notable of these translators were Drokmi and Marpa. Drokmi was the founder of the spiritual tradition embraced by Sakya monastery and the Sakyapa sect. Marpa's teachings formed the basis of the Kargyüpa Buddhist sect, the "Oral Tradition," which emphasizes direct instruction of a student by his master, as well as strict self-denial and intense meditational techniques. Through the disciples of Marpa's renowned student Milarepa, Tibet's poet-saint, six major monasteries and Kargyüpa subsects were founded in Central Tibet during the twelfth century, including Tsurphu, Taklung, Drigung, and Densathil monasteries.

Large monastic centers continued to flourish through the thirteenth and fourteenth centuries despite the constant political turmoil among them over the control of Tibet. In the mid-thirteenth century the Sakya *lamas* became administrators of the country with the help of the Mongol armies residing on the northern borders, the descendants of Genghis Khan. Eventually the Mongols became religious patrons of the Sakyapa sect under Kublai Khan, emperor of the Yuan dynasty in China, who handed over control of

Tibet to these *lamas*. The other great monasteries also sought patrons among different Mongol chiefs, leading to sporadic armed conflicts between the various factions. When the Yuan dynasty began to weaken, a powerful lord from the Yarlung Valley, Changchub Gyeltsen, successfully led his armies against Sakya in the mid-fourteenth century and became the new ruler of Tibet. His descendants, the Phakmodru family, ruled Tibet until the late fifteenth century, when their ministers, the Rimpung princes of Tsang Province, usurped control of the country.

During this time a respected Kadampa scholar named Tsong Khapa founded Ganden monastery. A firm believer in scholarship and strict monastic discipline, his uncompromising religious views quickly attracted many followers and patrons from the Lhasa area. Tsong Khapa's school of reformed teachings became known as the Gelukpa sect, the "Model of Virtue." Two of his main disciples founded Drepung and Sera monasteries near Lhasa. Despite their virtues, the Gelukpas didn't take long to become involved in worldly affairs, particularly politics.

The Rimpung princes were ousted by their own ministers, the governors of Tsang Province, in the 1560s. The new rulers were patrons of Tsurphu and Nenang monasteries, to the northwest of Lhasa. An intense rivalry between these Kargyüpa strongholds and the Gelukpa monasteries around Lhasa prompted the abbot of Drepung, Sonam Gyatsho, to seek foreign assistance. Late in the sixteenth century he met with Altan Khan, chief of the Mongol tribes, who were still based north of Tibet. The Khan and Sonam Gyatsho exchanged gifts and bestowed honorific titles upon each other; the abbot was given the title Ta-le (a Mongolian word meaning "ocean," now better known as Dalai, or Dalai Lama). As a result, the first two abbots of Drepung were retroactively named the First and Second Dalai Lama, and Sonam Gyatsho is revered as the third in this lineage. Following his death, a young boy was recognized as the spiritual incarnation of Sonam Gyatsho, establishing the tradition for choosing the Dalai Lama that exists to this day.

In the early seventeenth century a dispute between the kings of Tsang and the Gelukpas led to the sacking of Drepung and Sera monasteries. The Gelukpas retaliated, assisted by their Mongol patrons. The conflict reached its peak in the 1640s when the Mongols captured and killed the king of Tsang, and Tsurphu monastery was sacked. The head of the Gelukpa hierarchy at the time, the Fifth Dalai Lama, went on to become one of the most powerful and influential figures in Tibetan history; the Gelukpas were to maintain a religious domination over Tibet until the twentieth century.

The political role of the Gelukpas was more tenuous, especially following the death of the Fifth Dalai Lama. A Mongol army invaded in the early eighteenth century and established their general as the governor of Tibet. The Sixth Dalai Lama died mysteriously in the company of this general; a dispute over the boy chosen to be the next Dalai Lama encouraged the Chinese Manchu emperor to have his armies march on Lhasa. The Chinese delivered a boy who was grandly accepted by the Tibetan people as the Seventh Dalai Lama, but representatives of the Chinese emperor exerted varying degrees of control over Tibet's political affairs until the collapse of the Manchu dynasty. In 1911 the Thirteenth Dalai Lama expelled the Chinese from Tibet and reestablished the Gelukpa theocracy. The Gelukpas remained in control of Tibet until 1950, when Communist Chinese armies entered Lhasa. The Fourteenth Dalai Lama fled to India in 1959, establishing a Tibetan government-in-exile based in Dharamsala, to the north of Delhi. Monasteries that were destroyed during the Cultural Revolution are now slowly reestablishing themselves, sometimes with financial aid from the Chinese government, but the educational system that was so crucial to Tibetan Buddhism has been mostly dismantled. However, some of the religious traditions have managed to survive, and are now being taught by *lamas* living in exile in India.

OTHER RELIGIONS

What many people don't realize about Tibetan Buddhism is that it existed on two major, but very different, planes: as it was practiced by the monks, and the daily rituals of laypeople. Tibetan Buddhism is an amalgam of religious ideas, both indigenous and of foreign origin (mostly Indian), which matured and developed into a unique monastic culture. Tibetan Buddhism is also called Lamaism due to the importance of great monasteries and the vast numbers of monks. But when you see pilgrims burning incense at holy sites, pouring offerings of *tsampa* and *chang* onto the hearths, and walking around prayer walls, these are not purely Buddhist rituals but carryovers from the old folk religions that have persisted for millennia in Tibet. The Tibetans' lives are greatly influenced by their concern for appeasing the local deities residing in the ground, in springs, atop mountains, and within their homes. To anger these spirits could be disastrous; to propitiate them with the pleasant smells of incense bush and other offerings can bring harmony to their lives and family, good harvests, and safe crossings over the mountains. If you have the opportunity to drink *chang* in someone's home, watch what is done before the first sip: the ring finger is inserted into the *chang* and offering drops are flicked into the air. When the butter tea is being made, a dab of butter will be smudged onto the churn as an offering before it is served. Other ancient rituals are performed before a house can be built, before a new wife moves into her husband's home, and before the fields can be plowed. Such folk traditions are now an integral part of the Tibetan Buddhist religion.

The other main religion in Tibet is Bön. Many people assume it is the pre-Buddhist religion of Tibet, but this is only partially true. Bön as it is known today traces its origins to a Buddha-like historical figure named Tönpa Shenrab, who is said to have lived in a land to the west of Tibet, perhaps near present-day Iran. The religion has a bigger following in Northern and Eastern Tibet, though two large Bön monasteries, Menri and Yungdrungling, were established near Shigatse.

The pre-Buddhist Bön religion was not an organized monastic order, but rather a class of priests who specialized in funeral rites and sacrifices. All the Tibetan royal kings, even those who are said to have championed Buddhism, were buried at Chongye Valley and had funerals conducted by Bön priests. After the death of King Langdarma these priests seem to have disappeared; in about the eleventh century a new religion appeared that also called itself Bön, its followers the Bönpo. It differed from the religion of the older Bön priests, having many doctrinal similarities to the new Tantric schools of Buddhism that were being established in Tibet. Like the Guru Rimpoche cult of the Nyingmapa sect, the Bönpo developed a mythology and religious cult around Tönpa Shenrab.

Initially the Bön religion remained small, with individual *lamas* relying on the patronage of a few families. With the rapid growth of Buddhist monastic centers in Central Tibet, the Bönpo decided they too needed a major religious center and founded Menri *gompa* in the early fifteenth century. A canon of Bönpo texts, much like the Buddhist *Kangyur* and *Tengyur*, was compiled, and they also adopted pilgrimage circuits, prayer wheels, and *mani* walls. The Bönpo practitioners, however, spin the wheels and walk around sacred sites in a counterclockwise manner, opposite to the Buddhists; even the swastika they use is the reverse of the Buddhist symbol. In the Bön monasteries, the similarities to Buddhism are uncanny. The maroon-robed monks are nearly indistinguishable from their Buddhist counterparts, and the statue of Tönpa Shenrab on the main altar is almost identical to the Buddha, down to the blue head covering with the rounded protuberance on top. If you are interested in visiting a Bön monastery, see the details of an outing to Yungdrungling, near Shigatse, in the section "Day Hikes in and near Shigatse."

Conch-shell horns are sounded before the start of prayer ceremonies

Not to be forgotten are the Tibetan Muslims. Although Islam has never been a major religious force in Tibet, Turkestani, Kashmiri, and Chinese Muslim (Hui) traders have long lived in Tibet, selling goods in the bazaars alongside the Nepalese and Tibetans. Mostly through intermarriage, a population of Tibetan Muslims now resides in the larger cities, particularly in Lhasa. The city mosque is tucked into the maze of buildings to the east of the Barkor.

FESTIVALS

The Tibetan year is based upon a lunar calendar of twelve months, with the new year usually beginning sometime in February. Each month consists of thirty days, with the full moon on the 15th day and the new moon on the 30th day. The majority of Tibetan festivals are religious in nature. Also, on the 8th, 15th, and 30th of each month, most monasteries will have *tshok,* "offering ceremonies," for the Medicine Buddha, Öpame, and Sakyamuni, respectively; on the 25th day there is an offering to the *khandroma.* On the 10th day of every month the Nyingmapa sect celebrates special Guru Rimpoche days, the most important of these being in the sixth month to commemorate his birth. An informative Tibetan/Western pocket calendar with dates of the Tibetan festivals is printed annually by Rigpa UK, 330 Caledonian Road, London, England N1 1BB; email: 100564.2350 @compuserve.com.

First month, 1st to 3rd days: Losar, the Tibetan New Year. The largest and most popular nonreligious festival of the year, Losar is primarily a family-oriented festival celebrated in homes and with friends by eating special pastries and drinking plenty of *chang.* On the first day of the new year in Lhasa, pilgrims throng the Jokhang temple to offer butter in the burning lamps. The great incense kilns around the Barkor billow scented smoke as queues of worshipers wait to add offerings of juniper boughs. Everyone dresses in his or her finest clothes to parade around the Barkor. Early in the morning of the third day, pilgrims climb the hills around Lhasa to light fires of incense bush. In town, new colored prayer flags are hung out above each home and small incense fires burn everywhere.

First month, 4th to 26th days: Monlam Chenmo, the Great Prayer Festival. Founded in 1409 by Tsong Khapa to celebrate the miracles performed by Buddha at Sravasti in India, Monlam Chenmo is the greatest ritual event of the year. In former times as many as twenty thousand monks would crowd into Lhasa from the great Gelukpa monasteries for this festival. In the 1980s, more than a thousand monks came for the public and private prayer celebrations held in the Jokhang temple. Monlam Chenmo has been discontinued in Lhasa, but still is held in Amdo at both Labrang and Rongwo Göchen monasteries. But they celebrate it during the first month of the Chinese lunar calendar, not the Tibetan calendar.

First month, 15th day: Chotrül Düchen, the Butter Sculpture Festival. The first full moon of the new year is one of the four annual Great Festivals (*düchen*) celebrating events in the life of Buddha Sakyamuni; in this case it is the Great Miracle the Buddha performed at Sravasti, when he subdued the heretics and taught the *dharma*. In Lhasa, thousands of pilgrims came to see great sculptures made with colored yak butter that have been erected around the Barkor. The sculptures remained all night, then were removed before sunrise the following morning. Although this festival no longer occurs in Lhasa, pilgrims still throng the Barkor to perform *kora* on the first full moon of the year. The butter sculpture tradition remains an integral part of the Monlam Chenmo at Labrang and Rongwo Gönchen monasteries, in Amdo.

First Month, 25th Day: Jampa Dendren, Invitation to the Future Buddha. One of the last events of Monlam Chenmo is an offering to Gyelwa Jampa, the "Future Buddha," requesting his speedy arrival on earth. A silver image of Jampa, which is unveiled only once a year, was carried around the Barkor in a grand procession. In the past, the State Oracle would go into a trance and offer a *katak* to this statue.

Fourth month, 10th day: *Cham* (mask) dances at Tsurphu monastery. On the following day a large *köku* banner of the Buddha Sakyamuni is displayed.

Fourth month, 15th day: Saga Dawa, Buddha's Enlightenment and Ascent to Heaven. The Saga Dawa full moon is one of the four *düchen*, celebrating the enlightenment of Buddha and his attainment of nirvana upon his death. Thousands of pilgrims crowd into the Jokhang, and the Lingkor circumambulation route around Lhasa has a steady flow of worshipers for the entire day. Picnics are very popular, especially near the Lukhang, behind the Potala. In the past, government officials would be rowed in yak-leather coracles around the Lukhang, followed by the public. Many other pilgrimages occur on this day throughout Tibet, such as the circuit around Mount Zodang Gampori in Tsethang.

Fourth month, 15th to 18th days: Ta-gyuk, the Gyangtse Horse Racing Festival. The largest annual festival in Gyangtse, with horseracing, yak races, and *cham*. A fourteenth-century giant appliqué *köku* is hung one morning before sunrise from the tall display wall. This festival also marks the anniversary of the 1904 battle at Gyangtse between Tibetans and Colonel Younghusband's invading British troops.

Fifth month, 14th to 16th days: Tashilhumpo *Thangka* Festival. Immense silk appliqué *köku* banners of Dusum Sangye (the "Buddhas of the Three Times": Öpame, Sakyamuni, and Gyelwa Jampa) are displayed on three consecutive days at Tashilhumpo. *Cham* dancing may be held in the monastery's lower courtyard.

Fifth month, 15th day: Dzamling Chisang, the Universal Incense Offering. Commemoration of Guru Rimpoche subduing the obstructive deities and spirits in Tibet and converting them to protectors of Buddhism, in preparation for the founding of Samye,

Tibet's first Buddhist monastery. Incense billows throughout the country in offering to these deities. *Cham* dances are held at Samye.

Sixth month, 4th day: Drukwa Tsezhi (also called Chökor Düchen), the Fourth of the Sixth Month Festival. This celebration of Buddha "Turning the Wheel of Dharma" (by teaching his first sermon at Deer Park in Sarnath, after achieving enlightenment at Bodhgaya) is one of the four *düchen* and a day of pilgrimage. In Lhasa, a large procession of pilgrims journey from Phabongkha monastery across Phurbu Chokri to Sera Tse hermitage, and on to the Dode Valley. Others climb Gyaphelri, the holy mountain behind Drepung, to make offerings of incense and prayer flags on the summit. A giant silk appliqué *köku* may be displayed at Ganden monastery.

Sixth month, 30th day: Drepung monastery *Thangka* Festival. The huge *köku* is displayed for only a few hours early in the morning on a hill beside Drepung. This marks the start of Zhotön (see below); after the *thangka* comes down, the first opera dances are performed in the main courtyard. Sera monastery now displays a *köku* as well, starting about midday.

Seventh month, 1st to 7th days: Zhotön, the Yogurt (or Opera) Festival. Norbulingka is the scene of a week-long picnic of eating and drinking, with Ache Lhamo (Tibetan opera) performances in the gardens and at other venues around town for the entire week. Don't miss the yak races in the Lhasa stadium!

End of 7th month to middle of 8th month: Chabshuk, the Bathing Festival. Tibetans perform ritual bathing in rivers and lakes for purity and longevity in this thanksgiving festival. People erect tents and come to the rivers for plenty of fun and splashing. The festival starts when the constellation Pleiades (*mindruk*) rises at dawn above Mindruk Tsari, Lhasa's highest peak, converting water into *karchu*, a long-life "star water" ambrosia.

Fresco of Milarepa, Tibet's beloved poet-saint, Pelgyeling monastery

Nun on pilgrimage

Seventh month, 1st to 15th days: Ongkor, the Harvest Festival. Throughout Tibet farmers dress in their finest, carrying prayer texts in processions around the perimeter of their fields and making incense offerings for a good harvest. The day ends with dancing, drinking, and plenty of merriment.

Eighth month, 9th to 11th days: *Cham* **dances at Tashilhumpo.**

Ninth month, 22nd day: Lhabab Düchen, the Gods Descending Festival. One of the four major *düchen* festivals of the year, Lhabab Düchen celebrates Buddha's return to earth after spending three months in heaven teaching Buddhism to his mother and the gods. In Lhasa, throngs of worshipers vie to visit the Jokhang, and pilgrims circumambulate the Barkor and the Lingkor.

Tenth month, 15th day: Pelhe *Ritrö,* **the Pelden Lhamo Feast.** Celebration of the protectress Pelden Lhamo, with special prayer ceremonies at the Jokhang. One of the highlights is the procession around the Barkor with a Pelden Lhamo statue, which otherwise remains covered during the rest of the year.

Tenth month, 25th day: Ganden Ngamchö, the Twenty-fifth Day, the Festival of Lights. Lamps and candles are lit on the rooftops of monasteries and homes to celebrate the death and entry into nirvana of Tsong Khapa, the founder of the Gelukpa sect.

Twelfth month, 30th day: Banishing the Evil Spirits Festival. A day for exorcising the evils from the old year so the new year will begin on a good note. Tibetans busily clean their homes, chasing away the bad spirits to let the benevolent ones come in. *Cham* dances were traditionally held throughout the country on the 29th day; in Central Tibet they now seem to be confined to Tashilhumpo and Tsurphu monasteries on the 30th day, when Tsurphu also displays a giant *köku* banner of the protectors Gompo and Pelden Lhamo.

Ancient rock paintings at Tashi Do, near the shore of Nam Tsho

APPENDICES

A protector's image guarding the entrance to a gönkhang, *Taklung monastery*

APPENDIX A

TREKKING AND MOUNTAINEERING AGENCIES

China Golden Bridge Travel
Attn: Jiang Lin, General Manager
15th Floor, Tongmei Mansion, No. 76, Sect 01
North Jian She Road
Chengdu, Sichuan, People's Republic of China 610051
Phone: 86 28 2510483; Fax: 86 28 3397786

Chinese Mountaineering Association (CMA)
Attn: Ying Daoshui, Vice Secretary General
9 Tiyuguan Road
Beijing, People's Republic of China 100763
Phone: 86 10 67123796; Fax: 86 10 67111629; email: cma@sport.gov.cn

China Sichuan Mountaineering Association
Attn: Su Lihua or Wang Hua Shan
No. 1, Xiaotian Erlu
Chengdu, Sichuan, People's Republic of China 610041
Phone: 86 28 5588046, 5588047; Fax: 86 28 5588042; email: china@public.cd.sc.cn

High Asia Exploratory Mountain Travel Company
Attn: Jon Meisler
Chengdu Office: Phone/Fax: 86 28 5532663
USA Office: Phone/Fax 1-800-809-0034, outside USA 1-970-927-0423
Email: travel@highasia.com; http: www.highasia.com

Holyland Adventures (formerly CWTS-Tibet)
Attn: Thupten Gendun, Vice General Manager
No. 215 Beijing West Road
Lhasa, Tibet, People's Republic of China 850001
Phone/Fax: 86 891 6834472, 6836652; email: holyland@public.ls.xz.cn

Qinghai Mountaineering Association
Attn: Deng Haipong, Vice Secretary General
Number 1 Shan Shaan Tai
Xining, Qinghai, People's Republic of China 810000
Phone: 86 971 8238877, 8238909; Fax: 86 971 8238933

Shigatse Travels
Attn: Dorjee Tashi or Rene Sharma
c/o Yak Hotel, Beijing Dong Lu
Lhasa, Tibet, People's Republic of China 850000
Phone: 86 891 6330489, 6330483; Fax: 86 891 6330482
Email: stsad@public.ls.xz.cn or potala@usa.net

Tibet International Sports Travel (TIST)
Attn: Dawa, Sales and Marketing
No. 6 East Lingkor Road
Lhasa, Tibet, People's Republic of China 850000
Phone: 86 891 6334082, 6331421; Fax: 86 891 6334855
Email: TIST@public.ls.xz.cn

Tibet Mountaineering Association (TMA)
Attn: Yang Zhen, Sales and Marketing
No. 8 East Lingkor Road
Lhasa, Tibet, People's Republic of China 850000
Phone: 0086 891 6333720; Fax: 0086 891 6336366

Windhorse Adventure
Attn: G. T. Sonam, General Manager
No. 1 West Minzu Road
Lhasa, Tibet, People's Republic of China 850001
Phone: 86 891 6833009; Fax: 86 891 6836793
Email: wha@public.ls.xz.cn

Yunnan Mountaineering Association
Attn: Ms. Li Jin-qiu
Kunming, Yunnan, People's Republic of China
Phone: 86 871 3164626; Fax: 86 871 3135246

APPENDIX B

SUGGESTED READING

CULTURE AND RELIGION

Avedon, John. *In Exile from the Land of Snows*. London: Wisdom, 1985.

Chang, Garma C. C. *The Hundred Thousand Songs of Milarepa*. Boston: Shambala, 1989.

Dalai Lama. *Awakening the Mind, Lightening the Heart*. New York: Harper, 1995.

———. *Freedom in Exile: The Autobiography of the Dalai Lama*. London: Hodder and Stoughton, 1990.

Das, Lama Surya. *Awakening the Buddha Within: Tibetan Wisdom for the Western World*. New York: Broadway Books, 1997.

Govinda, Lama Anagarika. *The Way of the White Clouds*. Boston: Prajna, 1985.

Ricard, Mattieu. *The Life of Shabkar: The Autobiography of a Tibetan Yogin*. Albany, NY: State University of New York Press, 1994.

Richardson, Hugh. *Ceremonies of the Lhasa Year*. London: Serindia, 1993.

Vitali, Roberto. *Early Temples of Central Tibet*. London: Serindia, 1990.

Waddell, L. Austine. *Tibetan Buddhism*. New York: Dover, 1972.

GUIDEBOOKS

Armington, Stan, and Sushil Upadhyay. *Humla to Kailas: A Trek from Nepal into Tibet*. Kathmandu: Mandala Book Point, 1993.

Batchelor, Stephen. *The Tibet Guide: Central and Western Tibet*. Sommerville, Mass.: Wisdom, 1998.

Buckley, Michael. *Tibet Travel Adventure Guide*. Vancouver: ITMB, 1999.

Chan, Victor. *Tibet Handbook: A Pilgrimage Guide*. Chico, Calif.: Moon, 1994.

Dorje, Gyurme, ed. *Tibet Handbook*. Bath, England: Trade and Travel, 1999.

Dowman, Keith. *The Power Places of Central Tibet: The Pilgrim's Guide*. London: Routledge and Kegan Paul, 1988.

Mayhew, Bradley. *Tibet: A Lonely Planet Travel Survival Kit*. Sydney: Lonely Planet, 1999.

Pranavananda, Swami. *Kailas Manasarovar*. New Delhi, India, 1949.

HEALTH AND MEDICAL INFORMATION

Bezruchka, Steven. *The Pocket Doctor*, 3d ed. Seattle: The Mountaineers, 1999.

———. *First Aid: Quick Information for Mountaineering and Backcountry Use*. Seattle: The Mountaineers, 1988.

Wilkerson, James A., ed. *Medicine for Mountaineering*. 4th ed. Seattle: The Mountaineers, 1992.

HISTORY AND EXPLORATION

Allen, Charles. *A Mountain in Tibet*. London: Futura Macdonald & Co., 1983.

David-Neel, Alexandra. *My Journey to Lhasa*. London: Virago, 1983.

Goldstein, Melvyn C. *A History of Modern Tibet, 1913–1951: The Demise of the Lamaist State*. Los Angeles: University of California Press, 1989.

Harrer, Heinrich. *Seven Years in Tibet*. London: Pan Books, 1956.

Hopkirk, Peter. *Trespassers on the Roof of the World*. London: Oxford University Press, 1982.

Richardson, Hugh. *High Peaks, Pure Earth*. London: Serindia, 1998.

———. *Tibet and its History*. Boston: Shambala, 1984.

Rock, Joseph. "The Glories of Minya Konka." *National Geographic*, October 1930, 385–437.

Rowell, Galen. *Mountains of the Middle Kingdom*. San Francisco: Sierra Club Books, 1983.

Shakabpa, Tsepon, W. D. *Tibet: A Political History*. New Haven, Conn.: Yale University Press, 1967.

Snellgrove, David, and Hugh Richardson. *A Cultural History of Tibet*. Boulder, Colo.: Prajna Press, 1968.

Snelling, John. *The Sacred Mountain*. London, East West Publications, 1983.

Sutton, Stephanne Barry. *In China's Border Provinces: The Turbulent Career of Joseph Rock, Botanist-Explorer*. New York: Hastings House, 1974.

LANGUAGE BOOKS

Bell, Charles A. *English-Tibetan Colloquial Dictionary*. Calcutta: Firma KLM Pvt. Ltd., 1977.

Bloomfield, Andrew, and Tshering Yangki. *Tibetan Phrasebook*. Ithaca, NY: Snow Lion Publications, 1987. (Includes language cassettes.)

Lay, Dr. Nancy Duke. *Say It in Chinese (Mandarin)*. New York: Dover Publications, 1980.

Thonden, Losang. *Modern Tibetan Language*. 2 vols. Dharamsala, India: Library of Tibetan Works and Archives, 1984. (Language cassettes available separately.)

MOUNTAINEERING

Baume, Louis C. *Sivalaya: Explorations of the 8000-metre Peaks of the Himalaya*. Seattle: The Mountaineers, 1978.

Burdsall, Richard L. and Arthur B. Emmons. *Men Against the Clouds: The Conquest of Minya Konka*. Seattle: The Mountaineers, 1980 (reprint).

Fanshawe, Andy. *Coming Through: Expeditions to Chogolisa and Menlungtse*. London: Hodder and Stoughton, 1990.

Hall, Lincoln. *White Limbo*. Macmahon's Point, Australia: Weldons, 1985.

Howard-Bury, C. K. *Mount Everest: The Reconnaissance, 1921*. London: Edward Arnold, 1922.

Roskelley, John. *Last Days*. London: Hodder and Stoughton, 1992.

Scott, Doug, and Alex MacIntyre. *The Shishapangma Expedition*. Seattle: The Mountaineers, 1984.

Venables, Steven. *Everest: The Kangshung Face*. Bangalore, India: Arnold Publishers, 1989.

NATURAL HISTORY

De Schaunesee, Rudolphe Meyer. *The Birds of China*. Washington, D.C.: Smithsonian Institution Press, 1984.

Fleming, Robert Sr., Robert Fleming Jr., and Lain Singh Bangdel. *Birds of Nepal*. Kathmandu: Nature Himalayas, 1984.

Molnar, Peter. "The Geologic History and Structure of the Himalaya." *American Scientist* 74, (March-April 1986): 144–54.

Polunin, Oleg and Adam Stainton. *Concise Flowers of the Himalaya*. Delhi: Oxford University Press, 1987.

Schaller, George. *Tibet's Hidden Wilderness: Wildlife and Nomads of the Chang Tang Reserve*. New York: Harry N. Abrams, 1997.

———. *Wildlife of the Tibetan Steppe*. University of Chicago Press, 1998.

Vaurie, Charles. *Tibet and its Birds*. London: H. F. and G. Witherby, 1972.

APPENDIX C

GLOSSARY OF TIBETAN AND FOREIGN WORDS

ani	Buddhist nun
ani gompa	Buddhist nunnery
ba	nomadic herder tent made from woven yak hair
bodhisattva (Sanskrit)	(Tib., *changchub sempa*) an enlightened being who has devoted himself to freeing all other beings from suffering
bumpa	offering vase
chaktsal gang	special site where pilgrims prostrate
cham	religious mask dances performed by monks
chang	Tibetan beer, usually brewed from barley
chinlap	(Sanskrit, *prasad*) a blessing from a holy site
chörten	traditionally a domelike or conical monument, set on a square base and topped by a long spire; it may contain sacred objects, funeral remains, or *tsha-tshas*
chu	water, river, or stream
drokpa	nomadic herder
drubphuk	meditation cave
dukhang	assembly hall in a monastery for recitation of prayers
Dusum Sangye	the Buddhas of the Three Times (Past: Öpame; Present: Sakyamuni Buddha; Future: Gyelwa Jampa)
dzong	fortress
gompa	monastery
gönkhang	special place or protector's temple in a monastery where the *gompo* is worshipped
go-nyer	"door keeper" of a temple or monastery
Guru Tsengye	the eight manifestations of Guru Rimpoche
katak	silk offering scarf
khandroma	(Sanskrit, *dakini*) a female Buddhist spirit
khangtsen	monks' residence hall
köku	giant silk appliqué *thangka* displayed at religious festivals
kora	pilgrimage ritual of encircling a sacred place, such as a shrine, monastery, or mountain; used loosely in this text to refer to a route used by pilgrims
la	mountain pass
la-dze	votive pile of stones, often found on mountain passes
lama	highly educated monk
lhakhang	"house of the deity"; a temple
lu	serpent protectors residing in springs, rocks, and the earth
mandala (Sanskrit)	(Tib., *kyilkhor*; lit., magic circle) a geometric diagram used to worship deities or for meditation
mani	prayer, or related to prayers; also used as a term for a prayer wheel or a wall with carved prayer stones
mani khang	building with a revolving prayer wheel inside

mantra (Sanskrit)	(Tib., *ngak*) special type of sound, syllable, or oral prayer, usually associated with a specific Tantric ritual or deity
momo	steamed or boiled dumpling containing meat
Neten Chu-druk	The Sixteen *Arhats* (Elders), contemporaries of Sakyamuni Buddha who attained spiritual perfection
ngakpa	noncelibate Buddhist lay practitioner
Nye-we Sechen Gye	The Eight Great *Bodhisattvas* of Tibetan Buddhism, usually portrayed as standing figures flanking Sakyamuni Buddha
Om mani padme hum	"Hail to the jewel in the lotus"; the *mantra* of Chenrezik, the *Bodhisattva* of Compassion and Tibet's patron saint
phuk	cave
podrang	lit., palace; residence for the incarnate *lama* of a monastery
qu (Chi.)	(Tib. *chu*) former Chinese village-level administration center
rangjön	self-manifested; especially statues, or letters and words in rock
rimpoche	lit., precious; a title used for learned, often incarnate *lamas*
Risum Gompo	Protectors of the Three Families; a triad of *bodhisattvas* representing wisdom (Jampeyang), compassion (Chenrezik) and power (Chakna Dorje)
ritrö	hermitage or religious retreat
shang (Chi.)	lowest level of Chinese village administration
shuktri	the throne or raised platform for a *lama*
sung-jolma	something that possesses the power of speech (often a statue)
sungma	guardian protector of a building, temple or geographic area
tantra (Sanskrit)	(Tib., *gyu*; lit., thread or continuity) a specialized form of meditation and ritual teaching; a "quick path" to enlightenment
terma	hidden treasures, usually prayer texts or teachings
thangka	Tibetan scroll painting
thukpa	Tibetan stew, often with meat and some type of noodle
trülku	an incarnate *lama*
tsampa	toasted barley flour, the staple food for most Tibetans
tsha-tsha	a clay offering tablet often imprinted with religious figures
tsho	lake
xian (Chi.)	Chinese county-level administrative center
yab-se-sum	the "three fathers" of the Gelukpa sect, Tsong Khapa and his two main disciples, Gyeltsab Je and Khedrub Je
yab-yum	the union of male (*yab*) and female (*yum*) energy
yidam	a guardian deity for a person or a sect of Tibetan Buddhism
yuan (Chi.)	Chinese dollar
zhabje	footprint; a religiously significant print, often imbedded in rock

APPENDIX D

MOUNTAINEERING PEAKS IN TIBET

PEAKS IN THE TIBET AUTONOMOUS REGION (TAR)

THE MOUNT EVEREST-SHISHAPANGMA REGION (DINGRI/ NYELAM COUNTIES)

Mount Everest (Chomolangma; Chi., Qomolangma): 29,028 ft, 8848 m
Lhotse: 27,939 ft, 8516 m
Makalu: 27,765 ft, 8463 m
Cho Oyu (Jobo Uyok; Chi., Chowuyo): 26,748 ft, 8153 m
Shishapangma (Shixiapangma): 26,286 ft, 8012 m
Gyachung Gang (Gyelchongkang): 26,197 ft, 7985 m
Pholha Gangchen (Molamenchen): 25,272 ft, 7703 m
Changtse (Zhangzi or Jangzi): 24,747 ft, 7543 m
Lapchi Gang (Labchikang): 24,170 ft, 7367 m
Cho Oye (Cho Aui or Nangpai Gosum 2; Chi., Chowuyi): 24,117 ft, 7351 m
Mount Siguang: 23,976 ft, 7308 m
Shifeng (also Nubzi; possibly also known as Porong Ri): 23,924 ft, 7292 m
Gangbenchen (Kangbochen): 23,888 ft, 7281 m
Khartaphu (Mount Khadhaphu): 23,710 ft, 7227 m
Mount Nadhangri: 23,638 ft, 7205 m
Menlungtse (Meilongze): 23,559 ft, 7181 m
Pumori (Mount Phumari): 23,523 ft, 7170
Gauri Shankar (Jomo Tseringma; Chi., Mount Tashetseringma): 23,405 ft, 7134 m
Mount Lixin: 23,199 ft, 7071 m
Mount Chowusha: 23,038 ft, 7022 m
Mount Xiangdong: 23,025 ft, 7018 m
Mount Balung: 23,008 ft, 7013 m
Kelagangri (Telakangri): 21,870 ft, 6666 m
Mount Donakposang: 21,611 ft, 6587 m
Mount Namtshori: 21,443 ft, 6536 m
Tsangla (Zangia): 21,309 ft, 6495 m
Pulerri: 21,010 ft, 6404 m

SOUTHERN TIBET/BHUTAN BORDER REGION (LHODRAK/ TSONA COUNTIES)

Kula Gangri: 24,731 ft, 7538 m
Gangkeduo Rize (Kanggado; Kang To): 23,162 ft, 7060 m

NORTH OF LHASA (DAMZHUNG COUNTY)

Nyenchen Thanglha (Nychenthangla): 23,330 ft, 7111 m
Mount Samdinggangsar: 21,620 ft, 6590 m
Mount Khitsi: 20,361 ft, 6206 m
Mount Luktse: 20,190 ft, 6154 m

EAST OF LHASA (MINLIN COUNTY)
Gyalwa Peri (Mount Chialabailei): 23,481 ft, 7151 m

CENTRAL TIBET (NAKARTSE COUNTY)
Nechinkangsang (Nychenkangsa): 23,641 ft, 7206 m
Mount Lakuekangri: 21,184 ft, 6457 m
Jangsanglamo (Jiang Sanglamo): 20,748 ft, 6324 m
Jei Tongsusong (Jeidhongsusong): 20,485 ft, 6244 m
Mount Shiemakuo: 20,144 ft, 6140 m
Mount Khadhajopho: 20,052 ft, 6112 m

WESTERN TIBET (ALI, ZHONGBA, COQEN COUNTIES)
Gurla Mandata (Namonani): 25,242 ft, 7694 m
Mount Nobugangri (Loinbo Kangri): 23,277 ft, 7095 m
Shar Gang Sum (Mount Xiakangsum): 22,382 ft, 6822 m

PEAKS OF THE OUTER TIBETAN PLATEAU

QINGHAI PROVINCE
Buka Dabam (Mount Xinxing), Kun Lun Range: 22,506 ft, 6860 m
Mount Geladaindong, Tangula Range: 21,722 ft, 6621 m
Mount Gar Gangri, Tangula Range: 21,368 ft, 6513 m
Amnye Machen (Mount Machen Kangri), Kun Lun Range: 20,610 ft, 6282 m
Mount Tangula, Tangula Range: 20,357 ft, 6205 m

SICHUAN PROVINCE
Minyak Gangkar (Gongga Shan), Da Xue Range: 24,790 ft, 7556 m
Kula Shidak (Mount Siguniang), Qionglai Range: 20,505 ft, 6250 m
Mount Genyen, Shaluli Range: 20,357 ft, 6205 m
Trola (Que-er Shan/Chola Shan), Trola Range: 20,236 ft, 6168 m
Shar Dung Ri (Mount Xue Bao Ding), Min Shan Range: 18,333 ft, 5588 m

YUNNAN PROVINCE
Khawa Karpo (Mount Meili Xue Shan), Lu Shan Range: 22,113 ft, 6740m
Peak 6509 m, Lu Shan Range: 21,355 ft, 6509 m
Mount Larixiangka, Lu Shan Range: 20,928 ft, 6379 m
Peak 6145 m, Lu Shan Range: 20,160 ft, 6145 m
Yulong Xue Shan, Yu Ling Shan Range: 18,359 ft, 5596 m

INDEX

ABOUT THE MOUNTAINEERS

Founded in 1906, The Mountaineers is a Seattle-based nonprofit outdoor activity and conservation club with 15,000 members, whose mission is "to explore, study, preserve, and enjoy the natural beauty of the outdoors . . . . " The club sponsors many classes and year-round outdoor activities in the Pacific Northwest, and supports environmental causes by sponsoring legislation and presenting educational programs. The Mountaineers Books supports the club's mission by publishing travel and natural history guides, instructional texts, and works on conservation and history. For information, call or write The Mountaineers, Club Headquarters, 300 Third Avenue West, Seattle, Washington, 98119; (206) 284-6310.

ABOUT THE AUTHOR

Gary McCue is a freelance trekking guide in the Himalaya and Tibet. He has been based in Kathmandu since 1984, the same year he made the first of his many visits to Tibet. McCue's background in environmental science has served him in a variety of avocations, including working as a backcountry ranger, directing a recycling and environmental action center, teaching, and working as a whitewater rafting guide. His travels have taken him from the Rockies and the Sierras to South America, New Zealand, Australia, Indonesia, South East Asia, India, Pakistan, China, Mongolia, and many of the mountainous regions of the former Soviet Union.

(Photo by Kathy Butler)

Praise for
CAMPFIRE CHILLERS

"Campers who delight in sharing ghoulish tales around a crackling campfire can quench their most eerie thirsts with **Campfire Chillers.**"
—*McCall's* magazine

"A collection of nine tales you'll wish you hadn't read."
—The *Charlotte Observer*

"If your gang is running out of cliff-hanging stories around the campfire . . . take heart. . . . here's an aid you can whip out and read by firelight that'll scare 'em to death."
—*Four Wheeler* magazine

CAMPFIRE CHILLERS

THE CLASSICS
EDITED BY E. M. FREEMAN

The Globe Pequot Press

Old Saybrook, Connecticut

"Mrs. Amworth" appeared originally in *Visible and Invisible* by E. F. Benson. Reprinted with permission of A. P. Watt Ltd. and the estate of E. F. Benson.

"The Monkey's Paw" appeared originally in *Selected Short Stories* by W. W. Jacobs. Reprinted with permission of The Bodley Head.

"Where Angels Fear" by Manley Wade Wellman was published originally by Street & Smith Publications Inc., copyright © 1939. Copyright renewed in 1967 by Conde Nast Publications Inc. Reprinted with permission of Conde Nast Publications Inc.

"The Wendigo" appeared originally in *The Lost Valley and Other Stories* by Algernon Blackwood, copyright © 1917 by Alfred A. Knopf. Reprinted with permission of A. P. Watt Ltd. and the estate of Algernon Blackwood.

Library of Congress Cataloging-in-Publication Data

Campfire chillers : the classics / edited by E. M. Freeman.
    p.   cm.
  "An East Woods book."
  ISBN 1-56440-475-7
  1. Ghost stories, English.   2. Ghost stories, American.
3. Supernatural--Fiction. I. Freeman, E. M., 1949- .
PR1309.G5C3   1994
823' .0873308--dc20   94-1918
                                           CIP

Illustrations by Bill Reaske
Cover design by Schwartzman Graphic Design

♻ This book is printed on recycled paper.
Manufactured in the United States of America
Revised Edition/Sixth Printing

Contents

Introduction

No camping trip is complete without a "campfire chiller," a ghost story or tale of the supernatural which is shared around the campfire. Ghost stories are a campfire institution—like roasting marshmallows—appreciated by young and old alike.

This collection of classic tales has been compiled specifically for campers and those with a high tolerance for the bizarre. Several of the stories center around camping trips or occurrences experienced at night; they will all enhance your feeling of night-time isolation. You will find yourself listening intently to the sounds around you, your eyes will strain to see in the darkness, your pulse will quicken.

The stories vary in length, but most are ten to twelve pages and very suitable for story telling or reading aloud. Their power is heightened when presented in this manner.

A final note before you begin. Even with our monumental strides in science and technology, none of the events related in these classics has been explained. These tales may be classified as fiction . . . but in the woods, in the dark, strange things have been known to happen. Turn the page and begin reading and you will understand what we mean.

E. M. Freeman

THE BLACK CAT

Edgar Allan Poe (1809–1849)

The work of Edgar Allan Poe, American poet, storywriter, and essayist, reflects the tempestuous and tortured life that he led. Born in Boston to an American actor and English actress, he was early orphaned and spent a harsh and unloved childhood with adoptive parents. His adult life consisted of a constant struggle to maintain a balance of sanity; nevertheless, he managed to become one of America's foremost men of letters and is acknowledged as the founder of the modern detective story.

For the most wild yet most homely narrative which I am about to pen, I neither expect nor solicit belief. Mad indeed would I be to expect it, in a case where my very senses reject their own evidence. Yet, mad am I not—and very surely do I not dream. But to-morrow I die, and to-day I would unburden my soul. My immediate purpose is to place before the world, plainly, succinctly, and without comment, a series of mere household events. In their consequences, these events have terrified—have tortured—have destroyed me. Yet I will not attempt to expound them. To me, they have presented little but horror—to many they will seem less terrible than *baroques*. Hereafter, perhaps, some intellect may be found which will reduce my phantasm to the commonplace—some intellect more calm, more logical, and far less excitable than my own, which will perceive, in the circumstances I detail with awe, nothing more than an ordinary succession of very natural causes and effects.

From my infancy I was noted for the docility and humanity of my disposition. My tenderness of heart was even so conspicuous as to make me the jest of my companions. I was especially fond of animals, and was indulged by my parents with a great variety of pets. With these I spent most of my time, and never was so happy as when feeding and caressing them. This peculiarity of character grew with my growth, and, in my manhood, I derived from it one of my principal sources of pleasure. To those who have cherished an affection for a faithful and sagacious dog, I need hardly be at the trouble of explaining the nature or the intensity of the gratification thus derivable. There is something in the unselfish and self-sacrificing love of a brute, which goes directly to the heart of him who has had frequent occasion to test the paltry friendship and gossamer fidelity of mere *Man*.

I married early, and was happy to find in my wife a disposition not uncongenial with my own. Observing my partiality for domestic pets, she lost no opportunity of procuring those of the most agreeable kind. We had birds, gold-fish, a fine dog, rabbits, a small monkey, and a cat.

This latter was a remarkably large and beautiful animal, entirely black, and sagacious to an astonishing degree. In speaking of his intelligence, my wife, who at heart was not a little tinctured with superstition, made frequent allusion to the ancient popular notion, which regarded all black cats as witches in disguise. Not that she was ever *serious* upon this point—and I mention the matter at all for no better reason than that it happens, just now, to be remembered.

Pluto—this was the cat's name—was my favorite pet and playmate. I alone fed him, and he attended me wherever I went about the house. It was even with difficulty that I could prevent him from following me through the streets.

Our friendship lasted, in this manner, for several years, during which my general temperament and character—through the instrumentality of the Fiend Intemperance—had (I blush to confess it) experienced a radical alteration for the worse. I grew, day by day, more moody, more irritable, more regardless of the feelings of others. I suffered myself to use intemperate language to my wife. At length, I even offered her personal violence. My pets, of course, were made to feel the change in my disposition. I not only neglected, but ill-used them. For Pluto, however, I still retained sufficient regard to restrain me from maltreating him, as I made no scruple of maltreating the rabbits, the monkey, or even the dog, when, by accident, or through affection, they came in my way. But my disease grew upon me—for what disease is like Alcohol!—and at length even Pluto, who was now becoming old, and consequently somewhat peevish—even Pluto began to experience the effects of my ill temper.

One night, returning home, much intoxicated, from one of my haunts about town, I fancied that the cat avoided my presence. I seized him; when, in his fright at my violence, he inflicted a slight wound upon my hand with his teeth. The fury of a demon instantly possessed me. I knew myself no longer. My original soul seemed, at once, to take its flight from my body; and a more than fiendish malevolence, gin-nurtured, thrilled every fibre of my frame. I took from my waistcoat-pocket a penknife, opened it, grasped the poor beast by the throat, and deliberately cut one of its eyes from the socket! I blush, I burn, I shudder, while I pen the damnable atrocity.

When reason returned with the morning—when I had slept off the fumes of the night's debauch—I experienced a sentiment half of horror, half of remorse, for the crime of which I had been guilty; but it was, at best, a feeble and equivocal feeling, and the soul remained untouched. I again plunged into excess, and soon drowned in wine all memory of the deed.

In the meantime the cat slowly recovered. The socket of the lost eye presented, it is true, a frightful appearance, but he no longer appeared to suffer any pain. He went about the house as usual, but, as might be expected, fled in extreme terror at my approach. I had so much of my old heart left, as to be at first grieved by this evident dislike on the part of a creature which had once so loved me. But this feeling soon gave place to irritation. And then came, as if to my final and irrevocable overthrow, the spirit of PERVERSENESS. Of this spirit philosophy takes no account. Yet I am not more sure that my soul lives, than I am that perverseness is one of the primitive impulses of the human heart—one of the indivisible primary faculties, or sentiments, which give direction to the character of Man. Who has not, a hundred times, found himself committing a vile or a stupid action, for no other reason than because he knows he should *not*? Have we not a perpetual inclination, in the teeth of our best judgment, to violate that which is *Law*, merely because we understand it to be such? This spirit of perverseness, I say, came to my final overthrow. It was this unfathomable longing of the soul to vex *itself*—to offer violence to its own nature—to do wrong for the wrong's sake only—that urged me to continue and finally consummate the injury I had inflicted upon the unoffending brute. One morning, in cold blood, I slipped a noose about its neck and hung it to the limb of a tree;—hung it with the tears streaming from my eyes, and with the bitterest remorse at my heart;—hung it because I knew that it had loved me, and because I felt it had given me no reason of offense;—hung it because I knew that in so doing I was committing a sin—a deadly sin that would so jeopardize my immortal soul as to place it—if such a thing were possible—even beyond the reach of the infinite mercy of the Most Merciful and Most Terrible God.

On the night of the day on which this most cruel deed was done, I was aroused from sleep by the cry of fire. The curtains of my bed were in flames. The whole house was blazing. It was with great difficulty that my wife, a servant, and myself, made our escape from the conflagration. The destruction was complete. My entire worldly wealth was swallowed up, and I resigned myself thenceforward to despair.

I am above the weakness of seeking to establish a sequence of cause and effect between the disaster and the atrocity. But I am detailing a chain of facts—and wish not to leave even a possible link imperfect. On the day succeeding the fire, I visited the ruins. The walls, with one exception, had fallen in. This exception was found in a compartment wall, not very thick, which stood about the middle of my house, and against which has rested the head of my bed. The plastering had here, in great measure, resisted the action of the fire—a fact which I attributed to its having been recently spread. About this wall a dense crowd were collected, and many persons seemed to be examining a particular portion of it with very minute and eager attention. The words "strange!" "singular!" and other similar expressions, excited my curiosity. I approached and saw, as if graven in *bas-relief* upon the white surface, the figure of a gigantic cat. The impression was given with an accuracy truly marvellous. There was a rope about the animal's neck.

When I first beheld this apparition—for I could scarcely regard it as less—my wonder and my terror were extreme. But at length reflection came to my aid. The cat, I remembered, had been hung in a garden adjacent to the house. Upon the alarm of fire, this garden had been immediately filled by the crowd—by some one of whom the animal must have been cut from the tree and thrown through an open window, into my chamber. This had probably been done with the view of arousing me from sleep. The falling of other walls had compressed the victim of my cruelty into the substance of the freshly-spread plaster; the lime of which, with the flames, and the *ammonia* from the carcass, had then accomplished the portraiture as I saw it.

Although I thus readily accounted to my reason, if not altogether to my conscience, for the startling fact just detailed, it did not the less fail to make a deep impression upon my fancy. For months I could not rid myself of the phantasm of the cat; and, during this period, there came back into my spirit a half-sentiment that seemed, but was not, remorse. I went so far as to regret the loss of the animal, and to look about me, among the vile haunts which I now habitually frequented, for another pet of the same species, and of somewhat similar appearance, with which to supply its place.

One night as I sat, half stupefied, in a den of more than infamy, my attention was suddenly drawn to some black object, reposing upon the head of one of the immense hogsheads of gin, or of rum, which constituted the chief furniture of the apartment. I had been looking steadily at the top of this hogshead for some minutes, and what now caused me surprise was the fact that I had not sooner perceived the object thereupon. I approached it, and touched it with my hand. It was a black cat—a very large one— fully as large as Pluto, and closely resembling him in every respect but one. Pluto had not a white hair upon any portion of his body; but this cat had a large, although indefinite splotch of white, covering the whole region of the breast.

Upon my touching him, he immediately arose, purred loudly, rubbed against my hand, and appeared delighted with my notice. This, then, was the very creature of which I was in search. I at once offered to purchase it of the landlord; but this person made no claim to it—knew nothing of it—had never seen it before.

I continued my caresses, and when I prepared to go home, the animal evinced a disposition to accompany me. I permitted it to do so; occasionally stooping and patting it as I proceeded. When it reached the house it domesticated itself at once, and became immediately a great favorite with my wife.

For my own part, I soon found a dislike to it arising within me. This was just the reverse of what I had anticipated; but—I know not how or why it was—its evident fondness for myself rather disgusted and annoyed me. By slow degrees these feelings of disgust and annoyance rose into the bitterness of hatred. I avoided the creature; a certain sense of shame, and the remembrance of my former deed of cruelty, preventing me from physically abusing it. I did not, for some weeks, strike, or otherwise violently ill use it; but gradually—very gradually—I came to look upon it with unutterable loathing, and to flee silently from its odious presence, as from the breath of a pestilence.

What added, no doubt, to my hated of the beast, was the discovery, on the morning after I brought it home, that, like Pluto, it also had been deprived of one of its eyes. This circumstance, however, only endeared it to my wife, who, as I have already said, possessed, in a high degree, that humanity of feeling which had once been my distinguishing trait, and the source of many of my simplest and purest pleasures.

With my aversion to this cat, however, its partiality for myself seemed to increase. It followed my footsteps with a pertinacity which it would be difficult to make the reader comprehend. Whenever I sat, it would crouch beneath my chair, or spring upon my knees, covering me with its loathsome caresses. If I arose to walk it would get between my feet and thus nearly throw me down, or, fastening its long and sharp claws in my dress, clamber, in this manner, to my breast. At such times, although I longed to destroy it with a blow, I was yet withheld from so doing, partly by a memory of my former crime, but chiefly—let me confess it at once—by absolute *dread* of the beast.

This dread was not exactly a dread of physical evil—and yet I should be at a loss how otherwise to define it. I am almost ashamed to own—yes, even in this felon's cell, I am almost ashamed to own—that the terror and horror with which the animal inspired me, had been heightened by one of the merest chimeras it would be possible to conceive. My wife had called my attention, more than once, to the character of the mark of white hair, of which I have spoken, and which constituted the sole visible difference between the strange beast and the one I had destroyed. The reader will remember that this mark, although large, had been originally very indefinite; but, by slow degrees—degrees nearly imperceptible, and which for a long time my reason struggled to reject as fanciful—it had, at length, assumed a rigorous distinctness of outline. It was now the representation of an object that I shudder to name—and for this, above all, I loathed, and dreaded, and would have rid myself of the monster *had I dared*—it was now, I say, the image of a hideous—of a ghastly thing—of the GALLOWS!—oh, mournful and terrible engine of Horror and of Crime—of Agony and of Death!

And now was I indeed wretched beyond the wretchedness of mere Humanity. And *a brute beast*—whose fellow I had contemptuously destroyed—*a brute beast* to work for *me*—for me, a man fashioned in the image of the High God—so much of insufferable woe! Alas! neither by day nor by night knew I the blessing of rest anymore! During the former the creature left me no moment alone, and in the latter I started hourly from dreams of unutterable fear to find the hot breath of *the thing* upon my face, and its vast weight—an incarnate nightmare that I had no power to shake off—incumbent eternally upon my *heart!*

Beneath the pressure of torments such as these the feeble remnant of the good within me succumbed. Evil thoughts became my sole intimates—the darkest and most evil of thoughts. The moodiness of my usual temper increased to hatred of all things and of all mankind; while from the sudden, frequent, and ungovernable outbursts of a fury to which I now blindly abandoned myself, my uncomplaining wife, alas, was the most usual and the most patient of sufferers.

One day she accompanied me, upon some household errand, into the cellar of the old building which our poverty compelled us to inhabit. The cat followed me down the steep stairs, and nearly throwing me headlong, exasperated me to madness. Uplifting an axe, and forgetting in my wrath the childish dread which had hitherto stayed my hand, I aimed a blow at the animal, which, of course, would have proved instantly fatal had it descended as I wished. But this blow was arrested by the hand of my wife. Goaded by the interference into a rage more than demoniacal, I withdrew my arm from her grasp and buried the axe in her brain. She fell dead upon the spot without a groan.

The hideous murder accomplished, I set myself forthwith, and with entire deliberation, to the task of concealing the body. I knew that I could not remove it from the house, either by day or by night, without the risk of being observed by the neighbors. Many projects entered my mind. At one period I thought of cutting the corpse into minute fragments, and destroying them by fire. At another, I resolved to dig a grave for it in the floor of the cellar. Again, I deliberated about casting it in the well in the yard—about packing it in a box, as if merchandise, with the usual arrangements, and so getting a porter to take it from the house. Finally I hit upon what I considered a far better expedient than either of these. I determined to wall it up in the cellar, as the monks of the Middle Ages are recorded to have walled up their victims.

For a purpose such as this the cellar was well adapted. Its walls were loosely constructed, and had lately been plastered throughout with a rough plaster, which the dampness of the atmosphere had prevented from hardening. Moreover, in one of the walls was a projection, caused by a false chimney, or fireplace, that had been filled up and made to resemble the rest of the cellar. I made no doubt that I could readily displace the bricks at this point, insert the corpse, and wall the whole up as before, so that no eye could detect anything suspicious.

And in this calculation I was not deceived. By means of a crowbar I easily dislodged the bricks, and, having carefully deposited the body against the inner wall, I propped it in that position, while with little trouble I relaid the whole structure as it originally stood. Having procured mortar, sand, and hair, with every possible precaution, I prepared a plaster which could not be distinguished from the old, and with this I very carefully went over the new brick-work. When I had finished, I felt satisfied that all was right. The wall did not present the slightest appearance of having been disturbed. The rubbish on the floor was picked up with the minutest care. I looked around triumphantly, and said to myself: "Here at least, then, my labor has not been in vain."

My next step was to look for the beast which had been the cause of so much wretchedness; for I had, at length, firmly resolved to put it to death. Had I been able to meet with it at the moment, there could have been no doubt of its fate; but it appeared that the crafty animal had been alarmed at the violence of my previous anger, and forbore to present itself in my present mood. It is impossible to describe or to imagine the deep, the blissful sense of relief which the absence of the detested creature occasioned in my bosom. It did not make its appearance during the night; and thus for one night, at least, since its introduction into the house, I soundly and tranquilly slept; aye, *slept* even with the burden of murder upon my soul.

The second and the third day passed, and still my tormentor came not. Once again I breathed as a freeman. The monster, in terror, had fled the premises for ever! I should behold it no more! My happiness was supreme! The guilt of my dark deed disturbed me but little. Some few inquiries had been made, but these had been readily answered. Even a search had been instituted—but of course nothing was to be discovered. I looked upon my future felicity as secured.

Upon the fourth day of the assassination, a party of the police came, very unexpectedly, into the house, and proceeded again to make rigorous investigation of the premises. Secure, however, in the inscrutability of my place of concealment, I felt no embarrassment whatever. The officers bade me accompany them in their search. They left no nook or corner unexplored. At length, for the third or fourth time, they descended into the cellar. I quivered not a muscle. My heart beat calmly as that of one who slumbers in innocence. I walked the cellar from end to end. I folded my arms upon my bosom, and roamed easily to and fro. The police were thoroughly satisfied and prepared to depart. The glee at my heart was too strong to be restrained. I burned to say if but one word, by way of triumph, and to render doubly sure their assurance of my guiltlessness.

"Gentlemen," I said at last, as the party ascended the steps, "I delight to have allayed your suspicions. I wish you all health and a little more courtesy. By the bye, gentlemen, this—this is a very well-constructed house," (in the rabid desire to say something easily, I scarcely knew what I uttered at all),—"I may say an *excellently* well-constructed house. These walls—are you going gentlemen?—these walls are solidly put together;" and here, through the mere frenzy of bravado, I rapped heavily with a cane which I held in my hand, upon that very portion of the brick-work behind which stood the corpse of the wife of my bosom.

But may God shield and deliver me from the fangs of the Arch-Fiend! No sooner had the reverberation of my blows sunk into silence, than I was answered by a voice from within the tomb!—by a cry, at first muffled and broken, like the sobbing of a child, and then quickly swelling into one long, loud, and continuous scream utterly anomalous and inhuman—a howl—a wailing shriek, half of horror and half of triumph, such as might have arisen only out of hell, conjointly from the throats of the damned in their agony and the demons that exult in the damnation.

Of my own thoughts it is folly to speak. Swooning, I staggered to the opposite wall. For one instant the party on the stairs remained motionless, through extremity of terror and awe. In the next a dozen stout arms were toiling at the wall. It fell bodily. The corpse, already greatly decayed and clotted with gore, stood erect before the eyes of the spectators. Upon its head, with red extended mouth and solitary eye of fire, sat the hideous beast whose craft had seduced me into murder, and whose informing voice had consigned me to the hangman. I had walled the monster up within the tomb.

MRS. AMWORTH

E. F. Benson (1867–1940)

Born into an illustrious and well-to-do British family, E. F. Benson was a person of many and varied interests. While known primarily for his literary endeavors, he was a competent archeological scholar and an active local politician.

The village of Maxley, where, last summer and autumn, these strange events took place, lies on a heathery and pineclad upland of Sussex. In all England you could not find a sweeter and saner situation. Should the wind blow from the south, it comes laden with the spices of the sea; to the east high downs protect it from the inclemencies of March; and from the west and north the breezes which reach it travel over miles of aromatic forest and heather. The village itself is insignificant enough in point of population, but rich in amenities and beauty. Half-way down the single street, with its broad road and spacious areas of grass on each side, stands the little Norman Church and the antique graveyard long disused: for the rest there are a dozen small, sedate Georgian houses, red-bricked and long-windowed, each with a square of flower garden in front, and an ampler strip behind; a score of shops, and a couple of score of thatched cottages belonging to labourers on neighbouring estates, complete the entire cluster of its peaceful habitations. The general peace, however, is sadly broken on Saturdays and Sundays, for we lie on one of the main roads between London and Brighton and our quiet street becomes a race-course for flying motor-cars and bicycles. A notice just outside the village begging them to go slowly only seems to encourage them to accelerate their speed, for the road lies open and straight, and there is really no reason why they should do otherwise. By way of protest, therefore, the ladies of Maxley cover their noses and mouths with their handkerchiefs as they see a motor-car approaching, though, as the street is asphalted, they need not really take these precautions against dust. But late on Sunday night the horde of scorchers has passed, and we settle down again to five days of cheerful and leisurely seclusion. Railway strikes which agitate the country so much leave us undisturbed because most of the inhabitants of Maxley never leave it at all.

I am the fortunate possessor of one of these small Georgian houses, and consider myself no less fortunate in having so interesting and stimulating a neighbour as Francis Urcombe, who, the most confirmed of Maxleyites, has not slept away from his house, which stands just opposite to mine in the village street, for nearly two years, at which date, though still in middle life, he resigned his Physiological Professorship at Cambridge University, and devoted himself to the study of those occult and curious phenomena which seem equally to concern the physical and psychical sides of human nature. Indeed his retirement was not unconnected with his passion for the strange uncharted places that lie on the confines and borders of science, the existence of which is so stoutly denied by the more materialistic minds, for he advocated that all medical students should be obliged to pass some sort of examination in mesmerism, and that one of the tripos papers should be designed to test their knowledge in such subjects as appearances at time of death, haunted houses, vampirism, automatic writing, and possession.

"Of course they wouldn't listen to me," ran his account of the matter, "for there is nothing that these seats of learning are so frightened of as knowledge, and the road to knowledge lies in the study of things like these. The functions of the human frame are, broadly speaking, known. They are a country, anyhow, that has been charted and mapped out. But outside that lie huge tracts of undiscovered country, which certainly exist, and the real pioneers of knowledge are those who, at the cost of being derided as credulous and superstitious, want to push on into those misty and probably perilous places. I felt that I could be of more use by setting out without compass or knapsack into the mists than by sitting in a cage like a canary and chirping about what was known. Besides, teaching is very very bad for a man who knows himself only to be a learner: you only need to be a self-conceited ass to teach."

Here, then, in Francis Urcombe, was a delightful neighbour to one who, like myself, has an uneasy and burning curiosity about what he called the "misty and perilous places;" and this last spring we had a further and most welcome addition to our pleasant little community in the person of Mrs. Amworth, widow of an Indian civil servant. Her husband had been a judge in the North-West Provinces, and after his death at Peshawar she came back to England, and after a year in London found herself starving for the ampler air and sunshine of the country to take the place of the fogs and griminess of town. She had, too, a special reason for settling in Maxley, since her ancestors up till a hundred years ago had long been native to the place, and in the old churchyard, now disused, are many gravestones bearing her maiden name of Chaston. Big and energetic, her vigorous and genial personality speedily woke

Maxley up to a higher degree of sociality than it had ever known. Most of us were bachelors or spinsters or elderly folk not much inclined to exert ourselves in the expense and effort of hospitality, and hitherto the gaiety of a small tea party, with bridge afterwards and galoshes (when it was wet) to trip home in again for a solitary dinner, was about the climax of our festivities. But Mrs. Amworth showed us a more gregarious way, and set an example of luncheon parties and little dinners, which we began to follow. On other nights when no such hospitality was on foot, a lone man like myself found it pleasant to know that a call on the telephone to Mrs. Amworth's house not a hundred yards off, and an enquiry as to whether I might come over after dinner for a game of piquet before bedtime, would probably evoke a response of welcome. There she would be, with a comradelike eagerness for companionship, and there was a glass of port and a cup of coffee and a cigarette and a game of piquet. She played the piano, too, in a free and exuberant manner, and had a charming voice and sang to her own accompaniment; and as the days grew long and the light lingered late, we played our game in her garden, which in the course of a few months she had turned from being a nursery for slugs and snails into a glowing patch of luxuriant blossomings. She was always cheery and jolly; she was interested in everything; and in music, in gardening, in games of all sorts was a competent performer. Everybody (with one exception) liked her, everybody felt her to bring with her the tonic of a sunny day. That one exception was Francis Urcombe; he, though he confessed he did not like her, acknowledged that he was vastly interested in her. This always seemed strange to me, for pleasant and jovial as she was, I could see nothing in her that could call forth conjecture or intrigued surmise, so healthy and unmysterious a figure did she present. But of the genuineness of Urcombe's interest there could be no doubt; one could see him watching and scrutinizing her. In matter of age, she frankly volunteered the information that she was forty-five; but her briskness, her activity, her unravaged skin, her coal-black hair, made it difficult to believe that she was not adopting an unusual device, and adding ten years on to her age instead of subtracting them.

Often, also, as our quite unsentimental friendship ripened, Mrs. Amworth would ring me up and propose her advent. If I was busy writing, I was to give her, so we definitely bargained, a frank negative, and in answer I could hear her jolly laugh and her wishes for a successful evening of work. Sometimes, before her proposal arrived, Urcombe would already have stepped across from his house opposite for a smoke and a chat, and he, hearing who my intended visitor was, always urged me to beg her to come. She and I should play our piquet, said he, and he would look on, if we did not object, and learn something of the game. But I doubt whether he paid much attention to it, for nothing could be clearer than that, under that penthouse of forehead and thick eyebrows, his attention was fixed not on the cards, but on one of the players. But he seemed to enjoy an hour spent thus, and often, until one particular evening in July, he would watch her with the air of man who has some deep problem in front of him. She, enthusiastically keen about our game, seemed not to notice his scrutiny. Then came that evening when, as I see in the light of subsequent events, began the first twitching of the veil that hid the secret horror from my eyes. I did not know it then, though I noticed that thereafter, if she rang up to propose coming round, she always asked not only if I was at leisure, but whether Mr. Urcombe was with me. If so, she said, she would not spoil the hat of two old bachelors, and laughingly wished me good night. Urcombe, on this occasion, had been with me for some half-hour before Mrs. Amworth's appearance, and had been talking to me about the mediaeval beliefs concerning vampirism, one of those borderland subjects which he declared had not been sufficiently studied before it had been consigned by the medical profession to the dustheap of exploded superstitions. There he sat, grim and eager, tracing with that pellucid clearness which had made him in his Cambridge days so admirable a lecturer, the history of those mysterious visitations. In them all there were the same general features: one of those ghoulish spirits took up its abode in a living man or woman, conferring supernatural powers of bat-like flight and glutting itself with nocturnal blood-feasts. When its host died it continued to dwell in the corpse, which remained undecayed. By day it rested, by night it left the grave and went on its awful errands. No European country in the Middle Ages seemed to have escaped them; earlier yet, parallels were to be found in Roman and Greek and in Jewish history.

"It's a large order to set all that evidence aside as being moonshine," he said. "Hundreds of totally independent witnesses in many ages have testified to the occurrence of these phenomena, and there's no explanation known to me which covers all the facts. And if you feel inclined to say 'Why, then, if these are facts, do we not come across them now?' there are two answers I can make you. One is that there were diseases known in the Middle Ages, such as the black death, which were certainly existent then and which have become extinct since, but for that reason we do not assert that such diseases never existed. Just as the black death visited England and decimated the population of Norfolk, so here in this very district about three hundred years ago there was certainly an outbreak of vampirism, and Maxley was the centre of it. My second answer is even more convincing, for I tell you that vampirism is by no means extinct now. An outbreak of it certainly occurred in India a year or two ago."

At that moment I heard my knocker plied in the cheerful and peremptory manner in which Mrs. Amworth is accustomed to announce her arrival, and I went to the door to open it.

"Come in at once," I said, "and save me from having my blood curdled. Mr. Urcombe has been trying to alarm me."

Instantly her vital, voluminous presence seemed to fill the room.

"Ah, but how lovely!" she said. "I delight in having my blood curdled. Go on with your ghost story, Mr. Urcombe. I adore ghost stories."

I saw that, as his habit was, he was intently observing her.

"It wasn't a ghost story exactly," said he. "I was only telling our host how vampirism was not extinct yet. I was saying that there was an outbreak of it in India only a few years ago."

There was a more than perceptible pause, and I saw that, if Urcombe was observing her, she on her side was observing him with a fixed eye and parted mouth. Then her jolly laugh invaded that rather tense silence.

"Oh, what a shame!" she said. "You're not going to curdle my blood at all. Where did you pick up such a tale, Mr. Urcombe? I have lived for years in India and never heard a rumour of such a thing. Some storyteller in the bazaars must have invented it: they are famous at that."

I could see that Urcombe was on the point of saying something further, but checked himself.

"Ah! very likely that was it," he said.

But something had disturbed our usual peaceful sociability that night, and something had damped Mrs. Amworth's usual high spirits. She had no gusto for her piquet, and left after a couple of games. Urcombe had been silent too, indeed he hardly spoke again till she departed.

"That was unfortunate," he said, "for the outbreak of—of a very mysterious disease, let us call it, took place at Peshawar where she and her husband were. And—"

"Well?" I asked.

"He was one of the victims of it," said he. "Naturally I had quite forgotten that when I spoke."

The summer was unreasonably hot and rainless, and Maxley suffered from much drought, and also from a plague of big black night-flying gnats, the bite of which was very irritating and virulent. They came sailing in of an evening, settling on one's skin so quietly that one perceived nothing till the sharp stab announced that one had been bitten. They did not bite the hands or face, but chose always the neck and throat for their feeding-ground, and most of us, as the poison spread, assumed a temporary goitre. Then about the middle of August appeared the first of those mysterious cases of illness which our local doctor attributed to the long-continued heat coupled with the bite of these venomous insects. The patient was a boy of sixteen or seventeen, the son of Mrs. Amworth's gardener, and the symptoms were an anaemic pallor and a languid prostration, accompanied by great drowsiness and an abnormal appetite. He had, too, on his throat two small punctures where, so Dr. Ross conjectured, one of these great gnats had bitten him. But the odd thing was that there was no swelling or inflammation round the place where he had been bitten. The heat at this time had begun to abate, but the cooler weather failed to restore him, and the boy, in spite of the quantity of food which he so ravenously swallowed, wasted away to a skin-clad skeleton.

I met Dr. Ross in the street one afternoon about this time, and in answer to my enquiries about his patient he said that he was afraid the boy was dying. The case, he confessed, completely puzzled him: some obscure form of pernicious anaemia was all he could suggest. But he wondered whether Mr. Urcombe would consent to see the boy, on the chance of his being able to throw some new light on the case, and since Urcombe was dining with me that night, I proposed to Dr. Ross to join us. He could not do this, but said he would look in later. When he came, Urcombe at once consented to put his skill at the other's disposal, and together they went off at once. Being thus shorn of my sociable evening, I telephoned Mrs. Amworth to know if I might inflict myself on her for an hour. Her answer was a welcoming affirmative, and between piquet and music the hour lengthened itself into two. She spoke of the boy who was lying so desperately and mysteriously ill, and told me that she had often been to see him, taking him nourishing and delicate food. But today—and her kind eyes moistened as she spoke—she was afraid she had paid her last visit. Knowing the antipathy between her and Urcombe, I did not tell her he had been called into consultation; and when I returned home she accompanied me to my door, for the sake of a breath of night air, and in order to borrow a magazine which contained an article on gardening which she wished to read.

"Ah, this delicious night air," she said, luxuriously sniffing in the coolness. "Night air and gardening are the great tonics. There is nothing so stimulating as bare contact with rich mother earth. You are never so fresh as when you have been grubbing in the soil—black hands, black nails, and boots covered with mud." She gave her great jovial laugh.

"I'm a glutton for air and earth," she said. "Positively I look forward to death, for then I shall be buried and have the kind earth all round me. No leaden caskets for me—I have given explicit directions. But what shall I do about air? Well, I suppose one can't have everything. The magazine? A thousand thanks, I will faithfully return it. Good night: garden and keep your windows open, and you won't have anaemia."

"I always sleep with my windows open," said I.

I went straight up to my bedroom, of which one of the windows looks out over the street, and as I undressed I thought I heard voices talking outside not far away. But I paid no particular attention, put out my lights, and falling asleep plunged into the depths of the most horrible dream, distortedly suggested, no doubt, by my last words with Mrs. Amworth. I dreamed that I woke, and found that both my bedroom windows were shut. Half-suffocating, I dreamed that I sprang out of bed, and went across to open them. The blind over the first one was drawn down, and pulling it up I saw, with the indescribable horror of incipient nightmare, Mrs. Amworth's face suspended close to the pane in the darkness outside, nodding and smiling at me. Pulling down the blind again to keep that terror out, I rushed to the second window on the other side of the room, and there again was Mrs. Amworth's face. Then the panic came upon me in full blast; here was I suffocating in the airless room, and whichever window I opened Mrs. Amworth's face would float in, like those noiseless black gnats that bit before one was aware. The nightmare rose to screaming point, and with strangled yells I awoke to find my room cool and quiet with both windows open and blinds up and a half-moon high in its course, casting an oblong of tranquil light on the floor. But even when I was awake the horror persisted, and I lay tossing and turning. I must have slept long before the nightmare seized me for now it was nearly day, and soon in the east the drowsy eyelids of morning began to lift.

I was scarcely downstairs next morning—for after the dawn I slept late—when Urcombe rang up to know if he might see me immediately. He came in, grim and preoccupied, and I noticed that he was pulling on a pipe that was not even filled.

"I want your help," he said, "and so I must tell you first of all what happened last night. I went round with the little doctor to see his patient, and found him just alive, but scarcely more. I instantly diagnosed in my own mind what this anaemia, unaccountable by any other explanation, meant. The boy is the prey of a vampire."

He put his empty pipe on the breakfast table, by which I had just sat down, and folded his arms, looking at me steadily from under his overhanging brows.

"Now about last night," he said. "I insisted that he should be moved from his father's cottage into my house. As we were carrying him on a streatcher, whom should we meet but Mrs. Amworth? She expressed shocked surprise that we were moving him. Now why do you think she did that?"

With a start of horror, as I remembered my dream that night before, I felt an idea come into my mind so preposterous and unthinkable that I instantly turned it out again.

"I haven't the smallest idea," I said.

"Then listen, while I tell you about what happened later. I put out all light in the room where the boy lay, and watched. One window was a little open, for I had forgotten to close it, and about midnight I heard something outside, trying apparently to push it further open. I guessed who it was—yes, it was full twenty feet from the ground—and I peeped round the corner of the blind. Just outside was the face of Mrs. Amworth and her hand was on the frame of the window. Very softly I crept close, and then banged the window down, and I think I just caught the tip of one of her fingers."

"But it's impossible," I cried. "How could she be floating in the air like that? And what had she come for? Don't tell me such—"

Once more, with closer grip, the remembrance of my nightmare seized me.

"I am telling you what I saw," said he. "And all night long, until it was nearly day, she was fluttering outside, like some terrible bat, trying to gain admittance. Now put together various things I have told you."

He checked them off on his fingers.

"Number one," he said: "there was an outbreak of disease

similar to that which this boy is suffering from at Peshawar, and her husband died of it. Number two: Mrs. Amworth protested against my moving the boy to my house. Number three: she, or the demon that inhabits her body, a creature powerful and deadly, tries to gain admittance. And add this, too: in mediaeval times there was an epidemic of vampirism here at Maxley. The vampire, so the accounts run, was found to be Elizabeth Chaston . . . I see you remember Mrs. Amworth's maiden name. Finally, the boy is stronger this morning. He would certainly not have been alive if he had been visited again. And what do you make of it?"

There was a long silence, during which I found this incredible horror assuming the hues of reality.

"I have something to add," I said, "which may or may not bear on it. You say that the—the spectre went away shortly before dawn."

"Yes."

I told him of my dream, and he smiled grimly.

"Yes, you did well to awake," he said. "That warning came from your subconscious self, which never wholly slumbers, and cried out to you of deadly danger. For two reasons, then, you must help me: one to save others, the second to save yourself."

"What do you want me to do?" I asked.

"I want you first of all to help me in watching this boy, and ensuring that she does not come near him. Eventually I want you to help me in tracking the thing down, in exposing and destroying it. It is not human: it is an incarnate fiend. What steps we shall have to take I don't yet know."

It was now eleven of the forenoon, and presently I went across to his house for a twelve-hour vigil while he slept, to come on duty again that night, so that for the next twenty-four hours either Urcombe or myself was always in the room where the boy, now getting stronger every hour, was lying. The day following was Saturday and a morning of brilliant, pellucid weather, and already when I went across to his house to resume my duty the stream of motors down to Brighton had begun. Simultaneously I saw Urcombe with a cheerful face, which boded good news of his patient, coming out of his house, and Mrs. Amworth, with a gesture of salutation to me and a basket in her hand, walking up the broad strip of grass which bordered the road. There we all three met. I noticed (and saw that Urcombe noticed it too) that one finger of her left hand was bandaged.

"Good morning to you both," said she. "And I hear your patient is doing well, Mr. Urcombe. I have come to bring him a bowl of jelly, and to sit with him for an hour. He and I are great friends. I am overjoyed at his recovery."

Urcombe paused a moment, as if making up his mind, and then shot out a pointing finger at her.

"I forbid that," he said. "You shall not sit with him or see him. And you know the reason as well as I do."

I have never seen so horrible a change pass over a human face as that which now blanched hers to the colour of a grey mist. She put up her hand as if to shield herself from that pointing finger, which drew the sign of the cross in the air, and shrank back cowering on to the road. There was a wild hoot from a horn, a grinding of brakes, a shout—too late—from a passing car, and one long scream suddenly cut short. Her body rebounded from the roadway after the first wheel had gone over it, and the second followed it. It lay there, quivering and twitching, and was still.

She was buried three days afterwards in the cemetery outside Maxley, in accordance with the wishes she had told me that she had devised about her interment, and the shock which her sudden and awful death had caused to the little community began by degrees to pass off. To two people only, Urcombe and myself, the horror of it was mitigated from the first by the nature of the relief that her death brought; but, naturally enough, we kept our own counsel, and no hint of what greater horror had been thus averted was ever let slip. But, oddly enough, so it seemed to me, he was still not satisfied about something in connection with her, and would give no answer to my questions on the subject. Then as the days of a tranquil mellow September and the October that followed began to drop away like the leaves of the yellowing trees, his uneasiness relaxed. But before the entry of November the seeming tranquillity broke into hurricane.

I had been dining one night at the far end of the village, and about eleven o'clock was walking home again. The moon was of an unusual brilliance, rendering all that it shone on as distinct as in some etching. I had just come opposite the house which Mrs. Amsworth had occupied, where there was a board up telling that it was to let, when I heard the click of her front gate, and next moment I saw, with a sudden chill and quaking of my very spirit, that she stood there. Her profile, vividly illuminated, was turned to me, and I could not be mistaken in my identification of her. She appeared not to see me (indeed the shadow of the yew hedge in front of her garden enveloped me in its blackness) and she went swiftly across the road, and entered the gate of the house directly opposite. There I lost sight of her completely.

My breath was coming in short pants as if I had been running —and now indeed I ran, with fearful backward glances, along the hundred yards that separated me from my house and Urcombe's. It was to his that my flying steps took me, and next minute I was within.

"What have you come to tell me?" he asked. "Or shall I guess?"

"You can't guess," said I.

"No; it's no guess. She has come back and you have seen her. Tell me about it."

I gave him my story.

"That's Major Pearsall's house," he said. "Come back with me there at once."

"But what can we do?" I asked.

"I've no idea. That's what we have got to find out."

A minute later, we were opposite the house. When I had passed it before, it was all dark; now lights gleamed from a couple of windows upstairs. Even as we faced it, the front door opened, and next moment Major Pearsall emerged from the gate. He saw us and stopped.

"I'm on my way to Dr. Ross," he said quickly. "My wife has been taken suddenly ill. She had been in bed an hour when I came upstairs, and I found her white as a ghost and utterly exhausted. She had been to sleep, it seemed—But you will excuse me."

"One moment, Major," said Urcombe. "Was there any mark on her throat?"

"How did you guess that?" said he. "There was: one of those beastly gnats must have bitten her twice there. She was streaming with blood."

"And there's someone with her?" asked Urcombe.

"Yes, I roused her maid."

He went off, and Urcombe turned to me. "I know now what we have to do," he said. "Change your clothes, and I'll join you at your house."

"What is it?" I asked.

"I'll tell you on our way. We're going to the cemetery."

He carried a pick, a shovel, and a screwdriver when he rejoined me, and wore round his shoulders a long coil of rope. As we walked, he gave me the outlines of the ghastly hour that lay before us.

"What I have to tell you," he said, "will seem to you now too fantastic for credence, but before dawn we shall see whether it outstrips reality. By a most fortunate happening, you saw the spectre, the astral body, whatever you choose to call it, of Mrs. Amworth, going on its grisly business, and therefore, beyond doubt, the vampire spirit which abode in her during life animates her again in death. That is not exceptional—indeed, all these weeks since her death I have been expecting it. If I am right, we shall find her body undecayed and untouched by corruption."

"But she has been dead nearly two months," said I.

"If she had been dead two years it would still be so, if the vampire has possession of her. So remember: whatever you see done, it will be done not to her, who in the natural course would now be feeding the grasses above her grave, but to a spirit of untold evil and malignancy, which gives a phantom life to her body."

"But what shall I see done?" said I.

"I will tell you. We know that now, at this moment, the vampire clad in her mortal semblance is out; dining out. But it must get back before dawn, and it will pass into the material form that lies in her grave. We must wait for that, and then with your help I shall dig up her body. If I am right, you will look on her as she was in life, with the full vigour of the dreadful nutriment she has received pulsing in her veins. And then, when dawn has come, and the vampire cannot leave the lair of her body, I shall strike her with this"—and he pointed to his pick—"through the heart, and she, who comes to life again only with the animation the fiend gives her, she and her hellish partner will be dead indeed. Then we must bury her again, delivered at last."

We had come to the cemetery, and in the brightness of the moonshine there was no difficulty in identifying her grave. It lay some twenty yards from the small chapel, in the porch of which, obscured by shadow, we concealed ourselves. From there we had a clear and open sight of the grave, and now we must wait till its infernal visitor returned home. The night was warm and windless, yet even if a freezing wind had been raging I think I should have felt nothing of it, so intense was my preoccupation as to what the night and dawn would bring. There was a bell in the turret of the chapel that struck the quarters of the hour, and it amazed me to find how swiftly the chimes succeeded one another.

The moon had long set, but a twilight of stars shone in a clear sky, when five o'clock of the morning sounded from the turret. A few minutes more passed, and then I felt Urcombe's hand softly nudging me; and looking out in the direction of his pointing finger, I saw that the form of a woman, tall and large in build, was approaching from the right. Noiselessly, with a motion more of gliding and floating than walking, she moved across the cemetery to the grave which was the centre of our observation. She moved round it as if to be certain of its identity, and for a moment stood directly facing us. In the greyness to which now my eyes had grown accustomed, I could easily see her face, and recognise its features.

She drew her hand across her mouth as if wiping it, and broke into a chuckle of such laughter as made my hair stir on my head. Then she leaped into the grave, holding her hands high above her head, and inch by inch disappeared into the earth. Urcombe's hand now laid on my arm, in an injunction to keep still, but now he removed it.

"Come," he said.

With pick and shovel and rope we went to the grave. The earth was light and sandy, and soon after six struck we had delved down to the coffin lid. With his pick he loosened the earth round it, and, adjusting the rope through the handles by which it had been lowered, we tried to raise it. This was a long and laborious business, and the light had begun to herald day in the east before we had it out, and lying by the side of the grave. With his screwdriver he loosed the fastenings of the lid, and slid it aside, and standing there we looked on the face of Mrs. Amworth. The eyes, once closed in death, were open, the cheeks were flushed with colour, the red, full-lipped mouth seemed to smile.

"One blow and it is all over," he said. "You need not look."

Even as he spoke he took up the pick again, and, laying the point of it on her left breast, measured his distance. And though I knew what was coming I could not look away. . . .

He grasped the pick in both hands, raised it an inch or two for the taking of his arm, and then with full force brought it down on her breast. A fountain of blood, though she had been dead so long, spouted high in the air, falling with the thud of a heavy splash over the shroud, and simultaneously from those red lips came one long, appalling cry, swelling up like some hooting siren, and dying away again. With that, instantaneous as a lightning flash, came the touch of corruption on her face, the colour of it faded to ash, the plump cheeks fell in, the mouth dropped.

"Thank God, that's over," said he, and without pause slipped the coffin lid back into its place.

Day was coming fast now, and working like men possessed; we lowered the coffin into its place again, and shovelled the earth over it . . . The birds were busy with their earliest pipings as we went back to Maxley.

THE MONKEY'S PAW

W. W. Jacobs (1863–1943)

Born in London and educated in private schools, W. W. Jacobs first tried his hand at writing at the age of twenty. Jacobs was a humorist tale-teller whose stories dealt primarily with the adventures of seafaring men on shore. The more serious and horrific slant of The Monkey's Paw *is a notable exception to Jacobs's usual work.*

Without, the night was cold and wet, but in the small parlour of Labrunum Villa the blinds were drawn and the fire burned brightly. Father and son were at chess; the former, who possessed ideas about the game involving radical changes, putting his king into such sharp and unnecessary perils that it even provoked comment from the white-haired old lady knitting placidly by the fire.

"Hark at the wind," said Mr. White, who, having seen a fatal mistake after it was too late, was amiably desirous of preventing his son from seeing it.

"I'm listening," said the latter, grimly surveying the board as he stretched out his hand. "Check."

"I should hardly think that he'd come to-night," said his father, with his hand poised over the board.

"Mate," replied the son.

"That's the worst of living so far out," bawled Mr. White, with sudden and unlooked-for violence; "of all the beastly, slushy, out-of-the-way places to live in, this is the worst. Path's a bog, and the road's a torrent. I don't know what people are thinking about. I suppose because only two houses in the road are let, they think it doesn't matter."

"Never mind, dear," said his wife soothingly; "perhaps you'll win the next one."

Mr. White looked up sharply, just in time to intercept a knowing glance between mother and son. The words died away on his lips, and he hid a guilty grin in his thin grey beard.

"There he is," said Herbert White, as the gate banged to loudly and heavy footsteps came towards the door.

The old man rose with hospitable haste, and opening the door, was heard condoling with the new arrival. The new arrival also condoled with himself, so that Mrs. White said, "Tut, tut!" and coughed gently as her husband entered the room, followed by a tall, burly man, beady of eye and rubicund of visage.

"Sergeant-Major Morris," he said, introducing himself.

The sergeant-major shook hands, and taking the proffered seat by the fire, watched contentedly while his host got out whisky and tumblers and stood a small copper kettle on the fire.

At the third glass his eyes got brighter, and he began to talk, the little family circle regarding with eager interest this visitor from distant parts, as he squared his broad shoulders in the chair, and spoke of wild scenes and doughty deeds; of wars and plagues, and strange peoples.

"Twenty-one years of it," said Mr. White, nodding at his wife and son. "When he went away he was a slip of a youth in the warehouse. Now look at him."

"He don't look to have taken much harm," said Mrs. White politely.

"I'd like to go to India myself," said the old man, "just to look round a bit, you know."

"Better where you are," said the sergeant-major, shaking his head. He put down the empty glass, and sighing softly, shook it again.

"I should like to see those old temples and fakirs and jugglers," said the old man. "What was that you started telling me the other day about a monkey's paw or something, Morris?"

"Nothing," said the soldier hastily. "Leastways nothing worth hearing."

"Monkey's paw?" said Mrs. White curiously.

"Well, it's just a bit of what you might call magic, perhaps," said the sergeant-major off-handedly.

His three listeners leaned forward eagerly. The visitor absent-mindedly put his empty glass to his lips and then set it down again. His host filled it for him.

"To look at," said the sergeant-major, fumbling in his pocket. "it's just an ordinary little paw, dried to a mummy."

He took something out of his pocket and proffered it. Mrs. White drew back with a grimace, but her son, taking it, examined it curiously.

"And what is there special about it?" enquired Mr. White as he took it from his son, and having examined it, placed it upon the table.

"It had a spell put it by an old fakir," said the sergeant-major, "a very holy man. He wanted to show that fate ruled people's lives, and that those who interfered with it did so to their sorrow. He put a spell on it so that three separate men could each have three wishes from it."

His manner was so impressive that his hearers were conscious that their light laughter jarred somewhat.

"Well, why don't you have three, sir?" said Herbert White cleverly.

The soldier regarded him in the way that middle age is wont to regard presumptuous youth. "I have," he said quietly, and his blotchy face whitened.

"And did you really have the three wishes granted?" asked Mrs. White.

"I did," said the sergeant-major, and his glass tapped against his strong teeth.

"And has anybody else wished?" persisted the old lady.

"The first man had his three wishes. Yes," was the reply; "I don't know what the first two were, but the third was for death. That's how I got the paw."

His tones were so grave that a hush fell upon the group.

"If you've had your three wishes, it's no good to you now, then, Morris," said the old man at last. "What do you keep it for?"

The soldier shook his head. "Fancy, I suppose," he said slowly. "I did have some idea of selling it, but I don't think I will. It has caused enough mischief already. Besides, people won't buy. They think it's a fairy tale, some of them; and those who do think anything of it want to try it first and pay me afterward."

"If you could have another three wishes," said the old man, eyeing him keenly, "would you have them?"

"I don't know," said the other. "I don't know."

He took the paw, and dangling it between his forefinger and thumb, suddenly threw it upon the fire. White, with a slight cry, stooped down and snatched it off.

"Better let it burn," said the soldier solemnly.

"If you don't want it, Morris," said the other, "give it to me."

"I won't," said his friend doggedly. "I threw it on the fire. If you keep it, don't blame me for what happens. Pitch it on the fire again, like a sensible man."

The other shook his head and examined his new possession closely. "How do you do it?" he enquired.

"Hold it up in your right hand and wish aloud," said the sergeant-major, "but I warn you of the consequences."

"Sounds like the *Arabian Nights*," said Mrs. White, as she rose and began to set the supper. "Don't you think you might wish for four pairs of hands for me?"

Her husband drew the talisman from his pocket, and then all three burst into laughter as the sergeant-major, with a look of alarm on his face, caught him by the arm.

"If you must wish," he said gruffly, "wish for something sensible."

Mr. White dropped it back in his pocket, and placing chairs, motioned his friend to the table. In the business of supper the talisman was partly forgotten, and afterwards the three sat listening in an enthralled fashion to a second installment of the soldier's adventures in India.

"If the tale about the monkey's paw is not more truthful than those you have been telling us," said Herbert, as the door closed behind their guest, just in time to catch the last train, "we shan't make much out of it."

"Did you give him anything for it, father?" enquired Mrs. White, regarding her husband closely.

"A trifle," said he, colouring slightly. "He didn't want it, but I made him take it. And he pressed me again to throw it away."

"Likely," said Herbert, with pretending horror. "Why, we're going to be rich, and famous, and happy. Wish to be an emperor, father, to begin with; then you can't be henpecked."

He darted round the table, pursued by the maligned Mrs. White armed with an antimacassar.

Mr. White took the paw from his pocket and eyed it dubiously. "I don't know what to wish for, and that's a fact," he said slowly. "It seems to me I've got all I want."

"If you only cleared the house, you'd be quite happy, wouldn't you?" said Herbert, with his hand on his shoulder. "Well, wish for two hundred pounds, then; that'll just do it."

His father, smiling shamefacedly at his own credulity, held up the talisman, as his son, with a solemn face, somewhat marred by a wink at his mother, sat down at the piano and struck a few impressive chords.

"I wish for two hundred pounds," said the old man distinctly.

A fine crash from the piano greeted the words, interrupted by a shuddering cry from the old man. His wife and son ran toward him.

"It moved," he cried, with a glance of disgust at the object as it lay on the floor. "As I wished, it twisted in my hand like a snake."

"Well, I don't see the money," said his son, as he picked it up and placed it on the table, "and I bet I never shall."

"It must have been your fancy, father," said his wife, regarding him anxiously.

He shook his head. "Never mind, though; there's no harm done, but it gave me a shock all the same."

They sat down by the fire again while the two men finished their pipes. Outside, the wind was higher than ever, and the old man started nervously at the sound of a door banging upstairs. A silence unusual and depressing settled upon all three, which lasted until the old couple arose to retire for the night.

"I expect you'll find the cash tied up in a big bag in the middle of your bed," said Herbert, as he bade them good night, "and something horrible squatting up on top of the wardrobe watching you as you pocket your ill-gotten gains."

He sat alone in the darkness, gazing at the dying fire, and seeing faces in it. The last face was so horrible and so simian that he gazed at it in amazement. It got so vivid that, with a little uneasy laugh, he felt on the table for a glass containing a little water to throw over it. His hand grasped the monkey's paw, and with a little shiver he wiped his hand on his coat and went to bed.

II

In the brightness of the wintry sun next morning as it streamed over the breakfast table he laughed at his fears. There was an air of prosaic wholesomeness about the room which it had lacked on the previous night, and the dirty, shrivelled little paw was pitched on the side-board with a carelessness which betokened no great belief in its virtues.

"I suppose all soldiers are the same," said Mrs. White. "The idea of our listening to such nonsense! How could wishes be granted in these days? And if they could, how could two hundred pounds hurt you, father?"

"Might drop on his head from the sky," said the frivolous Herbert.

"Morris said the things happened so naturally," said his father, "that you might if you so wished attribute it to coincidence."

"Well, don't break into the money before I come back," said Herbert as he rose from the table. "I'm afraid it'll turn you into a mean avaricious man, and we shall have to disown you."

His mother laughed, and followed him to the door, watched him down the road; and returning to the breakfast table, was very merry at the expense of her husband's credulity. All of which did not prevent her from scurrying to the door at the postman's knock, nor prevent her from referring somewhat shortly to retired sergeant-majors of bibulous habits when she found that the post brought a tailor's bill.

"Herbert will have some more of his funny remarks, I expect, when he comes home," she said, as they sat at dinner.

"I dare say," said Mr. White, pouring himself out some beer; "but for all that, the thing moved in my hand; that I'll swear to you."

"You thought it did," said the old lady soothingly.

"I say it did," replied the other. "There was no thought about it; I had just—What's the matter?"

His wife made no reply. She was watching the mysterious movements of a man outside, who, peering in an undecided fashion at the house, appeared to be trying to make up his mind to enter. In mental connection with the two hundred pounds, she noticed that the stranger was well dressed, and wore a silk hat of glossy newness. Three times he paused at the gate, and then walked on again. The fourth time he stood with his hand upon it, and then with sudden resolution flung it open and walked up the path. Mrs. White at the same moment placed her hands behind her, and hurriedly unfastening the strings of her apron, put that useful article of apparel beneath the cushion of her chair.

She brought the stranger, who seemed ill at ease, into the room. He gazed at her furtively, and listened in a preoccupied fashion as the old lady apologized for the appearance of the room, and her husband's coat, a garment which he usually reserved for the garden. She then waited as patiently as her sex would permit, for him to broach his business, but he was at first strangely silent.

"I—was asked to call," he said at last, and stooped and picked a piece of cotton from his trousers. "I come from 'Maw and Meggins'."

The old lady started. "Is anything the matter?" she asked breathlessly. "Has anything happened to Herbert? What is it? What is it?"

Her husband interposed. "There, there, mother," he said hastily. "Sit down, and don't jump to conclusions. You've not brought bad news, I'm sure, sir;" and he eyed the other wistfully.

"I'm sorry—" began the visitor.

"Is he hurt?" demanded the mother wildly.

The visitor bowed in assent. "Badly hurt," he said quietly, "but he is not in any pain."

"Oh, thank God!" said the old woman, clasping her hands. "Thank God for that! Thank—"

She broke off suddenly as the sinister meaning of the assurance dawned upon her, and she saw the awful confirmation of her fears in the other's averted face. She caught her breath, and turning to her slower-witted husband, laid a trembling old hand upon his. There was a long silence.

"He was caught in the machinery," said the visitor at length in a low voice.

"Caught in the machinery," repeated Mr. White, in a dazed fashion, "yes."

He sat staring blankly out at the window, and taking his wife's hand between his own, pressed it as he had been wont to do in their old courting days nearly forty years before.

"He was the only one left to us," he said, turning gently to the visitor. "It is hard."

The other coughed, and rising, walked slowly to the window.

"The firm wished me to convey their sincere sympathy with you at your great loss," he said, without looking round. "I beg that you will understand I am only their servant and merely obeying orders."

There was no reply; the old woman's face was white, her eyes staring, and her breath inaudible; and on the husband's face was a look such as his friend the sergeant might have carried into his first action.

"I was to say that Maw and Meggins disclaim all responsibility," continued the other. "They admit no liability at all, but in consideration of your son's services, they wish to present you with a certain sum as compensation."

Mr. White dropped his wife's hand, and rising to his feet, gazed with a look of horror at his visitor. His dry lips shaped the words, "How much?"

"Two hundred pounds," was the answer.

Unconscious of his wife's shriek, the old man smiled faintly, put out his hands like a sightless man, and dropped, a senseless heap, to the floor.

III

In the huge new cemetery, some two miles distant, the old people buried their dead, and came back to the house steeped in shadow and silence. It was all over so quickly that at first they could hardly realise it, and remained in a state of expectation as though of something else to happen—something else which was to lighten this load, too heavy for old hearts to bear.

But the days passed, and expectation gave place to resignation —the hopeless resignation of the old, sometimes miscalled apathy. Sometimes they hardly exchanged a word, for now they had nothing to talk about and their days were long to weariness.

It was about a week after, that the old man, waking suddenly in the night, stretched out his hand and found himself alone. The room was in darkness, and the sound of subdued weeping came from the window. He raised himself in bed and listened.

"Come back," he said tenderly. "You will be cold.

"It is colder for my son," said the old woman, and wept afresh.

The sound of her sobs died away on his ears. The bed was warm, and his eyes heavy with sleep. He dozed fitfully, and then slept until a sudden wild cry from his wife awoke him with a start.

"*The paw!*" she cried wildly. "The monkey's paw!"

He started up in alarm. "Where? Where is it? What's the matter?"

She came stumbling across the room toward him. "I want it," she said quietly. "You've not destroyed it?"

"It's in the parlour, on the bracket," he replied, marveling. "Why?"

She cried and laughed together, and bending over, kissed his cheek.

"I only just thought of it," she said hysterically. "Why didn't I think of it before? Why didn't *you* think of it?"

"Think of what?" he questioned.

"The other two wishes," she replied rapidly. "We've only had one."

"Was not that enough?" he demanded fiercely.

"No," she cried triumphantly; "we'll have one more. Go down and get it quickly, and wish our boy alive again."

The man sat up in bed and flung the bedclothes from his quaking limbs. "Good God, you are mad!" he cried, aghast.

"Get it," she panted; "get it quickly, and wish—Oh my boy, my boy!"

Her husband struck a match and lit the candle. "Get back to bed," he said unsteadily. "You don't know what you are saying."

"We had the first wish granted," said the old woman feverishly; "why not the second?"

"A coincidence," stammered the old man.

"Go and get it and wish," cried his wife, quivering with excitement.

The old man turned and regarded her, and his voice shook. "He has been dead ten days, and besides he—I would not tell you else, but—I could only recognize him by his clothing. If he was too terrible for you to see then, how now?"

"Bring him back," cried the old woman, and dragged him toward the door. "Do you think I fear the child I have nursed?"

He went down in the darkness, and felt his way to the parlour, and then to the mantelpiece. The talisman was in its place, and a horrible fear that the unspoken wish might bring his mutilated son before him ere he could escape from the room seized upon him, and he caught his breath as he found that he had lost the direction of the door. His brow cold with sweat, he felt his way round the table, and groping along the wall until he found himself in the small passage with the unwholesome thing in his hand.

Even his wife's face seemed changed as he entered the room. It was white and expectant, and to his fears seemed to have an unnatural look upon it. He was afraid of her.

"Wish!" she cried, in a strong voice.

"It is foolish and wicked," he faltered.

"Wish!" repeated his wife.

He raised his hand. "I wish my son alive again."

The talisman fell to the floor, and he regarded it fearfully. Then he sank trembling into a chair as the old woman, with burning eyes, walked to the window and raised the blind.

He sat until he was chilled with the cold, glancing occasionally at the figure of the old woman peering through the window. The candle-end, which had burned below the rim of the china candlestick, was throwing pulsating shadows on the ceiling and walls, until, with a flicker larger than the rest, it expired. The old man, with an unspeakable sense of relief at the failure of the talisman, crept back to his bed, and a minute or two afterwards the old woman came silently and apathetically beside him.

Neither spoke, but lay silently listening to the ticking of the clock. A stair creaked, and a squeaky mouse scurried noisily through the wall. The darkness was oppressive, and after lying for some time screwing up his courage, he took the box of matches, and striking one, went downstairs for a candle.

At the foot of the stairs the match went out, and he paused to strike another; and at the same moment a knock, so quiet and stealthy as to be scarcely audible, sounded on the front door.

The matches fell from his hand and spilled in the passage. He stood motionless, his breath suspended until the knock was repeated. Then he turned and fled swiftly back to his room, and closed the door behind him. A third knock sounded through the house.

"*What's that?*" cried the old woman, starting up.

"A rat," said the old man in shaking tones—"a rat. It passed me on the stairs."

His wife sat up in bed listening. A loud knock resounded through the house.

"It's Herbert!" she screamed. "It's Herbert!"

She ran to the door, but her husband was before her, and catching her by the arm, held her tightly.

"What are you going to do?" he whispered hoarsely.

"It's my boy; it's Herbert!" she cried, struggling mechanically. "I forgot it was two miles away. What are you holding me for? Let go. I must open the door."

"For God's sake, don't let it in," cried the old man, trembling.

"You're afraid of your own son," she cried struggling. "Let me go. I'm coming, Herbert; I'm coming."

There was another knock, and another. The old woman with a sudden wrench broke free and ran from the room. Her husband followed to the landing, and called after her appealingly as she hurried downstairs. He heard the chain rattle back and the bottom bolt drawn slowly and stiffly from the socket. Then the old woman's voice, strained and panting.

"The bolt," she cried loudly. "Come down. I can't reach it."

But her husband was on his hands and knees groping wildly on the floor in search of the paw. If he could only find it before the thing outside got in. A perfect fusillade of knocks reverberated through the house, and he heard the scraping of a chair as his wife put it down in the passage against the door. He heard the creaking of the bolt as it came slowly back, and at the same moment he found the monkey's paw, and frantically breathed his third and last wish.

The knocking ceased suddenly, although the echoes of it were still in the house. He heard the chair drawn back, and the door open. A cold wind rushed up the staircase, and a long loud wail of disappointment and misery from his wife gave him courage to run down to her side, and then to the gate beyond. The street lamp flickering opposite shone on a quiet and deserted road.

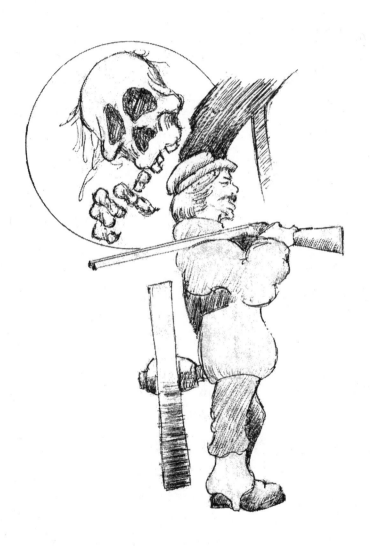

THE PHANTOM COACH

Amelia B. Edwards (1831–1892)

Equally talented in music and writing, this British author chose the latter career because she could earn money. She wrote several novels, two histories, and some poetry. After an extended visit to Egypt, she devoted her energies to the preservation of Egyptian antiquities, and it is for her contribution to modern archeology that she is best remembered.

The circumstances I am about to relate to you have truth to recommend them. They happened to myself, and my recollection of them is as vivid as if they had taken place only yesterday. Twenty years, however, have gone by since that night. During those twenty years I have told the story to but one other person. I tell it now with a reluctance which I find it difficult to overcome. All I entreat, meanwhile, is that you will abstain from forcing your own conclusions upon me. I want nothing explained away. I desire no arguments. My mind on this subject is quite made up, and, having the testimony of my own senses to rely upon, I prefer to abide by it.

Well! It was just twenty years ago, and within a day or two of the end of the grouse season. I had been out all day with my gun, and had had no sport to speak of. The wind was due east; the month, December; the place, a bleak wide moor in the far north of England. And I had lost my way. It was not a pleasant place in which to lose one's way, with the first feathery flakes of a coming snowstorm just fluttering down upon the heather, and the leaden evening closing in all around. I shaded my eyes with my hand, and stared anxiously into the gathering darkness, where the purple moorland melted into a range of low hills, some ten or twelve miles distant. Not the faintest smoke-wreath, not the tiniest cultivated patch, or fence, or sheep-track, met my eyes in any direction. There was nothing for it but to walk on, and take my chance of finding what shelter I could, by the way. So I shouldered my gun again and pushed wearily forward, for I had been on foot since an hour after daybreak and had eaten nothing since breakfast.

Meanwhile, the snow began to come down with ominous steadiness, and the wind fell. After this, the cold became more intense, and the night came rapidly up. As for me, my prospects darkened with the darkening sky, and my heart grew heavy as I thought how my young wife was already watching for me through the window of our little inn parlour, and thought of all the suffering in store for her throughout this weary night. We had been married four months, and, having spent out autumn in the Highlands, were now lodging in a remote little village situated just on the verge of the great English moorlands. We were very much in love, and, of course, very happy. This morning, when we parted, she had implored me to return before dusk, and I had promised her that I would. What would I not have given to have kept my word!

Even now, weary as I was, I felt that with a supper, an hour's rest, and a guide, I might still get back to her before midnight, if only guide and shelter could be found.

And all this time the snow fell and the night thickened. I

stopped and shouted every now and then, but my shouts seemed only to make the silence deeper. Then a vague sense of uneasiness came upon me, and I began to remember stories of travellers who had walked on and on in the falling snow until, wearied out, they were fain to lie down and sleep their lives away. Would it be possible, I asked myself, to keep on thus through all the long dark night? Would there not come a time when my limbs must fail, and my resolution give way? When I, too, must sleep the sleep of death. Death! I shuddered. How hard to die just now, when life lay all so bright before me! How hard for my darling, whose whole loving heart—but that thought was not to be borne! To banish it, I shouted again, louder and longer, and then listened eagerly. Was my shout answered, or did I only fancy that I heard a far-off cry? I hallooed again, and again the echo followed. Then a wavering speck of light came suddenly out of the dark, shifting, disappearing, growing momentarily nearer and brighter. Running towards it at full speed, I found myself, to my great joy, face to face with an old man and a lantern.

"Thank God!" was the exclamation that burst involuntarily from my lips.

Blinking and frowning, he lifted his lantern and peered into my face.

"What for?" growled he, sulkily.

"Well—for you. I began to fear I should be lost in the snow."

"Eh, then, folks do get cast away hereabouts fra' time to time, an' what's to hinder you from bein' cast away likewise, if the Lord's so minded?"

"If the Lord is so minded that you and I shall be lost together my friend, we must submit," I replied; "but I don't mean to be lost without you. How far am I now from Dwolding?"

"A gude twenty mile, more or less."

"And the nearest village?"

"The nearest village is Wyke, an' that's twelve miles t'other side."

"Where do you live, then?"

"Out yonder," said he, with a vague jerk of the lantern.

"You're going home, I presume?"

"Maybe I am."

"Then I'm going with you."

The old man shook his head, and rubbed his nose reflectively with the handle of the lantern.

"It ain't no use," growled he. "He 'ont let you in—not he."

"We'll see about that," I replied, briskly. "Who is he?"

"The master."

"Who is the master?"

"That's nowt to you," was the unceremonious reply.

"Well, well; you lead the way, and I'll engage that the master shall give me shelter and a supper tonight."

"Eh, you can try him!" muttered my reluctant guide; and, still shaking his head, he hobbled, gnome-like, away through the falling snow. A large mass loomed up presently out of the darkness, and a huge dog rushed out barking furiously.

"Is this the house?" I asked.

"Ay, it's the house. Down, Bey!" And he fumbled in his pocket for the key.

I drew up close behind him, prepared to lose no chance of entrance, and saw in the little circle of light shed by the lantern that the door was heavily studded with iron nails, like the door of a prison. In another minute he had turned the key and I had pushed past him into the house.

Once inside, I looked round with curiosity and found myself in a great raftered hall, which served, apparently, a variety of uses. One end was piled to the roof with corn, like a barn. The other was stored with flour-sacks, agricultural implements, casks, and all kinds of miscellaneous lumber; while from the beams overhead hung rows of hams, flitches, and bunches of dried herbs for winter use. In the centre of the floor stood some huge object gauntly dressed in a dingy wrapping-cloth, and reaching half way to the rafters. Lifting a corner of this cloth, I saw, to my surprise, a telescope of very considerable size, mounted on a rude movable platform, with four small wheels. The tube was made of painted wood bound round with bands of metal rudely fashioned; the speculum, so far as I could estimate its size in the dim light, measured at least fifteen inches in diameter. While I was yet examining the instrument, and asking myself whether it was not the work of some self-taught optician, a bell rang sharply.

"That's for you," said my guide, with a malicious grin. "Yonder's his room."

He pointed to a low black door at the opposite side of the hall. I crossed over, rapped somewhat loudly, and went in, without waiting for an invitation. A huge, white-haired old man rose from a table covered with books and papers, and confronted me sternly.

"Who are you?" said he. "How came you here? What do you want?"

"James Murray, barrister-at-law. On foot across the moor. Meat, drink, and sleep."

He bent his bushy brows into a portentous frown.

"Mine is not a house of entertainment." he said, haughtily. "Jacob, how dare you admit this stranger?"

"I didn't admit him," grumbled the old man. "He followed me over the muir, and shouldered his way in before me. I'm no match for six foot two."

"And pray, sir, by what right have you forced an entrance into my house?"

"The same by which I should have clung to your boat, if I were drowning. The right of self-preservation."

"Self-preservation?"

"There's an inch of snow on the ground already," I replied, briefly; "and it would be deep enough to cover my body before daybreak."

He strode to the window, pulled aside a heavy black curtain, and looked out.

"It is true," he said. "You can stay, if you choose, till morning. Jacob, serve the supper."

With this he waved me to a seat, resumed his own, and became at once absorbed in the studies from which I had disturbed him.

I placed my gun in a corner, drew a chair to the hearth, and examined my quarters at leisure. Smaller and less incongruous in its arrangements than the hall, this room contained, nevertheless, much to awaken my curiosity. The floor was carpetless. The whitewashed walls were in parts scrawled over with strange diagrams, and in others covered with shelves crowded with philosophical instruments, the uses of many of which were unknown to me. On one side of the fireplace stood a bookcase filled with dingy folios; on the other, a small organ, fantastically decorated with painted carvings of medieval saints and devils. Through the half-opened door of a cupboard at the further end of the room I saw a long array of geological specimens, surgical preparations, crucibles, retorts, and jars of chemicals; while on the mantelshelf beside me, amid a number of small objects stood a model of the solar system, a small galvanic battery, and a microscope. Every chair had its burden. Every corner was heaped high with books. The very floor was littered over with maps, casts, papers, tracings, and learned lumber of all conceivable kinds.

I stared about me with an amazement increased by every fresh object upon which my eyes chanced to rest. So strange a room I had never seen; yet seemed it stranger still, to find such a room in a lone farmhouse amid those wild and solitary moors! Over and over again I looked from my host to his surroundings, and from his surroundings back to my host, asking myself who and what he could be? His head was singularly fine; but it was more the head of a poet than of a philosopher. Broad in the temples, prominent over the eyes, and clothed with a rough profusion of perfectly white hair, it had all the ideality and much of the ruggedness that characterizes the head of Louis von Beethoven. There were the same deep lines about the mouth, and the same stern furrows in the brow. There was the same concentration of expression. While I was yet observing him, the door opened and Jacob brought in the supper. His master then closed his book, rose, and with more courtesy of manner than he had yet shown, invited me to the table.

A dish of ham and eggs, a loaf of brown bread, and a bottle of admirable sherry, were placed before me.

"I have but the homeliest farmhouse fare to offer you, sir," said my entertainer. "Your appetite, I trust, will make up for the deficiencies of our larder."

I had already fallen upon the viands, and now protested, with the enthusiasm of a starving sportsman, that I had never eaten anything so delicious.

He bowed stiffly, and sat down to his own supper, which consisted, primitively, of a jug of milk and a basin of porridge. We ate in silence, and, when we had done, Jacob removed the tray. I then drew my chair back to the fireside. My host, somewhat to my surprise, did the same, and turning abruptly towards me, said:

"Sir, I have lived here in strict retirement for three-and-twenty years. During that time I have not seen as many strange faces and I have not read a single newspaper. You are the first stranger who has crossed my threshold for more than four years. Will you favour me with a few words of information respecting that outer world from which I have parted company so long?"

"Pray interrogate me," I replied. "I am heartily at your service."

He bent his head in acknowledgment; leaned forward, with his elbows resting on his knees and his chin supported in the palms of his hands; stared fixedly into the fire; and proceeded to question me.

His inquiries related chiefly to scientific matters, with the later progress of which, as applied to the practical purposes of life, he was almost wholly unacquainted. No student of science myself, I replied as well as my slight information permitted; but the task was far from easy, and I was much relieved when, passing from interrogation to discussion, he began pouring forth his own conclusions upon the facts which I had been attempting to place before him. He talked, and I listened spellbound. He talked till I believe he almost forgot my presence, and only thought aloud. I had never heard anything like it then; I have never heard anything like it since. Familiar with all systems of all philosophies, subtle in analysis, bold in generalization, he poured forth his thoughts in an uninterrupted stream, and, still leaning forward in the same moody attitude with his eyes fixed upon the fire, wandered from topic to topic, from speculation to speculation, like an inspired dreamer. From practical science to mental philosophy; from electricity in the wire to electricity in the nerve; from Watts to Mesmer, from Mesmer to Reichenbach, from Reichenbach to Swedenborg, Spinoza, Condillac, Descartes, Berkeley, Aristotle, Plato, and the Magi and mystics of the East, were transitions which, however bewildering in their variety and scope, seemed easy and harmonious upon his lips as sequences in music. By and by—I forget now by what link of conjecture or illustration—he passed on to that field which lies beyond the boundary line or even conjectural philosophy, and reaches no man knows whither. He spoke of the soul and its aspirations; of the spirit and its powers; of second sight; of prophecy; of those phenomena which, under the names of ghosts, spectres, and supernatural appearances, have been denied by the sceptics and attested by the credulous, of all ages.

"The world," he said, "grows hourly more and more sceptical of all that lies beyond its own narrow radius; and our men of science foster the fatal tendency. They condemn as fable all that resists experiment. They reject as false all that cannot be brought to the test of the laboratory or the dissecting-room. Against what superstition have they waged so long and obstinate a war, as against the belief in apparitions? And yet what superstition has maintained its hold upon the minds of men so long and so firmly? Show me any fact in physics, in history, in archaeology, which is supported by testimony so wide and so various. Attested by all races of men, in all ages, and in all climates, by the soberest sages of antiquity, by the rudest savage of today, by the Christian, the Pagan, the Pantheist, the Materialist, this phenomenon is treated as a nursery tale by the philosophers of our century. Circumstantial evidence weighs with them as a feather in the balance. The comparison of causes with effects, however valuable in physical science, is put aside as worthless and unreliable. The evidence of competent witnesses, however conclusive in a court of justice, counts for nothing. He who pauses before he pronounces, is condemned as a trifler. He who believes, is a dreamer or a fool."

He spoke with bitterness, and, having said thus, relapsed for some minutes into silence. Presently he raised his head from his hands, and added, with an altered voice and manner:

"I, sir, paused, investigated, believed, and was not ashamed to state my convictions to the world. I, too, was branded as a visionary, held up to ridicule by my contemporaries, and hooted from that field of science in which I had laboured with honour during all the best years of my life. These things happened just three-

and-twenty years ago. Since then I have lived as you see me living now, and the world has forgotten me, as I have forgotten the world. You have my history."

"It is a very common one," he replied. "I have only suffered for the truth, as many a better and wiser man has suffered before me."

He rose, as if desirous of ending the conversation, and went over to the window.

"It has ceased snowing," he observed, as he dropped the curtain and came back to the fireside.

"Ceased!" I exclaimed, starting eagerly to my feet, "Oh, if it were only possible—but no! it is hopeless. Even if I could find my way across the moor, I could not walk twenty miles tonight."

"Walk twenty miles tonight!" repeated my host. "What are you thinking of?"

"Of my wife," I replied impatiently. "Of my young wife, who does not know that I have lost my way, and who is at this moment breaking her heart with suspense and terror."

"Where is she?"

"At Dwolding, twenty miles away."

"At Dwolding," he echoed, thoughtfully. "Yes, the distance, it is true, is twenty miles; but—are you so very anxious to save the next six or eight hours?"

"So very, very anxious, that I would give ten guineas at this moment for a guide and a horse."

"Your wish can be gratified at a less costly rate," said he, smiling. "The night mail from the north, which changes horses at Dwolding, passes within five miles of this spot, and will be due at a certain cross-road in about an hour and a quarter. If Jacob were to go with you across the moor and put you into the old coach-road, you could find your way, I suppose, to where it joins the new one?"

"Easily—gladly."

He smiled again, rang the bell, gave the old servant his directions, and, taking a bottle of whisky and wineglass from the cupboard in which he kept his chemicals said:

"The snow lies deep and it will be difficult walking tonight on the moor. A glass of usquebaugh before you start?"

I would have declined the spirit, but he pressed it on me, and I drank it. It went down my throat like liquid flame and almost took my breath away.

"It is strong," he said; "but it will help to keep out the cold. And now you have no moments to spare. Good night!"

I thanked him for his hospitality and would have shaken hands but that he had turned away before I could finish my sentence. In another minute I had traversed the hall, Jacob had locked the outer door behind me, and we were out on the wide white moor.

Although the wind had fallen, it was still bitterly cold. Not a star glimmered in the black vault overhead. Not a sound, save the rapid crunching of the snow beneath our feet, disturbed the heavy stillness of the night. Jacob, not too well pleased with his mission, shambled on before in sullen silence, his lantern in his hand and his shadow at his feet. I followed, with my gun over my shoulder, as little inclined for conversation as himself. My thoughts were full of my late host. His voice yet rang in my ears. His eloquence yet held my imagination captive. I remember to this day, with surprise, how my over-excited brain retained whole sentences and parts of sentences, troops of brilliant images, and fragments of splendid reasoning, in the very words in which he had uttered them. Musing thus over what I had heard, and striving to recall a lost link here and there, I strode on at the heel of my guide, absorbed and unobservant. Presently—at the end, as it seemed to me, of only a few minutes—he came to a sudden halt, and said:

"Yon's your road. Keep the stone fence to your right hand and you can't fail of the way."

"This, then, is the old coach-road?"

"Ay, 'tis the old coach-road."

"And how far do I go before I reach the cross-roads?"

"Nigh upon three mile."

I pulled out my purse, and he became more communicative.

"The road's a fair road enough," said he, "for foot passengers; but 'twas over-steep and narrow for the northern traffic. You'll mind where the parpet's broken away, close again' the signpost. It's never been mended since the accident."

"What accident?"

"Eh, the night mail pitched right over into the valley below—a gude fifty feet an' more—just at the worst bit o'road in the whole county."

"Horrible! Were many lives lost?"

"All. Four were found dead, and t'other two died next morning."

"How long is it since this happened?"

"Just nine year."

"Near the sign-post, you say? I will bear it in mind. Good night."

"Gude night, sir, and thankee." Jacob pocketed his half-crown, made a faint pretence of touching his hat, and trudged back by the way he had come.

I watched the light of his lantern till it quite disappeared, and then turned to pursue my way alone. This was no longer matter of the slightest difficulty, for, despite the dead darkness overhead, the line of stone fence showed distinctly enough against the pale gleam of the snow. How silent it seemed now, with only my footsteps to listen to; how silent and how solitary! A strange disagreeable sense of loneliness stole over me. I walked faster. I hummed a fragment of a tune. I cast up enormous sums in my head, and accumulated them at compound interest. I did my best, in short, to forget the startling speculations to which I had but just been listening, and, to some extent, I succeeded.

Meanwhile, the night air seemed to become colder and colder, and though I walked fast I found it impossible to keep myself warm. My feet were like ice. I lost sensation in my hands, and grasped my gun mechanically. I even breathed with difficulty, as though, instead of traversing a quiet North-country highway, I were scaling the uppermost heights of some gigantic alp. This last symptom became presently so distressing that I was forced to stop for a few minutes and lean against the stone fence. As I did so I chanced to look back up the road, and there, to my infinite relief, I saw a distant point of light, like the gleam of an approaching lantern. I at first concluded that Jacob had retraced his steps and followed me; but even as the conjecture presented itself, a second light flashed into sight—a light evidently parallel with the first, and approaching at the same rate of motion. It needed no second thought to show me that these must be the carriage-lamps of some private vehicle, though it seemed strange that any private vehicle should take a road professedly disused and dangerous.

There could be no doubt, however, of the fact, for the lamps grew larger and brighter every moment, and I even fancied I could already see the dark outline of the carriage between them. It was coming up very fast, and quite noiselessly, the snow being nearly a foot deep under the wheels.

And now the body of the vehicle became distinctly visible behind the lamps. It looked strangely lofty. A sudden suspicion flashed upon me. Was it possible that I had passed the cross-roads in the dark without observing the sign-post and could this be the very coach which I had come to meet?

No need to ask myself that question a second time, for here it came round the bend of the road, guard and driver, one outside passenger, and four steaming greys, all wrapped in a soft haze of light, through which the lamps blazed out, like a pair of fiery meteors.

I jumped forward, waved my hat, and shouted. The mail came down at full speed and passed me. For a moment I feared that I had not been seen or heard, but it was only for a moment. The coachman pulled up; the guard, muffled to the eyes in capes and comforters, and apparently sound asleep in the rumble, neither answered my hail nor made the slightest effort to dismount; the outside passenger did not even turn his head. I opened the door for myself, and looked in. There were but three travellers inside, so I stepped in, shut the door, slipped into the vacant corner, and congratulated myself of my good fortune.

The atmosphere of the coach seemed, if possible, colder than that of the outer air and was pervaded by a singularly damp and disagreeable smell. I looked round at my fellow-passengers. They were all three, men, and all silent. They did not seem to be asleep, but each leaned back in his corner of the vehicle, as if absorbed in his own reflections. I attempted to open a conversation.

"How intensely cold it is tonight," I said, addressing my opposite neighbour.

He lifted his head, looked at me, but made no reply.

"The winter," I added, "seems to have begun in earnest."

Although the corner in which he sat was so dim that I could distinguish none of his features very clearly, I saw that his eyes were still turned full upon me. And yet he answered never a word.

At any other time I should have felt, and perhaps expressed, some annoyance, but at the moment I felt too ill to do either. The icy coldness of the night air had struck a chill to my very marrow, and the strange smell inside the coach was affecting me with an intolerable nausea. I shivered from head to foot, and, turning to my left-hand neighbour, asked if he had any objection to an open window?

He neither spoke nor stirred.

I repeated the question somewhat more loudly, but with the same result. Then I lost my patience and let the sash down. As I did so, the leather strap broke in my hand, and I observed that the glass was covered with a thick coat of mildew, the accumulation, apparently, of years. My attention being thus drawn to the condition of the coach, I examined it more narrowly, and saw by the uncertain light of the outer lamps that it was in the last state of dilapidation. Every part of it was not only out of repair but in a condition of decay. The sashes splintered at a touch. The leather fittings were crusted over with mould, and literally rotting from the woodwork. The floor was almost breaking away beneath my feet. The whole machine, in short, was foul with damp, and had evidently been dragged from some outhouse in which it had been mouldering away for years, to do another day or two of duty on the road.

I turned to the third passenger, whom I had not yet addressed, and hazarded one more remark.

"This coach," I said, "is in deplorable condition. The regular mail, I suppose, is under repair."

He moved his head slowly, and looked me in the face, without speaking a word. I shall never forget that look while I live. I turned cold at heart under it. I turn cold at heart even now when I recall it. His eyes glowed with a fiery unnatural lustre. His face was livid as the face of a corpse. His bloodless lips were drawn back as if in the agony of death, and showed the gleaming teeth between.

The words that I was about to utter died upon my lips, and a strange horror—a dreadful horror—came upon me. My sight had by this time become used to the gloom of the coach and I could see with tolerable distinctness. I turned to my opposite neighbour. He, too, was looking at me with the same startling pallor in his face and the same stony glitter in his eyes. I passed my hand across my brow. I turned to the passenger on the seat beside my own, and saw—oh, Heaven! how shall I describe what I saw? I saw that he was no living man—that none of them were living men, like myself! A pale phosphorescent light—the light of putrefaction—played upon their awful faces; upon their hair, dank with the dews of the grave; upon their clothes, earth stained and dropping to pieces; upon their hands, which were as the hands of corpses long buried. Only their eyes, their terrible eyes, were living; and those eyes were all turned menacingly upon me!

A shriek of terror, a wild, unintelligible cry for help and mercy, burst from my lips as I flung myself against the door and strove in vain to open it.

In that single instant, brief and vivid as a landscape beheld in the flash of summer lightning, I saw the moon shining down through a rift of stormy cloud—the ghastly sign-post rearing its warning finger by the wayside—the broken parapet—the plunging horses—the black gulf below. Then the coach reeled like a ship at sea. Then came a mighty crash—a sense of crushing pain—and then darkness.

It seemed as if years had gone by when I awoke one morning from a deep sleep and found my wife watching by my bedside. I will pass over the scene that ensued and give you, in half a dozen words, the tale she told me with tears of thanksgiving. I had fallen over a precipice, close against the junction of the old coach-road and the new, and had only been saved from certain death by lighting upon a deep snowdrift that had accumulated at the foot of the rock beneath. In this snowdrift I was discovered at daybreak by a couple of shepherds, who carried me to the nearest shelter and brought a surgeon to my aid. The surgeon found me in a state of raving delirium, with a broken arm and a compound fracture of the skull. The letters in my pocket-book showed my name and address; my wife was summoned to nurse me; and, thanks to youth and a fine constitution, I came out of danger at last. The place of my fall, I need scarcely say, was precisely that at which a frightful accident had happened to the north mail nine years before.

I never told my wife the fearful events which I have just related to you. I told the surgeon who attended me; but he treated the whole adventure as a mere dream born of the fever in my brain. We discussed the question over and over again until we found that we could discuss it with temper no longer, and then we dropped it. Others may form what conclusions they please—I *know* that twenty years ago I was the fourth inside passenger in that Phantom Coach.

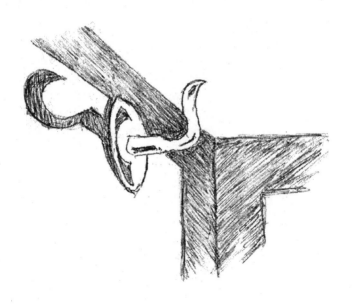

WHERE ANGELS FEAR

Manley Wade Wellman (1903–)

Manley Wade Wellman's early years were spent in Portugese Angola in West Africa with his physician father and missionary mother. After he returned to the States, he became a journalist and a prolific writer of books on American history, science fiction, and novels for young readers.

Half a mile from McCormack's cabin a paved highway crossed the rutted woodland road, and here a post held aloft in the misty darkness an electric light. Muriel Fisher paused in its brightest glow, and turned up her spectacled, good-humored young face. "Let's interview that whiskey, Scotty," she said.

McCormack smiled, and drew the silver flask from under the tail of his old shooting-coat. He was a tall, gaunt young man, made sturdy just now by rough, heavy clothes. Between his plaid scarf and the brim of his felt hat showed a fine, bony face, Gaelicly wide in jaw and brow, with a narrowness through the cheeks. "Drink," he invited, and drew the stopper for her.

She drank, with honest heartiness. Her bandanna-framed face, tilting back under the white light, seemed to have lost a touch of its healthy pink, but she looked ready enough in her tweed suit, turtle-neck brown sweater, woolen stockings and oxfords. "That braces me to the adventure," she said, handing back the flask. "This is like the beginning of a Sherlock Holmes story—old clothes, thick walking sticks, a bottle of liquor and a dark road to travel." Her spectacles turned to scan the extension of the road on the other side of the pavement. It seemed suddenly to dwindle, to become no more than a trail in the deepening fog. "Only," she added, "Sherlock Holmes was too rational to believe in haunted houses."

"His creator wasn't," said McCormack, and drank in turn. The potent whiskey cut from his mouth the savor of those sardines they had eaten together, just before starting into the night. "Conan Doyle believed in ghosts, fairies and God. What time is it, Muriel?"

She peeled down a knitted glove and looked at her wrist watch. "Twenty minutes after eleven. We'd better hurry if we reach this boogey-bin of yours before midnight."

They crossed the highway, and plunged into the half-gloom beyond. Only a narrow strip of the sky hung between the two blocky masses of trees, and from it there filtered a slaty-blue light. The moon would be full, or almost, but the wholly mistclouds obscured it. Underfoot the going was uneven and turfy, and the tip of McCormack's walking stick sent a pebble scuttling. Muriel started violently, laughed to deprecate her own nervousness, and fumbled for a cigarette. McCormack found himself grateful for the brief flare of her match.

"Tell me all about the house, Scotty," she begged.

"It's a treasure-trove of goblins, if it's authentic," he complied. "I've seen it only twice, and by daylight both times. It has the traditional look, all right—a big, square-roofed ruin, two stories high, on a rock above a stream. The local gossips tell me that it was built maybe sixty years ago, by a young couple who were found one morning in an upstairs room, hanging by their necks."

"Suicide," asked Muriel, "or murder?"

"Nobody's sure. After a while, some relatives moved in, a man with his wife and young son. During the first week, so I understand, the mother died suddenly and mysteriously. And the little boy was so scared by something that he had to be taken to a hospital. Next morning, the father was dangling and dead—in the same upstairs room. That was the last of regular residence at the place."

Muriel drew up her shoulders. "I don't wonder. What about the poor little boy?"

"He didn't entirely recover—the groceryman down at the village says he's at the State Hospital. Mental case—can't rightly remember who he is or how he got there. Quiet, harmless—but they don't dare leave as much as three feet of rope where he can get to it."

"And nobody's lived in the house since?" prompted the girl.

"Well—not lived in it," McCormack told her. "Once a convict escaped from the prison camp and ran away through the woods. That was year before last. I was spending the summer at my cabin. The State police tracked him to the house, and cut him down from the hook where he was hanging."

"Wooh!" gasped Muriel with shivery relish. "In the upstairs room?"

"In the upstairs room."

McCormack lighted his pipe. Its bowl sent forth a soft rose-colored glimmer, that relieved his strong, bony features with an impression of whimsical gentleness. The night was strangely still, except for the footfalls and respirations of man and woman. No insect chirped or creaked, the autumn leaves did not rustle on the branches. McCormack thought that cold perspiration was starting on his forehead, but perhaps it was the condensation of the mist.

"I dare hope that nobody knows we're out ghost-hunting," he

remarked. "Some heavy-handed jokester might dress up in a sheet and come to call."

"Have you brought any charms along?" his companion asked. "Wolfbane, crucifix, holy water—anything of that description?"

McCormack shook his head. "I'm out to see ghosts, not drive them away," he replied, and half smiled. He had an agreeable smile, but with his pipe-fire half screened in ashes, his face looked like a clay mask in the blue dimness. Muriel Fisher felt less cheerful than she had at the beginning of the walk, and far less skeptical of ghosts than when she and McCormack had shared sandwiches and coffee in his snug cabin. That cabin seemed far away just now, but she refused to wish herself back. She had come out here tonight expressly to see a haunted house.

"Where's the scene of all these Gothic horrors?" she asked after a time.

"Almost directly ahead," her companion informed her. "Yes, here's the creek, and the road ends. There was a bridge once, I daresay, but not now."

The trees shrank away from this spot, and the fog-strained moonlight was almost strong around the two adventurers. Before them, set deep between rocky banks, ran black, swift water. McCormack stepped cautiously to the very edge, peered down, and then across.

"It looked narrower by day. I must confess," he remarked. "However, I think I can jump it." He flung his walking stick to the far bank, gathered his body suddenly, and straddled his long legs into a skipping leap. He seemed to swing across the stream, gained the rough-looking rocks beyond, and turned back. His thin face was like a genial skull in the moonlight.

"If you go only a little way down, it's narrower," he called to Muriel.

But she, too, flung her stick across. "Don't coddle me," she cried gaily. "I can jump as far as you can."

She suited the action of the word, and bravely, but her stride could not match McCormack's, and her skirt hampered the scissory thrash of her legs. One blunt oxford touched the edge of the far bank, rock crunched and crumpled beneath it. She felt herself falling backward. McCormack moving quickly for so big a man, shot out a hand and clutched her by the wrist. With a mighty heave, he fairly whipped her to safety.

"Thanks, Scotty," she gasped, and straightened her spectacles, then the bandanna that was bound over her head and beneath her chin, peasant style. "You spared me a cold bath." They both smiled, and breathed deeply in mutual relief. "I take that escape as a good omen," she went on. "Now, is this the haunted house? It looks to be."

They had come into a larger clearing, but here the mist had thickened to a pearly cloud. In its heart rose a great cliff-like structure, with towering walls and a flat roof. The walls had weathered to a gloomy night-gray, in which shuttered windows formed indistinct deviations. A porch had once run the entire width of the front, but the roof was collapsed, the pillars fallen, and the floor all but in ruins.

"Isn't that a lightning-blasted oak in the front yard?" asked Muriel, pointing with her recovered stick. "I suppose owls hoot in its branches to foretell the death of the heir."

"There aren't any heirs," McCormack reminded her. "All of them died, or were hanged. Come around to the side. There's supposed to be an open window there."

He led the way, up a rise in the overgrown yard and through thickset brambles that may once have been a bank of roses. Three windows were ranged in line on the right side of the house, and the rearmost showed blacker than its fellows. McCormack pushed close to it, knee deep in rank shrubs that showed one or two wax-petaled flowers.

"No shutters," he reported, "and the glass is all broken out of the sash. Where are you, Muriel?"

"Right with you," came her reply from just behind his arm. He turned, set his hands to her waist, and lifted her lightly through the opening.

"Whee, it's dark," she cried in protest as her feet came to light on the dully-echoing floor. At once she struck a match. It gave blotchy glimpses of a big, crumbling room, apparently running all the way from front to back of this part of the house. McCormack struggled in through the gap where the window had been. His bracing fingers found the wood spongily dry, as if the house had been decaying for six centuries instead of sixty years.

"I brought no flashlight," he informed Muriel. "Only a candle."

"You did exactly right. Why chase away spirits with electricity?" She watched as he ignited the fat tallow cylinder, which yielded a clear, courageous tag of flame. "Now where?" she asked him.

"There should be stairs leading upward," he said, and moved across the room. Its boards creaked and buckled under his shoes, and crumbs of plaster fallen from the shattered ceiling made harsh, crunching noises. The candle showed them a doorway, through which they walked together.

Beyond, they found themselves in a central hall. Here was the flight of stairs they sought, its railings fallen away in a heap, and clotted blackness above. The plaster of the walls had broken away in sheets. Again they were aware of the presence in the house of decay's very soul.

"Do we go up?" inquired Muriel, her voice automatically hushed, and McCormack nodded and again led the way. His left hand held the candle high, his right clutched his stick tightly, as though to be ready to strike a blow. He could not have told what he feared to meet.

The upper landing was encircled with moldy-looking doors, two of them fallen from their hinges. McCormack went to each, Muriel close at his heels, and held in his candle for quick examination. He stopped at the right rear chamber, just above the window by which they had entered.

"Here's our haunted room," he announced. "See the hooks there, on the wall at the back?"

The hooks he mentioned were set well into the plaster, within inches of the ceiling. Strangely enough for that house of ruin and rot, they appeared to shine in the candlelight as if new and rustless. Elsewhere clung a strange pall of gloom, though the flaked and ragged wallpaper must have been reasonably light in color.

"I wonder if a hundred-watt lamp would help this room any," grunted the tall man. "It looks to be in mourning for the four who were hanged. But we'll douse the candle anyway, in a minute. Hold it, Muriel, while I spread something for us to sit down."

From a big pocket of his shooting-coat he fished a folded newspaper, and, spreading it out, covered a space against the wall directly beneath the hooks. "Now," he said, "light another cigarette if you like. I'll put a fresh fill in this pipe. Ready?"

He took back the candle and blew it out, and they sat down in the dark. After a blinded moment, they saw that a dim radiance stole into the room. There must be chinks in the window-shutter somewhere, and the moon, now close to zenith, was fighting its way through the mist so as to peer in. The two ghost-challengers sat shoulder to shoulder, each silently grateful for touch of the other. Muriel again peered at the illuminated dial of her watch.

"It lacks only seven or eight minutes of midnight," she announced in half a whisper. "Scotty, you're quite willing to stay?"

"Strange as it may seem," returned McCormack, "I'm suddenly quite willing to depart. But I won't. I came here to see ghosts, if there are any, and I don't intend to leave so close to the proverbial witching hour."

It was not much of a success as careless chatter. Silence fell again, and awkwardly. Muriel broke in, in a voice no louder than a sigh:

"Look—"

They both saw, or thought they saw, a stir in the soft shimmer of gauzy light. It might have been streaks of silent rain falling, had the roof been open. Again, it might have been the rhythmic creeping of long, spider-spare legs without a tangible body. McCormack felt something fasten tightly upon his biceps, and started violently; but it was Muriel's fingers, closing for comfort on his flesh. Her hand slid down into his own grasp. He, too, regained something of serenity and strength in being able to reassure her.

"Scotty," she was breathing at his ear, "I wonder if there's something the matter with the doorway. Is it closing?"

He stared. His eyes had grown more used to the almost-darkness.

"Not closing," he made easy-sounding reply. "The door's off the hinges, there it leans against the wall. But the opening does look smaller, somehow. Growing narrower."

"And lower," she added. "It's only an optical illusion, of course," and she chuckled nervously, "but I'd bet good money that you'd have to stoop to get through it."

Again the illusion of bandy leg-lines stirring in the room, this time very near. McCormack, at least, fancied that he heard something like a stealthy scramble, and once again he lifted the stick that had never quitted his strong right hand. His left squeezed

Muriel's wrist, trying to win back some of the calmness he had transmitted to her. But when he tried to fix his eyes on the spidery movement, it seemed to fade, to retreat. He echoed in his heart the words of his companion: optical illusion, of course—

"I'd have to stoop, too," Muriel was telling him. "It looks like the door to . . . to a doll house." Again her chuckle, more hysterical than before.

"Chin up," McCormack exhorted her. "When we get up from here and walk toward it, there'll be width and height enough."

"Are you . . . so anxious to see ghosts . . . now?" she fairly quavered.

McCormack did not wish to heighten her terror by denying; he did not wish to tempt any strange and sudden visitation by agreeing. He therefore kept his peace, and quartered the floor and walls with his straining eyes. Once again, something rustled near by, menacingly stealthy. He leaned hard against the wall, and drew up his legs so that his feet would come under him and bring him, if necessary, swiftly erect.

Too much imagination, he accused himself. This was undoubtedly the way that psychical investigators conditioned themselves to experience phenomena that never really happened. No wonder people had been frightened into hanging themselves on those hooks overhead. But he was too rational a being to be thus stampeded.

Optical illusion, he insisted once again to his thundering heart. At most, none of the things he almost saw or heard would be too terrible to face. A blow of his stick—but what if it lashed out and met no substance?

"I keep thinking I hear voices," Muriel said once again. "Not human voices—not exactly. They're too soft and—"

"Like whispers?" McCormack suggested, as casually as he could manage.

"No. Less audible than that. They're like an echo, a memory—they can be felt, not heard."

"Imagination," said McCormack, rather rudely. His eyes sought the door again.

There was no door. Only blank wall, solidly pale in the dimness. He felt a tightness on his heart and throat, and with real savagery tried to persuade himself that this was no more than curious—notable—absorbing.

"We're shut in," Muriel said aloud, and the ring of apprehension in her voice made him jump. Next moment a bell rang, clear and far away—rang again, again, again—

"It's midnight," he said briskly, and with the greatest relief he had known in years. "Hear that clock striking? Let's clear out, and head back to the cabin."

He rose to his feet, feeling unaccountably light, as though he had floated up. Once more he led the way, trying to make out the vanished door through which they had come short minutes ago.

Muriel's cry of agonized terror brought him up short.

"Scotty! *Look back there where we were sitting!*"

"What do you mean?" He spun around, still with that strange airy lightness.

Against the wall dangled two silent figures. Bands, or nooses of rope, held them by the necks to the gleaming hooks that jutted close to the ceiling. The figures hung limp, lank, unmistakenly dead.

One was long and thin, in rough coat and trousers. The other, smaller and unmistakenly feminine, wore a tweed suit and scuffed walking shoes.

To McCormack, those two corpses looked vaguely familiar.

Again Muriel's fear-loud cry beside him: "Scotty, I can't see you! Where have you gone?"

"I'm right here," he said hoarsely, and turned in the direction of her wail.

He could not see her either. He put out a hand to touch her. He could not see the hand.

Immediately he knew what man and woman were hanged on the wall of the haunted room.

WHAT WAS IT?

Fitz-James O'Brien (1828–1862)

Born in Ireland, Fitz-James O'Brien went to New York at age twenty-four. There he lived a bohemian life of alternating luxury and poverty, writing poetry and short stories for many magazines. He was talented but undisciplined, and his best work was in stories of the weird and uncanny.

It is, I confess, with considerable diffidence that I approach the strange narrative which I am about to relate. The events which I purpose detailing are of so extraordinary a character that I am quite prepared to meet with an unusual amount of incredulity and scorn. I accept all such beforehand. I have, I trust, the literary courage to face unbelief. I have, after mature consideration, resolved to narrate, in as simple and straightforward a manner as I can compass, some facts that passed under my observation, in the month of July last, and which, in the annals of the mysteries of physical science, are wholly unparalleled.

I live at No. — Twenty-sixth Street, in New York. The house is in some respects a curious one. It has enjoyed for the last two years the reputation of being haunted. It is a large and stately residence, surrounded by what was once a garden, but which is now only a green enclosure used for bleaching clothes. The dry basin of what has been a fountain, and a few fruit trees ragged and unpruned, indicate that this spot in past days was a pleasant, shady retreat, filled with fruits and flowers and the sweet murmur of waters.

The house is very spacious. A hall of noble size leads to a large spiral staircase winding through its centre, while the various apartments are of imposing dimensions. It was built some fifteen or twenty years since by Mr. A— —, the well-known New York merchant, who five years ago threw the commercial world into convulsions by a stupendous bank fraud. Mr. A— —, as every one knows, escaped to Europe, and died not long after, of a broken heart. Almost immediately after the news of his decease reached this country and was verified, the report spread in Twenty-sixth Street that No. — was haunted. Legal measures had dispossessed the widow of its former owner, and it was inhabited merely by a caretaker and his wife, placed there by the house agent into whose hands it had passed for the purposes of renting or sale. These people declared that they were troubled with unnatural noises. Doors were opened without any visible agency. The remnants of furniture scattered through the various rooms were, during the night, piled one upon the other by unknown hands. Invisible feet passed up and down the stairs in broad daylight, accompanied by the rustle of unseen silk dresses, and the gliding of viewless hands along the massive balusters. The caretaker and his wife declared they would live there no longer. The house agent laughed, dismissed them, and put others in their place. The noises and supernatural manifestations continued. The neighbourhood caught up the story, and the house remained untenanted for three years. Several persons negotiated for it; but, somehow, always before the bargain was closed they heard the unpleasant rumours and declined to treat any further.

It was in this state of things that my landlady, who at that time kept a boarding-house in Bleecker Street, and who wished to

move further up town, conceived the bold idea of renting No. —
Twenty-sixth Street. Happening to have in her house a rather
plucky and philosophical set of boarders, she laid her scheme
before us, stating candidly everything she had heard respecting
the ghostly qualities of the establishment to which she wished to
remove us. With the exception of two timid persons,—a sea-
captain and a returned Californian, who immediately gave notice
that they would leave,—all of Mrs. Moffat's guests declared that
they would accompany her in her chivalric incursion into the
abode of spirits.

Our removal was effected in the month of May, and we were
charmed with our new residence. The portion of Twenty-sixth
Street where our house is situated, between Seventh and Eighth
avenues, is one of the pleasantest localities in New York. The gardens back of the houses, running down nearly to the Hudson,
form, in the summer time, a perfect avenue of verdure. The air is
pure and invigorating, sweeping, as it does, straight across the
river from the Weehawken heights, and even the ragged garden
which surrounded the house, although displaying on washing
days rather too much clothesline, still gave us a piece of
greensward to look at, and a cool retreat in the summer evenings,
where we smoked our cigars in the dusk, and watched the fireflies
flashing their dark lanterns in the long grass.

Of course we had no sooner established ourselves at No. —
than we began to expect ghosts. We absolutely awaited their
advent with eagerness. Our dinner conversation was supernatural.
One of the boarders, who had purchased Mrs. Crowe's "Night
Side of Nature" for his private delectation, was regarded as a public enemy by the entire household for not having twenty copies.
The man led a life of supreme wretchedness while he was reading
this volume. A system of espionage was established, of which he
was the victim. If he incautiously laid the book down for an instant

and left the room, it was immediately seized and read aloud in secret places to a select few. I found myself a person of immense importance, it having leaked out that I was tolerably well versed in the history of supernaturalism, and had once written a story the foundation of which was a ghost. If a table or a wainscot panel happened to warp when we were assembled in the large drawing-room, there was an instant silence, and every one was prepared for an immediate clanking of chains and a spectral form.

After a month of psychological excitement, it was with the utmost dissatisfaction that we were forced to acknowledge that nothing in the remotest degree approaching the supernatural had manifested itself. Once the black butler asseverated that his candle had been blown out by some invisible agency while he was undressing himself for the night; but as I had more than once discovered this coloured gentleman in a condition when one candle must have appeared to him like two, I thought it possible that, by going a step further in his potations, he might have reversed this phenomenon, and seen no candle at all where he ought to have beheld one.

Things were in this state when an accident took place so awful and inexplicable in its character that my reason fairly reels at the bare memory of the occurrence. It was the tenth of July. After dinner was over I repaired, with my friend Dr. Hammond, to the garden to smoke my evening pipe. Independent of certain mental sympathies which existed between the Doctor and myself, we were linked together by a vice. We both smoked opium. We knew each other's secret, and respected it. We enjoyed together that wonderful expansion of thought, that marvellous intensifying of the perceptive faculties, that boundless feeling of existence when we seem to have points of contact with the whole universe,—in short, that unimaginable spiritual bliss, which I would not surrender for a throne, and which I hope you, reader, will never—never taste.

Those hours of opium happiness which the Doctor and I spent together in secret were regulated with a scientific accuracy. We did not blindly smoke the drug of paradise, and leave our dreams to chance. While smoking, we carefully steered our conversation through the brightest and calmest channels of thought. We talked of the East, and endeavoured to recall the magical panorama of its glowing scenery. We criticized the most sensuous poets,—those who painted life ruddy with health, brimming with passion, happy in the possession of youth and strength and beauty. If we talked of Shakespeare's "Tempest," we lingered over Ariel, and avoided Caliban. Like the Guebers, we turned our faces to the East, and saw only the sunny side of the world.

This skillful colouring of our train of thought produced in our subsequent visions of corresponding tone. The splendours of Arabian fairyland dyed our dreams. We paced the narrow strip of grass with the tread and port of kings. The song of the *rana arborea*, while he clung to the bark of the ragged plum-tree, sounded like the strains of divine musicians. Houses, walls, and streets melted like rain clouds, and vistas of unimaginable glory stretched away before us. It was a rapturous companionship. We enjoyed the vast delight more perfectly because, even in our most ecstatic moments, we were conscious of each other's presence. Our pleasures, while individual, were still twin, vibrating and moving in musical accord.

On the evening in question, the tenth of July, the Doctor and myself drifted into an unusually metaphysical mood. We lit our large meerschaums, filled with fine Turkish tobacco, in the core of which burned a little black nut of opium, that, like the nut in the fairy tale, held within its narrow limits wonders beyond the reach of kings; we paced to and fro, conversing. A strange perversity dominated the currents of our thought. They would *not* flow through the sun-lit channels into which we strove to divert them.

For some unaccountable reason, they constantly diverged into dark and lonesome beds, where a continual gloom brooded. It was in vain that, after our old fashion, we flung ourselves on the shores of the East, and talked of its gay bazaars, of the splendours of the time of Haroun, of harems and golden palaces. Black afreets continually arose from the depths of our talk, and expanded, like the one the fisherman released from the copper vessel, until they blotted everything bright from our vision. Insensibly, we yielded to the occult force that swayed us, and indulged in gloomy speculation. We had talked some upon the proneness of the human mind to mysticism, and the almost universal love of the terrible, when Hammond suddenly said to me, "What do you consider to be the greatest element of terror?"

The question puzzled me. That many things were terrible, I knew. Stumbling over a corpse in the dark; beholding, as I once did, a woman floating down a deep and rapid river, with wildly lifted arms, and awful, upturned face, uttering, as she drifted, shrieks that rent one's heart while we, spectators, stood frozen at a window which overhung the river at a height of sixty feet, unable to make the slightest effort to save her, but dumbly watched her last supreme agony and her disappearance. A shattered wreck, with no life visible, encountered floating listlessly on the ocean, is a terrible object, for it suggests a huge terror, the proportions of which are veiled. But it now struck me, for the first time, that there must be one great and ruling embodiment of fear,—a King of Terrors, to which all others must succumb. What might it be? To what train of circumstances would it owe its existence?

"I confess, Hammond," I replied to my friend, "I never considered the subject before. That there must be one Something more terrible than any other thing, I feel. I cannot attempt, however, even the most vague definition."

"I am somewhat like you, Harry," he answered. "I feel my

capacity to experience a terror greater than anything yet conceived by the human mind;—something combining in fearful and unnatural amalgamation hitherto supposed incompatible elements. The calling of the voices in Brockden Brown's novel of 'Wieland' is awful; so is the picture of the Dweller of the Threshold in Bulwer's 'Zanoni'; but," he added, shaking his head gloomily, "there is something more horrible than those."

"Look here, Hammond," I rejoined, "let us drop this kind of talk, for Heaven's sake! We shall suffer for it, depend on it."

"I don't know what's the matter with me tonight," he replied, "but my brain is running upon all sorts of weird and awful thoughts. I feel as if I could write a story like Hoffman, tonight, if I were only master of a literary style."

"Well, if we are going to be Hoffmanesque in our talk, I'm off to bed. Opium and nightmares should never be brought together. How sultry it is! Good night, Hammond."

"Good night, Harry. Pleasant dreams to you."

"To you, gloomy wretch, afreets, ghouls, and enchanters."

We parted, and each sought his respective chamber. I undressed quickly and got into bed, taking with me, according to my usual custom, a book, over which I generally read myself to sleep. I opened the volume as soon as I had laid my head upon the pillow, and instantly flung it to the other side of the room. It was Goudon's "History of Monsters"—a curious French work, which I had lately imported from Paris, but which, in the state of mind I had then reached, was anything but an agreeable companion. I resolved to go to sleep at once; so, turning down my gas until nothing but a little blue point of light glimmered on the top of the tube, I composed myself to rest.

The room was in total darkness. The atom of gas that still remained alight did not illuminate a distance of three inches round the burner. I desperately drew my arm across my eyes, as if to shut out even the darkness, and tried to think of nothing. It was in vain. The confounded themes touched on by Hammond in the garden kept obtruding themselves on my brain. I battled against them. I erected ramparts of would-be blankness of intellect to keep them out. They still crowded upon me. While I was lying still as a corpse, hoping that by a perfect physical inaction I should hasten mental repose, an awful incident occurred. A Something dropped, as it seemed, from the ceiling, plumb upon my chest, and the next instant I felt two bony hands encircling my throat, endeavouring to choke me.

I am no coward, and am possessed of considerable physical strength. The suddenness of the attack, instead of stunning me, strung every nerve to its highest tension. My body acted from instinct, before my brain had time to realize the terrors of my position. In an instant I wound two muscular arms around the creature, and squeezed it, with all the strength of despair, against my chest. In a few seconds the bony hands that had fastened on my throat loosened their hold, and I was free to breathe once more. Then commenced a struggle of awful intensity. Immersed in the most profound darkness, totally ignorant of the nature of the Thing by which I was so suddenly attacked, finding my grasp slipping every moment, by reason, it seemed to me, of the entire nakedness of my assailant, bitten with sharp teeth in the shoulder, neck, and chest, having every moment to protect my throat against a pair of sinewy, agile hands, which my utmost efforts could not confine,—these were a combination of circumstances to combat which required all the strength, skill, and courage that I possessed.

At last, after a silent, deadly, exhausting struggle, I got my assailant under by a series of incredible efforts of strength. Once pinned, with my knee on what I made out to be its chest. I knew that I was victor. I rested for a moment to breathe. I heard the creature beneath me panting in the darkness, and felt the violent throbbing of a heart. It was apparently as exhausted as I was; that was one comfort. At this moment I remembered that I usually placed under my pillow, before going to bed, a large yellow silk pocket handkerchief. I felt for it instantly; it was there. In a few seconds more I had, after a fashion, pinioned the creature's arms.

I now felt tolerably secure. There was nothing more to be done but to turn on the gas, and, having first seen what my midnight assailant was like, arouse the household. I will confess to being actuated by a certain pride in not giving the alarm before; I wished to make the capture alone and unaided.

Never losing my hold for an instant, I slipped from the bed to the floor, dragging my captive with me. I had but a few steps to make to reach the gas-burner; these I made with the greatest caution, holding the creature in a grip like a vice. At last I got within arm's length of the tiny speck of blue light which told me where the gas-burner lay. Quick as lightning I released my grasp with one hand and let on the full flood of light. Then I turned to look at my captive.

I cannot even attempt to give any definition of my sensations the instant after I turned on the gas. I suppose I must have shrieked with terror, for in less than a minute afterward my room was crowded with the inmates of the house. I shudder now as I think of that awful moment. *I saw nothing!* Yes; I had one arm firmly clasped round a breathing, panting, corporeal shape, my other hand gripped with all its strength a throat as warm, as apparently fleshy, as my own; and yet, with this living substance in my grasp, with its body pressed against my own, and all in the bright glare of a large jet of gas. I absolutely beheld nothing! Not even an outline, — a vapour!

I do not, even at this hour, realize the situation in which I found myself. I cannot recall the astounding incident thoroughly. Imagination in vain tries to compass the awful paradox.

It breathed. I felt its warm breath upon my cheek. It struggled fiercely. It had hands. They clutched me. Its skin was smooth, like my own. There it lay, pressed close up against me, solid as a stone, —and yet utterly invisible!

I wonder that I did not faint or go mad on the instant. Some wonderful instinct must have sustained me; for, absolutely, in place of loosening my hold on the terrible Enigma, I seemed to gain an additional strength in my moment of horror, and tightened my grasp with such wonderful force that I felt the creature shivering with agony.

Just then Hammond entered my room at the head of the household. As soon as he beheld my face—which, I suppose, must have been an awful sight to look at—he hastened forward, crying, "Great heaven, Harry! what has happened?"

"Hammond! Hammond!" I cried, "come here. O, this is awful! I have been attacked in bed by something or other, which I have hold of; but I can't see it, — I can't see it!"

Hammond, doubtless struck by the unfeigned horror expressed in my countenance, made one or two steps forward with an anxious yet puzzled expression. A very audible titter burst from the remainder of my visitors. This suppressed laughter made me furious. To laugh at a human being in my position! It was the worst species of cruelty. *Now*, I can understand why the appearance of a man struggling violently, as it would seem, with an airy nothing, and calling for assistance against a vision, should have appeared ludicrous. *Then*, so great was my rage against the mocking crowd that had I the power I would have stricken them dead where they stood.

"Hammond! Hammond!" I cried again, despairingly, "for God's sake come to me. I can hold the—the thing but a short while longer. It is overpowering me. Help me! Help me!"

"Harry," whispered Hammond, approaching me, "you have been smoking too much opium."

"I swear to you, Hammond, that this is no vision," I answered, in the same low tone. "Don't you see how it shakes my whole frame with its struggles? If you don't believe me, convince yourself. Feel it,—touch it."

Hammond advanced and laid his hand in the spot I indicated. A wild cry of horror burst from him. He had felt it!

In a moment he had discovered somewhere in my room a long piece of cord, and was the next instant winding it and knotting it about the body of the unseen being that I clasped in my arms.

"Harry," he said, in a hoarse, agitated voice, for though he preserved his presence of mind, he was deeply moved, "Harry, it's all safe now. You may let go, old fellow, if you're tired. The Thing can't move."

I was utterly exhausted, and I gladly loosed my hold.

Hammond stood holding the ends of the cord that bound the Invisible, twisted round his hand, while before him, self-supporting as it were, he beheld a rope laced and interlaced, and stretching tightly around a vacant space. I never saw a man look thoroughly stricken with awe. Nevertheless his face expressed all the courage and determination which I knew him to possess. His lips, although white, were set firmly, and one could perceive at a glance that, although stricken with fear, he was not daunted.

The confusion that ensued among the guests of the house who were witnesses of this extraordinary scene between Hammond and myself,—who beheld the pantomime of binding this struggling Something,—who beheld me almost sinking from physical exhaustion when my task of jailer was over,—the confusion and terror that took possession of the bystanders, when they saw all this, was beyond description. The weaker ones fled the apartment. The few who remained clustered near the door and could not be induced to approach Hammond and his Charge. Still incredulity broke out through their terror. They had not the courage to satisfy themselves, and yet they doubted. It was in vain that I begged of some of the men to come near and convince themselves by touch of the existence in that room of a living being which was invisible. They were incredulous, but did not dare to undeceive themselves. How could a solid, living, breathing body be invisible, they asked. My reply was this. I gave a sign to Hammond, and both of us—conquering our fearful repugnance to touch the invisible creature—lifted it from the ground, manacled as it was, and took it to my bed. Its weight was about that of a boy of fourteen.

"Now, my friends," I said, as Hammond and myself held the creature suspended over the bed, "I can give you self-evident proof that here is a solid, ponderable body, which, nevertheless, you cannot see. Be good enough to watch the surface of the bed attentively."

I was astonished at my own courage in treating this strange event so calmly; but I had recovered from my first terror, and felt a sort of scientific pride in the affair, which dominated every other feeling.

The eyes of the bystanders were immediately fixed on my bed. At a given signal Hammond and I let the creature fall. There was a dull sound of a heavy body alighting on a soft mass. The timbers of the bed creaked. A deep impression marked itself distinctly on the pillow, and on the bed itself. The crowd who witnessed this gave a low cry, and rushed from the room. Hammond and I were left alone with our Mystery.

We remained silent for some time, listening to the low, irregular breathing of the creature on the bed, and watching the rustle of the bedclothes as it impotently struggled to free itself from confinement. Then Hammond spoke.

"Harry, this is awful."

"Ay, awful."

"But not unaccountable."

"Not unaccountable! What do you mean; Such a thing has never occurred since the birth of the world. I know not what to think, Hammond. God grant that I am not mad, and that this is not an insane fantasy!"

"Let us reason a little, Harry. Here is a solid body which we touch, but which we cannot see. The fact is so unusual that it strikes us with terror. Is there no parallel, though, for such a phenomenon? Take a piece of pure glass. It is tangible and transparent. A certain chemical coarseness is all that prevents its being so entirely transparent as to be totally invisible. It is not *theoretically impossible*, mind you, to make a glass which shall not reflect a single ray of light,—a glass so pure and homogeneous in its atoms that the rays from the sun will pass through it as they do through the air, refracted but not reflected. We do not see the air, and yet we feel it."

"That's all very well, Hammond, but these are inanimate substances. Glass does not breathe, air does not breathe. *This* thing has a heart that palpitates,—a will that moves it,—lungs that play, and inspire and respire."

"You forget the phenomena of which we have so often heard of late," answered the Doctor, gravely. "At the meetings called 'spirit circles,' invisible hands have been thrust into the hands of those persons round the table,—warm, fleshy hands that seemed to pulsate with mortal life."

"What? Do you think, then, that this thing is—"

"I don't know what it is," was the solemn reply; "But please the gods I will, with your assistance, thoroughly investigate it."

We watched together, smoking many pipes, all night long, by the bedside of the unearthly being that tossed and panted until it was apparently wearied out. Then we learned by the low, regular breathing that it slept.

The next morning the house was all astir. The boarders congregated on the landing outside my room, and Hammond and myself were lions. We had to answer a thousand questions as to the state of our extraordinary prisoner, for as yet not one person in the house except ourselves could be induced to set foot in the apartment.

The creature was awake. This was evidenced by the convulsive manner in which the bedclothes were moved in its efforts to escape. There was something truly terrible in beholding, as it were, those second-hand indications of the terrible writhings and agonized struggles for liberty which themselves were invisible.

Hammond and myself had racked our brains during the long night to discover some means by which we might realize the shape and general appearance of the Enigma. As well as we could make out by passing our hands over the creature's form, its outlines and lineaments were human. There was a mouth; a round, smooth head without hair; a nose, which, however, was little elevated above the cheeks; and its hands and feet felt like those of a boy. At first we thought of placing the being on a smooth surface and tracing its outlines with chalk, as shoemakers trace the outline of the foot. This plan was given up as being of no value. Such an outline would give not the slightest idea of its conformation.

A happy thought struck me. We would take a cast of it in plaster of Paris. This would give us the solid figure, and satisfy all our wishes. But how to do it? The movements of the creature would disturb the setting of the plastic covering, and distort the mould. Another thought. Why not give it chloroform? It had respiratory organs,—that was evident by its breathing. Once reduced to a state of insensibility, we could do with it what we would. Doctor X— — was sent for; and after the worthy physician had recovered from the first shock of amazement, he proceeded to administer the chloroform. In three minutes afterward we were enabled to remove the fetters from the creature's body, and a modeller was busily engaged in covering the invisible form with the moist clay. In five minutes more we had a mould, and before evening a rough facsimile of the Mystery. It was shaped like a man,—distorted, uncouth, and horrible, but still a man. It was small, not over four feet and some inches in height, and its limbs revealed a muscular development that was unparalleled. Its face surpassed in hideousness anything I had ever seen. Gustav Doré, or Callot, or Tony Johannot, never conceived anything so horrible. There is a face in one of the latter's illustrations to *Un Voyage où il vous plaira*, which somewhat approaches the countenance of this creature, but does not equal it. It was the physiognomy of what I should fancy a ghoul might be. It looked as if it was capable of feeding on human flesh.

Having satisfied our curiosity, and bound every one in the house to secrecy, it became a question what was to be done with our Enigma? It was impossible that we should keep such a horror in our house; it was impossible that such an awful being should be let loose upon the world. I confess that I would have gladly voted for the creature's destruction. But who would shoulder the responsibility? Who would undertake the execution of this horrible semblance of a human being? Day after day this question was deliberated gravely. The boarders all left the house. Mrs. Moffat was in despair, and threatened Hammond and myself with all sorts of legal penalties if we did not remove the Horror. Our answer was, "We will go if you like, but we decline taking this creature with us. Remove it yourself if you please. It appeared in your house. On you the responsibility rests." To this there was, of course, no answer. Mrs. Moffat could not obtain for love or money a person who would even approach the Mystery.

The most singular part of the affair was that we were entirely ignorant of what the creature habitually fed on. Everything in the way of nutriment that we could think of was placed before it, but was never touched. It was awful to stand by, day after day, and see the clothes toss, and hear the hard breathing, and know that it was starving.

Ten, twelve days, a fortnight passed, and it still lived. The pulsations of the heart, however, were daily growing fainter, and had now nearly ceased. It was evident that the creature was dying for want of sustenance. While this terrible life-struggle was going on, I felt miserable. I could not sleep. Horrible as the creature was, it was pitiful to think of the pangs it was suffering.

At last it died. Hammond and I found it cold and stiff one morning in the bed. The heart had ceased to beat, the lungs to inspire. We hastened to bury it in the garden. It was a strange funeral, the dropping of that viewless corpse into the damp hole. The cast of its form I gave to Doctor X— —, who keeps it in his museum in Tenth Street.

As I am on the eve of a long journey from which I may not return, I have drawn up this narrative of an event the most singular that has ever come to my knowledge.

THE DAMNED THING

Ambrose Bierce (1842–1914)

Ambrose Bierce's career began in political journalism. In 1887 he became author of the "Prattler Column" in the San Francisco Examiner, and by the turn of the century, he was the literary dictator of the Pacific Coast, making and breaking reputations at will.

I
One Does Not Always Eat
What Is on the Table

By the light of a tallow candle which had been placed on one end of a rough table a man was reading something written in a book. It was an old account book, greatly worn; and the writing was not, apparently, very legible, for the man sometimes held the page close to the flame of the candle to get a stronger light on it. The shadow of the book would then throw into obscurity a half of the room, darkening a number of faces and figures; for besides the reader, eight other men were present. Seven of them sat against the rough log walls, silent, motionless, and the room being small, not very far from the table. By extending an arm any one of them could have touched the eighth man, who lay on the table, face upward, partly covered by a sheet, his arms at his sides. He was dead.

The man with the book was not reading aloud, and no one spoke; all seemed to be waiting for something to occur; the dead man only was without expectation. From the black darkness outside came in, through the aperture that served for a window, all the ever unfamiliar noises of night in the wilderness—the long nameless note of a distant coyote; the stilly pulsing trill of tireless insects in trees; strange cries of night birds, so different from those of the birds of day; the drone of great blundering beetles, and all that mysterious chorus of small sounds that seem always to have been but half heard when they have suddenly ceased, as if conscious of an indiscretion. But nothing of all this was noted in that company; its members were not overmuch addicted to idle interest in matters of no practical importance; that was obvious in every line of their rugged faces—obvious even in the dim light of the single candle. They were evidently men of the vicinity—farmers and woodsmen.

The person reading was a trifle different; one would have said of him that he was of the world, worldly, albeit there was that in his attire which attested a certain fellowship with the organisms of his environment. His coat would hardly have passed muster in San Francisco; his foot-gear was not of urban origin, and the hat that lay by him on the floor (he was the only one uncovered) was such that if one had considered it as an article of mere personal adornment he would have missed its meaning. In countenance the man was rather prepossessing, with just a hint of sternness; though that he may have assumed or cultivated, as appropriate to one in authority. For he was a coroner. It was by virtue of his office that he had possession of the book in which he was reading; it had been found among the dead man's effects—in his cabin, where the inquest was now taking place.

When the coroner had finished reading he put the book into his breast pocket. At that moment the door was pushed open and a young man entered. He, clearly, was not of mountain birth and breeding: he was clad as those who dwell in cities. His clothing was dusty, however, as from travel. He had, in fact, been riding hard to attend the inquest.

The coroner nodded; no one else greeted him.

"We have waited for you," said the coroner. "It is necessary to have done with this business to-night."

The young man smiled. "I am sorry to have kept you," he said. "I went away, not to evade your summons, but to post to my newspaper an account of what I suppose I am called back to relate."

The coroner smiled.

"The account that you posted to your newspaper," he said, "differs, probably, from that which you will give here under oath."

"That," replied the other, rather hotly and with a visible flush, "is as you please. I used manifold paper and have a copy of what I sent. It was not written as news, for it is incredible, but as fiction. It may go as a part of my testimony under oath."

"But you say it is incredible."

"That is nothing to you, sir, if I also swear that it is true."

The coroner was silent for a time, his eyes upon the floor. The men about the sides of the cabin talked in whispers, but seldom withdrew their gaze from the face of the corpse. Presently, the coroner lifted his eyes and said: "We will resume the inquest."

The men removed their hats. The witness was sworn.

"What is your name?" the coroner asked.

"William Harker."

"Age?"

"Twenty-seven."

"You knew the deceased, Hugh Morgan?"

"Yes."

"You were with him when he died?"

"Near him."

"How did that happen—your presence, I mean?"

"I was visiting him at this place to shoot and fish. A part of my purpose, however, was to study him and his odd, solitary way of life. He seemed a good model for a character in fiction. I sometimes write stories."

"I sometimes read them."

"Thank you."

"Stories in general—not yours."

Some of the jurors laughed. Against a somber background humor shows high lights. Soldiers in the intervals of battle laugh easily, and a jest in the death chamber conquers by surprise.

"Relate the circumstances of this man's death," said the coroner. "You may use any notes or memoranda that you please."

The witness understood. Pulling a manuscript from his breast pocket he held it near the candle and turning the leaves until he found the passage that he wanted began to read.

II
What May Happen in a Field of Wild Oats

" ... The sun had hardly risen when we left the house. We were looking for quail, each with a shotgun, but we had only one dog. Morgan said that our best ground was beyond a certain ridge that he pointed out, and we crossed it by a trail through the *chaparral*. On the other side was comparatively level ground, thickly covered with wild oats. As we emerged from the *chaparral* Morgan was but a few yards in advance. Suddenly we heard, at a little distance to our right and partly in a front, a noise as of some animal thrashing about in the bushes, which we could see were violently agitated.

" 'We've started a deer,' I said. 'I wish we had brought a rifle.'

"Morgan, who had stopped and was intently watching the agitated *chaparral*, said nothing, but had cocked both barrels of his gun and was holding it in readiness to aim. I thought him a trifle excited, which surprised me, for he had a reputation for exceptional coolness, even in moments of sudden and imminent peril.

" 'Oh, come,' I said, 'You are not going to fill up a deer with quail-shot are you?'

"Still he did not reply; but catching a sight of his face as he turned it slightly toward me I was struck by the intensity of his look. Then I understood that we had serious business in hand and my first conjecture was that we had 'jumped' a grizzly. I advanced to Morgan's side, cocking my piece as I moved.

"The bushes were now quiet and the sounds had ceased, but Morgan was as attentive to the place as before.

" 'What is it? What the devil is it?' I asked.

" 'That Damned Thing!' he replied, without turning his head. His voice was husky and unnatural. He trembled visibly.

"I was about to speak further, when I observed the wild oats near the place of the disturbance moving in the most inexplicable way. I can hardly describe it. It seemed as if stirred by a streak of wind, which not only bent it, but pressed it down—crushed it so that it did not rise; and this movement was slowly prolonging itself directly toward us.

"Nothing that I had ever seen had affected me so strangely as this unfamiliar and unaccountable phenomenon, yet I am unable to recall any sense of fear. I remember—and tell it here because, singularly enough, I recollected it then—that once in looking carelessly out of an open window I momentarily mistook a small tree close at hand for one of a group of larger trees at a little distance away. It looked the same size as the others but being more distinctly and sharply defined in mass and detail seemed out of harmony with them. It was a mere falsification of the law of aerial perspective, but it startled, almost terrified me. We so rely upon the orderly operation of familiar natural laws that any seeming suspension of them is noted as a menace to our safety, a warning of unthinkable calamity. So now the apparently causeless movement of the herbage and the slow, undeviating approach of the line of disturbances were distinctly disquieting. My companion appeared actually frightened, and I could hardly credit my senses when I saw him suddenly throw his gun to his shoulder and fire both barrels at the agitated grain! Before the smoke of the discharge had cleared away I heard a loud savage cry—a scream like that of a wild animal—and flinging his gun upon the ground Morgan sprang away and ran swiftly from the spot. At the same instant I was thrown violently to the ground by the impact of something unseen in the smoke—some soft, heavy substance that seemed thrown against me with great force.

"Before I could get upon my feet and recover my gun, which seemed to have been struck from my hands, I heard Morgan crying out as if in mortal agony, and mingling with his cries were such hoarse, savage sounds as one hears from fighting dogs. Inexpressibly terrified, I struggled to my feet and looked in the direction of Morgan's retreat; and may Heaven in mercy spare me from another sight like that! At a distance of less than thirty yards was my friend, down upon one knee, his head thrown back at a frightful angle, hatless, his long hair in disorder and his whole body in violent movement from side to side, backward and forward. His right arm was lifted and seemed to lack the hand—at least, I could see none. The other arm was invisible. At times, as my memory now reports this extraordinary scene, I could discern but a part of his body; it was as if he had been partly blotted out— I cannot otherwise express it—then a shifting of his position would bring it all into view again.

"All this must have occurred within a few seconds, yet in that time Morgan assumed all the postures of a determined wrestler vanquished by superior weight and strength. I saw nothing but him, and him not always distinctly. During the entire incident his shouts and curses were heard, as if through an enveloping uproar of such sounds of rage and fury as I had never heard from the throat of man or brute!

"For a moment only I stood irresolute, then throwing down my gun I ran forward to my friend's assistance. I had a vague belief that he was suffering from a fit, or some form of convulsion. Before I could reach his side he was down and quiet. All sounds had ceased, but with a feeling of such terror as even these awful events had not inspired I now saw again the mysterious movement of the wide oats, prolonging itself from the trampled area about the prostrate man toward the edge of a wood. It was only when it had reached the wood that I was able to withdraw my eyes and look at my companion. He was dead."

III
A Man Though Naked May Be in Rags

The coroner rose from his seat and stood beside the dead man. Lifting an edge of the sheet he pulled it away, exposing the entire body, altogether naked and showing in the candlelight a claylike yellow. It had, however, broad masculations of bluish black, obviously caused by extravasated blood from contusions. The chest and sides looked as if they had been beaten with a bludgeon. There were dreadful lacerations; the skin was torn in strips and shreds.

The coroner moved round to the end of the table and undid a silk handkerchief which had been passed under the chin and knotted on the top of the head. When the handkerchief was drawn away it exposed what had been the throat. Some of the jurors who had risen to get a better view repented their curiosity and turned away their faces. Witness Harker went to the open window and leaned out across the sill, faint and sick. Dropping the handker-chief upon the dead man's neck the coroner stepped to an angle of the room and from a pile of clothing produced one garment after another, each of which he held up a moment for inspection. All were torn, and stiff with blood. The jurors did not make a closer inspection. They seemed rather uninterested. They had, in truth, seen all this before; the only thing that was new to them being Harker's testimony.

"Gentlemen," the coroner said, "we have no more evidence, I think. Your duty has been already explained to you, if there is nothing you wish to ask you may go outside and consider your verdict."

The foreman rose—a tall, bearded man of sixty, coarsely clad.

"I should like to ask one question, Mr. Coroner," he said. "What asylum did this yer last witness escape from?"

"Mr. Harker," said the coroner, gravely and tranquilly, "from what asylum did you last escape?"

Harker flushed crimson again, but said nothing, and the seven jurors rose and solemnly filed out of the cabin.

"If you have done insulting me, sir," said Harker, as soon as he and the officer were left alone with the dead man, "I suppose I am at liberty to go."

"Yes."

Harker started to leave, but paused, with his hand on the door latch. The habit of his profession was strong in him—stronger than his sense of personal dignity. He turned about and said:

"The book that you have there—I recognize it as Morgan's diary. You seemed greatly interested in it; you read in it while I was testifying. May I see it? The public would like—"

"The book will cut no figure in this matter," replied the official, slipping it into his coat pocket; "all the entries in it were made before the writer's death."

As Harker passed out of the house the jury reentered and stood about the table, on which the now covered corpse showed under the sheet with sharp definition. The foreman seated himself near the candle, produced from his breast pocket a pencil and scrap of paper and wrote rather laboriously the following verdict, which with various degrees of effort all signed:

"We, the jury, do find that the remains come to their death at the hands of a mountain lion, but some of us thinks, all the same, they had fits."

IV
An Explanation from the Tomb

In the diary of the late Hugh Morgan are certain interesting entries having, possibly, a scientific value as suggestions. At the inquest upon his body the book was not put in evidence; possibly the coroner thought it not worth while to confuse the jury. The date of the first of the entries mentioned cannot be ascertained; the upper part of the leaf is torn away; the part of the entry remaining follows:

". . . would run in a half-circle, keeping his head turned always toward the center, and again he would stand still, barking furiously. At last he ran away into the brush as fast as he could go. I thought at first he had gone mad, but on returning to the house found no other alteration in his manner than what was obviously due to fear of punishment.

"Can a dog see with his nose? Do odors impress some cerebral center with images of the thing that emitted them? . . .

"Sept. 2—Looking at the stars last night as they rose above the crest of the ridge east of the house, I observed them successively disappear—from left to right. Each was eclipsed but an instant, and only a few at the same time, but along the entire length of the ridge all that were within a degree of two of the crest were blotted out. It was as if something had passed along between me and them; but I could not see it, and the stars were not thick enough to define its outline. Ugh! I don't like this."

Several weeks' entries are missing, three leaves being torn from the book.

"Sept. 27—It has been about here again—I find evidences of its presence every day. I watched again all last night in the same cover, gun in hand, double-charged with buckshot. In the morning the fresh footprints were there, as before. Yet I would have sworn that I did not sleep—indeed, I hardly sleep at all. It was terrible, insupportable! If these amazing experiences are real I shall go mad; if they are fanciful I am mad already.

"Oct. 3—I shall not go—it shall not drive me away. No, this is *my* house, *my* land. God hates a coward . . . .

"Oct. 5—I can stand it no longer; I have invited Harker to pass a few weeks with me—he has a level head. I can judge from his manner if he thinks me mad.

"Oct. 7—I have the solution of the mystery; it came to me last night—suddenly, as by revelation. How simple—how terribly simple!

"There are sounds that we cannot hear. At either end of the scale are notes that stir no chord of that imperfect instrument, the human ear. They are too high or too grave. I have observed a flock of blackbirds occupying an entire tree-top—the tops of several trees—and all in full song. Suddenly—in a moment—at absolutely the same instant—all spring into the air and fly away. How? They could not all see one another—whole tree-tops intervened. At no point could a leader have been visible to all. There must have been a signal of warning or command, high and shrill above the din, but by me unheard. I have observed, too, the same simultaneous flight when all were silent, among not only blackbirds, but other birds—quail, for example, widely separated by bushes—even on opposite sides of a hill.

"It is known to seamen that a school of whales basking or sporting on the surface of the ocean, miles apart, with the convexity of the earth between, will sometimes dive at the same instant—all gone out of sight in a moment. The signal has been sounded—too grave for the ear of the sailor at the masthead and his comrades on the deck—who nevertheless feel its vibrations in the ship as the stones of a cathedral are stirred by the bass of the organ.

"As with sounds, so with colors. At each end of the solar spectrum the chemist can detect the presence of what are known as 'actinic' rays. They represent colors—integral colors in the composition of light—which we are unable to discern. The human eye is an imperfect instrument; its range is but a few octaves of the real 'chromatic scale.' I am not mad; there are colors that we cannot see.

"And, God help me! the Damned Thing is of such a color!"

THE GHOST OF FEAR

H. G. Wells (1866–1946)

One of the most important and controversial writers of his age, England's H. G. Wells was both versatile and prolific. He was a novelist, historian, and scientific writer whose work was united by a plea for rational control of the material forces released by mankind. His extensive scientific endeavors did much to advance the actual and fictional aspects of that field.

"I can assure you," said I, "that it will take a very tangible ghost to frighten me." And I stood up before the fire with my glass in my hand.

"It is your own choosing," said the man with the withered arm, and glanced at me askance.

"Eight-and-twenty years," said I, "I have lived, and never a ghost have I seen as yet."

The old woman sat staring hard into the fire, her pale eyes wide open, "Ay," she broke in, "and eight-and-twenty years you have lived, never seen the likes of this house, I reckon. There's a many things to see, when one's still but eight-and-twenty." She swayed her head slowly from side to side. "A many things to see and sorrow for."

I half suspected these old people were trying to enhance the spectral terrors of their house by this droning insistence. I put down my empty glass on the table, and, looking about the room, caught a glimpse of myself, abbreviated and broadened to an impossible sturdiness, in the queer old mirror beside the china cupboard. "Well," I said, "if I see anything to-night, I shall be so much the wiser. For I come to the business with an open mind."

"It's your own choosing," said the man with the withered arm once more.

I heard the faint sound of a stick and a shambling step on the flags in the passage outside. The door creaked on its hinges as a second old man entered, more bent, more wrinkled, more aged even than the first. He supported himself by the help of a crutch, his eyes were covered by a shade, and his lower lip, half averted, hung pale and pink from his decaying yellow teeth. He made straight for an armchair on the opposite side of the table, sat down clumsily, and began to cough. The man with the withered hand gave the newcomer a short glance of positive dislike; the old woman took no notice of his arrival, but remained with her eyes fixed steadily on the fire.

"I said—it's your own choosing," said the man with the withered hand, when the coughing had ceased for a while.

"It's my own choosing," I answered.

The man with the shade became aware of my presence for the first time, and threw his head back for a moment, and sidewise, to see me. I caught a momentary glimpse of his eyes, small and bright and inflamed. Then he began to cough and splutter again.

"Why don't you drink?" said the man with the withered arm, pushing the beer toward him. The man with the shade poured out a glassful with a shaking hand, that splashed half as much again on the deal table. A monstrous shadow of him crouched upon the wall, and mocked his action as he poured and drank. I must confess I had scarcely expected these grotesque custodians. There is, to my mind, something inhuman in senility, something crouching and atavistic: the human qualities seem to drop from old people insensibly day by day. The three of them made me feel uncomfortable with their gaunt silences, their bent carriage, their evident unfriendliness to me and to one another. And that night, perhaps, I was in the mood for uncomfortable impressions. I resolved to get away from their vague foreshadowings of the evil things upstairs.

"If," said I, "you will show me to this haunted room of yours, I will make myself comfortable there."

The old man with the cough jerked his head back so suddenly that it startled me, and shot another glance of his red eyes at me from out of the darkness under the shade, but no one answered me. I waited a minute, glancing from one to the other. The old woman stared like a dead body, glaring into the fire with the lackluster eyes.

"If," I said, a little louder, "if you will show me to this haunted room of yours, I will relieve you from the task of entertaining me."

"There's a candle on the slab outside the door," said the man with the withered hand, looking at my feet as he addressed me. "But if you go to the Red Room to-night—"

"This night of all nights!" said the old woman, softly. "—You go alone."

"Very well," I answered shortly, "and which way do I go?"

"You go along the passage for a bit," said he, nodding his head on his shoulder at the door, "until you come to a spiral staircase; and on the second landing is a door covered with green baize. Go through that, and down the long corridor to the end, and the Red Room is on your left up the steps."

"Have I got that right?" I said, and repeated his directions.

He corrected me in one particular.

"And you are really going?" said the man with the shade, looking at me again for the third time with that queer, unnatural tilting of the face.

"This night of all nights!" whispered the old woman.

"It is what I came for," I said, and moved toward the door. As I did so, the old man with the shade rose and staggered round the table, so as to be closer to the others and to the fire. At the door I turned and looked at them, and saw they were all close together, dark against the firelight, staring at me over their shoulders, with an intent expression on their ancient faces.

"Good night," I said, setting the door open.

"It's your own choosing," said the man with the withered arm.

I left the door wide open until the candle was well alight, and then I shut them in, and walked down the chilly, echoing passage.

I must confess that the oddness of these three old pensioners in whose charge their ladyship had left the castle, and the deep-toned, old-fashioned furniture of the housekeeper's room, in which they forgathered, had affected me curiously in spite of my effort to keep myself at a matter-of-fact phase. They seemed to belong to another age, an older age, an age when things spiritual were indeed to be feared, when common sense was uncommon, an age when omens and witches were credible, and ghosts beyond denying. Their very existence, thought I, is spectral; the cut of their clothing, fashions born in dead brains; the ornaments and conveniences in the room about them even are ghostly—the thoughts of vanished men, which still haunt rather than participate in the world of to-day. And the passage I was in, long and shadowy, with a film of moisture glistening on the walls, was as gaunt and cold as a thing that is dead and rigid. But with an effort I sent such thoughts to the right-about. The long, drafty subterranean passage was chilly and dusty, and my candle flared and made the shadows cower and quiver. The echoes rang up and down the spiral staircase, and a shadow came sweeping up after me, and another fled before me into the darkness overhead. I came to the wide landing and stopped there for a moment listening to a rustling that I fancied I heard creeping behind me, and then, satisfied of the absolute silence, pushed open the unwilling baize-covered door and stood in the silent corridor.

The effect was scarcely what I expected, for the moonlight, coming in by the great window on the grand staircase, picked out everything in vivid black shadow or reticulated silvery illumination. Everything seemed in its proper position; the house might have been deserted on the yesterday instead of twelve months ago. There were candles in the sockets of the sconces, and whatever dust had gathered on the carpets or upon the polished flooring was distributed so evenly as to be invisible in my candlelight. A waiting stillness was over everything. I was about to advance, and stopped abruptly. A bronze group stood upon the landing hidden from me by a corner of the wall; but its shadow fell with marvelous distinctness upon the white paneling, and gave me the impression of someone crouching to waylay me. The thing jumped upon my attention suddenly. I stood rigid for half a moment, perhaps. Then, with my hand in the pocket that held the revolver, I advanced, only to discover a Ganymede and Eagle, glistening in the moonlight. That incident for a time restored my nerve, and a dim porcelain Chinaman on a buhl table, whose head rocked as I passed, scarcely startled me.

The door of the Red Room and the steps up to it were in a shadowy corner. I moved my candle from side to side in order to see clearly the nature of the recess in which I stood, before opening the door. Here it is, thought I, that my predecessor was found, and the memory of that story gave me a sudden twinge of apprehension. I glanced over my shoulder at the black Ganymede in the moonlight, and opened the door of the Red Room rather hastily, with my face half turned to the pallid silence of the corridor.

I entered, closed the door behind me at once, turned the key I found in the lock within, and stood with the candle held aloft surveying the scene of my vigil, the great Red Room of Lorraine Castle, in which the young Duke had died; or rather in which he had begun his dying, for he had opened the door and fallen headlong down the steps I had just ascended. That had been the end of his vigil, of his gallant attempt to conquer the ghostly tradition of the place, and never, I thought, had apoplexy better served the ends of superstition. There were other and older stories that clung to the room, back to the half-incredible beginning of it all, the tale of a timid wife and the tragic end that came to her husband's jest of frightening her. And looking round that huge shadowy room with its black window bays, its recesses and alcoves, its dusty brown-red hangings and dark gigantic furniture, one could well understand the legends that had sprouted in its black corners, its germinating darknesses. My candle was a little tongue of light in the vastness of the chamber; its rays failed to pierce to the opposite end of the room, and left an ocean of dull red mystery and suggestion, sentinel shadows and watching darknesses beyond its island of light. And the stillness of desolation brooded over it all.

I must confess some impalpable quality of that ancient room disturbed me. I tried to fight the feeling down. I resolved to make a systematic examination of the place, and so by leaving nothing to the imagination, dispel the fanciful suggestions of the obscurity before they obtained a hold upon me. After satisfying myself of the fastening of the door, I began to walk round the room, peering round each article of furniture, tucking up the valances of the bed and opening its curtain wide. In one place there was a distinct echo to my footsteps, the noises I made seemed so little that they enhanced rather than broke the silence of the place. I pulled up the blinds and examined the fastenings of the several windows. Attracted by the fall of a particle of dust, I leaned forward and looked up the blackness of the wide chimney. Then, trying to preserve my scientific attitude of mind, I walked round and began tapping the oak paneling for any secret opening, but I desisted before reaching the alcove. I saw my face in a mirror—white.

There were two big mirrors in the room, each with a pair of sconces bearing candles, and on the mantelshelf, too, were candles in china candlesticks. All these I lit one after the other. The fire was laid—an unexpected consideration from the old housekeeper—and I lit it, to keep down any disposition to shiver, and when it was burning well I stood round with my back to it and regarded the room again. I had pulled up a chintz-covered armchair and a table to form a kind of barricade before me. On this lay my revolver, ready to hand. My precise examination had done me a little good, but I still found the remoter darkness of the place and its perfect stillness too stimulating for the imagination. The echoing of the stir and cracking of the fire was no sort of comfort to me. The shadow in the alcove at the end of the room began to display that undefinable quality of a presence, that odd suggestion of a lurking living thing that comes so easily in silence and solitude. And to reassure myself, I walked with a candle into it and satisfied myself that there was nothing tangible there. I stood that candle upon the floor of the alcove and left it in that position.

By this time I was in a state of considerable nervous tension, although to my reason there was no adequate cause for my condition. My mind, however, was perfectly clear. I postulated quite unreservedly that nothing supernatural could happen, and to pass the time I began stringing some rhymes together, Ingoldsby fashion, concerning the original legend of the place. A few I spoke aloud, but the echoes were not pleasant. For the same reason I also abandoned, after a time, a conversation with myself upon the impossibility of ghosts and haunting. My mind reverted to the three old and distorted people downstairs, and I tried to keep it upon that topic.

The somber reds and grays of the room troubled me; even with its seven candles the place was merely dim. The light in the alcove flaring in a draft, and the fire flickering, kept the shadows and penumbra perpetually shifting and stirring in a noiseless flighty dance. Casting about for a remedy, I recalled the wax candles I had seen in the corridor, and, with a slight effort, carrying a candle and leaving the door open, I walked out into the moonlight, and presently returned with as many as ten. These I put in the various knick-knacks of china with which the room was sparsely adorned, and lit and placed them where the shadows had lain deepest, some on the floor, some in the window recesses, arranging and rearranging them until at last my seventeen candles were so placed that not an inch of the room but had the direct light of at least one of them. It occurred to me that when the ghost came I could warn him not to trip over them. The room was now quite brightly illuminated. There was something very cheering and reassuring in these little silent streaming flames, and to notice their steady diminution of length offered me an occupation and gave me a reassuring sense of the passage of time.

Even with that, however, the brooding expectation of the vigil weighed heavily enough upon me. I stood watching the minute hand of my watch creep towards midnight.

Then something happened in the alcove. I did not see the candle go out, I simply turned and saw that the darkness was there, as one might start and see the unexpected presence of a stranger. The black shadow had sprung back to its place. "By Jove," said I aloud, recovering from my surprise, "that draft's a strong one";

and taking the matchbox from the table, I walked across the room in a leisurely manner to relight the corner again. My first match would not strike, and as I succeeded with the second, something seemed to blink on the wall before me. I turned my head involuntarily and saw that the two candles on the little table by the fireplace were extinguished. I rose at once to my feet.

"Odd," I said. "Did I do that myself in a flash of absentmindedness?"

I walked back, relit one, and as I did so I saw the candle on the right sconce of one of the mirrors wink and go right out, and almost immediately its companion followed it. The flames vanished as if the wick had been suddenly nipped between a finger and thumb, leaving the wick neither glowing nor smoking, but black. While I stood gaping the candle at the foot of the bed went out, and the shadows seemed to take another step toward me.

"This won't do!" said I, and first one and then another candle on the mantleshelf followed.

"What's up?" I cried, with a queer high note getting into my voice somehow. At that the candle on the corner of the wardrobe went out, and the one I had relit in the alcove followed.

"Steady on!" I said, "those candles are wanted," speaking with a half-hysterical facetiousness, and scratching away at a match the while, "for the mantel candlesticks." My hands trembled so much that twice I missed the rough paper of the matchbox. As the mantel emerged from the darkness again, two candles in the remoter end of the room were eclipsed. But with the same match I also relit the larger mirror candles, and those on the floor near the doorway, so that for the moment I seemed to gain on the extinctions. But then in a noiseless volley there vanished four lights at once in different corners of the room, and I struck another match in quivering haste, and stood hesitating whither to take it.

As I stood undecided, an invisible hand seemed to sweep out

the two candles on the table. With a cry of terror I dashed at the alcove, then into the corner and then into the window, relighting three as two more vanished by the fireplace, and then, perceiving a better way I dropped matches on the iron-bound deedbox in the corner, and caught up the bedroom candlestick. With this I avoided the delay of striking matches, but for all that the steady process of extinction went on, and the shadows I feared and fought against returned, and crept in upon me, first a step gained on this side of me, then on that. I was now almost frantic with the horror of the coming darkness, and my self-possession deserted me. I leaped panting from candle to candle in a vain struggle against that remorseless advance.

I bruised myself in the thigh against a table, I sent a chair headlong, I stumbled and fell and whisked the cloth from the table in my fall. My candle rolled away from me and I snatched another as I rose. Abruptly this was blown out as I swung it off the table by the wind of my sudden movement, and immediately the two remaining candles followed. But there was light still in the room, a red light, that streamed across the ceiling and staved off the shadows from me. The fire! Of course I could still thrust my candle between the bars and relight it!

I turned to where the flames were still dancing between the glowing coals and splashing red reflections upon the furniture; made two steps toward the grate, and incontinently the flames dwindled and vanished, the glow vanished, the reflections rushed together and disappeared, and as I thrust the candle between the bars darkness closed upon me like the shutting of an eye, wrapped about me in a stifling embrace, sealed my vision, and crushed the last vestiges of self-possession from my brain. And it was not only palpable darkness, but intolerable terror. The candle fell from my hands. I flung out my arms in a vain effort to thrust that ponderous blackness away from me, and lifting up my voice, screamed with all my might, once, twice, thrice. Then I think I must have staggered to my feet. I know I thought suddenly of the moonlit corridor, and with my head bowed and my arms over my face, made a stumbling run for the door.

But I had forgotten the exact position of the door, and I struck myself heavily against the corner of the bed. I staggered back, turned, and was either struck or struck myself against some other bulky furnishing. I have a vague memory of battering myself thus to and fro in the darkness, of a heavy blow at last upon my forehead, of a horrible sensation of falling that lasted an age, of my last frantic effort to keep my footing, and then I remember no more.

I opened my eyes in daylight. My head was roughly bandaged, and the man with the withered hand was watching my face. I looked about me trying to remember what had happened, and for a space I could not recollect. I rolled my eyes into the corner and saw the old woman, no longer abstracted, no longer terrible, pouring out some drops of medicine from a little blue phial into a glass. "Where am I?" I said. "I seem to remember you, and yet I cannot remember who you are."

They told me then, and I heard of the haunted Red Room as one who hears a tale. "We found you at dawn," said he, "and there was blood on your forehead and lips."

I wondered that I had ever disliked him. The three of them in the daylight seemed commonplace old folk enough. The man with the green shade had his head bent as one who sleeps.

It was very slowly I recovered the memory of my experience. "You believe now," said the old man with the withered hand, "that the room is haunted." He spoke no longer as one who greets an intruder, but as one who condoles a friend.

"Yes," said I, "the room is haunted."

"And you have seen it. And we who have been here all our lives have never set eyes upon it. Because we have never dared.

Tell us, is it truly the old earl who—"

"No," said I, "it is not."

"I told you so," said the old lady, with the glass in her hand. "It is his poor young countess who was frightened—"

"It is not," I said. "There is neither ghost of earl nor ghost of countess in that room; there is not ghost there at all, but worse, far worse, something impalpable—"

"Well?" they said.

"The worst of all the things that haunt poor mortal men," said I; "and that is, in all its nakedness—'Fear!' Fear that will not have light nor sound, that will not bear with reason, that deafens and darkens and overwhelms. It followed me through the corridor, it fought against me in the room—"

I stopped abruptly. There was an interval of silence. My hand went up to my bandages. "The candles went out one after another, and I fled—"

Then the man with the shade lifted his face sideways to see me and spoke.

"That is it," said he. "I knew that was it. A Power of Darkness. To put such a curse upon a home! It lurks there always. You can feel it even in the daytime, even of a bright summer's day, in the hangings, in the curtains, keeping behind you however you face about. In the dusk it creeps into the corridor and follows you, so that you dare not turn. It is even as you say. Fear itself is in that room. Black Fear . . . And there it will be . . . so long as this house of sin endures."

THE WENDIGO

Algernon Blackwood (1869–1951)

This English mystic, novelist, and short story writer spent his early years as a journalist in Canada and New York. At age thirty, he returned to England and launched his career as a writer. His passion for nature and his conviction that man possessed strange powers pervaded his work, and toward the end of his life, he gained a considerable reputation as a terrifyingly effective teller of ghost stories on television.

I

A considerable number of hunting parties were out that year without finding so much as a fresh trail; for the moose were uncommonly shy, and the various Nimrods returned to the bosoms of their respective families with the best excuses the facts or their imaginations could suggest. Dr. Cathcart, among others, came back without a trophy; but he brought instead the memory of an experience which he declares was worth all the bull-moose that had ever been shot. But then Cathcart, of Aberdeen, was interested in other things besides moose—amongst them the vagaries of the human mind. This particular story, however, found no mention in his book on *Collective Hallucination* for the simple reason (so he confided once to a fellow colleague) that he himself played too intimate a part in it to form a competent judgement of the affair as a whole . . .

Besides himself and his guide, Hank Davis, there was young Simpson, his nephew, a divinity student destined for the "Wee Kirk" (then on his first visit to Canadian backwoods), and the latter's guide, Défago. Joseph Défago was a French "Canuck," who had strayed from his native Province of Quebec years before, and had got caught in Rat Portage when the Canadian Pacific Railway was a-building; a man who, in addition to his unparalleled knowledge of woodcraft and bush-lore, could also sing the old *voyageur* songs and tell a capital hunting yarn into the bargain. He was deeply susceptible, moreover, to that singular spell which the wilderness lays upon certain lonely natures, and he loved the wild solitudes with a kind of romantic passion that amounted almost to an obsession. The life of the backwoods fascinated him—whence, doubtless, his surpassing efficiency in dealing with their mysteries.

On this particular expedition he was Hank's choice. Hank knew him and swore by him. He also swore at him, "jest as a pal might," and since he had a vocabulary of picturesque, if utterly meaningless, oaths, the conversation between the two stalwart and hardy woodsmen was often of a rather lively description. This river of expletives, however, Hank agreed to dam a little out of respect for his old "hunting boss," Dr. Cathcart, whom of course he addressed after the fashion of the country as "Doc," and also because he understood that young Simpson was already a "bit of a parson." He had, however, one objection to Défago, and one only—which was, that the French Canadian sometimes exhibited what Hank described as "the output of a cursed and dismal mind," meaning apparently that he sometimes was true to type, Latin type, and suffered fits of a kind of silent moroseness when nothing could induce him to utter speech. Défago, that is to say, was imaginative and melancholy. And, as a rule, it was too long a spell of "civilization" that induced the attacks, for a few days of the wilderness invariably cured them.

This, then, was the party of four that found themselves in camp the last week in October of that "shy moose year" 'way up in the wilderness north of Rat Portage—a forsaken and desolate country. There was also Punk, an Indian, who had accompanied Dr. Cathcart and Hank on their hunting trips in previous years, and who acted as cook. His duty was merely to stay in camp, catch fish, and prepare venison steaks and coffee at a few minutes' notice. He dressed in the worn-out clothes bequeathed to him by former patrons, and except for his coarse black hair and dark skin, he looked in these city garments no more like a real redskin than a stage negro looks like a real African. For all that, however, Punk had in him still the instincts of his dying race; his taciturn silence and his endurance survived; also his superstition.

The party round the blazing fire that night were despondent, for a week had passed without a single sign of recent moose discovering itself. Défago had sung his song and plunged into a story, but Hank, in bad humour, reminded him so often that "he kep' mussing-up the fac's so, that it was 'most all nothin' but a petred-out lie," that the Frenchman had finally subsided into a sulky silence which nothing seemed likely to break. Dr. Cathcart and his nephew were fairly done after an exhausting day. Punk was washing up the dishes, grunting to himself under the lean-to of branches, where he later also slept. No one troubled to stir the slowly dying fire. Overhead the stars were brilliant in a sky quite wintry, and there was so little wind that ice was already forming stealthily along the shores of the still lake behind them. The silence of the vast listening forest stole forward and enveloped them.

Hank broke in suddenly with his nasal voice.

"I'm in favour of breaking new ground to-morrow, Doc," he

observed with energy, looking across at his employer. "We don't stand a dead Dago's chance about here."

"Agreed," said Cathcart, always a man of few words. "Think the idea's good."

"Sure pop, it's good," Hank resumed with confidence. "S'pose, now, you and I strike west, up Garden Lake way for a change! None of us ain't touched that quiet bit o' land yet—"

"I'm with you."

"And you, Défago, take Mr. Simpson along in the small canoe, skip across the lake, portage over into Fifty Island Water, and take a good squint down that thar southern shore. The moose 'yarded' there like hell last year, and for all we know they may be doin' it agin this year jest to spite us."

Défago, keeping his eyes on the fire, said nothing by way of reply. He was still offended, possibly, about his interrupted story.

"No one's been up that way this year, an' I'll lay my bottom dollar on *that*!" Hank added with emphasis, as though he had a reason for knowing. He looked over at his partner sharply. "Better take the little silk tent and stay away a couple o' nights," he concluded, as though the matter were definitely settled. For Hank was recognized as general organizer of the hunt, and in charge of the party.

It was obvious to any one that Défago did not jump at the plan, but his silence seemed to convey something more than ordinary disapproval, and across his sensitive dark face there passed a curious expression like a flash of firelight—not so quickly, however, that the three men had not time to catch it. "He funked for some reason, *I* thought," Simpson said afterwards in the tent he shared with his uncle. Dr. Cathcart made no immediate reply, although the look had interested him enough at the time for him to make a mental note of it. The expression had caused him a passing uneasiness he could not quite account for at the moment.

But Hank, of course, had been the first to notice it, and the odd thing was that instead of becoming explosive or angry over the other's reluctance, he at once began to humour him a bit.

"But there ain't no *speshul* reason why no one's been up there this year," he said with a perceptible hush in his tone; "not the reason *you* mean, anyway! Las' year it was the fires that kep' folks out, and this year I guess—I guess it jest happened so, that's all!" His manner was clearly meant to be encouraging.

Joseph Défago raised his eyes a moment, then dropped them again. A breath of wind stole out of the forest and stirred the embers into a passing blaze. Dr. Cathcart again noticed the expression in the guide's face, and again he did not like it. But this time the nature of the look betrayed itself. In those eyes, for an instant, he caught the gleam of a man scared in his very soul. It disquieted him more than he cared to admit.

"Bad Indians up that way?" he asked, with a laugh to ease matters a little, while Simpson, too sleepy to notice this subtle by-play, moved off to bed with a prodigious yawn; "or—or anything wrong with the country?" he added, when his nephew was out of hearing.

Hank met his eye with something less than his usual frankness.

"He's jest skeered," he replied good-humouredly, "Skeered stiff about some ole feery tale! That's all, ain't it, ole pard?" And he gave Défago a friendly kick in the moccasined foot that lay nearest the fire.

Défago looked up quickly, as from an interrupted reverie, a reverie, however, that had not prevented his seeing all that went on about him.

"Skeered—*nuthin'!*" he answered, with a flush of defiance. "There's nuthin' in the Bush that can skeer Joseph Défago, and don't you forget it!" And the natural energy with which he spoke made it impossible to know whether he told the whole truth or only a part of it.

Hank turned towards the doctor. He was just going to add something when he stopped abruptly and looked round. A sound close behind them in the darkness made all three start. It was old Punk, who had moved up from his lean-to while they talked and now stood there just behind the circle of firelight—listening.

" 'Nother time, Doc!" Hank whispered, with a wink, "when the gallery ain't stepped down into the stalls!" And, springing to his feet, he slapped the Indian on the back and cried noisily, "Come up t' the fire an' warm yer dirty red skin a bit." He dragged him towards the blaze and threw more wood on. "That was a mighty good feed you give us an hour or two back," he continued heartily, as though to set the man's thoughts on another scent, "and it ain't Christian to let you stand there freezin' yer soul to hell while we're gettin' all good an' toasted!" Punk moved in and warmed his feet, smiling darkly at the other's volubility which he only half understood, but saying nothing. And presently Dr. Cathcart, seeing that further conversation was impossible, followed his nephew's example and moved off to the tent, leaving the three men smoking over the now blazing fire.

It is not easy to undress in a small tent without waking one's companion, and Cathcart, hardened and warm-blooded as he was in spite of his fifty odd years, did what Hank would have described as "considerable of his twilight" in the open. He noticed, during the process, that Punk had meanwhile gone back to his lean-to, and that Hank and Défago were at it hammer and tongs, or rather, hammer and anvil, the little French Canadian being the anvil. It was all very like the conventional stage picture of Western melodrama: the fire lighting up their faces with patches of alternate red and black; Défago, in slouch hat and moccasins in the part of the "badlands" villain; Hank, open-faced and hatless, with that reckless fling of his shoulders, the honest and deceived hero; and old Punk, eavesdropping in the background, supplying the atmosphere of mystery. The doctor smiled as he noticed the details; but at the same time something deep within him—he hardly knew what—shrank a little, as though an almost imperceptible breath of warning had touched the surface of his soul and was gone again before he could seize it. Probably it was traceable to that "scared expression" he had seen in the eyes of Défago; "probably"—for this hint of fugitive emotion otherwise escaped his usually so keen analysis. Défago, he was vaguely aware, might cause trouble somehow . . . He was not as steady a guide as Hank, for instance . . . Further than that he could not get . . .

He watched the men a moment longer before diving into the stuffy tent where Simpson already slept soundly. Hank, he saw, was swearing like a mad African in a New York nigger saloon; but it was the swearing of "affection." The ridiculous oaths flew freely now that the cause of their obstruction was asleep. Presently he put his arm almost tenderly upon his comrade's shoulder, and they moved off together into the shadows where their tent stood faintly glimmering. Punk, too, a moment later followed their example and disappeared between his odorous blankets in the opposite direction.

Dr. Cathcart then likewise turned in, weariness and sleep still fighting in his mind with an obscure curiosity to know what it was had scared Défago about the country up Fifty Island Water way,—wondering, too, why Punk's presence had prevented the completion of what Hank had to say. Then sleep overtook him. He would know to-morrow. Hank would tell him the story while they trudged after the elusive moose.

Deep silence fell about the little camp, planted there so audaciously in the jaws of the wilderness. The lake gleamed like a sheet of black glass beneath the stars. The cold air pricked. In the draughts of night that poured their silent tide from the depths of the forest, with messages from distant ridges and from lakes just beginning to freeze, there lay already the faint, bleak odours of coming winter. White men, with their dull scent, might never have divined them; the fragrance of the wood-fire would have concealed from them these almost electrical hints of moss and bark and hardening swamp a hundred miles away. Even Hank and Défago, subtly in league with the soul of the woods as they were, would probably have spread their delicate nostrils in vain . . . .

But an hour later, when all slept like the dead, old Punk crept from his blankets and went down to the shore of the lake like a shadow—silently, as only Indian blood can move. He raised his head and looked about him. The thick darkness rendered sight of small avail, but, like the animals, he possessed other senses that darkness could not mute. He listened—then sniffed the air. Motionless as a hemlock-stem he stood there. After five minutes again he lifted his head and sniffed, and yet once again. A tingling of the wonderful nerves that betrayed itself by no outer sign, ran through him as he tasted the keen air. Then, merging his figure into the surrounding blackness in a way that only wild men and animals understand, he turned, still moving like a shadow, and went stealthily back to his lean-to and his bed.

And soon after he slept, the change of wind he had divined stirred gently the reflection of the stars within the lake. Rising among the far ridges of the country beyond Fifty Island Water, it came from the direction in which he had stared, and it passed over the sleeping camp with a faint and sighing murmur through the tops of the big tree that was almost too delicate to be audible. With it, down the desert paths of night, though too faint, too high even for the Indian's hair-like nerves, there passed a curious, thin odour, strangely disquieting, an odour of something that seemed unfamiliar—utterly unknown.

The French Canadian and the man of Indian blood each stirred uneasily in his sleep just about the time, though neither of them woke. Then the ghost of that unforgettably strange odour passed away and was lost among the leagues of tenantless forest beyond.

II

In the morning the camp was astir before the sun. There had been a light fall of snow during the night and the air was sharp. Punk had done his duty betimes, for the odours of coffee and fried bacon reached every tent. All were in good spirits.

"Wind's shifted!" cried Hank vigorously, watching Simpson and his guide already loading the small canoe. "It's across the lake—dead right for you fellers. And the snow'll make bully trails! If there's any moose mussing around up thar, they'll not get so much as a tail-end scent of you with the wind as it is. Good luck, Monsieur Défago!" he added, facetiously giving the name its French pronunciation for once, "*bonne chance!*"

Défago returned the good wishes, apparently in the best of spirits, the silent mood gone. Before eight o'clock old Punk had the camp to himself, Cathcart and Hank were far along the trail that led westwards, while the canoe that carried Défago and Simpson, with silk tent and grub for two days, was already a dark speck bobbing on the bosom of the lake, going due east.

The wintry sharpness of the air was tempered now by a sun that topped the wooded ridges and blazed with a luxurious warmth upon the world of lake and forest below; loons flew skimming through the sparkling spray that the wind lifted; divers shook their dripping heads to the sun and popped smartly out of sight again; and as far as eye could reach rose the leagues of endless, crowding Bush, desolate in its lonely sweep and grandeur, untrodden by foot of man, and stretching its mighty and unbroken carpet right up to the frozen shores of Hudson Bay.

Simpson, who saw it all for the first time as he paddled hard in the bows of the dancing canoe, was enchanted by its austere beauty. His heart drank in the sense of freedom and great spaces just as his lungs drank in the cool and perfumed wind. Behind him in the stern seat, singing fragments of his native chanties, Défago steered the craft of birchbark like a thing of life, answering cheerfully all his companion's questions. Both were gay and light-hearted. On such occasions men lose the superficial, worldly distinctions; they become human beings working together for a common end. Simpson, the employer, and Défago, the employed, among these primitive forces, were simply—two men, the "guider," and the "guided." Superior knowledge, of course, assumed control, and the younger man fell without a second thought into the quasi-subordinate position. He never dreamed of objecting when Défago dropped the "Mr.," and addressed him as "Say, Simpson," or "Simpson, boss," which was invariably the cast before they reached the farther shore after a stiff paddle of twelve miles against a head wind. He only laughed, and liked it; then ceased to notice it at all.

For this "divinity student" was a young man of parts and character, though as yet, of course, untravelled; and on this trip—the first time he had seen any country but his own and little Switzerland—the huge scale of things somewhat bewildered him. It was one thing, he realized, to hear about primeval forests, but quite another to see them. While to dwell in them and seek acquaintance with their wild life was, again, an initiation that no intelligent man could undergo without a certain shifting of personal values hitherto held for permanent and sacred.

Simpson knew the first faint indication of this emotion when he held the new .303 rifle in his hands and looked along its pair of faultless, gleaming barrels. The three days' journey to their headquarters, by lake and portage, had carried the process a stage farther. And now that he was about to plunge beyond even the fringe of wilderness where they were camped into the virgin heart of uninhabited regions as vast as Europe itself, the true nature of the situation stole upon him with an effect of delight and awe that his imagination was fully capable of appreciating. It was himself and Défago against a multitude—at least, against a Titan!

The bleak splendours of these remote and lonely forests rather overwhelmed him with the sense of his own littleness. That stern quality of the tangled backwoods which can only be described as merciless and terrible, rose out of these far blue woods swimming upon the horizon, and revealed itself. He understood the silent warning. He realized his own utter helplessness. Only Défago, as a symbol of a distant civilization where man was master, stood between him and a pitiless death by exhaustion and starvation.

It was thrilling to him, therefore, to watch Défago turn over the canoe upon the shore, pack the paddles carefully underneath, and then proceed to "blaze" the spruce stems for some distance on either side of an almost invisible trail, with the careless remark thrown in, "Say Simpson, if anything happens to me, you'll find the canoe all correc' by these marks;—then strike doo west into the sun to hit the home camp agin, see?"

It was the most natural thing in the world to say, and he said it without any noticable inflexion of the voice, only it happened to express the youth's emotions at the moment with an utterance that was symbolic of the situation and of his own helplessness as a factor in it. He was alone with Défago in a primitive world; that was all. The canoe, another symbol of man's ascendancy, was not to be left behind. Those small yellow patches, made on the trees by the axe, were the only indications of its hiding-place.

Meanwhile, shouldering the packs between them, each man carrying his own rifle, they followed the slender trail over rocks and fallen trunks and across half-frozen swamps; skirting numerous lakes that fairly gemmed the forest, their borders fringed with mist; and towards five o'clock found themselves suddenly on the edge of the woods, looking out across a large sheet of water in front of them, dotted with pine-clad islands of all describable shapes and sizes.

"Fifty Island Water," announced Défago wearily, "and the sun jest goin' to dip his bald old head into it!" he added, with unconscious poetry; and immediately they set about pitching camp for the night.

In a very few minutes, under those skillful hands that never made a movement too much or a movement too little, the silk tent stood taut and cosy, the beds of balsam boughs ready laid, and a brisk cooking-fire burned with the minimum of smoke. While the young Scotchman cleaned the fish they had caught trolling behind the canoe, Défago "guessed" he would "jest as soon" take a turn through the Bush for indications of moose. "*May* come across a trunk where they bin and rubbed horns," he said, as he moved off, "or feedin' on the last of the maple leaves,"—and he was gone.

His small figure melted away like a shadow in the dusk, while Simpson noted with a kind of admiration how easily the forest absorbed him into herself. A few steps, it seemed, and he was no longer visible.

Yet there was little underbrush hereabouts; the trees stood somewhat apart, well spaced; and in the clearings grew silver-birch and maple, spearlike and slender, against the immense stems of spruce and hemlock. But for occasional prostrate monsters, and the boulders of grey rock that thrust uncouth shoulders here and there out of the ground, it might well have been a bit of park in the Old Country. Almost, one might have seen in it the hand of man. A little to the right, however, began the great burnt section, miles in extent, proclaiming its real character—*brulé*, as it is called, where the fires of the previous year had raged for weeks, and the blackened stumps now rose gaunt and ugly, bereft of branches, like gigantic match-heads stuck into the ground, savage and desolate beyond words. The perfume of charcoal and rain-soaked ashes still hung faintly about it.

The dusk rapidly deepened; the glades grew dark; the crackling of the fire and the wash of little waves along the rocky lake shore were the only sounds audible. The wind had dropped with the sun, and in all that vast world of branches nothing stirred. Any moment, it seemed, the woodland gods, who are to be worshipped in silence and loneliness, might stretch their mighty and terrific outlines among the trees. In front, through doorways pillared by huge straight stems, lay the stretch of Fifty Island Water, a crescent-shaped lake some fifteen miles from tip to tip, and perhaps five miles across where they were camped. A sky rose and saffron, more clear than any atmosphere Simpson had ever known, still dropped its pale streaming fires across the waves, where the islands—a hundred, surely, rather than fifty—floated like the fairy barques of some enchanted fleet. Fringed with pines, whose crests fingered most delicately the sky, they almost seemed to move upwards as the light faded—about to weigh anchor and navigate the pathways of the heavens instead of the currents of their native and desolate lake.

And strips of coloured cloud, like flaunting pennons, signalled their departure to the stars. . . .

The beauty of the scene was strangely uplifting. Simpson smoked the fish and burnt his fingers into the bargain in his efforts to enjoy it and at the same time tend the frying-pan and the fire. Yet, ever at the back of his thoughts, lay that other aspect of the wilderness: the indifference to human life, the merciless spirit of desolation which took no note of man. The sense of his utter loneliness, now that even Défago had gone, came close as he looked about him and listened for the sound of his companion's returning footsteps.

There was pleasure in the sensation, yet with it a perfectly comprehensible alarm. And instinctively the thought stirred in him: "What should I—*could* I, do—if anything happened and he did not come back—?"

They enjoyed their well-earned supper, eating untold quantities of fish, and drinking unmilked tea strong enough to kill men who had not covered thirty miles of hard "going," eating little on the way. And when it was over, they smoked and told stories round the blazing fire, laughing, stretching weary limbs, and discussing plans for the morrow. Défago was in excellent spirits, though disappointed at having no signs of moose to report. But it was dark and he had not gone far. The *brulé*, too, was bad. His clothes and hands were smeared with charcoal. Simpson, watching him, realized with renewed vividness their position—alone together in the wilderness.

"Défago," he said presently, "these woods, you know, are a bit too big to feel quite at home in—to feel comfortable in, I mean! ... Eh?" He merely gave expression to the mood of the moment; he was hardly prepared for the earnestness, the solemnity even, with which the guide took him up.

"You've hit it right, Simpson, boss," he replied, fixing his searching brown eyes on his face, "and that's the truth, sure. There's no end to 'em—no end at all." Then he added in a lowered tone as if to himself, "There's lots found out *that*, and gone plumb to pieces!"

But the man's gravity of manner was not quite to the other's liking; it was a little too suggestive for this scenery and setting; he was sorry he had broached the subject. He remembered suddenly how his uncle had told him that men were sometimes stricken with a strange fever of the wilderness, when the seduction of the uninhabited wastes caught them so fiercely that they went forth, half fascinated, half deluded, to their death. And he had a shrewd idea that his companion held something in sympathy with that queer type. He led the conversation on to other topics, on to Hank and the doctor, for instance, and the natural rivalry as to who should get the first sight of moose.

"If they went doo west," observed Défago carelessly, "there's sixty miles between us now—with ole Punk at halfway house eatin' himself full to bustin' with fish and coffee." They laughed together over the picture. But the casual mention of those sixty miles again made Simpson realize the prodigious scale of this land where they hunted; sixty miles was a mere step; two hundred little more than a step. Stories of lost hunters rose persistently before his memory. The passion and mystery of homeless and wandering men, seduced by the beauty of great forests, swept his soul in a way too vivid to be quite pleasant. He wondered vaguely whether it was the mood of his companion that invited the unwelcome suggestion with such persistence.

"Sing us a song, Défago, if you're not too tired," he asked; "one of those old *voyageur* songs you sang the other night." He handed his tobacco pouch to the guide and then filled his own pipe, while the Canadian, nothing loth, sent his light voice across the lake in one of those plaintive, almost melancholy chanties with which lumbermen and trappers lessen the burden of their labour. There was an appealing and romantic flavour about it, something that recalled the atmosphere of the old pioneer days when Indians and wilderness were leagued together, battles frequent, and the Old Country farther off than it is to-day. The sound travelled pleasantly over the water, but the forest at their backs seemed to swallow it down with a single gulp that permitted neither echo nor resonance.

It was in the middle of the third verse that Simpson noticed something unusual—something that brought his thoughts back with a rush from far-away scenes. A curious change had come into the man's voice. Even before he knew what it was, uneasiness caught him, and looking up quickly, he saw that Défago, though still singing, was peering about him into the Bush, as though he heard or saw something. His voice grew fainter—dropped to a hush—then ceased altogether. The same instant, with a movement amazingly alert, he started to his feet and stood upright—*sniffing the air*. Like a dog scenting game, he drew the air into his nostrils in short, sharp breaths, turning quickly as he did so in all directions, and finally "pointing" down the lake shore, eastwards. It was a performance unpleasantly suggestive and at the same time singularly dramatic. Simpson's heart fluttered disagreeably as he watched it.

"Lord, man! How you made me jump!" he exclaimed, on his feet beside him the same instant, and peering over his shoulder into the sea of darkness. "What's up? Are you frightened—?"

Even before the question was out of his mouth he knew it was foolish, for any man with a pair of eyes in his head could see that the Canadian had turned white down to his very gills. Not even sunburn and the glare of the fire could hide that.

The student felt himself trembling a little, weakish in the knees. "What's up?" he repeated quickly. "D'you smell moose? Or anything queer, anything—wrong?" He lowered his voice instinctively.

The forest pressed round them with its encircling wall; the nearer tree-stems gleamed like bronze in the firelight; beyond that—blackness, and, so far as he could tell, a silence of death. Just behind them a passing puff of wind lifted a single leaf, looked at it, then laid it softly down again without disturbing the rest of the covey. It seemed as if a million invisible causes had combined just to produce that single visible effect. *Other* life pulsed about them—and was gone.

Défago turned abruptly; the livid hue of his face had turned to a dirty grey.

"I never said I heered—or smelt—nothin'," he said slowly and emphatically, in an oddly altered voice that conveyed somehow a touch of defiance. "I was only—takin' a look round—so to speak. It's always a mistake to be too previous with yer questions." Then he added suddenly with obvious effort, in his more natural voice, "Have you got the matches, Boss Simpson?" and proceeded to light the pipe he had half filled just before he began to sing.

Without speaking another word they sat down again by the fire, Défago changed his side so that he could face the direction the wind came from. For even a tenderfoot could tell that. Défago changed his position in order to hear and smell—all there was to be heard and smelt. And, since he now faced the lake with his back to the trees it was evidently nothing in the forest that had sent so strange and sudden a warning to his marvellously trained nerves.

"Guess now I don't feel like singing any," he explained presently of his own accord. "That song kinder brings back memories that's troublesome to me; I never oughter've begun it. It sets me on t'imagining things, see?"

Clearly the man was still fighting with some profoundly moving emotion. He wished to excuse himself in the eyes of the other. But the explanation, in that it was only a part of the truth, was a lie, and he knew perfectly well that Simpson was not deceived by it. For nothing could explain away the livid terror that had dropped over his face while he stood there sniffing the air. And nothing—no amount of blazing fire, or chatting on ordinary subjects—could make that camp exactly as it had been before. The shadow of an unknown horror, naked if unguessed, that had flashed for an instant in the face and gestures of the guide, had also communicated itself, vaguely and therefore more potently, to his companion. The guide's visible efforts to dissemble the truth only made things worse. Moreover, to add to the younger man's uneasiness, was the difficulty, nay, the impossibility he felt of asking questions, and also his complete ignorance as to the cause . . . Indians, wild animals, forest fires—all these, he knew, were wholly out of the question. His imagination searched vigorously, but in vain. . . .

Yet, somehow, or other, after another long spell of smoking, talking and roasting themselves before the great fire, the shadow that had so suddenly invaded their peaceful camp began to lift. Perhaps Défago's efforts, or the return of his quiet and normal attitude accomplished this; perhaps Simpson himself had exaggerated the affair out of all proportion to the truth; or possibly the vigorous air of the wilderness brought its own powers of healing. Whatever the cause, the feeling of immediate horror seemed to have passed away as mysteriously as it had come, for nothing occurred to feed it. Simpson began to feel that he had permitted himself the unreasoning terror of a child. He put it down partly to a certain subconscious excitement that this wild and immense scenery generated in his blood, partly to the spell of solitude, and partly to overfatigue. That pallor in the guide's face was, of course, uncommonly hard to explain, yet it *might* have been due in some way to an effect of firelight, or his own imagination . . . He gave it the benefit of the doubt; he was Scotch.

When a somewhat unordinary emotion has disappeared, the mind always finds a dozen ways of explaining away its causes . . . Simpson lit a last pipe and tried to laugh to himself. On getting home to Scotland it would make quite a good story. He did not realize that this laughter was a sign that terror still lurked in the recesses of his soul—that, in fact, it was merely one of the conventional signs by which a man, seriously alarmed, tries to persuade himself that he is *not* so.

Défago, however, heard that low laughter and looked up with surprise on his face. The two men stood, side by side, kicking the embers about before going to bed. It was ten o'clock—a late hour for hunters to be still awake.

"What's ticklin' yer?" he asked in his ordinary tone, yet gravely.

"I—I was thinking of our little toy woods at home, just at that moment," stammered Simpson, coming back to what really dominated his mind, and startled by the question, "and comparing them to—to all this," and he swept his arm round to indicate the Bush.

A pause followed in which neither of them said anything.

"All the same I wouldn't laugh about it, if I were you," Défago added, looking over Simpson's shoulder into the shadows. "There's places in there nobody won't never see into—nobody knows what lives in there either."

"Too big—too far off?" The suggestion in the guide's manner was immense and horrible.

Défago nodded. The expression on his face was dark. He, too, felt uneasy. The younger man understood that in a *hinterland* of this size there might well be depths of wood that would never in the life of the world be known or trodden. The thought was not exactly the sort he welcomed. In a loud voice, cheerfully, he suggested that it was time for bed. But the guide lingered, tinkering with the fire, arranging the stones needlessly, doing a dozen things that did not really need doing. Evidently there was something he wanted to say, yet found it difficult to "get at."

"Say, you, Boss Simpson," he began suddenly, as the last shower of sparks went up into the air, "you don't—smell nothing, do you—nothing pertickler, I mean?" The commonplace question, Simpson realized, veiled a dreadfully serious thought in his mind. A shiver ran down his back.

"Nothing but this burning wood," he replied firmly, kicking again at the embers. The sound of his own foot made him start.

"And all the evenin' you ain't smelt—nothing?" persisted the guide, peering at him through the gloom; "nothing extraordiny, and different to anything else you ever smelt before?"

"No, no, man; nothing at all!" he replied aggressively, half angrily.

Défago's face cleared. "That's good!" he exclaimed with evident relief. "That's good to hear."

"Have *you?*" asked Simpson sharply, and the same instant regretted the question.

The Canadian came closer in the darkness. He shook his head. "I guess not," he said, though without overwhelming conviction. "It must've been jest that song of mine that did it. It's the song they sing in lumber-camps and god-forsaken places like that, when they're skeered the Wendigo's somewhere around, doin' a bit of swift travellin'—"

"And what's the Wendigo, pray?" Simpson asked quickly, irritated because again he could not prevent that sudden shiver of the nerves. He knew that he was close upon the man's terror and the cause of it. Yet a rushing passionate curiosity overcame his better judgement, *and* his fear.

Défago turned swiftly and looked at him as though he were suddenly about to shriek. His eyes shone, but his mouth was wide open. Yet all he said, or whispered rather, for his voice sank very low, was—

"It's nuthin'—nuthin' but what those lousy fellers believe when they've bin hittin' the bottle too long—a sort of great animal that lives up yonder," he jerked his head northwards, "quick as lightning in its tracks, an' bigger'n anything else in the Bush, an' ain't supposed to be very good to look at—*that's all!*"

"A backwoods' superstition—" began Simpson, moving hastily towards the tent in order to shake off the hand of the guide that clutched his arm. "Come, come, hurry up for God's sake, and get the lantern going! It's time we were in bed and asleep if we're to be up with the sun to-morrow . . . ."

The guide was close on his heels. "I'm coming," he answered out of the darkness, "I'm coming." And after a slight delay he appeared with the lantern and hung it from a nail in the front pole of the tent. The shadows of a hundred trees shifted their places quickly as he did so, and when he stumbled over the rope, diving swiftly inside, the whole tent trembled as though a gust of wind struck it.

The two men lay down, without undressing, upon their beds of soft balsam boughs, cunningly arranged. Inside, all was warm and cosy, but outside the world of crowding trees pressed close about them, marshalling their million shadows, and smothering the little tent that stood there like a wee white shell facing the ocean of tremendous forest.

Between the two lonely figures within, however, there pressed another shadow that was *not* a shadow from the night. It was the Shadow cast by the strange Fear, never wholly exorcised, that had leaped suddenly upon Défago in the middle of his singing. And Simpson, as he lay there, watching the darkness through the open flap of the tent, ready to plunge into the fragrant abyss of sleep, knew first that unique and profound stillness of a primeval forest when no wind stirs . . . and when the night has weight and substance that enters into the soul to bind a veil about it . . . . Then sleep took him . . . .

III

Thus it seemed to him, at least. Yet it was true that the lap of water, just beyond the tent door, still beat time with his lessening pulses when he realized that he was lying with his eyes open and that another sound had recently introduced itself with cunning softness between the splash and murmur of the little waves.

And, long before he understood what this sound was, it had

stirred in him the centres of pity and alarm. He listened intently, though at first in vain, for the running blood beat all its drums too noisily in his ears. Did it come, he wondered, from the lake, or from the woods? . . .

Then, suddenly, with a rush and a flutter of the heart, he knew that it was close beside him in the tent; and, when he turned over for a better hearing, it focussed itself unmistakably not two feet away. It was a sound of weeping; Défago upon his bed of branches was sobbing in the darkness as though his heart would break, the blankets evidently stuffed against his mouth to stifle it.

And his first feeling, before he could think or reflect, was the rush of a poignant and searching tenderness. This intimate, human sound, heard amid the desolation about them, woke pity. It was so incongruous, so pitifully incongruous—and so vain! Tears—in this vast and cruel wilderness: of what avail? He thought of a little child crying in mid-Atlantic . . . . Then, of course, with fuller realization, and the memory of what had gone before, came the descent of the terror upon him, and his blood ran cold.

"Défago," he whispered quickly, "what's the matter?" He tried to make his voice very gentle. "Are you in pain—unhappy—?" There was no reply, but the sounds ceased abruptly. He stretched his hand out and touched him. The body did not stir.

"Are you awake?" for it occurred to him that the man was crying in his sleep. "Are you cold?" He noticed that his feet which were uncovered, projected beyond the mouth of the tent. He spread an extra fold of his own blankets over them. The guide had slipped down in his bed, and the branches seemed to have been dragged with him. He was afraid to pull the body back again, for fear of waking him.

One or two tentative questions he ventured softly, but though he waited for several minutes there came no reply, nor any sign of movement. Presently he heard his regular and quiet breathing, and putting his hand again gently on the breast, felt the steady rise and fall beneath.

"Let me know if anything's wrong," he whispered, "or if I can do anything. Wake me at once if you feel—queer."

He hardly knew quite what to say. He lay down again, thinking and wondering what it all meant. Défago, of course, had been crying in his sleep. Some dream or other had afflicted him. Yet never in his life would he forget that pitiful sound of sobbing, and the feeling that the whole awful wilderness of woods listened . . . .

His own mind busied itself for a long time with the recent events, of which *this* took its mysterious place as one, and though his reason successfully argued away all unwelcome suggestions, a sensation of uneasiness remained, resisting ejection, very deep-seated—peculiar beyond ordinary.

IV

But sleep, in the long run, proves greater than all emotions. His thoughts soon wandered again; he lay there, warm as toast, exceedingly weary; the night soothed and comforted, blunting the edges of memory and alarm. Half-an-hour later he was oblivious of everything in the outer world about him.

Yet sleep, in this case, was his great enemy, concealing all approaches, smothering the warning of his nerves.

As, sometimes, in a nightmare events crowd upon each others' heels with a conviction of dreadfullest reality, yet some inconsistent detail accuses the whole display of incompleteness and disguise, so the events that now followed, though they actually happened, persuaded the mind somehow that the detail which could explain them had been overlooked in the confusion, and that therefore they were but partly true, the rest delusion. At the back of the sleeper's mind something remains awake, ready to let slip the judgment, "All this is not *quite* real; when you wake up you'll understand."

And thus, in a way, it was with Simpson. The events, not wholly inexplicable or incredible in themselves, yet remain for the man who saw and heard them a sequence of separate acts of cold horror, because the little piece that might have made the puzzle clear lay concealed or overlooked.

So far as he can recall, it was a violent movement, running downwards through the tent towards the door, that first woke him and made him aware that his companion was sitting bolt upright beside him—quivering. Hours must have passed, for it was the pale gleam of the dawn that revealed his outline against the canvas. This time the man was not crying; he was quaking like a leaf; the trembling he felt plainly through the blankets down the entire length of his own body. Défago had huddled down against him for protection, shrinking away from something that apparently concealed itself near the door-flaps of the little tent.

Simpson thereupon called out in a loud voice some question or other—in the first bewilderment of waking he does not remember exactly what—and the man made no reply. The atmosphere and feeling of true nightmare lay horribly about him, making movement and speech both difficult. At first, indeed, he was not sure where he was—whether in one of the earlier camps, or at home in his bed at Aberdeen. The sense of confusion was very troubling.

And next—almost simultaneous with his waking, it seemed—the profound stillness of the dawn outside was shattered by a most uncommon sound. It came without warning, or audible approach; and it was unspeakably dreadful. It was a voice, Simpson declares, possibly a human voice; hoarse yet plaintive—a soft, roaring voice close outside the tent, overhead rather than upon the ground, of immense volume, while in some strange way most penetratingly and seductively sweet. It rang out, too, in three separate and distinct notes, or cries, that bore in some odd fashion a resemblance, far-fetched yet recognizable, to the name of the guide: "*Dé-fa-go!*"

The student admits he is unable to describe it quite intelligently, for it was unlike any sound he had ever heard in his life, and combined a blending of such contrary qualities. "A sort of windy, crying voice," he calls it, "as of something lonely and untamed, wild and of abominable power . . . ."

And, even before it ceased, dropping back into the great gulfs of silence, the guide beside him had sprung to his feet with an answering though unintelligible cry. He blundered against the tent-pole with violence, shaking the whole structure, spreading his arms out frantically for more room, and kicking his legs impetuously free of the clinging blankets. For a second, perhaps two, he stood upright by the door his outline dark against the pallor of the dawn; then, with a furious, rushing speed, before his companion could move a hand to stop him, he shot with a plunge through the flaps of canvas—and was gone. And as he went—so astonishingly fast that the voice could actually be heard dying in the distance—he called aloud in tones of anguished terror that at the same time held something strangely like the frenzied exultation of delight—

"Oh! oh! My feet of fire! My burning feet of fire! Oh! oh! This height and fiery speed!"

And then the distance quickly buried it, and the deep silence of very early morning descended upon the forest as before.

It had all come about with such rapidity that, but for the evidence of the empty bed beside him Simpson could almost have believed it to have been the memory of a nightmare carried over from sleep. He still felt the warm pressure of that vanished body against his side; there lay the twisted blankets in a heap; the very

tent yet trembled with the vehemence of the impetuous departure. The strange words rang in his ears, as though he still heard
them in the distance—wild language of a suddenly stricken mind.
Moreover, it was not only the senses of sight and hearing that
reported uncommon things to his brain, for even while the man
cried and ran, he had become aware that a strange perfume, faint
yet pungent, pervaded the interior of the tent. And it was at this
point, it seems, brought to himself by the consciousness that his
nostrils were taking this distressing odour down into his throat,
that he found his courage, sprang quickly to his feet—and went
out.

The grey light of dawn that dropped, cold and glimmering,
between the trees revealed the scene tolerably well. There stood
the tent behind him, soaked with dew; the dark ashes of the fire,
still warm; the lake, white beneath a coating of mist, the islands
rising darkly out of it like objects packed in wool; and patches of
snow beyond among the clearer spaces of the Bush—everything
cold, still, waiting for the sun. But nowhere a sign of the vanished
guide—still, doubtless, flying at frantic speed through the frozen
woods. There was not even the sound of disappearing footsteps,
nor the echoes of the dying voice. He had gone—utterly.

There was nothing; nothing but the sense of his recent presence, so strongly left behind about the camp; *and*—this penetrating, all-pervading odour.

And even this was now rapidly disappearing in its turn. In spite
of his exceeding mental perturbation, Simpson struggled hard to
detect its nature, and define it, but the ascertaining of an elusive
scent, not recognized subconsciously and at once, is a very subtle
operation of the mind. And he failed. It was gone before he could
properly seize or name it. Approximate description, even, seems
to have been difficult, for it was unlike any smell he knew. Acrid
rather, not unlike the odour of a lion, he thinks, yet softer and not

wholly unpleasing, with something almost sweet in it that reminded him of the scent of decaying garden leaves, earth, and the myriad, nameless perfumes that make up the odour of a big forest. Yet the "odour of lions" is the phrase with which he usually sums it all up.

Then—it was wholly gone, and he found himself standing by the ashes of the fire in a state of amazement and stupid terror that left him the helpless prey of anything that chose to happen. Had a musk-rat poked its pointed muzzle over a rock, or a squirrel scuttled in that instant down the bark of a tree, he would most likely have collapsed without more ado and fainted. For he felt about the whole affair the touch somewhere of a great Outer Horror . . . and his scattered powers had not as yet had time to collect themselves into a definite attitude of fighting self-control.

Nothing did happen, however. A great kiss of wind ran softly through the awakening forest, and a few maple leaves here and there rustled tremblingly to earth. The sky seemed to grow suddenly much lighter. Simpson felt the cool air upon his cheek and uncovered head; realized that he was shivering with the cold; and making a great effort, realized next that he was alone in the Bush—*and* that he was called upon to take immediate steps to find and succour his vanished companion.

Make an effort, accordingly, he did, though an ill-calculated and futile one. With that wilderness of trees about him, the sheet of water cutting him off behind, and the horror of that wild cry in his blood, he did what any other inexperienced man would have done in similar bewilderment: he ran about, without any sense of direction, like a frantic child, and called loudly without ceasing the name of the guide—

"Défago! Défago! Défago!" he yelled, and the trees gave him back the name as often as he shouted, only a little softened—"Défago! Défago! Défago!"

He followed the trail that lay for a short distance across the patches of snow, and then lost it again where the trees grew too thickly for snow to lie. He shouted till he was hoarse, and till the sound of his own voice in all that unanswering and listening world began to frighten him. His confusion increased in direct ratio to the violence of his efforts. His distress became formidably acute, till at length his exertions defeated their own object, and from sheer exhaustion he headed back to the camp again. It remains a wonder that he ever found his way. It was with great difficulty, and only after numberless false clues, that he at last saw the white tent between the trees, and so reached safety.

Exhaustion then applied its own remedy, and he grew calmer. He made the fire and breakfasted. Hot coffee and bacon put a little sense and judgment into him again, and he realized that he had been behaving like a boy. He now made another, and more successful attempt to face the situation collectedly, and a nature naturally plucky coming to his assistance, he decided that he must first make as thorough a search as possible, failing success in which, he must find his way to the home camp as best he could and bring help.

And this was what he did. Taking food, matches and rifle with him, and a small axe to blaze the trees against his return journey, he set forth. It was eight o'clock when he started, the sun shining over the tops of the trees in a sky without clouds. Pinned to a stake by the fire he left a note in case Défago returned while he was away.

This time, according to a careful plan, he took a new direction, intending to make a wide sweep that must sooner or later cut into indications of the guide's trail and, before he had gone a quarter of a mile he came across the tracks of a large animal in the snow, and beside it the light and smaller tracks of what were beyond question human feet—the feet of Défago. The relief he at once experienced was natural, though brief; for at first sight he saw in these tracks a simple explanation of the whole matter: these big marks had surely been left by a bull moose that, wind against it, had blundered upon the camp, and uttered its singular cry of warning and alarm the moment its mistake was apparent. Défago, in whom the hunting instinct was developed to the point of uncanny perfection, had scented the brute coming down the wind hours before. His excitement and disappearance were due, of course, to—to his—

Then the impossible explanation at which he gasped faded, as common sense showed him mercilessly that none of this was true. No guide, much less a guide like Défago, could have acted in so irrational a way, going off even without his rifle . . . ! The whole affair demanded a far more complicated elucidation, when he remembered the details of it all—the cry of terror, the amazing language, the grey face of horror when his nostrils first caught the new odour; that muffled sobbing in the darkness, and—for this, too, now came back to him dimly—the man's original aversion for this particular country . . . .

Besides, now that he examined them closer, these were not the tracks of a bull moose at all! Hank had explained to him the outline of a bull's hoofs, of a cow's or calf's, too, for that matter; he had drawn them clearly on a strip of birch bark. And these were wholly different. They were big, round, ample, and with no pointed outline as of sharp hoofs. He wondered for a moment whether bear-tracks were like that. There was no other animal he could think of, for caribou did not come so far south at this season, and, even if they did, would leave hoof-marks.

They were ominous signs—these mysterious writings left in the snow by the unknown creature that had lured a human being away from safety—and when he coupled them in his imagination with that haunting sound that broke the stillness of the dawn, a momentary dizziness shook his mind, distressing him again beyond belief. He felt the *threatening* aspect of it all. And, stooping down to examine the marks more closely, he caught a faint whiff of that sweet yet pungent odour that made him instantly straighten up again, fighting a sensation almost of nausea.

Then his memory played him another evil trick. He suddenly recalled those uncovered feet projecting beyond the edge of the tent, and the body's appearance of having been dragged towards the opening; the man's shrinking from something by the door when he woke later. The details now beat against his trembling mind with concerted attack. They seemed to gather in those deep spaces of the silent forest about him, where the host of trees stood waiting, listening, watching to see what he would do. The woods were closing round him.

With the persistence of true pluck, however, Simpson went forward, following the tracks as best he could, smothering these ugly emotions that sought to weaken his will. He blazed innumerable trees as he went, ever fearful of being unable to find the way back, and calling aloud at intervals of a few seconds the name of the guide. The dull tapping of the axe upon the massive trunks, and the unnatural accents of his own voice became at length sounds that he even dreaded to make, dreaded to hear. For they drew attention without ceasing to his presence and something was hunting himself down in the same way that he was hunting down another—

With a strong effort, he crushed the thought out the instant it rose. It was the beginning, he realized, of a bewilderment utterly diabolical in kind that would speedily destroy him.

Although the snow was not continuous, lying merely in shallow flurries over the more open spaces, he found no difficulty in following the tracks for the first few miles. They went straight as a ruled line wherever the trees permitted. The stride soon began to increase in length, till it finally assumed proportions that seemed absolutely impossible for any ordinary animal to have made. Like huge flying leaps they became. One of these measured, and though he knew that "stretch" of eighteen feet must be somehow wrong, he was at a complete loss to understand why he found no signs on the snow between the extreme points. But what perplexed him even more, making him feel his vision had gone utterly awry, was that Défago's stride increased in the same manner, and finally covered the same incredible distances. It looked as if the great beast had lifted him with it and carried him across these astonishing intervals. Simpson, who was much longer in the limb, found that he could not compass even half the stretch by taking a running jump.

And the sight of these huge tracks, running side by side, silent evidence of a dreadful journey in which terror or madness had urged to impossible results, was profoundly moving. It shocked him in the secret depths of his soul. It was the most horrible thing his eyes had ever looked upon. He began to follow them mechanically, absent-mindedly almost, ever peering over his shoulder to see if he, too, were being followed by something with a gigantic tread . . . . And soon it came about that he no longer quite realized what it was they signified—these impressions left upon the snow by something nameless and untamed, always accompanied by the footmarks of the little French Canadian, his guide, his comrade, the man who had shared his tent a few hours before, chatting, laughing, even singing by his side . . . .

V

For a man of his years and inexperience, only a canny Scot, perhaps, grounded in common sense and established in logic, could have preserved even that measure of balance that his youth somehow or other did manage to preserve through the whole adventure. Otherwise, two things, he presently noticed, while forging pluckily ahead, must have sent him headlong back to the comparative safety of his tent, instead of only making his hands close more tightly upon the rifle-stock, while his heart, trained for the Wee Kirk, sent a wordless prayer winging its way to heaven. Both tracks, he saw, had undergone a change, and this change, so far as it concerned the footsteps of the man, was in some undecipherable manner—appalling.

It was in the bigger tracks he first noticed this, and for a long time he could not quite believe his eyes. Was it the blown leaves that produced odd effects of light and shade, or that the dry snow, drifting like finely-grounded rice about the edges, cast shadows and high lights? Or was it actually the fact that the great marks had become faintly coloured? For round about the deep, plunging holes of the animal there now appeared a mysterious, reddish tinge that was more like an effect of light than of anything that dyed the substance of the snow itself. Every mark had it, and had it increasingly—this indistinct fiery tinge that painted a new touch of ghastliness into the picture.

But when, wholly unable to explain or credit it, he turned his attention to the other tracks to discover if they, too, bore similar witness, he noticed that these had meanwhile undergone a change that was infinitely worse, and charged with far more horrible suggestion. For, in the last hundred yards or so, he saw that they had grown gradually into the semblance of the parent tread. Imperceptibly the change had come about, yet unmistakably. It was hard to see where the change first began. The result, however, was beyond question. Smaller, neater, more cleanly modelled, they formed now an exact and careful duplicate of the larger tracks beside them. The feet that produced them had, therefore, also changed. And something in his mind reared up with loathing and with terror as he saw it.

Simpson, for the first time, hesitated; then, ashamed of his alarm and indecision, took a few hurried steps ahead; the next instant stopped dead in his tracks. Immediately in front of him all signs of the trail ceased; both tracks came to an abrupt end. On all sides, for a hundred yards and more, he searched in vain for the least indication of their continuance. There was—nothing.

The trees were very thick just there, big trees all of them, spruce, cedar, hemlock; there was no underbrush. He stood looking about him, all distraught; bereft of any power of judgment. Then he set to work to search again, and again, and yet again, but always with the same result: *nothing*. The feet that printed the surface of the snow thus far had now, apparently, left the ground!

And it was in that moment of distress and confusion that the whip of terror laid its most nicely calculated lash about his heart. It dropped with deadly effect upon the sorest spot of all, completely unnerving him. He had been secretly dreading all the time that it would come—and come it did.

Far overhead, muted by great height and distance, strangely thinned and wailing, he heard the crying voice of Défago, the guide.

The sound dropped upon him out of that still, wintry sky with an effect of dismay and terror unsurpassed. The rifle fell to his feet. He stood motionless an instant, listening as it were with his whole body, then staggered back against the nearest tree for support, disorganized hopelessly in mind and spirit. To him, in that moment, it seemed the most shattering and dislocating experience he had ever known, so that his heart emptied itself of all feeling whatsoever as by a sudden draught.

"Oh! oh! This fiery height! Oh, my feet of fire! My burning feet of fire . . . !" ran in far, beseeching accents of indescribable appeal this voice of anguish down the sky. Once it called—then silence through all the listening wilderness of trees.

And Simpson, scarcely knowing what he did, presently found himself running wildly to and fro, searching, calling, tripping over roots and boulders, and flinging himself in a frenzy of undirected pursuit after the Caller. Behind the screen of memory and emotion with which experience veils events, he plunged, distracted and half-deranged, picking up false lights like a ship at sea, terror in his eyes and heart and soul. For the Panic of the Wilderness had called to him in that far voice—the Power of untamed Distance—the Enticement of the Desolation that destroys. He knew in that moment all the pains of some one hopelessly and irretrievably lost, suffering the lust and travail of a soul in the final Loneliness. A vision of Défago, eternally hunted, driven and pursued across the skiey vastness of those ancient forests, fled like a flame across the dark ruin of his thoughts . . .

It seemed ages before he could find anything in the chaos of his disorganized sensations to which he could anchor himself steady for a moment, and think . . .

The cry was not repeated; his own hoarse calling brought no response; the inscrutable forces of the Wild had summoned their victim beyond recall—and held him fast.

Yet he searched and called, it seems, for hours afterwards, for it was late in the afternoon when at length he decided to abandon a useless pursuit and return to his camp on the shores of Fifty Island Water. Even then he went with reluctance, that crying voice still echoing in his ears. With difficulty he found his rifle and the homeward trail. The concentration necessary to follow the badly blazed trees, and a biting hunger that gnawed, helped to keep his mind steady. Otherwise, he admits, the temporary aberration he had suffered might have been prolonged to the point of positive disaster. Gradually the ballast shifted back again, and he regained something that approached his normal equilibrium.

But for all that the journey through the gathering dusk was

miserably haunted. He heard innumerable following footsteps; voices that laughed and whispered; and saw figures crouching behind trees and boulders, making signs to one another for a concerted attack the moment he had passed. The creeping murmur of the wind made him start and listen. He went stealthily, trying to hide where possible, and making as little sound as he could. The shadows of the woods, hitherto protective or covering merely, had now become menacing, challenging; and the pageantry in his frightened mind masked a host of possiblities that were all the more ominous for being obscure. The presentiment of a nameless doom lurked ill-concealed behind every detail of what had happened.

It was really admirable how he emerged victor in the end; men of riper powers and experience might have come through the ordeal with less success. He had himself tolerably well in hand, all things considered, and his plan of action proves it. Sleep being absolutely out of the question and travelling an unknown trail in the darkness equally impracticable, he sat up the whole of that night, rifle in hand, before a fire he never for a single moment allowed to die down. The severity of the haunted vigil marked his soul for life; but it was successfully accomplished; and with the very first signs of dawn he set forth upon the long return journey to the home-camp to get help. As before, he left a written note to explain his absence, and to indicate where he had left a plentiful *cache* of food and matches—though he had no expectation that any human hands would find them!

How Simpson found his way alone by the lake and forest might well make a story in itself, for to hear him tell it is to *know* the passionate loneliness of soul that a man can feel when the Wilderness holds him in the hollow of its illimitable hand—and laughs. It is also to admire his indomitable pluck.

He claims no skill, declaring that he followed the almost invisible trail mechanically, and without thinking. And this, doubtless, is the truth. He relied upon the guiding of the unconscious mind, which is instinct. Perhaps, too, some sense of orientation, known to animals and primitive men, may have helped as well, for through all that tangled region he succeeded in reaching the exact spot where Défago had hidden the canoe nearly three days before with the remark, "Strike doo west across the lake into the sun to find the camp."

There was not much sun left to guide him, but he used his compass to the best of his ability, embarking in the frail craft for the last twelve miles of his journey, with a sensation of immense relief that the forest was at last behind him. And, fortunately, the water was calm; he took his line across the centre of the lake instead of coasting round the shores for another twenty miles. Fortunately, too, the other hunters were back. The light of their fires furnished a steering-point without which he might have searched all night long for the actual position of the camp.

It was close upon midnight all the same when his canoe grated on the sandy cove, and Hank, Punk and his uncle, disturbed in their sleep by his cries, ran quickly down and helped a very exhausted and broken specimen of Scotch humanity over the rocks towards a dying fire.

VI

The sudden entrance of his prosaic uncle into this world of wizardry and horror that had haunted him without interruption now for two days and two nights, had the immediate effect of giving to the affair an entirely new aspect. The sound of that crisp "Hulloa, my boy! And what's up *now?*" and the grasp of that dry and vigorous hand introduced another standard of judgment. A revulsion of feeling washed through him. He realized that he had let himself "go" rather badly. He even felt vaguely ashamed of himself. The native hard-headedness of his race reclaimed him.

And that doubtless explains why he found it so hard to tell that group round the fire—everything. He told enough, however, for the immediate decision to be arrived at that a relief party must start at the earliest possible moment, and that Simpson, in order to guide it capably, must first have food and, above all, sleep. Dr. Cathcart observing the lad's condition more shrewdly than his patient knew, gave him a very slight injection of morphine. For six hours he slept like the dead.

From the description carefully written out afterwards by this student of divinity, it appears that the account he gave to the astonished group omitted sundry vital and important details. He declares that, with his uncle's wholesome matter-of-fact countenance staring him in the face, he simply had not the courage to mention them. Thus, all the search-party gathered, it would seem, was that Défago had suffered in the night an acute and inexplicable attack of mania, had imagined himself "called" by some one or something, and had plunged into the bush after it without food or rifle, where he must die a horrible and lingering death by cold and starvation unless he could be found and rescued in time. "In time," moreover, meant at once.

In the course of the following day, however—they were off by seven, leaving Punk in charge with instructions to have food and fire always ready—Simpson found it possible to tell his uncle a great deal more of the story's true inwardness, without divining that it was drawn out of him as a matter of fact by a very subtle form of cross-examination. By the time they reached the beginning of the trail, where the canoe was laid up against the return journey, he had mentioned how Défago spoke vaguely of "something he called a 'Wendigo'"; how he cried in his sleep; how he imagined an unusual scent about the camp; and had betrayed other symptoms of mental excitement. He also admitted the bewildering effect of "that extraordinary" odour upon himself, "pungent and acrid like the odour of lions." And by the time they were within an easy hour of Fifty Island Water he had let slip the further fact—a foolish avowal of his own hysterical condition, as he felt afterwards—that he heard the vanished guide call "for help." He omitted the singular phrases used, for he simply could not bring himself to repeat the preposterous language. Also, while describing how the man's footsteps in the snow had gradually assumed an exact miniature likeness of the animal's plunging tracks, he left out the fact that they measured a *wholly* incredible distance. It seemed a question, nicely balanced between individual pride and honesty, what he should reveal and what suppress. He mentioned the fiery tinge in the snow, for instance, yet shrank from telling that body and bed had been partly dragged out of the tent . . . .

With the net result that Dr. Cathcart, adroit psychologist that he fancied himself to be, had assured him clearly enough exactly where his mind, influenced by loneliness, bewilderment and terror, had yielded to the strain and invited delusion. While praising his conduct, he managed at the same time to point out where, when, and how his mind had gone astray. He made his nephew think himself finer than he was by judicious praise, yet more foolish than he was by minimizing the value of his evidence. Like many another materialist, that is, he lied cleverly on the basis of insufficent knowledge, *because* the knowledge supplied seemed to his own particular intelligence inadmissable.

"The spell of these terrible solitudes," he said, "cannot leave any mind untouched, any mind, that is, possessed of the higher imaginative qualities. It has worked upon yours exactly as it worked upon my own when I was your age. The animal that haunted your little camp was undoubtedly a moose, for the 'belling' of a moose may have, sometimes, a very peculiar quality of sound. The coloured appearance of the big tracks was obviously a defect of vision in your own eyes produced by excitement. The size and stretch of the tracks we shall prove when we come to them. But the hallucination of an audible voice, of course, is one of the commonest forms of delusion due to mental excitement— and excitement, my dear boy, perfectly excusable, and let me add, wonderfully controlled by you under the circumstances. For the rest, I am bound to say, you have acted with a splendid courage, for the terror of feeling oneself lost in this wilderness is nothing short of awful, and, had I been in your place, I don't for a moment believe I could have behaved with one quarter of your wisdom and decision. The only thing I find it uncommonly difficult to explain is—that—damned odour."

"It made me feel sick, I assure you," declared his nephew, "positively dizzy!" His uncle's attitude of calm omniscience, merely because he knew more psychological formulae, made him slightly defiant. It was so easy to be wise in the explanation of an experience one has not personally witnessed. "A kind of desolate and terrible odour is the only way I can describe it," he concluded, glancing at the features of the quiet, unemotional man beside him.

"I can only marvel," was the reply, "that under the circumstances it did not seem to you even worse." The dry words, Simpson knew, hovered between the truth, and his uncle's interpretation of "the truth."

And so at last they came to the little camp and found the tent still standing, the remains of the fire, and the piece of paper pinned to a stake beside it—untouched. The *cache*, poorly contrived by inexperienced hands, however, had been discovered and opened—by musk rats, mink and squirrel. The matches lay scattered about the opening, but the food had been taken to the last crumb.

"Well, fellers, he ain't here," exclaimed Hank loudly after his fashion, "And that's as sartain as the coal supply down below! But whar he's got to by this time is 'bout as unsartain as the trade in crowns in t'other place." The presence of a divinity student was no barrier to his language at such a time, though for the reader's sake it may be severely edited. "I propose," he added, "that we start out at once an' hunt for'm like hell!"

The gloom of Défago's probable fate oppressed the whole party with a sense of dreadful gravity the moment they saw the familiar signs of recent occupancy. Especially the tent, with the bed of balsam branches still smoothed and flattened by the pressure of his body, seemed to bring his presence near to them. Simpson, feeling vaguely as if his world were somehow at stake, went about explaining particulars in a hushed tone. He was much calmer now, though overwearied with the strain of his many journeys. His uncle's method of explaining—"explaining away," rather—the details still fresh in his haunted memory helped, too, to put ice upon his emotions.

"And that's the direction he ran off in," he said to his two companions, pointing in the direction where the guide had vanished that morning in the grey dawn. "Straight down there he ran like a deer, in between the birch and hemlock . . . ."

Hank and Dr. Cathcart exchanged glances.

"And it was about two miles down there, in a straight line," continued the other, speaking with something of the former terror in his voice, "that I followed his trail to the place where—it stopped—dead!"

"And where you heered him callin' an' caught the stench, an' all the rest of the wicked entertainment," cried Hank, with a volubility that betrayed his keen distress.

"And where your excitement overcame you to the point of producing illusions," added Dr. Cathcart under his breath, yet not so low that his nephew did not hear it.

It was early in the afternoon, for they had travelled quickly, and there were still a good two hours of daylight left. Dr. Cathcart and Hank lost no time in beginning the search, but Simpson was too exhausted to accompany them. They would follow the blazed marks on the trees, and where possible, his footsteps. Meanwhile the best thing he could do was to keep a good fire going, and rest.

But after something like three hours' search, the darkness already down, the two men returned to camp with nothing to report. Fresh snow had covered all signs, and though they had followed the blazed trees to the spot where Simpson had turned back, they had not discovered the smallest indication of a human being—or for that matter, of an animal. There were no fresh tracks of any kind; the snow lay undisturbed.

It was difficult to know what was best to do, though in reality there was nothing more they *could* do. They might stay and search for weeks without much chance of success. The fresh snow destroyed their only hope, and they gathered round the fire for supper, a gloomy and despondent party. The facts, indeed, were sad enough, for Défago had a wife at Rat Portage, and his earnings were the family's sole means of support.

Now that the whole truth in all its ugliness was out, it seemed useless to deal in further disguise or pretense. They talked openly of the facts and probabilities. It was not the first time, even in the experience of Dr. Cathcart, that a man had yielded to the singular seduction of the Solitudes and gone out of his mind; Défago, moreover, was predisposed to something of the sort, for he already had a touch of melancholia in his blood, and his fibre was weakened by bouts of drinking that often lasted for weeks at a time. Something on this trip—one might never know precisely what—had sufficed to push him over the line, that was all. And he had gone, off into the great wilderness of trees and lakes to die by starvation and exhaustion. The chances against his finding camp again were overwhelming; the delirium that was upon him would also doubtless have increased, and it was quite likely he might do violence to himself and so hasten his cruel fate. Even while they talked, indeed, the end had probably come. On the suggestion of Hank, his old pal, however, they proposed to wait a little longer and devote the whole of the following day, from dawn to darkness, to the most systematic search they could devise. They would divide the territory between them. They discussed their plan in great detail. All that men could do they would do.

And, meanwhile, they talked about the particular form in which the singular Panic of the Wilderness had made its attack upon the mind of the unfortunate guide. Hank, though familiar with the legend in its general outline, obviously did not welcome the turn the conversation had taken. He contributed little, though that little was illuminating. For he admitted that a story ran over all this section of country to the effect that several Indians had "seen the Wendigo" along the shores of Fifty Island Water in the "fall" of last year, and that this was the true reason of Défago's disinclination to hunt there. Hank doubtless felt that he had in a sense helped his old pal to death by over-persuading him. "When an Indian goes crazy," he explained, talking to himself more than to the others, it seemed, "it's always put that he's 'seen the Wendigo' An' pore old Défago was superstitious down to his very heels . . . !"

And then Simpson, feeling the atmosphere more sympathetic, told over again the full story of his astonishing tale; he left out no details this time; he mentioned his own sensations and gripping fears. He only omitted the strange language used.

"But Défago surely had already told you all these details of the

Wendigo legend, my dear fellow," insisted the doctor. "I mean, he had talked about it, and thus put into your mind the ideas which your own excitement afterwards developed?"

Whereupon Simpson again repeated the facts. Défago, he declared, had barely mentioned the beast. He, Simpson, knew nothing of the story, and, so far as he remembered, had never even read about it. Even the word was unfamiliar.

Of course he was telling the truth, and Dr. Cathcart was reluctantly compelled to admit the singular character of the whole affair. He did not do this in words so much as in manner, however. He kept his back against a good, stout tree; he poked the fire into a blaze the moment it showed signs of dying down; he was quicker than any of them to notice the least sound in the night about them—a fish jumping in the lake, a twig snapping in the bush, the dropping of occasional fragments of frozen snow from the branches overhead where the heat loosened them. His voice, too, changed a little in quality, becoming a shade less confident, lower also in tone. Fear, to put it plainly, hovered close about that little camp, and though all three would have been glad to speak of other matters, the only thing they seemed able to discuss was this—the source of their fear. They tried other subjects in vain; there was nothing to say about them. Hank was the most honest of the group; he said next to nothing. He never once, however, turned his back to the darkness. His face was always to the forest, and when wood was needed he didn't go farther than was necessary to get it.

VII

A wall of silence wrapped them in, for the snow, though not thick, was sufficient to deaden any noise, and the frost held things pretty tight besides. No sound but their voices and the soft roar of the flames made itself heard. Only, from time to time, something soft as the flutter of a pine-moth's wings went past them through the air. No one seemed anxious to go to bed. The hours slipped towards midnight.

"The legend is picturesque enough," observed the doctor after one of the longer pauses, speaking to break it rather than because he had anything to say, "for the Wendigo is simply the Call of the Wild personified, which some natures hear to their own destruction."

"That's about it," Hank said presently. "An' there's no misunderstandin' when you hear it. It calls you by name right 'nough."

Another pause followed. Then Dr. Cathcart came back to the forbidden subject with a rush that made the others jump.

"The allegory *is* significant," he remarked, looking about him into the darkness, "for the Voice, they say, resembles all the minor sounds of the Bush—wind, falling water, cries of the animals, and so forth. And, once the victim hears *that*—he's off for good, of course! His most vulnerable points, moreover, are said to be the feet and the eyes; the feet, you see, for the lust of wandering, and the eyes for the lust of beauty. The poor beggar goes at such a dreadful speed that he bleeds beneath the eyes, and his feet burn."

Dr. Cathcart, as he spoke, continued to peer uneasily into the surrounding gloom. His voice sank to a hushed tone.

"The Wendigo," he added, "is said to burn his feet—owing to the friction, apparently caused by its tremendous velocity—till they drop off, and new ones form exactly like its own."

Simpson listened in horrified amazement; but it was the pallor on Hank's face that fascinated him most. He would willingly have stopped his ears and closed his eyes, had he dared.

"It don't always keep to the ground neither," came in Hank's slow heavy drawl, "for it goes so high that he thinks the stars have set him all a-fire. An' it'll take great thumpin' jumps sometimes, an' run along the tops of the trees, carrying its partner with it, an' then droppin' him jest as a fish-hawk'll drop a pickerel to kill it before eatin'. An' its food, of all the muck in the whole Bush is— moss!" And he laughed, a short, unnatural laugh. "It's a moss-eater, is the Wendigo," he added, looking up excitedly into the faces of his companions. "Moss-eater," he repeated, with a string of the most outlandish oaths he could invent.

But Simpson now understood the true purpose of all this talk. What these two men, each strong and "experienced" in his own way, dreaded more than anything else was—silence. They were talking against time. They were also talking against darkness, against the invasion of panic, against the admission reflection might bring that they were in an enemy's country—against anything, in fact, rather than allow their inmost thoughts to assume control. He himself, already initiated by the awful vigil with terror, was beyond both of them in this respect. He had reached the stage where he was immune. But these two, the scoffing, analytical doctor, and the honest, dogged backwoodsman, each sat trembling in the depths of his being.

Thus the hours passed; and thus, with lowered voices and a kind of taut inner resistance of spirit, this little group of humanity sat in the jaws of the wilderness and talked foolishly of the terrible and haunting legend. It was an unequal contest, all things considered, for the wilderness had already the advantage of first attack— and of a hostage. The fate of their comrade hung over them with a steadily increasing weight of oppression that finally became insupportable.

It was Hank, after a pause longer than the preceding ones that no one seemed able to break, who first let loose all this pent-up emotion in very unexpected fashion, by springing suddenly to his feet and letting out the most ear-shattering yell imaginable into the night. He could not contain himself any longer, it seemed. To make it carry even beyond an ordinary cry he interrupted its rhythm by shaking the palm of his hand before his mouth.

"That's for Défago," he said, looking down at the other two with a queer, defiant laugh, "for it's my belief"—the sandwiched oaths may be omitted—"that my ole partner's not far from us at this very minute."

There was a vehemence and recklessness about his performance that made Simpson, too, start to his feet in amazement, and betrayed even the doctor into letting the pipe slip from between his lips. Hank's face was ghastly, but Cathcart's showed a sudden weakness—a loosening of all his faculties, as it were. Then a momentary anger blazed into his eyes, and he too, though with deliberation born of habitual self-control, got upon his feet and faced the excited guide. For this was unpermissable, foolish, dangerous, and he meant to stop it in the bud.

What might have happened in the next minute or two one may speculate about, yet never definitely know, for in the instant of profound silence that followed Hank's roaring voice, and as though in answer to it, something went past through the darkness of the sky overhead at terrific speed—something of necessity very large, for it displaced much air, while down between the trees there fell a faint and windy cry of a human voice, calling in tones of indescribable anguish and appeal—

"Oh, oh! This fiery height! Oh, oh! My feet of fire! My burning feet of fire!"

White to the very edge of his shirt, Hank looked stupidly about him like a child. Dr. Cathcart uttered some kind of unintelligible cry, turning as he did so with an instinctive movement of blind terror towards the protection of the tent, then halting in the act as though frozen. Simpson, alone of the three, retained his presence of mind a little. His own horror was too deep to allow of any immediate reaction. He had heard that cry before.

Turning to his stricken companions, he said almost calmly—
"That's exactly the cry I heard—the very words he used!"

Then, lifting his face to the sky, he cried aloud, "Défago, Défago! Come down here to us! Come down—!"

And before there was time for anybody to take definite action one way or another, there came the sound of something dropping heavily between the trees, striking the branches on the way down, and landing with a dreadful thud upon the frozen earth below. The crash and thunder of it was really terrific.

"That's him, s'help me the good Gawd!" came from Hank in a whispering cry half choked, his hand going automatically toward the hunting knife in his belt. "And he's coming! He's coming!" he added, with an irrational laugh of terror, as the sounds of heavy footsteps crunching over the snow became distinctly audible, approaching through the blackness towards the circle of light.

And while the steps, with their stumbling motion, moved nearer and nearer upon them, the three men stood round that fire, motionless and dumb. Dr. Cathcart had the appearance of a man suddenly withered; even his eyes did not move. Hank, suffering shockingly, seemed on the verge again of violent action; yet did nothing. He too, was hewn of stone. Like stricken children they seemed. The picture was hideous. and, meanwhile, their owner still invisible, the footsteps came closer, crunching the frozen snow. It was endless—too prolonged to be quite real—this measured and pitiless approach. It was accursed.

VIII

Then at length the darkness, having thus laboriously conceived, brought forth—a figure. It drew forward into the zone of uncertain light where fire and shadows mingled, not ten feet away; then halted, staring at them fixedly. The same instant it started forward again with the spasmodic motion as of a thing moved by wires, and coming up closer to them, full into the glare of the fire, they perceived then that—it was a man; and apparently that this man was—Défago.

Something like a skin of horror almost perceptibly drew down in that moment over every face, and three pairs of eyes shone through it as though they saw across the frontiers of normal vision into the Unknown.

Défago advanced, his tread faltering and uncertain; he made his way straight up to them as a group first, then turned sharply and peered close into the face of Simpson. The sound of a voice issued from his lips—

"Here I am, Boss Simpson. I heered some one calling me." It was a faint, dried-up voice, made wheezy and breathless as by immense exertion. "I'm havin' a reg'lar hell-fire kind of a trip, I am." And he laughed, thrusting his head forward into the other's face.

But that laugh started the machinery of the group of wax-work figures with the wax-white skins. Hank immediately sprang forward with a stream of oaths so far-fetched that Simpson did not recognize them as English at all, but thought he had lapsed into Indian or some other lingo. He only realized that Hank's presence, thrust thus between them, was welcome—uncommonly welcome. Dr. Cathcart, though more calmly and leisurely, advanced behind him, heavily stumbling.

Simpson seems hazy as to what was actually said and done in those next few seconds, for the eyes of that detestable and blasted visage peering at such close quarters into his own utterly bewildered his senses at first. He merely stood still. He said nothing. He had not the trained will of the older men that forced them into action in defiance of all emotional stress. He watched them moving as behind a glass, that half destroyed their reality; it was dreamlike; perverted. Yet, through the torrent of Hank's meaningless phrases, he remembers hearing his uncle's tone of authority—hard and forced—saying several things about food and warmth, blankets, whiskey and the rest; . . . and, further, that whiffs of that penetrating, unaccustomed odour, vile, yet sweetly bewildering, assailed his nostrils during all that followed.

It was no less a person than himself, however—less experienced and adroit than the others though he was—who gave indistinctive utterance to the sentence that brought a measure of relief into the ghastly situation by expressing the doubt and thought in each one's heart.

"It *is*—YOU, isn't it, Défago?" he asked under his breath, horror breaking his speech.

And at once Cathcart burst out with the loud answer before the other had time to move his lips. "Of course it is! Of course it is! Only—can't you see—he's nearly dead with exhaustion, cold and terror! Isn't *that* enough to change a man beyond all recognition?" It was said in order to convince himself as much as to convince the others. And continually, while he spoke and acted, he held a handkerchief to his nose. That odour pervaded the whole camp.

For the "Défago" who sat huddled by the big fire, wrapped in blankets, drinking hot whisky and holding food in wasted hands, was no more like the guide they had last seen alive than the picture of a man of sixty is like the daguerreotype of his early youth in the costume of another generation. Nothing really can describe that ghastly caricature, that parody, masquerading there in the firelight as Défago. From the ruins of the dark and awful memories he still retains, Simpson declares that the face was more animal than human, the features drawn about into wrong proportions, the skin loose and hanging, as though he had been subjected to extraordinary pressures and tensions. It made him think vaguely of those bladder-faces blown up by the hawkers on Ludgate Hill, that change their expression as they swell, and as they collapse emit a faint and wailing imitation of a voice. Both face and voice suggested some such abominable resemblance. But Cathcart long afterwards, seeking to describe the indescribable, asserts that thus might have looked a face and body that had been in air so rarefied that, the weight of atmosphere being removed, the entire structure threatened to fly asunder and become—*incoherent . . .*

It was Hank, though all distraught and shaking with a tearing volume of emotion he could neither handle nor understand, who brought things to a head without more ado. He went off to a little distance from the fire, apparently so that the light should not dazzle him too much, and shading his eyes for a moment with both hands, shouted in a loud voice that held anger and affection dreadfully mingled—

"You ain't Défago! You ain't Défago at all! I don't give a—damn, but that ain't you, my ole pal of twenty years!" He glared upon the huddled figure as though he would destroy him with his eyes. "An' if it is I'll swab the floor of hell with a wad of cotton-wool on a toothpick, s'help me the good Gawd!" he added, with a violent fling of horror and disgust.

It was impossible to silence him. He stood there shouting like one possessed, horrible to see, horrible to hear—*because it was the truth.* He repeated himself in fifty different ways, each more outlandish than the last. The woods rang with echoes. At one time it looked as if he meant to fling himself upon "the intruder," for his hand continually jerked towards the long hunting-knife in his belt.

But in the end he did nothing, and the whole tempest completed itself very nearly with tears. Hank's voice suddenly broke, he collapsed on the ground, and Cathcart somehow or other persuaded him at last to go into the tent and lie quiet. The remainder of the affair, indeed, was witnessed by him from behind the canvas, his white and terrified face peeping through the crack of the tent door-flap.

Then Dr. Cathcart, closely followed by his nephew who so far had kept his courage better than all of them, went up with a determined air and stood opposite to the figure of Défago huddled over the fire. He looked him squarely in the face and spoke. At first his voice was firm.

"Défago, tell us what's happened—just a little, so that we can know how best to help you?" he asked in a tone of authority, almost of command. And at that point, it *was* command. At once afterwards, however, it changed in quality, for the figure turned up to him a face so piteous, so terrible and so little like humanity, that the doctor shrank back from him as from something spiritually unclean. Simpson, watching close behind him, says he got the impression of a mask that was on the verge of dropping off, diabolical, revealed in utter nakedness. "Out with it, man, out with it!" Cathcart cried, terror running neck and neck with entreaty. "None of us can stand this much longer . . . !" It was the cry of instinct over reason.

And then "Défago," smiling *whitely*, answered in that thin and fading voice that already seemed passing over into a sound of quite another character—

"I seen that great Wendigo thing," he whispered, sniffing the air about him exactly like an animal. "I been with it too—"

Whether the poor devil would have said more or whether Dr. Cathcart would have continued the impossible cross-examination cannot be known, for at that moment the voice of Hank was heard yelling at the top of his voice from behind the canvas that concealed all but his terrified eyes. Such a howling was never heard.

"His feet! Oh Gawd, his feet! Look at his great changed—feet!"

Défago, shuffling where he sat, had moved in such a way that for the first time his legs were in full light and his feet were visible. Yet Simpson had no time, himself, to see properly what Hank had seen. And Hank has never seen fit to tell. That same instant, with a leap like that of a frightened tiger, Cathcart was upon him, bundling the folds of blanket about his legs with such speed that the young student caught little more than a passing glimpse of something dark and oddly massed where moccasined feet ought to have been, and saw even that but with uncertain vision.

Then, before the doctor had time to do more, or Simpson time to even think a question, much less ask it, Défago was standing upright in front of them, balancing with pain and difficulty, and upon his shapeless and twisted visage an expression so dark and so malicious that it was, in the true sense, monstrous.

"Now *you* seen it too," he wheezed, "you seen my fiery, burning feet! And now—that is, unless you kin save me an' prevent—it's 'bout time for—"

His piteous and beseeching voice was interrupted by a sound that was like the roar of wind coming across the lake. The trees overhead shook their tangled branches. The blazing fire bent its flames as before a blast. And something swept with a terrific, rushing noise about the little camp and seemed to surround it entirely in a single moment of time. Défago shook the clinging blankets from his body, turned towards the woods behind, and with the same stumbling motion that had brought him—was gone: gone, before any one could move muscle to prevent him, gone with an amazing, blundering swiftness that left no time to act. The darkness positively swallowed him; and less than a dozen seconds later, above the roar of the swaying trees and the shout of the sudden wind, all three men, watching and listening with stricken hearts, heard a cry that seemed to drop down upon them from a great height of sky and distance—

"Oh, oh! This fiery height! Oh, oh! My feet of fire! My burning feet of fire . . . !" then died away, into untold space and silence.

Dr. Cathcart—suddenly master of himself, and therefore of the others—was just able to seize Hank violently by the arm as he tried to dash headlong into the Bush.

"But I want ter know,—you!" shrieked the guide. "I want ter see! That ain't him at all, but some—devil that's shunted into his place . . . !"

Somehow or other—he admits he never quite knew how he accomplished it—he managed to keep him in the tent and pacify him. The doctor, apparently, had reached the stage where reaction had set in and allowed his own innate force to conquer. Certainly he "managed" Hank admirably. It was his nephew, however, hitherto so wonderfully controlled, who gave him most cause for anxiety, for the cumulative strain had now produced a condition of lachrymose hysteria which made it necessary to isolate him upon a bed of boughs and blankets as far removed from Hank as was possible under the circumstance.

And there he lay, as the watches of that haunted night passed over the lonely camp, crying startled sentences, and fragments of sentences, into the folds of his blankets. A quantity of gibberish about speed and height and fire mingled oddly with biblical memories of the class-room. "People with broken faces all on fire are coming at a most awful, awful, pace towards the camp!" he would moan one minute; and the next would sit up and stare into the woods, intently listening, and whisper, "How terrible in the wilderness are—are the feet of them that—" until his uncle came across to change the direction of his thoughts and comfort him.

The hysteria, fortunately, proved but temporary. Sleep cured him, just as it cured Hank.

Till the first signs of daylight came, soon after five o'clock, Dr. Cathcart kept his vigil. His face was the colour of chalk, and there were strange flushes beneath the eyes. An appalling terror of the soul battled with his will all through those silent hours. These were some of the outer signs . . .

At dawn he lit the fire himself, made breakfast, and woke the others, and by seven they were well on their way back to the home camp—three perplexed and afflicted men, but each in his own way having reduced his inner turmoil to a condition of more or less systematized order again.

IX

They talked little, and then only of the most wholesome and common things, for their minds were charged with painful thoughts that clamoured for explanation, though no one dared refer to them. Hank, being nearest to primitive conditions, was the first to find himself, for he was also less complex. In Dr. Cathcart "civilization" championed his forces against an attack singular enough. To this day, perhaps, he is not *quite* sure of certain things. Anyhow, he took longer to "find himself."

Simpson, the student of divinity, it was who arranged his conclusions probably with the best, though not most scientific, appearance of order. Out there, in the heart of unreclaimed wilderness, they had surely witnessed something crudely and essentially primitive. Something that had survived somehow the advance of humanity had emerged terrifically, betraying a scale of life still monstrous and immature. He envisaged it rather as a glimpse into prehistoric ages, when superstitions, gigantic and uncouth, still oppressed the hearts of men; when the forces of nature were still untamed, the Powers that may have haunted a primeval universe not yet withdrawn. To this day he thinks of what he termed years later in a sermon "savage and formidable Potencies lurking behind the souls of men, not evil perhaps in themselves, yet instinctively hostile to humanity as it exists."

With his uncle he never discussed the matter in detail, for the barrier between the two types of mind made it difficult. Only once, years later, something led them to the frontier of the subject—of a single detail of the subject rather—

"Can't you even tell me what—*they* were like?" he asked; and the reply, though conceived in wisdom, was not encouraging. "It is far better you should not try to know, or to find out."

"Well—that odour . . . ?" persisted the nephew. "What do you make of that?"

Dr. Cathcart looked at him and raised his eyebrows.

"Odours," he replied, "are not so easy as sounds and sights of telepathic communication. I make as much or as little, probably, as you do yourself."

He was not quite so glib as usual with his explanations. That was all.

At the fall of day, cold, exhausted, famished, the party came to the end of the long portage and dragged themselves into a camp that at first glimpse seemed empty. Fire there was none, and no Punk came forward to welcome them. The emotional capacity of all three was too over-spent to recognize either surprise or annoyance; but the cry of spontaneous affection that burst from the lips of Hank, as he rushed ahead of them towards the fireplace, came probably as a warning that the end of the amazing affair was not quiet yet. And both Cathcart and his nephew confessed afterwards that when they saw him kneel down in his excitement and embrace something that reclined, gently moving, beside the extinguished ashes, they felt in their very bones that this "something" would prove to be Défago—the true Défago, returned.

And, so, indeed, it was.

It is soon told. Exhausted to the point of emaciation, the

French Canadian—what was left of him, that is,—fumbled among the ashes, trying to make a fire. His body crouched there, the weak fingers obeying feebly the instinctive habit of a lifetime with twigs and matches. But there was no longer any mind to direct the simple operation. The mind had fled beyond recall. And with it, too, had fled memory. Not only recent events, but all previous life was a blank.

This time it was the real man, though incredibly and horribly shrunken. On his face was no expression of any kind whatever—fear, welcome, or recognition. He did not seem to know who it was that embraced him, or who it was that fed, warmed and spoke to him the words of comfort and relief. Forlorn and broken beyond all reach of human aid, the little man did meekly as he was bidden. The "something" that had constituted him "individual" had vanished for ever.

In some ways it was more terribly moving than anything they had yet seen—that idiot smile as he drew wads of coarse moss from his swollen cheeks and told them that he was "a damned moss eater"; the continued vomiting of even the simplest food; and, worst of all, the piteous and childish voice of complaint in which he told them that his feet pained him—"burn like fire"—which was natural enough when Dr. Cathcart examined them and found that both were dreadfully frozen. Beneath the eyes there were faint indications of recent bleeding.

The details of how he survived the prolonged exposure, of where he had been, or of how he covered the great distance from one camp to the other, including an immense detour of the lake on foot since he had no canoe—all this remains unknown. His memory had vanished completely. And before the end of the winter whose beginning witnessed this strange occurrence, Défago, bereft of mind, memory and soul, had gone with it. He lingered only a few weeks.

And what Punk was able to contribute to the story throws no further light upon it. He was cleaning fish by the lake shore about five o'clock in the evening—an hour, that is, before the search party returned—when he saw this shadow of the guide picking its way weakly into camp. In advance of him, he declares, came the faint whiff of a certain singular odour.

That same instant old Punk started for home. He covered the entire journey of three days as only Indian blood could have covered it. The terror of a whole race drove him. He knew what it all meant. Défago had "seen the Wendigo."

About the Editor

E. M. Freeman is a freelance editor and "ghost" writer. She is an avid hiker and camper and can make a canoe do everything but talk. Her interests led her to work on collecting the stories for this book. She is currently at work on a ghost story of her own.